Lecture Notes in Computer Science　　10666

Commenced Publication in 1973
Founding and Former Series Editors:
Gerhard Goos, Juris Hartmanis, and Jan van Leeuwen

More information about this series at http://www.springer.com/series/7412

Yao Zhao · Xiangwei Kong
David Taubman (Eds.)

Image
and Graphics

9th International Conference, ICIG 2017
Shanghai, China, September 13–15, 2017
Revised Selected Papers, Part I

 Springer

Editors
Yao Zhao
Beijing Jiaotong University
Beijing
China

Xiangwei Kong
Dalian University of Technology
Dalian
China

David Taubman
UNSW
Sydney, NSW
Australia

ISSN 0302-9743   ISSN 1611-3349 (electronic)
Lecture Notes in Computer Science
ISBN 978-3-319-71606-0   ISBN 978-3-319-71607-7   (eBook)
https://doi.org/10.1007/978-3-319-71607-7

Library of Congress Control Number: 2017960877

LNCS Sublibrary: SL6 – Image Processing, Computer Vision, Pattern Recognition, and Graphics

Printed on acid-free paper

This Springer imprint is published by Springer Nature
The registered company is Springer International Publishing AG
The registered company address is: Gewerbestrasse 11, 6330 Cham, Switzerland

Preface

These are the proceedings of the 8th International Conference on Image and Graphics (ICIG 2017), held in Shanghai, China, during September 13–15, 2017.

The China Society of Image and Graphics (CSIG) has hosted this series of ICIG conferences since 2000. ICIG is the biennial conference organized by the China Society of Image and Graphics (CSIG), focusing on innovative technologies of image, video, and graphics processing and fostering innovation, entrepreneurship, and networking. This time, Shanghai Jiaotong University was the organizer, and the Nanjing Technology University and Zong Mu Technology Ltd. Company were the co-organizers. Details about the past eight conferences, as well as the current one, are as follows:

Conference	Place	Date	Submitted	Proceeding
First (ICIG 2000)	Tianjin, China	August 16–18	220	156
Second (ICIG 2002)	Hefei, China	August 15–18	280	166
Third (ICIG 2004)	Hong Kong, China	December 17–19	460	140
4th (ICIG 2007)	Chengdu, China	August 22–24	525	184
5th (ICIG 2009)	Xi'an, China	September 20–23	362	179
6th (ICIG 2011)	Hefei, China	August 12–15	329	183
7th (ICIG 2013)	Qingdao, China	July 26–28	346	181
8th (ICIG 2015)	Tianjin, China	August 13–16	345	170
9th (ICIG 2017)	Shanghai, China	September 13–15	370	172

This time, the proceedings are published by Springer in the LNCS series. The titles, abstracts, and biographies of the three invited speakers of plenary talks are presented first. At ICIG 2017, 370 submissions were received, and 160 papers were accepted. To ease in the search of a required paper in these proceedings, the 160 regular papers have been arranged in alphabetical order according to their titles. Another 12 papers forming a special topic are included at the end.

Our sincere thanks go to all the contributors (around 200), who came from around the world to present their advanced works at this event. Special thanks go to the members of Technical Program Committee, who carefully reviewed every single submission and made their valuable comments for improving the accepted papers.

The proceedings could not have been produced without the invaluable efforts of the publication chairs, the web chairs, and a number of active members of CSIG.

September 2017

Yao Zhao
Xiangwei Kong
David Taubman

Organization

Honorary Chairs

Guanhua Xu	MOST, China
Yuan F. Zheng	Ohio State University, USA

General Chairs

Tieniu Tan	Chinese Academy of Sciences, China
Hongkai Xiong	Shanghai Jiaotong University, China
Zixiang Xiong	Texas A&M University, USA

Organizing Committee Chairs

Weiyao Lin	Shanghai Jiaotong University, China
Huimin Ma	Tsinghua University, China
Bo Yan	Fudan University, China

Technical Program Chairs

David Taubman	UNSW, Australia
Yao Zhao	Beijing Jiaotong University, China

Finance Chairs

Zhihua Chen	ECUST, China
Zhenwei Shi	Beihang University, China

Special Session Chairs

Jian Cheng	Chinese Academy of Sciences, China
Zhihai He	University of Missouri, USA
Z. Jane Wang	University of British Columbia, Canada

Award Chairs

Xin Li	West Virginia University, USA
Shiqiang Yang	Tsinghua University, China

Publicity Chairs

Mingming Cheng   Nankai University, China
Moncef Gabbouj   TUT, Finland

Exhibits Chairs

Zhijun Fang   Shanghai University of Engineering Science, China
Yan Lv   Microsoft Research, China

Publication Chairs

Xiangwei Kong   Dalian University of Technology, China
Jun Yan   Journal of Image and Graphics, China

International Liaisons

Xiaoqian Jiang   UCSD, USA
Huifang Sun   MERL, USA

Local Chairs

Wenrui Dai   UCSD, USA
Junni Zou   Shanghai Jiaotong University, China

Registration Chair

Chen Ye   Shanghai Jiaotong University, China

Webmasters

Chenglin Li   EPFL, Switzerland
Yangmei Shen   Shanghai Jiaotong University, China

Technical Program Committee

Ping An   Shanghai University, China
Ru An   Hohai University, China
Xiao Bai   Beijing University of Aeronautics and Astronautics, China
Lianfa Bai   Nanjing University of Science and Technology, China
Xiang Bai   Huazhong University of Science and Technology, China
Chongke Bi   Tianjin University, China
Hai Bian   Hangzhou Dica3d Technology Co., Ltd., China
Xiaochun Cao   Institute of Information Engineering,
            Chinese Academy of Sciences, China

Yan-Pei Cao	Tsinghua University, China
Chong Cao	Tsinghua University, China
Qi Chen	Hainan University, China
Kang Chen	Tsinghua University, China
Mingkai Chen	Nanjing University of Posts and Telecommunications, China
Mingming Cheng	Nankai University, China
Yue Dong	MSRA, China
Zhijun Fang	Shanghai University of Engineering Science, China
Qianjin Feng	Southern Medical University, China
Xiaoyi Feng	Northwestern Polytechnical University, China
Dongmei Fu	University of Science and Technology Beijing, China
Junying Gan	Wuyi University, China
Lin Gao	ICT, CAS, China
Yue Gao	Tsinghua University, China
Xinbo Gao	Xidian University, China
Zexun Geng	Information Engineering University, China
Guanghua Gu	Yanshan University, China
Lin Gu	National Institute of Informatics, Japan
Yanwen Guo	Nanjing University, China
Hu Han	Nanyang Technological University, Singapore
Xiaowei He	Northwest University, China
Qiming Hou	Zhejiang University, China
Dong Hu	Nanjing University of Posts and Telecommunications, China
Hua Huang	Beijing Institute of Technology, China
Haozhi Huang	Tsinghua University, China
Yongfeng Huang	Tsinghua University, China
Rongrong Ji	Xiamen University, China
Yunde Jia	Beijing Institute of Technology, China
Sen Jia	Shenzhen University, China
Xiuping Jia	University of New South Wales, USA
Zhiguo Jiang	Beijing University of Aeronautics and Astronautics, China
Zhaohui Jiang	Central South University, China
Xiaoqian Jiang	University of California, San Diego, USA
Lianwen Jin	South China University of Technology, China
Bin Kong	Institute of Intelligent Machines, Chinese Academy of Sciences, China
Xiangwei Kong	Dalian University of Technology, China
Dengfeng Kuang	Nankai University, China
Jianhuang Lai	Sun Yat-Sen University, China
Congyan Lang	Beijing Jiaotong University, China
Changhua Li	Xi'an University of Architecture and Technology, China
Chenglin Li	Swiss Federal Institute of Technology in Lausanne, Switzerland
Hua Li	Institute of Computing Technology, Chinese Academy of Sciences, China
Jiming Li	Zhejiang Police College, China

Qi Li	Peking University, China
Shutao Li	Hunan University, China
Xi Li	Zhejiang University, China
Jie Liang	China Aerodynamics Research and Development Center, China
Pin Liao	Nanchang University, China
Chunyu Lin	Beijing Jiaotong University, China
Xiaojing Liu	Qinghai University, China
Changhong Liu	Jiangxi Normal University, China
Bin Liu	University of Science and Technology of China, China
Bin Liu	Tsinghua University, China
Chenglin Liu	Institute of Automation, Chinese Academy of Sciences, China
Wenyu Liu	Huazhong University of Science and Technology, China
Yue Liu	Beijing Institute of Technology, China
Qingshan Liu	Nanjing University of Information Science and Technology, China
Hongbing Lu	Fourth Military Medical University, China
Hanqing Lu	Institute of Automation, Chinese Academy of Sciences, China
Jiwen Lu	Tsinghua University, China
Jianhua Ma	Southern Medical University, China
Huimin Ma	Tsinghua University, China
Weidong Min	Nanchang University, China
Xuanqin Mou	Xi'an Jiaotong University, China
Taijiang Mu	Tsinghua University, China
Feiping Nie	Northwestern Polytechnical University, China
Yongwei Nie	South China University of Technology, China
Zhigeng Pan	Hangzhou Normal University, China
Yanwei Pang	Tianjin University, China
Yuxin Peng	Peking University, China
Yuntao Qian	Zhejiang University, China
Bo Ren	Nankai University, China
Jun Sang	Chongqing University, China
Nong Sang	Huazhong University of Science and Technology, China
Yangmei Shen	Shanghai Jiaotong University, China
Yuying Shi	North China Electric Power University, China
Huifang Sun	Mitsubishi Electric Research Laboratories, USA
Jiande Sun	Shandong University, China
Linmi Tao	Tsinghua University, China
Lei Tong	Beijing University of Technology, China
Yunhai Wang	Shandong University, China
Qi Wang	Northwestern Polytechnical University, China
Cheng Wang	Xiamen University, China
Meng Wang	Hefei University of Technology, China
Hanzi Wang	Xiamen University, China
Peizhen Wang	Anhui University of Technology, China
Tianjiang Wang	Huazhong University of Science and Technology, China

Bin Wang	Tsinghua University, China
Lili Wang	Beihang University, China
Shigang Wang	Jilin University, China
Miao Wang	Tsinghua University, China
Yunhong Wang	Beijing University of Aeronautics and Astronautics, China
Chunhong Wu	University of Science and Technology Beijing, China
Hongzhi Wu	Zhejiang University, China
Xiaojun Wu	Jiangnan University, China
Fei Wu	Zhejiang University, China
Zhongke Wu	Beijing Normal University, China
Dingyuan Xia	Wuhan University of Technology, China
Hongkai Xiong	Shanghai Jiaotong University, China
Mingliang Xu	Zhengzhou University, China
Chunxu Xu	Tsinghua University, China
Kun Xu	Tsinghua University, China
Zengpu Xu	Tianjin University of Science and Technology, China
Jianru Xue	Xi'an Jiaotong University, China
Xiangyang Xue	Fudan University, China
Bo Yan	Fudan University, China
Ling-Qi Yan	UC Berkeley, USA
Xiao Yan	Tsinghua University, China
Jingwen Yan	Shantou University, China
Jun Yan	Institute of Remote Sensing and Digital Earth, Chinese Academy of Sciences, China
Jinfeng Yang	Civil Aviation University of China, China
Sheng Yang	Tsinghua University, China
Yongliang Yang	Bath University, UK
Shiqiang Yang	Tsinghua University, China
Tao Yang	Tsinghua University, China
Hongxun Yao	Harbin Institute of Technology, China
Yong Yin	Dalian Maritime University, China
Shiqi Yu	Shenzhen University, China
Nenghai Yu	University of Science and Technology of China, China
Yinwei Zhan	Guangdong University of Technology, China
Aiqing Zhang	Anhui Normal University, China
Wei Zhang	Shandong University, China
Daoqiang Zhang	Nanjing University of Aeronautics and Astronautics, China
Jiawan Zhang	Tianjin University, China
Lei Zhang	Beijing Institute of Technology, China
Song-Hai Zhang	Tsinghua University, China
Shiliang Zhang	Peking University, China
Xinpeng Zhang	Shanghai University, China
Yanci Zhang	Sichuan University, China
Yongfei Zhang	Beijing University of Aeronautics and Astronautics, China
Fang-Lue Zhang	Victoria University of Wellington, New Zealand
Guofeng Zhang	Zhejiang University, China

Qiang Zhang	Dalian University, China
Yun Zhang	Zhejiang University of Media and Communications, China
Liangpei Zhang	Wuhan University, China
Shengchuan Zhang	Xiamen University, China
Xiaopeng Zhang	Shanghai Jiaotong University, China
Sicheng Zhao	Tsinghua University, China
Yao Zhao	Beijing Jiaotong University, China
Jieyu Zhao	Ningbo University, China
Chunhui Zhao	Harbin Engineering University, China
Ying Zhao	Central South University, China
Wei-Shi Zheng	Sun Yat-Sen University, China
Ping Zhong	National University of Defense Technology, China
Quan Zhou	China Academy of Space Technology, Xi'an, China
Jun Zhou	Griffith University, Australia
Liang Zhou	Nanjing University of Posts and Telecommunications, China
Linna Zhou	University of International Relations, China
Tao Zhou	Ningxia Medical University, China
Wengang Zhou	University of Science and Technology of China, China
Zhe Zhu	Duke University, USA
Wang-Jiang Zhu	Tsinghua University, China
Yonggui Zhu	Communication University of China, China

Contents – Part I

Contents – Part II

Compression, Transmission, Retrieval

5G Multimedia Communications

Artificial Intelligence

Biological and Medical Image Processing

Color and Multispectral Processing

Contents – Part III

Computer Graphics and Visualization

Hyperspectral Image Processing

Multi-view and Stereoscopic Processing

Representation, Analysis and Applications of Large-Scale 3D Multimedia Data

Security

Surveillance and Remote Sensing

S2DLDP with its Application to Palmprint Recognition

Ligang Liu[1], Jianxin Zhang[1(✉)], and Yinghua Jiang[2]

[1] Key Lab of Advanced Design and Intelligent Computing, Ministry of Education,
Dalian University, Dalian, People's Republic of China
zjx99326@163.com
[2] Information and Engineering College, Dalian University,
Dalian, People's Republic of China

Abstract. In this paper, we introduce the sparse two-dimensional local discriminant projections (S2DLDP) algorithm into palmprint recognition, and give an exactly recognition performance evaluation of the S2DLDP algorithm on public PolyU palmprint database. S2DLDP algorithm applies the idea of sparse for 2DLDP, possessing advantages of high computational efficiency and recognition performance. We perform the algorithm using various non-zero elements and image sizes, and then compare it with LDA, LPP and DLPP algorithm. The optimal recognition rate obtained by S2DLDP is 99.5%, which is significantly higher than the other three methods. Experiment results illuminate the excellent effectiveness of the S2DLDP algorithm for palmprint recognition.

Keywords: S2DLDP · Sparse projection · Palmprint recognition

1 Introduction

Palmprint recognition is regarded as a potential biometric recognition technology. It has the advantages of low capture cost and high recognition accuracy, and can be widely applied to employees' attendance system, building security control, automatic teller machines and ID card [1–4].

Palmprint recognition mainly includes two key steps, i.e., feature extraction and classifier construction [4]. Generally, feature extraction algorithms have great influence to the recognition accuracy. Due to the characteristics of highly descriptive, low computational cost and well separability, the subspace-based feature extraction methods have been widely researched for palmprint recognition. The main idea of subspace recognition methods is to put the high dimensional matrix projection into a low dimensional space, thereby reducing the processing dimension and obtaining the recognition features. The subspace algorithms maintain the specific characteristic of the palmprint with lower dimensional vectors or matrices. Currently, the main subspace projection methods include principal component analysis (PCA), linear discriminant analysis (LDA), locality preserving projection (LPP) [5] and discriminant locality preserving projections (DLPP) [6], etc. Although PCA and LDA have been widely used in image processing field, they have some obvious disadvantages for recognition. PCA and LDA consider global statistical properties based on the training data, while ignore the local nature of

© Springer International Publishing AG 2017
Y. Zhao et al. (Eds.): ICIG 2017, Part I, LNCS 10666, pp. 1–10, 2017.
https://doi.org/10.1007/978-3-319-71607-7_1

the sample data. For palmprint recognition, as the original sample data form is matrix, LDA and DLPP need to transform image matrix into a long vector form, which breaks the continuity properties of the image data in a certain degree. Also, this increases the time complexity due to the high dimension vector, and generates small sample problems. Therefore, some scholars propose some typical two-dimensional subspace methods, such as two-dimensional principal component analysis (2DPCA) [7], two-dimensional linear discriminant analysis (2DLDA) [8] two-dimensional locality preserving projections (2DLPP) [9] and two-dimensional discriminant locality preserving projections (2DDLPP) based on the comprehensive of sample class information.

However, at the point of the extracted features in a low-dimensional subspace, the greatest disadvantage of all methods mentioned above is that the learned projection axes are linear combination of all the original features. So, it is difficult to physically interpret the extracted features. In order to solve this problem, Zuo et al. [10] proposed sparse principle components analysis (SPCA) that uses the least angle regression [11, 12] and the Elastic Net [13]. Zhao et al. [14] proposed a spectral bounds framework for sparse subspace, and they also proposed sparse PCA and sparse LDA (SLDA). The sparse subspace algorithm has been widely studied. Though SPCA and SLDA can directly operate on the high dimensional vectors, they have two limitations. One limitation is time-consuming when the dimension of the features is very high. Another one is some manifold structural information embedded in the two-dimensional images may be lost. Recently, Lai et al. [15] introduced the idea of sparse into 2DDLPP and proposed a novel and effective image feature extraction method named sparse two-dimensional local discriminant projections (S2DLDP). The S2DLDP method shows well recognition performance for face recognition. This paper studies the application of S2DLDP methods in palmprint recognition.

The rest of the paper is organized as follows: Sect. 2 describes the algorithm theory of S2DLDP. Section 3 presents the experimental results and gives some analysis of them. Section 4 offers our conclusions.

2   Palmprint Feature Extraction Based S2DLDP

Research results have proven that discriminative features play an important role in recognition and classification problems, and sparse-based feature extraction method can achieve better recognition performance [16]. In essence, the S2DLDP algorithm is 2DLDP form of sparse representation. This algorithm uses a direct sparse regression approach instead of the palm image matrix. It not only has high computational efficiency, but also can get more intuitive sparse projection matrix.

2.1   Two-Dimensional Discriminant Locality Preserving Projections (2DDLPP)

The main idea of 2DDLPP is projecting $m \times n$ image matrix A_i to the w by a linear transformation $y_i = A_i w$, and to get an m-dimensional column vector y_i, which is called the projection feature vector of image A_i. Given the projection vector P_Φ, sample array

$B_1, B_2, \ldots, B_M$ can be mapped to a set of d dimensional Euclidean space points $Z_1, Z_2, \ldots, Z_M$, where $Z_i^T = P_\Phi^T B_i, i = 1, \ldots, M$.

To resolve optimal projection vector P_Φ, we can turn 2DDLPP into the minimization of following function:

$$\sum_{i,j=1}^{M} \left\| Z_i - Z_j \right\|^2 W(i,j) \tag{1}$$

However, the issue can be transformed into a generalized eigenvalue problem:

$$P_\Phi^T S_L P_\Phi = \lambda P_\Phi^T S_L P_\Phi \Rightarrow S_L P_\Phi = \lambda S_D P_\Phi \tag{2}$$

S_D, S_W and S_L are respectively defined as:

$$S_D = \sum_{i=1}^{M} B_i B_i^T D_{ii}, S_w = \sum_{i,j=1}^{M} B_i B_j^T D_{ij}, S_L = S_D - S_W$$

S_L is the 2D Laplacian matrix. The larger value of D_{ii}, the more important of the position B_i, and the position of the projection results Z_i is more important. The optimal feature vectors $P_{\Phi_1}, \ldots, P_{\Phi d}$ should be the eigenvectors corresponding to a group of the smallest eigenvalues $\lambda_1, \lambda_2, \ldots, \lambda_d$ from the characteristic Eq. (2), and then we can get all features matrix of the sample to complete the feature extraction.

$$Z_i^T = \left[Z_i^{(1)}, \ldots, Z_i^{(d)} \right]^T = P^T B_i, i = 1, \ldots, M \tag{3}$$

2DDLPP avoids the singular value problem exists in DLPP to obtain the final matrix. Meanwhile, it possesses the characteristics of simple calculation, simple application and keeps the characteristics of nonlinear local retention from DLPP.

2.2 Sparse Two-Dimensional Local Discriminant Projections (S2DLDP)

Optimal projection from local feature extraction method, basing on image matrix, is often obtained by solving the eigenvalue equation. According to supervised learning representative model and unsupervised learning representative model, Lai [15] summarizes 2D projection learning framework as:

$$X^T \left(L_b \otimes I_{n1} \right) X\varphi = \lambda X^T \left(L_w \otimes I_{n1} \right) X\varphi \tag{4}$$

L_b and L_w represent image diagonal weighting matrices, and I_{n1} is an identity matrix of order n_1. The operator $\otimes$ is kronecker product of the matrices. Note that there are two obvious limitations in 2D projection learning framework. One is the high computational complexity due to the calculations of $X^T \left(L_b \otimes I_{n1} \right) X\varphi$ and $X^T \left(L_w \otimes I_{n1} \right) X\varphi$. Another is that learned projection axes are the linear combination of all the original features, which is difficult to semantically explain the extracted features. Therefore, the idea of sparsity is introduced.

To solve sparse problems, so far, researchers have put forward a lot of regression method for fitting data, which is representative of the Ridge regression, Lasso regression and Elastic Net regression. In this paper, we use Elastic Net regression to resolve the above equation. The two-dimensional representation of Elastic Net regression method is given:

$$\varphi = \arg\min_{\varphi} \left(\sum_{i=1}^{m} \sum_{h=1}^{n_1} (X_i(h,:) \times \varphi - y_i)^2 + a \sum_{j=1}^{n_2} \overline{\varphi}_j^2 + \beta \sum_{j=1}^{n_2} \left| \overline{\varphi}_j \right| \right) \quad (5)$$

Elastic net regression is widely used for feature extraction, which compounds Ridge regression and Lasso regression. It also introduces the l_1 norm and l_2 norm, and overcomes the limitations of Lasso regression. The selected features of elastic net regression, unaffected by sample restrictions on the number, effectively choose the characteristics of the groups [17–19]. In this paper, the S2DLDP algorithm is implemented in this way. After the algorithm introduces sparse limit, Lai [15] draws the following algorithm model framework:

$$\begin{cases} X^T \left(L_b \otimes I_{n1} \right) X\varphi = \lambda X^T \left(L_w \otimes I_{n1} \right) X\varphi \\ subject \ to \ Card(\varphi) \leq K \end{cases} \quad (6)$$

Among them, $Card(\varphi)$ is the number of non-zero elements contained in vectors φ, K is a positive integer not greater than the dimension of the image matrix.

3   The Experimental Results and Analysis

To test the application efficiency of S2DLDP in palmprint recognition, we perform the algorithm in PolyU palmprint database and give an exactly comparison with several typical subspace methods. PolyU palmprint database is the largest and most widely used palmprint database with the original palmprint image size of 384 * 284 pixels. Our experiment is tested on a subset of the PolyU database. The subset consists of 1000 images form 100 palms. We segment the region of interest (ROI) in these images, and then the image size is 128 * 128 pixels. In the experiment, we select the top four images of each person as the training image, and the remained six images as test set. In recognition phase, the Euclidean distance is employed to calculate the similarity between palmprint features (Fig. 1).

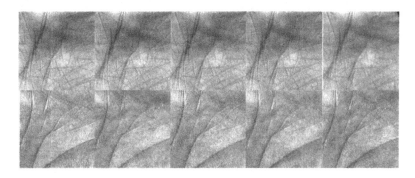

Fig. 1. Typical palmprint ROI images in PolyU database

3.1 The Non-zero Number Test Result

From Eq. 6 we can get that non-zero $Card(\varphi)$ in vector has the function of sparse restriction in image. The feature corresponding to the non-zero element is important, and influences the objective function. Based on this conclusion, to some extent, we discovery the features play a key role in the palmprint recognition. So it is not necessary to use the whole features, but only the key features. This has certain guidance in terms of the acquired characteristics. Therefore, studying the number of non-zero elements $Card(\varphi)$ under circumstances may achieve better recognition results.

At first, the eigen-palms learned by S2DLDP with $Card(\varphi) = 1:4:20$ are shown in Fig. 2, where the eigen-palms are much clearer. This indicates that non-zero elements automatically form the palm profiles in the metrics of the S2DLDP algorithm. Thus S2DLDP can learn a set of semantic palm contours. This method not only gives a meaningful and intuitive explanation on the learned subspace, but also shows us the more discriminative feature subspace for palmprint recognition.

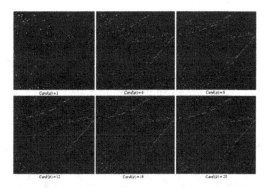

Fig. 2. Eigen-palm using various $Card(\varphi)$

$Card(\varphi) = 4:8:40$ are taken to experiment, and we calculate the recognition rate under various $Card(\varphi)$. Then, we draw recognition rate in different experiments plotted in the same figure for comparison in Fig. 3, where the horizontal axes d, varying from 1 to 50 with one step, denotes the various dimension of features.

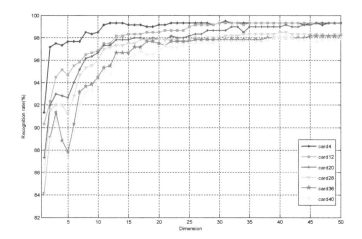

Fig. 3. Comparative palmprint recognition rate with various $Card(\varphi)$

In Fig. 3, recognition result gradually deteriorates with the increase of value $Card(\varphi)$. To achieve better recognition results, the number of non-zero should take a smaller value, and we set the value with 4. Note that when the number of non-zero elements is more, the effectiveness to enhance identify is not obvious. This experiment indicates that the sparse-palms with a large $Card(\varphi)$ are not necessary to obtain higher recognition rates. The above two figures show us an insightful understanding of the appearance-based 2D palm image representation and recognition.

3.2 The Image Size Test Result

After repeated experiments, the S2DLDP algorithm achieves optimal performance with $Card(\varphi) = 4$ and nearest neighbor number k = 1. Therefore, under the above conditions, we evaluate the effectiveness of recognition rate using various sub-image sizes of 32×32, 64×64, 128×128 pixels, respectively. Then, some different eigen-palms are given in Fig. 4 and comparison results are illustrated in Fig. 5, in which we take $d = 1: 1: 100$ as horizontal axes.

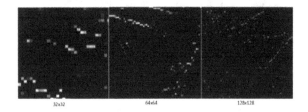

Fig. 4. Comparative eigen-palms based on different sub image size

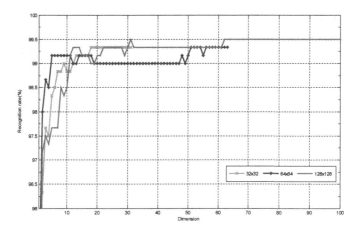

Fig. 5. Comparative recognition rate result based on different sub-image size

In Fig. 5, the recognition rate under different sub image size shows a trend of growth with the increase of the dimension size image characteristics, and gradually stabilizes. Meanwhile, curve clearly shows that S2DLDP algorithm achieves better recognition rate in dealing with a larger image, and the recognition rate can reach 99.5%. What is more, when image size is 32×32 pixel, recognition rate has no obvious descend, as the change of dimension.

3.3 The Comparative Test Result with LDA, LPP and DLPP

To further illustrate the effectiveness of the algorithm which is used to identify, experiment changes the number of training samples, using the top three and five palmprint images of each person as the training image, the remained images as the test images.

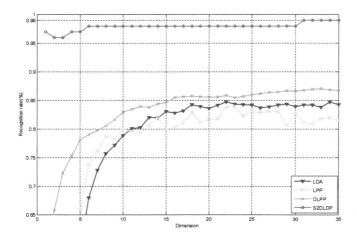

Fig. 6. The comparison of recognition rate for 3 training samples

For S2DLDP algorithm, the parameters do not change. In order to save computation time, all of the images are resized to 32 * 32 pixels. The comparative test results are given in Figs. 6 and 7 in which we take $d = 1: 1: 35$ as horizontal axes. The best recognition performance under corresponding feature dimension is shown in Table 1.

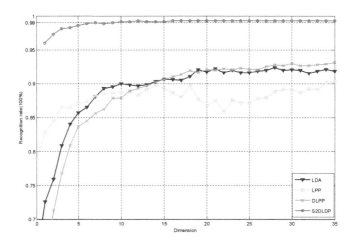

Fig. 7. The comparison result of recognition rate for 5 training samples

Table 1. The optimal recognition rate results with feature dimension of the four methods on the PolyU palmprint database

Methods	3 training samples		5 training samples	
	Recognition rate (%)	Dimension	Recognition rate (%)	Dimension
LDA	85%	22	92%	20
LPP	84%	23	90%	18
DLPP	87%	33	93%	30
S2DLDP	99%	31	99.5%	6

In Figs. 6 and 7, the recognition rates of S2DLDP are significantly higher than other methods. S2DLDP not only gives an intuitively semantic interpretation of the learned subspace, but also shows that palm profile subspace is more discriminative for palmprint recognition.

4   Conclusions

In this paper, the S2DLDP algorithm is introduced into palmprint recognition, and achieves the optimal recognition rate of 99.5%. The S2DLDP algorithm fully integrates the local separability, sample information and inherent attribute of two-dimensional images. To a certain extent, it reduces the complexity of calculation and improves the recognition rate. This algorithm provides intuitive, semantics, and interpretable palmprint feature space, and the palmprint features extracted have strong distinction. The experimental results show that the sparse projection in the process of feature extraction and dimensionality reduction realizes the function of feature selection, also proves its validity application for palmprint recognition.

Acknowledgments. The work is supported by the Natural Science Foundation of Liaoning Province (No. 201602035) and the High-level Talent Innovation Support Program of Dalian City (No. 2016RQ078).

References

1. Tamrakar, D., Khanna, P.: Noise and rotation invariant RDF descriptor for palmprint identification. Multimedia Tools Appl. **75**, 5777–5794 (2016)
2. Leng, L., Li, M., Kim, C., et al.: Dual-source discrimination power analysis for multi-instance contactless palmprint recognition. Multimedia Tools Appl. **76**, 333–354 (2017)
3. Guo, Z.H., Zhang, D., Zhang, L., et al.: Feature band selection for online multispectral palmprint recognition. IEEE Trans. Inf. Forensics Secur. **7**, 1094–1099 (2012)
4. Li, H., Zhang, J., Wang, L.: Robust palmprint identification based on directional representations and compressed sensing. Multimedia Tools Appl. **70**, 2331–2345 (2012)
5. Yang, J., Zhang, D., Yang, J.Y., et al.: Globally maximizing, locally minimizing: unsupervised discriminant projection with applications to face and palm biometrics. IEEE Trans. Pattern Anal. Mach. Intell. **29**, 650–664 (2004)
6. Zhong, F., Zhang, J., Li, D.: Discriminant locality preserving projections based on L1-norm maximization. IEEE Trans. Neural Networks Learn. Syst. **25**, 2065–2074 (2014)
7. Yang, J., Zhang, D., Frangi, A.F., et al.: Two-dimensional PCA: a new approach to appearance-based face representation and recognition. IEEE Trans. Pattern Anal. Mach. Intell. **26**, 131–137 (2004)
8. Li, M., Yuan, B.: 2D-LDA: a statistical linear discriminant analysis for image matrix. Pattern Recogn. Lett. **26**, 527–532 (2005)
9. Hu, D., Feng, G., Zhou, Z.: Two-dimensional locality preserving projections (2DLPP) with its application to palmprint recognition. Pattern Recogn. **40**, 339–342 (2008)
10. Zou, H., Hastie, T., Tibshirani, R.: Sparse principal component analysis. J. Comput. Graph. Stat. **15**, 265–286 (2006)
11. Gluhovsky, I.: Multinomial least angle regression. IEEE Trans. Neural Networks Learn. Syst. **23**, 169–174 (2012)
12. Hagiwara, K.: Least angle regression in orthogonal case. In: Loo, C.K., Yap, K.S., Wong, K.W., Teoh, A., Huang, K. (eds.) ICONIP 2014. LNCS, vol. 8835, pp. 540–547. Springer, Cham (2014). https://doi.org/10.1007/978-3-319-12640-1_65
13. Wang, L., Cheng, H.: Robust sparse PCA via weighted elastic net. Pattern Recogn. **321**, 88–95 (2012)
14. Zhao, Q., Meng, D., Xu, Z.: Robust sparse principal component analysis. Sci. Chin. Inf. Sci. **57**, 1–14 (2014)
15. Lai, Z., Wan, M., Jin, Z., et al.: Sparse two-dimensional local discriminant projections for feature extraction. Neurocomputing **74**, 629–637 (2011)
16. Wagner, A., Wright, J., Ganesh, A., et al.: Toward a practical face recognition system: robust alignment and illumination by sparse representation. IEEE Trans. Pattern Anal. Mach. Intell. **34**, 372–386 (2012)

17. Li, C.N., Shao, Y.H., Deng, N.Y.: Robust L1-norm two-dimensional linear discriminant analysis. Neural Netw. Official J. Int. Neural Netw. Soc. **65**, 92–104 (2015)
18. Wang, J., Lu, C., Wang, M., et al.: Robust face recognition via adaptive sparse representation. IEEE Trans. Cybern. **44**, 2368–2378 (2014)
19. Zhong, F., Zhang, J.: Linear discriminant analysis based on L1-norm maximization. IEEE Trans. Image Process. **22**, 3018–3027 (2013)

A Hierarchical Voting Scheme for Robust Geometric Model Fitting

Fan Xiao[1], Guobao Xiao[1,2], Xing Wang[1], Jin Zheng[3], Yan Yan[1], and Hanzi Wang[1(✉)]

[1] Fujian Key Laboratory of Sensing and Computing for Smart City,
School of Information Science and Engineering, Xiamen University,
Xiamen 361005, China
wang.hanzi@gmail.com
[2] School of Aerospace Engineering, Xiamen University, Xiamen 361005, China
[3] Beijing Key Laboratory of Digital Media,
School of Computer Science and Engineering, Beihang University,
Beijing 100191, China

Abstract. In this paper, we propose an efficient and robust model fitting method, called Hierarchical Voting scheme based Fitting (HVF), to deal with multiple-structure data. HVF starts from a hierarchical voting scheme, which simultaneously analyses the consensus information of data points and the preference information of model hypotheses. Based on the proposed hierarchical voting scheme, HVF effectively removes "bad" model hypotheses and outliers to improve the efficiency and accuracy of fitting results. Then, HVF introduces a continuous relaxation based clustering algorithm to fit and segment multiple-structure data. The proposed HVF can effectively estimate model instances from the model hypotheses generated by random sampling, which usually includes a large proportion of "bad" model hypotheses. Experimental results show that the proposed HVF method has significant superiority over several state-of-the-art fitting methods on both synthetic data and real images.

Keywords: Geometric model fitting · Multiple-structure data
Hierarchical voting scheme

1 Introduction

Geometric model fitting addresses the basic task of estimating the number and the parameters of model instances and it has various applications in computer vision such as camera calibration, 3D reconstruction and motion segmentation. It is particularly challenging to determine the correct model instances from multiple-structure data in the presence of severe outliers and noises. Recently, many robust model fitting methods have been proposed, including AKSWH [1], T-linkage [2], MSH [3], RansaCov [4] and SDF [5].

© Springer International Publishing AG 2017
Y. Zhao et al. (Eds.): ICIG 2017, Part I, LNCS 10666, pp. 11–22, 2017.
https://doi.org/10.1007/978-3-319-71607-7_2

Conventionally, a "hypothesize-and-verify" framework has been widely adopted to fit models by firstly verifying a set of model hypotheses generated from data points and then selecting the best model hypothesis satisfying some specific criteria. The representative work of such a framework is RANSAC [6], which shows favorable robustness and simplicity for single model estimation. The variants of RANSAC (e.g., [7–9]) deal with multiple-structure data in a sequential manner, where one model instance can be estimated in each round and then the corresponding inliers are removed for the model estimation in the next round. However, the verifying criteria of these methods generally require to give one threshold related to the inlier noise scale, whose value is non-trivial to be determined. In addition, since the intersecting parts of different model instances are probably removed during the sequential fitting procedure, the fitting performance of these methods is constrained.

Some other robust fitting methods adopts the voting scheme. Unlike the verifying procedure, the voting scheme simultaneously select all the potential model instances. For example, HT [10] and its variant RHT [11] are the representative methods. After mapping data points into the parameter space, each data point is converted into a set of votes for the corresponding model hypotheses. However, when searching for the model hypotheses with the most number of votes as the underlying model instances, the quantization may be ambiguous and high-dimensional data may lead to prohibitive computation as well.

Inspired by the clustering algorithms, a "voting-and-clustering" framework is widely used in geometric model fitting recently. In terms of different voting schemes, the methods based on this framework can be divided into the consensus analysis based voting (referred to as the consensus voting) methods and the preference analysis based voting (referred to as the preference voting) methods. The methods based on the consensus voting (e.g., AKSWH and MSH) endow each model hypothesis votes coming from the corresponding inliers and then cluster the model hypotheses according to the consensus information. On the other hand, the methods based on the preference voting (e.g., KF [12], J-linkage [13] and T-linkage), the model hypotheses vote for the data points within the respective inlier noise scale, and then the data points are clustered to obtain the model instances. However, there are some limitations in these methods unilaterally based on consensus or preference analysis. For the consensus voting based methods, how to distinguish the correct model instances from the redundant and invalid model hypotheses is difficult. For the preference voting based methods, the "bad" model hypotheses may cause incorrect analysis of the data points, which leads to the fitting failure. Besides, the intersection of the model instances may be dealt with unfavorably for the preference voting based methods [4].

To benefit from the superiorities and alleviate the deficiencies of the consensus voting scheme and the preference voting scheme, we propose a Hierarchical Voting scheme based Fitting method (HVF) which effectively combines both voting schemes. Specifically, we firstly apply the consensus voting scheme as the first step of the hierarchical voting scheme to distinguish the "good" model hypotheses from the "bad" model hypotheses. Then for the second step

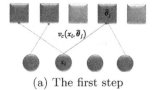

(a) The first step

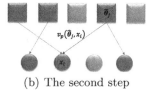

(b) The second step

Fig. 1. An illustration of the hierarchical voting scheme, where the squares represent the model hypotheses and the circles represent the data points. (a) The first step includes the consensus voting scheme: the vote $v_c(x_i, \hat{\boldsymbol{\theta}}_j)$ from the i−th data point x_i is given to the j−th model hypothesis $\hat{\boldsymbol{\theta}}_j$, which removes the "bad" model hypotheses (green squres). (b) The second step includes the preference voting scheme: the vote $v_p(\hat{\boldsymbol{\theta}}_j, x_i)$ from the j−th model hypothesis $\hat{\boldsymbol{\theta}}_j$ is given to the i−th data point x_i, which removes outliers (green circles). (Color figure online)

of the hierarchical voting scheme, the model hypotheses that are prone to be the "good" model hypotheses are retained for more precise preference voting to the data points, which contributes to the gross outliers removal. Finally, the data points are clustered into the sets corresponding to the true model instances. An illustration of the hierarchical voting scheme is depicted in Fig. 1.

Compared with the state-of-the-art model fitting methods, the proposed method HVF has three advantages: Firstly, HVF can simultaneously estimate the number and the parameters of multiple model instances in challenging multiple-structure data (e.g. with intersecting parts or a large number of outliers and noises). Secondly, the hierarchical voting scheme, combining the consensus voting and preference voting schemes, effectively improves the fitting accuracy and robustness by comprehensive analysis. Thirdly, HVF successfully reduces the negative influence of "bad" model hypotheses and gross outliers, which shows high computational efficiency.

The rest of the paper is organized as follows: We detail the specific two steps of the hierarchical voting scheme and present the overall HVF method in Sect. 2. We provide the extensive experimental results compared with several state-of-the-art methods on both synthetic data and real images in Sect. 3, and then draw conclusions in Sect. 4.

2   A Hierarchical Voting Scheme for Model Fitting

In this section, we describe the proposed hierarchical voting scheme at first, and then present the complete model fitting method HVF based on this voting scheme. From a set of N data points in d dimensions $\boldsymbol{X} = \{x_i\}_{i=1}^{N} \in \mathbb{R}^d$, we randomly sample M p-subsets (p is the minimum number of data points required to estimate a model hypothesis) to generate model hypotheses $\hat{\boldsymbol{\Theta}} = \{\hat{\boldsymbol{\theta}}_j\}_{j=1}^{M} \in \mathbb{R}^p$. Some other sampling methods [14,15] have been proposed to produce as many all-inlier p-subsets as possible and they are easy to be employed in our method as well. Here we put emphasis on the model selection process and only use random sampling for the generation of model hypotheses for simplicity. For the i-th data point, its absolute residual set $\boldsymbol{r}_i = \{r_i^1, \ldots, r_i^M\}$ is measured with regard to all the model hypotheses by computing the Simpson distance, where r_i^j represents the residual of the i-th data point to the j-th model hypothesis.

2.1   The Consensus Voting of the Hierarchical Voting Scheme

The qualities of model hypotheses depend on their similarities to the true model instances. A "good" model hypothesis, similar to the corresponding true model instance, holds a larger proportion of true inliers and compacts the corresponding inliers more tightly than the other "bad" model hypotheses. The "bad" model hypotheses, however, are very likely to mislead the preference analysis. Therefore, the first step of the hierarchical voting scheme is constructed to alleviate the negative effects of the "bad" model hypotheses.

Following the idea of the conventional consensus voting schemes [1,10,11], each generated model hypothesis acts as a model hypothesis candidate while each data point acts as a voter. Basically, we make an inlier vote for the model hypotheses it closely relates to. In this paper, we introduce a biased measurement to assign continuous values for the consensus voting and enlarge the differences between the "good" and "bad" model hypotheses. Unlike the binary voting in RANSAC and HT/RHT, a continuous value gives detailed information about the disparities between different data points with regard to the evaluation of a model hypothesis. Furthermore, the consensus analysis scheme simply based on the number of the inliers in [6,17] is sensitive to a threshold related to the inlier noise scale and is not discriminative enough for dichotomizing model hypotheses. Therefore, we consider the voting details from two aspects. On one hand, since the relationships between data points and model hypotheses are reflected on the distribution of data points, votes from different data points contribute to the model hypotheses in different degrees. Specifically, the closer a data point is to a model hypothesis, the greater contributions it gives to this model hypothesis in the voting. On the other hand, the model hypotheses with all the inliers in smaller deviations are more close to the underlying model instances than the others. Hence, we get these model hypotheses to accept the support from the data points in different degrees. Specifically, the model hypotheses which compact the inliers more tightly are endowed with greater acceptance of the votes.

To achieve the above idea, here we use the concept of the variable bandwidth kernel desity estimation [20,21] to design the voting formulation. Similar to the Gaussian kernel function, we combine the density estimation of model hypotheses and the residuals of data points with respect to model hypotheses. Thus each model hypothesis is endowed with a discriminative vote value which takes the information of both model hypotheses and data points into consideration. In addition, we restrain the model hypotheses with large inlier noise scales. To this end, the consensus vote value of the j-th model hypothesis from the i-th data point is defined as:

$$v_c(\hat{\boldsymbol{\theta}}_j, x_i) = \begin{cases} \dfrac{1}{N * \hat{s}_j} \, e^{-(r_i^j)^2/2h^2} & r_i^j < \alpha \hat{s}_j, \\ 0 & otherwise, \end{cases} \tag{1}$$

where $\hat{s}_j$ is the inlier noise scale of the j-th model hypotheses estimated by IKOSE [1], h is the bandwidth used in computing the variable bandwidth kernel density, and α is a constant (98% of inliers of a Gaussian distribution are included when α is set to 2.5).

After all the data points give their votes to the generated model hypotheses, each model hypothesis gathers the support from all the data points. Therefore, the voting score of the j-th model hypothesis from all the data points is calculated as follows:

$$V_c^j = \sum_{i=1}^{N} v_c(\hat{\boldsymbol{\theta}}_j, x_i). \tag{2}$$

Based on the above formulation, the "good" model hypotheses, which possesses more inliers, denser inlier distribution and smaller inlier noise scale, tend to have significantly higher voting scores than the "bad" model hypotheses. Thus, we retain the "good" model hypotheses with significantly higher voting scores as $\hat{\boldsymbol{\Theta}}^* = \{\hat{\boldsymbol{\theta}}_j^*\}_{j=1}^{m}$ (m is the number of the retained model hypotheses), and filter out the "bad" model hypotheses. Similar to [1], we adopt an adaptive model hypothesis selection method based on the information theory to decide the cut-off boundary using the voting scores.

2.2   The Preference Voting of the Hierarchical Voting Scheme

The above-mentioned consensus voting to the model hypotheses step effectively eliminates the "bad" model hypotheses. Thus the influence of "bad" model hypotheses, which often leads to the failure in the estimation of model instances, is significantly reduced. However, as for the data points, there are still a great number of gross outliers that need to be removed. As a supplementary of the first step, we also use the affinity information in the second step to handle this problem. Each data point is supported by the model hypotheses with close affinities in the form of votes. Since the retained model hypotheses generally include redundancy, which means several model hypotheses correspond to the same model instance, the true inliers receive much more votes from multiple model hypotheses (corresponding to the same model instance) than the gross outliers. In addition, in the case of the intersecting models, the inliers located in the intersection receive the votes from multiple model hypotheses (corresponding to the multiple intersecting model instances). Hence, the differences between the true inliers and the gross outliers can be easily discriminated by utilizing these observations in the preference voting. To this end, the preference vote value of the i-th data point voted by the j-th model hypothesis is defined as:

$$v_p(x_i, \hat{\boldsymbol{\theta}}_j^*) = \begin{cases} \xi(x_i, \hat{\boldsymbol{\theta}}_j^*) & r_i^j < \alpha \hat{s}_j, \\ 0 & otherwise, \end{cases} \tag{3}$$

where $\xi(x_i, \hat{\boldsymbol{\theta}}_j^*)$ is a function that calculates the value of a valid vote from the j-th retained model hypothesis to the i-th data points based on the affinity information. Various functions can be used as the function $\xi(x_i, \hat{\boldsymbol{\theta}}_j^*)$, such as the Gaussian function and the exponential function. Since the consensus voting in the first step removes a great number of "bad" model hypotheses, the retained model hypotheses are relatively reliable in the preference analysis of data points and have discriminative residuals for the inliers and the outliers. For simplicity and effciency, we employ a function similar to the one used in J-linkage [2], which sets the valid vote $\xi(x_i, \hat{\boldsymbol{\theta}}_j^*)$ to 1. Then the voting score of a data point can be computed as the sum of all the votes from the retained model hypotheses, which can be written as follows:

$$V_p^i = \sum_{j=1}^{m} v_p(x_i, \hat{\boldsymbol{\theta}}_j^*). \tag{4}$$

The retained model hypotheses that are close to the true model instances, give plenty of votes to the inliers but only few votes to the outliers. Therefore, we can derive a set of filtered points X^* of which the voting scores are larger than a cut-off threshold. For the outlier-free data or the data with a small proportion of outlier, it is unlikely to wrongly remove the inliers when the cut-off threshold is fixed to 0. For the data with severe outlier contamination, the outlier removal results are more accurate when the cut-off threshold is fixed to 5%–10% of the number of the retained model hypotheses. Here we set the threshold to 0 to filter out the outliers without any support from the retained model hypotheses.

Note that the preference voting step removes most gross outliers in the given data by utilizing the retained model hypotheses. Some experiments on the performance of the outlier removal are demonstrated in Sect. 3.1.

2.3 The Complete Method

With all the components of the hierarchical voting scheme mentioned above, we present the complete proposed method HVF, summarized in Algorithm 1. The proposed hierarchical voting scheme acts as the key step of HVF to sequentially evaluate model hypotheses and data points. Specifically, the first step of HVF differentiates the "bad" model hypotheses from the "good" model hypotheses by using the consensus voting. And then HVF removes the "bad" model hypotheses. Benefiting from this step, HVF not only reduces the influence of the "bad" model hypotheses in terms of the preference analysis, but also removes the unnecessary computation on the evaluation of data points using "bad" model hypotheses. The second step of HVF utilizes the preference information to eliminate outliers, which narrows the range of clustering data points in the next step and reduces the influence of outliers. After the hierachichal voting procedure, a bottom-up clustering method similar to [2] is applied to the filtered data points using the preference information. With the help of the hierarchical voting scheme, the clustering step is carried out with more accurate preference analysis and less computational complexity. Finally, the estimated model instances can be derived from the clusters obtained on the filtered data points.

Algorithm 1. Hierarchical voting scheme based fitting method

Input: A set of data points X and the number of model hypotheses M.
Output: The model instances in data and the corresponding inliers.
1: Generate the model hypotheses $\hat{\Theta}$ by randomly sampling M p-subsets from X.
2: Vote for the model hypotheses according to the biased values computed by Eq. (1), which is based on the consensus information of data points.
3: Retain the "good" model hypotheses $\hat{\Theta}^*$ from $\hat{\Theta}$ according to the scores of the model hypotheses computed by Eq. (2).
4: Vote for the data points with the biased values computed by Eq. (3), which is based on the preference information from the remained model hypotheses.
5: Remove the outliers from the data points to yield the filtered data points X^* according to the scores of the data points computed by Eq. (4).
6: Cluster the data points in X^* based on the preference information related to $\hat{\Theta}^*$.
7: Derive the parameters of the model instances and find the corresponding inliers.

---

3   Experiments

In this section, we evaluate the proposed model fitting method HVF on synthetic data and real images. Four state-of-the-art model fitting methods—KF [12], AKSWH [1], J-linkage [13] and T-linkage [2] (HVF takes some inspiration from these methods and has some similarities to them in terms of voting schemes), are used for performance comparison. For fairness, we implement each experiment 50 times with the best tuned settings. We generate 5000 model hypotheses for line fitting, 10000 for homography based segmentation and two-view based motion segmentation. Intuitively, we show some fitting results obtained by HVF and list the average performance statistics obtained by the five competing methods. We conduct all the experiments in MATLAB on the Windows system with Inter Core i7-4790 CPU 3.6 GHz and 16 GB RAM. The fitting error is computed as [2,18], which equals to the proportion of the misclassified points in all the data points. The outlier removal error is calculated as the proportion of the incorrectly dichotomized inliers and outliers in all the data points.

3.1   Line Fitting and Outlier Removal

For line fitting, the five model fitting methods are tested on several synthetic data and some datasets from [12,19]. The gross outlier proportions of these data range from 0 to 80%. To investigate the effectiveness of the hierarchical voting scheme, we test the performance of outlier removal on the data of line fitting. As shown in Fig. 2, HVF is compared with the other three methods (AKSWH is not evaluated since it focuses on the model hypotheses selecting and clustering without explicit outlier removal) in the line fitting task in terms of the outlier removal results. These data respectively consist of 2, 4 and 6 lines. It can be seen that HVF achieves the lowest outlier removal errors among the four methods or equivalent low outlier removal errors compared with J-linkage and T-linkage

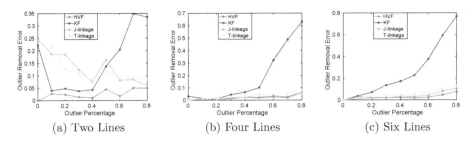

Fig. 2. The average results of outlier removal in line fitting obtained by KF (blue lines), J-linkage (green lines), T-linkage (cyan lines) and HVF (red lines). (Color figure online)

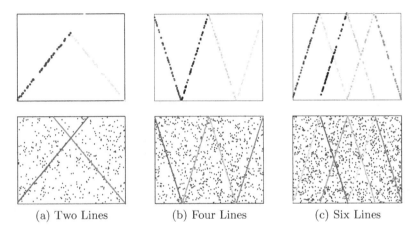

Fig. 3. Some outlier removal results and fitting results obtained by HVF on the line fitting. The top row shows the outlier removal results where the yellow dots are outliers. The bottom row shows the line fitting results where the blue dots are outliers. Each of the other colors represents a model instance. (Color figure online)

under most conditions. This is due to that the number and the quality of the model hypotheses and the data points are progressively refined by using the hierarchical voting scheme. We show some outlier removal results and fitting results obtained by HVF for line fitting in Fig. 3. The gross outlier proportions of these three data are 80%. We can see that HVF successfully removes most of the outliers although the outlier proportions are high. In addition, HVF can favorably deal with the multiple-structure data for line fitting even if there exist intersections between the model instances.

3.2   Homography Based Segmentation

In terms of homography based segmentation, we test the performance of the five model fitting methods on 10 data from the AdelaideRMF [16] dataset. The segmentation results for 4 data and the performance for the 10 data are respectively

(a) Elderhalla   (b) Oldclassicswing   (c) Elderhallb   (d) Johnsona

Fig. 4. Some results obtained by HVF on 4 data for homography based segmentation. The top row and the bottom row show the ground truth (i.e., Elderhalla, Oldclassic-swing, Elderhallb and Johnsona) and the fitting results obtained by HVF, respectively. The red dots represent the outliers. Each of the other colors represents a model instance. (Color figure online)

shown in Fig. 4 and Table 1. From Fig. 4 and Table 1, we can see that the proposed HVF achieves the lowest fitting errors and the least computational time on all the data among the five methods. HVF achieves better accuracy than the AKSWH and T-linkage which have already achieved quite good results in some data. The improvement of speed of HVF is quite obvious due to the proposed hierarchical voting scheme (at least equivalent to AKSWH in the "Johnsona" or at most 25 times faster than the T-linkage in the "Hartley"). T-linkage improves the accuracy of the preference analysis compared with J-linkage at the cost of prohibitive computational time. KF obtains the worst performance due to its sensitivity to the parameters.

Table 1. The average fitting errors (%) and the CPU time (in seconds) of HVF on 10 data for homography based segmentation. The best results are boldfaces.

Data	Elderhalla	Hartley	Ladysymon	Library	Neem	Nese	Oldclassic-swing	Sene	Elderhallb	Johnsona
KF	40.93	16.27	19.33	39.52	19.74	8.91	7.47	37.76	26.98	21.47
	(1.76)	(3.55)	(5.09)	(2.57)	(10.57)	(4.76)	(10.58)	(1.88)	(3.55)	(17.38)
AKSWH	2.26	9.73	13.67	5.50	19.27	3.76	4.50	5.67	19.25	18.66
	(1.70)	(1.90)	(2.03)	(3.16)	(2.07)	(2.72)	(2.58)	(3.22)	(1.99)	(2.56)
J-linkage	7.75	8.64	11.53	6.99	9.88	2.54	3.99	0.97	16.51	7.00
	(1.91)	(2.03)	(6.98)	(2.02)	(5.68)	(13.02)	(23.92)	(5.84)	(1.81)	(4.06)
T-linkage	4.03	8.37	10.86	6.84	14.59	1.07	3.69	0.94	18.31	9.30
	(11.25)	(20.86)	(12.19)	(9.03)	(10.92)	(14.97)	(29.38)	(13.18)	(14.16)	(32.54)
HVF	**1.40**	**8.13**	**10.68**	**3.26**	**9.76**	**0.46**	**3.48**	**0.78**	**16.43**	**5.17**
	(1.05)	**(0.83)**	**(1.06)**	**(0.74)**	**(1.14)**	**(1.25)**	**(1.83)**	**(0.84)**	**(0.99)**	**(2.47)**

3.3 Two-View Based Motion Segmentation

For two-view based motion segmentation, we evaluate the competing methods on 8 pairs of images in the AdelaideRMF dataset. The segmentation results for 4 data and the performance for the 8 data are respectively shown in Fig. 5 and Table 2. As we can see, the proposed HVF achieves the fastest computational speed in all the 8 data among the five competing methods, the lowest fitting errors in 6 out of the 8 data, and the second lowest fitting errors in the "Biscuit-book" and "Cubechips" data (still close to the lowest fitting errors obtained by T-linkage, which clusters all the data points with slightly higher clustering precision, but consumes much more computational cost). KF and AKSWH achieve unsatisfactory performance on some data. KF is prone to be disturbed by "bad" model hypotheses because it is difficult to generate sufficient clean subsets in the task of two-view based motion segmentation. AKSWH may wrongly remove "good" model hypotheses, which causes errors in the final estimation. J-linkage and T-linkage are based on the preference analysis, and thus the "bad" model hypotheses may affect the accuracy of the preference description and the final estimation. The improvement on speed obtained by the proposed HVF is remarkable compared with the other four methods, for the reason that the removal of "bad" model hypotheses and outliers accelerates the clustering. Specifically, the speed of HVF is at least equivalent to KF in the "Breadtoycar" or at most 15 times faster than T-linkage in the "Cubebreadtoychips".

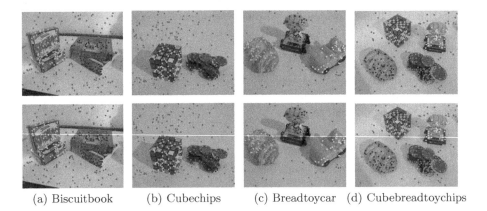

(a) Biscuitbook   (b) Cubechips   (c) Breadtoycar   (d) Cubebreadtoychips

Fig. 5. Some results obtained by HVF on 4 data for two-view based motion segmentation. The top row and the bottom row show the ground truth (i.e., Biscuitbook, Cubechips, Breadtoycar and Cubebreadtoychips) and the fitting results obtained by HVF, respectively. The red dots represent the outliers. Each of the other colors represents a model instance. (Color figure online)

Table 2. The average fitting errors (%) and the CPU time (in seconds) of HVF on 8 data for two-view based motion segmentation. The best results are boldfaces.

Data	Biscuitbook	Cubechips	Gamebiscuit	Breadtoy	Breadtoycar	Toycubecar	Breadcar-toychips	Cubebread-toychips
KF	13.60	29.35	15.76	22.17	47.87	27.63	39.38	51.19
	(2.70)	(4.23)	(3.03)	(1.97)	(1.48)	(2.09)	(3.61)	(4.20)
AKSWH	14.14	28.27	32.27	47.38	47.17	46.34	51.00	58.43
	(2.20)	(4.26)	(13.71)	(24.53)	(3.54)	(4.37)	(2.87)	(7.32)
J-linkage	2.54	16.01	16.98	7.81	27.69	19.68	28.59	26.21
	(5.66)	(11.52)	(15.36)	(3.05)	(4.15)	(7.69)	(4.42)	(12.20)
T-linkage	**1.69**	**4.70**	16.70	14.17	19.05	18.56	18.19	25.75
	(25.82)	(19.03)	(17.70)	(14.66)	(7.51)	(6.37)	(15.33)	(30.30)
HVF	2.05	6.41	**13.26**	**6.63**	**15.66**	**15.55**	**17.30**	**17.80**
	(1.44)	(1.29)	(1.30)	(1.50)	(1.09)	(1.02)	(1.48)	(2.00)

4 Conclusion

We propose a multiple-structure fitting method (HVF) based on a hierarchical voting scheme. The hierarchical voting scheme comprehensively utilizes both the consensus information of data points and the preference information of model hypotheses, to remove a large proportion of "bad" model hypotheses and gross outliers. Based on the hierarchical voting scheme, HVF is able to successfully estimate the number and the parameters of model instances simultaneously for multiple-structure data contaminated with a large number of outliers and noises. Especially, HVF can effectively select the model instances from the model hypotheses of uneven quality generated by random sampling with noticeable acceleration. This is because that the effective removal of "bad" model hypotheses and outliers. The experimental results have shown that HVF has significant superiority in robustness, accuracy and efficiency compared with several state-of-the-art fitting methods.

Acknowledgments. This work was supported by the National Natural Science Foundation of China under Grants U1605252, 61472334, and 61571379, by the National Key Research and Development Plan (Grant No. 2016YFC0801002), and by the Natural Science Foundation of Fujian Province of China under Grant 2017J01127.

References

1. Wang, H., Chin, T.J., Suter, D.: Simultaneously fitting and segmenting multiple-structure data with outliers. IEEE Trans. Pattern Anal. Mach. Intell. **34**(6), 1177–1192 (2012)
2. Magri, L., Fusiello, A.: T-linkage: a continuous relaxation of j-linkage for multi-model fitting. In: IEEE Conference on Computer Vision and Pattern Recognition, pp. 3954–3961 (2014)
3. Wang, H., Xiao, G., Yan, Y., Suter, D.: Mode-seeking on hypergraphs for robust geometric model fitting. In: IEEE International Conference on Computer Vision, pp. 2902–2910 (2015)

4. Magri, L., Fusiello, A.: Multiple model fitting as a set coverage problem. In: IEEE Conference on Computer Vision and Pattern Recognition, pp. 3318–3326 (2016)
5. Xiao, G., Wang, H., Yan, Y., Suter, D.: Superpixel-based two-view deterministic fitting for multiple-structure data. In: European Conference on Computer Vision, pp. 517–533 (2016)
6. Fischler, M.A., Bolles, R.C.: Random sample consensus: a paradigm for model fitting with applications to image analysis and automated cartography. Commun. ACM **24**(6), 381–395 (1981)
7. Torr, P.H.: Geometric motion segmentation and model selection. Philos. Trans. R. Soc. London A: Math. Phys. Eng. Sci. **356**(1740), 1321–1340 (1998)
8. Vincent, E., Laganire, R.: Detecting planar homographies in an image pair. In: International Symposium on Image and Signal Processing and Analysis, pp. 182–187 (2001)
9. Zuliani, M., Kenney, C.S., Manjunath, B.S.: The multi-RANSAC algorithm and its application to detect planar homographies. In: IEEE International Conference on Image Processing, pp. III-153 (2005)
10. Duda, R.O., Hart, P.E.: Use of the Hough transformation to detect lines and curves in pictures. Commun. ACM **15**(1), 11–15 (1972)
11. Xu, L., Oja, E., Kultanen, P.: A new curve detection method: Randomized Hough Transform (RHT). Pattern Recogn. Lett. **11**(5), 331–338 (1990)
12. Chin, T.J., Wang, H., Suter, D.: Robust fitting of multiple structures: the statistical learning approach. In: IEEE International Conference on Computer Vision, pp. 413–420 (2009)
13. Toldo, R., Fusiello, A.: Robust multiple structures estimation with J-linkage. In: European Conference on Computer Vision, pp. 537–547 (2008)
14. Tran, Q.H., Chin, T.J., Chojnacki, W., Suter, D.: Sampling minimal subsets with large spans for robust estimation. Int. J. Comput. Vis. **106**(1), 93–112 (2014)
15. Pham, T.T., Chin, T.J., Yu, J., Suter, D.: The random cluster model for robust geometric fitting. IEEE Trans. Pattern Anal. Mach. Intell. **36**(8), 1658–1671 (2014)
16. Wong, H.S., Chin, T.J., Yu, J., Suter, D.: Dynamic and hierarchical multi-structure geometric model fitting. In: IEEE International Conference on Computer Vision, pp. 1044–1051 (2011)
17. Chen, T.C., Chung, K.L.: An efficient randomized algorithm for detecting circles. Comput. Vis. Image Underst. **83**(2), 172–191 (2001)
18. Mittal, S., Anand, S., Meer, P.: Generalized projection-based M-estimator. IEEE Trans. Pattern Anal. Mach. Intell. **34**(12), 2351–2364 (2012)
19. Magri, L., Fusiello, A.: Robust multiple model fitting with preference analysis and low-rank approximation. In: British Machine Vision Conference, pp. 1–12 (2015)
20. Silverman, B.W.: Density Estimation for Statistics and Data Analysis. CRC Press, Boca Raton (1986)
21. Wand, M.P., Jones, M.C.: Kernel Smoothing. CRC Press, Boca Raton (1994)

Multi-kernel Hashing with Semantic Correlation Maximization for Cross-Modal Retrieval

Guangfei Yang, Huanghui Miao, Jun Tang, Dong Liang, and Nian Wang[✉]

School of Electronics and Information Engineering, Anhui University, Hefei, China
yanggfahu@163.com, miaohhahu@163.com, tangjunahu@163.com,
dliang@ahu.edu.cn, wangnianahu@126.com

Abstract. Cross-modal hashing aims to facilitate approximate nearest neighbor search by embedding multimedia data represented in high-dimensional space into a common low-dimensional Hamming space, which serves as a key part in multimedia retrieval. In recent years, kernel-based hashing methods have achieved impressive success in cross-modal hashing. Enlightened by this, we present a novel multiple kernel hashing method, where hash functions are learned in the kernelized space using a sequential optimization strategy. Experimental results on two benchmark datasets verify that the proposed method significantly outperforms some state-of-the-art methods.

Keywords: Cross-modal hashing · Multimedia retrieval
Kernel-based hashing · Multiple kernels

1 Introduction

Nowadays, the amount of multimedia data grows explosively with the rapid development of information technology, consequently making the hashing based approximate nearest neighbor (ANN) search technique in great demand. The basic idea of hashing methods is to embed original high-dimensional data into compact binary codes, which can lead to fast computation of Hamming distances by hardware accelerated bit-wise XOR operation.

Most previous hashing methods focused on single-modal data. One of the most well-known work is locality sensitive hashing (LSH) [3], which projects data samples from original feature space to Hamming feature space while preserving their similarity as much as possible. To achieve better retrieval performance, various extensions of LSH were proposed to design more compact hashing, such as PCA based hashing [14], manifold learning based hashing [7], and kernel learning based hashing [5,6,13,19]. Spectral Hashing (SH) [16] generates hash codes by thresholding a subset of eigenvectors of graph Laplacian constructed on data samples. Co-Regularized Hashing (CRH) [22] presents a boosted co-regularized framework to learn hashing functions for each bit. Supervised Hashing with Pseudo Labels (SHPL) [10] uses the cluster centers of training data to generate pseudo labels, which is utilized to enhance the discrimination of hash codes.

© Springer International Publishing AG 2017
Y. Zhao et al. (Eds.): ICIG 2017, Part I, LNCS 10666, pp. 23–34, 2017.
https://doi.org/10.1007/978-3-319-71607-7_3

Supervised Hashing with Kernels (KSH) [6] try to construct the hash functions by optimizing the code inner products.

These aforementioned methods are only applicable for single modality. However, most data in real-world applications are in the form of multiple modalities. For instance, a web page may contain both images and text and a YouTube video often has relevant tags. Consequently, more and more research interest has been devoted to cross-modal hashing. CMFH [2] was among the first to learn cross-modal hash functions using collective matrix factorization, and it aims to generate unified hash codes for each instance. In [20], Zhang and Li proposed an algorithm with linear-time complexity to learn hash functions, which can be used for large-scale data. Quantized Correlation Hashing (QCH) [17] aims to jointly learn binary codes learning and minimize the quantization loss. Kernelized Cross-Modal Hashing for Multimedia Retrieval (KCH) [11] maps data from different modalities into a common kernel space by canonical correlation analysis. Notably, multi-kernel learning has emerged as an effective approach to cross-modal hashing, as the utilization of multiple kernels can explore the complementary property of each single kernel. In [24], Zhou et al. proposed an kernelized cross-modal hashing algorithm embedded in boosting framework, but it only utilizes single kernel. Boosting Multi-kernel Locality-Sensitive Hashing (BMKLSH) [18] uses multi-kernel learning to produce hash codes, and the experimental results show its superiority over KLSH [5] based on single kernel learning.

Motivated by the great success of multi-kernel learning, we propose a supervised cross-modal hashing approach based on multi-kernel learning, which is named Multiple Kernel with Semantic Correlation Hashing (MKSH). Unlike the existing single-kernel methods [4,6,21,23], we aim to learn multi-kernel hash functions. Moreover, differing from the existing multi-kernel hashing approaches [15] that assign the same weight to each kernel in a brute-force way, we utilize an alternated optimization strategy to simultaneously learn the kernel combination coefficients and hash functions that can lead to higher retrieval accuracy. Our contributions are summarized as follows:

– We propose a novel cross-modal hashing algorithm utilizing multi-kernel learning.
– In order to find the optimal allocation of different kernels, we propose an iterative method to solve the objective function.
– To further enhance the algorithm performance, we utilize a sequential strategy to learn hash functions.

2   Proposed Algorithm

In this section, we detail the procedure of our hashing approach. Let $O = \{o_i\}_{i=1}^n$ denote a set of multi-view samples and $\mathbf{X} = \{x_i\}_{i=1}^n$, $\mathbf{Y} = \{y_j\}_{j=1}^n$ represent two different views of O, where $\mathbf{X} \in \Re^{d_x}$ and $\mathbf{Y} \in \Re^{d_y}$. The goal of MKSH is to learn two hash functions for each modality respectively: $f(x) = \left[f_{(1)}(x), f_{(2)}(x), \ldots, f_{(k)}(x)\right] : \Re^{d_x} \rightarrow \{-1, 1\}^k$ and $g(y) =$

$\left[g_{(1)}(y), g_{(2)}(y), \ldots, g_{(k)}(y) \right]$: $\Re^{d_y} \rightarrow \{-1, 1\}^k$, where k denotes the length of hash codes.

2.1   Learning Hash Functions

We use multiple kernels to define the mapping function in each modality as:

$$\begin{cases} K(x_i) = \left[\mu_1 K_1(x_i^{(1)}) + \mu_2 K_2(x_i^{(2)}) \ldots \mu_M K_M(x_i^{(M)}) \right] \\ K(y_j) = \left[\mu_1 K_1(y_j^{(1)}) + \mu_2 K_2(y_j^{(2)}) \ldots \mu_M K_M(y_j^{(M)}) \right] \end{cases} \quad (1)$$

where M indicates the number of kernels, and $K_M(x_i^{(M)})$ is defined as $K_M(x_i^{(M)}) = k_M(\bar{x}_i, x_j)$ $(K_M(y_j^{(M)}) = k_M(\bar{y}_i, y_j))$, and $\bar{x} \in \mathbf{X}$ $(\bar{y} \in \mathbf{Y})$ are landmarks. We can use clustering methods to obtain landmarks. Then we define a prediction function with kernel as follows:

$$p(x) = \sum_{j=1}^{m} K(x_j) w_j - b \quad (2)$$

where m is the number of landmarks, and $b \in \Re$ is the bias, $w_i \in \Re$ is the coefficient. As a fast alternative to the median, following [6], we set $b = \frac{1}{n} \sum_{i=1}^{n} \sum_{j=1}^{m} K(x_j) w_j$. Then we have:

$$\begin{aligned} p(x) &= \sum_{j=1}^{m} \left(K(x_j) - \frac{1}{n} \sum_{i=1}^{n} K(x_j) \right) w_j \\ &= \mathbf{W}^T K(x). \end{aligned} \quad (3)$$

The hashing functions are defined as follows:

$$\begin{cases} f(x) = \text{sgn}\left(\mathbf{W}_x^T K(x) \right) \\ g(y) = \text{sgn}\left(\mathbf{W}_y^T K(y) \right) \end{cases} \quad (4)$$

where $\text{sgn}(u)$ is set to 1 if $u > 0$, otherwise -1, and $\mathbf{W}_x \in \Re^{d_x \times k}$ represent the projection matrices. We utilize the cosine similarity between the semantic label vectors to construct the pairwise semantic similarity $\tilde{\mathbf{S}}_{ij}$, where $\tilde{\mathbf{S}}_{ij} = (l_i \cdot l_j)/(\|l_i\|_2 \|l_j\|_2)$, l_i and l_j are label vectors. We also use L to store label information, with $L_{ij} = l_{i,j}/\|l_i\|_2$, where L_{ij} denotes the element at the ith row and the jth column in the matrix $\mathbf{L}$, then we write $\tilde{\mathbf{S}}_{ij} = \mathbf{L} * \mathbf{L}^T$, finally, we perform element wise linear transformation on $\tilde{\mathbf{S}}_{ij}$ to get semantic similarity matrix $\mathbf{S}_{ij}$ as follows:

$$\mathbf{S}_{ij} = 2\mathbf{L} * \mathbf{L}^T - 1_n 1_n^T. \quad (5)$$

where $\mathbf{S}_{ij} \in [-1, 1]$ is the semantic similarity matrix, and $\mathbf{1}_n$ is an all-one column vector. Then we define the objective function minimizing the squared error as follows:

$$\min_{f,g} \sum_{i,j} \left(f(x_i)^T g(y_j) - \mathbf{S}_{ij} \right)^2 \tag{6}$$

Eq. (6) can be rewritten as:

$$\min_{\mathbf{W}_x, \mathbf{W}_y} \left\| \operatorname{sgn} \left(K(x)\mathbf{W}_x \right) \operatorname{sgn} \left(K(y)\mathbf{W}_y \right)^T - \mathbf{S}_{ij} \right\|_F^2. \tag{7}$$

2.2 Learning Projection Matrices

The problem described in Eq. (7) is NP hard. However, we can use spectral relaxation to obtain a close-formed solution. We rewrite Eq. 7 as follows:

$$\min_{\mathbf{W}_x, \mathbf{W}_y} \left\| K(x)\mathbf{W}_x \left(K(y)\mathbf{W}_y \right)^T - \mathbf{S}_{ij} \right\|_F^2 \tag{8}$$

$$s.t. \quad \begin{cases} \mathbf{W}_x^T K(x)^T K(x)\mathbf{W}_x = n\mathbf{I}_c \\ \mathbf{W}_y^T K(y)^T K(y)\mathbf{W}_y = n\mathbf{I}_c \end{cases}$$

Removing the constant, then we have:

$$\max_{\mathbf{W}_x, \mathbf{W}_y} tr \left(\mathbf{W}_x^T K(x)^T \mathbf{S}_{ij} K(y)\mathbf{W}_y \right) \tag{9}$$

$$s.t. \quad \begin{cases} \mathbf{W}_x^T K(x)^T K(x)\mathbf{W}_x = n\mathbf{I}_c \\ \mathbf{W}_y^T K(y)^T K(y)\mathbf{W}_y = n\mathbf{I}_c \end{cases}$$

In Eq. (9), $\mathbf{I}_c$ denotes an identity matrix of size $c \times c$, the term $K(x)^T SK(y)$ can be regarded as to weigh the relationship between two different modalities. If we define $C_{xy} = K(x)^T SK(y)$ and $C_{xx} = K(x)^T SK(x)$ and $C_{yy} = K(y)^T SK(y)$, then the problem (9) can be viewed as a generalized eigenvalue problem. Consequently, we can get the optimal value of W_x and W_y by eigen-decomposition.

Some literatures have experimentally verified that orthogonal constraints are helpless to produce discriminative hash codes [14]. Following the idea in [20], we turn to use a sequential optimization strategy to learn hash functions. Suppose that the latter projection is related to the former, we solve hashing functions by defining a residue. The residue matrix $\mathbf{V}_t$ is denoted by:

$$\mathbf{V}_t = \mathbf{S} - \sum_{k=1}^{t-1} \operatorname{sgn} \left(K(x)\mathbf{W}_x^{(k)} \right) \operatorname{sgn} \left(K(y)\mathbf{W}_y^{(k)} \right)^T \tag{10}$$

Algorithm 1. Sequential Learning Algorithm for MKSH

Require: The kernel matrices in different views $K_m(x), K_m(y), m = 1, \ldots M$ and the similarity matrix **S**.

Ensure: The kernel weights vector μ, the projection matrices $\mathbf{W}_x$ and $\mathbf{W}_y$.

1: Initialize μ with equal weights, and utilize Eq. (1) to calculate the initial kernel matrices $K(x)$ and $K(y)$.

2: **repeat**

3:   Update $\mathbf{W}_x, \mathbf{W}_y$ by Eq. (11).

4:   Update μ by Eq. (12).

5:   Update $K(x)$ and $K(y)$ according to Eq. (1).

6: **until** convergence.

7: $f(x) = \text{sgn}(\mathbf{W}_x^T K(x))$, $g(y) = \text{sgn}(\mathbf{W}_y^T K(y))$.

Then $\mathbf{C}_{xy}$ can be computed by:

$$\mathbf{C}_{xy}^t = K(x)^T \mathbf{V}_t K(y)$$

$$= K(x)^T \mathbf{S} K(y) - \sum_{k=1}^{t-1} K(x)^T \text{sgn}\left(K(x)\mathbf{W}_x^{(k)}\right) \text{sgn}\left(K(y)\mathbf{W}_y^{(k)}\right)^T K(y)$$

$$= \mathbf{C}_{xy}^{(t-1)} - K(x)^T \text{sgn}\left(K(x)\mathbf{W}_x^{(t-1)}\right) \text{sgn}\left(K(y)\mathbf{W}_y^{(t-1)}\right)^T K(y)$$

We rewrite Eq. (8) as follows:

$$\max_{\mathbf{W}_x, \mathbf{W}_y} \left\| \left(K(x)\mathbf{W}_x^{(t)}\right) \left(K(y)\mathbf{W}_y^{(t)}\right)^T - \mathbf{V}_t \right\|_F^2 \tag{11}$$

Once the optimal value of Eq. (11) is obtained we can get the projections of two modalities $\mathbf{W}_x$ and $\mathbf{W}_y$.

2.3   Optimizing the Weights of Multiple Kernels

The objective function is written as:

$$L(\mathbf{S}, \mathbf{W}_x, \mathbf{W}_y, \mu) = \frac{1}{2}\mu^T F \mu \tag{12}$$

$$s.t. \quad \sum_{m=1}^{M} \mu_m = 1, \mu_m \geqslant 0$$

where $F = tr\left(\mathbf{W}_x^T K(x)^T \mathbf{S} K(y) \mathbf{W}_y\right)$. If $\mathbf{W}_x$ and $\mathbf{W}_y$ are available, Eq. (12) can be regarded as a quadratic programming problem.

The overall algorithm is summarized in Algorithm 1.

3   Experiments

In this section, we conduct experiments on two benchmark datasets to verify the effectiveness of our approach.

3.1 Datasets

The used datasets are the Wiki dataset [8] and the NUS-WIDE dataset [1].

The Wiki dataset contains 2866 image-text pairs. Each image is represented by a SIFT feature vector with 1000-dimensional Bag-of-Visual-Words SIFT histogram, and each text is represented by an index vector of the top 5000 most frequent tags. There are 10 categories in the Wiki dataset.

The NUS-WIDE dataset contains 269648 images collected from Flickr. Following the experimental protocol in [12], we choose a subset comprising the most frequently-used 10 classes. Each image is represented by a 500-dimensional bag-of-visual-words SIFT histogram, and each text is represented by a Bag-of-Words feature vector with top 1000 most frequent tags. In the subset, we randomly choose 5000 image-tag pairs as the training set, and randomly choose 1866 image-text pairs from the remaining documents as the test set. Table 1 shows the details of the evaluated datasets in our experiments.

Table 1. The details of the evaluated datasets

Dataset	Wiki	NUS-WIDE
Image modality	BoVW(1000-D)	BoVW(500-D)
Text modality	BoW(5000-D)	BoW(1000-D)
Dataset size	2866	186577
Training set size	2173	5000
Testing set size	693	1866
Num. of categories	10	10

3.2 Experimental Setup

We perform two cross-modal retrieval tasks on the NUS-WIDE and the Wiki datasets respectively, i.e., 'img to text' and 'text to img'. We compare MKSH to six state-of-the-art cross-modal hashing methods, i.e., LCMH [25], LSSH [23], SCM-Seq [20], CMFH [2], RCMH [9], and KSH-CV [24]. We employ the mean Average Precision (mAP) to evaluate the retrieval performance. The average precision is defined as: $AP = \frac{1}{N}\sum_{i=1}^{R} P(i) \times \delta(i)$, where $P(i)$ means the retrieval accuracy of top i retrieved documents, and $\delta(i)$ is an indicator function, if the i-th rank is a relevant instance, $\delta(i) = 1$, otherwise $\delta(i) = 0$. N is the number of relevant instances in the training set.

In our experiment, we choose the Gaussian RBF kernel $K(x,y) = \exp(-\frac{\|x-y\|^2}{2\varepsilon^2})$, the sigmoid kernel $K(x,y) = tanh(\alpha xy + c)$ and the exponential kernel $K(x,y) = \exp(-\frac{\|x-y\|}{2\lambda^2})$ as kernel functions, and set $R = 50$.

3.3   Experimental Results

We compare the mAP values of all the methods on the Wiki and NUS-WIDE datasets, and the code length ranges from 16 to 64. The detailed results are reported in Tables 2 and 3. Figure 1 shows the precision-recall curves of two query tasks on the Wiki dataset. We also compare the performance of our method using multiple kernels and single kernel respectively, and the results are plotted in Figs. 2 and 3.

Table 2. mAP results on Wiki dataset.

Task	Methods	Hash code length			
		16 bits	32 bits	48 bits	64 bits
Img to text	LCMH	0.1166	0.1354	0.1440	0.1489
	LSSH	0.1959	0.1801	0.1854	0.1821
	SCM-Seq	0.1837	0.1902	0.1751	0.1880
	CMFH	0.1627	0.1627	0.1626	0.1635
	RCMH	0.1584	0.1600	0.1603	0.1670
	KSH-CV	0.1674	0.1765	0.1718	0.1717
	MKSH	**0.2192**	**0.2125**	**0.2249**	**0.2161**
Text to img	LCMH	0.1296	0.1365	0.1378	0.1457
	LSSH	0.1625	0.1584	0.1524	0.1609
	SCM-Seq	0.1711	0.1708	0.1673	0.1705
	CMFH	0.1577	0.1580	0.1560	0.1561
	RCMH	0.1535	0.1572	0.1618	0.1571
	KSH-CV	0.1923	0.1901	0.1885	0.1825
	MKSH	**0.2048**	**0.2079**	**0.2184**	**0.2348**

We can draw two conclusions from the aforementioned experimental results. Firstly, MKSH outperforms the alternatives, which shows its superiority over the compared methods. Secondly, MKSH shows its consistent advantage when the length of hash codes become longer, which can be owed to its sequential optimization strategy.

From Fig. 1 we also have two observations. Firstly, MKSH outperforms the compared methods. Secondly, we can find that RCMH and LCMH are not applicable for large-scale cross-modal retrieval due to their poor performance.

3.4   Parameters Sensitivity Study

According to our experimental study, the four parameters, including ε, α, c and λ, have a slight influence on the performance, so we set $\varepsilon = 0.6$, $\alpha = 9$,

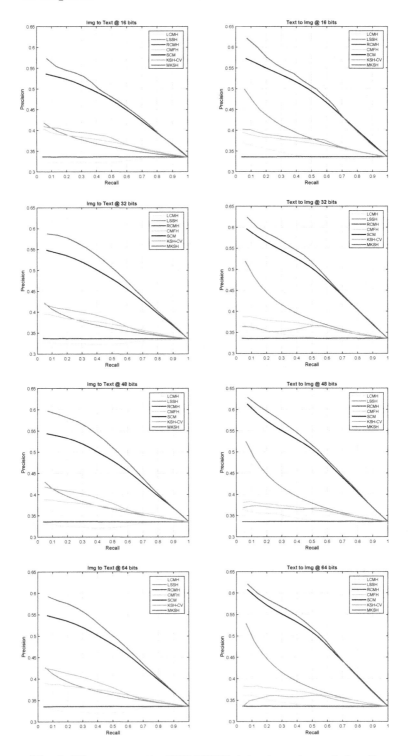

Fig. 1. PR-curves on the NUS-WIDE dataset varying code length

Table 3. mAP results on NUS-WIDE dataset.

Task	Methods	Hash code length			
		16bits	32bits	48bits	64bits
Img to text	LCMH	0.3376	0.3763	0.3783	0.3745
	LSSH	0.4746	0.4920	0.4903	0.4915
	SCM-Seq	0.5739	0.5941	0.5920	0.5962
	CMFH	0.4741	0.4886	0.4871	0.4853
	RCMH	0.3817	0.3820	0.3847	0.3817
	KSH-CV	0.4609	0.4678	0.4648	0.4692
	MKSH	**0.6075**	**0.6303**	**0.6537**	**0.6487**
Text to img	LCMH	0.4108	0.4183	0.3964	0.3877
	LSSH	0.5827	0.6142	0.6125	0.6119
	SCM-Seq	0.6159	0.6501	0.6668	0.6658
	CMFH	0.4636	0.4781	0.4839	0.4884
	RCMH	0.3822	0.3835	0.3806	0.3807
	KSH-CV	0.4220	0.4177	0.4111	0.4022
	MKSH	**0.6890**	**0.7003**	**0.7135**	**0.6684**

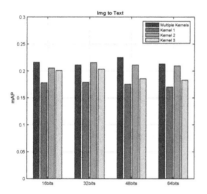 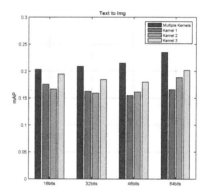

Fig. 2. Compare mAP on multiple kernels and single kernels (Wiki)

$c = -0.1$ and $\lambda = 0.8$. The generation of the kernel matrix depends on the number of landmarks. Figure 4 shows the performance when varying the number of landmarks on the WIKI and NUS-WIDE datasets respectively. We can observe that the precision almost remain the same with the variation of the number of landmarks. Therefore, we can learn that the number of landmarks is not a sensitive parameter.

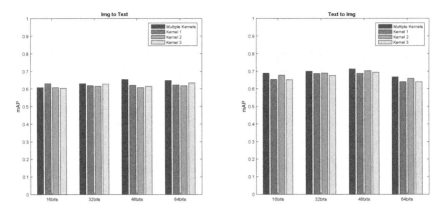

Fig. 3. Compare mAP on multiple kernels and single kernels (NUS-WIDE)

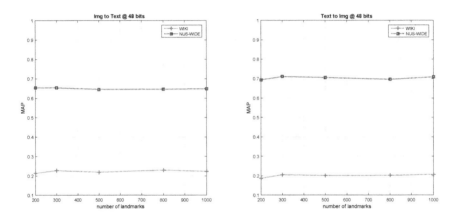

Fig. 4. The effect of landmarks on MKSH

4   Conclusions

In this paper, we have proposed a novel algorithm for cross-modal hashing named MKSH. Multi-kernel learning and a sequential optimization strategy are used to achieve better performance. Experimental results on the Wiki and the NUS-WIDE datasets show that our method outperforms several state-of-the-art methods.

Acknowledgements. This work is supported by the Key Projects of Outstanding Youth Talent Support Program of Anhui Provincial Universities under Grant gxyqZD2016012, and the Natural Science Foundation of China under Grant 61672032.

References

1. Chua, T.S., Tang, J., Hong, R., Li, H., Luo, Z., Zheng, Y.: NUS-WIDE: a real-world web image database from national university of Singapore. In: Proceedings of the ACM International Conference on Image and Video Retrieval, p. 48. ACM (2009)
2. Ding, G., Guo, Y., Zhou, J.: Collective matrix factorization hashing for multimodal data. In: Proceedings of the IEEE Conference on Computer Vision and Pattern Recognition, pp. 2075–2082 (2014)
3. Gan, J., Feng, J., Fang, Q., Ng, W.: Locality-sensitive hashing scheme based on dynamic collision counting. In: Proceedings of the 2012 ACM SIGMOD International Conference on Management of Data, pp. 541–552. ACM (2012)
4. Jiang, K., Que, Q., Kulis, B.: Revisiting kernelized locality-sensitive hashing for improved large-scale image retrieval. In: Computer Vision and Pattern Recognition, pp. 4933–4941 (2014)
5. Kulis, B., Grauman, K.: Kernelized locality-sensitive hashing for scalable image search. In: 2009 IEEE 12th International Conference on Computer Vision, pp. 2130–2137. IEEE (2009)
6. Liu, W., Wang, J., Ji, R., Jiang, Y.G., Chang, S.F.: Supervised hashing with kernels. In: 2012 IEEE Conference on Computer Vision and Pattern Recognition (CVPR), pp. 2074–2081. IEEE (2012)
7. Liu, W., Wang, J., Kumar, S., Chang, S.F.: Hashing with graphs. In: Proceedings of the 28th International Conference on Machine Learning (ICML 2011), pp. 1–8 (2011)
8. Lu, X., Wu, F., Tang, S., Zhang, Z., He, X., Zhuang, Y.: A low rank structural large margin method for cross-modal ranking. In: International ACM SIGIR Conference on Research and Development in Information Retrieval, pp. 433–442 (2013)
9. Moran, S., Lavrenko, V.: Regularised cross-modal hashing. In: Proceedings of the 38th International ACM SIGIR Conference on Research and Development in Information Retrieval, pp. 907–910. ACM (2015)
10. Song, J., Gao, L., Yan, Y., Zhang, D., Sebe, N.: Supervised hashing with pseudo labels for scalable multimedia retrieval, pp. 827–830 (2015)
11. Tan, S., Hu, L., Wang-Xu, A., Tang, J., Jia, Z.: Kernelized cross-modal hashing for multimedia retrieval. In: 2016 12th World Congress on Intelligent Control and Automation (WCICA), pp. 1224–1228. IEEE (2016)
12. Tang, J., Wang, K., Shao, L.: Supervised matrix factorization hashing for cross-modal retrieval. IEEE Trans. Image Process. **25**(7), 3157–3166 (2016)
13. Tian, J., Liu, C., Li, Y.Q., Qin, B., Zha, Y.F.: Kernelized supervised context hashing. IET Image Process. **10**(12), 986–995 (2016)
14. Wang, J., Kumar, S., Chang, S.F.: Semi-supervised hashing for scalable image retrieval. In: 2010 IEEE Conference on Computer Vision and Pattern Recognition (CVPR), pp. 3424–3431. IEEE (2010)
15. Wang, S., Jiang, S., Huang, Q., Tian, Q.: S3MKL: scalable semi-supervised multiple kernel learning for image data mining. In: Proceedings of the 18th ACM International Conference on Multimedia, pp. 163–172. ACM (2010)
16. Weiss, Y., Torralba, A., Fergus, R.: Spectral hashing. In: Advances in Neural Information Processing Systems, pp. 1753–1760 (2009)
17. Wu, B., Yang, Q., Zheng, W.S., Wang, Y., Wang, J.: Quantized correlation hashing for fast cross-modal search. In: IJCAI, pp. 3946–3952 (2015)

18. Xia, H., Wu, P., Hoi, S.C., Jin, R.: Boosting multi-kernel locality-sensitive hashing for scalable image retrieval. In: Proceedings of the 35th International ACM SIGIR Conference on Research and Development in Information Retrieval, pp. 55–64. ACM (2012)
19. Xie, B., Zheng, S.: Kernelized locality-sensitive hashing for semi-supervised agglomerative clustering. Comput. Sci. (2013)
20. Zhang, D., Li, W.J.: Large-scale supervised multimodal hashing with semantic correlation maximization. In: Twenty-Eighth AAAI Conference on Artificial Intelligence, pp. 2177–2183 (2014)
21. Zhang, Y., Lu, W., Liu, Y., Wu, F.: Kernelized sparse hashing for scalable image retrieval. Neurocomputing **172**(C), 207–214 (2016)
22. Zhen, Y., Yeung, D.Y.: Co-regularized hashing for multimodal data. In: Advances in Neural Information Processing Systems, pp. 1376–1384 (2012)
23. Zhou, J., Ding, G., Guo, Y.: Latent semantic sparse hashing for cross-modal similarity search. In: Proceedings of the 37th International ACM SIGIR Conference on Research & Development in Information Retrieval, pp. 415–424. ACM (2014)
24. Zhou, J., Ding, G., Guo, Y., Liu, Q., Dong, X.: Kernel-based supervised hashing for cross-view similarity search. In: 2014 IEEE International Conference on Multimedia and Expo (ICME), pp. 1–6. IEEE (2014)
25. Zhu, X., Huang, Z., Shen, H.T., Zhao, X.: Linear cross-modal hashing for efficient multimedia search. In: Proceedings of the 21st ACM International Conference on Multimedia, pp. 143–152. ACM (2013)

Preprocessing and Segmentation Algorithm for Multiple Overlapped Fiber Image

Xiaochun Chen[1], Yanbin Zhang[1,2(✉)], Shun Fu[1,3], Hu Peng[1,3], and Xiang Chen[3]

[1] Key Laboratory of EDA, Research Institute of Tsinghua University in Shenzhen,
Shenzhen 518057, China
zhangyanbin1990@live.com
[2] Harbin Institute of Technology (Shenzhen), Shenzhen 518055, China
[3] Sun Yat-sen University, Guangzhou 510275, China

Abstract. In the fiber image recognition system, pinpoint segmentation is critical for fiber feature extraction and further identification. In the case of fiber image taken by the optical microscope, the overlapped types are complicate which deteriorates the accuracy of segmentation. In order to get the concise and clear fiber contour curve for later process, a pretreatment method combined the curve fitting and complex domain filtering is designed in this paper. A novel technology for the concave points matching is also applied to the segmentation. The essence of the segmentation is to construct a virtual fiber boundary on the fiber contour which is obtained though the fiber image preprocessing approach presented in this article, the virtual boundary will connect the concave points to be matched so that the overlapped fibers are separated into independent individuals. Whether or not the virtual boundary is successfully restored is judged by the triangular area consisted of a given concave point, its precursor point (or subsequent point) and the target point, as well as the characteristic relationship between concave points in the bounded closed corners set of the fiber contour curves. The experimental result shows that the overlapped fibers can be segmented without changing any morphological parameter, and the fiber segmentation approach is suitable for complex scenes such as fiber adhesion or cross with each other and has a high segmentation accuracy.

Keywords: Concave points matching · Fiber image preprocessing
Overlapped fibers · Fiber segmentation

1 Introduction

The composition and content of fibers are important in the import and export trade of textiles or clothing products. In order to guarantee the quality of products and protect the interests of consumers, the composition and content of fibers need to be strictly controlled. The longitudinal and cross-sectional features are important parameters for the automatic identification of different types of fibers [1, 2]. These indicators are often depended on the precise measurement of single fiber. However, multiple overlapped or adhesive fibers are often found in the practical application scenarios, which brings the

© Springer International Publishing AG 2017
Y. Zhao et al. (Eds.): ICIG 2017, Part I, LNCS 10666, pp. 35–47, 2017.
https://doi.org/10.1007/978-3-319-71607-7_4

difficulty to the extraction of the key parameters of the fibers. So it is necessary to study how to segment the overlapped fibers [3, 4].

The traditional method of fiber image segmentation has morphological image processing [5], watershed transform [6] and separation method based on branch slope at each intersection [7]. The morphology method obtains the contour curve of fibers by means of dilation and erosion, but the number of times needs to be specified manually, resulting in the deformation of the contour in the fiber image. The watershed method is simple and accurate, but it is too sensitive to noise and often produces serious over-segmentation results. The method based on the cross-branch slope is to match edges with similar slope, but the correctness will significantly reduce when the number of cross fibers is high. As a result, these methods are not practical in the actual application scenario.

Researchers have found that human vision has the ability to quickly search for a target of interest. If the target fiber can be accurately positioned during the pretreatment process, the interference of the image background can be reduced when extracting the fiber contour. Based on the significance theory [9], the image pretreatment method is proposed to extract the fiber contour curves. The second stage of this methodology is to detect the corners on the curves and locate the concave points in the corners set. The third stage is the matching process advanced in the paper with concave points obtained from the second stage. The final stage is to segment the overlapped fibers using the matching points. In this stage, we also perform comprehensive experiments using different types of overlapped fibers to demonstrate the usefulness of our approach and its generalization power.

2 Fiber Image Preprocessing

When the system receives the fiber grayscale images, the gray level of the edge contour is similar to that of the background noise, causing the contour of the fibers discontinuous. For avoiding the digital error and noise effects, the fiber images have to be denoised [8] before extracting the fiber contour.

As discussed in the introduction, the common methods of image preprocessing cannot clear up noise completely, so it is not trivial to distill the clear fiber contour curve. In order to achieve the purpose of getting the clear and accurate fiber target, the B-spline curve fitting and complex domain nonlinear anisotropic diffusion process are used here to obtain the edge of fiber image.

2.1 Target Fiber Protrusion Method by Visual Significance Theory

In this section, the B-spline surface fitting method is used to obtain the closed background of the image [10, 11], then subtract the fitting background from the original fiber image to obtain the target fiber image, this process also can solve the image illumination unevenness. B-spline function has the advantages of good smoothness after fitting and has a high fitting precision, thus is often applied for surface fitting. Considering the practical problems such as the timeliness and calculation of the algorithm, the cubic B-spline function is usually chosen. The cubic B-spline function is widely used because of its low computational cost and good stability when fitting the surface. Therefore, under the constraint of the least squares criterion, the cubic B-spline surface is used to fit the background.

The gray-scale fiber image of m * n size is represented as $G(x_i, y_j, z_i)$, $1 \leq i \leq m$, $1 \leq j \leq n$, $z_{ij} = z(x_i, y_i)$ is the gray value of the gray-scale image at the point (x_i, y_j). With interval π_u: $0 < u < 1$, π_v: $0 < v < 1$. For the sake of convenience, use $F_i(u)$ to denote $(m + 1)$ B-spline functions on π_u, $(n + 1)$ cubic B-spline functions on u are denoted by $F_j(v)$. As a result, the fitting background can be represented as follows:

$$S_{mn}: F(u, v) = \sum_{i=0}^{m+1} \sum_{j=0}^{n+1} F_i(u) F_j(v) P_{ij} \tag{1}$$

u, v is obtained by normalization. $P_{i,j}$ is the control of the vertex. $F_i(u)$ and $F_j(v)$ is the cubic B-spline base function, defined as:

$$F_i(X) = \frac{1}{N!} \sum_{k=0}^{N-i} (-1)^k C_{N+1}^k (X + N - i - k)^N, 0 \leq X \leq 1 \tag{2}$$

If we set $(m + 1) * (n + 1)$ control vertices and arrange them as a matrix of $(m + 1) * (n + 1)$ size, when $m = n = 3$, feature grid of the double cubic B-spline surface is constructed, and the corresponding matrix form of the formula (1) is expressed as:

$$S_{mn}: r(u, v) = UAPA^T V^T \tag{3}$$

where $U = [u^3, u^2, v, 1]$, $V = [v^3, v^2, v, 1]$,

$$A = \frac{1}{6} \begin{bmatrix} -1 & 3 & -3 & 1 \\ 3 & -6 & 3 & 0 \\ -3 & 0 & 3 & 0 \\ 1 & 4 & 1 & 0 \end{bmatrix}; P = \begin{bmatrix} P_{11} & P_{12} & P_{13} & P_{14} \\ P_{21} & P_{22} & P_{23} & P_{24} \\ P_{31} & P_{32} & P_{33} & P_{34} \\ P_{41} & P_{42} & P_{43} & P_{44} \end{bmatrix}$$

In order to control the fitting accuracy, use formula (4) to calculate the feature control vertices reversely. The least squares solution of $P_{i,j}$ is obtained as follows:

$$F_{obj} = \sum_{i=0}^{m+1} \sum_{j=0}^{n+1} |z(x_i, y_j) - r(u_i, v_j)| \tag{4}$$

Use the above formula for P derivative, and set it to zero. We can obtain the least squares solution of $P_{i,j}$, and finally get the image of the least squares fitting surface, that is the background of the image.

The presence of image noise reduces the image quality and affects the result of segmentation. The improved complex domain anisotropic diffusion filter [12, 13] not only has the ability to suppress noise, but also has a high edge detection accuracy.

With the Laplacian operator adjacent to the discrete, the processed image can be expressed as:

$$I_{i,j}^{t+1} = I_{i,j}^t + \lambda[c_N \cdot \partial_N I + c_S \cdot \partial_S I + c_E \cdot \partial_E I + c_W \cdot \partial_W I] \tag{5}$$

where $\lambda = 0.2$, $I_{i,j}^t$ is the original image, C_n, C_s, C_e, C_w are diffusion coefficients, the C(x) is expressed as: $C(x) = 1/(1 + (x/k)^2)$. Where x is the gradient of the image in all directions, k is the edge threshold. The image gradients in all directions is defined as:

$$\partial_N I_{i,j} = I_{i-1,j}^t - I_{i,j}^t, \ \partial_S I_{i,j} = I_{i+1,j}^t - I_{i,j}^t$$
$$\partial_E I_{i,j} = I_{i,j+1}^t - I_{i,j}^t, \ \partial_W I_{i,j} = I_{i,j-1}^t - I_{i,j}^t \tag{6}$$

In Eq. (6), α represents the difference operation of two pixels.

2.2 Contour Extraction of Target Fiber Image

After the B-spline surface fitting and diffusion treatment, a clear fiber structure can be obtained. In order to meet demand for subsequent corner extraction, the fiber must be morphologically operated [14]. The morphology process uses the Set Theory to analysis and research the image, mainly through the intersection and set operations between structural elements and images, so the selection of structural elements counts a great deal. The expansion of corrosion is applied to the fiber image, and then the noise in the image can be removed. At last, a perfect fiber binary image is obtained after morphological filling processing.

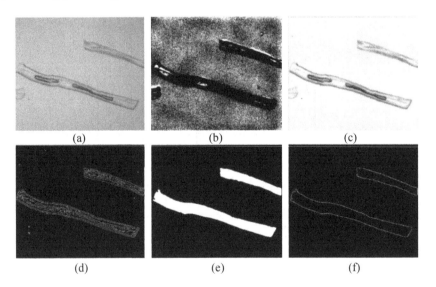

(a)   (b)   (c)

(d)   (e)   (f)

Fig. 1. Fiber image preprocessing. (a) Gray scale image; (b) fitting background; (c) clear fiber image after preprocessing; (d) edge detection of (c); (e) fiber binary image after morphological process; (f) binary image of fiber contours;

As is shown in Fig. 1(b), the fitting image background is obtained by processing Fig. 1(a) using double cubic B-spline surface fitting under the constraint of the least squares criterion [15] and the complex domain filtering method; Subtracting the fitting background from the original gray-scale fiber image, the target fiber image is obtained just as Fig. 1(c); the binary image of the target image is extracted shown in Fig. 1(d), then the mathematical morphology method and fiber internal filling are used to eliminate the false edge inside the fiber. After the above processing, the fiber binary image with smooth edge can be obtained shown in Fig. 1(e). In order to detect the corners in the binary fiber contour image is extracted from Fig. 1(e), as is shown in Fig. 1(f).

3   Concave Points Matching and Fiber Segmentation Algorithm

The connection locations produced by the crossed boundaries of fibers are often embodied in the form of concave points. There may be numerous concave points generated by two overlapped fibers, but the concave points only in the same fiber boundary can be used for fiber segmentation. In this paper, the features of concave points and the variation regulation of triangle area are used to find the matching concave points. These matching points are used to segment the overlapped fibers at last.

3.1   Extraction Method of Fiber Contour Concave Points

The points having the maximum bending degree on the curve also have the local maximum curvature, called contour corners. For a digital curve composed of pixels with integer coordinates, it is not easy to get the curvature of the points on the curve directly. To this end, we need to establish a mathematical method to calculate the discrete curvature of each corner point, the general process is as follows:

(1)   Select a suitable scale to measure the discrete curvature;
(2)   Design a measurement method of discrete curvature and calculate the discrete curvature of each point on the curve;
(3)   Determine the absolute value of the discrete curvature maxima;
(4)   Set a threshold, the point that has the curvature value beyond the threshold is recognized as a corner.

There are many contour corners detection algorithms [16–18]. Because of the advantages of low complexity and computational cost, K cosine curvature algorithm [19, 20] is used to detect the corner points on the contour curve. The t-th contour is expressed as:

$$L_t = \{P_t(x_i, y_i) | i = 1, 2, 3 \dots n\} \tag{7}$$

where n is the number of contour points on the t-th contour curve. For point $P_i(x_i, y_i)$, $P_{i-k}(x_{i-k}, y_{i-k})$ and $P_{i+k}(x_{i+k}, y_{i+k})$. The k-vectors at point P_i are define as:

$$\vec{\alpha}_i(k) = (x_{i+k} - x_i, y_{i+k} - y_i)$$
$$\vec{\beta}_i(k) = (x_{i-k} - x_i, y_{i-k} - y_i)$$

We compute the k-cosine, which is the cosine of the angle between the two k-vectors above, as follows:

$$C_i(k) = \cos \vartheta_i = \frac{\vec{\alpha}_i(k) \cdot \vec{\beta}_i(k)}{\left|\vec{\alpha}_i(k)\right|\left|\vec{\beta}_i(k)\right|} \tag{8}$$

The cosine of the angle between two vectors formed by P_i and all the points on both sides of P_i can be calculated through this method. The largest cosine can be selected from all the cosine values, which is named as C_{max} and the current K is denoted as K_M. Satisfy $C_{i+Km}(K)$ with the largest cosine value.

The points with curvature maxima should also have the local maximum of the cosine. The point with the cosine value over C_T will be regarded as the point of maximum curvature. In this paper, a point with a vector angle below 165° is regarded as a corner, namely the range of C_i should be [−0.9, 1) (Fig. 2).

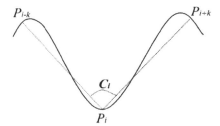

Fig. 2. The schematic of K-Cosine curvature algorithm

The corners in the fiber contour image includes concave points and convex points. Determination of concave points of corner points by vector angle method [21]. The vectors of P_i and P_{i-k} and P_{i+k} are shown in Fig. 3. P_i is the point which is located on the contour curve L, and takes the preceding P_{i-k} and succeeding P_{i+k} with a distance of k pixels from the point P_i.

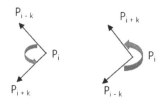

Fig. 3. The judgment of concave points

The pixels of the fiber contour stored in counter-clockwise direction in this paper, V_t is the threshold of the angle formed by the concave point with its preceding and succeeding point. If the angle formed from the vector P_iP_{i-k} along the anticlockwise direction to the vector P_iP_{i+k} is less than or equal to V_t, then the corner P_i is judged as a concave point, otherwise P_i is a judged as a convex point. All concave points on each region can be obtained by traversing all corners. Obviously, V_t should be set as $180°$ in this paper.

3.2 Concave Points Matching Method

Algorithm Implementation. From the above discussion and other features of the concave point of the overlapped fibers, the following steps are used to achieve the matching process:

(1) For the concave point P_i on the contour curve, firstly, its coordinate and serial number should be obtained on the contour curve, then point $P_j(i \neq j)$ and the following method is adopted to determine if P_i and P_j have the possibility of matching: If there are other corners between P_i and P_j, P_i and P_j may be the matching points and then we can use the next step for further judgement; Otherwise the matching is not successful, continue to match with the next concave point P_{j+1}.
(2) If the intermediate point on the curve of between P_i and P_j is inside the contour of the fiber, proceed to the next step. Otherwise, regard that the matching is not successful, continue to match with the next concave point.
(3) Using the area value of the triangular support region form by the concave point, its precursor point (subsequent point) and the target concave point to determine whether P_i and P_j are on the same fiber contour. The matched concave points are divided into two types of matching set. There are total four matching points for the overlapped fiber set, and two matching points for the adhesive fiber set.
(4) Examination: In order to prevent interference from other incoherent concave points, the matching points are placed in the same set in counterclockwise direction, and if the number of matching concave points in the set exceeds four, it means the error concave points are chosen and placed in. If the distance between the two concave points is far more than the distance among other two matching concave points, the matching concave points should also be removed.
(5) Repeat the above steps, all the concave points will be matched.

Algorithm Description. The intersection of two convex polygons in the plane is still a convex polygon, that is to say, the overlapped region of two fiber contours is a convex polygon, and the cross points in the vertex set is the concave point of the fiber contour. Since the contour curve between two adjacent concave points contains at least one convex polygon boundary, thereby there is at least one concave point between two adjacent concave points belonging to the same contour at the fiber overlapped region.

In the convex polygon, the midpoint of the two vertexs must be inside the polygon. Therefore, the midpoint of two matching concave points in the overlapped region is bounded to be inside the fiber contour curve.

The concave points are always located in the intersection of two contour curves. Take $P_i(x, y)$ as the current detecting point, $P_L(x_{j-m}, y_{j-m})$ is the precursor point of P_i. According to the order in which pixels are stored, in the same way, $P_R(x_{j+m}, y_{j+m})$ is the subsequent point of P_i.

The triangle $\triangle P_i P_L P_j$ is constructed by P_i, P_L and P_j, and the distance D_{IL} between P_i and P_L, the distance D_{IJ} between P_i and P_j, and the distance D_{JL} between P_L and P_j are calculated. The Helen formula is also used here to calculate the area of the triangle supporting region.

$$A = (D_{IL} + D_{IJ} + D_{JL})/2 \tag{9}$$

$$S_{iL} = \sqrt{A(A - D_{IL})(A - D_{IJ})(A - D_{JL})} \tag{10}$$

Obviously, when the area S_{iL} is closer to 0, indicating the connection line of P_i, P_L and P_j is closer to a straight line, in this case, P_i and P_j may be on the same contour. On the contrary, the larger the area S_{iL} is, the less likely P_i and P_j are on the same contour.

Similarly, we can make P_i, P_R and P_j form a triangle $\triangle P_i P_R P_j$, the calculation method of the area of the triangle is as follows:

$$S_{iR} = \sqrt{A(A - D_{IR})(A - D_{IJ})(A - D_{JR})} \tag{11}$$

the same method can be used to judge whether P_i or P_j is on the same contour or not. An experiment is carried out to illustrate the procedure just as Fig. 4.

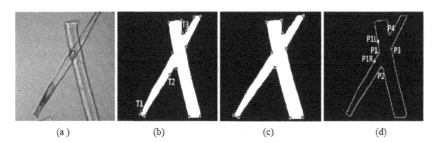

(a)   (b)   (c)   (d)

Fig. 4. Matching process of concave points. (a) The gray-scale fiber image; (b) the fiber binary image with false corners; (c) the fiber binary image after removing false corners; (d) fiber contour curve

The original fiber image is shown in Fig. 4(a), after the image preprocessing, the binarized fiber image is obtained. There are concave points, convex points, false concave points and false convex points in the binary image. Using the appropriate method to remove the false corner points, and then extract the edge of the fiber with a clear binary contour, as shown in Fig. 4(b)–(d).

In Fig. 4(d), the contour points P_1 and P_2 belong to the same fiber contour. On the left side of P_1, take the precursor point P_{1L}, and take the subsequent point P_{1R} on the other side of P_1. Using P_{1L}, P_1 and P_2 to form a triangle $\triangle P_1 P_{1L} P_2$, because of the three vertices are on the same fiber contour curve, the area of $\triangle P_1 P_{1L} P_2$ satisfy: $S_{1L} < T$,

Where T is the threshold. The area of the triangular formed by P_1, P_{1L} and P_3 are greater than the threshold T, denoting that they are not on the same side of contour curve. It can be seen that the introduction of P_{1L} let P_1 find its matching point P_2. Similarly, $\triangle P_1 P_{1R} P_4$ is constructed, so that P_1 can find its another matching point P_4. The area threshold is set here to find the points on the same line. In theory the smaller the better, 0 is an ideal value. However, the outline of the fiber boundaries may have a certain degree of distortion. The magnification of the fiber image used in this paper is 200 times, by means of a large number of testing, the threshold in this paper is set to about 15.

By way of the above algorithm, the matching point pair is obtained as: $\{P_1, P_2\}$, $\{P_1, P_4\}$, $\{P_2, P_3\}$, $\{P_3, P_4\}$. Then the segmentation method can be adopted to segment the overlapped fiber in the binary image, and finally get two independent fibers.

3.3 Fiber Image Segmentation Method Based on Concave Points Matching

In the previous section, the concave points in the binary fiber image has been matched. And the subsequent work is to separate the fiber image using the matching points.

Determine whether there is a crossed or adhesive set on the fiber contour. If it does not exist, it means that the fiber is independent one. After separation of individual fibers, there are only crossed or adhesive fibers left in the image.

Then the concave points are classified as cross and adhesive set. The adhesive fibers can be separated by the adhesive-typed matching points. After the completion of this step, there are only cross-typed fibers in the image. The segmentation of overlapped fiber of the cross-type is based on the four matching concave points in the intersection area. Draw lines between two adjacent points and we can segment the crossed fibers.

Figure 5 provides the separation process of two adhesive fibers. The preprocessing process of the image is same as Fig. 4 above. The concave points of two adhesive fibers can be detected by K-cosine curvature algorithm and the vector angle method, and then use the matching algorithm described in this article to verify whether they are matched to each other. Then use the segmentation method to segment the adhesive fibers, and finally get two independent fibers.

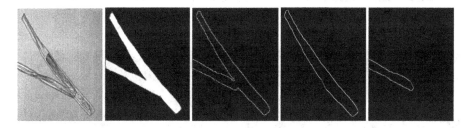

Fig. 5. The segmentation of adhesive fibers

4   Experimental Results

4.1   The Basic Morphology of Overlapped Fiber Images

The samples in this paper is provided by Shenzhen Entry-Exit Inspection and Quarantine Bureau. Each sample image contains more than two fibers. These fibers exist mainly in three ways: independent, crossed, or adhesive ones.

The independent fibers are easy to mark, but those overlapped fibers must be separated into individual ones before they are correctly marked. Figure 4 provides the basic morphology of crossed fiber image. After removing the noise and extracting the contour, the crossed position of the image includes four concave points. In order to restore the original outline shape of the two fibers, the concave points matching algorithms have to be used here. Figure 5 provides another basic morphology of adhesive fiber image. The adhesive position of the image includes two concave points.

4.2   Discussion of Matching and Segmentation Results

Figures 6 and 7 shows the segment process of more than two fibers. As the B-spline curve fitting and complex domain filtering is used, the clear contours are obtained here. Figure 6 contains three crossed fibers, with two crossed positions and eight concave points. The tests show that the fiber contours are extracted accurately based on the preprocessing algorithm described above and the concave points in this image are identified correctly. The individual fibers, obtained by the segmentation method after the matching process, are separated without any deformation.

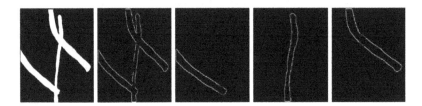

Fig. 6. Three fibers segmentation of the crossed type

Fig. 7. The fiber segmentation of the mixed type

Figure 7 shows the segmentation process of four fibers, one of which is a separate isolated fiber and the other three cross or adhere each other. For the isolated fiber, we can use the principle of connecting domain to identify it. For the other three overlapped fibers, use the algorithm described in this paper to find the matching points, and then through segmentation method to achieve image segmentation effect.

In order to test the effect of algorithm, some sample are used here. The fibers segmentation accuracy of the crossed type, adhesive type as well as the mixed type of cross and adhesion are calculated as Table 1. The crossed type of each sample only has two fibers and the adhesive type has two to four fibers. The number of mixed type of each sample range from three to seven.

Table 1. The fibers segmentation accuracy

Overlapped type	Numbers of samples	Result (%)
Crossed	25	100
Adhesive	35	82.86
Crossed and adhesive	50	76

4.3 Matching Error and Resolvent

In Fig. 7(a), there are actually five adherent fibers, but actually six fibers are separated. Due to the fact that the contours on both sides of two concave points (point 2 and point 8 in Fig. 7(c)) which should not match are similar. What's worse, they are also concentrated in a narrow area, causing the line connected by P_2, P_8 and their precursor point or subsequent point close to a straight line, resulting in matching error. At last, the number of fibers separated is greater than the actual number of fibers.

Figure 7(b) actually include five adherent fibers, but only four were separated. The reason for this is that the distance between the two concave points (P1, P4) is too long compared with the others. what's worse, the triangle area formed with the forward point (or the successor point) at point P_1 and the target point is too big in the process of concave points matching, resulting in the failure of the algorithm used in this paper (Fig. 8).

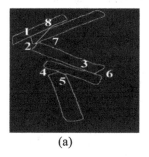 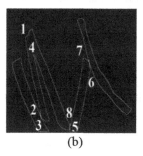

(a)   (b)

Fig. 8. False segmentation caused by matching errors. (a) Over-segmentation (b) under-segmentation

According to the algorithm of this paper, we can store the matching concave points in a counterclockwise order such as {left, right, right, upper}, we can obtain {P_1, P_2, P_7, P_8}. What's more, prohibits the separation of fibers from non-adjacent concave points, because P_1 and P_7 or P_2 and P_8 are not adjacent, they cannot be used for segmentation, so the problem in Fig. 7(a) is solved. The expansion process of the image preprocessing in Fig. 7(b) results in the small area being smoothed and filled so that the concave point feature is weakened. Therefore, in the image preprocessing, the number of times of mathematical morphology should be minimized when using B-spline to obtain the contour.

5   Conclusions and Perspectives

In this paper, we have presented a fiber segmentation method, which classified corners of the overlapped fiber image into concave points and convex points. By using the characteristic relationship between the concave points and the Helen formula to calculate the area of the triangle supporting region to judge whether two points are belonging to the same fiber contour. The experimental results show that the algorithm can resolve the problem that the multiple fibers are not easily separated and the inaccurate segmentation when multiple fibers crossed or adhered each other. The algorithm is not only suitable for extracting the concave points at the corresponding overlapped boundary in the fiber image, but also can realize the segmentation of the overlapped fibers by the matching algorithm.

The proposed image segmentation approach has been inspired by the corner property of fiber contours. As a result, this framework may be suitable for separating other Fibrous objects. An interesting topic is whether this framework could be used to distinguish different fiber kinds, e.g. cotton and fibrilia, or wool and cashmere. From the results of segmentation, the next step will make use of the separated fibers to measure the diameters or other important features. This will be investigated in the future.

Acknowledgments. The authors would like to thank the Science, Technology and Innovation Commission of Shenzhen Municipality (No. JCYJ20160429170032960) and Guangdong Province and Ministry of Education (No. 2012B091100495). The authors would also like to thank Shenzhen Entry-Exit Inspection and Quarantine Bureau Testing for providing the samples.

References

1. Zhao, X., Li, D., Yang, B.: An efficient and effective automatic recognition system for online recognition of foreign fibers in cotton. IEEE Access (99), 1 (2016)
2. Yang, C., Zhang, Z.: Research on image recognition method of foreign fibers in lint. In: IEEE ICACI, pp. 52–56 (2015)
3. Li, Y., Yan, W., Xin, L.: Segmentation of fiber image based on GVF snake model with clustering method. In: IEEE ICICTA, pp. 1182–1186 (2011)
4. Chen, L., Chen, X., Wang, S.: Foreign fiber image segmentation based on maximum entropy and genetic algorithm. J. Comput. Commun. 3(11), 1–7 (2015)
5. Peng, Q.: A novel algorithm for the extraction of machining areas based on morphological image processing. Int. J. Comput. Integr. Manuf. 28(12), 1350–1359 (2015)
6. Grau, V., Mewes, A., Alcaniz, M.: Improved watershed transform for medical image segmentation using prior information. IEEE Trans. Med. Imaging 23(4), 447–458 (2004)

7. Rizvandi, N.B., Pižurica, A., Philips, W.: Automatic individual detection and separation of multiple overlapped nematode worms using skeleton analysis. In: Campilho, A., Kamel, M. (eds.) ICIAR 2008. LNCS, vol. 5112, pp. 817–826. Springer, Heidelberg (2008). https://doi.org/10.1007/978-3-540-69812-8_81

8. Laparra, V., Gutiérrez, J.: Image denoising with kernels based on natural image relations. J. Mach. Learn. Res. **11**(1), 873–903 (2016)

9. Vikram, T., Tscherepanow, M., Wrede, B.: A saliency map based on sampling an image into random rectangular regions of interest. Pattern Recogn. **45**(9), 3114–3124 (2012)

10. Bharati, N., Khosla, A., Sood, N.: Image reconstruction using cubic B-Spline interpolation. In: IEEE INDICON, pp. 1–5 (2011)

11. Li, W., Xu, S., Zheng, J.: Target curvature driven fairing algorithm for planar cubic B-Spline curves. Comput. Aided Geom. Des. **21**(5), 499–513 (2004)

12. Liao, Z., Hu, S., Sun, D.: Enclosed laplacian operator of nonlinear anisotropic diffusion to preserve singularities and delete isolated points in image smoothing. Math. Problems Eng. **2011**(1024-123X), 34–35 (2011)

13. Qian, W., Liu, R.: The anisotropic diffusion methods based on the directions of the image feature. J. Image Graph. **11**(6), 818–822 (2006)

14. Rebhi, A., Abid, S., Fnaiech, F.: Fabric defect detection using local homogeneity and morphological image processing. In: IEEE IPAS, pp. 1–5 (2016)

15. Doranga, S., Wu, C.Q.: Parameter identification for nonlinear dynamic systems via multilinear least square estimation. In: Foss, G., Niezrecki, C. (eds.) Special Topics in Structural Dynamics. CPSEMS, vol. 6, pp. 169–182. Springer, Cham (2014). https://doi.org/10.1007/978-3-319-04729-4_14

16. Zhang, W., Wang, F., Zhu, L.: Corner detection using gabor filters. Iet Image Process. **8**(11), 639–646 (2014)

17. Liao, B., Xu, J., Sun, H., Chen, H.: Robust corner detection based on bilateral filter in direct curvature scale space. In: Tan, Y., Shi, Y., Buarque, F., Gelbukh, A., Das, S., Engelbrecht, A. (eds.) ICSI 2015. LNCS, vol. 9142, pp. 357–365. Springer, Cham (2015). https://doi.org/10.1007/978-3-319-20469-7_38

18. Awrangjeb, M., Lu, G.: Robust image corner detection based on the chord-to-point distance accumulation technique. IEEE Trans. Multimedia **10**(6), 1059–1072 (2008)

19. Rosenfeld, A., Johnston, E.: Angle detection on digital curves. IEEE Trans. Comput. **22**(9), 875–878 (1973)

20. Sun, T.: K-cosine corner detection. J. Comput. **3**(7), 16–22 (2008)

21. Liang, J.: Intelligent splitting in the chromosome domain. Pattern Recogn. **22**(5), 519–532 (1989)

Action Graph Decomposition Based on Sparse Coding

Wengang Feng[✉], Huawei Tian, Yanhui Xiao, Jianwei Ding,
and Yunqi Tang

School of Investigation and Anti-Terrorism,
People's Public Security University of China, Beijing 100038, China
fengwengang@ppsuc.edu.cn

Abstract. A video can be thought of as a visual document which may be represented from different dimensions such as frames, objects and other different levels of features. Action recognition is usually one of the most important and popular tasks, and requires the understanding of temporal and spatial cues in videos. What structures do the temporal relationships share in common inter- and intra-classes of actions? What is the best representation for those temporal relationships? We propose a new temporal relationship representation, called action graphs based on Laplacian matrices and Allen's temporal relationships. Recognition framework based on sparse coding, which also mimics human vision system to represent and infer knowledge. To our best knowledge, "action graphs" is put forward to represent the temporal relationships. we are the first using sparse graph coding for event analysis.

Keywords: Action graph · Sparse coding · Event analysis

1 Introduction

A video can be thought of as a visual document which may be represented from different dimensions such as frames, objects and other different levels of features. Since the proposal of corner points in 1980s, local features have been designed and applied in image and video analysis with great success for many tasks. For video activity analysis in real scenarios, it is crucial to explore beyond the simple use of local features. Two trends for action representation are becoming evident: (1) instead of using signal-level features for recognition, higher-level features [1] and/or semantics and attributes [2] become common choice of features; (2) the temporal/spatial relationship between features are attracting increasing attention and efforts [3, 4]. Both are efforts for analysis of activities in more complex settings.

With the prevalence of video-related applications across different domains such as surveillance, human machine interaction and movie narration, automatically analyzing video content has attracted attention from both research and industry. Action recognition is usually one of the most important and popular tasks, and requires the understanding of temporal and spatial cues in videos.

Efforts have been taken to build models for representation and inference for action recognition. Models at the early stage used local features, and achieved success under

© Springer International Publishing AG 2017
Y. Zhao et al. (Eds.): ICIG 2017, Part I, LNCS 10666, pp. 48–57, 2017.
https://doi.org/10.1007/978-3-319-71607-7_5

some specific conditions. To represent the actions in a video, many of them applied the bag-of-features scheme and neglected the spatial or temporal relationships between the local features. Since the same set of local features can represents different actions, this scheme is hard to handle complex scenarios.

Action recognition has put special emphasis on the representation of the spatial and temporal relationships between low-level or mid-level features. Graphical models are the choice for most work. Such models build a graph for higher-level or global action recognition based on lower-level features. Examples of such models include hidden Markov models, dynamic Bayesian networks among others. Recently, deep learning approaches construct a multi-layer graphical model to learn the representation from videos automatically, and achieve state-of-the-art performance.

Motivated by graphical models to preserve the structure of the signals, we propose an action graph-based sparse coding framework. Most models of sparse coding are based on a linear combination of dictionary signals to approximate the input, and the signals are usually n-dimensional vectors. Differing from traditional use, we apply sparse coding to action graphs, which are represented by n × n dimensional matrices. Such an extension keeps the spatio-temporal structure at the signal level, and the sparse coding problem still remains tractable and has effective solvers.

1.1   Sparse Coding for Visual Computing

Sparse coding and dictionary learning have attracted interests during the last decade, as reviewed in [5]. Originated from computational neuroscience, sparse coding is a class of algorithms for finding a small set of basis functions that capture higher-level features in the data, given only unlabeled data [6]. Since its introduction and promotion by Olshausen and Field [7], sparse coding has been applied into many fields such as image/video/audio classification, image annotation, object/speech recognition and many others.

Zhu et al. encode local 3D spatial-temporal gradient features with sparse codes for human action recognition [8]. [9] uses sparse coding for unusual events analysis in video by learning the dictionary and the codes without supervision. It is worth noting that all of these approaches use vectorized features as input without consideration on the structure information among the features. [10] combines the geometrical structure of the data into sparse coding framework, and achieves better performance in image classification and clustering. Further, [11] proposes tensor sparse coding for positive definite matrices as input features. This motivates this work by combining graph representation of actions [12] with sparse coding.

Differing from most existing research, the elementary objects of dictionary learning and sparse coding operations are graphs in our approach. More specifically, it is the graphs that describe the temporal relationships that comprise our mid-level features. Graphs have been used in the activity analysis in literature. Gaur et al. [13] proposed a "string of feature graphs" model to recognize complex activities in videos. The string of feature graphs (SFGs) describe the temporally ordered local feature points such as spatio-temporal interest points (STIPs) within a time window. Ta et al. [14] provide ad similar idea but using hyper-graphs to represent the spatio-temporal relationship of more than two STIPs. The recognition in both works is fulfilled by graph matching.

Using individual STIPs to construct the nodes can result in unstable graphs and performance. A study similar to ours is that of Brendel and Todorovic [15], who built a spatio-temporal graph based on segmented videos.

2 Action Graph from Dense Trajectories

In this section, we describe the construction of action graphs. Dense trajectories [16] are employed as low-level features from which we extract meaningful local action descriptors (referred to as actionlets hereafter). The action graphs describe the temporal relations between actionlets, and are used as features in the sparse coding framework in Sect. 2.3.

(a) Lifting   (b) Running

(c) Swimming   (d) Swinging

Fig. 1. Illustration on trajectory grouping based on spatio-temporal proximity

2.1 Grouping Dense Trajectories

The dense trajectories in [16] are extracted from multiple spatial scales based on dense optical field. Abrupt change and stationary trajectories are removed from the final results. For each trajectory, the descriptor combines trajectory shape, appearance (HoG), and motion (HoF and MBH) information. Therefore, the feature vector for a single trajectory is in the form of

$$Q = \left(S, HoG, HoF, MBH_x, MBH_y \right)$$

where $S = \frac{(\Delta P_q, \ldots, \Delta P_{q+L-1})}{\sum_{i=q}^{q+L-1} \|\Delta P_i\|}$ is the normalized shape vector, and its dimension L is the length of the trajectory. MBH is divided into MBH_x and MBH_y to describe the motion in x and y direction respectively.

The trajectories are clustered into groups based on their descriptors, and each group consists of spatio-temporally similar trajectories which characterize the motion of a particular object or its part. Given two trajectories q_1 and q_2, the distance between them is

$$d(q_1, q_2) = \frac{1}{L} d_S(q_1, q_2) \cdot \bar{d}_{spatial}(q_1, q_2) \cdot d_q(q_1, q_2)$$

where d_S is the Euclidean distance between the shape vectors of q_1 and q_2, $\bar{d}_{spatial}(q_1, q_2)$ is the mean spatial distance between corresponding trajectory points, and $d_q(q_1, q_2)$ indicates the temporal distance. Trajectories are grouped based on a graph clustering algorithm. Figure 1 shows examples of grouped trajectories with background motion removed for some sample videos.

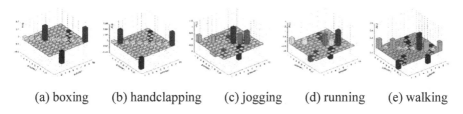

(a) boxing   (b) handclapping   (c) jogging   (d) running   (e) walking

Fig. 2. Laplacian matrix of action graphs for overlaps of five different actions in KTH dataset. The X and Y axes are different types of actionlets

The trajectories provide low level description to the action content in a video. A mean feature vector, $x_i \in R^d$, is obtained for all the trajectories in the same group. Because of the large motion variation even in the same type of actions, our model clusters these trajectory groups using K-means over $x_i \in R^d$'s to generate a set of prototypes of trajectory clusters, which describes different types of local actions.

2.2   Action Graphs

Based on the bag-of-groups representation, our model develops the statistical temporal relations between the "groups". We categorize Allen's temporal relationships into two classes: overlaps (O) and separates (S), and construct two types of action graphs. It is also possible too use the original thirteen relations to construct action graphs. Because the procedure is the same, we use the two categorized relations for simplicity.

For each type of action, the temporal relationship between pairs of group words is modelled by an action graph, which is a two-dimensional histogram. Each histogram shows the frequencies with which the relation is true between a pair of group words. That is, a temporal relation $R^i \in \{O, S\}$, $R^i(x, y)$ is the frequency of $xR^i y$ between two group words x and y. In our model, we construct the temporal relations for each type of action in a supervised manner. Figure 2 shows an example of overlaps for different actions in one testing dataset. It can be observed that different actions exhibit different histograms, and similar actions have similar histograms. Examining each of the histograms shows which temporal relation (such as overlaps for boxing) has a stronger response for some pairs of group words than the others. This implies the major relation between actionlets.

2.3   Action Graph Representation with Sparse Coding

Given actionlets and their temporal relationship, we precede here to present a sparse coding approach which is based on the temporal relationship graphs, and apply it for video action recognition. Let $Y = [y_1, \ldots, y_n] \in R^{d \times n}$ denote the data matrix of a video clip, where $y_i \in R^d$ denotes each actionlet descriptor. For the temporal relationships separate (S) and overlap (O), each is represented by an undirected action graph for this study. Therefore $K = 2$ action graphs $G_{k=1}^K$ are employed to cover all the cases using a 1-of-K coding scheme. If actionlets a_i and a_j has a temporal relationship R_k, then edge (a_i, a_j) exists in graph G_k. For each type of graph, sparse coding analysis is performed separately, and then the codes are combined to form the feature representation of a video clip for tasks such as classification.

In this section, we describe the Laplacian matrix of action graphs in Sect. 2.3.1, followed by discussion on sparse coding framework in Sects. 2.3.2 and 2.3.3.

2.3.1   Laplacian Matrix of Action Graphs

As representation of action graphs, the adjacency matrices are not an ideal choice to be adapted in a sparse coding framework. As shown in the following sections, symmetric positive definite matrices are desirable to compare action graphs and reduce the problem to a classic form. In this work, we use the Laplacian matrix, L, to represent the action graphs. This is mainly because the Laplacian matrix of a graph is always symmetric positive semi-definite (SPSD), i.e. $\forall y, y^T L y \geq 0$.

There exists an easy conversion between the Laplacian matrix of a graph and its adjacency or incidence matrix. For adjacency matrix A representation of action graphs, its Laplacian matrix $L = D - A$ where D is diagonal degree matrix. However, construction of Laplacian matrix from adjacency matrices only apply for simple graphs which are undirected without loops or multiple edges between two actionlets. Another way to obtain Laplacian matrix of a graph is through incidence matrices. Suppose $M_{|V| \times |E|}$ is the incidence matrix, then $L = MM^T$. For an undirected graph, we can use its oriented incidence matrix by arbitrarily defining an order of the actionlets; it is straightforward to get M and thus L for a directed graph. We use the incidence matrix of a graph to obtain its Laplacian matrix for further extension although we use undirected graphs in this work.

To make the matrices of action graphs strictly positive definite (SPD), we regularize the Laplacian matrices by adding a small multiple of the identity matrix. Without further explanation, all the action graphs below are represented by regularized Laplacian matrices, including the dictionary and the action graph to be approximated.

2.3.2 Sparse Coding for Action Graphs

Action graphs describe the temporal relationship among the actionlets, and each is represented by a Laplacian matrix. For each of the two relationships, we collect several action graphs from different videos of the same type. For example, graph O describes the "overlap" relationship between any two actionlets. If there exists a pair of actionlets a_i and a_j in a video whose time intervals overlap, then there is an edge between nodes a_i and a_j in the graph O, and the weight is the normalized frequency of a_iOa_j.

Given a set of video clips, an action graph A_i is constructed for each of them. For localization and precise detection purpose, A_i's are constructed from short clips or results after shot detection on an entire video. Let $D = \left[A_1, A_2, \ldots, A_p\right] \in R^{(n \times n) \times p}$ be the dictionary of the action graphs, and A_i be an $n \times n$ basis relationship, where n is the total number of actionlet types across different actions. For given videos, let $G = [G_1, G_2, \ldots, G_m] \in R^{(n \times n) \times m}$ be the action graphs extracted from them. Based on the dictionary, we decompose each graph G_i into the linear combination of the basis relationships

$$G_i \approx \hat{G}_i = s_{i1}A_1 + s_{i2}A_2 + \ldots + s_{ip}A_p \triangleq s_iD$$

where s_i is the coefficient vector for action graph G_i. Let $S = [S_1, S_2, \ldots, S_m]$ be the coefficient matrix for G.

The empirical loss function $l(G, S) = \sum_{i=1}^{m} d(G_i, s_iD)$ evaluates the decomposition error by representing G using S based on dictionary $D. d(\cdot, \cdot)$ measures the distortion of the approximation $\hat{G}_i$ to its original action graph G_i, which can be evaluated by the distance between two matrices. The objective function can then be formulated as in

$$\min_{S} \sum_{i=1}^{m} d(G_i, s_iD) + \beta \|S_i\|_1$$

where $\|\cdot\|_1$ denotes L_1 norm. $\|S_i\|_1$ is the sparsity term, and β is a parameter which trades off between the empirical loss and sparsity.

2.3.3 Distance Between Action Graphs

To evaluate the empirical loss, different distance metrics between action graphs, $d(\cdot, \cdot)$, could be used. Let S_{++}^n denote the set of symmetric positive definite (SPD) matrices.

Given $A, B \in S_{++}^n$, in this paper we use the Logdet divergence [67] as the distortion measurement because it results in a tractable convex optimization problem. The Logdet divergence between $A, B \in S_{++}^n$ is defined by

$$D_{ld}(A, B) = tr(AB^{-1}) - \log \det(AB^{-1}) - n$$

The Logdet is convex in A, and therefore A can be G_i which is the true action graph we need to estimate based on a sparse combination of the basis action graphs in the dictionary D. Following a similar procedure as in [120], we transform $D_{ld}(A, B)$ to convert into a known determinant maximization problem. The objective function becomes

$$\min_{S} \sum_{i=1}^{m} tr\left(s_i^Q \varepsilon\right) - \log \det\left(s_i \hat{D}\right), \quad s.t. \ s_i \geq 0, \ s_i \hat{D} \succ 0$$

where $\hat{D}$ is transformed dictionary tuned according to the action graph to approximate, G_i, i.e., $\hat{D} = \left[\hat{A}_j\right]_{j=1}^{p}$ with $\hat{A}_j = G_i^{-1/2} A_j G_i^{-1/2}$. ε is the vector of the traces of dictionary $\hat{D}: \varepsilon_i = tr\hat{A}_i + \beta$.

This is a convex optimization problem on $\{s_i | s_i D \succ 0\}$ known as max-det problem [17], which has an efficient interior-point solution. We use the cvx modeling framework 1 to get the optimal values for S.

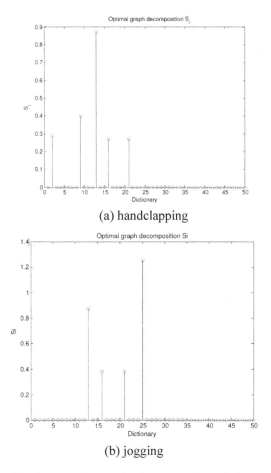

(a) handclapping

(b) jogging

Fig. 3. Plot of the optimal sparse coding solutions

Notice the sparseness of the coefficients.

2.4   Experimental Results

We use the KTH dataset to evaluate our approach. We split the videos of each category into training and testing, and build the dictionary D from the training dataset. Action graphs are constructed for each video, and we randomly select k ($p = Nk$, where N is the number of actions) action graphs from each category and assemble them to obtain the dictionary D. Therefore, the dictionary is in the form of

$$D = [A_{11}, \ldots, A_{1k}] \ldots, [A_{N1}, \ldots, A_{Nk}]$$

For any given video, its action graph is decomposed using the dictionary and represented by the decomposition coefficients, s_i. Figure. 3 shows two examples of the coefficients of two videos of different actions. For classification purpose, we get the maximum of decomposition coefficients of each category, a, and label the video with the category having the maximum coefficient as shown in the following equation:

$$a^* = \arg \max_a \{\max\{s_{ai}\}\}$$

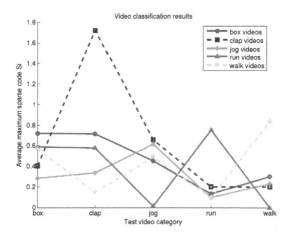

Fig. 4. Average sparse coding coefficients s_i for each category of videos

Figure 4 shows the result from sparse coding optimization. For each testing video of categories shown in x-axis, we take the maximum optimized coefficients sa^* for each category a, $a \in \{box, clap, jog, run, walk\}$, i.e. $sa^* = \max\{s_{a\cdot}\}$, and then average it over all the videos in the same category to obtain $[\bar{s}_a^*]$. Each vector $[\bar{s}_{box}^*, \ldots, \bar{s}_{walk}^*]$ corresponds to one curve in the figure. For each curve, we can see the peak of the coefficients is always consistent with its actual type of actions. Figure 5 shows the decomposition coefficients from some sample videos. The shaded cells denote that the corresponding videos do not have the maximum coefficient and thus will be misclassified.

action	box (s1)					clap (s2)				walk (s5)		
videos	V11	V12	V13	V14	V15	V21	V22	V23	V24	V51	V52	V53
max{s1}	0.83	0.68	0.68	0.74	0.68	0.34	0.72	0	0.57	0.62	0.55	0.55
max{s2}	0	0.63	0.63	1.69	0.63	2.64	1.08	1.88	1.27	0.45	0	0
max{s3}	0.66	0.37	0.37	0.51	0.37	0.38	0.58	1.18	0.49	0.54	0.54	0.4
max{s4}	0.13	0.14	0.14	0.13	0.14	0.01	0.29	0.25	0.26	0	0	0.29
max{s5}	0.89	0.17	0.17	0.12	0.17	0.19	0.07	0.43	0.11	0.85	1.43	0.23

action	jog (s3)						run (s4)					
videos	V31	V32	V33	V34	V35	V36	V41	V42	V43	V44	V45	V46
max{s1}	0.02	0	0.47	0.3	0.4	0.54	0.75	0.68	0.21	0	0.73	0.72
max{s2}	0	0.49	0.39	0.33	0.29	0.54	0.14	0.66	0.59	1.83	0.11	0.16
max{s3}	0.94	0.55	0.56	0.54	0.56	0.55	0	0	0.09	0	0	0
max{s4}	0	0.08	0.14	0.13	0.24	0	0.43	0	0.65	2.4	0.62	0.85
max{s5}	0	1.18	0	0.22	0	0	0	0	0	0	0	0

Fig. 5. The maximum coefficients from the sparse coding

3 Summary

We present a sparse coding approach to decompose action graphs for analysing activities in videos. The action in a video is characterized by an action graph, which describe the temporal relationships between different types of mid-level trajectory clusters. The use of graphs instead of vectors as features keeps better structure information about the components of actions. The difficulty with variation in graphs is handled by using tensor sparse coding.

Acknowledgement. This paper is supported by the National Natural Science Foundation of China (Grant Nos. 61501467, 61402484, 61503387 and 61503387).

References

1. Yuan, F., Xia, G.-S., Sahbi, H., Prinet, V.: Mid-level features and spatio-temporal context for activity recognition. Pattern Recogn. **45**(12), 4182–4191 (2012)
2. Liu, J., Kuipers, B., Savarese, S.: Recognizing human actions by attributes. In: IEEE Conference on Computer Vision and Pattern Recognition (CVPR), pp. 3337–3344 (2011)
3. Cheng, Y., Fan, Q., Pankanti, S., Choudhary, A.: Temporal sequence modeling for video event detection. In: 2014 IEEE Conference on Computer Vision and Pattern Recognition (CVPR), pp. 2235–2242 (2014)
4. Mikolov, T., Sutskever, I., Chen, K., Corrado, G.S., Dean, J.: Distributed representations of words and phrases and their compositionality. In: Advances in Neural Information Processing Systems, pp. 3111–3119 (2013)
5. Wright, J., Ma, Y., Mairal, J., Sapiro, G., Huang, T.S., Yan, S.: Sparse representation for computer vision and pattern recognition. Proc. IEEE **98**(6), 1031–1044 (2010)
6. Lee, H.: Unsupervised feature learning via sparse hierarchical representations, Ph.D. thesis, Stanford University (2010)
7. Olshausen, B.A., et al.: Emergence of simple-cell receptive field properties by learning a sparse code for natural images. Nature **381**(6583), 607–609 (1996)

8. Zhu, Y., Zhao, X., Fu, Y., Liu, Y.: Sparse coding on local spatial-temporal volumes for human action recognition. In: Kimmel, R., Klette, R., Sugimoto, A. (eds.) ACCV 2010. LNCS, vol. 6493, pp. 660–671. Springer, Heidelberg (2011). https://doi.org/10.1007/978-3-642-19309-5_51

9. Zhao, B., Fei-Fei, L., Xing, E.P.: Online detection of unusual events in videos via dynamic sparse coding. In: IEEE Conference on Computer Vision and Pattern Recognition (CVPR), pp. 3313–3320 (2011)

10. Zheng, M., Jiajun, B., Chen, C., Wang, C., Zhang, L., Qiu, G., Cai, D.: Graph regularized sparse coding for image representation. IEEE Trans. Image Process. **20**(5), 1327–1336 (2011)

11. Sivalingam, R., Boley, D., Morellas, V., Papanikolopoulos, N.: Tensor sparse coding for positive definite matrices. IEEE Trans. Pattern Anal. Mach. Intell. (TPAMI) **36**(3), 592–605 (2014)

12. Cheng, G., Wan, Y., Santiteerakul, W., Tang, S., Buckles, B.: Action recognition with temporal relationships. In: IEEE Conference on Computer Vision and Pattern Recognition Workshops (CVPRW), pp. 671–675 (2013)

13. Gaur, U., Zhu, Y., Song, B., Roy-Chowdhury, A.: A string of feature graphs model for recognition of complex activities in natural videos. In: IEEE International Conference on Computer Vision (ICCV), pp. 2595–2602 (2011)

14. Ta, A.P., Wolf, C., Lavoue, G., Baskurt, A.: Recognizing and localizing individual activities through graph matching. In: IEEE International Conference on Advanced Video and Signal Based Surveillance (AVSS), pp. 196–203 (2010)

15. Brendel, W., Todorovic, S.: Learning spatiotemporal graphs for human activities. In: IEEE Conference on Computer Vision and Pattern Recognition (CVPR), pp. 778–785 (2011)

16. Wang, H., Kläser, A., Schmid, C., Liu, C.L.: Action recognition by dense trajectories. In: IEEE Conference Computer Vision on Pattern Recognition (CVPR), pp. 3169–3176 (2011)

17. Vandenberghe, L., Boyd, S., Shaopo, W.: Determinant maximization with linear matrix inequality constraints. SIAM J. Matrix Anal. Appl. **19**(2), 499–533 (1998)

An Unsupervised Change Detection Approach for Remote Sensing Image Using Visual Attention Mechanism

Lin Wu[✉], Guanghua Feng, and Jiangtao Long

Chongqing Communication College, Chongqing, 400035, China
`wulin@buaa.edu.cn`

Abstract. In this paper, we propose a novel approach for unsupervised change detection by integrating visual attention mechanism which has the ability to find the real changes between two images. The approach starts by generating a difference image using the differential method. Subsequently, an entropy-based saliency map is generated in order to highlight the changed regions which are regarded as salient regions. Thirdly, a fusion image is generated using difference image and entropy-based saliency map. Finally, the K-means clustering algorithm is used to segment the fusion image into changed and unchanged classes. To demonstrate the effect of our approach, we compare it with the other four state-of-the-art change detection methods over two datasets, meanwhile extensive quantitative and qualitative analysis of the change detection results confirms the effectiveness of the proposed approach, showing its capability to consistently produce promising results on all the datasets without any priori assumptions.

Keywords: Change detection · Remote sensing image · Visual attention
Saliency map

1 Introduction

With the development of remote sensing technology, the land changes could now automatically be observed through multi-temporal remote sensing images. Within the past three decades, many change detection methods have been proposed, which could be categorized as either supervised or unsupervised according to the nature of data processing [1]. The former is not widely used because of the absence of ground truth; the latter is thus the focus of change detection study. Unsupervised change detection is a process that conducts a direct comparison of multi-temporal remote sensing images acquired on the same geographical area in order to identify changes that may have occurred [2, 3]. We briefly describe some typical and popular unsupervised methods as well as their limitations in the following.

In general, the widely used unsupervised change detection methods include image differencing [4], image rationing [5], image regression [6], change vector analysis (CVA) [7], etc. Only a single spectral band of the multi-spectral images is taken into account in image differencing, image rationing and image regression methods, while several spectral bands are used at each time in the CVA method. In spite of their relative simplicity and widespread usage, the aforementioned change detection methods exhibit

© Springer International Publishing AG 2017
Y. Zhao et al. (Eds.): ICIG 2017, Part I, LNCS 10666, pp. 58–69, 2017.
https://doi.org/10.1007/978-3-319-71607-7_6

a major limitation: the lack of automatic and non-heuristic techniques for the analysis of the difference image. In fact, in these methods, such an analysis is performed by thresholding the difference image according to empirical strategies [8] or manual trial-and-error procedures, which significantly affect the reliability and accuracy of the final change detection results.

As a result, Bruzzone and Prieto proposed two automatic change detection techniques based on the Bayesian theory in analyzing difference image [9]. The first technique, which is referred to as the expectation maximization (EM-based) approach, allows automatic selection of decision threshold for minimizing the overall change detection error under the assumption that the pixels in difference image are spatially independent. The second technique, which is referred to as the Markov random field (MRF-based) approach, analyzes the difference image by considering the spatial contextual information included in the neighborhood of each pixel. The EM-based approach parameter-free, whereas the MRF-based approach is parameter-dependent and the spatial contextual information may be affected in the change detection process. Another approach in [10] follows the similar way as in [9]. They analyze difference image in a pixel-by-pixel manner with a complex mathematical model. As the model is too complex, such approaches are not feasible in high resolution remote sensing images.

Afterwards, in [11], a multiscale-based change detection approach was proposed for difference image analysis, which is computed in spatial domain from multi-temporal images and decomposed using undecimated discrete wavelet transform (UDWT). For each pixel in difference image, a multiscale feature vector is extracted using the subbands of the UDWT decomposition and the difference image itself. The final change detection result is obtained by clustering the multiscale feature vectors using the k-means algorithm into two disjoint classes: changed and unchanged. This method, generally speaking, performs well, particularly on detecting adequate changes under strong noise contaminations. However, as it directly uses subbands from the UDWT decompositions, this approach has problems in detecting accurate boundaries between changed and unchanged regions. In addition, this method highly depends on the number of scales used in the UDWT decomposition. In [12], an unsupervised change detection approach which is based on fuzzy clustering approach and takes into account spatial correlation between neighboring pixels of the difference image was proposed. Two fuzzy clustering algorithms, namely fuzzy c-means (FCM) and Gustafson-Kessel clustering (GKC) algorithms have been used for classifying the pixels into changed and unchanged clusters. For clustering purpose, various image features are extracted using the neighborhood information of pixels. Hybridization of FCM and GKC with two other optimization techniques, genetic algorithm (GA) and simulated annealing (SA), is adopted to further enhance the change detection performance. The proposed approach does not require any priori knowledge of distributions of changed and unchanged pixels, but instead it is very sensitive to noise.

More recent studies not only focus on improving existing unsupervised change detection methods but also aim for proposing novel unsupervised change detection methods. In [13], an improved approach based on principal component analysis (PCA) and GA is proposed. It firstly applies the PCA to the difference image to enhance the change information and eliminate noise, subsequently computes significance index of each principal component for selecting the principal components which contain predominant change information based on Gaussian mixture model. Then the unsupervised change detection in PCA difference image is implemented and the resultant optimal binary change detection mask is obtained by minimizing a MSE-based fitness function using GA. This approach is applicable for unsupervised change detection in different types of remote sensing images without any priori assumptions. However, the convergence speed of GA in this work is too slow and therefore, unpractical. In [14], a novel approach for unsupervised change detection based on parallel binary particle swarm optimization (PBPSO) was proposed. This approach operates on a difference image, which is created by using a novel fusion algorithm on multi-temporal remote sensing images, by iteratively minimizing a cost function with PBPSO to produce a final binary change detection mask representing changed and unchanged pixels. Each BPSO of parallel instances is run on a separate processor and initialized with a different starting population representing a set of change detection masks. A communication strategy is applied to transmit data between BPSOs running in parallel. This approach takes the full advantage of parallel processing to improve both the convergence rate and change detection performance. However, the parallel processing using for change detection is expensive and therefore, unattractive.

Almost all the aforementioned unsupervised change detection methods suffer from one limitation listed as follows. Firstly, many methods highly depend on the priori assumption in modeling the difference image data, which limit the further improvement of change detection accuracy. Secondly, with the increase of the remote sensing data acquisition channels and the scope of remote sensing applications, the now available thresholding methods will be more arduous to establish suitable models or the clustering methods will be more sensitive to noise.

Consequently, within this paper, we aim to propose a general unsupervised change detection approach, which has strong adaptation and robustness with better change detection performance than the conventional unsupervised ones, by utilizing visual attention mechanism. It is generally known that human visual attention system has the ability to find the real changes between two images. In recent years, the research of visual attention model has been greatly developed in the field of computer vision and pattern recognition. By imitating human visual characteristic, the region of interest observed by human eye can be extracted from an image. In addition, the changed regions usually cover less than the unchanged ones for remote sensing image change detection. Thus, the changed regions can be regarded as salient regions and further highlighted by visual attention model, that motivates us to solve the change detection problem based on visual attention mechanism. We empirically test the effectiveness using two real-world multi-temporal remote sensing image datasets.

The remainder of this paper is organized as follows. Section 2 describes the proposed change detection approach. Section 3 provides some experimental results of the proposed approach and compares with some state-of-the-art change detection methods. Finally, this paper is concluded in Sect. 4.

2 Methodology

In this section, we first give an overview of the proposed change detection approach. Afterwards, the key steps of our approach will be described in detail.

2.1 An Overview of the Approach

The procedure of the proposed approach is illustrated in Fig. 1. To sum up, the proposed approach is separated into the following major steps: (1) Generating difference image; (2) Generating saliency map; (3) Generating entropy-based saliency map; (4) Generating fusion image; (5) Segmenting the fusion image. Among them, generating the saliency map and entropy-based saliency map are the core parts of our approach.

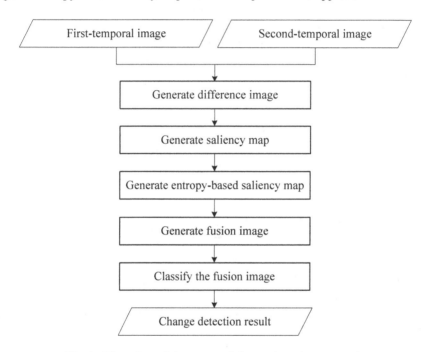

Fig. 1. Flow chart of the proposed change detection approach.

2.2 Key Steps of the Approach

Generating Difference Image. Suppose that there are multi-temporal remote sensing images $I_1 = \{I_1(i, j) | 1 \leq i \leq H, 1 \leq j \leq W\}$ and $I_2 = \{I_2(i, j) | 1 \leq i \leq H, 1 \leq j \leq W\}$ acquired on the same geographical area at two different timestamps t_1 and t_2 respectively, where H and W are height and width of both images, respectively. Then the difference image I_D can be formulated as,

$$I_D(i,j) = |I_1(i,j) - I_2(i,j)| \tag{1}$$

Generating Saliency Map. After generating the difference image, the frequency-tuned (FT) saliency region detection algorithm [15] is applied to the different image to generate saliency map. The FT algorithm computes saliency for image pixels using low level features of color and luminance in the Lab color space [16], which is easy to implement, fast, and provides full resolution saliency map. The resulting saliency map is better suited to salient object segmentation. The specific steps are shown as follows.

(1) The Gauss filter is utilized to smooth the difference image I_D which is generated in Eq. 1; the resulting image is denoted by I_G and formulated as,

$$I_G(i,j) = I_D(i,j) \otimes G \tag{2}$$

where $\otimes$ denotes convolution, G is Gauss filter operator. Within our experiments shown in Sect. 3, we choose G to be a 3×3 neighborhood.

(2) Convert image I_G from the RGB color space to the Lab color space, thus luminance feature L and color features a, b of each pixel are generated.

(3) Compute the mean value of features L, a and b, and the formulas are shown as follows,

$$\mu_L = \frac{1}{H \times W} \sum_{i=1}^{H} \sum_{j=1}^{W} L(i,j) \tag{3}$$

$$\mu_a = \frac{1}{H \times W} \sum_{i=1}^{H} \sum_{j=1}^{W} a(i,j) \tag{4}$$

$$\mu_b = \frac{1}{H \times W} \sum_{i=1}^{H} \sum_{j=1}^{W} b(i,j) \tag{5}$$

where μ_L is the mean value of feature L, μ_a is the mean value of feature a, μ_b is the mean value of feature b, respectively.

(4) Compute saliency value of a pixel in the Lab color space. Specifically, the saliency of a pixel is a distance metric between itself and the image and defined by using its luminance and color features contrast to all other pixels in the image, i.e.,

$$S_L(i,j) = \left(L(i,j) - \mu_L\right)^2 \tag{6}$$

$$S_a(i,j) = \left(a(i,j) - \mu_a\right)^2 \tag{7}$$

$$S_b(i,j) = \left(b(i,j) - \mu_b\right)^2 \tag{8}$$

where $S_L(i,j)$ is the saliency value at position (i,j) for luminance feature L, $S_a(i,j)$ is the saliency value at position (i,j) for color feature a, $S_b(i,j)$ is the saliency value at position (i,j) for color feature b, respectively.

(5) Normalize the saliency values of S_L, S_a and S_b, and the formulas are shown as follows,

$$S'_L = \frac{S_L - \min(S_L)}{\max(S_L) - \min(S_L)} \tag{9}$$

$$S'_a = \frac{S_a - \min(S_a)}{\max(S_a) - \min(S_a)} \tag{10}$$

$$S'_b = \frac{S_b - \min(S_b)}{\max(S_b) - \min(S_b)} \tag{11}$$

where S'_L, S'_a and S'_b are the normalization value of S_L, S_a and S_b, respectively.

(6) Compute the final saliency value of a pixel. Specifically, the final saliency of a pixel is a fusion value and defined as,

$$S(i,j) = \omega_L \times S'_L(i,j) + \omega_a \times S'_a(i,j) + \omega_b \times S'_b(i,j) \tag{12}$$

$$\omega_L + \omega_a + \omega_b = 1 \tag{13}$$

where $S(i, j)$ is the final saliency value at position (i, j) in the Lab color space; ω_L, ω_a and ω_b are weights of S'_L, S'_a and S'_b, respectively. Within our experiments shown in Sect. 3, the values of ω_L, ω_a and ω_b are 1/3. Thus, the saliency map is obtained and denoted by I_S.

The aforementioned approach of generating saliency map is no need to utilize down sampling. Thus, the size of the resulting saliency map is same to the size of the original image. Besides, this approach retains all spatial frequency information and the whole salient regions with much richer change information can be extracted.

Generating Entropy-Based Saliency Map. After generating the saliency map, our approach will compute local entropy of the saliency map, and the specific steps are shown as follows.

(1) Determine the size of local window. The width and height of this window are M and N, respectively. Within our experiments shown in Sect. 3, the size of local window is 5×5.

(2) Compute the gray distribution value of a pixel in saliency map according to the size of local window. The gray distribution value is denoted by p_{ij} and formulated as,

$$p_{ij} = I_S(i,j) / \sum_{i=1}^{M} \sum_{j=1}^{N} I_S(i,j) \tag{14}$$

where $I_S(i, j)$ is the gray value at position (i, j) in the saliency map.

(3) Compute the local entropy of a pixel in saliency map according to the size of local window. The local entropy is denoted by E and formulated as,

$$E = -\sum_{i=1}^{M}\sum_{j=1}^{N} p_{ij} \log p_{ij} \tag{15}$$

(4) For each pixel in the saliency map, compute its local entropy and the entropy-based saliency map denoted by I_E is obtained.

Generating Fusion Image. In order to generate a difference image with not only clear change regions but also much richer detail and edge information, in our approach, we generate a fusion image of the difference image I_D and entropy-based saliency map I_H using wavelet transform method. Wavelet transform is a multi-scale analysis method, which has the characteristics of time-frequency localization and multi-resolution, so it can be analyzed in time domain and frequency domain simultaneously [17]. The proposed fusion approach can reduce the correlation among different layers and obtain the desired fusion effect.

(1) Apply Mallat wavelet transform algorithm [18] to the difference image I_D and entropy-based saliency map I_H, respectively. Within our experiments shown in Sect. 3, the haar wavelet basis function is selected for 2-level wavelet transform. Suppose that F_1 and F_2 are mirror conjugate filters used for wavelet transform in our approach, n is the wavelet decomposition level, thus the wavelet decomposition can be formulated as,

$$\begin{cases} A_{j+1} = F_{1r}F_{1c}A_j \\ D^1_{j+1} = F_{1r}F_{2c}A_j \\ D^2_{j+1} = F_{2r}F_{1c}A_j \\ D^3_{j+1} = F_{2r}F_{2c}A_j \end{cases} \tag{16}$$

where $0 \le j \le n-1$; F_{1r} and F_{1c} are line and column components of mirror conjugate filter F_1; F_{2r} and F_{2c} are line and column components of mirror conjugate filter F_2; A_j is wavelet decomposition scale coefficient of the jth layer; A_{j+1} is wavelet decomposition scale coefficient of the $(j+1)$th layer; D^1_{j+1} is wavelet decomposition horizontal detail coefficient of the $(j+1)$th layer; D^2_{j+1} is wavelet decomposition column detail coefficient of the $(j+1)$th layer; D^3_{j+1} is wavelet decomposition diagonal detail coefficient of the $(j+1)$th layer. Most of all, A_0 is the original image.

(2) Generate a fusion image based on the aforementioned wavelet transform results. The weighted average method is used for scale coefficient fusion, i.e.,

$$A_n(I_F) = \alpha \times A_n(I_D) + (1-\alpha) \times A_n(I_E) \tag{17}$$

where $0 < \alpha < 1$ and the value of α is 0.70 within our experiments shown in Sect. 3; $A_n(I_F)$ is wavelet decomposition scale coefficient of the nth layer of the fusion image; $A_n(I_D)$ is wavelet decomposition scale coefficient of the nth layer of the difference image; $A_n(I_E)$ is wavelet decomposition scale coefficient of the nth layer of the entropy-based saliency map.

The detail coefficients of the entropy-based saliency map I_E are used for detail coefficients of the fusion image I_F, and the detail coefficients of the difference image I_D will not be considered.

(3) Generate the final fusion image by wavelet reconstruction which can be formulated as,

$$A_j = F_{1r}^* F_{1c}^* A_{j+1} + F_{1r}^* F_{2c}^* D_{j+1}^1 + F_{2r}^* F_{1c}^* D_{j+1}^2 + F_{2r}^* F_{2c}^* D_{j+1}^3 \tag{18}$$

where $0 \leq j \leq n - 1$; F_{1r}^*, F_{1c}^*, F_{2r}^* and F_{2c}^* are conjugate transpose matrix of F_{1r}, F_{1c}, F_{2r} and F_{2c}, respectively.

Segmenting Fusion Image. After generating the fusion image, we segment the fusion image into changed and unchanged classes by using K-means clustering algorithm [19], which is widely used in image processing and has robust performance, thus the final change detection result is obtained.

3   Experimental Results and Analysis

In order to test the effectiveness and adaptability of our approach, experiments are carried out on two publicly available remote sensing image datasets of different sensors.

3.1   Experimental Datasets

The first dataset shown in Fig. 2(a) and (b) is composed of two remote sensing images with 400×400 pixels acquired over the region of Mount Hillers, Utah, America, by the ASTER sensor. The first image was acquired on May 6, 2005; the other was acquired on July 19, 2005, and the main changes between them are that snow on the peaks disappeared owing to the temperature rose.

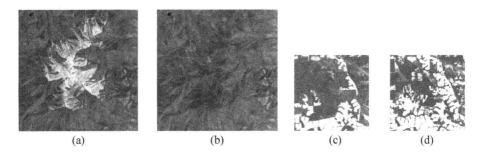

| (a) | (b) | (c) | (d) |

Fig. 2. Datasets used in the experiments.

The second dataset shown in Fig. 2(c) and (d) is composed of two remote sensing images with 250×250 pixels acquired over the region of Brazil, by the LandSat sensor in 2000 and 2005, respectively. The main changes between them are that some forests loss or gain owing to human activities and climate change.

3.2   Change Detection Results and Analysis

In this part, we compare the proposed change detection approach with the following state-of-the-art change detection methods: EM-based method [9], MRF-based method [9], Multiscale-based method [11] and FCM-based method [12]. The quantitative and qualitative change detection results, i.e. false alarm rate, missed alarm rate, total error rate [11], obtained from different methods are tabulated in Tables 1 and 2 and shown in Figs. 3 and 4, respectively.

Table 1. Quantitative study for the results of the first dataset.

Method	FA	MA	TE	P_{FA}	P_{MA}	P_{TE}
EM	33020	25	33045	24.35%	0.10%	20.65%
MRF	9200	32	9232	6.79%	0.13%	5.77%
Multiscale	8035	97	8132	5.93%	0.40%	5.08%
FCM	35355	1175	36530	26.08%	4.81%	22.83%
Proposed	**4873**	**1690**	**6563**	**3.59%**	**6.92%**	**4.10%**

Table 2. Quantitative study for the results of the second dataset.

Method	FA	MA	TE	P_{FA}	P_{MA}	P_{TE}
EM	4207	53	4260	8.34%	0.44%	6.82%
MRF	5609	254	5863	11.12%	2.11%	9.38%
Multiscale	3849	19	3868	7.63%	0.16%	6.19%
FCM	4274	37	4311	8.47%	0.31%	6.90%
Proposed	**1013**	**794**	**1807**	**2.01%**	**6.59%**	**2.89%**

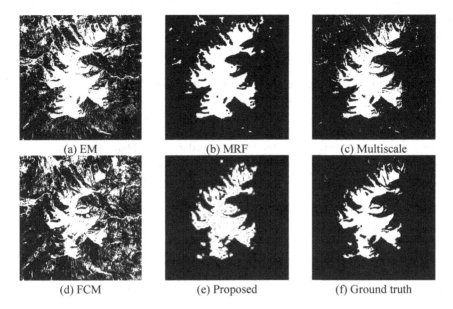

(a) EM   (b) MRF   (c) Multiscale

(d) FCM   (e) Proposed   (f) Ground truth

Fig. 3. Qualitative change detection results of the first dataset.

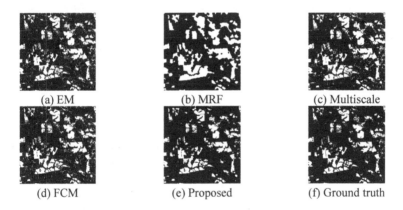

(a) EM   (b) MRF   (c) Multiscale

(d) FCM   (e) Proposed   (f) Ground truth

Fig. 4. Qualitative change detection results of the second dataset.

(1) Results of the First Dataset

In the ground truth of the first dataset, there are 24440 changed and 135560 unchanged pixels, respectively. The quantitative and qualitative change detection results obtained from different methods for the first dataset are shown in Table 1 and demonstrated in Fig. 3, respectively. The proposed approach achieves 4.10% total error rate (P_{TE}), i.e. 95.90% correct detection rate. The change detection result from the Multiscale-based method is very close to that of ours. The correct detection rate of MRF-based method is about 1.67% lower than that of ours. Meanwhile, the change detection results from the EM-based and the FCM-based methods are noisy and are about 17.64% lower than that of ours.

(2) Results of the Second Dataset

In the ground truth of the second dataset, there are 12053 changed and 50447 unchanged pixels, respectively. The quantitative and qualitative change detection results obtained from different methods for the second dataset are shown in Table 2 and demonstrated in Fig. 4, respectively. Our approach achieves 2.89% total error rate (P_{TE}), i.e. 97.11% correct detection rate. The Multiscale-based method obtains suboptimal change detection result with 3.30% lower than ours. The EM-based and the FCM-based methods obtain very similar change detection results with about 3.97% lower than ours. Meanwhile, the change detection result from the MRF-based method is rich in false alarms and is about 6.49% lowers than ours.

In summary, the four change detection methods exhibit different performances and none of them can perform well for all the experimental datasets. For example, the EM-based method performs bad for the first dataset, mainly due to the fact that the unimodal Gaussian model employed in modeling the difference image data fails to provide accurate data model; the FCM-based method performs bad for the first dataset, mainly due to the fact that its performance highly depends on the quality of the initialization data and it easily obtains local optimal solution. In contrast, it is very clear from the aforementioned results on all the datasets that the proposed change detection approach obtains the binary change detection mask more accurately than other methods and does not need any prior knowledge about data distribution. Our approach utilizes a novel implementation strategy by integrating visual attention mechanism for remote sensing change detection and the change detection accuracy has been significantly improved.

4   Conclusions

In this paper, we proposed a novel unsupervised change detection approach by integrating visual attention mechanism for remote sensing images. We compared our approach with series of other state-of-the-art methods in the aspect of change detection over two real-world datasets. Empirical results demonstrated that the proposed approach is robust to noise and can consistently produce excellent change detection results on all the datasets without any priori assumptions. Hence, our approach shows a great potential advantages and applications for remote sensing change detection.

As part of our future work, we intend to discuss ways to further reduce the missed alarms and missed alarm rate in the proposed approach and extract the change information directly from the original images rather than the difference image.

References

1. Lu, D., Mausel, P., Brondizio, E., Moran, E.: Change detection techniques. Int. J. Remote Sens. **25**(12), 2365–2401 (2004)

2. Melgani, F., Bazi, Y.: Markovian fusion approach to robust unsupervised change detection in remotely sensed imagery. IEEE Trans. Geosci. Remote Sens. Lett. **3**, 457–461 (2006)
3. Bazi, Y., Melgani, F., Al-Sharari, D.: Unsupervised change detection in multi-spectral remotely sensed imagery with level set methods. IEEE Trans. Geosci. Remote Sens. **48**, 3178–3187 (2010)
4. Kapur, J.N., Sahoo, P.K., Wong, A.K.C.: A new method for gray-level picture thresholding using the entropy of the histogram. Comput. Vis. Graph. Image Process **29**, 273–285 (1985)
5. Stow, D.A.: Reducing the effects of misregistration on pixel-level change detection. Int. J. Remote Sens. **20**, 2477–2483 (1999)
6. Jha, C.S., Unni, N.V.M.: Digital change detection of forest conversion of a dry tropical Indian forest region. Int. J. Remote Sens. **15**, 2543–2552 (2007)
7. Nackaerts, K., Vaesen, K., Muys, B., Coppin, P.: Comparative performance of a modified change vector analysis in forest change detection. Int. J. Remote Sens. **26**, 839–852 (2005)
8. Fung, T., LeDrew, E.: The determination of optimal threshold levels for change detection using various accuracy indices. Photogram. Eng. Remote Sens. **54**, 1449–1454 (1988)
9. Bruzzone, L., Prieto, D.: Automatic analysis of the difference image for unsupervised change detection. IEEE Trans. Geosci. Remote Sens. **38**, 1171–1182 (2000)
10. Kasetkasem, T., Varshney, P.: An image change detection algorithm based on Markov random field models. IEEE Trans. Geosci. Remote Sens. **40**, 1815–1823 (2002)
11. Celik, T.: Multiscale change detection in multitemporal satellite images. IEEE Trans. Geosci. Remote Sens. Lett. **6**, 820–824 (2009)
12. Ghosh, A., Mishra, N.S., Ghosh, S.: Fuzzy clustering algorithms for unsupervised change detection in remote sensing images. Inf. Sci. **181**, 699–715 (2011)
13. Wu, L., Wang, Y.H., Long, J.T., Liu, Z.S.: An unsupervised change detection approach for remote sensing image using principal component analysis and genetic algorithm. In: Zhang, Y.J. (ed.) Image and Graphics. LNCS, vol. 9217, pp. 589–602. Springer, Cham (2015). https://doi.org/10.1007/978-3-319-21978-3_52
14. Kusetogullari, H., Yavariabdi, A., Celik, T.: Unsupervised change detection in multi-temporal multispectral satellite images using parallel particle swarm optimization. IEEE J. Sel. Top. Appl. Earth Observations Remote Sens. **8**, 2151–2164 (2015)
15. Achanta, R., Hemami, S., Estrada, F., Susstrunk, S.: Frequency-tuned salient region detection. Comput. Vis. Patt. Recogn. **22**, 1597–1604 (2009)
16. Zhai, Y., Mubarak, S.: Visual attention detection in video sequences using spatiotemporal cues. In: ACM Multimedia, pp. 23–27 (2006)
17. Arivazhagan, S., Ganesan, L.: Texture classification using wavelet transform. Patt. Recogn. Lett. **24**, 1513–1521 (2003)
18. Mallat, S.G.: A theory for multiresolution signal decomposition: the wavelet representation. IEEE Trans. Pattern Anal. Mach. Intell. **11**(7), 674–693 (1989)
19. Hind, R.M., Abbas, F., Abdulkarem, A.: Performance evaluation of K-mean and fuzzy C-mean image segmentation based clustering classifier. Int. J. Adv. Comput. Sci. Appl. **6**(12), 176–183 (2015)

An Efficient and Robust Visual Tracking via Color-Based Context Prior Model

Chunlei Yu, Baojun Zhao$^{(\boxtimes)}$, Zengshuo Zhang, and Maowen Li

Beijing Key Laboratory of Embedded Real-time Information Processing
Technique, Beijing Institute of Technology, Beijing 100081, China
Chunlei_Yu@126.com,
{zbj,zhangzengshuo,limaowen}@bit.edu.cn

Abstract. Real-time object tracking has been widely applied to time-critical multimedia fields such as surveillance and human-computer interaction. It is a challenge to balance accuracy and speed in tracking. Spatio-Temporal Context tracker (STC) formulates the spatio-temporal relationship between the object and its surrounding background, and achieves good performance in accuracy and speed. However, the context prior model only utilizes the grayscale feature which is not efficient. When the target is not obvious in the context, or the context exists a similar interference compared to the target, STC tracker drifts from the target. To solve the problem, we exploit the standard color histograms of the context to build a discriminative context prior model. More specifically, we utilize an effective lookup-table to compute the prior context model at a low computational cost. Finally, extensive experiments on challenging sequences show the effectiveness and robustness of our proposed method.

Keywords: Visual object tracking · Spatio-Temporal Context · Prior model
Color histogram · Lookup-table

1 Introduction

Visual Object Tracking is a hot topic in the field of computer vision. Based on image sequences, visual object tracking has been widely applied to intelligent robots, monitoring, factory automation, man-machine interface, vehicle tracking to name a few. However, there is still a challenge in visual tracking for many factors such as illumination variation, deformation, occlusion, scale variation and fast motion, etc.

Generally visual object tracking is divided into two categories: generative model methods and discriminative model methods. Generative models [1, 2] learn a representative appearance model to identify the target, and search the best-matching windows. On the other hand, discriminative models [3, 4] focus on training a classifier which aims at distinguishing the target and the background. The biggest difference of generative and discriminative models is that discriminative models use the background information. Background information is advantageous for effective tracking [5, 6], thus the discriminative methods are generally better than the generative methods. However, the discriminative methods have some shortcomings, such as lack of samples. Besides, speed is a very important metric in practical application. Trackers that run at a low

© Springer International Publishing AG 2017
Y. Zhao et al. (Eds.): ICIG 2017, Part I, LNCS 10666, pp. 70–84, 2017.
https://doi.org/10.1007/978-3-319-71607-7_7

speed with expensive computing cost have no practical value. Therefore, study on fast and robust tracking methods is valuable.

Correlation filter (CF) based trackers have got much attention for their good performance both in speed and accuracy. CF based trackers use a learned filter to localize the target in the next frame by confirming the position of maximal response. Spatio-Temporal Context (STC) [7] tracker follows a similar workflow as CF based trackers. There exists a strong spatio-temporal relationship between the scenes containing the object in consecutive frames. STC exploits the context information, and performs favorably in IV or OCC scenarios. But when the target is not obvious in the context, or the context exist a similar interference compared to the target, STC has drifting problem for its prior model only use the grayscale features. In this paper, we utilize the color histograms to get the saliency object likelihood scores in a context tracking framework, and take it as the context prior model, as shown in Fig. 1. The object region is more significant in proposed prior model compared with the STC prior model. Our model is well applied to time-critical applications for the favorable simplicity of our representation.

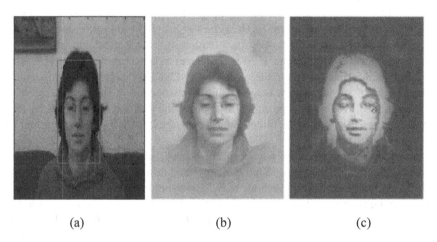

(a)   (b)   (c)

Fig. 1. The proposed prior model using color histogram to distinguish object from background. (a) is the original context image. (b) is the STC prior model. (c) is the proposed saliency prior model. (Color figure online)

Our contributions are as follows: we propose a discriminative context prior model to distinguish the object region from the background. It relies on standard color histograms and achieves good performance on a variety of challenging sequences. More specifically, we utilize an effective lookup-table to compute the context prior model over a large search region at a low computational cost. Finally, we extensively evaluate our method on benchmark datasets to prove its good performance compared with other state-of-the-art trackers.

The rest of this paper is organized as follows: First, we introduce the related work in Sect. 2. Then our tracking method is described in Sect. 3. Extensive experiments are conducted to evaluate the proposed method compared with other state-of the-art methods in Sect. 4. Section 5 concludes the paper.

2 Related Work

In this section, we provide a brief overview of trackers, and discuss the methods closely related to our proposed method (CF based trackers).

Generative trackers describe the target with an appearance model. They search the best matched region by the updated generative model. Examples of this category include mean shift tracker [8], incremental tracker (IVT) [9], multi-task tracker (MTT) [2], and object tracker via structured learning [10] to name a few. Discriminative trackers treat the object tracking as a classification problem. They use a classifier to predict the foreground and background. Examples of this category include multiple instance learning (MIL) [11], correlation filter (CF) based trackers and so on.

CF based trackers design correction filters to produce correction peak for the tracking target, but generating low response to the background. Correction filters only use a small part of the computational power. They adapt the product of FFT domain to replace the convolution of spatial domain, and achieve hundreds of frame per second. The proposal of Minimum Output Sum of Squared Error (MOSSE) [12] makes the correction filters appropriate for online tracking. Many improvements have been made based on the framework of MOSSE. Henriques *et al.* [13] proposed using correction filter in a kernel space based on exploiting the circulant structure of tracking-by-detection with kernels (CSK). CSK uses a dense sampling strategy, which can extract all information of the target. Although CSK has made gratifying achievements in terms of speed, the grayscale feature is insufficient in the description of the target appearance. KCF [14] is proposed to improve the performance of CSK by using of HOG features. By further handling the scale changes, SAMF [15] is proposed and achieve good performance.

Context information has already been considered in many tracking methods. In general, they extract key points around the target and describe them with SURF, SIFT or other descriptors. But these methods may ignore the crucial information and spend much computational cost. Zhang *et al.* efficiently adapt the context information in filter learning and model the scale based on the correlation response. Robust feature representation plays important role in visual tracking [16]. While in STC, the tracker uses grayscale features, which lack of description of the appearance. Our saliency context prior model makes full use of color information to make the target saliency from the background. Besides, to reduce the cost of computing, we utilize an effective lookup-table over a large search region at a low computational cost. The proposed prior model will be introduced below.

3 The Proposed Method

3.1 Dense Spatio-Temporal Context Prior Model

STC tracker can be treated as calculating the possibility that a target appears at a sampling area. It computes a confidence map which estimates the object location likelihood:

$$c(\mathbf{x}) = P(\mathbf{x}|o) \tag{1}$$

where $\mathbf{x}$ is the object location and o denotes the object present in the scene. The maxing $c(\mathbf{x})$ is the target location. Equation (1) can be expressed as

$$c(\mathbf{x}) = \sum\nolimits_{c(\mathbf{z}) \in X^c} P(\mathbf{x}, c(\mathbf{z})|o) = \sum\nolimits_{c(\mathbf{z}) \in X^c} P(\mathbf{x}|c(\mathbf{z}), o)P(c(\mathbf{z})|o) \tag{2}$$

In Eq. (2), $\mathbf{c(z)}$ means the feature set of the context. $P(\mathbf{x}|\mathbf{c(z)}, o)$ is the spatial context model, which means the relationship between the target and surrounding points in the context. $P(\mathbf{c(z)}|o)$ is the context prior model, which expresses the exterior feature of points in the context. STC tracker is to locate the target by designing the prior probability $P(\mathbf{c(z)}|o)$ and updating the spatial context model $P(\mathbf{x}|\mathbf{c(z)}, o)$.

The conditional probability function $P(\mathbf{x}|\mathbf{c(z)}, o)$ in Eq. (2) is described as

$$P(\mathbf{x}|\mathbf{c(z)}, o) = h^{sc}(\mathbf{x} - \mathbf{z}) \tag{3}$$

where $h^{sc}(\mathbf{x} - \mathbf{z})$ means the relative distance and direction between object location $\mathbf{x}$ and its local context location $\mathbf{z}$, presenting the relationship between an object and its spatial context.

The context prior probability is

$$P(\mathbf{c(z)}|o) = I(z)\omega_\sigma(\mathbf{z} - \mathbf{x}^*) \tag{4}$$

where $I(\mathbf{z})$ is image grayscale, and $\omega_\sigma(\mathbf{z} - \mathbf{x}^*)$ is weighting function defined by

$$\omega_\sigma(\mathbf{z}) = ae^{-\frac{|\mathbf{x}|^2}{\sigma^2}} \tag{5}$$

In Eq. (5), a is a normalization constant restricts $P(\mathbf{c(z)}|o)$ to range from 0 to 1. σ is a scale parameter.

3.2 The Proposed Saliency Prior Model

STC tracker utilizes the grayscale features. When the target is not obvious in the context, or the context exist a similar interference compared to the target, STC has the tracking drift problem. To distinguish object region from background, we employ a color histogram on the current image I with Bayesian classifier. Let $b_\mathbf{x}$ denotes the bin b assigned to the color components of context. For an object region O and its surrounding region S, we get the object likelihood as:

$$P(\mathbf{x} \in O|O, S, b_\mathbf{x}) = \frac{P(b_\mathbf{x}|\mathbf{x} \in O)P(\mathbf{x} \in O)}{P(b_\mathbf{x}|\mathbf{x} \in S)P(\mathbf{x} \in S)} \tag{6}$$

Let $H^I_\Omega(b_\mathbf{x})$ means the b-th bin of the non-normalized histogram H of region Ω. We estimate the likelihood with the color histogram. i.e. $P(b_\mathbf{x}|\mathbf{x} \in O) \approx \frac{H^I_O(b_\mathbf{x})}{|O|}$ and

$P(b_x|\mathbf{x} \in S) \approx \frac{H_S^l(b_x)}{|S|}$. The $|\cdot|$ means the number of pixels of a region. Furthermore, the prior probability can be estimated as $P(b_x|\mathbf{x} \in O) \approx \frac{|O|}{|S|}$. Then Eq. (6) can be simplified to

$$P(\mathbf{x} \in O|O, S, b_x) = \begin{cases} \frac{H_O^l(b_x)}{H_S^l(b_x)} & I(x) \in S \\ 0.5 & \text{otherwise} \end{cases} \tag{7}$$

This discriminative model allows us to distinguish object and background pixels. In Eq. (7), the object likelihood scores can be computed via an efficient lookup-table, which can greatly reduce the computational cost. We updated the object model on a regular basis using the linear interpolation:

$$P_{1:t}(\mathbf{x} \in O|b_x) = \eta P(\mathbf{x} \in O|b_x) + (1 - \eta)P_{1:t-1}(\mathbf{x} \in O|b_x) \tag{8}$$

where η means the learning rate.

In our method, the object model $P(\mathbf{x} \in O|O, S, b_x)$ is treated as the context prior probability. As with Eq. (4), then the context prior probability becomes

$$P(c(\mathbf{x})|O) = P(\mathbf{x} \in O|O, S, b_x)\omega_\sigma(\mathbf{x} - \mathbf{x}^*) \tag{9}$$

As the framework of STC, The confidence map is

$$c(\mathbf{x}) = P(\mathbf{x}|O) = be^{-|\frac{\mathbf{x}-\mathbf{x}^*}{\alpha}|^\beta} \tag{10}$$

where b is a normalization constant, α is a scale parameter and β is a shape parameter. Associate Eqs. (3) and (9), the confidence map is

$$\mathbf{c}_{t+1}(\mathbf{x}) = F^{-1}\left(F\left(H_{t+1}^{stc}(\mathbf{x})\right) \odot F\left(P_{t+1}(x)\omega_{\sigma_t}\left(\mathbf{x} - \mathbf{x}_t^*\right)\right)\right) \tag{11}$$

Therefore, the spatial context model is

$$h^{sc}(\mathbf{x}) = F^{-1}\left(\frac{F\left(be^{-|\frac{\mathbf{x}-\mathbf{x}^*}{\alpha}|^\beta}\right)}{F(P(\mathbf{x})\omega_\sigma(\mathbf{x} - \mathbf{x}^*))}\right) \tag{12}$$

The object location $\mathbf{x}_{t+1}^*$ in the $(t + 1)$-th frame is determined by maximizing the new confidence map

$$\mathbf{x}_{t+1}^* = \arg \max_{\mathbf{x} \in \Omega_c(\mathbf{x}_t^*)} \mathbf{c}_{t+1}(\mathbf{x}) \tag{13}$$

The spatio-temporal context model id undated by

$$H_{t+1}^{stc} = (1 - \rho)H_t^{stc} + \rho h_t^{sc} \tag{14}$$

where ρ denotes learning parameter and h_t^{sc} is the spatial context computed by Eq. (12) at the t-th frame.

3.3   Lookup-Table Update Scheme

To reduce the amount of computational cost, we adapt a lookup-table to calculate the object likelihood score. Here we will introduce how to get the lookup-table from a context and its update scheme.

For a given context, there exist three color components. Each component ranges from 0 to 255. We can get the index of the component of each pixel. The index ranges from 1 to 256^3. So it will cost a large computational cost to get the color histogram. To reduce the computational cost, we divide the pixel from 256 to 16 levels. The index range will be reduced from 256^3 to 16^3. Then the histogram of object region $H_O^l(\boldsymbol{b_x})$ and the histogram of surrounding background region $H_S^l(\boldsymbol{b_x})$ can be calculated. We can get the object likelihood $P(\mathbf{x} \in O|O, S, b_x)$ according to Eq. (7). The lookup-table is updated by Eq. (8).

For grayscale sequences, the computational cost is not as large as color sequences, and to better distinguish the object and background, we compute the histogram on 256 grayscale levels directly.

3.4   Scale Update Scheme

As with STC, The scale parameter is updated with the maximum of confidence map. The scale update scheme as

$$\begin{cases} s_t' = \sqrt{\dfrac{c_t(x_t^*)}{c_{t-1}(x_{t-1}^*)}} \\ \overline{s_t} = \dfrac{1}{n}\sum_{i=1}^n s_{t-i}' \\ s_{t+1} = (1 - \lambda)s_t + \lambda\overline{s_t} \\ \sigma_{t+1} = s_t\sigma_t \end{cases} \tag{15}$$

In Eq. (15), $\mathbf{c_t}(\mathbf{x_t^*})$ is the confidence map and s_t' is the estimated scale between two consecutive frames. The estimated target scale s_{t+1} is obtained through filtering in which $\overline{s_t}$ is the average of estimated scales from n consecutive frames, and λ is a fixed filter parameter.

The procedure of our algorithm is shown in Algorithm 1.

Algorithm 1   Proposed Algorithm for Object Tracking

1: Initial target bounding box $b_0 = [x_0, y_0, w_0, h_0]$ and tracking parameters.

2: Compute the pre-computed confidence map $\mathbf{c(x)}$.

3: **repeat**

4:        Compute the normalized **weight window** ω_σ.

5:        Crop out context window and target window, then compute **object likelihood**
          $P(\mathbf{x} \in O | O, S, \boldsymbol{b_x})$ via the lookup-table.

6:        Update the **lookup-table**.

7:        Get the **context prior model** $P(\mathbf{c(x)}|O)$.

8 :   **If frame > 1**

9:        Calculate the response of **the confidence map** $c_{t+1}(\mathbf{x})$.

10:       Get the location of the **maximal response** in $c_{t+1}(\mathbf{x})$, and compute the **location** of
          target on current frame.

11:       Crop out context window and target window, and compute the **context prior model**.

12:       Compute the response of **the confidence map** and **update scale** via Eq.(15).

13:    **End**

14:       Update the **lookup-table**.

15:       Compute **the context prior model** and **the spatial context model**.

16:       Update **the Spatio-Temporal Context Model** via Eq.(14).

17: **End**

4   Experimental Results and Analysis

In this section, we evaluate the performance of proposed tracker on 17 challenging sequences provided on Online Test Benchmark [5]. The challenges involve 10 common attributes: illumination variation, out-of-plane rotation, scale variation, occlusion, deformation, motion blur, fast motion, in-plane-rotation, background clutter and low resolution.

The proposed tracker is compared with 11 state-of-the-art tracking methods in recent years. They are sparse collaborative appearance (SCM), the structured output tracker (Struck), tracking learning detection (TLD), CSK tracker, KCF tracker, STC tracker, deep learning tracker (DLT), Multi-Instance Learning (MIL), L1 tracker (L1APG), adaptive structural local sparse appearance model (ASLA) and Compressive Tracker (CT).

4.1   Experimental Setup

The proposed tracker is implemented in Matlab R2015a and runs at 137 frames per second results on Intel i5 2.5 GHz CPU, 4G RAM, Win7 system. We test 17 sequences on total 4200 frames. And the proceeding speed is 137 frames per second. The state of the target in the first frame is given by the ground truth. The parameter σ_t in Eq. (12) is set to $\sigma_1 = \frac{h_0 + w_0}{2}$, where h_0 and w_0 are height and width of the initial tracking rectangle. The scale parameter s_t is set to $s_1 = 1$. The number of frames n for updating scale in Eq. (15) is set to 5. The parameter λ in Eq. (15) is set to 0.25. The parameter α is set to 2.25 and β is set to 1. The learning parameter ρ in Eq. (11) is set to 0.025. The learning rate of object model η in Eq. (15) is set to 0.03. All the parameters are fixed for all experiments.

4.2   Evaluation Metrics

For quantitative evaluations, we use the center location error (CLE), the success plot and the precision plot. The CLE metric is defined as:

$$\text{CLE} = \frac{1}{N}\sum_{i=1}^{N} \sqrt{\left|x_t^i - x_g^i\right|^2 + \left|y_t^i - y_g^i\right|^2} \tag{16}$$

The success plot is based on the overlap ratio. The success plot is defined as $S = \frac{area\left(R_t \cap R_g\right)}{area\left(R_t \cup R_g\right)}$, where R_t is a tracked bounding box and R_g is the ground truth bounding box, and the result of one frame is considered as a success if $S > 0.5$. The area under curve (AUC) of each success plot serves as the second measure to rank the tracking algorithms. Meanwhile, the precision plot illustrates the percentage of frames whose tracked locations are within the given threshold distance to the ground truth. A representative precision score with the threshold equal to 20 is used to rank the trackers.

4.3   Quantitative Comparisons

(1) Overall Performance: Fig. 2 shows the overall performance of the 12 tracking algorithm in terms of success and precision plots. Note that all the plots are generated using the code library from the benchmark evaluation and the results of KCF are provided by the authors. In the success plot, the proposed algorithm achieve the AUC of 0.580, ranking second in the 12 trackers, which outperforms the STC method by 15.6%. Meanwhile, in the precision plot, the precision score of the proposed method is ranking first in the 12 trackers, and outperforms the STC method by18.6%.

Table 1 shows the CLE of the 17 sequences. In general our proposed method is ranking first and KCF is ranking second among 12 trackers, and ranking second both in the success rate and overlap rate, as shown in Table 2 and Table 3.

(2) Attribute-based Performance: To analyze the strength and weakness of the proposed method, we evaluate the trackers on sequences with 10 attributes. We focus on 5 of 10 attributes. Figure 3 shows the success plots of views with 5 attributes and Fig. 4 shows the corresponding precision plots. In the following, we analyze the results based on scores of success plots which is more informative than the score at one position in the precision plot.

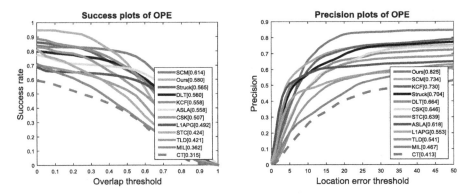

Fig. 2. The success plot and precision plot of OPE for 12 trackers. The performance score of success plot is the AUC value. The performance score of precision plot is at error threshold of 20 pixels.

Table 1. Center location error (in pixels). The red fonts indicate the best performance. The green fonts indicate the second performance.

Sequence	SCM	Struck	TLD	CSK	KCF	STC	DLT	MIL	L1APG	ASLA	CT	Ours
CarDark	1.1	1.0	27.5	3.2	6.0	2.8	18.4	43.5	1.4	1.0	119.2	4.7
Car4	4.0	8.7	12.8	19.1	9.9	10.7	2.5	50.8	77.0	2.0	86.0	6.3
David2	4.3	1.5	5.0	2.3	2.1	5.6	2.6	10.9	1.3	1.8	76.7	2.5
Trellis	7.7	6.9	31.1	18.8	7.8	33.8	81.6	71.5	62.3	8.3	41.7	8.0
Mhyang	2.6	2.6	9.5	3.6	2.4	4.5	2.8	20.4	3.3	2.6	13.3	12.6
Singer1	3.3	14.5	8.0	14.0	12.8	5.8	4.1	16.4	53.2	3.7	15.5	10.5
Bolt	455.1	398.8	90.9	429.4	153.4	139.8	NaN	393.5	409.0	373.8	363.8	5.5
Boy	51.2	3.8	4.5	20.1	2.9	25.9	2.2	12.8	7.0	106.3	9.0	5.2
Crossing	1.4	2.8	24.3	9.0	2.2	34.1	1.8	3.2	62.9	1.4	3.6	2.5
Football	16.8	17.3	14.3	16.2	14.6	16.1	192.3	12.1	15.0	15.5	11.9	6.1
Girl	2.9	2.6	9.8	19.3	11.9	21.8	10.8	13.7	2.8	3.1	18.9	7.1
Walking2	2.7	11.2	44.6	17.9	29.0	13.8	2.9	60.6	4.5	38.5	58.5	12.6
Walking	2.5	4.6	10.2	7.2	4.0	7.2	16.4	3.4	2.9	2.6	6.9	5.8
MountainBike	10.4	8.6	216.1	6.5	7.7	7.0	14.2	73.0	8.5	8.8	214.3	7.5
Woman	7.8	4.2	139.9	207.3	10.1	28.5	5.2	125.3	128.3	140.9	114.5	12.8
Faceocc1	11.9	18.8	27.4	11.9	16.0	250.4	19.6	29.9	17.8	78.3	25.8	13.1
Basketball	53.2	118.3	213.9	6.5	7.9	75.3	12.0	91.9	137.7	82.7	89.1	6.4
Average	37.6	36.8	52.3	47.8	17.7	40.2	24.3	60.8	58.5	51.2	74.6	7.6

For the sequences with the deformation and in-plane rotation, the proposed algo-rithm ranks first among all evaluated trackers. The object color doesn't change with deformation or rotation. So the proposed model can distinguishes object region from surrounding background, which make the tracking stable and drifting problem is avoided.

Table 2. Scores of success rate. The result of one frame is considered as a success if S > 0.5. The red fonts indicate the best performance. The green fonts indicate the second performance.

Sequence	SCM	Struck	TLD	CSK	KCF	STC	DLT	MIL	L1APG	ASLA	CT	Ours
CarDark	0.997	1	0.529	0.992	0.692	0.997	0.679	0.178	1	1	0.003	0.677
Car4	0.973	0.398	0.792	0.276	0.364	0.225	1	0.276	0.296	1	0.275	0.545
David2	0.911	1	0.952	1	1	0.752	0.994	0.324	1	0.946	0.002	0.713
Trellis	0.854	0.784	0.473	0.591	0.84	0.58	0.329	0.244	0.153	0.858	0.35	0.965
Mhyang	0.997	1	0.893	1	1	0.86	1	0.389	0.97	1	0.73	0.698
Singer1	1	0.299	0.991	0.296	0.276	0.507	1	0.276	0.379	1	0.248	0.504
Bolt	0.014	0.017	0.146	0.017	0.003	0.043	0.043	0.011	0.011	0.014	0.006	0.943
Boy	0.439	0.975	0.935	0.842	0.992	0.663	1	0.385	0.899	0.439	0.688	0.636
Crossing	1	0.942	0.517	0.317	0.95	0.175	0.992	0.983	0.25	1	0.983	1
Football	0.586	0.66	0.412	0.657	0.702	0.619	0.296	0.738	0.669	0.652	0.785	0.793
Girl	0.882	0.98	0.764	0.398	0.742	0.302	0.606	0.294	0.97	0.906	0.178	0.634
Walking2	1	0.434	0.34	0.388	0.38	0.442	1	0.38	0.976	0.398	0.384	0.614
Walking	0.959	0.566	0.383	0.519	0.515	0.721	0.447	0.541	0.998	0.998	0.502	0.973
MountainBike	0.961	0.855	0.259	1	0.987	0.873	0.36	0.575	0.921	0.899	0.171	0.614
Woman	0.858	0.935	0.166	0.245	0.936	0.258	0.864	0.188	0.196	0.194	0.159	0.549
Faceocc1	1	1	0.834	1	1	0.243	0.928	0.765	1	0.311	0.854	0.957
Basketball	0.611	0.102	0.025	0.874	0.898	0.236	0.599	0.274	0.286	0.556	0.259	0.927
Average	0.826	0.703	0.554	0.612	0.722	0.500	0.714	0.401	0.646	0.716	0.387	0.750

With the sequences with attributes of out-of-plane rotation and occlusion, the proposed algorithm ranks second among the evaluated methods with a narrow margin (less than 1%) to the best performing methods, corresponding to KCF and SCM respectively. The KCF method utilizes HOG features to describe the target and its local context region. SCM employ local features extracted from the local image patches, and utilize the target template from the first frame to handle the drift problem. Our method computes the object likelihood with the color histogram, and can track on the object whose color has little change.

For the videos with illumination variation, our method ranks fifth while SCM performs well. In illumination variation sequences, the color component of target changes, but the lookup-table is also corresponding to the target before illumination occurs. The object region may not be prominent in the proposed prior model.

In next section, we will illustrate the comparisons between the proposed method and other state-of-the-art method on the 17 sequences in Table 1.

Table 3. Scores of overlap rate. The red fonts indicate the best performance. The green fonts indicate the second performance.

Sequence	SCM	Struck	TLD	CSK	KCF	STC	DLT	MIL	L1APG	ASLA	CT	Ours
CarDark	0.828	0.872	0.443	0.744	0.608	0.738	0.562	0.198	0.864	0.832	0.003	0.686
Car4	0.745	0.490	0.626	0.468	0.485	0.358	0.866	0.265	0.246	0.741	0.213	0.556
David2	0.733	0.854	0.684	0.807	0.813	0.583	0.821	0.452	0.841	0.878	0.002	0.550
Trellis	0.665	0.610	0.481	0.479	0.624	0.468	0.260	0.251	0.212	0.788	0.341	0.687
Mhyang	0.794	0.803	0.627	0.782	0.798	0.680	0.861	0.507	0.813	0.897	0.596	0.624
Singer1	0.852	0.365	0.714	0.364	0.361	0.530	0.838	0.362	0.284	0.778	0.355	0.474
Bolt	0.016	0.014	0.159	0.019	0.015	0.040	0.036	0.010	0.012	0.011	0.010	0.702
Boy	0.370	0.747	0.653	0.646	0.762	0.536	0.815	0.491	0.721	0.362	0.586	0.574
Crossing	0.769	0.667	0.399	0.480	0.698	0.248	0.722	0.715	0.209	0.773	0.674	0.728
Football	0.484	0.530	0.489	0.545	0.547	0.507	0.239	0.582	0.544	0.528	0.604	0.650
Girl	0.672	0.734	0.566	0.372	0.542	0.340	0.521	0.402	0.719	0.700	0.314	0.537
Walking2	0.803	0.510	0.307	0.458	0.401	0.518	0.806	0.285	0.745	0.370	0.265	0.592
Walking	0.701	0.569	0.447	0.534	0.528	0.592	0.414	0.543	0.741	0.758	0.519	0.622
MountainBike	0.664	0.700	0.198	0.702	0.700	0.581	0.462	0.448	0.726	0.711	0.142	0.555
Woman	0.653	0.721	0.131	0.193	0.694	0.365	0.614	0.154	0.159	0.146	0.129	0.475
Faceocc1	0.780	0.718	0.581	0.780	0.742	0.213	0.679	0.592	0.740	0.325	0.630	0.682
Basketball	0.459	0.206	0.022	0.697	0.669	0.290	0.508	0.220	0.227	0.381	0.257	0.621
Average	0.646	0.595	0.443	0.534	0.587	0.446	0.590	0.381	0.518	0.587	0.332	0.607

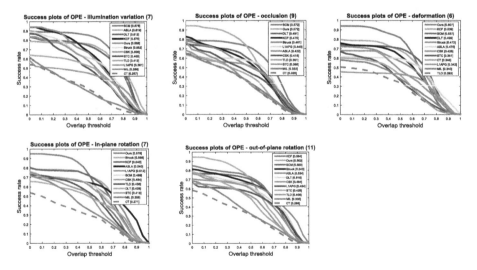

Fig. 3. The success plots of videos with 5 attributes. The number in the title indicates the number of sequences. Best viewed on color display.

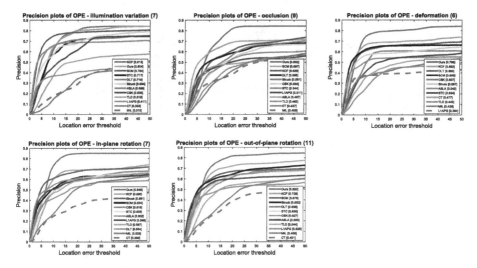

Fig. 4. The precision plots of videos with 5 attributes. The number in the title indicates the number of sequences. Best viewed on color display.

4.4 Qualitative Comparisons

(1) Deformation: Figure 5 shows some screenshots of the tracking results in three challenging sequences where the target objects undergo large shape deformation. In the Bolt sequence, the appearance of target and disturbance change due to shape deformation and fast motion. Only our method can track the target well. The CT, KCF, MIL, ASLA and L1APG methods undergo large drift at the beginning of the video (e.g. #10). The TLD method begins to drift at frame #80. After frame #150, only our method tracks the target well until to the end of the Bolt sequence. The target object in the Basketball sequence undergoes significant appearance variation duo to non-rigid body deformation. The TLD and Struck methods lose target at frame #30. L1APG and MIL algorithm lose track of target after frame #294. ALSA method begins to lose at frame #470. Only KCF, and our method perform well at all frames.

(2) Illumination Variation: Figure 6 shows some sampled results in three sequences in which the target objects undergo large illumination changes. In the Car4 sequence, the moving car passes under a bridge and trees. Despite large illumination variation at frame #180, #200 and #240, the proposed method is able to track well. The CT, L1APG and MIL methods drift away from the target objects when sudden illumination variation occurs at frame #240. ALSA, DLT and SCM method handle scale variation well (e.g. #400, #500, #600). The object appearance in the Trellis sequence changes significantly due to variations in illumination and pose. Only KCF and our method perform well, and never lose from beginning to the end of sequence. CT, CSK, Struck and TLD methods lose the target during the tracking process, but when target moves close to their location, they keep up with the target again (e.g. #423, #569).

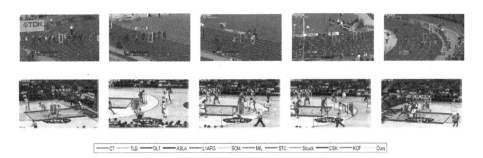

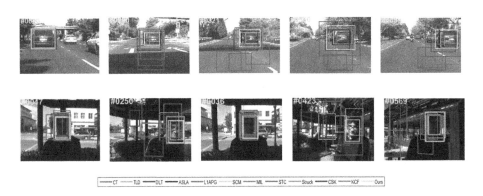

Fig. 5. Qualitative results of the 12 trackers over sequence Bolt and basketball, in which the targets undergo deformation. Best viewed on color display.

Fig. 6. Qualitative results of the 12 trackers over sequence Trellis and Car4, in which the targets undergo illumination variation. Best viewed on color display.

(3) Heavy Occlusion: Figure 7 shows sampled results of three sequences where the targets undergo heavy occlusions. In the Football sequence, the target is almost fully occluded in the frame #292. Our method is able to locate on the target when it appears on the screen (# 362). In the FaceOcc1 sequence, the target is frequently occluded by a book (#237, #553, #745, and so on). STC, ASLA and MIL methods begin to fail track on the target on frame #237. TLD tracks on part of the target on frame #553. Struck, DLT, KCF and our method perform well in the entire sequence.

(4) In- Plane Rotation and Out-of-Plane Rotation: During the tracking process, rotation will result in shape deformation and visual changes. Figure 8 shows sampled results of sequences where the targets undergo both in-plane rotation and out-of plane rotation, the same as Bolt sequence in Fig. 4. The proposed method is always tracking on the object in the whole sequence.

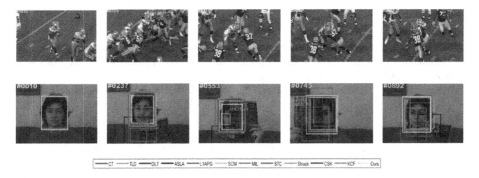

Fig. 7. Qualitative results of the 12 trackers over sequence Football and FaceOcc1, in which the targets undergo occlusion. Best viewed on color display.

Fig. 8. Qualitative results of the 12 trackers over sequence MountainBike and David2, in which the targets undergo in- plane rotation and out-of-plane rotation. Best viewed on color display.

5   Conclusion

In this paper, we propose a robust object tracking approach based on color-based context prior model. We exploit the standard color histograms to distinguish the target from background, and build a discriminative context prior model. Our method refers to the STC tracking framework and scale update scheme. More specifically, to reduce the amount of calculation, we adapt an effective lookup-table, which can compute at a low computational cost. Moreover, numerous experiments are conducted to compare the proposed method with other relevant state-of-the-art trackers. Both quantitative and qualitative evaluations further demonstrate the effectiveness and robustness of the proposed method.

Acknowledgements. This work is supported by the Chang Jiang Scholars Programme (Grant No. T2012122), and 111 Project of China under Grant B14010.

References

1. Sevilla-Lara, L., Learned-Miller, E.: Distribution fields for tracking. In: IEEE Conference on Computer Vision and Pattern Recognition, vol. 157, pp. 1910–1917. IEEE Computer Society (2012)
2. Ahuja, N., Liu, S., Ghanem, B., Zhang, T.: Robust visual tracking via multi-task sparse learning. In: Computer Vision and Pattern Recognition, vol. 157, pp. 2042–2049. IEEE (2012)
3. Hare, S., Saffari, A., Torr, P.H.S.: Struck: structured output tracking with kernels. In: IEEE International Conference on Computer Vision, vol. 23, pp. 263–270. IEEE (2012)
4. Wang, Q., Chen, F., Xu, W., Yang, M.H.: Object tracking with joint optimization of representation and classification. IEEE Trans. Circ. Syst. Video Technol. **25**(4), 638–650 (2015)
5. Wu, Y., Lim, J., Yang, M.H.: Online object tracking: a benchmark. In: IEEE Conference on Computer Vision and Pattern Recognition, vol. 9, pp. 2411–2418. IEEE Computer Society (2013)
6. Wu, Y., Lim, J., Yang, M.H.: Object tracking benchmark. IEEE Trans. Pattern Anal. Mach. Intell. **37**(9), 1834 (2015)
7. Zhang, K., Zhang, L.: Fast tracking via spatio-temporal context learning. Comput. Sci. (2013)
8. Comaniciu, D., Ramesh, V., Meer, P.: Kernel-based object tracking. IEEE Trans. Pattern Anal. Mach. Intell. **25**(5), 564–575 (2003)
9. Cauwenberghs, G., Poggio, T.: Incremental and decremental support vector machine learning. In: Advances in Neural Information Processing Systems 13, vol. 1, pp. 409–415 (2001)
10. Zhang, T., Ghanem, B., Xu, C., Ahuja, N.: Object tracking by occlusion detection via structured sparse learning, vol. 71, no. 4, pp. 1033–1040 (2013)
11. Babenko, B., Yang, M. H., Belongie, S.: Visual tracking with online multiple instance learning. In: IEEE Conference on Computer Vision and Pattern Recognition, CVPR 2009, vol. 33, pp. 983–990. IEEE (2009)
12. Bolme, D.S., Beveridge, J.R., Draper, B.A., Lui, Y.M.: Visual object tracking using adaptive correlation filters. In: Computer Vision and Pattern Recognition, vol. 119, pp. 2544–2550. IEEE (2010)
13. Henriques, J.F., Caseiro, R., Martins, P., Batista, J.: Exploiting the circulant structure of tracking-by-detection with kernels. In: Fitzgibbon, A., Lazebnik, S., Perona, P., Sato, Y., Schmid, C. (eds.) ECCV 2012. LNCS, vol. 7575, pp. 702–715. Springer, Heidelberg (2012). https://doi.org/10.1007/978-3-642-33765-9_50
14. Henriques, J.F., Caseiro, R., Martins, P., Batista, J.: High-speed tracking with kernelized correlation filters. IEEE Trans. Pattern Anal. Mach. Intell. **37**(3), 583–596 (2014)
15. Li, Y., Zhu, J.: A scale adaptive kernel correlation filter tracker with feature integration. In: Agapito, L., Bronstein, M., Rother, C. (eds.) ECCV 2014 Workshops. LNCS, vol. 8926, pp. 254–265. Springer, Cham (2015). https://doi.org/10.1007/978-3-319-16181-5_18
16. Han, Y., Deng, C., Zhang, Z., Li, J., Zhao, B.: Adaptive feature representation for visual tracking. arXiv preprint arXiv:1705.04442 (2017)

Non-local L_0 Gradient Minimization Filter and Its Applications for Depth Image Upsampling

Hang Yang[1($\boxtimes$)], Xueqi Sun[2], Ming Zhu[1], and Kun Wu[1]

[1] Changchun Institute of Optics, Fine Mechanics and Physics,
Chinese Academy of Science, Changchun 130033, China
yanghang@ciomp.ac.cn, zhuming@163.com, wukun_ciomp@126.com
[2] Changchun University of Science and Technology, Changchun 130022, China
xueqiSun@163.com

Abstract. In this work, we propose a non-local L_0 gradient minimization filter. The nonlocal idea is to restore an unknown pixel using other similar pixels, and the nonlocal gradient model has been verified for feature and structure-preserving. We introduce the nonlocal idea into a L_0 gradient minimization approach, which is effective for preserving major edges while eliminating the low-amplitude structures. An optimization framework is designed for achieving this effort. Many optimized based filters do not have the property of joint filtering, so they can not be used in many problems, such as joint denoising, joint upsampling, while the proposed filter not only inherits the advantages of the L_0 gradient minimization filter, but also has the property of the joint filtering. So our filter can be applied to joint super resolution. With the guidance of the high-resolution image, we propose upsampling the low-resolution depth image with the proposed filter. Experimental results demonstrate the effectiveness of our method both qualitatively and quantitatively compared with the state-of-the-art methods.

Keywords: L_0 norm · Non-local · Joint filtering · Edge-preserving

1 Introduction

Edge-aware image processing technique is broadly studied for smoothing images without destroying different levels of structures. It is wildly applied for computer graphics community. Edge-preserving filters can be broadly divided into two broad categories: average based approaches and optimization based approaches.

The methods of first class smooth images by taking a weighted average of nearby pixels, where the weights depend on the intensity/color difference. Average based filters include bilateral filter [17], nonlocal means filter [1], guided image filter [8] and rolling guidance filter [23]. They often use guidance image to

H. Yang—Thanks to the National Science Foundation of China under Grant (No. 61401425) for providing support.

define the similarity between pixels. The main drawback of these filters is that they will produce the halo effect near the edge.

The total variation (TV) model [15], L_0 gradient minimization filter (L_0 filter) [20], weighted least squares (WLS) [3] and curvature filter [7] belong to the optimization based methods. These approaches smooth images by optimizing objective functions containing terms defined in L_p norm ($p = 0, 1, 2$). Although the optimization based methods can avoid the halo effect along salient edges and often generate high quality results, it does not have the property of joint filtering with reference image, and this shortcoming limits their applications.

Recently, the nonlocal framework has been extensively studied by many scholars as a regularization term to overcome the staircase effect and obtain better performance. Gilboa and Osher defined a variational functional based nonlocal TV operators [6]. Zhang et al. [24] proposed a fast split Bregman iteration for this nonlocal TV minimization. Lately, the nonlocal regularizations are extended to process more general inverse problems in [12]. However, they penalize large nonlocal gradient magnitudes, and it possibly influence contrast during smoothing.

In summary, most image smooth models aim to preserve edges from noise and textures, and each of them has its limitations. In this work, we present a new edge-preserving filter based on an optimization framework, which incorporates the nonlocal strategy into the L_0 gradient minimization model and takes advantage of both variational models and spatial filters. This notion leads to an unconventional global optimization process involving discrete metrics, whose solution is able to manipulate the edges in a variety of ways depending on the saliency.

The proposed framework is general and can be used for several applications. Different from other optimization based methods, the proposed algorithm can use the reference image for joint filtering.

The depth images captured by 3D scanning devices such as ToF camera or Kinect camera may be highly degraded, which have limited resolution and low quality. As a result, it's hard to recover high quality depth maps from single depth image. Fortunately, the depth map is often coupled by high resolution (HR) color image which shows the same scene and they have strong structural similarities [4,19,22]. In recently, deep learn based depth upsampling methods [5,9,11,16] achieve well results. These methods produce the end-to-end upsampling networks, which learn high-resolution features in the intensity image and supplement the low-resolution depth structures in the depth map.

So this paper applies the proposed filter for depth image super resolution and treats the natural image as the reference image. With the guidance of the high-resolution RGB image, the proposed algorithm is well suited for upsampling the low-resolution depth image and it can not only reduce noises, but also preserve the sharp edges during super resolution. With simulations, the experimental results demonstrate that the proposed approach is promising, and it does significantly improve the visual quality of the low-resolution depth image compared with the existing upsampling methods.

2   Non-local L_0 Gradient Minimization

Different from the definition of gradient, the nonlocal gradient $\nabla_\omega S_p$ of each pixel p on the image S is defined as follows:

$$\nabla_\omega S_p = \{S_p(q), \forall q \in \Omega_p\} \tag{1}$$

where

$$S_p(q) = (S_q - S_p)\sqrt{\omega(p,q)} \tag{2}$$

and $S_p(q)$ is the vector element corresponding to q, $\omega(p,q)$ is the weight function, which is assumed to be nonnegative and symmetric, it measures the similarity features between two patches (the size is $m \times m$) centered at the pixels p and q, Ω_p is a search window centered at the pixel p (the size of Ω_p is $n \times n$) [12,24]. The weight function $\omega(p,q)$ in Ω_p has the form:

$$\omega(p,q) = \frac{1}{C_p}\exp(-\frac{(G_a*\mid J(p+\cdot)-J(q+\cdot)\mid^2)(0)}{h^2}) \tag{3}$$

and the normalizing factor C_p is

$$C_p = \sum_{q\in\Omega_p}\exp(-\frac{(G_a*\mid J(p+\cdot)-J(q+\cdot)\mid^2)(0)}{h^2}) \tag{4}$$

where G_a is the Gaussian kernel with standard deviation a, h is a smoothing parameter, and J is a reference image which can be chosen according to different applications.

In this work, we denote the input image and filtered image as I and S, respectively. Our nonlocal gradient measure is written as

$$C(S) = \sharp\{p \mid\parallel \nabla_\omega S_p \parallel_1 \neq 0\} \tag{5}$$

It counts p whose magnitude

$$\sum_{q\in\Omega_p}\mid (S_q - S_p)\sqrt{\omega(p,q)}\mid$$

is not zero. Based on this definition, we can estimate S by solving:

$$\min_S\{\parallel S - I\parallel_2^2 + \lambda C(S)\} \tag{6}$$

The first term constrains image structure similarity.

It is a discrete counting metric involved in Eq. (6). These two terms describe the pixel-wise difference and global discontinuity respectively, it is commonly regarded as computationally intractable. In this work, we introduce an auxiliary variable based on the half-quadratic splitting method, which can expand the original terms and update them iteratively. This approach leads to an alternating optimization strategy.

Due to the discrete nature, our method contains new subproblems, and it is different from other L_0-norm regularized optimization problems. Although the proposed method can only approximate the solution of Eq. (6), but it can make the original problem easier to handle and inherit the property to maintain salient structures [20].

The auxiliary variables $\mathbf{d}_p$ are introduced, and they are corresponding to $\nabla_\omega S_p$. We can rewrite the cost function as

$$\min_{S,\mathbf{d}}\{\sum_p (S_p - I_p)^2 + \lambda C(\mathbf{d}_p) + \beta \parallel \mathbf{d}_p - \nabla_\omega S_p \parallel_2^2\} \tag{7}$$

where $C(\mathbf{d}) = \sharp\{p \parallel \parallel \mathbf{d}_p \parallel_1 \neq 0\}$, and β is a an automatically adapting controlling parameter.

Our split variables approaches motivate us to propose this iterative method. In practice, a good result can be obtained by solving the following two subproblems iteratively.

Subproblem 1: computing S

$$S = \arg\min_S\{\sum_p (S_p - I_p)^2 + \beta \parallel \mathbf{d}_p - \nabla_\omega S_p \parallel_2^2\} \tag{8}$$

Now, the subproblem for S consists in solving the linear equations

$$(S - I) - \beta div_\omega(\nabla_\omega S - \mathbf{d}) = 0 \tag{9}$$

which provides

$$S = (1 - \beta \Delta_\omega)^{-1}(I - \beta div_\omega \mathbf{d}) \tag{10}$$

Here, $div_\omega \mathbf{d}$ is defined as the divergence of $\mathbf{d}$, and its discretization at p can be written as

$$div_\omega \mathbf{d}_p = \sum_{q \in \Omega_p} (\mathbf{d}_p(q) - \mathbf{d}_q(p))\sqrt{\omega(p,q)} \tag{11}$$

The non-local Laplacian Δ_ω is defined as

$$\Delta_\omega S = div_\omega \nabla_\omega S = \sum_{q \in \Omega_p} (S_q - S_p)\omega(p,q) \tag{12}$$

Since the non-local Laplacian is negative semi definite, the operator $1 - \Delta_\omega$ is diagonally dominant. Therefore we can solve S by a Gauss-Seidel algorithm.

Subproblem 2: computing d

$$\mathbf{d} = \arg\min_{\mathbf{d}}\{\sum_p \parallel \mathbf{d}_p - \nabla_\omega S_p \parallel_2^2 + \frac{\lambda}{\beta}C(\mathbf{d}_p)\} \tag{13}$$

This subproblem can be solved efficiently because the Eq. (13) can be spatially decomposed where $\mathbf{d}_p$ are estimated individually. It is the main benefit of the proposed scheme, which makes the altered problem empirically solvable. Equation (13) is accordingly decomposed to:

$$E_p = \| \mathbf{d}_p - \nabla_\omega S_p \|_2^2 + \frac{\lambda}{\beta} H(\mathbf{d}_p) \tag{14}$$

where $H(\mathbf{d}_p)$ is a binary function returning 1 if $\| \mathbf{d}_p \|_1 \neq 0$ and 0 otherwise.

Equation (14) reaches its minimum E_p^* under the condition

$$\mathbf{d}_p = \begin{cases} \mathbf{0}, & \| \nabla_\omega S_p \|_2^2 \leq \lambda/\beta \\ \nabla_\omega S_p, & otherwise \end{cases} \tag{15}$$

Proof: (1) When $\lambda/\beta \geq \| \nabla_\omega S_p \|_2^2$, non-zero $\mathbf{d}_p$ yields

$$E(p) = \| \mathbf{d}_p - \nabla_\omega S_p \|_2^2 + \lambda/\beta \tag{16}$$
$$\geq \lambda/\beta \tag{17}$$
$$\geq \| \nabla_\omega S_p \|_2^2 \tag{18}$$

Note that $\mathbf{d}_p = \mathbf{0}$ leads to

$$Ep = \| \nabla_\omega S_p \|_2^2 \tag{19}$$

Comparing Eq. (16), the minimum energy $E_p = \| \nabla_\omega S_p \|_2^2$ is produced when $\mathbf{d}_p = \mathbf{0}$.

(2) When $\lambda/\beta < \| \nabla_\omega S_p \|_2^2$, Eq. (19) still holds. But when $\mathbf{d}_p = \nabla_\omega S_p$, E_p has its minimum value λ/β. Comparing these two values, the minimum energy E_p is produced when $\mathbf{d}_p = \nabla_\omega S_p$.

Parameter β is automatically adapted in iterations starting from a small value, it is multiplied by 2 each time. This scheme is effective to speed up convergence [20].

Continuous nonlocal gradient L_1 norm was enforced in nonlocal total variation (NLTV) [24] smoothing to suppress noise. In our method, strong smoothing inevitably curtails originally salient edges to penalize their magnitudes. In this framework, large nonlocal gradient magnitudes are allowed by nature with our discrete counting measure.

In Fig. 1, we show a natural image smoothing example compared with other competitive algorithms. One can see that L_0 filter [20] ($\lambda = 0.035$) generates a sharp but not completely smooth image which is shown in Fig. 1(b). Many details are still retained after filtering, such as flower diameter and butterfly, it is not good enough for applications. The result obtained by NLTV [24] ($\lambda = 0.05$) is shown in Fig. 1(c), in the case of overall non-local gradients with small energies, the edges are not sharp, which makes them difficult to distinguish low contrast details around. In Fig. 1(d), our result ($\lambda = 0.05$) contains the most significant structures, which are slightly sharper as the nonlocal gradient energy increases.

Fig. 1. Visual quality comparison of image smoothing. (a) original image, (b) the result of L_0 filter, (c) the result of NLTV, (d) the result of our method.

Our alternating minimization method is described in Algorithm 1.

Algorithm 1. Non-local L_0 Gradient Minimization

---

1. Input: image I, reference image J, smoothing weight λ , parameters β
2. Initialization: $S^0 = I$, compute $\omega(\cdot, \cdot)$ using Eqs. (3)–(4).
3. for $i = 0 : MaxIters$
    With S^i, solve for $\mathbf{d}^i$ in Eq. (15);
    With $\mathbf{d}^i$, solver for S^{i+1} with Eq. (12).
    end
4. Output: result image $S^{MaxIters}$.

In [14], Petschnigg *et al.* proposed to denoise a no-flash image with its flash version as the reference image. In Fig. 2, we show a comparison of using the joint bilateral filter (JBF) [14], NLTV [24] and our method. Although JBF works well, from the Fig. 2(b), one can find that the gradient inversion artifacts are significant near some edges. And NLTV does not obtain a satisfactory result. Our result is sharper and contains few noise, which is shown in Fig. 2(d).

Fig. 2. Visual quality comparison of flash/no flash denoising. (a) original flash/no flash image pair, (b) the result of JBF, (c) the result of NLTV, (d) the result of our method.

3   Depth Image Upsampling

In this application, we upscale a single depth image d (size of $m \times n$) which is guided by a high-resolution natural image T (size of $M \times N$). One can see that depth images are textureless compared with natural images and have quite sparse gradients. However, according to the statistics of depth image gradient [21], the sparse gradient assumption is not accurate enough. That is to say, most gradient values of depth image are not always 0 but rather very small.

The proposed nonlocal L_0 gradient regularization can reduce the penalty for small elements, because we deal with the nonlocal gradient of the image as a whole, take into account the energy sum of the multi-directional weighted gradients, and avoid to obtain an overly smooth result.

In the first step, we upsample the depth image d to the size of $M \times N$ with nearest neighbor interpolation, and obtain an initial image D. In the second step, we compute the weights $\omega(p, q)$ with the high-resolution natural image T in Eqs. (3) and (4), that is to say, T is used as the reference image. In the last step, we use D as the input image and solve the minimization problem Eq. (7). The result of Eq. (7) is the final joint upsampling image.

Table 1. PSNR (in dB) comparison on middlebury 2007 datasets with added noise for magnification factors (×4, ×8).

	Art		Books		Moebius	
	×4	×8	×4	×8	×4	×8
He et al. [8]	29.98	**27.72**	33.94	31.99	32.23	30.22
Park et al. [13]	29.69	27.42	34.36	32.28	33.28	31.12
Chan et al. [2]	29.88	27.15	33.82	31.12	32.46	29.51
SRF [10]	29.79	26.94	33.13	31.92	31.43	29.86
Ours	**30.46**	27.53	**35.98**	**33.20**	**34.41**	**31.32**

Table 2. SSIM comparison on middlebury 2007 datasets with added noise for magnification factors (×4, ×8).

	Art		Books		Moebius	
	×4	×8	×4	×8	×4	×8
He et al. [8]	0.84	0.78	0.80	0.74	0.78	0.71
Park et al. [13]	0.92	0.88	0.89	0.84	0.90	0.83
Chan et al. [2]	0.80	0.71	0.91	0.89	0.91	0.87
SRF [10]	0.82	0.72	0.74	0.64	0.73	0.62
Ours	0.97	0.94	0.96	0.93	0.97	0.94

We show some experimental evaluations of our algorithm compared with the competitive methods for depth image upsampling. We work on 3 depth images from Middlebury 2007 datasets [4] with the scaling factors of 4 and 8, respectively. To simulate the acquisition process, these depth images are added Gaussian noise [13].

The numerical results for this experiment in terms of the PSNR are shown in Table 1. In our experiments, our method clearly outperforms the other four methods in the most cases.

The numerical results for this experiment in terms of the Peak Signal Noise Ratio (PSNR) are shown in Table 1 and Structural Similarity (SSIM) [18] in Table 2. From the Table 1, one can see that our method clearly outperforms the other four method in the most cases. In Table 2, the proposed method achieve significant SSIM improvements over other leading methods. In average, our algorithm outperforms other methods by 0.05 for the SSIM comparison.

To show the visual comparison clearly, we show some results of experiments in Fig. 3. One can find that our method can enhance edges and reduce noise better, whereas other algorithms suffer from edge blurring or noise. From Table 1 and Figs. 3, 4 and 5 one can observe that the proposed approach is effective for noisy complex scenes and can obtain clearer high resolution depth images.

In order to show the stability of the proposed deconvolution algorithm, we give the convergence curve of the alternative optimization in Fig. 6. We plot the

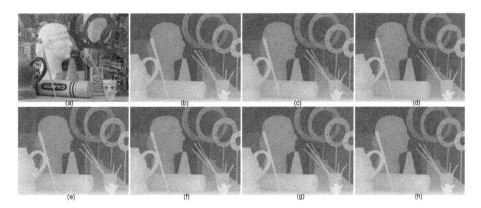

Fig. 3. Joint upsampling on "Art" image. (a) high-resolution RGB image, (b) original depth map, (c) low-resolution and noisy depth image (enlarged using nearest neighbor upsampling), (d) He et al. [8], (e) Park et al. [13], (f) Chan et al. [2], (g) SRF [10], (h) our method.

Fig. 4. Joint upsampling on "Books" image. (a) high-resolution RGB image, (b) original depth map, (c) low-resolution and noisy depth image (enlarged using nearest neighbor upsampling), (d) He et al. [8], (e) Park et al. [13], (f) Chan et al. [2], (g) SRF [10], (h) our method.

histories of the relative error $\mid S^{k+1} - S^k \mid$. Three depth images (*Art*, *Book* and *Moebius*) are used and the scaling factor is 8. It is noticeable that the proposed method is stable.

In order to improve computational time and storage efficiency, we only compute the "best" neighbors, that is, for each pixel p, we only include the 10 best neighbors in the searching window of 7×7 centered at p and the size of patch is 5×5, the parameters a and h are empirically set to 0.5 and 0.25, respectively. 7–10 iterations are generally performed in our algorithm.

For computational time, the proposed approach takes about 2.3 s for a computer which runs Windows 7 64bit version with Intel Core i5 CPU and 8 GB RAM to construct the weight function of a 256×256 image in Matlab 2010b.

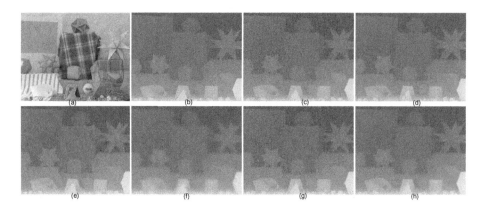

Fig. 5. Joint upsampling on "Moebius" image. (a) high-resolution RGB image, (b) original depth map, (c) low-resolution and noisy depth image (enlarged using nearest neighbor upsampling), (d) He et al. [8], (e) Park et al. [13], (f) Chan et al. [2], (g) SRF [10], (h) our method.

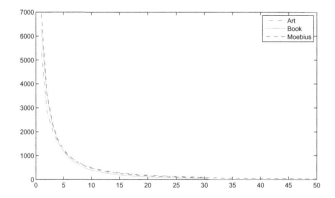

Fig. 6. Convergence curves of the alternative optimization.

Once the weight is constructed, the iteration of our method is comparable to ROF [15] in speed. The computation speed depends on the number of iterations. In general, it takes around 3.5 s for 10 iterations.

4   Conclusion

In this work, we propose a solution for nonlocal L_0 gradient minimization and show its applications for depth image upsampling. We propose an effective smoothing approach based on minimizing discretely counting nonlocal spatial changes. Different from many optimized based filters, the proposed method has the property of joint filtering, so our filter can be used for many applications. In particular, it achieves good performance in the depth image super resolution.

Treating the high-resolution RGB image as a reference image, the proposed algorithm is well suited for upsampling the low-resolution depth image. The experimental results demonstrate that the proposed approach is promising, and it has better objective performance compared to the existing upsampling methods.

References

1. Buades, A., Coll, B., Morel, J.M.: A non-local algorithm for image denoising. In: Conference on Computer Vision and Pattern Recognition, vol. 2, pp. 60–65. IEEE (2005)
2. Chan, D., Buisman, H., Theobalt, C., Thrun. S.: A noise-aware filter for real-time depth upsampling. In: The Workshop on Multi-camera Multi-modal Sensor Fusion Algorithms Applications (2008)
3. Farbman, Z., Fattal, R., Lischinski, D., Szeliski, R.: Edge-preserving decompositions for multi-scale tone and detail manipulation. ACM Trans. Graph. **27**, 67 (2008)
4. Ferstl, D., Reinbacher, C., Ranftl, R., Ruether, M., Bischof, H.: Guided depth upsampling using anisotropic total generalized variation. IEEE International Conference on Computer Vision, pp. 993–1000. IEEE (2013)
5. Ferstl, D., Ruther, M., Bischof, H.: Variational depth superresolution using example-based edge representations. In: IEEE International Conference on Computer Vision (ICCV), pp. 513–521. IEEE (2015)
6. Gilboa, G., Osher, S.: Nonlocal operators with applications to image processing. Multiscale Model. Simul. **7**, 1005–1028 (2008)
7. Gong, Y.: Bernstein filter: a new solver for mean curvature regularized models. In: IEEE International Conference on Acoustics, Speech and Signal Processing (ICASSP), pp. 1701–1705. IEEE (2016)
8. He, K., Sun, J., Tang, X.: Guided image filtering. IEEE Trans. Pattern Anal. Mach. Intell. **35**, 1397–1409 (2013)
9. Hornacek, M., Rhemann, C., Gelautz, M., Rother, C.: Depth super resolution by rigid body self-similarity in 3D. In: Proceedings of the IEEE Conference on Computer Vision and Pattern Recognition (CVPR), pp. 1123–1130. IEEE (2013)
10. Huang, J.B., Singh, A., Ahuja, N.: Single image super-resolution from transformed self-exemplars. In: Proceedings of the IEEE Conference on Computer Vision and Pattern Recognition (CVPR), pp. 5197–5206. IEEE (2015)
11. Hui, T.-W., Loy, C.C., Tang, X.: Depth map super-resolution by deep multi-scale guidance. In: Leibe, B., Matas, J., Sebe, N., Welling, M. (eds.) ECCV 2016. LNCS, vol. 9907, pp. 353–369. Springer, Cham (2016). https://doi.org/10.1007/978-3-319-46487-9_22
12. Lou, Y., Zhang, X., Osher, S.: Image recovery via nonlocal operators. J. Sci. Comput. **42**, 185–197 (2010)
13. Park, J., Kim, H., Tai, Y.W., Brown, M.S., Kweon, I.: High quality depth map upsampling for 3D-TOF cameras. In: IEEE International Conference on Computer Vision (ICCV), pp. 1623–1630. IEEE (2011)
14. Petschnigg, G., Szeliski, R., Agrawala, M.: Digital photography with flash and no-flash image pairs. ACM Trans. Graph. (TOG) **23**, 664–672 (2004)
15. Rudin, L., Osher, S., Fatemi, E.: Nonlinear total variation based noise removal algorithms. Physica D: Nonlinear Phenom. **60**, 259–268 (1992)

16. Song, X., Dai, Y., Qin, X.: Deep depth super-resolution: learning depth super-resolution using deep convolutional neural network. arXiv preprint arXiv:1607.01977 (2016)
17. Tomasi, C., Manduchi, R.: Bilateral filtering for gray and color images. In: International Conference on Computer Vision, pp. 839–846. IEEE (1998)
18. Wang, Z., Bovik, A.C., Sheikh, H.R.: Image quality assessment: from error visibility to structural similarity. IEEE Trans. Image Process. **13**, 600–612 (2004)
19. Xie, J., Feris, R.S., Sun, M.T.: Edge-guided single depth image super resolution. IEEE Trans. Image Process. **25**, 428–438 (2016)
20. Xu, L., Lu, C., Xu, Y., Jia, J.: Image smoothing via L_0 gradient minimization. ACM Trans. Graph. **30**, 174 (2011)
21. Xue, H., Zhang, S., Cai, D.: Depth image inpainting: improving low rank matrix completion with low gradient regularization. arXiv preprint arXiv:160405817 (2016)
22. Yang, J., Ye, X., Li, K., Hou, C., Wang, Y.: Color-guided depth recovery from RGB-D data using an adaptive autoregressive model. IEEE Trans. Image Process. **23**, 3443–3458 (2014)
23. Zhang, Q., Shen, X., Xu, L., Jia, J.: Rolling guidance filter. In: Fleet, D., Pajdla, T., Schiele, B., Tuytelaars, T. (eds.) ECCV 2014. LNCS, vol. 8691, pp. 815–830. Springer, Cham (2014). https://doi.org/10.1007/978-3-319-10578-9_53
24. Zhang, X., Burger, M., Bresson, X.: Bregmanized nonlocal regularization for deconvolution and sparse reconstruction. SIAM J. Imaging Sci. **3**, 253–276 (2010)

Salient Object Detection via Google Image Retrieval

Weimin Tan and Bo Yan$^{(\boxtimes)}$

Shanghai Key Laboratory of Intelligent Information Processing,
School of Computer Science, Fudan University, Shanghai, China
byan@fudan.edu.cn

Abstract. Among trillions of images available online, there likely exists images whose content is visually similar to the query image (source image). Based on this observation, we propose a novel approach for salient object detection with the help of retrieved images returned by Google image search. We take the regional saliency of the source image as the frequency of occurrences in the retrieved images. The procedure of our saliency estimation approach is as follows. Firstly, given a query (source image) we extract N similar images from the retrieved result returned by Google. Then, we conduct matching between the source image and the extracted retrieval images in order to detect the repetitive region among them. Simultaneously, we segment the source image into several distinctive regions using superpixel segmentation and fusion. Finally, we derive the saliency map from the matching on the segmented regions. Experimental results demonstrate that compared with other methods, the proposed approach consistently achieves higher saliency detection performance in terms of subjective observations and objective evaluations.

Keywords: Saliency estimation · Google image search
Superpixel fusion

1 Introduction

Saliency detection plays an important role in image understanding, analysis, and processing. Its goal is to identify salient object region in an image. The detected region captures the attention of humans at the first sight of an image. As shown in many previous works, salient object detection has been applied to a variety of applications including image segmentation [23], object recognition and understanding [20], content-aware image/video retargeting [13,24], content-based image retrieval [7], and image/video compression [9], *etc.*

In the past decade, a number of saliency detection approaches have been proposed to model the human vision system. These models try to use the global

B. Yan—This work was supported in part by NSFC (Grant Nos.: 61370158; 61522202).

© Springer International Publishing AG 2017
Y. Zhao et al. (Eds.): ICIG 2017, Part I, LNCS 10666, pp. 97–107, 2017.
https://doi.org/10.1007/978-3-319-71607-7_9

Retrieved   Source images   Our saliency maps
images

Fig. 1. Illustration of our approach to salient object detection. (Color figure online)

statistical features of the image, including color contrast [3,12], edges and gradients [10], spectral analysis [1], and histograms [3]. In saliency detection, an important work is the one from Itti *et al.* [10], which detects salient region using central-surrounded differences across multi-scale image features. Achanta *et al.* [1] propose a frequency tuned approach that directly defines a pixel saliency based on the difference between the pixel color and the average color of the image. Hou and Zhang [8] propose a frequency domain analysis method that employs the spectral residual of the amplitude spectrum of Fourier transform to generate the saliency map. However, these approaches only take into account the intrinsic information of the image while ignore the extrinsic information, which can be insufficient to deal with the complex scene variations common in natural images.

In this paper, we propose a radically different saliency detection approach inspired by the works on content-based image retrieval [11,19]. Our new approach is built upon a key observation that among trillions of images available online, there likely exist images that are visually similar to the query image (source image). Instead of just relying on the intrinsic information of the source image, we propose to "learn" the relevant knowledge from visually similar images returned by Google image search, as illustrated in Fig. 1.

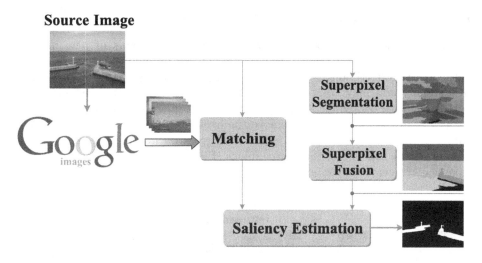

Fig. 2. Overview of our approach. (Color figure online)

2   Our Proposed Approach

The procedure of our proposed saliency detection approach is shown in Fig. 2. Firstly, the source image as query searches visually similar images from trillions of online images using Google image search. The returned retrieval results by Google usually have visual appearance and semantic concept close to that of the query but objects may significantly differ among them. So we remove the images that are irrelevant to the source image in the retrieved top N_{top} images, and reserve N images that have similar foreground with the source image, but differ from background areas. Then, we leverage this in the matching step by performing SIFT matching [16] and RANSAC verification [6] between the reserved retrieval images and the source image. Due to the similarity of the foreground and the variability of the background between the source image and the retrieved images, the saliency (foreground) naturally collects more matching feature points. In other words, it is common with respect to the foregrounds in the retrieved images.

Simultaneously, since the SIFT descriptor only represents a feature region, and our goal is to detect the salient object region in the source image, we need to segment the source image into several distinctive regions and map the matched SIFT feature points to the segmented regions. To address this, the source image is first abstracted as a set of superpixels using segmentation algorithm [14]. Then, we propose to automatically fuse the initial segmentation regions with similar color and texture features, which helps to make the estimated saliency more consistent with the object in the source image.

Finally, we count the number of matching feature points in each fusion region of the source image, and obtain a matching vector (each dimension of the vector represents the number of matching feature points in a fusion region). The saliency map of the source image is then calculated based on the normalized version of this vector and the number of fusion regions.

2.1   Google Image Search

There is an enormous amount of web images with millions of new images uploaded every month. Google image search can quickly find the similar images to the query from trillions of web images. Due to the returned images by Google are diversity and may not contain similar objects to the query, we reserve N retrieval images containing similar objects to the query (source image) in the retrieved top N_{top} images, and remove the irrelevant images making no contribution to saliency detection. These reserved retrieval images are used to help estimating the saliency of the source image. Figure 3 shows retrieval results for a particular query (source image).

Fig. 3. Illustration of retrieval results for a particular query (source image). These retrieved images are used to help estimating the saliency of the source image. (Color figure online)

2.2   Matching

After obtaining the relevant retrieval images for a source image, we exploit them to detect the repetitive region between the source image and the retrieved images. From Fig. 3, we can observe that these retrieved images have significant differences with respect to the source image in terms of color, illumination, and viewpoint. Therefore, simply using global features such as color or texture is difficult to detect the repetitiveness among them. Fortunately, the research of local feature descriptors has made great progress in recent years. Many powerful local descriptors have been proposed to improve the accuracy and efficiency of matching. One of the most widely used local feature descriptors is SIFT [16], which is proved to be robust to changes in illumination, noise, and minor changes in viewpoint [16].

Therefore, we employ SIFT descriptor to conduct matching between the source image and each retrieved image for detecting the repetitive feature region. Specifically, we first extract SIFT descriptors from the source image and the retrieved images. Then, we match the source image to the retrieved images using their SIFT descriptors with nearest neighbor distance ratio 0.8. Finally, we perform RANSAC [6] to the previous matching results. All the matches verified by RANSAC are considered to be correct matching.

Figure 4 shows an intuitive example, where the blue line represents the matching between the background area of the source image and the retrieved images; the yellow line represents the matching between the foreground area of the source image and the retrieved images. Due to the retrieved images containing objects similar to the source image, and having different backgrounds among them, the number of correct matching points in the foreground region of the source image is usually more than that of the background area. In other words, the foreground region of the source image appears more frequently in the retrieved images than that of the background.

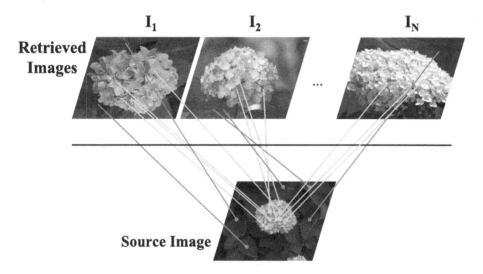

Fig. 4. An intuitive matching example that using the SIFT matching verified by RANSAC between the source image and the retrieved images detects the repetitive feature region among them. (Color figure online)

2.3   Superpixel Segmentation and Fusion

Although in the previous matching step we have found the repetitive feature region in the source image, SIFT descriptor only represents a feature region instead of object region, *i.e.*, typically, the SIFT feature region is not geometrically well aligned with the object region in the source image. If we directly use the repetitiveness of SIFT feature region to compute the saliency of the source image, the estimated saliency will be poor. To address this issue, we need to segment the source image into several distinctive regions and map the matched SIFT feature points to the segmented regions.

Superpixel Segmentation: To segment the source image, we first abstract the source image as a set of superpixels using Liu's algorithm [14] (we use a MATLAB implementation from http://mingyuliu.net/), which is fast and robust for images with different natural scenes. The number of superpixels in [14] is manually set. Generally, too few superpixels lead to insufficient segmentation, making the foreground and background of the source image fusion together; too many superpixels cause the foreground and background of the source image segmenting into multiple parts, making the estimated saliency inconsistent. Empirically, we find 30 superpixels are enough for images in SED1 dataset [2].

Superpixel Fusion: After superpixel segmentation, we propose to automatically fuse the superpixels produced by previous step with similar CIE-Lab color and texture features. The texture feature is obtained using Gabor filter with response of eight orientations. Both the bandwidth and the extracted scale are set to one. When the feature contrast of two neighboring superpixels is less than a threshold T_{Fusion}, these two superpixels are fused into a new large superpixel. The threshold T_{Fusion} is defined as:

$$T_{Fusion} = mean(C_{sp}) - std(C_{sp})/2 \qquad (1)$$

where C_{sp} denotes the feature contrast of neighboring superpixels in the CIE-Lab color and texture feature space. $mean(C_{sp})$ and $std(C_{sp})$ denote the mean and the standard deviation of C_{sp}, respectively. We use N_{sp} to denote the number of fused regions.

Figure 5 illustrates how the superpixel fusion affects the saliency estimation. The estimated saliency with fusion is capable of providing more consistent with the object in the source image than without fusion.

2.4   Saliency Estimation

After the source image is segmented into a number of distinctive regions, we map the matched SIFT features obtained in the matching step to their respective fusion region, and obtain a matching vector $\mathbf{V} \in \Re^{N_{sp}}$ (each dimension of vector $\mathbf{V}$ represents the number of matched SIFT features in a fusion region). This vector is used to estimate the saliency of the source image. Besides, we also consider another factor that affects the estimated saliency, that is, the number of fused regions N_{sp}. When N_{sp} is small, *i.e.*, less than a threshold T_{sp}, the object in the source image is usually not segmented into multiple parts. Considering the number of fused regions in the saliency calculation is helpful in detecting clean saliency object.

The saliency value S_i of the ith region, $i = 1, 2, \ldots, N_{sp}$, in the source image is calculated as follows:

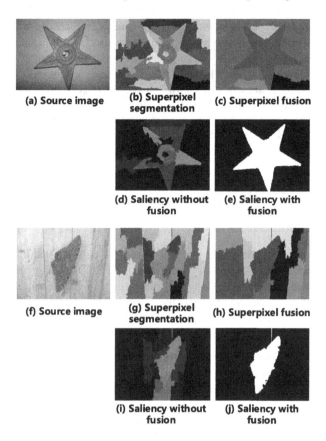

Fig. 5. Illustration of the importance of superpixel fusion. Left: source images; middle: superpixel segmentation images and corresponding saliency maps without fusion; right: superpixel fusion images and corresponding saliency maps with fusion. Without fusion, the obtained saliency map of simple superpixel segmentation is both more scattered and misaligned relative to the source image than with fusion.

$$S_i = \begin{cases} \delta\left[V_i - max(\boldsymbol{V})\right] & if \ N_{sp} \leq T_{sp} \\ \dfrac{V_i}{\|\boldsymbol{V}\|_2} & if \ N_{sp} > T_{sp} \end{cases} \tag{2}$$

where $\delta\left(.\right)$ is the Kronecker delta function. We empirically set $T_{sp} = 5$.

From Eq. (2), we observe that the saliency value S depends on the number of fusion regions N_{sp} and the matching vector $\boldsymbol{V}$. When N_{sp} is less than T_{sp}, the saliency value of the region with the largest V value, *i.e.*, containing the most number of matching points, is equal to one, and the rest of the region's value is zero. When N_{sp} is greater than T_{sp}, the saliency S is equal to the normalized matching vector.

Besides, we need to choose a value of N_{top} and N, which denotes the number of retrieved top images and the number of them used in our approach, respectively. We set $N_{top} = 100$. In addition, clearly, with increasing values of N, the number of matching points in each fused region is increased. The increased number of matching points in salient fusion region is typically more than other regions. Thus, a large value of N helps to discriminate the saliency of regions in the source image, but it also increases the computation time in the matching step. Empirically, we find that N within [5, 15] is enough for saliency estimation in our approach.

3   Experimental Results

3.1   Experimental Setup

Dataset: We provide a comparison of our approach to several saliency detection approaches on SED1 [2] with binary ground truth. SED1 is a subset of the SED dataset [2], and consists of 100 images. Each image in SED1 dataset contains a human-labeled foreground mask used as ground truth for salient object detection. This dataset contains many images with different natural scenes making it challenging for saliency detection.

Evaluation criterion: In our experiments, we adopt five criteria to evaluate the quantitative performance of different approaches: receiver operating characteristic (ROC) curve, mean absolute error (MAE) [18], mean precision, mean recall, and F-measure. The ROC curve plots the true positive rate against the false positive rate and presents a robust evaluation of saliency detection performance. The ROC curve is obtained by thresholding the saliency map using a series of fixed integers from 0 to 255. MAE is proposed by [18], which provides a better estimate of the dissimilarity between the saliency map and ground truth. It calculates the mean absolute error between the estimated saliency map and the binary ground truth (GT). Furthermore, we use F-measure to evaluate the overall performance.

3.2   Comparison of Approaches

In the experiments, we qualitatively compare the proposed approach with IT [10], FT [1], Paria [17], SeR [21], SR [8], SWD [4], COV [5], FES [22], LPS [15], and HDCT [12]. These ten approaches are implemented using their either publicly available source code or original saliency detection results from the authors.

Figure 6(a) shows the comparison results of the proposed approach against other competing approaches in the ROC curve on the SED1 dataset. From Fig. 6(a), we observe that given a fixed false positive rate, the proposed approach obtains a higher true positive rate than other approaches in most cases, and achieves a competitive performance compared to HDCT [12].

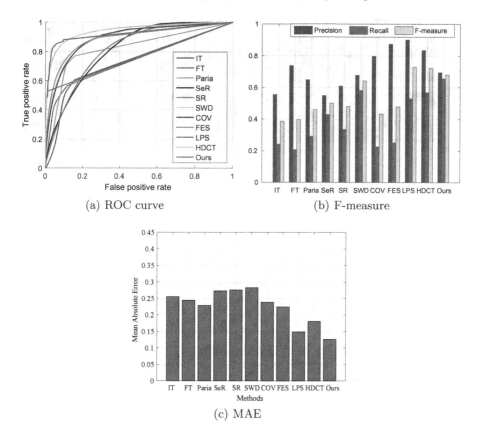

Fig. 6. Objective comparison of saliency detection methods on SED1 dataset. Clearly, our approach outperforms other methods in terms of ROC curve, F-measure, and MAE objective evaluation.

Figure 6(b) shows the comparison of average F-measure. It reports that our approach achieves the best F-measure performance on the SED1 dataset [2], except for LPS [15] and HDCT [12]. Result demonstrates that our approach is able to generate overall better quality of saliency maps.

Figure 6(c) demonstrates the MAE comparison results between our approach and other methods. Results in Fig. 6(c) show that our approach outperforms other saliency detection methods by a large margin. Similar conclusions are also observed in the MAE comparison. It well demonstrates that the estimated saliency maps obtained by our approach are the most similar to the ground truth.

More experimental results for various approaches are shown in Fig. 7. On most images, our approach is capable of producing saliency maps that cover the entire foregrounds, while other methods only detect parts of foregrounds.

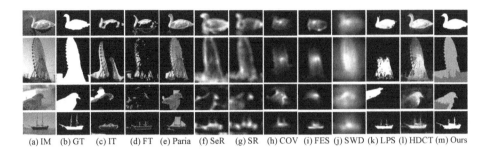

(a) IM (b) GT (c) IT (d) FT (e) Paria (f) SeR (g) SR (h) COV (i) FES (j) SWD (k) LPS (l) HDCT (m) Ours

Fig. 7. Visual comparison of saliency detection on SED1 dataset. (a) images (IM), (b) ground truths (GT), (c)–(l) saliency maps produced using different methods, and (m) our approach.

4 Conclusion

In this paper, we have presented a novel approach for salient object detection. We consider saliency to be a repetitiveness with respect to the retrieved images returned by Google image search. The proposed approach is simple, effective, and yields visually pleasing saliency maps. We believe applying the result of image retrieval to saliency estimation or other research fields is a promising direction. In the future, we plan to extend the proposed approach to feature saliency estimation for improving the accuracy of recognition.

References

1. Achanta, R., Hemami, S., Estrada, F., Susstrunk, S.: Frequency-tuned salient region detection. In: CVPR 2009, pp. 1597–1604, June 2009
2. Alpert, S., Galun, M., Brandt, A., Basri, R.: Image segmentation by probabilistic bottom-up aggregation and cue integration. IEEE Trans. Pattern Anal. Mach. Intell. (TPAMI) **34**, 315–327 (2012)
3. Cheng, M., Mitra, N.J., Huang, X., Torr, P.H., Hu, S.: Global contrast based salient region detection. IEEE Trans. Pattern Anal. Mach. Intell. (TPAMI) **37**(3), 569–582 (2015)
4. Duan, L., Wu, C., Miao, J., Qing, L., Fu, Y.: Visual saliency detection by spatially weighted dissimilarity. In: IEEE Conference on Computer Vision and Pattern Recognition (CVPR 2011), pp. 473–480 (2011)
5. Erdem, E., Erdem, A.: Visual saliency estimation by nonlinearly integrating features using region covariances. J. Vis. **13**(4), 11 (2013)
6. Fischler, M.A., Bolles, R.C.: Random sample consensus: a paradigm for model fitting with applications to image analysis and automated cartography. Commun. ACM **24**(6), 381–395 (1981)
7. Fu, H., Chi, Z., Feng, D.: Attention-driven image interpretation with application to image retrieval. Pattern Recogn. **39**, 1604–1621 (2006)
8. Hou, X., Zhang, L.: Saliency detection: a spectral residual approach. In: CVPR 2007, pp. 1–8, June 2007

9. Itti, L.: Automatic foveation for video compression using a neurobiological model of visual attention. IEEE Trans. Image Process. (TIP) **13**, 1304–1318 (2004)

10. Itti, L., Koch, C., Niebur, E.: A model of saliency-based visual attention for rapid scene analysis. IEEE Trans. Pattern Anal. Mach. Intell. **20**, 1254–1259 (1998)

11. Ke, Y., Sukthankar, R., Huston, L.: Efficient near-duplicate detection and sub-image retrieval. In: ACM Multimedia, vol. 4, p. 5 (2004)

12. Kim, J., Han, D., Tai, Y.-W., Kim, J.: Salient region detection via high-dimensional color transform and local spatial support. IEEE Trans. Image Process. (TIP) **25**(1), 9–23 (2016)

13. Li, Z., Qin, S., Itti, L.: Visual attention guided bit allocation in video compression. Image Vis. Comput. **29**, 1–14 (2011)

14. Liu, M.-Y., Tuzel, O., Ramalingam, S., Chellappa, R.: Entropy rate superpixel segmentation. In: CVPR 2011, pp. 2097–2104, June 2011

15. Liu, Z., Zou, W., Le Meur, O.: Saliency tree: a novel saliency detection framework. IEEE Trans. Image Process. (TIP) **23**(5), 1937–1952 (2014)

16. Lowe, D.: Distinctive image features from scale-invariant keypoints. IJCV **60**, 91–110 (2004)

17. Mehrani, P., Veksler, O.: Saliency segmentation based on learning and graph cut refinement. In: Proceedings of the British Machine Vision Conference, pp. 110.1–110.12 (2010)

18. Perazzi, F., Krahenbuhl, P., Pritch, Y., Hornung, A.: Saliency filters: contrast based filtering for salient region detection. In: CVPR 2012, pp. 733–740, June 2012

19. Philbin, J., Chum, O., Isard, M., Sivic, J., Zisserman, A.: Object retrieval with large vocabularies and fast spatial matching. In: IEEE Conference on Computer Vision and Pattern Recognition (CVPR 2007), pp. 1–8 (2007)

20. Rutishauser, U., Walther, D., Koch, C., Perona, P.: Is bottom-up attention useful for object recognition? In: CVPR'2004, vol. 2, pp. II-37–II-44 (2004)

21. Seo, H.J., Milanfar, P.: Static and space-time visual saliency detection by self-resemblance. J. Vis. **9**, 15 (2009)

22. Tavakoli, H.R., Rahtu, E., Heikkilä, J.: Fast and efficient saliency detection using sparse sampling and kernel density estimation. In: Image Analysis, pp. 666–675 (2011)

23. Wang, L., Xue, J., Zheng, N., Hua, G.: Automatic salient object extraction with contextual cue. In: ICCV 2011, pp. 105–112 (2011)

24. Yan, B., Li, K., Yang, X., Hu, T.: Seam searching-based pixel fusion for image retargeting. IEEE Trans. Circ. Syst. Video Technol. (TCSVT) **25**, 15–23 (2015)

Abnormal Gait Detection in Surveillance Videos with FFT-Based Analysis on Walking Rhythm

Anqin Zhang[1,2], Su Yang[1(✉)], Xinfeng Zhang[1], Jiulong Zhang[3], and Weishan Zhang[4]

[1] Shanghai Key Laboratory of Intelligent Information Processing, School of Computer Science, Fudan University, Shanghai, China
suyang@fudan.edu.cn
[2] School of Computer and Information Engineering, Shanghai University of Electric Power, Shanghai, China
[3] School of Computer Science, Xi'an University of Technology, Xi'an, China
[4] Department of Software Engineering, China University of Petroleum, Qingdao 266580, China

Abstract. For abnormal gait detection in surveillance videos, the existing methods suffer from that they are unable to recognize novel types of anomalies if the corresponding prototypes have not been included in the training data for supervised machine learning but it is impractical to foresee all types of anomalies. This research aims to solve the problem in an unsupervised manner, which does not rely on any prior knowledge regarding abnormal prototypes and avoids time-consuming machine learning over large-scale high-dimensional features. The intuition is that normal gait is nearly periodic signal and anomalies may disturb such periodicity. Hence, the time-varying ratio of width to height of a walking person is transformed to frequency domain using Fast Fourier Transform (FFT), and the standard deviation over spectrum is used as an indicator of anomalies, subject to any sudden change to break the normally periodical walking rhythm. The experimental results demonstrate its precision.

Keywords: Anomaly detection over time series · Abnormal gait detection Unsupervised learning · Aspect ratio · Fast Fourier transform

1 Introduction

Gait is a very common behavior of people in daily life [1, 2] to exhibit the physical and psychological states of people. In the existing researches, gait is treated as a biometric feature for automatic identification and verification of human identities [3, 4, 5, 6, 7]. However, gait can disclose more than identity and it provides an informative indication of the physical condition of a person, such as tumbles, jumps, and limps, which are regarded abnormal gait patterns.

A couple of clinical gait analysis studies have shown that abnormal gait can reflect a person's physical problems or the deterioration of a patient's health [17, 18, 19]. So, computer-aided gait analysis provides decision support to doctors for more reliable and

© Springer International Publishing AG 2017
Y. Zhao et al. (Eds.): ICIG 2017, Part I, LNCS 10666, pp. 108–117, 2017.
https://doi.org/10.1007/978-3-319-71607-7_10

accurate diagnosis of a disease. Moreover, it acts as an essential means in terms of healthcare for elder people, which can alarm physical problems of elder people in early time.

Depending on the sensors to collect the motion profiles of people, the existing researches in terms of abnormal gait detection can be sorted into two categories: Wearable device-based and video surveillance-based.

For wearable sensor-based abnormal gait detection, in [8], the gait data are acquired using six body-worn tags and wall-mounted sensors and a classifier is adopted for recognition of health problems in the context of machine learning. In [9], the falling-down detection is performed based on a system of wearable sensors. In [10], some fine-grained gait features representing stability, symmetry, and harmony are extracted from plantar pressure data collected from the sensors placed under toes and heels, and finally the gait patterns of Parkinson's disease are identified by employing Back Propagation (BP) Neural Network. Wearable devices require people to carry some extra equipment and most people are unwilling to wear all day. So, the scenarios of applications are limited.

For abnormal gait detection in surveillance videos, first, gait silhouettes of human bodies should be detected, and then motion features should be extracted from gait silhouettes for anomaly detection. In [11], a system to recognize abnormal activities for elderly care is developed based on R-transform and kernel discriminant. In [12], grid-based partition of body silhouettes is applied to detect abnormal gait patterns with support vector machine. In [13], the authors characterize gait patterns using silhouette-masked flow histograms. In [14], the gait patterns are classified as normal and abnormal using K-Nearest-Neighbor (KNN) classifier.

All of the aforementioned works suffer from the following problems:

(1) The methodology in terms of supervised machine learning relies on learning the prototypes of a couple of known types of anomalies. However, it is not practical to foresee or include all types of anomalies in the training data. Once some novel types of anomalies appear, the prototypes of which have never been applied to the classifier before, the anomaly detection system will fail to recognize such novel patterns.

(2) To render a high-precision anomaly detection system in the framework of supervised machine leaning, a large-scale training data is usually needed, which incurs time-consuming machine learning over large-scale high-dimensional data.

In view of the limits of the existing works, our work is based on such an intuition that normal gait is nearly periodic signal and anomalies usually disturb such periodicity. By evaluating whether the signal of working rhythm is periodical in terms of signal processing, the proposed method does not need any machine learning. As a one-dimensional statistic over FFT to measure anomalies in the present of a periodical signal, the proposed method is non-parametric and quite efficient.

The contribution of the proposed method is as follows:

(1) Abnormal gait detection is formulated as an unsupervised leaning problem and solved in the context of outlier detection over time series, which is different from the existing researches based on supervised machine learning. Such a solution is

more practical in that no prior knowledge regarding the prototypes of abnormal walking patterns is required and the anomalies not consistent with the known prototypes can also be detected.

(2) The time-varying ratio of width to height of a walking person forms a time series to characterize the rhythm of walking, namely, aspect ratio [16]. Then, we transform the time series of the aspect ratio to frequency domain using Fast Fourier Transform (FFT) and compute the standard deviation of the corresponding spectral magnitude as an indicator for anomaly detection, which is subject to any sudden change or strong pulse-like disturbance in the normally periodical time series of aspect ratio. Such a scheme for change detection in time series has a solid background in terms of signal processing.

Since only one-dimensional measure is applied to anomaly detection, the proposed solution is non-parametric and quite efficient in contrast to supervised machine learning, which rely on large-scale training data and time-consuming machine learning over large-scale high-dimensional data.

The experimental results show that the method promises high precision in detecting abnormal gait patterns from normal cases even in the case that the walking subjects exhibit a variety of abnormal gait motions, where no training data is required and the computational load is low.

2   The Proposed Method

Although there are many researches on gait based on computer vision, the most researches are focus on automatic identification and verification of human identities. There are few researches on the analysis and recognition of abnormal gait by computer vision technology. The main purpose of our work is to realize the abnormal gait recognition by analyzing the gait, so as to infer whether the individual is in an abnormal state.

In the literature, the time series of aspect ratio [16] is an important feature of human gait, which is the ratio of width to height changing over time to reflect the walking rhythm. Intuitively, the time series of aspect ratio can be regarded as a pseudo periodical signal for normal gait, and the periodicity of the aspect ratio should be unstable in case any abnormal gait appears.

The proposed method begins with extraction of human silhouettes from input videos using background subtraction. Then we use bounding box to enclose human gait silhouette in each frame and get the aspect ratio of the gait silhouette. So we can get the aspect ratio time series from input videos. Using Fast Fourier transform, we can observe and analyze the time series of aspect ratio in the frequency domain. Finally, we use the standard deviation of spectral magnitude to distinguish abnormal gaits from normal ones.

In Fig. 1, the whole procedure of the pipelined processing for feature extraction is illustrated.

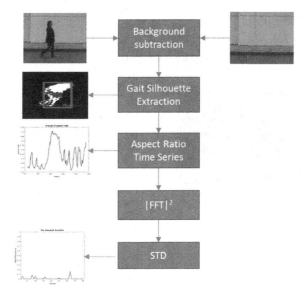

Fig. 1. Flowchart of the proposed method.

2.1 Gait Silhouette Extraction

The proposed method begins with extraction of human silhouettes from input videos. Here, the environment is continuously monitored by a stationary video camera, which provides the required input for gait detection. The input video is segmented into clips, each of which is composed of a couple of continuous frames of images for further processing. Initially, a background model of the environment is obtained and then, every frame in the video sequence is subtracted by the background model [15] to obtain the foreground image as shown in Fig. 2.

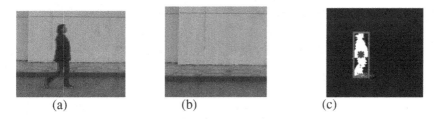

| (a) | (b) | (c) |

Fig. 2. Gait silhouette extraction: (a) Original image; (b) Background image; (c) Human silhouette.

In Fig. 2, (a) is a frame of video, (b) is the background image obtained from the first 100 frames of the video sequence, (c) is the human silhouette obtained by the differential processing.

2.2   Aspect Ratio

In Fig. 3, we use bounding box to enclose human gait silhouette, so we can get the width and height of the gait silhouette of interest.

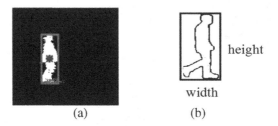

(a)   (b)

Fig. 3. Aspect ratio: (a) Bounding box of gait silhouette; (b) Width and height of the silhouette to compute aspect ratio.

Then, the aspect ratio [16] is defined as the ratio of the width of the person to the height of the person in Eq. (1), which is one of the most important features of human gait.

$$\text{Aspect Ratio} = \text{Width/Height} \tag{1}$$

The aspect ratio of the human body in a single frame image is a single value. Therefore, we need to extract gait silhouette from the video sequence, according to the changes of gait in the process of dynamic change of human walking, and extract the characteristic of the aspect ratio of the human silhouette in each frame. When the aspect ratio time series of the human silhouette is obtained, we focus on the change of the aspect ratio time series of the human body in the video sequence. In Fig. 4 shows the variation of the aspect ratio in a video sequence.

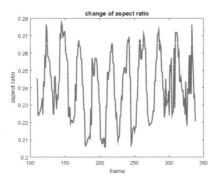

Fig. 4. The aspect ratio time series of the normal gait.

As can be seen from Fig. 4, the aspect ratio of the normal gait shows a quasi- periodic variation with time evolution with regular rhythm of peaks and bottoms to appear.

Examples of four types of gaits are shown in Fig. 5, which are normal, tumble, jump and limp.

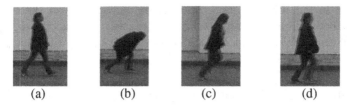

Fig. 5. Examples of four types of gaits: (a) Normal; (b) Tumble; (c) Jump; (d) Limp

The corresponding silhouettes, aspect ratio, and standard deviation of the spectral representation of aspect ratio are shown in Fig. 6.

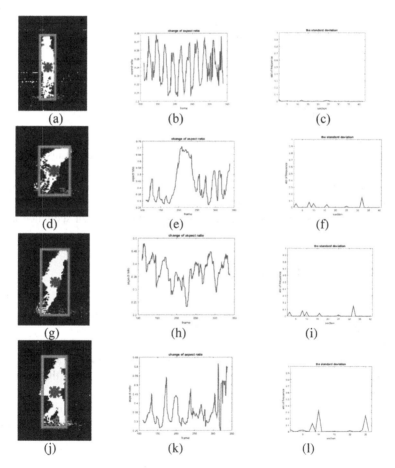

Fig. 6. The exemplar silhouettes, aspect ratio, and standard deviation of spectral magnitude of aspect ratio for four types of gaits: (a), (b), (c): normal; (d), (e), (f): tumble; (g), (h), (i): jump; (j), (k), (l): limp. Here, (a), (d), (g), (j) are the silhouettes; (b), (e), (h), (k) are the corresponding aspect ratio changing over time; (c), (f), (i), (l) are the standard deviations of the frequency.

As shown in Fig. 6(b), the aspect ratio of the moving human silhouette shows periodic variation with time with regular rhythm of peaks and bottoms to appear. For the abnormal cases shown in Fig. 6(e), (h), (k), it can be observed that the periodicity of the time series of aspect ratio is disturbed.

2.3   Statistic over FFT Regarding Periodicity

Using Fast Fourier transform, we can observe and analyze the time series of aspect ratio in the frequency domain. It is well-known that by means of FFT, any periodical signal can be decomposed into a couple of basic periodical signals in terms of sine or cosine waveforms with different frequencies. So, FFT is a primary analytical tool to observe periodicity of signals in frequency domain. This motivates us to use the standard deviation of spectral magnitude to distinguish abnormal gaits from normal ones. In our method, the aspect ratio time series is first segmented according to the extreme value, and then the fast Fourier transform is performed on each segment. Finally, the standard deviation of each segment is obtained.

3   Experiments

3.1   Data Collection

Since there is no benchmark for abnormal gait detection in unsupervised manner, For performance evaluation, we collect video data to do research by ourselves. In the experiment, the camera is fixed to observe the lateral image of human walking. In total, eight subjects are required to walk across the same background both normally and in an unusual way, such as tumble, skip, and limp. Some sample images are shown in Fig. 5. The data sets include 32 sequences, and an average length of each sequence is about 300 frames.

3.2   Performance Evaluation

As shown in Fig. 6, we can observe a strong regularity from the periodicity of normal gait. In such a case, the standard deviation of the spectral magnitude is relatively small, and on the contrary, the feature of abnormal gaits is large.

Figure 7 shows that the normal and abnormal gaits correspond with smaller and bigger standard deviation, respectively. The X axis in the figure is a section of the aspect ratio time series according to the extreme value. The Y axis in the figure is the standard deviation of the frequency of each segment.

For performance evaluation, the accuracy of the detection results is defined as the ratio of the correctly detected anomalies to the number of all anomalies as follows:

$$Accuracy = \frac{1}{N} \sum_{i=1}^{N} \delta(F_i > \theta) \tag{2}$$

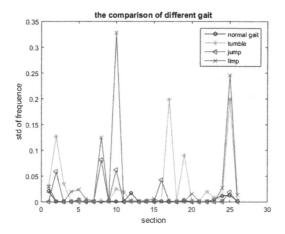

Fig. 7. Comparison of the FFT features of different gaits.

where Fi represents the FFT feature of the ith gait sample, N the number of all abnormal gait samples, θ a predefined threshold, and $\delta(Fi > \theta) = 1$ if $Fi > \theta$, which functions to count the correct hits of anomalies. The setting of parameter θ can affect the accuracy of abnormal gait detection. Figure 8 shows the effects of different parameter values on the detection results, where the parameter θ is assumed to be between 0.00009 and 0.004. Note that the detection results can reach 100% if the parameter value is properly set.

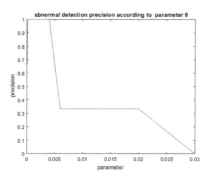

Fig. 8. Precision of anomaly detection against parameter θ.

Similar to our works, the accuracy of the detection method using KNN classifier in work [14] is 77%, and the method in [13] using silhouette-masked flow histograms to analyze abnormal walking gait, the accuracy is 90%. Obviously, the accuracy of our algorithm is higher.

The proposed method is implemented on a computer configured with Core i5 and 8 GB RAM. As our method does not need any training, the processing time for each frame is 256 ms under MATLAB, which is obviously efficient.

4 Conclusions

Human gait contains a lot of information, and gait characteristics of human are diffi-cultly to disguise and are easily to obtain. Gait can exhibit the physical and psycho-logical states of people to some degree. Abnormal gait may represent some problems of the physical and psychological states of people, so it is very important to detect abnormal gait rapidly, for treatment diseases or prevention threats to public safety.

In this paper, An unsupervised approach for abnormal gait detection is proposed, which requires no prior knowledge regarding prototypes of abnormal gaits, nor any machine learning. Here, the periodicity of the time series of aspect ratio is measured in frequency domain as the standard deviation of the spectral magnitude, which acts as the indicator of how the nearly periodical walking rhythm in normal case is disturbed. The experimental results show that the proposed method is not only promising in terms of precision but also efficient due to the one-dimensional non-parametric feature adopted. The method has the potential to be applied to a variety of applications, including unobtrusive clinical gait analysis and automated video surveillance.

Currently, our methods cannot solve the problems in different scales and the camera motion. In the future, we will work to study the problem in different, unconstrained real world settings. In addition, we are working to adopt our approach to situations with several people and find the method to extract and analyze several silhouettes simultaneously.

Acknowledgments. This work is supported by NSFC (Grant No. 61472087).

References

1. Cutting, J., Kozlowski, L.: Recognizing friends by their walk: gait perception without familiarity cues. Bull. Psychon. Soc. **9**(5), 353–356 (1977)
2. Sudeep, S., Jonathon, P.P., Zongyi, L., et al.: The human ID gait challenge problem: data sets, performance, and analysis. IEEE Trans. Pattern Anal. Mach. Intell. **27**(2), 162–177 (2005)
3. Nixon, M.S., Carter, J.N.: Advances in automatic gait recognition. In: IEEE International Conference on Automatic Face and Gesture Recognition, pp. 11–16 (2004)
4. Han, J., Bhanu, B.: Individual recognition using gait energy image. IEEE Trans. Pattern Anal. Mach. Intell. **28**(2), 316–322 (2006)
5. He, Q., Debrunner. C.: Individual recognition from periodic activity using hidden Markov models. The Workshop on Human Motion, pp. 47–52 (2000)
6. Wang, L., Tan, T., Ning, H., et al.: Silhouette analysis-based gait recognition for human identification. IEEE Trans. Pattern Anal. Mach. Intell. **25**(12), 1505–1518 (2004)
7. Bashir, K., Xiang, T., Gong, S.: Gait recognition without subject cooperation. Pattern Recogn. Lett. **31**(13), 2052–2060 (2010)
8. Pogorelc, B., Bosnić, Z., Gams, M.: Automatic recognition of gait-related health problems in the elderly using machine learning. Multimedia Tools Appl. **58**(2), 333–354 (2012)
9. Huynh, Q.T., Nguyen, U.D., Irazabal, L.B., Ghassemian, N., Tran, B.Q.: Optimization of an accelerometer and gyroscope-based fall detection algorithm. J. Sens. **2015**, 1–8 (2015)

10. Wang, T., Zhang, D., Wang, Z., et al.: Recognizing gait pattern of parkinson's disease patients based on fine-grained movement function features. In: IEEE International Conference on Ubiquitous Intelligence and Computing, pp. 1–10 (2015)
11. Khan, Z.A., Sohn, W.: Abnormal human activity recognition system based on R-transform and kernel discriminant technique for elderly home care. IEEE Trans. Consum. Electron. **57** (4), 1843–1850 (2011)
12. Bauckhage, C., Tsotsos, J.K., Bunn, F.E.: Automatic detection of abnormal gait. Image Vis. Comput. **27**(1–2), 108–115 (2009)
13. Wang, L.: Abnormal walking gait analysis using silhouette-masked flow histograms, vol. 3, pp. 473–476 (2006)
14. Fathima, S.M.H.S.S., Banu, R.S.D.W.: Abnormal gait classification using silhouettes. ARPN J. Eng. Appl Sci. **10**(8), 3761–3765 (2015)
15. Zivkovic, Z., van der Heijden, F.: Efficient adaptive density estimation per image pixel for the task of background subtraction. Pattern Recogn. Lett. **27**(7), 773–780 (2006)
16. Lin, K.W., Chung, P.C.: Aspect ratio waves for gait analysis. In: International Conference on Intelligent Information Hiding and Multimedia Signal Processing, pp. 118–121 (2009)
17. Vaught, S.L.: Gait, balance, and fall prevention. Ochsner J. **3**(2), 94–97 (2001)
18. Chang, F.M., Rhodes, J.T., Flynn, K.M., et al.: The role of gait analysis in treating gait abnormalities in cerebral palsy. Orthop. Clin. N. Am. **41**(4), 489–506 (2010)
19. Jamshidi, N., Rostami, M., Najarian, S., et al.: Differences in centre of pressure trajectory between normal and steppage gait. J. Res. Med. Sci. **15**(1), 33–40 (2010)

Uncooperative Gait Recognition Using Joint Bayesian

Chao Li[1($\boxtimes$)], Kan Qiao[2], Xin Min[1], Xiaoyan Pang[2], and Shouqian Sun[1]

[1] College of Computer Science and Technology, Zhejiang University,
Hangzhou 310027, China
{superli,minx,ssq}@zju.edu.cn
[2] Sir Run Run Shaw Hospital, Zhejiang University, Hangzhou 310027, China
{qiaok,pangxiaoy}@srrsh.com

Abstract. Human gait, as a soft biometric, helps to recognize people by walking without subject cooperation. In this paper, we propose a more challenging uncooperative setting under which views of the gallery and probe are both unknown and mixed up (uncooperative setting). Joint Bayesian is adopted to model the view variance. We conduct experiments to evaluate the effectiveness of Joint Bayesian under the proposed uncooperative setting on OU-ISIR Large Population Dataset (OULP) and CASIA-B Dataset (CASIA-B). As a result, we confirm that Joint Bayesian significantly outperform the state-of-the-art methods for both identification and verification tasks even when the training subjects are different from the test subjects. For further comparison, the uncooperative protocol, experimental results, learning models, and test codes are available.

Keywords: Gait recognition · Joint Bayesian
Uncooperative gait recognition

1 Introduction

Biometrics refers to the use of intrinsic physical or behavioral traits in order to identify humans. Besides regular features (face, fingerprint, iris, DNA and retina), human gait, which can be obtained from people at larger distances and at low resolution without subjects' cooperation has recently attracted much attention. It also has a vast application prospect in crime investigation and wide-area surveillance. For example, criminals usually wear gloves, dark sun-glasses, and face masks to invalidate finger print, eyes, and face recognition. In such scenarios, gait recognition is the only useful and effective identification method. Previous research [1,2] has shown that human gait, specifically the walking pattern, is difficult to disguise and unique to each people.

In general, video sensor-based gait recognition methods are divided into two families: appearance-based [3–5] and model-based [6–8]. In the appearance-based methods, it focus on the motion of human body and usually operate

© Springer International Publishing AG 2017
Y. Zhao et al. (Eds.): ICIG 2017, Part I, LNCS 10666, pp. 118–126, 2017.
https://doi.org/10.1007/978-3-319-71607-7_11

on silhouettes of gait. They extract gait descriptors from the silhouettes. The general framework of appearance-based methods usually consists of silhouette extraction, period detection, representation generation, and recognition. A typical example is gait energy image (GEI) [3] which is proposed as a mixture of dynamic and static features. In model-based gait recognition, it focus more on the extraction of the stride parameters of subject that describe the gait by using the human body structure. The model-based methods usually require high resolution images as well as are computationally expensive while gait recognition needs to be real-time and effective at low resolution. However, the performance of gait recognition is often influenced by several variations such as clothing, walking speed, observation views, and carrying bags. For appearance-based methods, view changes are the most problematic variations.

A. Joint Bayesian for modeling view variance

When dealing with view change problems, many appearance-based methods are proposed: (1) view transformation model (VTM) based generative approaches [9,10]. (2) view-invariant feature-based approaches [11]. (3) multi-view gallery-based approaches [12]. (4) subspace-based view-invariant discriminative approaches [13–15]. However, VTM-based approaches(e.g. TCM+ [10], wQVTM [9]) as well as some discriminative approaches (GMMFA [13]) often require view information for a matching pair, while the information usually can't be obtained easily without subject's cooperate.

So, we introduce Joint Bayesian to model the view variance which differs from the above approaches, and the commonly used GEI is adopted as the input gait representation. After the training process, the proposed method can be easily used without any view information in advance.

B. Uncooperative gait recognition and transform learning

Most exist cross-view gait recognition methods [9,10,13] are based on the assumption that gallery and probe views are known as a priori or fixed (cooperative setting) while this assumption is often not valid in practice.

Usually, the gallery and probe view are often unknown and mixed up (uncooperative setting). However, to the best of our knowledge, only a few studies [11,14,15] focus on uncooperative gait recognition. In [14,15], the uncooperative setting just consider two different views every time while our proposed setting consider four different views and is more complex. Our proposed uncooperative setting is same with [11], but they just conduct experiments on OU-ISIR Large Population Dataset (OULP) [16] while we also use the famous CASIA-B Dataset (CASIA-B) [17] as a benchmark. Additionally, the training subjects are often different from the test subjects, so that transfer learning is performed [14,15].

2   Gait Recognition

Usually, gait recognition can be divided into two major tasks: gait verification and gait identification as in face recognition [18–20]. Gait verification is used for verifying whether two input gait sequences (Gallery, Probe) belong to the same subject. In this paper, we calculated the similar score ($SimScore$) using Joint Bayesian to evaluate the similarity of two given sequences. Euclidean distance was also adopted as a baseline method for comparison. In gait identification, a set of subjects are gathered (The gallery), and it aims to decide which of the gallery identities are similar to the probe at test time. Under the closed set identification condition, a probe sequence is compared with all the gallery identities, then identity which has the largest $SimScore$ is the final result.

2.1   Gait Verification Using Joint Bayesian

In this paper, we modeled gait representations by summing two independent Gaussian variables as:

$$x = \mu + \varepsilon \tag{1}$$

where x represents a mean-subtracted representation vector. For a better performance, L_2 - normalization was applied for gait representations. μ is gait identity following a Gaussian distribution $N(0, S_\mu)$. ε stands for different gait variations (e.g., view, clothing and carrying bags etc.) following a Gaussian distribution $N(0, S_\varepsilon)$. Joint Bayesian models the joint probability of two gait representations using the intra-class variation (I) or inter-class variance (E) hypothesis, $P(x_1, x_2|H_I)$ and $P(x_1, x_2|H_E)$. Given the above prior from Eq. 1 and the independent assumption between μ and ε, the covariance matrix of $P(x_1, x_2|H_I)$ and $P(x_1, x_2|H_E)$ can be derived separately as:

$$\Sigma_I = \begin{bmatrix} S_\mu + S_\varepsilon & S_\mu \\ S_\mu & S_\mu + S_\varepsilon \end{bmatrix} \tag{2}$$

$$\Sigma_E = \begin{bmatrix} S_\mu + S_\varepsilon & 0 \\ 0 & S_\mu + S_\varepsilon \end{bmatrix} \tag{3}$$

S_μ and S_ε are two unknown covariance matrices which can be learned from the training set using EM algorithm. During the testing phase, the likelihood ratio ($r(x1, x2)$) is regarded as the similar score ($SimScore$):

$$SimScore(x_1, x_2) = r(x_1, x_2) = log \frac{P(x_1, x_2|H_I)}{P(x_1, x_2|H_E)} \tag{4}$$

$r(x_1, x_2)$ is efficient to obtained with the following closed-form process:

$$r(x_1, x_2) = x_1^T A x_1 + x_2^T A x_2 - 2x_1^T G x_2 \tag{5}$$

where A and G are two final result model, which can be obtained by using simple algebra operations between S_μ and S_ε. Please refer to [21] for more details. We also public our trained model (A and G) and testing codes in https://pan.baidu. com/s/1qYk9HoC for further comparison.

2.2   Gait Identification Using Joint Bayesian

For gait identification, the probe sample x_p is classified as class i, if the final *SimScore* with all the gallery (x_i) is the maximum as shown in Eq. 6.

$$i = arg \max_{i \in [0, N_{gallery}-1]} SimScore(x_i, x_p) \tag{6}$$

where $N_{gallery}$ is the number of training subjects. In the experiments, we just used the first period of the gait sequence.

3   Experiments

To evaluate the performance of Joint Bayesian under uncooperative setting [11,14,15], extensive experiments have been carried out on the two largest public gait dataset: OU-ISIR Large Population Dataset (OULP) [16] and CASIA-B Dataset (CASIA-B) [17]. For comparison, we just considered four different views on OULP (55°, 65°, 75°, 85°) and CASIA-B (36°, 54°, 72°, 90°), respectively.

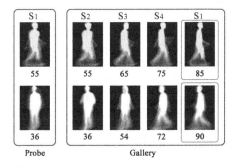

Fig. 1. Examples of GEIs from different people in OULP (top) and CASIA-B (bottom) under four different view conditions. The first S1 appears to be the best match to S2, because they are under the same view, which can easily lead to a wrong match.

Table 1. Comparison of rank-1 (%) and EERs (%) with other existent methods on OULP in uncooperative setting.

	Joint Bayesian	GEINet	LDA	1NN
Rank-1 [%]	96.81 ± 0.60	89.70	91.09 ± 0.89	21.62 ± 1.44
EERs [%]	1.58 ± 0.14	1.60	4.11 ± 0.24	31.53 ± 0.95

Table 2. Comparison of rank-1 (%) and EERs (%) with other existent methods on CASIA-B in uncooperative setting.

	Joint Bayesian	RankSVM	LDA	1NN
Rank-1 [%]	86.4 ± 2.78	72.2 ± 3.80	76.0 ± 3.56	12.9 ± 3.8
EERs [%]	8.3 ± 1.58	15.5 ± 1.72	12.6 ± 1.34	42.5 ± 3.79

3.1   Experiments Settings

Gait Features. We first computed gait periods in each gait sequence and then extracted the most commonly used gait energy image (GEI) [3] which is proposed as a mixture of dynamic and static features. GEI is calculated by averaging gait silhouettes over a gait cycle. If the gait sequence has more than one cycle, we just chose the first one. For preprocessing, gait silhouette images were scaled to 64×44 pixel-sized images and PCA was adopted to preserve 95% of the variance before Joint Bayesian was applied. GEIs under four view conditions are shown in Fig. 1.

Uncooperative Setting. All experiments are carried out following the uncooperative protocol as follows unless otherwise specified. First of all, the whole set of gait sequences is equally and randomly divided into two groups of the same number of subjects, one for training and the other for testing, i.e. the subjects in the two groups are different and transfer learning is performed. Secondly, the test data is further split into a gallery set and a probe set as the following steps: (1) A gallery view of each subject is drawn randomly from four different views; (2) A probe view of corresponding subject is randomly chosen from the other three views. We have made public details of our division for all the experiments in https://pan.baidu.com/s/1qYk9HoC.

Benchmarks. On the two gait datasets, two commonly used methods are adopted as baseline methods. They are : (1) 1 Nearest Neighbor classifier (1NN). The original gait representation (GEI) are used in this method, and it has a relatively high dimensionality ($64 \times 44 = 2816$); (2) Linear Discriminant Analysis (LDA): Firstly, PCA is adopted along with LDA to achieve the best performance as in [14,15].

Additionally, on CASIA-B, RankSVM [14,15] achieves the best performance under uncooperative setting while they just consider two different views every time. RanSVM are so computationally expensive when the training subjects increase that it is not suitable for OULP which has a large training population (956 subjects). On OULP, GEINet [11] is the state-of-the-art method which uses the deep learning method and the performance is dependent on the number of training subjects, so that it is not suitable for CASIA-B. RankSVM and GEINet are also adopted as the comparison methods separately on the two datasets. The results of GEINet are provided by the authors while RankSVM are implemented by ourselves.

Evaluation Criteria. The recognition performance is evaluated using four metrics: (1) cumulative match characteristics (CMC) curve, (2) rank-1 identification rates, (3) the receiver operating characteristic (ROC) curve of false acceptance rates (FAR) and false rejection rates (FRR), and (4) equal error rates (EERs). CMC curve, and rank-1 identification rates are used for identification task while ROC curve and EERs are used for verification task.

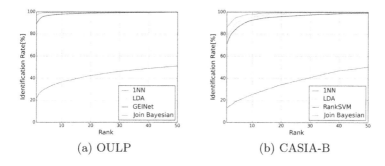

(a) OULP   (b) CASIA-B

Fig. 2. CMC curves of two different datasets in uncooperative setting.

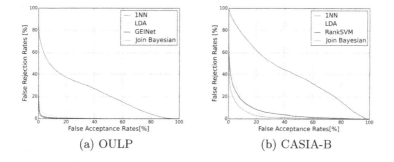

(a) OULP   (b) CASIA-B

Fig. 3. ROC curves of two different datasets in uncooperative setting.

3.2   Experimental Results on OULP

The OULP has nearly 4000 subjects, and because of the largest population, experimental results can be calculated in a statistically reliable way. Each subject has two video sequences (Gallery, Probe) and is at four view angles (55°, 65°, 75°, 85°). GEIs at different views with four sample subjects are shown in Fig. 1.

We used a subset (1912 subjects) of OULP following the uncooperative protocol of [11] and the subset was further divided into two groups of the same number of subjects, one for training while the other one for testing. To reduce any effect of random grouping, five 2-fold cross validations were performed. During each train phase, $956 * (956 - 1) = 912980$ intra-class samples and $956 * 1 = 956$ inter-class samples were used for training Joint Bayesian. For preprocessing, gait silhouette images were scaled to 64×44 pixel-sized images and PCA was adopted to preserve 95% of the variance.

We summarize rank-1 identification rate and EERs in Table 1. Furthermore, Figs. 2a, and 3a show more details of CMC and ROC curves. We find that our proposed method significantly outperforms the benchmarks with respect to rank-1 and EERs under uncooperative setting. More specifically, compared with the state-of-the-art method (GEINet), rank-1 identification rates of Joint Bayesian improves from 89.70% to 96.81%; for verification task, our proposed method also achieve a competitive result with respect to EERs. We can also find that learning based method (1NN PCA+LDA) significantly outperforms the existing template matching methods (1NN).

3.3   Experimental Results on CASIA-B

In CASIA-B, totally 124 subjects gait data are captured from 11 views $(0°–180°)$. Between two nearest view directions, the interval angle is $18°$. Three covariate condition changes, i.e., clothing, carrying, and view angle are all considered. In this dataset, each subject has 10 gait sequences: 6 normal walking sequences (nm), 2 carrying-bag sequences (bg), and 2 wearing-coat sequences (cl).

For consistency with the result of OULP, we just considered the view covariate condition change (6 nm sequences), and four similar views $(36°, 54°, 72°, 90°)$ were selected. Following the uncooperative protocol, the dataset was also divided into two groups of the same number of subjects, on for training and one for testing. As in Sect. 3.2, five repeated experiments performed. As a result 5 2-fold cross validations were performed, and the same processing are adopted as in 3.2.

We summarize the rank-1 identification rate and EERs in Table 2. CMC and ROC curves are also shown in Figs. 2b and 3b. They show similar trends as those in the OULP experiments that Joint Bayesian achieves the best results for both the identification and verification tasks. We can also find that: (1) the corresponding methods perform better on OULP than on CASIA-B due to OULP's cleaner silhouettes and larger training subjects; (2) RankSVM loses it's stronger power than in [14,15] because our proposed uncooperative setting is more challenging; (3) the insufficient dataset leads to volatile results for all the methods.

4   Conclusion

In this paper, Joint Bayesian is used for model the view variance for uncooperative gait recognition. Extensive experiments have been conducted to validate the effectiveness of our method particularly under our proposed more challenging uncooperative setting. Our proposed method which learns transferable information independent of the identity of people achieved state-of-the-art results for both the identification and verification tasks through experiments on OULP and CASIA-B datasets. What's more important, Joint Bayesian can be trained from different subjects and performs better which makes it more generally applicable.

In our future works, we will evaluate our proposed method with a wider view variation, or other variations (e.g. clothing, carrying bags). Additionally, cross-dataset gait recognition will be evaluated and the novel deep convolutional features will also be considered.

Acknowledgments. The authors would like to thank OU-ISIR and CBSR for providing access to the OULP and CASIA-B. This study is partly supported by the National Natural Science Foundation of China (Nos. 61303137, 61402141, 61562072), and Specialized Research Fund for the Doctoral Program of Higher Education (No. 20130101110148).

References

1. Murray, M.P., Drought, A.B., Kory, R.C.: Walking patterns of normal men. J. Bone Joint Surg. Am. **46**(2), 335–360 (1964)
2. Cutting, J.E., Kozlowski, L.T.: Recognizing friends by their walk: gait perception without familiarity cues. Bull. Psychon. Soc. **9**(5), 353–356 (1977)
3. Liu, Z., Sarkar, S.: Simplest representation yet for gait recognition: averaged silhouette. In: Proceedings of 2004 International Conference on Pattern Recognition, pp. 211–214. IEEE Press, New York (2004)
4. Lam, T.H., Cheung, K.H., Liu, J.N.: Gait flow image: a silhouette-based gait representation for human identification. Pattern Recogn. **44**(4), 973–987 (2011)
5. Bashir, K., Xiang, T., Gong, S.: Gait recognition using gait entropy image. In: Proceedings of 3rd International Conference on Crime Detection and Prevention, pp. 1–6. IEEE Press, New York (2009)
6. Luo, J., Tang, J., Tjahjadi, T., Xiao, X.: Robust arbitrary view gait recognition based on parametric 3D human body reconstruction and virtual posture synthesis. Pattern Recogn. **60**, 361–377 (2016)
7. Bhanu, B., Han, J.: Model-based human recognition 2D and 3D gait. In: Bhanu, B., Han, J. (eds.) Human Recognition at a Distance in Video. Advances in Pattern Recognition, pp. 65–94. Springer, Heidelberg (2010). https://doi.org/10.1007/978-0-85729-124-0_5
8. Nixon, M.S., Carter, J.N., Cunado, D., Huang, P.S., Stevenage, S.: Automatic gait recognition. In: Jain, A.K., Bolle, R., Pankanti, S. (eds.) Biometrics, pp. 231–249. Springer, Boston (1996). https://doi.org/10.1007/0-306-47044-6_11
9. Muramatsu, D., Makihara, Y., Yagi, Y.: View transformation model incorporating quality measures for cross-view gait recognition. IEEE Trans. Cybern. **46**(7), 1602–1615 (2016)
10. Muramatsu, D., Makihara, Y., Yagi, Y.: Cross-view gait recognition by fusion of multiple transformation consistency measures. IET Biometrics **4**(2), 62–73 (2015)
11. Shiraga, K., Makihara, Y., Muramatsu, D., Echigo, T., Yagi, Y.: GEINet: view-invariant gait recognition using a convolutional neural network. In: 2016 International Conference on Biometrics, pp. 1–8. IEEE Press, New York (2016)

12. Iwashita, Y., Baba, R., Ogawara, K., Kurazume, R.: Person identification from spatio-temporal 3D gait. In: 2010 International Conference on Emerging Security Technologies, pp. 30–35. IEEE Press, New York (2010)
13. Sharma, A., Kumar, A., Daume, H., Jacobs, D.W.: Generalized multiview analysis: a discriminative latent space. In: 2012 IEEE Conference on Computer Vision and Pattern Recognition, pp. 2160–2167. IEEE Press, New York (2012)
14. Martín-Félez, R., Xiang, T.: Gait recognition by ranking. In: Fitzgibbon, A., Lazebnik, S., Perona, P., Sato, Y., Schmid, C. (eds.) ECCV 2012. LNCS, vol. 7572, pp. 328–341. Springer, Heidelberg (2012). https://doi.org/10.1007/978-3-642-33718-5_24
15. Martín-Félez, R., Xiang, T.: Uncooperative gait recognition by learning to rank. Pattern Recogn. **47**(12), 3793–3806 (2014)
16. Iwama, H., Okumura, M., Makihara, Y., Yagi, Y.: The OU-ISIR gait database comprising the large population dataset and performance evaluation of gait recognition. IEEE Trans. Inf. Forensics Secur. **7**(5), 1511–1521 (2012)
17. Yu, S., Tan, D., Tan, T.: A framework for evaluating the effect of view angle, clothing and carrying condition on gait recognition. In: 2006 International Conference on Pattern Recognition, pp. 441–444. IEEE Press, New York (2006)
18. Sun, Y., Wang, X., Tang, X.: Deep learning face representation from predicting 10,000 classes. In: Proceedings of 2014 IEEE Conference on Computer Vision and Pattern Recognitionm, pp. 1891–1898. IEEE Press, New York (2014)
19. Sun, Y., Chen, Y., Wang, X., Tang, X.: Deep learning face representation by joint identification-verification. In: Advances in Neural Information Processing Systems, pp. 1988–1996. IEEE Press, New York (2014)
20. Sun, Y., Wang, X., Tang, X.: Deeply learned face representations are sparse, selective, and robust. In: Proceedings of the IEEE Conference on Computer Vision and Pattern Recognition, pp. 2892–2900. IEEE Press, New York (2015)
21. Chen, D., Cao, X., Wang, L., Wen, F., Sun, J.: Bayesian face revisited: a joint formulation. In: Fitzgibbon, A., Lazebnik, S., Perona, P., Sato, Y., Schmid, C. (eds.) ECCV 2012. LNCS, vol. 7574, pp. 566–579. Springer, Heidelberg (2012). https://doi.org/10.1007/978-3-642-33712-3_41

Pedestrian Detection via Structure-Sensitive Deep Representation Learning

Deliang Huang[1], Shijia Huang[2], Hefeng Wu[2(✉)], and Ning Liu[1]

[1] School of Data and Computer Science, Sun Yat-sen University,
Guangzhou, China
`huangdl007@qq.com`, `liuning2@mail.sysu.edu.cn`
[2] School of Information Science and Technology,
Guangdong University of Foreign Studies, Guangzhou, China
`huangshijia_gia@qq.com`, `wuhefeng@gmail.com`

Abstract. Pedestrian detection is a fundamental task in a wide range of computer vision applications. Detecting the head-shoulder appearance is an attractive way for pedestrian detection, especially in scenes with crowd, heavy occlusion or large camera tilt angles. However, the head-shoulder part contains less information than the full human body, which requires better feature extraction to ensure the effectiveness of the detection. This paper proposes a head-shoulder detection method based on the convolutional neural network (CNN). According to the characteristics of the head and shoulders, our method integrates a structure-sensitive ROI pooling layer into the CNN architecture. The proposed CNN is trained in a multi-task scheme with classification and localization outputs. Furthermore, the convolutional layers of the network are pre-trained using a triplet loss to capture better features of the head-shoulder appearance. Extensive experimental results demonstrate that the average accuracy of the proposed method is 89.6% when the IoU threshold is 0.5. Our method obtains close results to the state-of-the-art method Faster R-CNN while outperforming it in speed. Even when the number of extracted candidate regions increases, the increased detection time is negligible. In addition, when the IoU threshold is greater than 0.6, the average accuracy of our method is higher than that of Faster R-CNN, which indicates that our results have higher IoU with ground truth.

1 Introduction

Pedestrian detection has gained great attention in the past few decades due to its important role in many computer vision applications [1–4]. Head-shoulder detection is one of the active ways for the pedestrian detection task [5–7]. There are two main motivations for choosing the head-shoulder part as the target. For one thing, head-shoulder detection is more reliable than detection of full pedestrian body. In complex and dynamic scenes, many challenging factors like posture change and occlusion would seriously interfere with the human body but less with the head and shoulders which would still have high consistency

© Springer International Publishing AG 2017
Y. Zhao et al. (Eds.): ICIG 2017, Part I, LNCS 10666, pp. 127–138, 2017.
https://doi.org/10.1007/978-3-319-71607-7_12

under different postures. When the pedestrian is occluded, head and shoulders are more likely to be detected. For another thing, because of the diversity of the head shape, hair style and hair color, it is difficult to achieve ideal results of head detection. However, with a larger part composed of head and shoulders, we can extract more valuable features.

Many works have been presented for exploiting the head-shoulder appearance for pedestrian detection [6–8]. Hand-crafted features are conventionally combined with classifiers in the field of machine learning to complete the detection task. Histogram of Oriented Gradients (HOG) is a typical feature that can describe the shape and edge information of the object, which was introduced by Dalal and Triggs [9] for pedestrian detection. Later, Li et al. [6] applied HOG features to the detection of head and shoulders. Local Binary Pattern (LBP) is also a widely applied descriptor in object detection. Wang et al. [10] gained improved results of pedestrian detection with the combination of HOG and LBP features. Zeng and Ma [7] presented a discriminative multi-level HOG-LBP feature for head-shoulder detection. Besides the commonly used support vector machine (SVM) classifiers, Viola-Jones classifiers and AdaBoost classifiers are also often employed due to their property of fast computation [5,11]. However, traditional methods cannot well capture the rich information conveyed by images and have very limited generalization ability for various application environments.

Recently, deep learning methods have been actively applied in diverse tasks for their ability of learning features directly from images. Many deep learning models, commonly based on convolutional neural networks (CNN), have been presented for object detection [12–16]. Among them, R-CNN [12] performed feature extraction without any sharing for the calculation of each candidate region. SPPnet [13] introduced adaptively-sized pooling on shared convolutional feature maps for efficient region-based object detection. Afterwards, end-to-end detector training on shared convolutional features was achieved by Fast R-CNN [14], and Faster R-CNN [15] incorporated region proposals to form an efficient unified network. Inspired by these deep learning methods, we exploit the powerful representation learning ability of deep learning models for the head-shoulder detection task.

In order to extract reliable head-shoulder characteristic for detecting pedestrians in complex and challenging environments, this paper introduces a head-shoulder detection method based on the convolutional neural network. The proposed model combines candidate region extraction, head-shoulder classification and location prediction by sharing parameters. We propose a novel structure-sensitive neural network method by embedding head-shoulder structure information, which can add translation variability to better predict head-shoulder location. Specifically, we construct structure-sensitive convolutional feature maps behind the shared convolutional layers, and use a structure-sensitive pooling method to integrate the location information of head and shoulders into the feature of the candidate region. In this way, the pedestrians will be localized more accurately and the Intersection-over-Union (IoU) between the detection bounding box and the ground truth box is higher. Meanwhile, to improve the effectiveness of our model, we pre-train the shared convolutional layers with a triplet loss for the initialization of the head-shoulder detection network model. The experimental results demonstrate that the performance of our method is close to that of Faster R-CNN [15] while running faster than it with higher IoU. Besides, when the number of Regions-of-Interest (RoIs) is increased, the increased detection time can be ignored.

2   Proposed Method

The framework of our method is illustrated in Fig. 1. The lower part of Fig. 1 shows the detection process. First, The high-level convolutional features of the image are extracted via the shared convolutional subnet. Second, the image candidate regions that may contain head-shoulders will be generated. Third, structure-sensitive pooling is performed for each candidate region. Finally, with the pooled feature, the predictors will classify a candidate and find the accurate location. Furthermore, to improve the effectiveness of our model, we pre-train the shared convolutional subnet with a triplet loss, as shown in the upper part of Fig. 1.

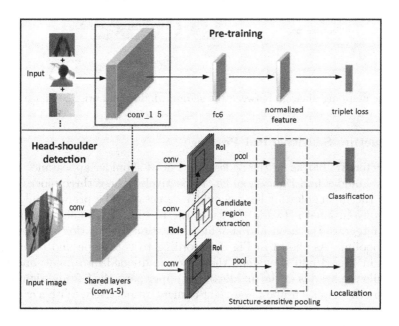

Fig. 1. The framework of the proposed method for head-shoulder detection.

2.1   Candidate Region Extraction

We utilize a candidate region extraction method based on sliding window. All image patches will be enumerated by the sliding window and they will be classified as foreground objects or background. Only the foreground patches will be considered as candidate regions and be further processed. The image patches are generated based on the feature maps output by the shared convolutional subnet. For simplicity, the size of the sliding window is fixed to 3 × 3 and the stride is set to 1. Meanwhile, in order to handle objects of different sizes, we introduce a multi-scale mapping strategy. That is, a window on the feature map corresponds to multiple image regions of different sizes on the original image. Here we use the combination of different scales and aspect ratios. According to the shape characteristic of head-shoulders, we define three scales $\{100^2, 150^2, 200^2\}$ and three aspect ratios $\{3:4, 4:4, 5:4\}$. Therefore, each sliding window maps to nine image regions of different sizes, illustrated in Fig. 2. We use the softmax classifier to pick out all foreground regions as the candidates.

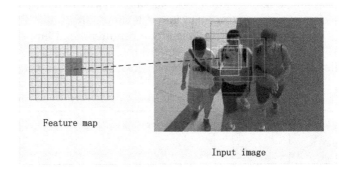

Feature map

Input image

Fig. 2. The mapping diagram between the sliding window and original image regions.

2.2 Structure-Sensitive RoI Pooling

The characteristic blocks on the pedestrian's head-shoulder appearance contain head, left shoulder and right shoulder, respectively. These three blocks can be viewed as the main roles for head-shoulder detection. The proposed algorithm uses the convolutional network to extract the feature of head-shoulder appearance and integrate the head and shoulders' location information via structure-sensitive pooling. As shown in Fig. 3, according to the shape and positions of a pedestrian's head and shoulders, the region is divided into upper and lower parts. While the head is at the middle of the upper part, the left and right shoulders occupy the lower left and lower right corners, respectively. With a candidate region of size $w \times h$ and the coordinates of the top left corner to be (x_0, y_0), the head block is defined as $\{x_0 + w/4 \le x < x_0 + 3w/4, y_0 \le y < y_0 + h/2\}$, the left shoulder block is $\{x_0 \le x < x_0 + w/2, y_0 + h/2 \le y < y_0 + h\}$, and the right shoulder block is $\{x_0 + w/2 \le x < x_0 + w, y_0 + h/2 \le y < y_0 + h\}$.

A convolutional layer is used to output $3k$ feature maps, with k feature maps for each characteristic block. Then the pooling for each block is formulated as:

$$r(i|\theta) = \sum_{(x,y)\in R(i), ik\le j<(i+1)k} z_j(x_0 + x, y_0 + y)/n, \tag{1}$$

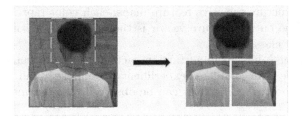

Fig. 3. Division diagram of pedestrian's head and shoulders.

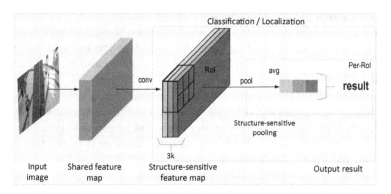

Fig. 4. Illustration of the structure-sensitive pooling operation.

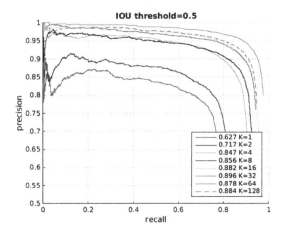

Fig. 5. The performance under different values of k.

where $r(i|\theta)$ denotes the pooled feature for the ith ($i = 0, 1, 2$) characteristic block, $R(i)$ denotes the corresponding region of the ith characteristic block in the given RoI, z_j denotes the jth feature map for the ith block, (x_0, y_0) refers to the coordinates of the top left corner of the RoI, and n represents the number of pixels. The structure-sensitive pooling operation is illustrated in Fig. 4. In the head-shoulder structure-sensitive feature maps, each color represents a characteristic block. The output feature vector is then fed into the softmax classifier for head-shoulder classification.

The parameter k has an important impact on the performance of the proposed method. We have conducted experiments to analyze it and the experimental results are reported in Fig. 5. It can be observed that our method performs the best when $k = 32$.

2.3 Multi-task Loss with Classification and Localization

Due to the coherent relationship between object classification and location prediction and to reduce computational complexity, we use multi-task learning to achieve our goal. As shown in Fig. 1, the high-level image features will be only extracted once, and then they will be used by the object classifier and the object position regressor concurrently.

For each RoI, the classifier will output its probability of different categories. We only define two categories: head-shoulder and non head-shoulder. We denote p_0 as the probability of non head-shoulder class and p_1 as the other. The output of the classifier is $P = (p_0, p_1)$. With the softmax classifier [14], the loss function is formulated as:

$$L_{cls}(P, u) = -\log(p_u) \tag{2}$$

where u represents the true category of RoI, $u = 1$ indicates head-shoulder and $u = 0$ otherwise. If a RoI belongs to the head-shoulder class, the location predictor will output the relative location information in RoI:

$$\begin{cases} t_x = gt_x/R_w, \\ t_y = gt_y/R_h, \\ t_w = gt_w/R_w, \\ t_h = gt_h/R_h, \end{cases} \tag{3}$$

where R_w and R_h refer to the width and height of RoI, and gt_x, gt_y, gt_w and gt_h represent the coordinates of the upper left corner, width and height of the true target rectangle in RoI. In order to predict these target values, it is also necessary to select an appropriate regression function and we select the smooth $L1$ function which is insensitive to outliers. And the regression error of the target location is the cumulative error of these target values:

$$smoothL_1(x) = \begin{cases} 0.5x^2, & \text{if } ||x|| < 1, \\ ||x|| - 0.5, & \text{otherwise,} \end{cases} \tag{4}$$

$$L_{loc}(t, v) = \sum_{i \in \{x, y, w, h\}} smoothL_1(t_i - v_i). \tag{5}$$

where t refers to the true output, and v is the predicted output. Thus the multi-task loss function of object classification and location regression is:

$$L(P, u, t, v) = L_{cls}(P, u) + \gamma[u = 1]L_{loc}(t, v) \tag{6}$$

where γ is used to balance the weights between the classification loss and the location regression loss, and $[u = 1]$ is 1 when $u = 1$ and 0 otherwise, which indicates that the location regression loss is calculated only if the true category of RoI is head-shoulder.

2.4 Pre-training with Triplet Loss

In order to improve the performance of our head-shoulder detection network model, we pre-train the shared convolutional subnet to improve its representation ability on the head-shoulder, which is used for the initialization of the detection network model, as illustrated in Fig. 1. The shared subnet is appended with a fully connected layer, a normalization layer and a triplet loss layer, and this network is denoted as the pre-model.

The training data are prepared in triplets (x_i^a, x_i^p, x_i^n), $i = 1, \ldots, N$, with an anchor image x_i^a (head-shoulder), a positive sample x_i^p (head-shoulder) and a negative sample x_i^n (non head-shoulder). The triplet loss aims to minimize the distance between an anchor and a positive and maximize the distance between the anchor and a negative. Similar to [17], the triplet loss function is formulated as:

$$\sum_i \left[\|f(x_i^a) - f(x_i^p)\|_2^2 - \|f(x_i^a) - f(x_i^n)\|_2^2 + \alpha \right]_+, \tag{7}$$

where $f(x)$ is the output feature of image x, α is an enforced margin between positive and negative pairs, and $[z]_+$ equals z when $z > 0$ and 0 otherwise.

3 Experiments

Dateset. In the camera view of large tilt angles, pedestrians' heads and shoulders are visible even if inter-occlusion exists among them. But in the camera view of small tilt angles, the heads and shoulders of occluded pedestrians are often invisible. Therefore, applying head-shoulder detection to camera views of large tilt angles is more appropriate. But up to now we have not found similar public datasets, so we need to collect our own dataset to verify the effectiveness of the proposed method. First, we shoot the pedestrian videos under different scenarios such as stations, markets and campuses. Then each pedestrian's head-shoulders in selected video frames is marked with a rectangular bounding box, and the coordinates of the top left corner and the lower right corner are saved. Eventually, the collected dataset contains six scenes with a total of 5,196 images, each with the size of 640×360, and the dataset is divided into training and test sets. The training set contains 4,196 images of pedestrians, with a total of 38,246 positive samples, while the test set contains 1,000 images, with a total of 12,831 positive samples.

Network details. The shared convolutional subnet (conv 1–5) has the same structure of the first five convolutional layers of Fast R-CNN [14]. The network structure of candidate region extraction, similar to the Region Proposal Network [15], includes a conv layer with kernel 3×3, stride 1 and 512 feature maps, a conv layer with kernel 1×1, stride 1 and 18 feature maps, and a softmax layer. The network structure of object classification contains a conv layer with kernel 1×1 and stride 1, a structure-sensitive pooling layer and a softmax layer, while the structure of location prediction contains a conv layer with kernel 1×1, stride 1 and $24k$ feature maps, a structure-sensitive pooling layer and a output layer with 8 neurons.

We conduct extensive experiments to verify the proposed head-shoulder detection network model on the test dataset.

3.1   Experimental Results

Some representative pedestrian detection results of our method under different scenarios are illustrated in Fig. 6. It can be observed that our method performs robustly in different scenes under various background and illumination conditions. Even in the cases where pedestrians are occluded, our method can also detect pedestrians' head-shoulder parts accurately.

To further evaluate the performance of our detection model, we compare our method with several state-of-the-art detection methods, including two traditional methods (the HOG feature based method [9] and the DPM method [18]) and the deep learning based method Faster R-CNN [15]. In the experiments, the proposed method and the compared methods are trained using the same training dataset, and then they are tested on the same test dataset. Under the condition

Fig. 6. Example pedestrian detection results of our model under different scenarios.

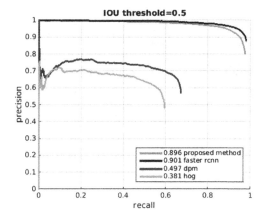

Fig. 7. Comparison with state-of-the-art methods.

that IoU is equal to 0.5, the evaluation results are presented in Fig. 7. It can be observed that the performance of the proposed model is close to Faster R-CNN's, and the quantitative difference of mAP between the two is merely about 0.5%. However, the results of the two traditional detection methods (HOG and DPM) are very unsatisfactory compared with those based on deep learning. It can be inferred that, in this task, the features extracted by the deep learning based methods are more excellent than the traditional hand-crafted features.

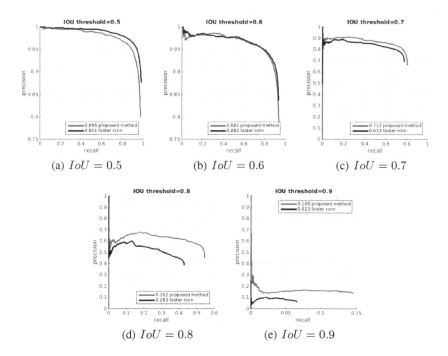

Fig. 8. Comparison results under different IoU thresholds

3.2 Results with Different IoU Thresholds

When testing the proposed model, in order to verify that our model can locate the pedestrians more close to the ground-truth bounding boxes, we set various IoU thresholds and compare the results between the proposed method and Faster R-CNN. The results are reported in Fig. 8. It shows that when the IoU threshold is 0.5 or 0.6, the results of the proposed model are similar to those of Faster R-CNN. But if the threshold is greater than 0.6, the results of our method are all superior to those of Faster R-CNN. In particular, when the IoU threshold is 0.9, the mAP of our model is 0.106 while the other is only 0.023. These results demonstrate that our method can make the detection bounding box more accurate to ground truth.

3.3 Detection Speed Analysis

The detection procedure of the proposed method and Faster R-CNN both include the extraction of candidate regions and the calculation for each candidate region, so the detection time is determined by the performance of the detection module as well as the number of extracted candidate regions. To compare the detection speed of the two methods comprehensively, it is necessary not only to measure the detection time at different image sizes when extracting equal number of candidate regions, but also to measure the detection time when different numbers of candidate regions are extracted under the same image size. When the number of extracted candidates is fixed to 300, the detection time at different image sizes is shown in Table 1. When the image size is fixed to 640×360, the detection time for different numbers of candidates (300, 1000 and 2000) are reported in Table 2.

As observed in Table 1, the detection time of the proposed model and the Faster R-CNN model increases with the increment of image sizes. However, at the same image size, the time that the proposed model consumes is less than the other. Table 2 reports that the consumed time for the proposed model is all less than that of Faster R-CNN in the situation of various candidate numbers. The detection time of our model increases in a very small scale with the rising

Table 1. The detection time (in seconds) with various image sizes

Image scale	480×272	640×360	1280×720	1920×1080
Faster R-CNN	0.044	0.056	0.081	0.084
Proposed model	0.025	0.037	0.062	0.064

Table 2. The detection time (in seconds) with various numbers of RoIs

Number of RoIs	300	1000	2000
Faster R-CNN	0.056	0.088	0.138
Proposed model	0.037	0.038	0.039

number of candidate regions, which can be ignored when compared with the Faster R-CNN model.

4   Conclusion

This paper has presented a novel pedestrian detection method by detecting head-shoulder based on the convolutional neural network. The head-shoulder detection network model integrates candidate region extraction, object classification and location prediction in the form of sharing convolutional features. To embed translation variability into the model, we construct head-shoulder structure-sensitive convolutional feature maps and introduce structure-sensitive pooling. Furthermore, to improve the representation ability of our network model on pedestrians' head-shoulders, we pre-train the shared convolutional subnet with a triplet loss, whose parameters are used for the initialization of the head-shoulder detection network model. The experimental results demonstrate that the proposed method has similar performance to the Faster R-CNN model, while achieving higher detection speed as well as higher IoU.

Acknowledgement. This research is supported by Natural Science Foundation of Guangdong Province (2014A030310348, 2014A030313154), National Natural Science Foundation of China (61472455, 61402120), Guangdong Provincial Department of Science and Technology (GDST16EG04) 2016A050503024, and the Startup Program in Guangdong University of Foreign Studies (299-X5122029).

References

1. Liu, N., Wu, H., Lin, L.: Hierarchical ensemble of background models for PTZ-based video surveillance. IEEE Trans. Cybern. **45**, 89–102 (2015)
2. Dollár, P., Wojek, C., Schiele, B., Perona, P.: Pedestrian detection: an evaluation of the state of the art. IEEE Trans. Pattern Anal. Mach. Intell. **34**, 743–761 (2012)
3. Wu, H., Liu, N., Luo, X., Su, J., Chen, L.: Real-time background subtraction-based video surveillance of people by integrating local texture patterns. Sig. Image Video Process. **8**, 665–676 (2014)
4. Teichman, A., Thrun, S.: Practical object recognition in autonomous driving and beyond. In: Advanced Robotics and its Social Impacts (ARSO), pp. 35–38 (2011)
5. Li, M., Zhang, Z., Huang, K., Tan, T.: Rapid and robust human detection and tracking based on omega-shape features. In: IEEE International Conference on Image Processing, pp. 2545–2548 (2010)
6. Li, M., Zhang, Z., Huang, K., Tan, T.: Estimating the number of people in crowded scenes by MID based foreground segmentation and head-shoulder detection. In: International Conference on Pattern Recognition, pp. 1–4 (2008)
7. Zeng, C., Ma, H.: Robust head-shoulder detection by PCA-based multilevel HOG-LBP detector for people counting. In: International Conference on Pattern Recognition, pp. 2069–2072 (2010)
8. Wu, B., Nevatia, R.: Tracking of multiple humans in meetings. In: IEEE Conference on Computer Vision and Pattern Recognition Workshop, p. 143 (2006)

9. Dalal, N., Triggs, B.: Histograms of oriented gradients for human detection. In: IEEE Conference on Computer Vision and Pattern Recognition (CVPR), pp. 886–893 (2005)

10. Wang, X., Han, T.X., Yan, S.: An HOG-LBP human detector with partial occlusion handling. In: IEEE International Conference on Computer Vision (ICCV), pp. 32–39 (2010)

11. Zhu, Q., Yeh, M.C., Cheng, K.T., Avidan, S.: Fast human detection using a cascade of histograms of oriented gradients. In: IEEE Conference on Computer Vision and Pattern Recognition (CVPR), pp. 1491–1498 (2006)

12. Girshick, R., Donahue, J., Darrell, T., Malik, J.: Rich feature hierarchies for accurate object detection and semantic segmentation. In: IEEE Conference on Computer Vision and Pattern Recognition (CVPR), pp. 580–587 (2013)

13. He, K., Zhang, X., Ren, S., Sun, J.: Spatial pyramid pooling in deep convolutional networks for visual recognition. IEEE Trans. Pattern Anal. Mach. Intell. **37**, 1904–1916 (2015)

14. Girshick, R.: Fast R-CNN. In: IEEE International Conference on Computer Vision (ICCV), pp. 1440–1448 (2015)

15. Ren, S., He, K., Girshick, R.B., Sun, J.: Faster R-CNN: towards real-time object detection with region proposal networks. IEEE Trans. Pattern Anal. Mach. Intell. **39**, 1137–1149 (2017)

16. Sermanet, P., Eigen, D., Zhang, X., Mathieu, M., Fergus, R., Lecun, Y.: Overfeat: integrated recognition, localization and detection using convolutional networks. arXiv:1312.6229 (2015)

17. Schroff, F., Kalenichenko, D., Philbin, J.: Facenet: a unified embedding for face recognition and clustering. In: IEEE Conference on Computer Vision and Pattern Recognition (CVPR), pp. 815–823 (2015)

18. Felzenszwalb, P.F., Girshick, R.B., McAllester, D.A., Ramanan, D.: Object detection with discriminatively trained part-based models. IEEE Trans. Pattern Anal. Mach. Intell. **32**, 1627–1645 (2010)

Two-Stage Saliency Fusion for Object Segmentation

Guangling Sun, Jingru Ren, Zhi Liu[(⊠)], and Wei Shan

School of Communication and Information Engineering,
Shanghai University, Shanghai 200444, China
sunguangling@shu.edu.cn, claudiaruru@126.com,
liuzhisjtu@163.com, shanwei1993@126.com

Abstract. This paper proposes an effective two-stage saliency fusion method to generate the fusion map, which is used as a prior for object segmentation. Given multiple saliency maps generated by different saliency models, the first stage is to produce two fusion maps based on average and min-max statistics, respectively. The second stage is to perform the Fourier transform (FT) on the two fusion maps, and to combine the amplitude spectrum of average fusion map and the phase spectrum of min-max fusion map, so as to reform the spectrum, and the final fusion map is obtained by using the inverse FT on the reformed spectrum. Last, object segmentation is performed under graph cut by using the final fusion map as a prior. Extensive experiments on three public datasets demonstrate that the proposed method facilitates to achieve the better object segmentation performance compared to using individual saliency map and other fusion methods.

Keywords: Object segmentation · Saliency fusion · Statistical fusion
Fourier transform

1 Introduction

Automatic object segmentation is a key requirement in a number of applications [1]. Some object/background prior is necessary for object segmentation, and undoubtedly, saliency map is an effective option. Saliency models that generate saliency maps can be classified into two categories. One is concerned with predicting human fixation, and the pioneer work of this category originated from [2]. The other one tries to detect salient objects with well-defined boundaries to highlight the complete objects. Obviously, the latter one is a more suitable prior for object segmentation. Fortunately, plenty of saliency models with high performances are developed in the recent years [3]. Especially, integrating multiple features, multiple levels, multiple scales, multiple stages and multiple saliency maps have demonstrated the effectiveness for improving saliency detection performance, such as multiple kernel boosting on multiple features [4] and Bayesian integration of low-level and mid-level cues [5]. In [6], the stacked denoising autoencoders are used to model background and generate deep reconstruction residuals at multiple scales and directions, and then the residual maps are integrated to obtain the saliency map. In [7], four Mahalanobis distance maps based on the four spaces of background-based distribution are first integrated, and then are enhanced within Bayesian

© Springer International Publishing AG 2017
Y. Zhao et al. (Eds.): ICIG 2017, Part I, LNCS 10666, pp. 139–148, 2017.
https://doi.org/10.1007/978-3-319-71607-7_13

perspective and refined with geodesic distance to generate the saliency map. In [8], the sum fusion method is evaluated and the results verify that combining several best saliency maps can actually enhance saliency detection performance. A data-driven saliency aggregation approach under the conditional random field framework is proposed in [9], which focuses on modeling the contribution of individual saliency map. Besides, the work in [10] integrates different saliency maps for fixation prediction and also demonstrates the performance improvement. A selection framework from multiple saliency maps adaptive to the input image is proposed in [11].

In this paper, we focus on fusion of multiple saliency maps, and specifically, the fused saliency map is used as an object prior for effective object segmentation. A high-quality saliency map for segmentation should effectively highlight object pixels and suppress background pixels, i.e., the contrast of saliency values between object pixels and background pixels should be as high as possible. For this purpose, the proposed saliency fusion method has the following two main contributions, which makes it different from the previous works: (1) The saliency fusion is performed in both spatial domain and frequency domain; (2) The fusions in the two domains are implemented in two stages in sequel to achieve a controllable SNR-contrast trade-off. Specifically, in the first stage, based on the statistics in the spatial domain, the average fusion map and min-max fusion map are generated. In particular, the saliency values of potential object pixels and background pixels are increased and decreased, respectively, as much as possible by using the min-max fusion. In the second stage, the above two fusion maps are further fused in the frequency domain. Specifically, the amplitude spectrum of average fusion map and the phase spectrum of min-max fusion map are integrated to reduce the errors and preserve the prominent contrast between object and background simultaneously.

2   Proposed Saliency Fusion for Object Segmentation

An overview of the proposed two-stage saliency fusion for object segmentation is illustrated in Fig. 1. Given the input image in Fig. 1(a), a number of existing saliency models are exploited to generate multiple saliency maps as shown in Fig. 1(b). For example, we can use the top six high-performing saliency models as reported in [3] to generate six saliency maps for the input image. The proposed two-stage saliency fusion method sequentially performs fusion in spatial domain and frequency domain, which are described in Sects. 2.1 and 2.2, respectively. Then the fusion map is used as a prior to perform object segmentation, which is described in Sect. 2.3.

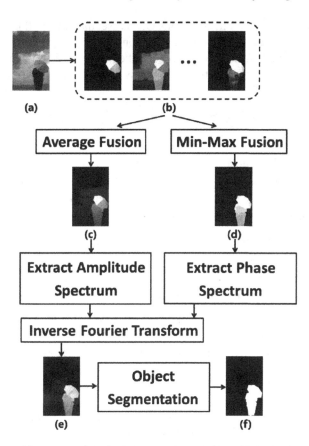

Fig. 1. Overview of the proposed method. (a) Input image; (b) multiple saliency maps generated by using different saliency models; (c) average fusion (AF) map; (d) min-max fusion (MMF) map; (e) AAPMF map by integrating the amplitude spectrum of AF map and the phase spectrum of MMF map; (f) segmentation result via graph cut.

2.1   Fusion Based on Average and Min-Max Statistics

The average statistics is one widely used statistics, and it is effective to average all saliency maps at pixel level for improving saliency detection performance [8]. Therefore we use the average operation to first generate the average fusion (AF) map as shown in Fig. 1(c). Although the AF map achieves performance improvement, it is not always a good candidate of prior for segmentation due that it cannot sufficiently highlight object pixels and suppress background pixels. In other words, the AF map generally weakens the contrast between object pixels and background pixels. Therefore, as a complement, we propose a novel fusion scheme which relies on the minimum and maximum of all saliency values. Specifically, the fusion value of each pixel is adaptive to the corresponding pixel's value in the AF map and a threshold. For each pixel, if its corresponding pixel's value in the AF map is less than a threshold, the pixel will be determined to be a potential background pixel, and the minimum among all saliency values of the pixel will be assigned to the pixel's fusion value. Otherwise, the pixel will be determined to be a potential object pixel, and the maximum among all saliency values of the pixel will be assigned to the pixel's fusion value. We term the fusion result as the min-max fusion (MMF) map, and the min-max statistical fusion is fusion defined as follows:

$$F_{MMF}(p) = \begin{cases} \min_{i=1,2,\cdots N} [S_i(p)], & \text{if } F_{AF}(p) \le T \\ \max_{i=1,2,\cdots N} [S_i(p)], & \text{otherwise} \end{cases}, \tag{1}$$

where $S_i(p)$ denotes the saliency value of each pixel p in the ith saliency map, and N is the total number of saliency maps. F_{MMF} and F_{AF} denote the MMF map and the AF map, respectively. For each saliency map S_i, the Otsu's method [12] is applied to obtain the threshold T_i, and the average of all N thresholds is assigned to the threshold T, i.e., $T = \sum_{i=1}^{N} T_i/N$. For the multiple saliency maps shown in Fig. 1(b), the corresponding MMF map is shown in Fig. 1(d).

2.2   Fusion Based on Fourier Transform of AF Map and MMF Map

Depending on the min-max operation, it is understandable that the MMF map owns the expected property of highlighting potential object pixels and suppressing potential background pixels, respectively, as intensively as possible. However, the MMF map will inevitably falsely highlight some background pixels and/or suppress some object pixels. Therefore, the AF map is exploited to alleviate such errors via the use of Fourier Transform (FT).

As we know, saliency map is in nature a grey-scale map, so its signal-noise ratio (SNR) is reflected in the amplitude spectrum and the boundaries between object regions and background regions are reflected in the phase spectrum. The two spectrums are obtained via FT on AF map and MMF map. The SNR of AF map is higher than that of MMF map since the AF map is the average of multiple saliency maps, while the MMF map contains more noises introduced by the min-max operation including wrongly judged object pixels and background pixels. On the other hand, the contrast between object pixels and background pixels in the MMF map are higher than that in the AF map, also due to the min-max operation for generating MMF map. Obviously, the higher the contrast between object pixels and background pixels is, the more complete boundaries between object regions and background regions will be preserved. Therefore, we choose the amplitude spectrum of AF map and the phase spectrum of MMF map to reform a new spectrum so as to obtain a better SNR-contrast trade-off than both AF map and MMF map.

The inverse FT (IFT) is performed on the reformed spectrum to obtain the final fusion map, which is abbreviated to AAPMF (Amplitude spectrum of AF map and Phase spectrum of MMF map based Fusion) map, as follows:

$$F_{AAPMF} = \text{IFT}\left[\mathbf{A}(F_{AF}), \mathbf{P}(F_{MMF})\right], \tag{2}$$

where **A** refers to extracting the amplitude spectrum and **P** refers to exacting the phase spectrum. The AAPMF map as shown in Fig. 1(e) is used as a prior for object segmentation.

To further verify the reasonableness and effectiveness of the proposed spectrum integration strategy, we also generate the fusion map by reforming the new spectrum with the amplitude spectrum of MMF map and the phase spectrum of AF map, and similarly, we denote it as AMPAF map. Some examples of AF, MMF, AAPMF and AMPAF maps are shown in Fig. 2. It can be seen from Fig. 2 that AAPMF maps can highlight object regions and suppress background regions better than the other maps, and the corresponding segmentation results using AAPMF maps also achieve the better quality than the other segmentation results. Therefore, the AAPMF map can serve as the better prior for object segmentation.

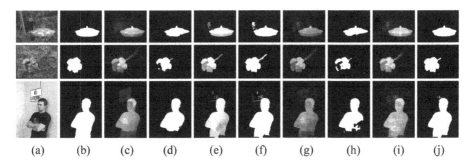

(a)   (b)   (c)   (d)   (e)   (f)   (g)   (h)   (i)   (j)

Fig. 2. The impact of amplitude spectrum and phase spectrum of saliency map. (a) Input image; (b) ground truth; (c) AF map; (d) segmentation result using (c); (e) MMF map; (f) segmentation result using (e); (g) AMPAF map; (h) segmentation result using (g); (i) AAPMF map; (j) segmentation result using (i).

2.3   Object Segmentation

Given the saliency prior such as AAPMF map, the object segmentation is formulated as assigning labels to each pixel by solving an energy minimization problem under the framework of graph cut [13]. As a result, each pixel p gets its label $L_p \in \{0, 1\}$, where $L_p = 1$ denotes object and $L_p = 0$ denotes background. The energy function is defined as follows:

$$E = \sum_p D(L_p) + \lambda \sum_{\substack{(p,q)\in\Omega \\ L_p \neq L_q}} \theta(L_p, L_q)$$

$$D(L_p) = \begin{cases} S_F(p), & L_p = 0 \\ 1 - S_F(p), & L_p = 1 \end{cases} \qquad (3)$$

$$\theta(L_p, L_q) = \exp\left[-\frac{(I_p - I_q)^2}{2\sigma^2}\right] \cdot \frac{1}{dist(p,q)},$$

where $D(\cdot)$ is the data term, $\theta(\cdot)$ is the smoothness term, and Ω is the set of pairs of neighboring pixels. The parameter λ is used to balance the two terms, and is set to 0.1 for a moderate effect of smoothness. S_F denotes the saliency prior, which uses the AAPMF map here. In the smoothness term, I_p denotes the color feature of the pixel p, the parameter σ^2 is set to 2.5, and $disp(p, q)$ is the Euclidean distance between a pair of pixels, p and q. The max-flow algorithm [14] is adopted to minimize the energy function and obtain the labels of pixels, which represent the object segmentation result. For example, Fig. 1(f) is the object segmentation result by using AAPMF map as the saliency prior.

3   Experimental Results

3.1   Experimental Setting

To verify the effectiveness of the proposed saliency fusion method for object segmentation, we evaluated its performance on the three public benchmark datasets including MSRA10 K [15], ECSSD [16] and PASCAL-S [17], with 10000, 1000 and 850 images, respectively. For each image in the three datasets, the manually annotated pixel-level binary ground truth of objects is provided. According to the benchmark [3], we selected the top six saliency models with the highest performances, i.e., DRFI [18], QCUT [19], RBD [20], ST [21], DSR [22] and MC [23], to generate saliency maps. In addition to AAPMF map, we also tested AF map, MMF map and AMPAF map, and compared with the other two fusion methods, *i.e.* maximum and multiplication, which generate MaxF map using the pixel-wise maximum of all saliency values as the fusion value and PF map using the pixel-wise multiplication of all saliency values as the fusion value, respectively. We specified S_F in Eq. (3) with each of the above mentioned saliency maps and fusion maps to obtain the corresponding object segmentation results.

3.2   Quantitative Comparison

We evaluated all segmentation results using the conventional F-measure defined as follows:

$$F_\beta = \frac{(1 + \beta^2)\, Precision \times Recall}{\beta^2 Precision + Recall},\tag{4}$$

and the weighted F-measure, which is recently introduced in [24], as follows:

$$F_\beta^\omega = \frac{(1 + \beta^2)\, Precision^\omega \times Recall^\omega}{\beta^2 Precision^\omega + Recall^\omega},\tag{5}$$

where $Precision^\omega$ and $Recall^\omega$ (namely weighted $Precision$ and weighted $Recall$) are computed by the extended basic quantities including true positive, true negative, false positive and false negative, which are weighted according to the pixels' location and neighborhood. The coefficient β^2 is set to 0.3 indicating more importance of precision than recall as suggested in [3]. Here we compute all measures for each image and then obtain the average on all images in a given dataset for performance comparison. All results are listed in Table 1. In each row of Table 1, the 1st, 2nd and 3rd place of performance are marked with red, green and blue, respectively. It can be observed that in terms of F-measure and weighted F-measure, AAPMF map consistently performs best on all datasets. This objectively reveals the overall better performance of AAPMF map as a prior for object segmentation. Particularly, the advantage of AAPMF map over AF map, MMF map and AMPAF map further demonstrates the reasonableness of reforming the spectrum by combining the amplitude spectrum of AF map and the phase spectrum of MMF map.

Table 1. Average F-measure (F) and average F_β^ω-measure (F_β^ω) of object segmentation results on three public benchmark datasets (D) consisting of MSRA10 K (M), ECSSD (E) and PASCAL-S (P).

D	Metric	Top Six Saliency Models						Saliency Fusion Methods					AAPMF (proposed)
		DRFI	DSR	MC	QCUT	RBD	ST	MaxF	PF	AF	MMF	AMPAF	
M	F	.856	.784	.784	.728	.816	.844	.836	.505	.861	.874	.845	.880
	F_β^ω	.839	.777	.774	.735	.808	.820	.783	.525	.856	.846	.840	.861
E	F	.740	.651	.647	.604	.645	.708	.715	.356	.734	.756	.709	.760
	F_β^ω	.715	.638	.621	.604	.619	.667	.642	.377	.717	.711	.694	.723
P	F	.617	.541	.553	.511	.580	.600	.628	.279	.629	.651	.597	.652
	F_β^ω	.583	.517	.525	.503	.544	.555	.552	.292	.601	.598	.575	.606

*For Table 1, in the first column, D denotes Datasets, M, E and P denote MSRA10K, ECSSD and PASCAL-S dataset, respectively; in the second column, F and F_β^ω denotes F-measure and F_β^ω-measure, respectively.

3.3 Qualitative Comparison

Some object segmentation results are shown in Fig. 3 for a qualitative comparison. Overall, the segmentation results with AAPMF maps show the best visual quality compared to others. Besides, it can be seen from Fig. 3(c)–(h) that the segmentation results with the saliency maps may miss some object regions and/or contain some background regions. The results with MaxF maps shown in Fig. 3(i) usually introduce some irrelevant regions, while the results with PF maps shown in Fig. 3(j) usually miss some portions of object regions. Compared to the results with AF, MMF and AMPAF maps shown in Fig. 3(k)–(m), the results with AAPMF maps shown in Fig. 3(n) can generally segment more complete objects with more accurate boundaries.

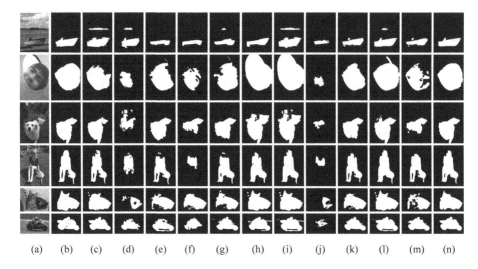

(a)   (b)   (c)   (d)   (e)   (f)   (g)   (h)   (i)   (j)   (k)   (l)   (m)   (n)

Fig. 3. Object segmentation results of sample images from MSRA10 K (the first two rows), ECSSD (the middle two rows) and PASCAL-S (the bottom two rows). (a) original images; (b) ground truths; (c)–(h) segmentation results with DRFI, DSR, MC, QCUT, RBD and ST; (i)–(j) segmentation results with MaxF and PF; (k)-(m) segmentation results with AF, MMF and AMPAF; (n) segmentation results with AAPMF (our results).

3.4   Computation Cost

Our method is implemented using Matlab on a PC with an Intel Core i7 4.0 GHz CPU and 16 GB RAM. The average processing time for an image with a resolution of 400×300 is 0.88 s excluding the generation of saliency map. The first-stage fusion takes 0.51 s, the second-stage fusion takes 0.06 s, and the object segmentation takes 0.31 s. It can be seen that the two-stage saliency fusion is computationally efficient. The other saliency fusion methods are also computationally efficient. Specifically, MaxF, PF, AF, MMF and AMPAF take 0.02 s, 0.03 s, 0.03 s, 0.48 s and 0.58 s, respectively, to generate saliency fusion maps. The object segmentation based on these saliency fusion maps also takes about 0.31 s.

3.5   Discussion

Since the saliency fusion heavily depends on the individual saliency maps involved in the fusion, the proposed method will fail once all the individual saliency maps are insufficient to highlight salient objects. Some failure examples from the PASCAL-S dataset, which is a more challenging dataset for object segmentation, are shown in Fig. 4. Nonetheless, the results reported in Table 1 indicate that even in the PASCAL-S dataset with more challenging images, the segmentation performance using AAPMF map as a prior is still better than the results using individual saliency maps, MaxF, PF, AF, MMF and AMPAF maps as a prior.

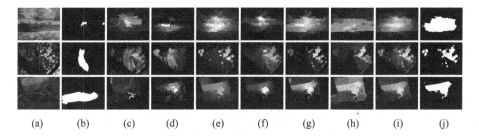

Fig. 4. Failure examples of the proposed method. (a) Input images; (b) ground truths; (c)–(h) saliency maps generated by the top six models: DRFI, DSR, MC, QCUT, RBD and ST; (i) AAPMF maps generated by the proposed fusion method; (j) our segmentation results by using AAPMF map as a prior.

4 Conclusion

This paper proposes a novel approach to fuse multiple saliency maps in two stages for object segmentation. In the first stage, the AF map and MMF map are obtained based on the average and min-max statistics, respectively. In the second stage, the amplitude spectrum of AF map and the phase spectrum of MMF map are integrated to generate the AAPMF map via the use of FT and IFT. Experimental results demonstrate that the two-stage saliency fusion as a prior actually boosts the performance of object segmentation.

Acknowledgements. This work was supported by the National Natural Science Foundation of China under Grant No. 61471230, Shanghai Municipal Natural Science Foundation under Grant No. 16ZR1411100, and the Program for Professor of Special Appointment (Eastern Scholar) at Shanghai Institutions of Higher Learning.

References

1. Hu, S.M., Chen, T., Xu, K., Cheng, M.M., Martin, R.R.: Internet visual media processing: a survey with graphics and vision applications. Vis. Comput. **29**(5), 393–405 (2013)
2. Itti, L., Koch, C., Niebur, E.: A model of saliency-based visual attention for rapid scene analysis. IEEE Trans. Pattern Anal. Mach. Intell. **20**(11), 1254–1259 (1998)
3. Borji, A., Cheng, M.M., Jiang, H., Li, J.: Salient object detection: a benchmark. IEEE Trans. Image Process. **24**(12), 5706–5722 (2015)
4. Zhou, X., Liu, Z., Sun, G., Ye, L., Wang, X.: Improving saliency detection via multiple kernel boosting and adaptive fusion. IEEE Sig. Process. Lett. **23**(4), 517–521 (2016)
5. Xie, Y., Lu, H., Yang, M.H.: Bayesian saliency via low and mid-level cues. IEEE Trans. Image Process. **22**(5), 1689–1698 (2013)
6. Han, J., Zhang, D., Hu, X., Guo, L., Ren, J., Wu, F.: Background prior based salient object detection via deep reconstruction residual. IEEE Trans. Circuits Syst. Video Technol. **25**(8), 1309–1321 (2015)
7. Zhao, T., Li, L., Ding, X., Huang, Y., Zeng, D.: Saliency detection with spaces of background-based distribution. IEEE Sig. Process. Lett. **23**(5), 683–687 (2016)

8. Borji, A., Sihite, D.N., Itti, L.: Salient object detection: a benchmark. In: Fitzgibbon, A., Lazebnik, S., Perona, P., Sato, Y., Schmid, C. (eds.) ECCV 2012. LNCS, pp. 414–429. Springer, Heidelberg (2012). https://doi.org/10.1007/978-3-642-33709-3_30
9. Mai, L., Niu, Y., Liu, F.: Saliency aggregation: a data-driven approach. In: 26th IEEE Conference on Computer Vision and Pattern Recognition, pp. 1131–1138. IEEE Press, Portland (2013)
10. Le Meur, O., Liu, Z.: Saliency aggregation: does unity make strength? In: Cremers, D., Reid, I., Saito, H., Yang, M.-H. (eds.) ACCV 2014. LNCS, vol. 9006, pp. 18–32. Springer, Cham (2015). https://doi.org/10.1007/978-3-319-16817-3_2
11. Zhang, C.Q., Tao, Z.Q., Wei, X.X., Cao, X.C.: A flexible framework of adaptive method selection for image saliency. Pattern Recognit. Lett. **63**(1), 66–70 (2015)
12. Otsu, N.: A threshold selection method from gray-level histograms. IEEE Trans. Syst. Man Cybern. **9**(1), 62–66 (1979)
13. Boykov, Y., Jolly, M.: Interactive graph cuts for optimal boundary and region segmentation of objects in n-d images. In: 8th IEEE International Conference on Computer Vision, pp. 105–112. IEEE Press, Vancouver (2001)
14. Boykov, Y., Kolmogorov, V.: An experimental comparison of min-cut/max-flow algorithms for energy minimization in vision. IEEE Trans. Pattern Anal. Mach. Intell. **26**(9), 1124–1137 (2004)
15. THUR15000. http://mmcheng.net/gsal/
16. Yan, Q., Xu, L., Shi, J., Jia, J.: Hierarchical image saliency detection on extended CSSD. IEEE Trans. Pattern Anal. Mach. Intell. **38**(4), 717–729 (2015)
17. Li, Y., Hou, X., Koch, C., Rehg, J.M., Yuille, A.L.: The secrets of salient object segmentation. In: 27th IEEE Conference on Computer Vision and Pattern Recognition, pp. 280–287. IEEE Press, Columbus (2014)
18. Jiang, H., Wang, J., Yuan, Z., Wu, Y., Zheng, N., Li, S.: Salient object detection: a discriminative regional feature integration approach. In: 26th IEEE Conference on Computer Vision and Pattern Recognition, pp. 2083–2090. IEEE Press, Portland (2013)
19. Aytekin, C., Kiranyaz, S., Gabbouj, M.: Automatic object segmentation by quantum cuts. In: 22th IEEE International Conference on Pattern Recognition, pp. 112–117. IEEE Press, Stockholm (2014)
20. Zhu, W., Liang, S., Wei, Y., Sun, J.: Saliency optimization from robust background detection. In: 27th IEEE Conference on Computer Vision and Pattern Recognition, pp. 2814–2821. IEEE Press, Columbus (2014)
21. Liu, Z., Zou, W., Le Meur, O.: Saliency tree: a novel saliency detection framework. IEEE Trans. Image Process. **23**(5), 1937–1952 (2014)
22. Li, X., Lu, H., Zhang, L., Ruan, X., Yang, M.H.: Saliency detection via dense and sparse reconstruction. In: 14th IEEE International Conference on Computer Vision, pp. 1937–1952. IEEE Press, Sydney (2013)
23. Jiang, B., Zhang, L., Lu, H., Yang, C., Yang, M.H.: Saliency detection via absorbing Markov chain. In: 14th IEEE International Conference on Computer Vision, pp. 2979–2983. IEEE Press, Sydney (2013)
24. Margolin, R., Zelink-Manor, L., Tal, A.: How to evaluate foreground maps? In: 27th IEEE Conference on Computer Vision and Pattern Recognition, pp. 248–255. IEEE Press, Columbus (2014)

Recognition of Offline Handwritten Mathematical Symbols Using Convolutional Neural Networks

Lanfang Dong$^{(\boxtimes)}$ ⓘ and Hanchao Liu ⓘ

School of Computer Science and Technology,
University of Science and Technology of China, Hefei, China
lfdong@ustc.edu.cn, lhanchao@mail.ustc.edu.cn

Abstract. This paper presents a method of Convolutional Neural Networks (CNN) to recognize offline handwritten mathematical symbols. In this paper, we propose a CNN model called HMS-VGGNet, in which the Batch Normalization and Global Average Pooling methods and only very small, specifically, 1×1 and 3×3 convolutional filters are applied. HMS-VGGNet uses only offline features of the symbols and has achieved the state-of-the-art accuracies in Competition on Recognition of Online Handwritten Mathematical Expressions (CROHME) 2014 test set and HASYv2 dataset. In CROHME 2016 test set, our result is only 0.39% less than the winner of CROHME 2016 who has used both online and offline features. The models proposed in this paper are accurate yet slim, which will be shown in our experiments.

Keywords: Batch normalization · Global average pooling
Very small convolutional filters · CROHME · HASYv2

1 Introduction

Handwritten mathematical symbols recognition is an essential component of handwritten mathematical expressions recognition which could convert the handwritten mathematical symbols images or traces to specific styles which could be shown and edited in computers, for example LATEX. This task, which has both offline and online model, is still a great challenge owning to its large scale classes, great differences in handwritten styles and very similar symbols. The input of online handwritten mathematical symbols recognition is the timing sampling point sequences gotten from pen-based or touch-based devices, such as smartphones and tablets, while in offline model the input is the images of symbols after written.

Currently, online handwritten mathematical symbols recognition has been studied widely and has achieved great performance. Competition on Recognition of Online Handwritten Mathematical Expressions (CROHME) has been held 5 times from 2011 to 2016 [1–3], attracting the researchers around the world. CROHME represents the highest performance of online handwritten mathematical expression recognition. Recognition of handwritten mathematical symbols has become an isolated task of the competition since CROHME 2014. Owning to the available tracing information, online

© Springer International Publishing AG 2017
Y. Zhao et al. (Eds.): ICIG 2017, Part I, LNCS 10666, pp. 149–161, 2017.
https://doi.org/10.1007/978-3-319-71607-7_14

data can be converted to offline images. In recent years, researchers used the offline features extracted from the symbol images as an auxiliary to recognize the online mathematical symbols and got great achievements. Álvaro et al. [2, 4] combined 9 offline features including PRHLT and FKI features and 7 online features extracted from symbol images and the original online data separately. They used the Bidirectional Long Short Term Memory Recurrent Neural Networks (BLSTM) to classify the features and achieved 91.24% recognition rate in CROHME 2014. Dai et al. [5] used Convolutional Neural Network (CNN) and BLSTM to classify the symbol images and online data separately and combined the results and got 91.28% in CROHME 2014 test set. Davila et al. [6] also used a combination of online features such as normalized line length and covariance of point coordinates and offline features such as 2D fuzzy histograms of points and fuzzy histograms of orientations of the lines to recognize online symbols. MyScript [3], the winner of CROHME 2016 also extracted both online and offline features and processed with a combination of Deep MLP and Recurrent Neural Networks. MyScript achieved 92.81% in CROHME 2016 test set and this is the best result in that set as far as we know.

Nevertheless, researchers didn't give much attention on the recognition of offline handwritten mathematical symbols and little work was published. Since the datasets of offline handwritten mathematical symbols are rare, online data of CROHME were used by Ramadhan et al. [7] to generate symbol images for offline symbol recognition. Ranadhan et al. designed a CNN model that was trained using the images converted from CROHME 2014 training set and got 87.72% accuracy in CROHME 2014 test images drawn from online data [7]. However, due to the absence of the features of online data and the rough designed network architecture, the accuracy of [7] is obviously lower compared to the online handwritten mathematical symbols recognition results.

In recent years, convolutional neural network that was proposed by LeCun [8] for offline handwritten digits recognition has enjoyed a great success in lots of computer vision tasks, such as image recognition [9–12], object detection [13, 14] and semantic segmentation [14]. In this paper, we apply CNN to the recognition of offline handwritten mathematical symbols. And we design a deep and slim CNN architecture denoted as HMS-VGGNet. Previous research results have shown that the deeper the network is, the better results the network gets [9–12]. However, when the network goes deeper, it becomes harder to train and the model size usually grows larger. To overcome the difficulties of training and to keep the model size reasonable HMS-VGGNet which is elaborately designed for the recognition of offline handwritten mathematical symbols has applied Batch Normalization (BN) [15], Global Average Pooling (GAP) [16] and very small convolutional kernels. Considering the lack of offline data and for the convenience of comparing results, we use both the images drawn from CROHME dataset and the data of HASYv2 [17] to train and evaluate our models. As shown in our experiments, HMS-VGGNet raises the accuracy of offline handwritten mathematical symbols recognition significantly.

The rest of the paper is organized as follows. In Sect. 2, we give a brief introduction to BN, GAP and the benefits of 1×1 and 3×3 convolutional kernels. The details of the datasets used in our experiments are shown in Sect. 3, and our network configurations are present in Sect. 4. In Sect. 5, our training methods, experiments results and analyses are presented. Section 6 concludes the paper.

2 A Brief Introduction of BN, GAP and Very Small Convolutional Kernels

2.1 Batch Normalization

In the training process of CNN, it is especially hard when the network goes deeper by the fact that the inputs to each layer are affected by the parameters of all preceding layers [15]. Each layer in the network needs to adapt to the change of the inputs distribution, making the training process difficult and slow. Batch Normalization with benefits of accelerating training and achieving better performance is a solution of this problem by guaranteeing the inputs distribution of each layer stable.

In order to achieve the goal, BN takes two steps of input data processing. Firstly, BN normalizes the inputs distribution of each layer in every training step to make it with the mean of 0 and the variance of 1. For one dimension $x^{(k)}$ of the input x, BN normalizes the input by

$$\hat{x}^{(k)} = \frac{x^{(k)} - E[x^{(k)}]}{\sqrt{Var[x^{(k)}]}} \qquad (1)$$

where $E[x^{(k)}]$ and $Var[x^{(k)}]$ are the mean and variance of $x^{(k)}$. However, this normalization step may destroy what the preceding layer can represent. To recover the features that should be learnt by the preceding layer, BN sets two parameters γ and β to learn in the second step. By the processing of

$$y^{(k)} = \gamma^{(k)} \hat{x}^{(k)} + \beta^{(k)} \qquad (2)$$

BN can finally make the inputs distribution of layers stable.

2.2 Global Average Pooling

Fully connected layers, following the convolutional or pooling layers, are common in classical CNN models such as LeNet-5 [8], AlexNet [9] and VGGNet [11]. However, fully connected layers are easy to overfit because of the huge number of parameters. In 2013, Lin et al. [16] proposed a new method called global average pooling to replace fully connected layers. In the layer of global average pooling, all the parameters in one feature map are averaged to generate the result, as illustrated in Fig. 1.

GAP layers have 3 benefits: (1) There are no extra parameters in GAP layers thus overfitting is avoided at GAP layers; (2) Since the output of GAP is the average of the whole feature map, GAP will be more robust to spatial translations; (3) Because of the huge number of parameters in fully connected layers which usually take over 50% in all the parameters of the whole network, replacing them by GAP layers can significantly reduce the size of the model, and this makes GAP very popular in model compression [18].

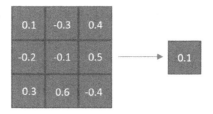

Fig. 1. Process of global average pooling

2.3   1 × 1 and 3 × 3 Convolutional Kernels

In recent years, 1 × 1 and 3 × 3 filters are widely used in new CNN models [10–12, 18, 19] for their benefits of reducing computations, pruning parameters and improving accuracies.

As a result of keeping the size of feature maps and reducing the number of feature maps with little effect on accuracies, 1 × 1 convolutional layers were used to reduce parameters and avoid computational blow up in [10, 19]. At the same time, 3 × 3 filters are the smallest filters that could capture the notion of left/right, up/down and center. Although the receptive fields of 3 × 3 filters are small, a few continuous 3 × 3 layers can get the same receptive field of bigger filters, for example, a stack of two 3 × 3 convolutional layers has an effective receptive field of 5 × 5, with the advantages of deeper layers and fewer parameters [11, 19].

3   Datasets

In our experiments we use the images converted from CROHME online data and the images of HASYv2 dataset to train and evaluate our models for the lack of offline data and the convenience of comparing results. CROHME is the most commonly used dataset when recognizing handwritten mathematical symbols and HASYv2 which has 151 k handwritten mathematical symbol images is the biggest public offline handwritten mathematical symbols dataset to our best knowledge.

3.1   CROHME Offline Data Generation

There are 101 different classes of mathematical symbol in CROHME 2016 dataset. The online data is given in Ink Markup Language (InkML) [20]. In the InkML file, a symbol S is consisted with a set of trances $\{T_1, T_2, \ldots, T_n\}$. Each trace $T_i(i = 1, \ldots, n)$ consists of a set of timing sampling points $\{p_{i1}, p_{i2}, \ldots, p_{im}\}$, and each point $p_{ij}(i = 1, \ldots, n; j = 1, \ldots, m)$ records its position. When generating symbol images from online data, we connect the points p_{ij} and p_{ij+1} from the same trace with a single line and finish the generation after all the traces from the same symbol are drawn. Due to the different data acquisition devices used in CROHME, the size of symbols differs a lot. In our generation approach, as shown in Algorithm 1, we normalize the symbols size.

Since the aspect ratio, which is an important feature of symbols, differs a lot from different mathematical symbols, the longer side of the images we get from Algorithm 1 is 70 pixels while the shorter is different from each other. We expand image I with white pixels to make its size to 70×70. Taking into account that 'COMMA', '.' and '\prime' are relatively small in real handwritten symbol images, the longer side are fixed to 16 pixels when drawing these symbol images. After generation we expand these images with white pixels to 70×70 pixels. At last we resize the images generated from online data to 48×48. The first row in Fig. 2 shows some samples of the generated images.

Algorithm 1. Symbol image generation from online data of CROHME

Input: Online data of Symbol $S = \{T_1, T_2, ..., T_n\}$, where $T_i = \{p_{i1}, p_{i2}, ..., p_{im}\}, i = 1, ..., n$

Output: Symbol image I

1. Find the maximum and minimum horizontal and vertical axis of the points in S, presenting them by $x_{min}, y_{min}, x_{max}, y_{max}$;
2. For every point in S, convert the original position $p_{ij\_0}(x_{ij\_0}, y_{ij\_0})$ to a new position $p_{ij\_1}(x_{ij\_1}, y_{ij\_1})$, where $x_{ij\_1} = x_{ij\_0} - x_{min}$, $y_{ij\_1} = y_{ij\_0} - y_{min}$;
3. Compare $height = y_{max} - y_{min}$ and $width = x_{max} - x_{min}$ and name the longer one as L;
4. Scale every sampling point $p_{ij\_1}(x_{ij\_1}, y_{ij\_1})$ obtained in step 2 to get the new position $p_{ij2}(64 * x_{ij\_1}/L, 64 * y_{ij\_1}/L)$;
5. For every T_i in S :
   Connect the adjacent points p_{ij_2} and p_{ij+1_2} with a line whose thickness is 2 pixels;
6. Extend 3 pixels around the image generated in step 5.

3.2   Data Enrichment

As a result of the expressive power of deep networks, overfitting is a common problem that is hard to deal. Researchers have proposed some methods to prevent overfitting such as Dropout [21] and Batch Normalization. However, the most effective way to prevent overfitting is enriching the training set to make the networks learn more universal features. In the training set of CROHME 2016 there are only 85802 symbols and there are 369 classes of 151 k training samples in HASYv2. In addition to the lack of training samples, the distributions of training set of CROHME and HASYv2 are also bias, for example the sample number of symbol '-' is 8390 and there are only 2 samples of '∃' in the training set of CROHME 2016. These drawbacks of the datasets will pull the accuracies down.

To avoid the drawbacks we use elastic distortion [22] to enrich our training set. There are two random matrices $\Delta x(x, y) = rand(-1, 1)$ and $\Delta y(x, y) = rand(-1, 1)$ representing the horizontal and vertical axis displacement of the pixel (x, y) in elastic distortion algorithm. The matrices are convolved with a Gaussian kernel, whose size is $n \times n$ and standard deviation is σ. All the pixels in the original image are moved following the convolution results $\Delta conv\_x$ and $\Delta conv\_y$. After the movements we rotate the images by a random angle θ. In this paper, $\sigma = 5$, n = 11 and θ is in the range of $-25° \sim 25°$. Using elastic distortion, we have enriched the samples of each class to about 4000 and 1000 in CROHME and HASYv2 training sets. The second and third rows in Fig. 2 show several samples generated by elastic distortion.

As HASYv2 covers most of the CROHME symbol classes, we use the samples of HASYv2 whose class is also included in CROHME when conducting the experiments of CROHME. Since the size of images in HASYv2 is 32×32, the images from HASYv2 used in CROHME experiments are resized to 48×48. We use the symbols of CROHME 2013 test set as the validation set and the test set of CROHME 2014 and 2016 to evaluate our models in CROHME experiments. In HASYv2 experiments, we use cross validation as suggested in [17]. Table 1 shows the details of the datasets used in our experiments.

Fig. 2. Samples of the dataset used in our experiments. The first row shows the images drawn from online data, the second and third rows are the samples generated by elastic distortion. Samples of the second and third rows are generated by the images of the first row in the same column.

Table 1. Datasets used in our experiments

Experiments	Usage	Dataset	Image size	Dataset scale	
				Before distortion	After distortion
CROHME	Train	CROHME 2016 train + HASYv2 (part)	48×48	132120	403729
	Validation	CROHME 2013 test	48×48	6081	–
	Test	CROHME 2014 test	48×48	10061	–
		CROHME 2016 test	48×48	10019	–
HASYv2	Train	HASYv2 train	32×32	151406 ± 166	366566 ± 1356
	Test	HASYv2 test	32×32	16827 ± 166	–

4 Network Configurations

In order to make the effects of BN, GAP and small kernels clear, we have designed four networks with similar architecture and the details of these networks are shown in Table 2. Network C is the baseline of our contrast experiments. Network A uses fully connected layers while global average pooling layers are used in C. The only difference of B and C is that C uses Batch Normalization while B doesn't. Compared to C, D adds two extra 1×1 convolutional layers to reduce the dimension.

In Table 2, the convolutional layer parameters are denoted as "Conv-(filter size)-(number of filters)-(stride of filters)-(padding pixels)". All max-pooling layers in our network are performed over 2×2 pixel window, with stride 2. All convolutional/fully connected layers are equipped with the rectification non-linearity. And all convolutional layers are equipped with Batch Normalization before ReLU except those in network B. We omit the ReLU and BN for brevity in Table 2. The ratios of all the Dropout operations used in our networks are 0.5.

Table 2. HMS-VGGNet configurations (shown in columns). The detailed differences are shown in the contents of this section.

Input: 48×48 (CROHME)/32×32 (HASYv2) RGB images			
A	B	C	D
Conv-3-32-1-1 Conv-3-32-1-1			
MaxPool			
Conv-3-64-1-1 Conv-3-64-1-1			
MaxPool			
Conv-3-128-1-1 Conv-3-128-1-1			Conv-3-128-1-1 Conv-1-64-1-0 Conv-3-128-1-1
MaxPool			
Conv-3-256-1-1 Conv-3-256-1-1			Conv-3-256-1-1 Conv-1-128-1-0 Conv-3-256-1-1
MaxPool	MaxPool Dropout		
FC-512 Dropout	Conv-1-101-1-0 (CROHME)/		
FC-512 Dropout	Conv-1-369-1-0 (HASYv2)		
FC-101 (CROHME)/ FC-369 (HASYv2)	AveragePool		
Softmax			

The architecture of the networks, which is denoted as HMS-VGGNet, is inspired by VGGNet [11]. However, there are several improvements in our networks for the handwritten mathematical symbols recognition task compared with the original VGGNet. Firstly, the images of handwritten symbol images are much smaller and simpler than the natural images used in VGGNet, so we have pruned several layers and filters to fit our task. The second improvement is that Batch Normalization layers are added after all the convolutional layers of Net A, C and D to accelerate the training process and improve the accuracies. Thirdly, we use global average pooling layers to replace the fully connected layers in B, C and D and reduced the model size by a large margin. Besides, we also apply 1×1 filters which could reduce the model size further and effect the accuracy negligibly to Network D. All the conclusions above will be proven in the experiments of Sect. 5.

5   Experiments

5.1   Experiments in CROHME Dataset

Training Methods. Our experiments were conducted on Caffe framework [23] using a GTX 1060 GPU card. The training used stochastic gradient descent with 0.9 momentum. The initial learning rate was 0.01 and reduced to 10% every 40k iterations. The batch size was set to 40 and the training stopped after 202k iterations (around 20 epochs). Besides, we used the "xavier" algorithm to initialize the weights of all the convolutional layers in our networks.

Results and Analyses. In the CROHME experiments, we use the symbols of CROHME 2013 test set as the validation set. And we use the test sets of CROHME 2014 and 2016 to evaluate the models. Table 3 shows the results of the four networks in these datasets.

All the four networks have achieved great performance in the three datasets. The Top-1 recognition rates of Network C in the CROHME 2014 and CROHME 2016 test sets are about 0.5% to 1% higher than those of Network A and B, while the Top-3 and Top-5 accuracies are also have an improvement about 0.1%–0.5% compared with Network A and B. The gaps between the recognition results of C and D are rather small. C has a 0.39% and 0.15% higher Top-1 performance than D in CROHME 2014 and 2016. And the gaps of Top-3 and Top-5 recognition rates don't exceed 0.1%. These results give strong evidence that the usage of BN and GAP can get better accuracies.

Table 4 elaborates the parameter scales of the four models. Replacing the fully connected layers by global average pooling layers has a sharp decrease of model size. The number of parameters of C is only 44.92% of that of A. After applying the 1×1 convolutional layers, D has a further reduced model size than C and it doesn't have much effect on accuracies compared to C, as illustrated in Tables 3 and 4.

Combining isolated classifiers is an effective way to raise the accuracies which is also used in [4, 5, 9–12]. In order to increase recognition rates further, we have combined network C with D. The ensemble method is averaging the results of the two models. The results of our methods and existing systems in CROHME are shown in

Table 3. Accuracies of our models in CROHME datasets

Dataset	CROHME 2013 test			CROHME 2014 test			CROHME 2016 test		
Network	Top-N accuracies (%)			Top-N accuracies (%)			Top-N accuracies (%)		
	Top-1	Top-3	Top-5	Top-1	Top-3	Top-5	Top-1	Top-3	Top-5
A	**88.46**	99.14	99.62	90.93	98.20	99.04	91.63	98.66	99.41
B	87.80	**99.23**	99.65	90.85	98.32	99.05	91.32	98.71	99.44
C	88.11	99.18	99.62	**91.81**	98.67	**99.18**	**92.16**	99.08	99.51
D	88.39	99.19	**99.67**	91.42	**98.76**	99.12	92.01	**99.16**	**99.52**

Table 5. Our networks outperform all the other systems in CROHME 2014 test set with a 91.82% Top-1 recognition rate. In CROHME 2016 test set, our networks have achieved the second place with 0.39% less than MyScript, the winner of CROHME 2016, who has used both online and offline features. The accuracies of our networks have a significant increase compared with the existing methods that use offline features only in CROHME dataset as shown in Table 5.

Table 6 shows the average computational time of our four networks. Although network C and D spend more time than network A and B, our four networks are all quite fast in our CROHME and HASYv2 experiments.

Table 4. Parameter Scales of HMS-VGGNets. The model size is the size of caffemodel file generated by Caffe. Since the only difference of B and C is the usage of BN, the parameter scales of B and C are the same.

Network	Number of parameters	Model size
A	2.67 M	10.7 MB
B	1.20 M	4.8 MB
C	1.20 M	4.8 MB
D	**0.87 M**	**3.5 MB**

Although we have achieved rather good results in CROHME dataset, there are two questions shown in our experiments.

Question 1: Why the results of A and B in CROHME 2013 (validation set) are only slightly lower or even higher than those of C and D? There are some symbol classes difficult or even impossible to discriminate without context information due to the very confusable handwritten styles, such as 'x-X-×', '1-|', '0-o-O'. We have analyzed the test sets of CROHME 2013, 2014 and 2016 and find 24 symbol classes that are difficult to classify. The percentage of these classes of CROHME 2013 test set is higher than those of CROHME 2014 and 2016 test sets, as shown in Table 7. This makes it harder to classify in CROHME 2013 test set, so the gaps of recognition rates of A, B, C and D are relatively small. This is also the reason why the Top-1 accuracy is significantly lower than Top-3 and Top-5 accuracies. Some misclassified symbols are illustrated in Fig. 3.

Table 5. Top-1 accuracies of our networks compared with other systems on CROHME. Top 3 accuracies in each dataset are bolded.

System	CROHME 2014 test top-1 accuracy	CROHME 2016 test top-1 accuracy	Features used
MyScript [2, 3]	91.04% [2]	**92.81%** [3]	Online + Offline
Alvaro [2, 4]	91.24% [2]	–	Online + Offline
Dai (1) [5]	89.39% [5]	–	Offline
Dai (2) [3, 5]	91.28% [5]	**92.27%** [3]	Online + Offline
Davila [2, 3, 6]	88.66% [2]	88.85% [3]	Online + Offline
Ramadhan [7]	87.72% [7]	–	Offline
Ours C	**91.81%**	92.16%	Offline
Ours D	**91.42%**	92.01%	Offline
Ours C + D	**91.82%**	**92.42%**	Offline

Table 6. Computational time of our networks in our experiments

Network	CROHME test	HASYv2 test
A	1.40 ms	1.31 ms
B	1.61 ms	1.52 ms
C	1.38 ms	1.25 ms
D	0.91 ms	0.81 ms
C + D	2.84 ms	2.59 ms

Question 2: Why the results of our methods are still less than that of MyScript? Since online data has the tracing information while offline data doesn't, online data has advantages when classifying symbols who have similar shapes and different writing processes such as '5' and 's'. Our networks only use offline features so it is hard for them to classify those symbols.

Table 7. Percentage of symbols hard to classify. These symbol classes are 'COMMA, (, 0, 1, 9, c, C, ., g, 1,/, o, p, P, \prime, q, s, S, \times, v, V, |, x, X'

Datasets	Total	Symbols hard to classify	Percentage
CROHME 2013 test	6081	1923	31.62%
CROHME 2014 test	10061	2776	27.59%
CROHME 2016 test	10019	2762	27.57%

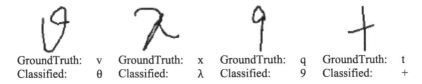

GroundTruth:	v	GroundTruth:	x	GroundTruth:	q	GroundTruth:	t
Classified:	θ	Classified:	λ	Classified:	9	Classified:	+

Fig. 3. Misclassified Samples of our networks

5.2 Experiments in HASYv2 Dataset

When conducting experiments in HASYv2 dataset, we have used cross validation to test our models as suggested by [17]. There are 10 folds in HASYv2, so we have evaluated 10 times using different folds in our experiments. The training method is almost the same as that in Sect. 5.1. We totally trained 185 k iterations (around 20 epochs) and divided the learning rate by 10 after every 35 k iterations.

Since the HASYv2 dataset is proposed lately, the other experiments on HASYv2 are still rare. We have compared our results with the model baselines in [17], as shown in Table 8. All the four networks proposed in this paper have higher accuracies than the baselines. Besides, the parameter scales of our networks are significantly smaller than TF-CNN which keeps the highest accuracy in the baselines due to the usage of small convolutional filters, GAP and well-designed architectures. Our models have achieved the state-of-the-art accuracy in HASYv2 dataset to our best knowledge.

Table 8. Accuracies of our networks compared with the model baseline of HASYv2

Classifiers	Top-N accuracies			Number of parameters
	Top-1	Top-3	Top-5	
TF-CNN [17]	81.0%	–	–	4.59 M
Random forest [17]	62.4%	–	–	–
MLP (1 layer) [17]	62.2%	–	–	–
Ours A	84.70%	97.15%	98.33%	2.15 M
Ours B	84.40%	97.14%	98.35%	1.27 M
Ours C	84.90%	97.25%	98.41%	1.27 M
Ours D	84.81%	97.26%	98.48%	0.94 M
Ours C + D	**85.05%**	**97.38%**	**98.52%**	2.20 M

There are 369 classes in HASYv2 dataset and it has more classes that are hard to discriminate than CROHME, such as $\mathcal{H}$, $\mathbb{H}$ and H; $\rightarrow$, $\mapsto$, $\rightharpoonup$, and $\hookrightarrow$. Besides, some symbols are even difficult to tell in printed form, such as \Sigma and \sum. These difficulties make great challenges for our task, so our four networks perform similarly and don't get better accuracies any more.

6 Conclusion

In this paper, we have elaborately designed a CNN architecture called HMS-VGGNet for offline handwritten mathematical symbols recognition. Experiments show that our models have achieved very competitive results in CROHME (91.82% and 92.42% Top-1 accuracy in CROHME 2014 and 2016 and around 99% Top-3 and Top-5 accuracies for both datasets) and HASYv2 (85.13% Top-1 accuracy, 97.38% Top-3 accuracy and 98.52% Top-5 accuracy) datasets using this slim and deep architecture. From our experiments results we also analyse the benefits of BN, GAP and very small filters. We will use these networks in our offline handwritten mathematical expression recognition system in the future. Since online data can generate offline images, our networks can also be used as an auxiliary method for online handwritten mathematical symbols recognition to improve accuracies further.

References

1. Mouchère, H., Zanibbi, R., Garain, U., et al.: Advancing the state of the art for handwritten math recognition: the CROHME competitions, 2011–2014. Int. J. Doc. Anal. Recogn. **19**(2), 173–189 (2016)
2. Mouchere, H., Viard-Gaudin, C., Zanibbi, R., et al.: ICFHR 2014 competition on recognition of on-line handwritten mathematical expressions (CROHME 2014). In: 14th International Conference on Frontiers in Handwriting Recognition, pp. 791–796. IEEE Press, Crete (2014)
3. Mouchère, H., Viard-Gaudin, C., Zanibbi, R., et al.: ICFHR 2016 CROHME: competition on recognition of online handwritten mathematical expressions. In: 15th International Conference on Frontiers in Handwriting Recognition, Shenzhen, pp. 607–612 (2016)
4. Álvaro, F., Sánchez, J.A., Benedí, J.M.: Offline features for classifying handwritten math symbols with recurrent neural networks. In: 2014 22nd International Conference on Pattern Recognition, pp. 2944–2949. IEEE Press, Stockholm (2014)
5. Dai, N.H., Le, A.D., Nakagawa, M.: Deep neural networks for recognizing online handwritten mathematical symbols. In: 2015 3rd IAPR Asian Conference on Pattern Recognition, pp. 121–125. IEEE Press, Kuala Lumpur (2015)
6. Davila, K., Ludi, S., Zanibbi, R.: Using off-line features and synthetic data for on-line handwritten math symbol recognition. In: 2014 14th International Conference on Frontiers in Handwriting Recognition, pp. 323–328. IEEE Press, Crete (2014)
7. Ramadhan, I., Purnama, B., Al, F.S.: Convolutional neural networks applied to handwritten mathematical symbols classification. In: 2016 4th International Conference on Information and Communication Technology, pp. 1–4. IEEE Press, Bandung (2016)
8. LeCun, Y., Bottou, L., Bengio, Y., et al.: Gradient-based learning applied to document recognition. Proc. IEEE **86**(11), 2278–2324 (1998)
9. Krizhevsky, A., Sutskever, I., Hinton, G.E.: ImageNet classification with deep convolutional neural networks. In: Proceedings of Advances in Neural Information Processing Systems, Lake Tahoe, pp. 1097–1105 (2012)
10. Szegedy, C., Liu, W., Jia, Y., et al.: Going deeper with convolutions. In: IEEE Conference on Computer Vision and Pattern Recognition, Boston, pp. 1–9 (2015)
11. Simonyan, K., Zisserman, A.: Very deep convolutional networks for large-scale image recognition (2014). arXiv:1409.1556
12. He, K., Zhang, X., Ren, S., et al.: Deep residual learning for image recognition. In: IEEE Conference on Computer Vision and Pattern Recognition, Las Vegas, pp. 770–778 (2016)
13. Girshick, R., Donahue, J., Darrell, T., et al.: Rich feature hierarchies for accurate object detection and semantic segmentation. In: IEEE Conference on Computer Vision and Pattern Recognition, Columbus, pp. 580–587 (2014)
14. He, K., Gkioxari, G., Dollár, P., et al.: Mask R-CNN (2017). arXiv:1703.06870
15. Ioffe, S., Szegedy, C.: Batch normalization: accelerating deep network training by reducing internal covariate shift (2015). arXiv:1502.03167
16. Lin, M., Chen, Q., Yan, S.: Network in network (2013). arXiv:1312.4400
17. Thoma, M.: The HASYv2 dataset (2017). arXiv:1701.08380

18. Iandola, F.N., Han, S., Moskewicz, M.W., et al.: SqueezeNet: AlexNet-level accuracy with 50x fewer parameters and < 0.5 MB model size (2016). arXiv:1602.07360

19. Szegedy, C., Vanhoucke, V., Ioffe, S., et al.: Rethinking the inception architecture for computer vision. In: IEEE Conference on Computer Vision and Pattern Recognition, Las Vegas, pp. 2818–2826 (2016)

20. Ink markup language. http://www.w3.org/TR/InkML/. Accessed 06 Apr 2017

21. Hinton, G.E., Srivastava, N., Krizhevsky, A., et al.: Improving neural networks by preventing co-adaptation of feature detectors (2012). arXiv:1207.0580

22. Simard, P.Y., Steinkraus, D., Platt, J.C.: Best practices for convolutional neural networks applied to visual document analysis. In: 2003 International Conference on Document Analysis and Recognition, Edinburgh, vol. 3, pp. 958–962 (2003)

23. Jia, Y., Shelhamer, E., Donahue, J., et al.: Caffe: convolutional architecture for fast feature embedding. In: ACM Proceedings of the 22nd International Conference on Multimedia, Orlando, pp. 675–678 (2014)

4D ISIP: 4D Implicit Surface Interest Point Detection

Shirui Li[1,2,3(✉)], Alper Yilmaz[4], Changlin Xiao[4], and Hua Li[1,2,3]

[1] Key Laboratory of Intelligent Information Processing,
Chinese Academy of Sciences, Beijing, China
lishiruilishirui@gmail.com
[2] Institute of Computing Technology, Chinese Academy of Sciences,
Beijing, China
lihua@ict.ac.cn
[3] University of Chinese Academy of Sciences, Beijing, China
[4] The Ohio State University, Columbus, USA
yilmaz.15@osu.edu, xiao.157@buckeyemail.osu.edu

Abstract. In this paper, we proposed a new method to detect 4D spatiotemporal interest point called 4D-ISIP (4 dimension implicit surface interest point). We implicitly represent the 3D scene by 3D volume which has a truncated signed distance function (TSDF) in every voxel. The TSDF represents the distance between the spatial point and object surface which is a kind of implicit surface representation. The basic idea of 4D-ISIP detection is to detect the points whose local neighborhood has significant variations along both spatial and temporal dimensions. In order to test our 4D-ISIP detection, we built a system to acquire 3D human motion dataset using only one Kinect. Experimental results show that our method can detect 4D-ISIP for different human actions.

Keywords: Non-rigid motion 3D reconstruction and tracking
Spatiotemporal interest point dectection · Human action recognition
3D human motion dataset · Kinect · Depth sensor

1 Introduction

Interest point detection has been a hot topic in computer vision field for a number of years. It's a fundamental research problem in computer vision, which plays a key role in many high-level problems, such as activity recognition, 3D reconstruction, image retrieval and so on. In this paper we proposed a new method to robustly detect interest point in 4D spatiotemporal space (x, y, z, t) for human action recognition.

3D spatiotemporal interest point (3D STIP) have been shown to perform well for activity recognition and event recognition [22,30]. It used RGB video to detect interest point, which RGB image is sensitive to color and illumination changes, occlusions, as well as background clutters. With the advent of 3D acquisition equipment, we can easily get the depth information. Depth data can

© Springer International Publishing AG 2017
Y. Zhao et al. (Eds.): ICIG 2017, Part I, LNCS 10666, pp. 162–173, 2017.
https://doi.org/10.1007/978-3-319-71607-7_15

significantly simplify the task of background subtraction and human detection. It can work well in low light conditions, giving a real 3D measure invariant to surface color and texture, while resolving silhouette pose ambiguities.

The depth data provided by Kinect, however, is noisy, which may have an impact on interest point detection [30]. In order to resolve this problem, we acquire a non-noisy human 3D action representation by fusing the depth data stream into global TSDF volume which can be useful for detecting robust interest points. Then, we introduced a new 4D implicit surface interest point (4D-ISIP) as an extension to 3D-STIP for motion recognition, especially for human actions recognition.

2   Related Work

Interest point is usually required to be robust under different image transformations and is typically the local extrema point of some domain. There are a number of interest point detectors [8,14,19,20] for static images. They are widely used for image matching, image retrieval and image classification. For the activity recognition, the spatiotemporal interest points (STIP) detected from a sequence of images is shown to work effectively. The widely used STIP detectors include three main approaches: (1) Laptev [12] detected the spatiotemporal volumes with large variation along spatial and temporal directions in a video sequence. A spatiotemporal second-moment matrix is used to model a video sequence. The interest point locations are determined by computing the local maxima of the response function $H = det(M) - k \cdot trace^3(M)$, We will give details about this method in Sect. 3.2 (2) Dollár et al. [5] proposed a cubed detector computing the interest point by the local maxima of the response function R, which is defined as: $R = (I * g * h_{ev})^2 + (I * g * h_{od})^2$ where g is the 2D gaussian smoothing kernel, h_{ev} and h_{od} are a quadrature pair of 1D Gabor filters. (3) Willems et al. [26] proposed the Hessian detector, which measures the strength of each interest point using the Hessian matrix. The response function is defined as $S = |det(\Gamma)|$, where Γ is the Hessian matrix.

The above methods detect the interest points from RGB images. Compared to depth data RGB images they are sensitive to illumination changes, occlusions, and background clutter. As the development of the depth sensor, many STIP detectors had been extended to the depth data. Xia and Aggarwal [27] presented a filtering method to extract STIPs from depth videos called DSTIP. Zhang and Parker [28] extracted STIPs by calculating a response function from both depth and RGB channels.

All the above methods only use partial view of the human body. Holte et al. [9] used multi-cameras to construct the 3D human action and then detected STIPs in every single camera view. Following that, they projected STIPs to 3D space to find 4D (x, y, z, t) spatiotemporal interest points. Cho et al. [3] proposed a volumetric spatial feature representation (VSFR) to measure the density of 3D point clouds for view-invariant human action recognition from depth sequence images. Kim et al. [10] extracted 4D spatiotemporal interest points (4D-STIP) in

3D space volume sequence reconstructed from multi-views. They detected interest points having large variations in (x, y, z) space firstly, then they check if those interest points have a significant variation in time axis. Kim et al. [10] used binary volume to represent the whole 3D human and calculate the partial derivatives.

In this paper, We only use one Kinect to get non-noisy 3D human motion, which is more practical in real applications. We use implicit surface (TSDF volume) to represent the whole 3D human, which provides a way to robustly calculate the partial derivative in 4 directions (x, y, z, t). We directly calculated the 4D ISIP in (x, y, z, t) space and choose the points which simultaneously have large variations in different four directions.

Utilizing a single Kinect to accurately recover 3D human action is an active and challenging research topic in recent years. Many methods [1,2,25] get 3D human model based on a trained human template, but those methods can't be used to reconstruct the human body with clothes. Zhang et al. [29] reconstructed human body with clothes. However all of those methods require the reconstructed human to stay still during acquisition, which is not possible in reality. Newcombe et al. [15] proposed a real-time method to reconstruct dynamic scenes without any prior templates. But it is not capable of long term tracking, because of growing warp field and error accumulation. Guo et al. [7] introduced a novel L_0 based motion regularizer with an iterative optimization solver, which can robustly reconstruct non-rigid geometries and motions from single view depth input. In this paper, we combine Newcombe et al. [15] and Guo et al. [7] to build a system to construct 3D human motion dataset for 4D ISIP detection.

3   Method

Before we introduce 4D-ISIP we introduce how to represent and acquire human action dataset firstly. We adopt the volumetric truncated signed distance function (TSDF) [4] to represent the 3D scene. We combine Newcombe et al. [15] and Guo et al. [7] to build a system to construct 3D human motion dataset for 4D ISIP detection. Then, we gave a detail about the 3D spatial temporal interest points below. Lastly, we will introduce how to extended 3D-STIP to 4D-ISIP.

3.1   Acquisition of 3D Human Motion Dataset

Upon acquisition of every input depth data, we first estimate the ground plane using RANSAC to segment human body from the ground. This is followed by point neighborhood statistics to filter noise outlier data.

DynamicFusion [15] can reconstruct non-rigidly deforming scenes in real-time by fusing RGBD scans acquired from commodity sensors without any template. It can generate denoised, detailed and complete reconstructions. But it is not capable of long term tracking, because of growing warp field and error accumulation. The method proposed by Guo et al. [7] provides long term tracking using a human template. We use DynamicFusion to get a complete human body mesh by rotating our body in front of the Kinect as the template. Then we use Shi and Tomasi [20] to track human motion with partial data input.

Lastly, We generated the same topology mesh for every motion frame. Then we transformed those mesh into TSDF representation. In Fig. 1, we illustrate how we use TSDF to implicitly represent an arbitrary surface as zero crossings within the volume. The whole scene is represented by a 3D volume with a TSDF value in each voxel. TSDF is the truncated distance between spatial point and object surface.

$$\Psi(\eta) \begin{cases} min(1, \frac{\eta}{\tau}) & \text{if } \eta \geq -\tau \\ -1 & \text{otherwise} \end{cases} \tag{1}$$

where τ is the threshold distance and η is the distance to surface, $\Psi(\eta)$ is the truncated signed distance.

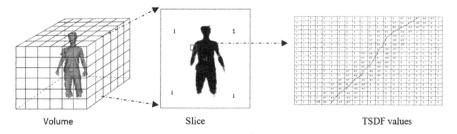

| Volume | Slice | TSDF values |

Fig. 1. TSDF volume

3.2 3D Spatial Temporal Interest Points

In order to model a spatial-temporal image sequence, Laptev [12] used a function $f : \mathbb{R}^2 \times \mathbb{R} \mapsto \mathbb{R}$ and constructed its linear scale-space representation $L : \mathbb{R}^2 \times \mathbb{R} \times \mathbb{R}_+^2 \mapsto \mathbb{R}$ by convolution of f with an anisotropic Gaussian kernel with independent spatial variance σ_s^2 and temporal variance σ_t^2:

$$L(x, y, t; \sigma_s^2, \sigma_t^2) = g(x, y, t; \sigma_s^2, \sigma_t^2) * f(x, y, t), \tag{2}$$

where the spatiotemporal separable Gaussian kernel is defined as:

$$g(x, y, t; \sigma_s^2, \sigma_t^2) = \frac{1}{\sqrt{(2\pi)^3 \sigma_s^4 \sigma_t^2}} \times exp(\frac{-(x^2 + y^2)}{2\sigma_s^2} - \frac{t^2}{2\sigma_t^2}), \tag{3}$$

where $\sigma_{s'}^2 = l\sigma_s^2$ and $\sigma_{t'}^2 = l\sigma_t^2$. Then they define a spatiotemporal second-moment matrix as:

$$M = g(\cdot; \sigma_{s'}^2, \sigma_{t'}^2) * \begin{pmatrix} L_x^2 & L_x L_y & L_x L_t \\ L_x L_y & L_y^2 & L_y L_t \\ L_x L_t & L_y L_t & L_t^2 \end{pmatrix}. \tag{4}$$

The first-order derivatives of f are given by:

$$L_x(\cdot; \sigma_s^2, \sigma_t^2) = \partial_x(g * f)$$
$$L_y(\cdot; \sigma_s^2, \sigma_t^2) = \partial_y(g * f). \tag{5}$$
$$L_t(\cdot; \sigma_s^2, \sigma_t^2) = \partial_t(g * f)$$

For detecting interest points, search for region in f having significant eigenvalues $\lambda_1, \lambda_2, \lambda_3$ of M. Laptev [12] calculate H by combining the determinant and the trace of M. And select the point with a large H value as the STIP:

$$H = det(M) - k \cdot trace^3(M) = \lambda_1 \lambda_2 \lambda_3 - k(\lambda_1 + \lambda_2 + \lambda_3)^3, \qquad (6)$$

where $k = 0.04$ is an empirical value.

3.3   4D Implicit Surface Interested Points

We define $p : \mathbb{R}^3 \times \mathbb{R} \mapsto \mathbb{R}$ as a truncated signed distance function which is the shortest distance to surface point. This can be regarded as an implicit surface representation. In this paper, our goal is to find interest points that have significant variation in (x, y, z, t) directions. Firstly, we do a Gaussian filtering for the complete 3D motion sequences. Considering that spatial and temporal directions have different noise and scale characteristics, we use $\bar{\sigma}_s^2$ for spatial space scale and $\bar{\sigma}_t^2$ for temporal scale:

$$\bar{L}(x, y, z, t; \bar{\sigma}_s^2, \bar{\sigma}_t^2) = \bar{g}(x, y, z, t; \bar{\sigma}_s^2, \bar{\sigma}_t^2) * p(x, y, z, t), \qquad (7)$$

which results in 4D Gaussian given by:

$$\bar{g}(x, y, z, t; \bar{\sigma}_s^2, \bar{\sigma}_t^2) = \frac{1}{\sqrt{(2\pi)^3 \bar{\sigma}_s^6 \bar{\sigma}_t^2}}$$
$$\times \ exp(-\frac{(x^2 + y^2 + z^2)}{2\bar{\sigma}_s^2} - \frac{t^2}{2\bar{\sigma}_t^2}) \qquad (8)$$

After filtering, we define a spatiotemporal second-moment matrix, which is a 4-by-4 matrix composed of first order of spatial and temporal derivatives averaged by Gaussian weighting function:

$$\bar{M} = \bar{g}(\cdot; \bar{\sigma}_{s'}^2, \bar{\sigma}_{t'}^2) * \begin{pmatrix} \bar{L}_x^2 & \bar{L}_x \bar{L}_y & \bar{L}_x \bar{L}_z & \bar{L}_x \bar{L}_t \\ \bar{L}_x \bar{L}_y & \bar{L}_y^2 & \bar{L}_y \bar{L}_z & \bar{L}_y \bar{L}_t \\ \bar{L}_x \bar{L}_z & \bar{L}_y \bar{L}_z & \bar{L}_z^2 & \bar{L}_z \bar{L}_t \\ \bar{L}_x \bar{L}_t & \bar{L}_y \bar{L}_t & \bar{L}_z \bar{L}_t & \bar{L}_t^2 \end{pmatrix}, \qquad (9)$$

where $\bar{\sigma}_{s'}^2 = l' \bar{\sigma}_s^2$ and $\bar{\sigma}_{t'}^2 = l' \bar{\sigma}_t^2$. l' is an empirical value, in our experiments we set $l' = 2$.

$$\bar{L}_x(\cdot; \bar{\sigma}_s^2, \bar{\sigma}_t^2) = \partial_x(\bar{g} * p),$$
$$\bar{L}_y(\cdot; \bar{\sigma}_s^2, \bar{\sigma}_t^2) = \partial_y(\bar{g} * p),$$
$$\bar{L}_z(\cdot; \bar{\sigma}_s^2, \bar{\sigma}_t^2) = \partial_z(\bar{g} * p), \qquad (10)$$
$$\bar{L}_t(\cdot; \bar{\sigma}_s^2, \bar{\sigma}_t^2) = \partial_t(\bar{g} * p).$$

In order to extract interest points, we search for regions in p having significant eigenvalues $\bar{\lambda}_1 < \bar{\lambda}_2 < \bar{\lambda}_3 < \bar{\lambda}_4$ of $\bar{M}$. Similar to the Harris corner function and STIP function, we define a function as follows:

$$\bar{H} = det(\bar{M}) - k * trace^4(\bar{M})$$
$$= \bar{\lambda}_1 \bar{\lambda}_2 \bar{\lambda}_3 \bar{\lambda}_4 - k(\bar{\lambda}_1 + \bar{\lambda}_2 + \bar{\lambda}_3 + \bar{\lambda}_4)^4. \qquad (11)$$

letting the ratios $\alpha = \bar{\lambda}_2/\bar{\lambda}_1$, $\beta = \bar{\lambda}_3/\bar{\lambda}_1$, $\gamma = \bar{\lambda}_3/\bar{\lambda}_1$, we re-write H as

$$\bar{H} = \bar{\lambda}_1^4(\alpha\beta\gamma - k(1 + \alpha + \beta + \gamma)^4), \tag{12}$$

where $\bar{H} \geq 0$, we have $k \leq \alpha\beta\gamma/(1 + \alpha + \beta + \gamma)^4$. Suppose $\alpha = \beta = \gamma = 23$, we get $k \leq 0.0005$. In our experiment we use $k = 0.0005$. We select point with a $\bar{H}$ value bigger than a threshold value $\bar{H}_t$ as the candidate. At last, we select the points with the local maxima $\bar{H}$ as the 4D ISIPs.

4   Experiments

4.1   3D Human Action Reconstruction

There are a number of datasets for human action recognition. Some of those datasets [11,16–18,21] are captured by single RGB camera. Some of those datasets [6,24] are captured by multiple view RGB cameras, which can provide 3D human motion. However, the acquired 3D models are not accuracy enough. There are also some datasets [13,23] captured by single Kinect. But those datasets have an only partial view data with high noise.

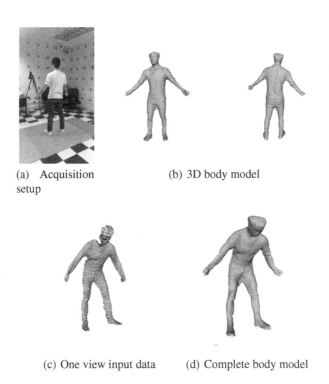

(a) Acquisition setup   (b) 3D body model

(c) One view input data   (d) Complete body model

Fig. 2. Reconstruction setup (a) and reconstruction results (b). The complete 3D body model (d) is driven by the input one view data (c)

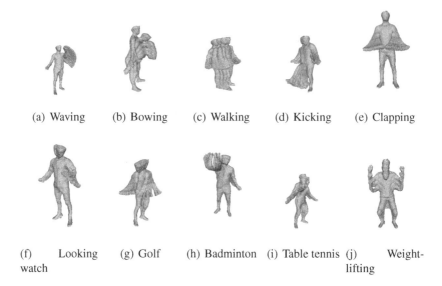

(a) Waving   (b) Bowing   (c) Walking   (d) Kicking   (e) Clapping

(f)   Looking   (g) Golf   (h) Badminton   (i) Table tennis   (j)   Weight-
watch   lifting

Fig. 3. Action dataset includes ten actions

We constructed a 3D human action dataset using single fixed Kinect. In order to generate a 3D whole body, we rotate the body in front of the Kinect without required of a rigid body motion, as shown in Figure 2(a). Then we use this model as a template to do tracking. As shown in Fig. 2(c), with just one view input we can get a complete body model. Figure 3 show the sequences of reconstructed action dataset. We put a couple of frames together, so we can see the animation. This dataset includes 10 kinds of human action class: waving, walking, bowing, clapping, kicking, looking watch, weight-lifting, golf swinging, playing table tennis and badminton.

4.2   4D-ISIP Detection

Upon the generated human motion sequences, we can extract 4D-ISIPs. In our experiments we set the resolution of volume is $128 * 128 * 128$, $\bar{\sigma}_s = 2$ and $\bar{\sigma}_t = 1$. We normalized the value of $\bar{H}$ by $\bar{H} = (\bar{H} - \bar{H}_{min})/(\bar{H}_{max} - \bar{H}_{min})$. Apparently, we will get different results by setting different threshold. Figure 4(a, b, c) are the point clouds of action sequences. The red points in the those point clouds are the 4D ISIPs. As increasing the value of threshold the number of 4D-ISIPs is decreasing. Figure 4(d) is the 3D mesh of the kicking sequence. In order to extract sparse 4D-ISIPs, we set $\bar{H}_t = 0.6$ in following experiments.

As Fig. 5 shows that we can robustly detect the changing motion directions, which suggests that 4D ISIP can represent the human motion. It can be used to describe trajectory of human action which can be used for action recognition. The red points in point cloud denote the detected 4D ISIP. The corresponding mesh models are also shown on the left. Here are more 4D ISIPs detection results in Fig. 6.

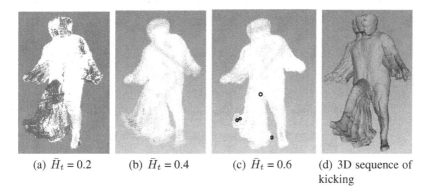

(a) $\bar{H}_t = 0.2$ (b) $\bar{H}_t = 0.4$ (c) $\bar{H}_t = 0.6$ (d) 3D sequence of
                                                                                        kicking

Fig. 4. Selection of threshold value $\bar{H}_t$. (a) (b) (c) are the point clouds of the action sequence, (d) is the 3D mesh of the action sequence. (Color figure online)

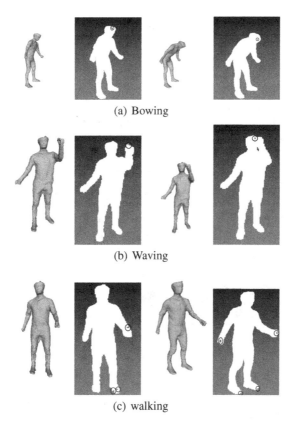

(a) Bowing

(b) Waving

(c) walking

Fig. 5. 4D-ISIP detection results on dataset (Color figure online)

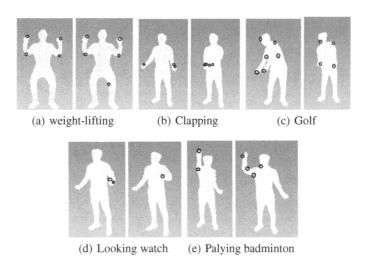

(a) weight-lifting   (b) Clapping   (c) Golf

(d) Looking watch   (e) Palying badminton

Fig. 6. More results of 4D-ISIP detection

4.3   Comparison with 3D STIP

Technically, 3D STIP [12] detect interest point in (x, y, t) space which can't describe the real 3D motion. It can't handle motion occlusion and illumination change problems. For instance STIP can't handle the motion of waving hand back and forth. Because this kind of motions has slight variations in image content. However, this motion have a significant variations in 3D (x, y, z) and 4D (x, y, z, t) space. The proposed 4D ISIP approach can work in this situation. As shown in Fig. 7.

Furthermore, 4D-ISIP is robust to illumination change, which is important for action recognition. As shown in Fig. 8. The 3D STIP is sensitive to illumination change. Because it extracts the interest points on RGB image which is sensitive to illumination change.

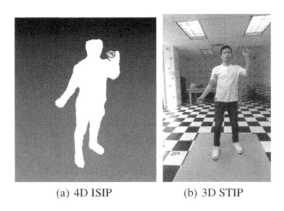

(a) 4D ISIP   (b) 3D STIP

Fig. 7. 4D ISIPs can be detected even there is a slightly change in image content.

(a) 3D STIP   (b) 4D ISIP

Fig. 8. Illumination change, 3D STIP is sensitive to illumination change, (a) show the 3D STIPs on the image sequence under the illumination change. Meanwhile, 4D ISIP is robust to the illumination change, (b) is the 4D ISIP on point cloud

5   Conclusions

In this paper, we built a system to acquire 3D human motion using one only Kinect. We proposed a new 4D ISIP(4D implicit surface interest point detection) which is the keypoint of the motion. It can be used for motion recognition, especially for human action recognition. We use the TSDF volume as implicit surface representation to represent the reconstructed 3D body. This results in a non-noisy human 3D action representation by fusing the depth data stream into global TSDF volume which can be useful for getting a robust interest point detection. Our approach doesn't use the image information and only uses the pure 3D geometric information to detect the interest points which has a sort of advantages. It's robust to the illumination change, occlusion, and noise caused by RGB or depth data stream. In the future work, we expected that the proposed 4D-ISIP could be used in human action recognition dealing with scale and view-invariant problems.

Acknowledgements. This work was funded by Natural Science Foundation of China (61227802, 61379082) and China Scholarship Council.

References

1. Bogo, F., Black, M.J., Loper, M., Romero, J.: Detailed full-body reconstructions of moving people from monocular RGB-D sequences. In: Proceedings of the IEEE International Conference on Computer Vision, pp. 2300–2308 (2015)
2. Chen, Y., Liu, Z., Zhang, Z.: Tensor-based human body modeling. In: Proceedings of the IEEE Conference on Computer Vision and Pattern Recognition, pp. 105–112 (2013)
3. Cho, S.S., Lee, A.R., Suk, H.I., Park, J.S., Lee, S.W.: Volumetric spatial feature representation for view-invariant human action recognition using a depth camera. Opt. Eng. **54**(3), 033102 (2015)
4. Curless, B., Levoy, M.: A volumetric method for building complex models from range images. In: Proceedings of the 23rd Annual Conference on Computer Graphics and Interactive Techniques, pp. 303–312. ACM (1996)
5. Dollár, P., Rabaud, V., Cottrell, G., Belongie, S.: Behavior recognition via sparse spatio-temporal features. In: 2nd Joint IEEE International Workshop on Visual Surveillance and Performance Evaluation of Tracking and Surveillance, pp. 65–72. IEEE (2005)

6. Gkalelis, N., Kim, H., Hilton, A., Nikolaidis, N., Pitas, I.: The i3DPost multi-view and 3D human action/interaction database. In: Conference for Visual Media Production, CVMP 2009, pp. 159–168. IEEE (2009)

7. Guo, K., Xu, F., Wang, Y., Liu, Y., Dai, Q.: Robust non-rigid motion tracking and surface reconstruction using L0 regularization. In: Proceedings of the IEEE International Conference on Computer Vision, pp. 3083–3091 (2015)

8. Harris, C., Stephens, M.: A combined corner and edge detector. In: Alvey Vision Conference, vol. 15, p. 50. Citeseer (1988)

9. Holte, M.B., Chakraborty, B., Gonzalez, J., Moeslund, T.B.: A local 3-D motion descriptor for multi-view human action recognition from 4-D spatio-temporal interest points. IEEE J. Sel. Top. Signal Process. **6**(5), 553–565 (2012)

10. Kim, S.J., Kim, S.W., Sandhan, T., Choi, J.Y.: View invariant action recognition using generalized 4D features. Pattern Recogn. Lett. **49**, 40–47 (2014)

11. Kuehne, H., Jhuang, H., Garrote, E., Poggio, T., Serre, T.: HMDB: a large video database for human motion recognition. In: 2011 IEEE International Conference on Computer Vision (ICCV), pp. 2556–2563. IEEE (2011)

12. Laptev, I.: On space-time interest points. Int. J. Comput. Vis. **64**(2–3), 107–123 (2005)

13. Li, W., Zhang, Z., Liu, Z.: Action recognition based on a bag of 3D points. In: 2010 IEEE Computer Society Conference on Computer Vision and Pattern Recognition Workshops (CVPRW), pp. 9–14. IEEE (2010)

14. Lowe, D.G.: Distinctive image features from scale-invariant keypoints. Int. J. Comput. Vis. **60**(2), 91–110 (2004)

15. Newcombe, R.A., Fox, D., Seitz, S.M.: DynamicFusion: reconstruction and tracking of non-rigid scenes in real-time. In: Proceedings of the IEEE Conference on Computer Vision and Pattern Recognition, pp. 343–352 (2015)

16. Niebles, J.C., Chen, C.-W., Fei-Fei, L.: Modeling temporal structure of decomposable motion segments for activity classification. In: Daniilidis, K., Maragos, P., Paragios, N. (eds.) ECCV 2010. LNCS, vol. 6312, pp. 392–405. Springer, Heidelberg (2010). https://doi.org/10.1007/978-3-642-15552-9_29

17. Reddy, K.K., Shah, M.: Recognizing 50 human action categories of web videos. Mach. Vis. Appl. **24**(5), 971–981 (2013)

18. Rodriguez, M.D., Ahmed, J., Shah, M.: Action mach a spatio-temporal maximum average correlation height filter for action recognition. In: IEEE Conference on Computer Vision and Pattern Recognition, CVPR 2008, pp. 1–8. IEEE (2008)

19. Rosten, E., Porter, R., Drummond, T.: Faster and better: a machine learning approach to corner detection. IEEE Trans. Pattern Anal. Mach. Intell. **32**(1), 105–119 (2010)

20. Shi, J., Tomasi, C.: Good features to track. In: 1994 IEEE Computer Society Conference on Computer Vision and Pattern Recognition, Proceedings CVPR 1994, pp. 593–600. IEEE (1994)

21. Tran, D., Sorokin, A.: Human activity recognition with metric learning. In: Forsyth, D., Torr, P., Zisserman, A. (eds.) ECCV 2008. LNCS, vol. 5302, pp. 548–561. Springer, Heidelberg (2008). https://doi.org/10.1007/978-3-540-88682-2_42

22. Wang, H., Ullah, M.M., Klaser, A., Laptev, I., Schmid, C.: Evaluation of local spatio-temporal features for action recognition. In: BMVC 2009-British Machine Vision Conference, pp. 124–131. BMVA Press (2009)

23. Wang, J., Liu, Z., Wu, Y., Yuan, J.: Mining actionlet ensemble for action recognition with depth cameras. In: 2012 IEEE Conference on Computer Vision and Pattern Recognition (CVPR), pp. 1290–1297. IEEE (2012)

24. Weinland, D., Boyer, E., Ronfard, R.: Action recognition from arbitrary views using 3D exemplars. In: IEEE 11th International Conference on Computer Vision, 2007, ICCV 2007, pp. 1–7. IEEE (2007)
25. Weiss, A., Hirshberg, D., Black, M.J.: Home 3D body scans from noisy image and range data. In: 2011 IEEE International Conference on Computer Vision (ICCV), pp. 1951–1958. IEEE (2011)
26. Willems, G., Tuytelaars, T., Van Gool, L.: An efficient dense and scale-invariant spatio-temporal interest point detector. In: Forsyth, D., Torr, P., Zisserman, A. (eds.) ECCV 2008. LNCS, vol. 5303, pp. 650–663. Springer, Heidelberg (2008). https://doi.org/10.1007/978-3-540-88688-4_48
27. Xia, L., Aggarwal, J.: Spatio-temporal depth cuboid similarity feature for activity recognition using depth camera. In: Proceedings of the IEEE Conference on Computer Vision and Pattern Recognition, pp. 2834–2841 (2013)
28. Zhang, H., Parker, L.E.: 4-dimensional local spatio-temporal features for human activity recognition. In: 2011 IEEE/RSJ International Conference on Intelligent Robots and Systems (IROS), pp. 2044–2049. IEEE (2011)
29. Zhang, Q., Fu, B., Ye, M., Yang, R.: Quality dynamic human body modeling using a single low-cost depth camera. In: 2014 IEEE Conference on Computer Vision and Pattern Recognition (CVPR), pp. 676–683. IEEE (2014)
30. Zhu, Y., Chen, W., Guo, G.: Evaluating spatiotemporal interest point features for depth-based action recognition. Image Vis. Comput. **32**(8), 453–464 (2014)

Integrative Embedded Car Detection System with DPM

Wei Zhang, Lian-fa Bai, Yi Zhang, and Jing Han[✉]

School of Electronic Engineering and Optoelectronic Technology,
Nanjing University of Science and Technology, Nanjing 210094, China
hajlyx@foxmail.com

Abstract. In this paper a embedded system based on CPU and FPGA integration is presented for car detection with the improved Deformable Part Model (Deformable Part Model, DPM). Original images are computed and layered into multi-resolution HOG feature pyramid on CPU, and then transmitted to FPGA for fast convolution operations, and finally return to CPU for statistical matching and display. Due to the architecture of the DPM algorithm, combined with the hardware characteristics of the embedded system, the overall algorithm frameworks are simplified and optimized. According to the mathematical derivation and statistical rules, the feature dimensions and the pyramid levels of the model descend without sacrificing the accuracy, which effectively reduce the amount of calculation and data transmission. The advantages of parallel processing and pipeline design of FPGA are made full used to achieve the acceleration of convolution computation, which significantly reduce the running time of the program. Several experiments have been done for visible images in the unmanned aerial vehicle's view and the driver assistance scene, and infrared images captured in an overlooking perspective are also tested and analyzed. The result shows that the system has good real-time and accuracy performance in different situations.

Keywords: DPM · Convolution acceleration · Vehicle detection
Fast feature Pyramid

1 Introduction

Vehicle detection is mainly used for traffic safety and UAV surveillance, which has aroused widespread concern of many scholars [1]. Most researches used various sensors to design intelligent system. Although the current GPS and radar sensors have been developed and had a good performance in obstacle avoidance, but the amount of information they provided is far less than visual sensors. With the development of the visual sensors, the cost and size of them are greatly reduced, which make them become more and more convenient in kinds of applications, such as vehicle driving assist system and unmanned airborne systems. At the same time, the chip technology has made considerable progress, which enables some complex algorithms to be implemented on embedded platform. A multi-feature fusion method was proposed to identify the UAV aerial image in [1]. Although this method had good accuracy, the real-time performance was to poor to carry on the unmanned airborne systems.

© Springer International Publishing AG 2017
Y. Zhao et al. (Eds.): ICIG 2017, Part I, LNCS 10666, pp. 174–185, 2017.
https://doi.org/10.1007/978-3-319-71607-7_16

For the static detection of vehicles, most of the current algorithms were based on the shape feature [2], such as HOG-LBP, Haar-like-Adaboost, DPM-SVM and so on. In order to solve the problem that the accuracy and the real-time is not strong enough in the moving vehicle detection, [3] presented a new detector based on the improved Adaboost algorithm and the inter-frame difference method. [4] combined HOG and SVM for vehicle detection in the outdoor environment, which improved the success rate of classification by adjusting the SVM parameters. Based on the characteristics of HOG, [5] proposed a two stages car detection method using DPM with composite feature sets, which can identify many kinds of vehicles in different viewing angles.

After a comprehensive comparison of the approaches proposed in the literature, aiming at the issues of poor real-time performance, narrow detection range and low accuracy in complex environment, we regard the deformable part model (DPM) as our research direction.

As for the embedded implementation of DPM algorithm, many kinds of vehicle detection system architectures exist in the literature. Most of these methods are entirely based on FPGA, which means that all the steps of the algorithm were implemented on FPGA. These approaches focus on the details of hardware design and optimization, without considering the hardware characteristics and the algorithm structure, which lead to its poor performance in flexibility and adaptability. In order to solve this problem, we decide to use CPU and FPGA embedded system platform to realize vehicle detection algorithm.

2   Algorithm and Implementation of Detection System

2.1   DPM Algorithm Overview

The Fig. 1 shows that the overall algorithm flow of DPM. DPM is a very successful target detection algorithm, which has become an important part of many classifiers, segmentation, human posture and behavior classification. DPM can be regarded as the expansion of the HOG algorithm. Firstly, the histogram of gradient direction is calculated, and then the gradient models are obtained by SVM. These trained models can be used to detect the target directly. However, the single model matching is falling far short of need of multi-view vehicle detection, so the multiple model matching is necessary. Considering the spatial correspondence among multiple models, we add the position offset between the part model and the root model as cost, that is to say, subtract the offset cost then get the composite score. It is essentially a spatial prior knowledge of the part model and the root model. In this way, we can get the final result of the target detection according to the statistic of response of each model and target.

Through analysis on the flowchart of DPM algorithm, we notice that the convolution response between each model and image in which a large mount of computation should be carried out is basically a simple iterative calculation. On the contrary, the extraction of image features and the calculation of feature pyramid need little computing resources, which are the most complex parts of algorithm. According to the character-istics of structure of the DPM, we decided to design an embedded platform composed of CPU and FPGA to implement the vehicle detection in different scenarios.

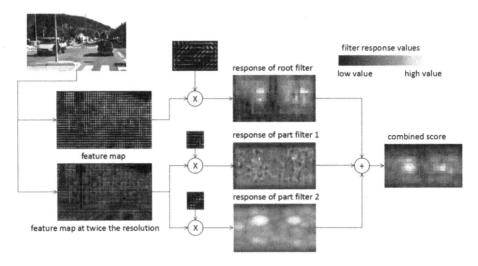

Fig. 1. The overall algorithm flow of DPM

2.2 System Architecture

In order to implement the DPM algorithm in Advanced Driver Assistant Systems (ADAS) and unmanned aerial system, the consumption and volume of the hardware platform must meet the requirements. Low-power FPGA chip has strong parallel processing ability, which is suitable for the calculation of convolution. It is possible to improve the uptime of the whole algorithm by utilizing pipeline architecture of FPGA. Tegra X1 combines the NVIDIA Maxwell GPU architecture with an ARM CPU cluster to deliver the performance and power efficiency required by computer graphics and artificial intelligence. Designed for power and space constrained applications, Tegra X1 has many kinds of peripherals and interfaces. So we built a embedded image processing system based on NVIDIA Tegra X1 and XILINX Spatan6 XC6SLX100T.

The overall overview of the whole system is shown in Fig. 2. Tegra X1 is responsible for acquiring the video stream through the USB port, image preprocessing and scaling, generating feature pyramid of image, reducing feature dimensions and pyramid levels. Feature images selected transmit to FPGA convolution via ethernet for calculation, and then the images sorted return to Tegra X1 for statistical matching and stream out the results to the HDMI. Due to the complexity of DPM algorithm and the whole system requirements, we need to consider some detail designs in specific implementation of the system. The difficulties in the realization of the system and the specific solutions are described below (Fig. 3).

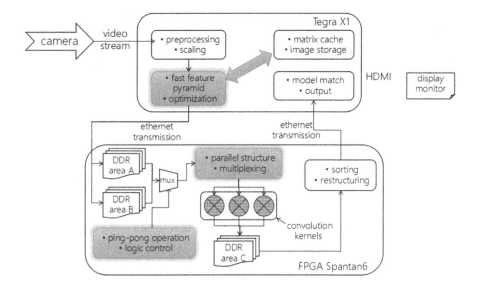

Fig. 2. The whole architecture of image processing system

Fig. 3. The detection system hardware

2.3   Feature Pyramid and Optimization

After the original construction of feature pyramid, the different scale images acquired exceed dozens of layers. If these layers are directly calculated by the HOG feature and carried out the subsequent convolution operations, the amount of computation required will be too large, resulting in severe time consuming in the whole system, which means that real-time will be seriously affected. In order to deal with this problem, we should reduce the levels of pyramid as far as possible without affecting detection accuracy. [8] presented a method based on statistical characteristics of fast feature construction of pyramid. The key sight of it was that one may compute finely sampled feature pyramids at a fraction of the cost, without sacrificing performance: for a broad family of features they found that features computed at octave-spaced scale intervals were sufficient to approximate features on a finely-sampled pyramid. This method greatly reduced the levels of pyramid which need to be calculated entirely. The core idea can be described by the following formula:

$$C_s = \Omega(I_s) \tag{1}$$

As is said above, I represents the original image and C represents the feature image. Let I_s denote I captured at scale s and $R(C, s)$ denote I resampled by s. As long as $C = \Omega(I)$ is computed, we can predict the image $C_s = \Omega(I_s)$ at a new scale s using only C. Instead of computing $C_s = \Omega(R(C, s))$, we propose a new approximation below:

$$C_s \approx R(C, s)s^{-\lambda_\Omega} \tag{2}$$

Figure 4 shows a visual demonstration of Eq. (2). After the original image is scaled to 1/2 resolution, we calculated the HOG features of these two images. By interpolation and scaling these two feature maps we get the other layers of pyramid.

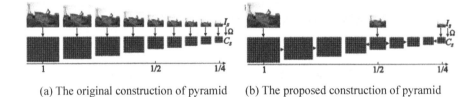

(a) The original construction of pyramid   (b) The proposed construction of pyramid

Fig. 4. The construction of fast feature pyramid

2.4   Convolution of Feature Matrix

Convolution calculation is implemented on the FPGA. The main method to implement FPGA design efficiently focus on the buffer scheme and the improvement of the convolution kernel module. Following is the specific implementation process:

Convolution Accelerator. According to the algorithm needs, we design two sizes of convolution kernel (6 * 6 and 15 * 5), the number of 6 * 6 kernel is 16 and the other is 2. The parallel computation of convolution is realized by shift registers multiplexing and module cascade. The design of the convolution architecture is shown in Fig. 5. The whole convolution accelerator works as follows: buffer the incoming pixel sequence in shift registers, start calculating convolution when first pixel arrive in the first kernel. The outputs of convolution kernel enter the next shift register and control logic module simultaneously. On the one hand the pixel sequence continues to be transmitted to shift register and calculated in convolution kernel, on the other hand it is also transmitted to control logic module for sorting and restructuring. The circulation has been in progress until the first pixel complete calculation in last convolution kernel, at the same time the pixel sequence of the second row and the third row are also done computation in corresponding kernel. These results enter control logic module, sorted by specific rules and output to next module.

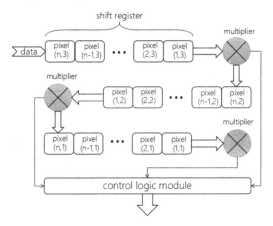

Fig. 5. The framework of convolution accelerator

Buffer Scheme. FIFO and DDR3 are used to cache the data in order to ensure timing requirement. The main function of FIFO is to maintain the continuity and integrity of data when the data is transmitted. DDR3 is mainly for the realization of the ping-pong operation shown in Fig. 6, with the aim of hiding the data transfer time to the computation time. Figure 6(a) denotes the initial state. The incoming data is stored in A area of DDR3 until this area is full, and then the address control module sends a signal that changes the storage path to the B area. Meanwhile, read the data stored in A area to convolution kernel for computation, this is working state 1. Once B area is full, address control module holds incoming data waiting for the convolution kernel to completed calculation, at this time the system is in working state 2. When convolution kernel finishes all calculations, address control module switches read address and write address, this is working

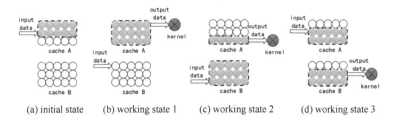

(a) initial state   (b) working state 1   (c) working state 2   (d) working state 3

Fig. 6. The ping-pong operation

state 3. And then cycle three working states above. It appears the data is continuously carrying on transmission and processing from the data input and output.

Logical Architecture and Data Reuse. Prior to discussion of data reuse, it is necessary to consider the computation to communication ratio that features the DRAM traffic needed by a kernel in a specific system implementation, used to describe the computation operations per memory access. The data reuse optimization can reduce the total number of memory access, improving computation to communication ratio. Under the premise of limited bandwidth and limited on-chip resources, we design corresponding data multiplexing architectures for different sizes of convolution kernels respectively. In order to save the shift register resources, we designed a shift register multiplexing module, effectively reducing the number of shift register.

2.5   Communication

The communication between FPGA and Tegra X1 is based on ethernet. Due to the large amount of data to be transmitted and the high stability requirements, there will be serious packet loss and poor data transmission stability if we simply use the UDP/IP protocol to transmit. Although TCP/IP protocol can solve the problem of packet loss, the data transmission speed can not reach the extent of the algorithm needs. After a careful study of our algorithm, we write a protocol that preserves both the stability of TCP and the speed of UDP. We carried out the pseudo TCP coding of the transmitted data over the UDP protocol, which made a speed-stability trade off.

3   Experiments and Evaluation

In order to evaluate the adaptability and accuracy of the proposed image processing system in various situations, we have done a lot of experiments and tests. We test UAV aerial images in different heights, aiming to assess the effectiveness of the system for the detection of targets at different scales. For the driver's view, we use the KITTI data sets for test, which basically meet the requirements of the auxiliary driving scene. We also test our system with infrared images.

3.1   Assessment Architecture

Precision and recall are two quality indicators used to evaluate the performance of vehicle detection, defined respectively as:

$$precision = \frac{true\ positives}{true\ positives + false\ positives} \tag{3}$$

$$recall = \frac{true\ positives}{true\ positives + false\ negatives} \tag{4}$$

Precision indicates the percentage of detected cars out of the total number of detected objects, which can measure the accuracy of the algorithm. Recall represents the ability of the algorithm to detect all the targets in the image. Therefore, these two indicators constitute a complete architecture.

3.2 Results

A total of the 408 frames UAV aerial images with a resolution of 640 * 480 were collected from in 60 m and 100 m height. We selected different sizes of positive and negative samples from these images, training in the semi-supervised way with Matlab. Testing the trained models many times, we set the parameter of NARC (number of aspect ratio cluster to use) to 2, so that the trained models can achieve an optimal balance between speed and accuracy.

Table 1 shows a comparison of the proposed system with other systems. The vehicle detection system we presented is better than [6, 7] in precision and recall index, we can find from Fig. 7 that the background is very complex and numerous cars are shaded. In such a complicated environment our system still have good precision and recall, reflecting the advantage of our method strongly. [9] is slightly better than our system, the following discussion may be the main reason:

- The algorithm proposed by [9] was implemented on a Intel i5 processor at 3.4 GHz while ours was carried on embedded system. There is a marked difference in the aspect of hardware.
- The images tested in [9] have few vehicles with very clear background, on the contrary, images detected in this paper have a number of vehicles and some of them were partial occluded, which increase the difficulty of detection to a certain extent.

Table 1. Comparison of UAV images test

	Proposed	[6]	[7]	[9]
Precision	84.3%	75.0%	83.7%	91.3%
Recall	81.7%	65.0%	51.3%	90.0%

As for the problem of insufficient hardware, we can make full use of the Tegra X1 GPU to accelerate the construction of pyramid, improving the performance of detection. For the vehicle detection in complex environment, an effective solution is to strengthen the depth of the training sets, the specific approach is to increase the parameter of NARC or increase the number of training samples.

The test images in KITTI have a total of 379 frames with a resolution of 1392 * 512. We use Matlab to intercepted a large number of positive and negative samples for training. The parameter of NARC is set to 4.

The overall difficulty of detection in driver's view is higher than that of the UAV aerial view. Due to the various sizes of the vehicle targets in this scenario and the differences among vehicles will be more obvious, so we need more samples to be trained, which greatly increase the complexity of the training sets. Furthermore, environmental

(a) Flight altitude at 60m   (b) Flight altitude at 60m

(c) Flight altitude at 100m   (d) Flight altitude at 100m

Fig. 7. Results of unmanned aerial vehicle test

conditions such as Light difference, shadows of obstructions and perplexing objects also decrease the accuracy of detection.

Figure 8(b) shows the Precision-Recall curve obtained after a large number of experimental tests. As can be seen from the graph, the system proposed in this paper is slightly

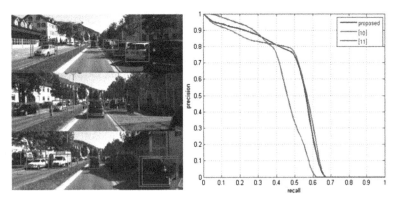

Fig. 8. Results of KITTI test

higher than that of [10] in precision when recall is between 0–0.4, and it is almost the same as the [10] while the recall is above 0.4. In view of the overall situation, the performance of our system is slightly better than [10]. Precision of proposed system is slightly inferior to [11] when recall is low but it is significantly higher than that of [11] at higher recall rate. On the whole the system we presented has strong adaptability in a variety of situations.

In order to evaluate the performance of detection with infrared images, we retrain our models to fit the infrared objection. As the infrared images are monochrome images with a limited gray level, the information extracted from them is much less than visible images, leading to a slight decrease in accuracy. As we can see from Fig. 9 that our algorithm still has a good recognition in this situation.

Fig. 9. Detection with infrared images

The convolution acceleration module of the system is implemented on FPGA with ISE Design Suite 14.7, and the layout and routing are provided by the ISE toolkit. ISE will also generate resource occupancy report, as shown in Table 2. As can be seen that the use of FPGA hardware resources for the design of the convolution accelerator is quite adequate.

Table 2. FPGA resource occupancy report

XC6SLX100T	Used	Available	Percentage
Flip-flops	86262	126576	68.2%
LUTs	57352	63288	90.6%
Block RAM	148	268	55.2%
DSP slices	164	180	91.1%

In order to evaluate the overall performance of the system, we have done extensive test in different hardware systems, choosing some important indicators to assess. With the bandwidth of 20 MByte/s, according to the total clock cycle of FPGA and the total time spent on Tegra X1 for program we can calculate a theoretical processing time. As shown in Table 3, compared to the other two kinds of hardware our system has a significant advantage in power consumption, and the loss of frame rate and resolution is acceptable, the overall performance is good enough to meet the needs of most application scenarios.

Table 3. Comparison of performance and consumption

Hardware/Performance	Processing time (ms)	Resolution (pixels)
Intel i5 2.4 GHz with original DPM	650	640 * 480
Intel i5 2.4 GHz with optimized DPM	185	640 * 480
Proposed (UAV)	65	640 * 480
Proposed (KITTI)	110	1392 * 512

4 Conclusion

In this article we discuss the various methods of vehicle detection, describing the advantages of DPM algorithm in specific applications. With detailed analysis on algorithm we decompose it into several modules to be implemented in the embedded platform. In this paper, a vehicle detection system composed of Tegra X1 and FPGA Spatan 6 is presented, which makes full use of the powerful floating-point computing ability of CPU and the fast parallel processing ability of FPGA. Compared to the traditional CPU and GPU platform, the embedded system proposed has low power consumption, good performance of detection and fabulous mobility and adaptability that other system can not achieve. For the further optimization and promotion scheme of the system, a method that worth trying is adding GPU accelerator to the whole calculation of the system to further improve the calculation speed and detection performance.

Acknowledgements. This work was supported by the Natural Science Foundations of China (61231014, 61373061 and 61501235) and Fundamental Research Funds for the Central Universities (30915011335).

References

1. Wang, J.R.: Research on Multi-feature Fusion of Aerial Photography Image Recognition taken by UAV. Chengdu University of Technology, Chengdu (2015)
2. Yang, X.F., Yang, Y.: A method of efficient vehicle detection based on HOG-LBP. Comput. Eng. **40**(9), 210–214 (2014)
3. Liu, Y., Wang, H.H., Xiang, Y.L., Lu, P.L.: An approach of real-time vehicle detection based on improved adaboost algorithm and frame differencing rule. J. Huazhong Univ. Sci. Technol. **41**(S1), 379–382 (2013)
4. Guzmán, S., Gómez, A., Diez, G., Fernández, D.S.: Car detection methodology in outdoor environment based on histogram of oriented gradient (HOG) and support vector machine (SVM). In: Networked and Electronic Media (LACNEM), Medellin, Colombia, pp. 1–4. IET (2015)
5. Xu, H., Huang, Q., Jay Kuo, C.C.: Car detection using deformable part models with composite features. In: Image Processing (ICIP), Phoenix, AZ, USA, pp. 3812–3816. IEEE (2016)

6. Rosenbaum, D., Charmette, B., Kurz, F., Suri, S., Thomas, U., Reinartz, P.: Automatic traffic monitoring from an airborne wide angle camera system. ISPRS Arch. **37**(B3b), 557–562 (2008)
7. Maria, G., Baccaglini, E., Brevi, D., Gavelli, M., Scopigno, R.: A drone-based image processing system for car detection in a smart transport infrastructure. In: Electrotechnical Conference (MELECON), Lemesos, Cyprus, pp. 1–5. IEEE (2016)
8. Dollár, P., Appel, R., Belongie, S., Perona, P.: Fast feature Pyramids for object detection. IEEE Trans. Pattern Anal. Mach. Intell. **36**(8), 1532–1545 (2014)
9. Qu, Y.Y., Jiang, L., Guo, X.P.: Moving vehicle detection with convolutional networks in UAV videos. In: Control, Automation and Robotics (ICCAR), Hong Kong, China, pp. 225–229. IEEE (2016)
10. Yebes, J., Bergasa, L., Arroyo, R., Lázaro, A.: Supervised learning and evaluation of KITTI's cars detector with DPM. In: Intelligent Vehicles Symposium Proceedings, Dearborn, MI, USA, pp. 768–773. IEEE (2014)
11. Felzenszwalb, P., Girshick, R., McAllester, D.: Cascade object detection with deformable part models. In: Computer Vision and Pattern Recognition (CVPR), San Francisco, CA, USA, pp. 2241–2248. IEEE (2010)
12. Kadota, R., Sugano, H., Hiromoto, M., Ochi, H., Miyamoto, R., Nakamura, Y.: Hardware architecture for hog feature extraction. In: Intelligent Information Hiding and Multimedia Signal Processing, Kyoto, Japan, pp. 1330–1333. IEEE (2009)
13. Ma, X., Najjar, W., Chowdhury, A.R.: High-throughput fixed-point object detection on FPGAs. In: Field Programmable Custom Computing Machines, Boston, MA, USA, p. 107. IEEE (2014)
14. Negi, K., Dohi, K., Shibata, Y., Oguri, K.: Deep pipelined one-chip FPGA implementation of a real-time image-based human detection algorithm. In: Field Programmable Technology (FPT), New Delhi, India, pp. 1–8. IEEE (2011)

Online Fast Deep Learning Tracker Based on Deep Sparse Neural Networks

Xin Wang$^{(\boxtimes)}$ ⓘ, Zhiqiang Hou, Wangsheng Yu, and Zefenfen Jin

Information and Navigation College, Air Force Engineering University,
Xi'an 710077, China
wangxiin@foxmail.com, hou-zhq@sohu.com

Abstract. Deep learning can explore robust and powerful feature representa-tions from data and has gained significant attention in visual tracking tasks. However, due to its high computational complexity and time-consuming training process, the most existing deep learning based trackers require an offline pre-training process on a large scale dataset, and have low tracking speeds. Therefore, aiming at these difficulties of the deep learning based trackers, we propose an online deep learning tracker based on Sparse Auto-Encoders (SAE) and Rectifier Linear Unit (ReLU). Combined ReLU with SAE, the deep neural networks (DNNs) obtain the sparsity similar to the DNNs with offline pre-training. The inherent sparsity make the deep model get rid of the complex pre-training process and can be used for online-only tracking well. Meanwhile, the technique of data augmentation is employed in the single positive sample to balance the quantities of positive and negative samples, which improve the stability of the model to some extent. Finally, in order to overcome the problem of randomness and drift of particle filter, we adopt a local dense sampling searching method to generate a local confidence map to locate the target's position. Moreover, several corresponding update strategies are proposed to improve the robustness of the proposed tracker. Extensive experimental results show the effectiveness and robustness of the proposed tracker in challenging environment against state-of-the-art methods. Not only the proposed tracker leaves out the complicated and time-consuming pre-training process efficiently, but achieves an online fast and robust tracking.

Keywords: Visual tracking · Online fast tracking · Deep sparse neural networks
Rectifier Linear Unit (ReLU) · Local confidence maps

1 Introduction

Visual tracking technology is one of the hot research directions in computer vision field, which is widely used in military and civil fields [1, 2].

In recent years, a large number of tracking algorithms have been proposed. Existing tracking algorithms can be divided into two categories [3]: generative methods and discriminative methods. The generative methods, e.g., IVT [4] (incremental visual tracking), L1T [5] (the l_1 tracker), and MTT [6] (multitask tracking), establish the appearance model of the target, and then search the most similar candidate samples as current tracking result. The discriminative methods treat the tracking problem as a

© Springer International Publishing AG 2017
Y. Zhao et al. (Eds.): ICIG 2017, Part I, LNCS 10666, pp. 186–198, 2017.
https://doi.org/10.1007/978-3-319-71607-7_17

binary classification of the target and background. Some popular discriminative trackers include MIL [7] (multiple instance learning), TLD [8] (tracking-learning-detection), and Struck [9]. Although the above trackers have achieved good results under simple controlled conditions, these trackers based on hand-crafted features are still facing enormous challenges in complex environments, *e.g.*, illumination variation, severe occlusion, and background clutters.

Due to Deep Neural Networks (DNNs) [10] can exploit robust and powerful feature representations automatically using its deep structure, the deep learning based tracking algorithms have gained significant attention in visual tracking tasks. Combined offline pre-training with online fine-tuning, Wang and Yeung [11] first applied the stacked denoising auto-encoders (SDAE) architecture to the visual tracking tasks, and achieved a robust tracking performance in some complicated scenarios. Li et al. [12] applied a single-CNN (Convolutional Neural Network) on visual tracking, and combined with multiple image cues to improve the tracking success rate. In [13], Zhang et al. propose a CNT tracker, which take the advantage of local structure feature and global geometric information to improve the tracking performance. Ma et al. [14] utilized hierarchical features with CNNs and gained a state-of-the-art result in complicated tracking situations. With the fast development of deep learning, the trackers based on deep learning outperform the traditional tracking algorithms significantly in tracking success rate and accuracy.

However, there are still several difficulties of the deep learning based trackers that are desired to be solved. (i) A complex and time-consuming offline pre-training process is indispensable to most existing deep learning based trackers. The offline pre-training process requires an auxiliary large scale dataset and the learned generic representations from the auxiliary dataset may not be suitable to track a specific object. (ii) The traditional nonlinear activation functions like *sigmoid* or *tanh* have complex mathematical expressions. It results in high computational complexity in error back propagation (BP) during the training of deep networks and will reduce the tracking speed. (iii) The trackers like DLT or CNT use the particle filter to obtain the candidate samples. The bad particles will affect the tracking performance and easily cause the tracking drift. Meanwhile, the randomness of the particles will result in the inconsistency of the tracking results in the repeat experimentations.

In this work, we propose an online fast deep learning tracker to solve the above problems. The main contributions of our works can be summarized as follows:

(1) We adopt Rectifier Linear Unit (ReLU) as the activation function of Sparse Auto-Encoders (SAE) and build a simple yet effective Deep Sparse Neural Network (DSNN) for tracking. The ReLU and sparsity constraint make DSNN highly sparse and get rid of the complex pre-training process. It makes the proposed tracker achieve an online-only training and tracking. Meanwhile, the simple mathematical expression reduces the computational complexity in training and improves the tracking speed.

(2) In order to overcome the problem of randomness and drift of particle filter, we adopt a local dense sampling searching method to generate a local confidence map. By searching the maximum confidence value, the current position of target is located accurately. In addition, in order to balance the quantities of positive and

negative samples, a technique of data augmentation is employed for the single positive sample.

(3) We present an online adaptive model update strategy aiming at the long-term tracking tasks. By establishing a sliding time window and adaptively adjusting the local searching area, the update strategy improves the robustness of the proposed tracker in challenging environment.

Extensive experimental results on OTB2013 [15] show that the proposed tracker is effective and efficient in challenging environment against state-of-the-art methods. Not only the proposed tracker leaves out the complicated and time-consuming pre-training process efficiently, but achieves an online fast and robust tracking.

2 Deep Sparse Neural Network for Tracking

The sparsity of neural networks means that the features of the input layer are represented by the least hidden neurons. It is actually to look for a set of "overcomplete" basis vectors to represent the data efficiently and has better sparsity and expressiveness.

2.1 Sparse Auto-Encoders with ReLU

Sparse Auto-Encoder (SAE) [16] is an unsupervised learning model, which is one basic algorithm in deep learning. By using the "Layer-by-Layer Greedy Algorithm" to stack multiple SAEs, we obtain a deep sparse networks. Figure 1(a) shows the basic structure of stacked-SAEs. Let $\hat{x}_i$ denote the reconstruction of the input data x_i, W and W' denote the weight matrix of encoder and decoder respectively, and b denote the bias vector of encoder. In our work, the loss function of the stacked-SAEs is defined as:

$$L(W, b) = \sum_{i=1}^{m} \|x_i - \hat{x}_i\|_2^2 + \lambda \left(\|W\|_F^2 + \|W'\|_{\mathcal{F}}^2 \right) + \mu H(\rho \| \hat{\rho}) \tag{1}$$

where m is the number of samples, λ is a penalty factor which balances the reconstruction loss and weights, μ is the sparsity penalty factor, and $\|\cdot\|_F$ denotes the Frobenius norm. The cross-entropy $H(\rho \| \hat{\rho})$ is given as:

$$H(\rho \| \hat{\rho}) = - \sum_{j=1}^{n} \left[\rho log \left(\hat{\rho}_j \right) + (1 - \rho) log \left(1 - \hat{\rho}_j \right) \right] \tag{2}$$

$$\hat{\rho}_j = \frac{1}{m} \sum_{i=1}^{m} \left[h_j(x_i) \right] \tag{3}$$

where k and n are the number of neurons in input and hidden layer respectively. $h_j(x_i)$ denotes the activation value in the jth hidden layer to the input x_i. The sparsity target ρ is close to 0, and it is set to 0.05 in our experiments.

In order to obtain the robust and powerful capacity of extracting features, the offline pre-training on a large scale dataset is usually used in deep networks. The key of pre-training is to obtain the sparse distributed representation of deep networks [17]. Rectifier Linear Unit (ReLU) [18, 19] is a sparse activation function. As shown in Fig. 1(b), the rectifier function ReLU(x) = max(0, x) is a one-side activation function, which enforces hard zeros in the learned feature representation and leads to the sparsity of hidden units. So we adopt ReLU as an activation function to the aforementioned stacked-SAEs to improve the sparsity of the DNN. The variant of stacked-SAEs with ReLU is shown in Fig. 1(c).

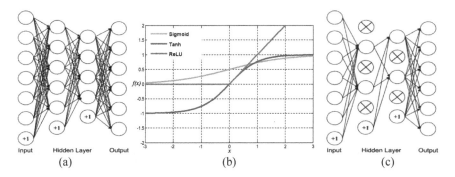

Fig. 1. The basic stacked-SAEs and its variant with ReLU: (a) basic stacked-SAEs, (b) activation function curves, and (c) the variant of stacked-SAEs with ReLU.

It is proven in [19, 20] that ReLU will bring the inherent sparsity to DNNs, which let the pre-training become less effective for DNNs with the activation function of ReLU. So the usage of ReLU as activation function leaves out the offline pre-training process of DNN. It will solve the over-fitting problem in pre-training well. Meanwhile, the unilateral activation side of ReLU is an unsaturated linear function, which effectively solves the problem of gradient vanishing in the training process. Moreover, since the gradient of ReLU is the fixed value of 1 or 0, it isn't necessary to perform complex gradient calculation in the network training. This reduces the computational complexity and improves the training speed effectively.

2.2 Online Tracking Network

In order to achieve the purpose of tracking, we add a *softmax* classifier as the last layer to the stacked-SAEs to classify learned features. The logistic regression is included in the *softmax* classifier:

$$l_\theta(t) = \frac{1}{1 + e^{-\theta^T t}} \tag{4}$$

where $l_\theta(x)$ is a value in [0, 1], *i.e.* represents the probability of the sample t as the true target; θ is the model parameters. The final model of deep sparse neural networks for tracking is shown in Fig. 2.

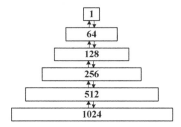

Fig. 2. The model of tracking network. The number in each layer denotes the number of neurons in this layer.

3 Proposed Tracking Algorithm

Based on the aforementioned deep sparse neural networks, we propose an online fast deep learning tracker. In this Section, we will describe our proposed tracking algorithm in detail.

3.1 Initialization of the Tracking Network

Given the initial state $s_0 = \{x_0, y_0, w_0, h_0\}$ of target, we can obtain a single positive sample patch by sampling at the initial frame, where (x_0, y_0) denotes the initial position, w_0 and h_0 denote the initial width and height, respectively. Meanwhile, we also obtain 100 negative sample patches by random sampling around (x_0, y_0). Normalizing all patches, we can get the standard gray-scale images of 32×32 pixels as the input data for the tracking network.

Meanwhile, considering the imbalance between positive and negative will affect the robustness of the tracking network, so we need to augment the quantity of positive samples to balance the quantity of positive and negative samples. A method of sampling within 2 pixels near the positive sample to data augmentation was proposed in [11]. However, this method is prone to accumulate the error and affect the tracking results. In [21], new data was created by transforming the images such as scaling, translation, rotation, noising, changing brightness, mirroring and cropping to expand the quantity of samples. We extend the single positive sample in initial frame to 10 samples by changing the brightness, contrast, noise, and smoothing and mirroring. The results are shown in Fig. 3.

Using these 10 positive samples and 100 negative samples as the label data, we can get the tracking network parameters corresponding to the specific task by training the tracking network of Fig. 2.

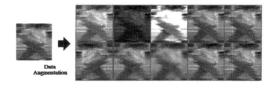

Fig. 3. Data augmentation for single positive sample.

3.2 Local Confidence Maps

During the tracking process, each sample patch can get a value into [0, 1] through the *softmax* classifier in the tracking network. The value reflects the probability that the sample patch is a positive sample (*i.e.* the target), and we call it "confidence value" of the sample patch. In our proposed algorithm, we use local dense sampling method to sample all the pixels in the candidate area as the sampling center. Sending all the sample patches to the tracking network, we can get the confidence value of all the pixels in the candidate area. As is shown in Fig. 4, the local confidence map of the candidate area can be obtained by visualizing all the confidence value, which can intuitively reflect the possible position of the target in local area.

According to Eq. (5), the sample patch with the highest confidence is determined as the tracking result in current frame.

$$s_t = arg\ max(\varsigma_i) \tag{5}$$

where ς_i denotes the confidence value of the i th sample patch, $s_t = \{x_t, y_t, w_t, h_t\}$, *i.e.* the target state in frame t.

In addition, we add a random disturbance (w_r, h_r) to the size (w_i, h_i) of the sample patch to accommodate the scale change of the target during tracking. In this paper, both w_r and h_r follow a normal distribution with mean of 0 and variance of 0.1.

(a) Baketball   (b) Car4   (c) MountainBike   (d) Suv   (e) Trellis

Fig. 4. Local confidence maps of some videos. The darker the red denote the higher confidence value. (Color figure online)

3.3   Online Adaptive Model Update

In the long-term tracking, the target is susceptible to the illumination variation, deformation, background clutter and so on, and it is easy to cause tracking drifting. At this time, the tracking network parameters need to be updated. The update criteria of tracking network are as follows:

$$max(\varsigma_i) < \tau_1 \, || \, fn \geq \eta \tag{6}$$

where τ_1 is the threshold of network update, fn is the number of cumulative frames after the last update, and η is the maximum of cumulative frames.

The update strategy is to establish a sliding time window of positive samples [22] and put the tracking results of current frame and its adjacent 9 frames into the sliding window, which is shown in Fig. 5. And the positive samples in the sliding window are replaced and updated in real time. When Eq. (6) is satisfied, we resample 100 negative samples in current frame, and take them together with 10 positive samples of the initial frame and 10 positive samples of the sliding time window as the label data to train the tracking network and update the network parameters.

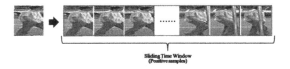

Fig. 5. Sliding time window of positive samples.

Meanwhile, the initial local searching area may not detect the correct target when the target is occluded, so the searching area is needed to expand that the target can be tracked correctly. The update criteria of searching area are as follows:

$$max(\varsigma_i) < \tau_2 \tag{7}$$

where τ_2 is the threshold of searching area updating.

The searching area is updated as follows:

$$N = N + \delta \tag{8}$$

where N is the length of square searching area, and the initial N is set to 10 pixels. δ is the increment of N.

3.4   Overall Process of Proposed Algorithm

We present the main steps of the proposed tracking algorithm in Table 1. The flow chart as shown in Fig. 6.

Table 1. The main steps of DLST algorithm.

Input: Image sequences, initial target state s_0 and initial searching area N.	
Output: Tracking result for each frame, *i.e.* the estimated state $\hat{s}_t$ of target.	
Initialize the tracking model	
Repeat:	
1	Determine local searching area based on s_{t-1} and N;
2	Local dense sample in the searching area and get the local confidence map;
3	Estimate current state $\hat{s}_t$ of target using Eq.(5);
4	Add the tracking result $\hat{s}_t$ to the sliding time window of positive samples;
5	Update the tracking model based on Eq. (6), (7), and (8)
Until *End of image sequences.*	

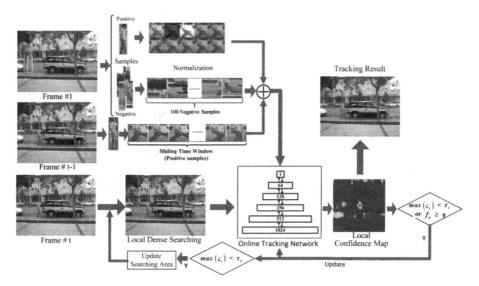

Fig. 6. Flow chart of the proposed tracking algorithm.

4 Experiments

The proposed tracking algorithm is realized in MATLAB under the experimental platform of CPU (Intel Xeon 2.4 GHz) and GPU (TITAN X). We empirically compare our tracker with some state-of-the-art trackers using the OTB2013 benchmark dataset [15], which includes 51 fully-annotated sequences. These trackers are: SST [23], SCM [24], Struck [9], DLT [11], LLC [25], CN [26], MIL [7], and NRMLC [27]. The results of these trackers are provided by their authors.

The setting of experimental parameters of our tracker are as follows: $\lambda = 0.005$, $\mu = 0.2$, $\eta = 50$, $\tau_1 = 0.9$, $\tau_2 = 0.5$, $\delta = 5$. In experiments, we use the OPE evaluate method of and the evaluation indicators mentioned in [15].

4.1 Qualitative Comparison

We use all 51 sequences of OTB2013 in our experiments. Some tracking results of the 9 challenging sequences are shown in Fig. 7. Then we analyse the performance in the following different scenarios:

(1) Illumination variation: There are severe illumination changing in "Car4", "Singer2", and "Trellis". Compared with other trackers, the proposed tracker tracks the targets more accurately. And in "Car4", our tracker can better adapt to the scale changing of target along the whole sequence.

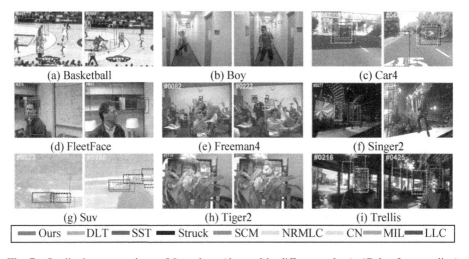

(a) Basketball   (b) Boy   (c) Car4

(d) FleetFace   (e) Freeman4   (f) Singer2

(g) Suv   (h) Tiger2   (i) Trellis

| Ours   DLT   SST   Struck   SCM   NRMLC   CN   MIL   LLC |

Fig. 7. Qualitative comparison of 9 trackers (denoted in different colors). (Color figure online)

(2) Occlusion and Rotation: The targets are partially or completely occluded in "Suv" and "Tiger2". Our tracker always tracks the target continuously from beginning to end. In "Fleetface" and "Tiger2", out-of-plane or in-plane rotation increase the difficulty of tracking, yet our tracker can still provide accurate results relatively.

(3) Fast motion and Motion blur: In "Boy" and "Basketball", the motion of target is very fast and even causes the motion blur. The proposed tracker has the capacity to track the target more reliably and accurately than others.

(4) Deformation and Background clutter: There are deformation and similar background to target in "Basketball" and "Freeman4". This is a challenge to the robustness of the features extracted by trackers. From the tracking results, our tracker explores more robust and powerful features to track the correct target stably.

4.2 Quantitative Comparison

For quantitative comparison, the precision plots and success plots of these trackers for all 51 sequences on OTB2013 are given respectively in Fig. 8. Our tracker ranks 1st for both plots and outperforms these state-of-the-art trackers in overall performance. For precision plots, our tracker achieves 0.660 which is higher than DLT (the similar deep learning based tracker) by 12.4%. For success plots, our tracker achieves 0.501 which is improved by 14.9% over DLT tracker.

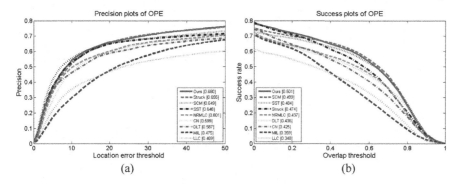

Fig. 8. Precision plots and success plots of 9 trackers on OTB2013.

Tables 2 and 3 show the precision values and success rates of 9 trackers on 11 different attributes, respectively. In both tables, these abbreviations represent different attributes which are defined in [15]: IV-Illumination Variation, SV-Scale Variation, OCC-Occlusion, BC-Background Clutters, DEF-Deformation, MB-Motion Blur, FM-Fast Motion, IPR-In Plane Rotation, OPR-Out of Plane Rotation, OV-Out of View, LR-Low Resolution. The number below the abbreviation represents the quantity of sequences within this attribute in OTB2013. The best results are in red and the second

Table 2. The precision values of 9 trackers on 11 attributes.

	Ours	DLT	SST	Struck	SCM	NRMLC	CN	MIL	LLC
IV(25)	0.633	0.534	0.603	0.558	0.594	0.437	0.532	0.349	0.423
SV(28)	0.659	0.590	0.688	0.639	0.672	0.597	0.554	0.471	0.494
OCC(29)	0.645	0.574	0.588	0.564	0.640	0.583	0.582	0.427	0.455
BC(21)	0.583	0.495	0.644	0.585	0.578	0.497	0.642	0.456	0.383
DEF(19)	0.644	0.563	0.487	0.521	0.586	0.541	0.523	0.455	0.323
MB(12)	0.482	0.453	0.408	0.551	0.339	0.378	0.396	0.357	0.299
FM(17)	0.503	0.446	0.425	0.604	0.333	0.397	0.416	0.396	0.290
IPR(31)	0.634	0.548	0.630	0.617	0.597	0.511	0.615	0.453	0.515
OPR(39)	0.656	0.561	0.599	0.597	0.618	0.546	0.605	0.466	0.498
OV(6)	0.641	0.444	0.406	0.539	0.429	0.492	0.434	0.393	0.240
LR(4)	0.402	0.396	0.527	0.545	0.305	0.542	0.405	0.171	0.319

Table 3. The success rates of 9 trackers on 11 attributes.

	Ours	DLT	SST	Struck	SCM	NRMLC	CN	MIL	LLC
IV(25)	0.489	0.405	0.459	0.428	0.473	0.341	0.390	0.311	0.311
SV(28)	0.492	0.455	0.504	0.425	0.518	0.427	0.363	0.335	0.360
OCC(29)	0.487	0.423	0.436	0.413	0.487	0.437	0.404	0.335	0.342
BC(21)	0.440	0.339	0.489	0.458	0.450	0.370	0.453	0.373	0.298
DEF(19)	0.469	0.394	0.391	0.393	0.448	0.392	0.388	0.369	0.258
MB(12)	0.380	0.363	0.313	0.433	0.298	0.303	0.329	0.282	0.253
FM(17)	0.417	0.360	0.340	0.462	0.296	0.334	0.334	0.326	0.257
IPR(31)	0.480	0.411	0.451	0.444	0.458	0.367	0.437	0.340	0.373
OPR(39)	0.489	0.412	0.437	0.432	0.470	0.389	0.418	0.350	0.354
OV(6)	0.535	0.367	0.347	0.459	0.361	0.410	0.410	0.382	0.255
LR(4)	0.349	0.346	0.407	0.372	0.279	0.428	0.311	0.153	0.256

best in green. From Tables 2 and 3, we observe that our tracker ranks the optimal or suboptimal results on 8 attributes. Only on two attributes of BC and LR, our tracker doesn't rank the top 3. These data show that our tracker has a favorable performance on different challenging environments against the contrast trackers.

4.3   Tracking Speed Comparison

FPS (frames per second) measures the tracking speed and represents the time complexity of the tracker. Table 4 show the tracking speed of 9 trackers. From that, we find that our proposed tracker achieves average 16.5 FPS in our experimental environment. It is faster than DLT and other similar deep learning based trackers like DeepTrack (2.5 FPS) [28].

Table 4. The tracking speed comparison for the 9 trackers.

Tracker	Ours	DLT	SST	Struck	SCM	NRMLC	CN	MIL	LLC
FPS	16.5	15	2.2	20.2	0.51	–	100	28.06	–

5   Conclusions

In this paper, we propose a robust and fast visual tracking algorithm based on deep sparse neural networks. Combined ReLU with stacked-SAEs, the deep sparse network avoids the complex and time-consuming pre-training, and realizes online-only training and tracking. Data augmentation of single positive sample relieves the imbalance between positive and negative samples, which improves the reliability of deep networks. Meanwhile, the local dense searching method and adaptive update strategy solve the problem of particle drift and randomness. A lot of experimental results on OTB2013 dataset show that our proposed algorithm achieves state-of-the-art results in complicated environment and realize a practical tracking speed.

However, there are still several possible research directions to improve our algorithm. For example, it is not robust enough for our tracker when the target's scale changes significantly or the complete occlusion sustains too long time. Therefore, the problem of scale adaptability and long-time occlusion will be the focus of our future work.

Acknowledgments. This research has been supported by the National Natural Science Foundation of China (No. 61473309) and the Natural Science Foundation of Shaanxi Province (No. 2016JM6050).

References

1. Smeulders, A.W.M., Chu, D.M., Cucchiara, R., et al.: Visual tracking: an experimental survey. IEEE Trans. Pattern Anal. Mach. Intell. **36**(7), 1442–1468 (2014)
2. Yilmaz, A., Javed, O., Shah, M.: Object tracking: a survey. ACM Comput. Surv. **38**(4), 1–45 (2006)
3. Li, X., Hu, W.M., Shen, C.H., et al.: A survey of appearance models in visual object tracking. ACM Trans. Intell. Syst. Technol. **4**(4), Article 58 (2013)
4. Ross, D.A., Lim, J., Lin, R.S.: Incremental learning for robust visual tracking. Int. J. Comput. Vis. **77**(1–3), 125–141 (2008)
5. Mei, X., Ling, H.: Robust visual tracking using l1 minimization. In: IEEE International Conference on Computer Vision, pp. 1436–1443. IEEE, Washington, D.C. (2009)
6. Zhang, T.Z., Ghanem, B., Liu, S., et al.: Robust visual tracking via multi-task sparse learning. In: IEEE Conference on Computer Vision and Pattern Recognition, pp. 2042–2049. IEEE, Washington, D.C. (2012)
7. Babenko, B., Yang, M.H., Belongie, S.: Robust object tracking with online multiple instance learning. IEEE Trans. Pattern Anal. Mach. Intell. **33**(8), 1619–1632 (2011)
8. Kalal, Z., Mikolajczyk, K., Matas, J.: Tracking-learning-detection. IEEE Trans. Pattern Anal. Mach. Intell. **34**(7), 1409–1422 (2012)
9. Hare, S., Saffari, A., Torr, P.H.: Struck: structured output tracking with kernels. In: IEEE International Conference on Computer Vision, pp. 263–270. IEEE, Washington, D.C. (2011)
10. Lecun, Y., Bengo, Y., Hinton, G.: Deep learning. Nature **521**(7553), 436–444 (2015)
11. Wang, N.Y., Yeung, D.: Learning a deep compact image representation for visual tracking. In: Advances in Neural Information Processing Systems, pp. 809–817. IMLS, Nevada (2013)
12. Li, H., Li, Y., Porikli, F.: Robust online visual tracking with a single convolutional neural network. In: Cremers, D., Reid, I., Saito, H., Yang, M.-H. (eds.) ACCV 2014. LNCS, vol. 9007, pp. 194–209. Springer, Cham (2015). https://doi.org/10.1007/978-3-319-16814-2_13
13. Zhang, K.H., Liu, Q.S., Wu, Y., et al.: Robust visual tracking via convolutional networks. IEEE Trans. Image Process. **25**(4), 1779–1792 (2015)
14. Ma, C., Huang, J.B., Yang, X.K., et al.: Hierarchical convolutional features for visual tracking. In: IEEE International Conference on Computer Vision, pp. 3074–3082. IEEE, Washington, D.C. (2015)
15. Wu, Y., Lim, J., Yang, M.H.: Online object tracking: a benchmark. IEEE Trans. Pattern Anal. Mach. Intell. **37**(9), 1834–1848 (2015)
16. Wang, X., Hou, Z., Yu, W., et al.: Robust visual tracking via multiscale deep sparse networks. Opt. Eng. **56**(4), 043107 (2017)

17. Arpit, D., Zhou, Y., Ngo, H., et al.: Why regularized auto-encoders learn sparse representation? In: International Conference on Machine Learning, pp. 134–144. IMLS, Nevada (2015)
18. Nair, V., Hinton, G.,: Rectified linear units improve restricted Boltzmann machines. In: International Conference on Machine Learning, pp. 807–814. IMLS, Nevada (2010)
19. Glorot, X., Bordes, A., Bengio, Y.: Deep sparse rectifier neural networks. In: International Conference on Artificial Intelligence and Statistics, pp. 315–323. Microtome, Brookline (2011)
20. Li, J., Zhang, T., Luo, W., et al.: Sparseness analysis in the pretraining of deep neural networks. IEEE Trans. Neural Netw. Learn. Syst. **PP**(99), 1–14 (2016)
21. Eigen, D., Puhrsch, C., Fergus, R.: Depth map prediction from a single image using scale deep network. In: IEEE Conference on Computer Vision and Pattern Recognition, pp. 2366–2374. IEEE, Washington, D.C. (2014)
22. Gao, C., Chen, F., Yu, J.G., et al.: Robust visual tracking using exemplar-based detectors. IEEE Trans. Circ. Syst. Video Technol. **27**(2), 300–312 (2016)
23. Zhang, T.Z., Liu, S., Xu, C.S., et al.: Structural sparse tracking. In: IEEE Conference on Computer Vision and Pattern Recognition, pp. 150–158. IEEE, Washington, D.C. (2015)
24. Zhong, W., Lu, H., Yang, M.H.: Robust object tracking via sparsity-based collaborative model. In: IEEE Conference on Computer Vision and Pattern Recognition, pp. 1838–1845. IEEE, Washington, D.C. (2012)
25. Wang, G.F., Qin, X.Y., Zhong, F., et al.: Visual tracking via sparse and local linear coding. IEEE Trans. Image Process. **24**(11), 3796–3809 (2015)
26. Danelljan, M., Khan, F.S., Felsberg, M., et al.: Adaptive color attributes for real-time visual tracking. In: IEEE Conference on Computer Vision and Pattern Recognition, pp. 1090–1097. IEEE, Washington, D.C. (2014)
27. Liu, F., Zhou, T., Yang, J., et al.: Visual tracking via nonnegative regularization multiple locality coding. In: IEEE International Conference on Computer Vision Workshop, pp. 912–920. IEEE, Washington, D.C. (2016)
28. Li, H., Li, Y., Porikli, F.: DeepTrack: learning discriminative feature representations by convolutional neural networks for visual tracking. In: British Machine Vision Conference, pp. 1–12 (2014)

Affine-Gradient Based Local Binary Pattern Descriptor for Texture Classification

You Hao[1,2(✉)], Shirui Li[1,2], Hanlin Mo[1,2], and Hua Li[1]

[1] Key Laboratory of Intelligent Information Processing,
Institute of Computing Technology, Chinese Academy of Sciences, Beijing, China
{haoyou,mohanlin,lihua}@ict.ac.cn, lishiruilishirui@gmail.com
[2] University of Chinese Academy of Sciences, Beijing, China

Abstract. We present a novel Affine-Gradient based Local Binary Pattern (AGLBP) descriptor for texture classification. It is very hard to describe complicated texture using single type information, such as Local Binary Pattern (LBP), which just utilizes the sign information of the difference between pixel and its local neighbors. Our descriptor has three characteristics: (1) In order to make full use of the information contained in the texture, the Affine-Gradient, which is different from Euclidean-Gradient and invariant to affine transformation, is incorporated into AGLBP. (2) An improved method is proposed for rotation invariance, which depends on the reference direction calculating respect to local neighbors. (3) Feature selection method, considering both the statistical frequency and the intraclass variance of the training dataset, is also applied to reduce the dimensionality of descriptors. Experiments on three standard texture datasets, Outex12, Outex10 and KTH-TIPS2, are conducted to evaluate the performance of AGLBP. The results show that our proposed descriptor gets better performance comparing to some state-of-the-art rotation texture descriptors in texture classification.

Keywords: AGLBP · Affine-Gradient · Texture descriptor
Feature selection · Invariant

1 Introduction

Texture is the most fundamental information on which the majority of all living organisms base their visual cognition and is a key component of computer vision system [11]. Basically, all the digital images can be regarded as texture. Texture analysis has been applied to many visual problems such as material categorization, surface inspection, medical image analysis, object recognition, image segmentation, pedestrian detection, face analysis and so on.

Over the years, lots of texture descriptors have been proposed [12,20,22,28]. Among these descriptors, local patterns have achieved good performance in most texture applications [3,15,18]. In particular, LBP is an efficient descriptor for describing local structures [18]. LBP descriptors have already demonstrated powerful discriminative capability, low computational complexity, and

© Springer International Publishing AG 2017
Y. Zhao et al. (Eds.): ICIG 2017, Part I, LNCS 10666, pp. 199–210, 2017.
https://doi.org/10.1007/978-3-319-71607-7_18

low sensitivity to illumination variation. For further improving the discrimination of LBP, a large number of LBP variants have been proposed [14]. Most of these changes make efforts on the following three directions.

First is to utilize different forms of information from the original textures. Guo et al. proposed Complete LBP which utilized the sign and magnitude information of local neighborhood in the descriptor [9]. Some other methods concentrate on the local derivative information respected to a local region, such as LDP [30], CLDP [29], LDDP [8], POEM [27] and so on. Second is rotation invariance, which is an important topic in texture classification. Many methods have been proposed to achieve rotation invariance, such as SRP [13,24], SIFT [15] and so on. Third is feature selection. The exponential increasing in the number of features with the patch size is a limitation for the traditional LBP. The uniform LBP descriptor proposed by Ojala et al. [18] is the first attempt to solve this problem.

The main contributions of the paper are threefold. Firstly, we propose the Affine-Gradient based method to describe texture information. Affine-Gradient (AG) has some properties that Euclidean-Gradient (EG) does not have, which will be elaborated detailedly in the following. Secondly, an improved method for determining the local reference direction is proposed to reach rotation invariance, which is fast to compute and effective for the rotation transformations. Finally, we propose a simple but effective feature selection method considering both the distribution of patterns and the intraclass variance on the training datasets. Experiments show that the proposed feature selection method not only increases the discriminative power but also reduce the dimension of descriptor effectively.

2   Affine-Gradient Based Local Pattern Descriptor

In this section we elaborate our approach in detail. First, we give a brief review of LBP. Second, we discuss how to make full use of multi-information, especially Affine-Gradient (AG), for texture classification. The properties of AG are discussed in detail. Then we discuss the method we proposed to achieve the rotation invariance. Finally, the criterion for feature selection are discussed.

2.1   Overview of LBP Method

The traditional LBP operator extracts information that is invariant to local grayscale variations in the image. It is computed at each pixel location, considering the values of a small circular neighborhood around the central pixel q_c. Then, the LBP is defined as following:

$$LBP_{R,P} = \sum_{p=0}^{P-1} s(g_p - g_c) \cdot 2^p \qquad s(x) = \begin{cases} 1, x \geq 0 \\ 0, x < 0 \end{cases} \qquad (1)$$

where g_c is the central pixel and g_p are the values of its neighbors. p is the index of the neighbor, R is the radius of the circular neighborhood and P is the number of pixels in the neighborhood. Then the histogram of these patterns is used to describe the texture of the image.

There are three obvious disadvantages of LBP. First, it has no rotation invariance. Second, it is just 1-th order sign information used in the descriptor. Third is the exponentially length increasing with the parameter R. The proposed method has been improved in these three direction.

2.2   Affine-Gradient Based Descriptors

In here, we propose the method based on the AG information to increase the discrimination of the descriptor. The Euclidean Gradient (EG) can be defined as $G = \sqrt{I_x^2 + I_y^2}$. It is 2-norm of gradient in Euclidean space that remains invariant only under Euclidean transformation.

Olver et al. [19] proposed that there are two basic relative affine differential invariant of 2-order in two-dimensional affine spaces as following:

$$H = I_{xx}I_{yy} - I_{xy}^2 \tag{2}$$
$$J = I_{xx}I_y^2 - 2I_xI_yI_{xy} + I_x^2I_{yy} \tag{3}$$

All other 2-order differential invariants can be made up of these two expressions. And their ratios constitute absolute invariant of differential in affine space. The affine gradient magnitude $(affG)$ can be defined as Eq. (4). In order to avoid the calculation fault of zero-denominator, we can make some changes to the definition as $affG'$.

$$affG = \left| \frac{H}{J} \right|, \qquad affG' = \sqrt{\frac{H^2}{J^2 + 1}} \tag{4}$$

The Affine-Gradient is superior than Euclidean-Gradient (EG), because AG is invariant for the affine transformation, and the EG just remains invariant under Euclidean transformation. Using the AG information can improve the robustness of descriptor for the geometric transformation. Ge et al. constructed a new descriptor using the AG to replace the EG in SIFT, which get much better performance than the original SIFT [4]. The gradient and AG information are shown in Fig. 1.

(a)　　　　　　(b)　　　　　　(c)　　　　　　(d)

Fig. 1. The EG and AG information of image example: (a) image example; (b) EG magnitudes of example; (c) AG of example range in (0–0.2); (d) AG of example range in (0.2–1).

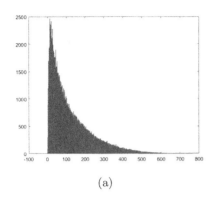
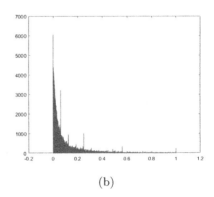

(a)   (b)

Fig. 2. The histogram of EG and AG: (a) histogram of the gradient; (b) histogram of the AG.

In Fig. 2(a) and (b), we can see that the histogram of EG is much more continuous and smooth than that of AG. In fact, the range of AG is from 0 to 162, not limited to 0 to 1 corresponding to Fig. 2(b). It's just more sparse where the value bigger than 1. But the distribution of EG just ranges form 0 to 763 corresponding to Fig. 2(a). So intuitively, the information of AG ranging (0,1) probably corresponding to that of EG as shown in Fig. 1(b) and (c). And there are some local extreme information in the AG as shown in Fig. 1(d).

For further verification of the validity of AG, experiments are conducted on Outex12 dataset. The Local Gradient Pattern (LGP) and Local Affine-Gradient Patter (LAGP) can be defined as

$$LGP_{R,P} = \sum_{p=0}^{P-1} s(G_p - G_c) \qquad (5)$$

$$LAGP_{R,P} = \sum_{p=0}^{P-1} s(affG'_p - affG'_c) \qquad (6)$$

The s function is defined in Eq. (1). The Multi-Information based descriptor MI-G, can be defined as the concatenation of LGP and LBP. Similarly, MI-AG is the concatenation of LAGP and LBP. Then the experimental results are listed in Table 1.

Table 1. Results of Multi-information based descriptors on Outex12

Problem	Form	LBP	MI-G	MI-AG
Outex12	*original*	55.26	58.04	**58.69**
	ri	71.37	73.49	**79.28**
	u2	56.98	58.03	**60.02**
	riu2	65.09	77.62	**77.65**

From the results, we can see that the Multi-Information descriptor based on Affine-Gradient get the best performance in all scenarios. It was demonstrated that the AG information can substantially increase the discriminative power of the descriptors.

2.3   Rotation Invariance

Mehta and Egiazarian [16] proposed a method that quantizing the directions into P discrete values, then make direction with the maximum magnitude of the difference as the reference direction. The definition of can be defined as [16]:

$$D = \underset{p \in (0,1,...,P-1)}{\arg\max} |g_p - g_c| \tag{7}$$

But this definition discard the sign information of the magnitude and will assign the opposite directions into the same one. In this paper, we take both the sign and magnitude of the discrete directions into consideration. The reference direction can be defined as:

$$Ds = (D + \frac{P}{2} \cdot s(g_D - g_c)) \mod P \tag{8}$$

where s is the sign function defined in Eq. (1). The proposed descriptor is computed by rotating the weights with respect to the reference direction. The rotation invariance LBP (roLBP) can be defined as

$$roLBP_{R,P} = \sum_{p=0}^{P-1} s(g_p - g_c) \cdot 2^{(p-Ds) \mod P} \tag{9}$$

In the above definition, the weight term $(p - Ds) \mod P$ depends on Ds. Thus, the mod operator circularly shifts the weights with respect to the reference direction Ds.

To illuminate the advantage of the proposed method, both roLBP and RLBP are evaluated on the Outex12 dataset and the results are shown in Table 2. Considering the computational complexity, both of the methods are applied feature selection method proposed in [16] to reduce the length of descriptors, which called DRLBP and DroLBP as shown in Table 2. The DroLBP get best performance in scale $(3, 16)$. We can see that our method get better performance in a larger scale, because our method is closer to ground-truth gradient direction. And the gradient direction has little effect in a very small scale. Use approximate gradient direction as the reference direction may get better result in a lager scale, which needs further validation.

Applying the reference direction selection method to the LAGP descriptor. We can get the rotation invariant descriptor roLAGP as following:

$$roLAGP_{R,P} = \sum_{p=0}^{P-1} s(affG'_p - affG'_c) \cdot 2^{(p-Ds) \mod P} \tag{10}$$

Table 2. Experiment results of different reference direction selection descriptors on Outex12

Problem	(R, P)	$DRLBP$	$DroLBP$
Outex12	$(1, 8)$	74.7685	71.6667
	$(2, 12)$	93.8079	93.1713
	$(3, 16)$	96.2616	**96.4815**

Then the final descriptor AGLBP can be defined as the concatenation of roLBP and roLAGP.

$$AGLBP_{R,P} = roLBP_{R,P\_}roLAGP_{R,P} \tag{11}$$

2.4   Feature Selection

It is observed the dimensionality of descriptors also increases exponentially with the number of neighboring pixels. In [16], proposed a method depending on the distribution of patterns in the training dataset. Besides, some patterns may be negative to the final classification result. So in our method, the intraclass variance of training datasets is also chosen as the evaluation for feature selection.

In the statistical description, variance is defined as $\frac{1}{n-1}\sum(X - \mu)^2$, where μ is mean value of the array. The distribution of the intraclass variance of all patterns are computed from the training dataset, as shown in Fig. 3.

The bins of the histogram are sorted in descending order. Then there will be two method for feature selection. One selects the top N patterns in the ordered list, the other selects bins which is less than a threshold ϕ as the final descriptor. The final patterns selected depend on the threshold parameter N or ϕ and the training datasets. The final dimensionality of the descriptor is not constant. It

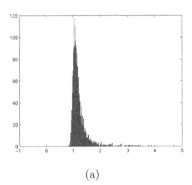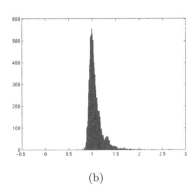

(a)   (b)

Fig. 3. The intraclass variance distribution for roLBP on Outex12 dataset: (a) The variance distribution of roLBP in Outex12 training dataset; (b) The variance distribution of roLAGP in Outex12 training dataset.

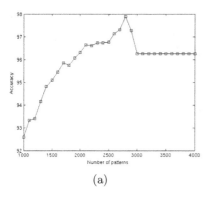
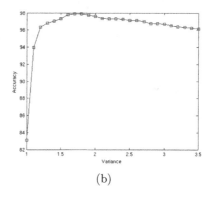

(a)   (b)

Fig. 4. The accuracy-parameter curve for roLBP on Outex12 dataset: (a) the accuracy-N curve of roLBP on Outex12 dataset; (b) the accuracy-ϕ curve of roLBP on Outex12 dataset.

varies across different datasets. The accuracy-parameter curve of the two method for roLBP on Outex12 dataset are plotted in Fig. 4.

It can be observed in Fig. 4(b) that the classification accuracy reach the peak with the threshold value almost between 1.6–2.0, just over the peak of distribution corresponding to Fig. 3(a). This values results in a significant reduction of the dimensionality.

Thus, the proposed approach consider both the statical frequency and the intraclass variance of the training textures, which not only reduces the dimensionality of descriptors, but also improves the classification accuracy. The effective of the proposed approach will be demonstrated in next section.

2.5   Classification Method

Some state-of-the-art methods, such as artificial neural network (ANN), SVM, AdaBoost, can achieve outstanding classification performance, but these methods require complex learning procedure and may influence analysis of discriminative capabilities of features. To make a fair comparison with some other approaches, the Nearest Neighbor (NN) classifier based on the Chi-Square distance was performed as our classification method. The effectiveness of the Chi-Square distance for classification is demonstrated in [7,8].

3   Experiments

To evaluate the proposed descriptor (AGLBP), three experiments are conducted on texture datasets: Outex10, Outex12 and KTH-TIPS2. Outex10 and Outex12 datasets are for rotation invariant texture classification with rotation and illumination deformations. The KTH-TIPS2 is for material categorization and includes scale and viewpoints variations. The parameter ϕ of proposed method is set to 2 in all our experiments. Some state-of-the-art descriptors have been implemented and compared on each dataset, such as *LBP-HF* [1], *LBPV* [10], *LDDP* [8], *LCP* [6], *VZ_MR8* [25], *VZ_joint* [26], *PLBP* [21], *MDLBP* [23], *FBLLBP* [7], *BIF* [2,5], *LEP* [31], *DRLBP* [16].

3.1   Outex12

Outex is a framework for empirical evaluation of texture classification algorithms [17]. First we conduct experiment on the Outex12 dataset. It consists of 9120 images, which are separated into 24 different texture classes captured with different illuminations and rotations. This dataset contains 20 training images and 360 ($2*9*20$) testing images under two different illumination and 9 different orientation for each class. In experiment, following two problem proposed in the dataset [17], problem 000 and 001. Considering the length of the final descriptor is depending on the parameter (R, P), we use a conservative setting of the parameter as $(1, 8)$, $(2, 12)$ and $(3, 16)$. All the LBP-based methods were performed and the results are shown in Table 3.

LBP
   Among these methods, the proposed method with setting $(3, 16)$ has achieved the highest accuracy of 97.84% for problem 000 and 97.38% for problem 001. For further analysis, we compare our method with some other state-of-the-art methods. The results are shown in Table 4. It can be seen that the proposed descriptor achieves the best result, the close second is *DRLBP*, which get the accuracy 97.15% for problem 000 and 95.37% for problem 001. Another interesting result is that the proposed method with setting $(1, 8)$ not only not improving the performance, but getting a lower accuracy. It may be the pattern types of setting $(1, 8)$ is not enough to describe the texture information, so there is no need for feature selection. So feature selection is only applicable when the descriptor dimension is too long.

Table 3. Experiment results of LBP based methods on different datasets

Problems	(R, P)	LBP	LBP^{u2}	LBP^{ri}	LBP^{riu2}	LBP-HF	$LBPV$	$AGLBP$
Outex10	(1, 8)	50.20	57.44	82.78	74.38	72.03	91.40	63.72
	(2, 12)	-	59.62	91.48	86.74	90.52	92.18	**95.43**
	(3, 16)	-	61.35	95.76	88.92	97.03	94.37	**99.22**
Outex12-000	(1, 8)	54.21	55.81	72.26	65.93	70.85	76.41	61.99
	(2, 12)	-	57.85	86.78	82.66	88.49	86.80	**93.31**
	(3, 16)	-	58.56	93.50	83.98	91.08	90.85	**97.84**
Outex12-001	(1, 8)	56.32	58.15	70.39	64.26	77.24	77.08	67.50
	(2, 12)	-	57.08	84.77	75.86	91.34	84.09	**94.83**
	(3, 16)	-	59.49	92.97	79.63	92.40	84.76	**97.38**
KTH-TIPS2	(1, 8)	90.97	85.85	83.65	82.78	88.73	78.98	81.28
	(2, 12)	-	87.92	89.75	87.95	90.87	83.00	**95.23**
	(3, 16)	-	91.95	94.36	91.52	91.85	85.10	**97.12**

Table 4. Experiment results of descriptors on different datasets

Problems	LBP^{ri}	LDDP	LCP	LBP-HF	LBPV	VZ_MR8	VZ_Joint
Outex10	95.76	73.16	74.12	97.03	94.37	93.59	92.00
Outex12-000	93.50	63.48	70.16	91.08	90.85	91.34	90.46
Outex12-001	92.97	68.48	68.48	92.40	84.76	92.83	91.74
KTH-TIPS2	94.36	92.74	92.15	91.85	85.10	93.50	95.46
Problems	PLBP	MDLBP	FBLLBP	BIF	LEP	DRLBP	AGLBP
Outex10	96.64	95.34	98.68	-	-	99.19	**99.22**
Outex12-000	82.79	93.96	88.38	-	-	97.15	**97.84**
Outex12-001	90.08	89.94	92.17	-	-	95.37	**97.38**
KTH-TIPS2	-	-	-	98.50	96.41	96.78	**97.12**

3.2 Outex10

Then experiment is conducted on the Outex10 dataset, which includes 4320 images of 24 different classes. These images are captured under the same illumination but rotated at nine different angles. There are 20 images at each angle for each class. Following the problem proposed in the dataset [17], 480 images captured at angle $0°$ are taken as the training set and the rest 3840 images captured at other angles used for testing.

The results with various setting are shown in Table 3. For further analysis, AGLBP are compared with some other state-of-the-art approaches. The result of these methods are also shown in Table 4. It can be observed that AGLBP performs well under various rotation deformations. The problem for our method with setting $(1, 8)$ also exists, but among all, our method with setting $(3, 16)$ has achieved the highest accuracy 99.22%, better than the results of 99.19%, which achieved by $DRLBP$.

3.3 KTH-TIPS2 Dataset

Experiment on the KTH-TIPS2 dataset has also been conducted for material classification. The KTH-TIPS2 database contains 11 texture classes with different materials. For each class, the images are captured from 4 different samples of materials. And for each sample, 9 different scales with 4 different illumination and 3 different poses are conducted for the imaging. In this experiment, following problem proposed in most research [6,10], images of one random sample are selected from each class are taken as the training dataset, images from the other samples are taken as the testing dataset.

All the methods were performed and the results are shown in Table 3. As the same, AGLBP is also compared with some other state-of-the-art approaches. The result of these methods are shown in Table 4. The proposed descriptor outperforms all other descriptors again. It can be concluded that our method is effective for texture classification.

4 Conclusion

In this paper we have proposed an Affine-Gradient based Local Binary Pattern (AGLBP) descriptor for texture classification. Affine-Gradient is different from the Euclidean-Gradient and has been proved to have a good improvement for texture classification. In addition, we have proposed an improved method for determining the local reference direction to reach rotation invariance. Importantly, the dimension increasing bringing by multi-information is also alleviated by proposed feature selection method, which considering both the statistical frequency and the intraclass variance of the training texture. Three extensive experiments have been conducted on texture datasets including rotating, scaling and viewpoint deformations. The results demonstrate that the AGLBP performed better than some state-of-the-art approaches for texture classification. The AGLBP utilize the Affine-Gradient which has been demonstrated robust for the viewpoint deformation. For further research, information invariant for projective transformation should be utilized to enhance the robustness to viewpoint deformation.

Acknowledgments. This work is supported by the National Science Foundation of China under Grant Nos. 61379082 and 61227802.

References

1. Ahonen, T., Matas, J., He, C., Pietikäinen, M.: Rotation invariant image description with local binary pattern histogram fourier features. In: Salberg, A.-B., Hardeberg, J.Y., Jenssen, R. (eds.) SCIA 2009. LNCS, vol. 5575, pp. 61–70. Springer, Heidelberg (2009). https://doi.org/10.1007/978-3-642-02230-2_7
2. Crosier, M., Griffin, L.D.: Using basic image features for texture classification. Int. J. Comput. Vis. **88**(3), 447–460 (2010)
3. Dalal, N., Triggs, B.: Histograms of oriented gradients for human detection. In: Computer Vision and Pattern Recognition. In: IEEE Computer Society Conference on CVPR 2005, vol. 1, pp. 886–893. IEEE (2005)
4. Ge, J., Cao, W., Zhou, W., Gong, M., Liu, L., Li, H.: A local feature descriptor under color affine trans-formation. J. Comput.-Aided Des. Comput. Graph. **25**(1), 25–33 (2013). (in Chinese)
5. Griffin, L.D., Lillholm, M.: Feature category systems for 2nd order local image structure induced by natural image statistics and otherwise. In: Electronic Imaging 2007, p. 649209. International Society for Optics and Photonics (2007)
6. Guo, Y., Zhao, G., Pietikäinen, M.: Texture classification using a linear configuration model based descriptor. In: BMVC, pp. 1–10 (2011)
7. Guo, Y., Zhao, G., Pietikäinen, M., Xu, Z.: Descriptor learning based on fisher separation criterion for texture classification. In: Kimmel, R., Klette, R., Sugimoto, A. (eds.) ACCV 2010. LNCS, vol. 6494, pp. 185–198. Springer, Heidelberg (2011). https://doi.org/10.1007/978-3-642-19318-7_15
8. Guo, Z., Li, Q., You, J., Zhang, D., Liu, W.: Local directional derivative pattern for rotation invariant texture classification. Neural Comput. Appl. **21**(8), 1893–1904 (2012)

9. Guo, Z., Zhang, L., Zhang, D.: A completed modeling of local binary pattern operator for texture classification. IEEE Trans. Image Process. **19**(6), 1657–1663 (2010)

10. Guo, Z., Zhang, L., Zhang, D.: Rotation invariant texture classification using LBP variance (LBPV) with global matching. Pattern Recogn. **43**(3), 706–719 (2010)

11. Haindl, M., Filip, J.: Visual Texture: Accurate Material Appearance Measurement, Representation and Modeling. Springer, London (2013). https://doi.org/10.1007/978-1-4471-4902-6

12. Haralick, R.M., Shanmugam, K.: Textural features for image classification. IEEE Trans. Syst. Man Cybern. **3**(6), 610–621 (1973)

13. Liu, L., Fieguth, P., Clausi, D., Kuang, G.: Sorted random projections for robust rotation-invariant texture classification. Pattern Recogn. **45**(6), 2405–2418 (2012)

14. Liu, L., Fieguth, P., Guo, Y., Wang, X., Pietikäinen, M.: Local binary features for texture classification: taxonomy and experimental study. Pattern Recogn. **62**, 135–160 (2017)

15. Lowe, D.G.: Distinctive image features from scale-invariant keypoints. Int. J. Comput. Vis. **60**(2), 91–110 (2004)

16. Mehta, R., Egiazarian, K.: Dominant rotated local binary patterns (DRLBP) for texture classification. Pattern Recogn. Lett. **71**, 16–22 (2016)

17. Ojala, T., Maenpaa, T., Pietikainen, M., Viertola, J., Kyllonen, J., Huovinen, S.: Outex-new framework for empirical evaluation of texture analysis algorithms. In: 16th International Conference on Pattern Recognition, Proceedings, vol. 1, pp. 701–706. IEEE (2002)

18. Ojala, T., Pietikainen, M., Maenpaa, T.: Multiresolution gray-scale and rotation invariant texture classification with local binary patterns. IEEE Trans. Pattern Anal. Mach. Intell. **24**(7), 971–987 (2002)

19. Olver, P.J., Sapiro, G., Tannenbaum, A.: Affine invariant detection: edge maps, anisotropic diffusion, and active contours. Acta Applicandae Mathematicae **59**(1), 45–77 (1999)

20. Porter, R., Canagarajah, N.: Robust rotation-invariant texture classification: wavelet, Gabor filter and GMRF based schemes. IEE Proc.-Vis. Image Sig. Process. **144**(3), 180–188 (1997)

21. Qian, X., Hua, X.S., Chen, P., Ke, L.: PLBP: an effective local binary patterns texture descriptor with pyramid representation. Pattern Recogn. **44**(10), 2502–2515 (2011)

22. Qian, X., Liu, G., Guo, D., Li, Z., Wang, Z., Wang, H.: Object categorization using hierarchical wavelet packet texture descriptors. In: 11th IEEE International Symposium on Multimedia, ISM 2009, pp. 44–51. IEEE (2009)

23. Schaefer, G., Doshi, N.P.: Multi-dimensional local binary pattern descriptors for improved texture analysis. In: 2012 21st International Conference on Pattern Recognition (ICPR), pp. 2500–2503. IEEE (2012)

24. Skibbe, H., Reisert, M., Schmidt, T., Brox, T., Ronneberger, O., Burkhardt, H.: Fast rotation invariant 3D feature computation utilizing efficient local neighborhood operators. IEEE Trans. Pattern Anal. Mach. Intell. **34**(8), 1563–1575 (2012)

25. Varma, M., Zisserman, A.: A statistical approach to texture classification from single images. Int. J. Comput. Vis. **62**(1), 61–81 (2005)

26. Varma, M., Zisserman, A.: A statistical approach to material classification using image patch exemplars. IEEE Trans. Pattern Anal. Mach. Intell. **31**(11), 2032–2047 (2009)

27. Vu, N.S., Caplier, A.: Enhanced patterns of oriented edge magnitudes for face recognition and image matching. IEEE Trans. Image Process. **21**(3), 1352–1365 (2012)
28. Wu, W.R., Wei, S.C.: Rotation and gray-scale transform-invariant texture classification using spiral resampling, subband decomposition, and hidden Markov model. IEEE Trans. Image Process. **5**(10), 1423–1434 (1996)
29. Yin, S., Dai, X., Ouyang, P., Liu, L., Wei, S.: A multi-modal face recognition method using complete local derivative patterns and depth maps. Sensors **14**(10), 19561–19581 (2014)
30. Zhang, B., Gao, Y., Zhao, S., Liu, J.: Local derivative pattern versus local binary pattern: face recognition with high-order local pattern descriptor. IEEE Trans. Image Process. **19**(2), 533–544 (2010)
31. Zhang, J., Liang, J., Zhao, H.: Local energy pattern for texture classification using self-adaptive quantization thresholds. IEEE Trans. Image Process. **22**(1), 31–42 (2013)

Deep Convolutional Neural Network for Facial Expression Recognition

Yikui Zhai[1], Jian Liu[1], Junying Zeng[1(✉)], Vincenzo Piuri[2],
Fabio Scotti[2], Zilu Ying[1], Ying Xu[1], and Junying Gan[1]

[1] School of Electronic and Information on Engineer, Wuyi University,
Jiangmen 529020, China
`yikuizhai@163.com, iamjianliu@163.com,`
`zengjunying@126.com, ziluy@163.com, xuying117@163.com,`
`junyinggan@163.com`
[2] Department of Computer Science,
Università degli Studi di Milano, 26013 Crema, Italy
`{vincenzo.piuri,fabio.scotti}@unimi.it`

Abstract. In this paper, a deep convolutional neural network model and the method of transfer learning are used to solve the problems of facial expression recognition (FER). Firstly, the method of transfer learning was adopted and face recognition net was transferred into facial expression recognition net. And then, in order to enhance the classification ability of our proposed model, a modified Softmax loss function (Softmax-MSE) and a double activation layer (DAL) are proposed. We performed our experiment on enhanced SFEW2.0 dataset and FER2013 dataset. The experiments have achieved overall classification accuracy of 48.5% and 59.1% respectively, which achieved the state-of-art performance.

Keywords: Facial expression recognition (FER)
Deep convolutional neural network · Transfer learning

1 Introduction

Deep Convolutional Neural Networks (DCNN) are playing a more and more important role in most artificial intelligence domains such as face recognition [1], facial expression recognition [2], etc. Based on their large-scale databases, deep convolutional neural networks have achieved good performance on these subjects.

However, there are few datasets on facial expression recognition tasks and it is unrealistic to build a large-scale FER dataset. To resolve this problem, many researchers turned to using the method of transfer learning for answers. Because in related domains (such as face recognition and facial expression recognition), the pre-learned features from the first layers have almost the same generality. Most of researchers utilize transfer learning by fine-tuning a pre-trained model from other areas and have achieved great performance [3, 4].

Although the great progress has been made, the problems on facial expression recognition are still severe. Because usually facial expression recognition task has 6 or 7 classes, features generated from the first layers of pre-trained model are often too big and have lots of redundant information. The problem of over-fitting still remains.

© Springer International Publishing AG 2017
Y. Zhao et al. (Eds.): ICIG 2017, Part I, LNCS 10666, pp. 211–223, 2017.
https://doi.org/10.1007/978-3-319-71607-7_19

In this paper, we use deep convolutional neural network model to classify facial expressions. Like the mostly used method, we firstly use transfer learning method to fine-tune a face recognition model into facial expression model on FER datasets. To restrain the over-fitting problem, we first did data augmentation on SFEW2.0 dataset and then we propose double activation layer (DAL) and Softmax-MSE loss function in our proposed network. We performed our experiments on both SFEW2.0 and FER 2013 datasets and achieved state-of-art performance.

The rest of this paper is organized as follows. Section 2 introduces the related works, the main algorithms are detailed in Sect. 3, experiments and conclusions are described in Sects. 4 and 5 respectively.

2   Related Works

In [5], Ekman and Friesen developed Facial Action Coding System (FACS) which can divide human faces into several independent and interrelated action units. They classified human facial expressions into 6 basic ones: "happy", "sad", "surprise", "fear", "anger" and "disgust" and they built a facial expression dataset based on these 6 facial expressions. Ekman and Friesen's work gave a basic description of facial expressions. Motivated by their work, Lien and Kanade [6] developed a system that can automatically recognizes uncorrelated action units using Hidden Markov Models (HMMs). Other researchers did facial expression recognition by applying Gaussian Mixture Model (GMM) [7–9].

Recently, the rapid development of machine learning especially the development of DCNN brought a new direction to facial expression recognition. Lecun et al. [10] proposed Convolutional Neural Networks which is the first successful learning algorithm for multi-layer networks. As a kind of depth learning model, DCNN improves the training performance of the back propagation by reducing the number of parameters to be trained through local spatial mapping. Many researchers adapted DCNN framework in their facial expression recognition research and achieved good performance. Burkert et al. [11] proposed a DCNN framework for facial expression recognition which is irrelevant to any manual feature extraction and it outperforms earlier DCNN based methods. Yu and Zhang [12] put forward a DCNN facial expression recognition framework which gathers three state-of-art neural networks. The structure of this DCNN framework is made up of three state-of-art face detectors and a classification model that ensembles multiple DCNN. The framework was tested on SFEW 2.0 dataset and achieved good performance.

DCNN networks are suitable for tasks that have large databases in that deep convolutional neural networks have large amount of parameters and large database can fit them well. While in facial expression recognition task, it is impractical to have large database on FER tasks. Transfer learning solved this problem for its usage of other related knowledge. In [13] Zhang settled the problems of facial feature fusion and the relations of multiple action units (AUs) in building robust expression recognition systems by utilizing two transfer learning algorithms – multi-kernel learning and multi-task learning. In [14], Chen et al. used the method of transfer learning to train a person-specific FER model by utilizing the informative knowledge from other people.

Learning a FER model using transfer learning only consume a small amount of data. Because there is a great relevance between face recognition tasks and facial expression recognition tasks, many researchers used transfer learning method to train facial expression recognition based on the knowledge of face recognition tasks like in [3, 4].

3 Proposed Approach

3.1 Convolutional Neural Networks

Convolutional neural networks have been used for classification tasks for many years. Recently the rapid development of DCNN have greatly promoted the classification performance. DCNN mainly applied on two methods: Local Receptive Fields (LRF) and Sharing Weights.

General neural networks adopted fully-connected design between input layers and hidden layers. It is feasible to calculate the feature of the whole image when the image is in small size. But when the image becomes bigger, the calculation will be more time-consuming. Convolutional layer is the way to solve this problem. It restricts the connections between the input units and hidden units to make each hidden units only connect to a small area of input units.

Sharing weights is another strategy to save training expenditure. DCNN combines several convolutional layers and pooling layers, and then implement mapping between input matrix and output matrix in fully-connected layers. Each convolutional layer and pooling layer contains several feature mapping, and each feature maps a "plane" which consists of multiple neurons. Each "plane" extracts a kind of feature from input using convolutional filter. In our expression net, the size of input image is $144 * 144 * 3$, the size of filter in this net is $5 * 5 * 3$, the pad of convolutional operation is 2.

3.2 Transfer Face Net to Exp Net

In this paper, a representative transfer learning method in [15] was adopted. We transfer face recognition network in [16] to facial expression recognition network. There are two networks in [16] and we adopted Net B.

To apply the knowledge of face recognition network to facial expression network, we modify the architecture of face net into expression recognition net. First we changed the number of outcomes in fully-connected layers of the original face net and then kept the other parameters in face net invariable. For there are only 7 classes in facial expression recognition task while there are far more than 7 classes in face net, so we changed the number of outcomes in the last fully-connected layer into 7.

After modifying face net into expression recognition net, we append double activation layer on the last convolutional layer and input the outputs of the double activation layer to the loss layer.

3.3 Modified Softmax Loss Function (Softmax-MSE)

There are mainly two issues in transferring face net into facial expression recognition net. The first one is that the transferred face net may still contains information which is still helpful for face identification because of the big quantitative difference between face dataset and facial expression dataset. The second one is that the fine-tuned face net is so huge for FER tasks, so the over-fitting problem couldn't be solved appropriately.

In order to overcome these problems, we proposed a modified Softmax loss function (Softmax-MSE) which is a cost-sensitive learning method that takes classification error into consideration. At present, the existing Softmax loss function is a non-cost-sensitive function. Experimental results indicate that Softmax loss function would achieve better performance in some tasks such as face recognition which do not care the correlations of outcomes, but cost-sensitive function like Euclidean loss function would achieve better regressive performance on tasks that require high correlation of outcomes. Furthermore, our proposed Softmax-MSE loss function absorb their advantages and weaken their shortcomings. The function is detailed as follows.

Suppose that input neurons and output neurons have the same number of m, and the input of loss layer is m, and the input of loss layer is $X = \{x_0, x_1, \ldots, x_{m-1}\}$, then the Softmax function output of the kth neuron of the layer is defined as:

$$p_k = \frac{e^{x_k - \max(X)}}{\sum\limits_{i=0}^{m-1} e^{x_i - \max(X)}} \tag{1}$$

where $k \in [0, m-1]$. If the batch size of the net is n, $p_k = \max([p_0, p_1, \ldots, p_{m-1}])$, the regressive prediction value is:

$$\hat{y}_j = \sum_{k=0}^{m-1} k p_k \tag{2}$$

Softmax-MSE loss value of the nth image is:

$$L = \frac{1}{n} \sum_{j=0}^{n-1} (\hat{y}_j - y_j)^2 \tag{3}$$

where y_j is the expectation value of $\hat{y}_j$, and it is also the label value of the jth image.

In order to maintain the advantage of Softmax loss function, we used the gradient of Softmax loss function in Softmax-MSE layer:

$$\frac{\partial L_j}{\partial x_i} = \begin{cases} p_i - 1, & i = y_j \\ p_i, & i \neq y_j \end{cases} \tag{4}$$

To illustrate the proposed Softmax-MSE function more clearly, we made two comparative experiments, one of which is based on implementing proposed Net B_DAL network on enhanced SFEW 2.0 dataset and the other is based on implementing proposed Net B_DAL_MSE network on enhanced SFEW 2.0 dataset. The experiments results will be detailed in part 5.

3.4 Double Activation Layer

In [16], both Net A and Net B employ Maxout activation method in all their layers and achieved relatively good results. Motivated by this, we modified Net B by appending Double Activation Layer (DAL) on fully-connected layer to enhance the performance of the network.

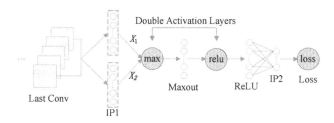

Fig. 1. The architecture of DAL layers

As shown in Fig. 1, DAL adapt Maxout + ReLU architecture by utilizing the nonlinearity of Maxout and the sparseness of ReLU function to make the network obtain its global optimal result. Specifically, there are two groups of inner product layer which are connected to the last convolutional layers of the network. Then the outputs of those two inner product layers are pumped into max-out layers which find the bigger output. During the last layer in double activation layers, "relu" layer get the maxout as input. In Fig. 1, "IP1" and "IP2" are inner product layers.

Suppose that the input of activation layer is X, then the output of ReLU layer is:

$$Y = \max(0, X) \tag{5}$$

In proposed network, there are two sets of inner product layers in IP1 layer and one set of inner product layer in IP2 layer. As depicted in Fig. 1, the outputs of last convolutional layers are the input of the two sets of inner product layers respectively.

Assume that the outputs of two sets of inner product layers in IP1 layer are X1 and X2, then the output of Maxout is:

$$Y = \max(X_1, X_2) \tag{6}$$

After the max function, then the output of relu layer is input to IP2 layer. Lastly, the output of IP2 layer is input to loss layer.

4 Experiments

4.1 Preprocessing on SFEW 2.0 New and FER2013

We did our experiments on SFEW 2.0 dataset [17] and FER2013 dataset [18]. Both the two datasets have 7 classes: "Angry", "Disgust", "Fear", "Happy", "Sad", "Surprise" and "Neutral".

The original SFEW dataset has 958 face images in training set and it is insufficient for fine-tuning a face net to expression net. So we did data augmentation on the training set of SFEW dataset by adding random information to three channels of the colored face image and remain the test set of SFEW dataset unchanged. To make the performance of expression net better, we did selective measures on the training set of SFEW dataset by excluding noisy image. These images either contain no human face or the face in the image could not be detected by face detector. In the next paper, we refer the processed SFEW dataset as enhanced dataset.

The detailed information about these two datasets is described in Table 1. "SFEW2.0 new" refers to data-augmented SFEW2.0 dataset. The numbers of images in each class is showing in Table 1.

Table 1. The information about FER2013 and SFEW2.0 new datasets

	Ang	Dis	Fear	Happy	Neural	Sad	Surprise
SFEW2.0 new	356	180	327	773	580	593	385
FER2013	3995	436	4097	7215	4965	4830	3171

Before training expression net, as shown in Fig. 2, we first applied Viola and Jones [19] face detector for face detection. Then we detected 5 basic facial key points in the image and crop the human face in the image into size of 144 * 144 based on these facial key points and set images gray.

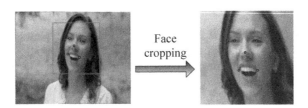

Fig. 2. The preprocessing on SFEW2.0 dataset

Because our fine-tuning is based on a pre-trained face net, it gave a good starting point of training stage. According to the experimental results, we set the base learning rate as 10e−5 and the learning policy as "fix" mode, besides we set the momentum as 0.9, gamma as 5 * 10e−6 and power as 0.75. The other parameters in the solver file are set based on the true conditions of expression dataset. The training is implemented on deep learning framework Caffe [20]. In the training stage on FER2013 dataset, we also adopted the same solving parameters of training on SFEW new dataset. We didn't do data augmentation on FER2013 dataset because it has enough training images.

4.2   Experiments and Results on SFEW2.0 and FER2013

The experiments are implemented on SFEW 2.0 new dataset and FER 2013 dataset respectively. Firstly, we adopted the network described in Sect. 3.4 and set it as Net B, then we employed DAL to Net B by appending DAL to the first fully-connected layer and called the net as Net B_DAL. At last, we changed the Softmax layer in Net B_DAL into Softmax-MSE loss layer and call the changed net as Net B_DAL_MSE. Secondly, we trained these three networks on both SFEW dataset and FER 2013 dataset using fine-tuning method. The overall average accuracy is shown in Table 2.

Table 2. The overall average accuracy

Methods	Average accuracy	Datasets
AUDN [21]	26.14%	SFEW 2.0
STM-ExpLet [22]	31.73%	
Inception [23]	47.70%	
Mapped LBP [24]	41.92%	
Train from scratch	39.55%	
VGG fine-tune	41.23%	
Transfer learning [25]	48.50%	SFEW2.0 + FER2013
Multiple deep network [12]	52.29%	
Net B	46.52%	SFEW2.0 new
Net B_DAL	45.64%	
Net B_DAL_MSE	48.51%	
Net B	60.91%	FER2013
Net B_DAL	58.33%	
Net B_DAL_MSE	59.15%	

From Figs. 3, 4 and 5 report the confusion matrix of experiments on fine-tuning Net B, Net B_DAL and Net B_DAL_MSE on SFEW 2.0 new dataset respectively. Figures 6, 7 and 8 report the confusion matrix of experiments of fine-tuning Net B, Net B_DAL and Net B_DAL_MSE on FER 2013 dataset respectively. The diagonals in the pictures show the rates of correct classification rate of 7 facial expressions. The boxes in the figures are covered gray, the more dark the box, the more higher the correct classification rate.

In the three figures above, comparing Figs. 4 and 5 with Fig. 3, we can see that although the overall average accuracy of Net B_DAL and Net B_DAL_MSE are lower than Net B, some expression's accuracy in Net B_DAL and Net N_DAL_MSE are higher than its counterparts in Net B. For example, the accuracy of Neutral expression in Net B_DAL_MSE is 3% higher than Net B. In FER tasks, the expression of Disgust

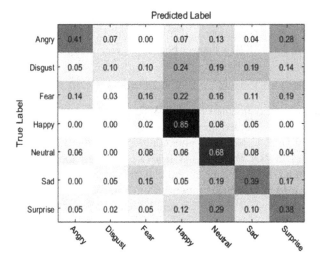

Fig. 3. The confusion matrix of Net_B on SFEW2.0 new

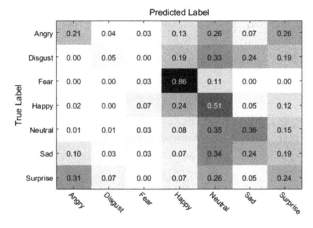

Fig. 4. The confusion matrix of Net B_DAL on SFEW2.0 new

and Neutral are the most two difficult ones to classify. Besides, SFEW dataset is built in unconstrained conditions, experiments on SFEW dataset are harder than the experiments on other datasets.

Figures 6, 7 and 8 below report the confusion matrix of experiments Net B, Net B_DAL and Net B_DAL_MSE fine-tuning on FER 2013 dataset respectively. For FER 2013 dataset contains more pictures of 7 facial expression classes than in SFEW 2.0 dataset, the experiments on FER 2013 dataset are more comprehensive. The experimental results draw the same conclusions as in experiments on SFEW2.0 new dataset.

The curve of train accuracy and test accuracy with iterations is shown in Figs. 9 and 10. Here test accuracy means validation accuracy. Both the two experiments are

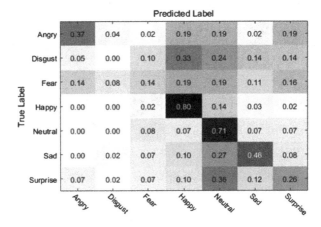

Fig. 5. The confusion matrix of Net B_DAL_MSE on SFEW2.0 new

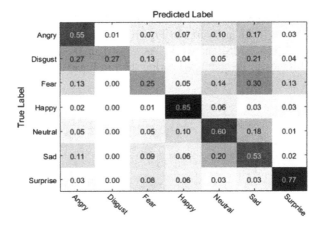

Fig. 6. The confusion matrix of Net_B on FER2013

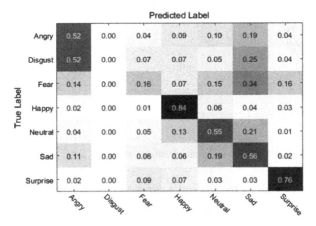

Fig. 7. The confusion matrix of Net B_DAL on FER2013

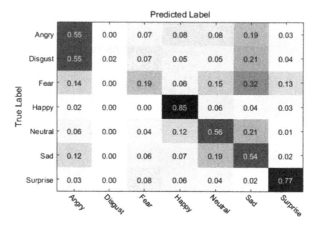

Fig. 8. The confusion matrix of Net B_DAL_MSE on FER2013

experimented on the SFEW 2.0 new dataset. In Fig. 9, the train and test process are conducted using Net B_DAL network. In Fig. 10, the train and test process are conducted using Net B_DAL_MSE network. As shown in these two figures, the test accuracy in Fig. 9 tends to be stabilized earlier than in Fig. 10.

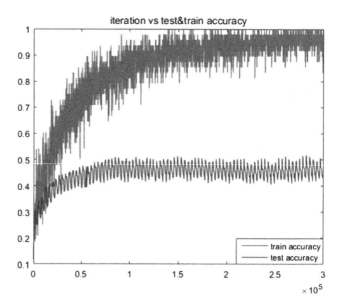

Fig. 9. The curve of test and train accuracy of Net B_DAL on SFEW2.0 new

Another statement about the shape the curves goes has to be made. As can be seen in Figs. 9 and 10, the test accuracy curves and train accuracy curves are jagged. The reason for this phenomenon is that the SFEW 2.0 new dataset contains few pictures.

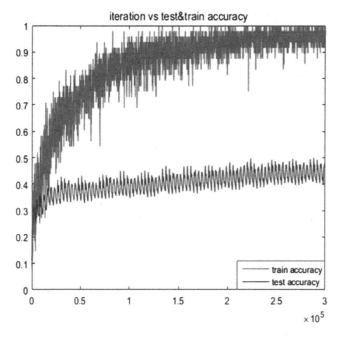

Fig. 10. The curve of test and train of Net B_DAL_MSE on SFEW2.0 new

5   Conclusions and Future Works

In this paper, we proposed double activation layer (DAL) and Softmax-MSE loss function to overcome the over-fitting problem. Based on Net B, we proposed Net B_DAL and Net B_DAL_MSE and did experiments of fine-tuning Net B, Net B_DAL and Net B_DAL_MSE on SFEW 2.0 new dataset and FER 2013 dataset respectively. The experiments achieved state-of-art performance. But the accuracies on Disgust and Neutral are not as good as expected. In future, we plan to work on improving the accuracy on these two expressions.

Acknowledgment. This work is supported by NNSF (No. 61372193), Guangdong Higher Education Outstanding Young Teachers Training Program Grant (No. SYQ2014001), Characteristic Innovation Project of Guangdong Province (Nos. 2015KTSCX 143, 2015KTSCX145, 2015KTSCX148), Youth Innovation Talent Project of Guangdong Province (Nos. 2015K QNCX172, 2016KQNCX171), Science and Technology Project of Jiangmen City (Nos. 20150 1003001556, 201601003002191), and China National Oversea Study Scholarship Foundation.

References

1. Sun, Y., Wang, X., Tang, X.: Deep convolutional network cascade for facial point detection. In: Proceedings of the IEEE Conference on Computer Vision and Pattern Recognition, pp. 3476–3483 (2013)

2. Kahou, S.E., Pal, C., Bouthillier, X., et al.: Combining modality specific deep neural networks for emotion recognition in video. In: Proceedings of the 15th ACM on International Conference on Multimodal Interaction, pp. 543–550. ACM (2013)

3. Ding, H., Zhou, S.K., Chellappa, R.: FaceNet2ExpNet: regularizing a deep face recognition net for expression recognition. arXiv preprint arXiv:1609.06591 (2016)

4. Wang, F., Xiang, X., Liu, C., et al.: Transferring face verification nets to pain and expression regression. arXiv preprint arXiv:1702.06925 (2017)

5. Ekman, P., Friesen, W.V.: Facial action coding system (1977)

6. Lien, J.J., Kanade, T., Cohn, J.F., et al.: Automated facial expression recognition based on FACS action units. In: International Conference on Face & Gesture Recognition, p. 390. IEEE Computer Society (1998)

7. Yang, J.: Maximum margin GMM learning for facial expression recognition. In: IEEE International Conference and Workshops on Automatic Face and Gesture Recognition, pp. 1–6. IEEE (2013)

8. Tariq, U., Yang, J., Huang, T.S.: Maximum margin GMM learning for facial expression recognition (2013)

9. Rong, L.I., Wang, H.J., Yan-Hua, X.U., et al.: A face expression recognition method based on fusion of supervised super-vector encoding and adaptive GMM model. Comput. Mod. 02, 15–20 (2016)

10. Lecun, Y., Boser, B., Denker, J.S., et al.: Backpropagation applied to handwritten zip code recognition. Neural Comput. 1(4), 541–551 (2008)

11. Burkert, P., Trier, F., Afzal, M.Z., et al.: DeXpression: deep convolutional neural network for expression recognition. Comput. Sci. 22(10), 217–222 (2015)

12. Yu, Z., Zhang, C.: Image based static facial expression recognition with multiple deep network learning. In: Proceedings of the 2015 ACM on International Conference on Multimodal Interaction, pp. 435–442. ACM (2015)

13. Zhang, X.: Facial expression analysis via transfer learning. Dissertations & Theses - Gradworks (2015)

14. Chen, J., Liu, X., Tu, P., et al.: Person-specific expression recognition with transfer learning. In: IEEE International Conference on Image Processing, pp. 2621–2624. IEEE (2012)

15. Girshick, R., Donahue, J., Darrell, T., et al.: Rich feature hierarchies for accurate object detection and semantic segmentation. In: Proceedings of the IEEE Conference on Computer Vision and Pattern Recognition, pp. 580–587 (2014)

16. Wu, X., He, R., Sun, Z.: A lightened CNN for deep face representation. Comput. Sci. (2015)

17. Dhall, A., Goecke, R., Lucey, S., et al.: Static facial expressions in the wild: data and experiment protocol. CVHCI

18. Goodfellow, I.J., Erhan, D., Luc, C.P., et al.: Challenges in representation learning: a report on three machine learning contests. Neural Netw. 64, 59–63 (2015)

19. Viola, P., Jones, M.: Robust real-time face detection. Int. J. Comput. Vis. 57(2), 137–154 (2004)

20. Jia, Y., Shelhamer, E., et al.: Caffe: convolutional architecture for fast feature embedding. Eprint ArXiv, pp. 675–678 (2014)

21. Liu, M., Li, S., Shan, S., et al.: AU-inspired deep networks for facial expression feature learning. Neurocomputing 159(C), 126–136 (2015)

22. Liu, M., Shan, S., Wang, R., et al.: Learning expressionlets on spatio-temporal manifold for dynamic facial expression recognition. In: IEEE Conference on Computer Vision and Pattern Recognition, pp. 1749–1756. IEEE (2014)

23. Mollahosseini, A., Chan, D., Mahoor, M.H.: Going deeper in facial expression recognition using deep neural networks. Comput. Sci., 1–10 (2015)
24. Levi, G., Hassner, T.: Emotion recognition in the wild via convolutional neural networks and mapped binary patterns. In: ACM on International Conference on Multimodal Interaction, vol. 2015, pp. 503–510. ACM (2015)
25. Ng, H.W., Nguyen, V.D., Vonikakis, V., et al.: Deep learning for emotion recognition on small datasets using transfer learning. In: ACM International Conference on Multimodal Interaction, vol. 2015, pp. 443–449. ACM (2015)

A New Framework for Removing Impulse Noise in an Image

Zhou Yingyue[1(✉)], Xu Su[1], Zang Hongbin[2], and He Hongsen[1]

[1] Robot Technology Used for Special Environment Key Laboratory of Sichuan Province, School of Information Engineering, Southwest University of Science and Technology, Mianyang 621010, China
zhouyingyue@swust.edu.cn,
4571122@qq.com, 78056970@qq.com
[2] School of Manufacturing Science and Engineering,
Southwest University of Science and Technology, Mianyang 621010, China
11016936@qq.com

Abstract. Nonlocal means filter (NLMF) or sparse representation based denoising technology has the remarkable performance in image denoising. In order to combine the advantages of the two methods together, a new image denoising framework is proposed. In this framework, the image containing impulse noise is processed firstly by NLMF to obtain a good temporary denoised image. Based on it, a number of patches are extracted for training a redundant dictionary which is adapted to the target signal. Finally, each noisy image patch in which the impulse noise is replaced by the values from the temporary denoised image is coded sparsely over the dictionary. Then, a clean image patch is reconstructed by multiplying the code efficient and the redundant dictionary. Verified by the extensive experiments, this denoising framework can not only obtain the better performance than that after use individually NLMF or sparse representation technology, but also get an obvious promotion in denoising texture images.

Keywords: Image denoising · Impulse noise · Nonlocal means filter
Sparse representation

1 Introduction

Image denoising is always a hot research problem in the low-level visual information processing. During digital image requiring, storing and transferring, some noise may disturb the image. Therefore, the researchers try to remove the existing noise and at the same time keep the key features of the original image as much as possible [1, 2]. Besides, some new techniques and methods are employed into image denoising to verify the feasibility and effectiveness. In the practice, Gaussian noise, impulse noise and multiplicative noise are usually used to model the practical noise. Among them, impulse noise is special because it just corrupts the image pixels with a certain proportion and the remaining pixels are kept same with the original values [3]. Therefore, an image corrupted by impulse noise is usually treated as disturbed by "outliers" and

© Springer International Publishing AG 2017
Y. Zhao et al. (Eds.): ICIG 2017, Part I, LNCS 10666, pp. 224–237, 2017.
https://doi.org/10.1007/978-3-319-71607-7_20

removing the outliers will help for image understanding. There are some typical techniques to remove impulse noise such as median filter [4], adaptive center weighted median filter (ACWMF) [5], directional weighted median filter [6], the trilateral filter based on the rank-ordered absolutely difference (ROAD) [7], detailed preserving variational model (DPVM) [8], decision based DPVM [9–11] and so on. These methods are effective to denoise to some extent. However, some drawbacks still exist. For example, when the noise level is higher than 30%, the most widely used ACWMF will generate a very low noise detection ratio. Similarly, in the trilateral filter based on ROAD, the insufficiency of useful pixels for filtering will result in a bad denoising performance. DPVM is very effective to remove outliers, but it has no ability to use the texture features when the objective image has abundant textures. In recent years, some novel methods are employed in image denoising, such as non-local means filter (NLMF) [12, 13], sparse representation based denoising techniques (SRDT) [3, 14–16], BM3D [17], neural network based denoising method [18] and so on. These new methods are verified better than some traditional methods.

In this paper, we propose an image denoising framework which skillfully combines NLMF with SRDT together to remove impulse noise in an image. The input noisy image is filtered by NLMF firstly. Different from NLMF under Gaussian noisy circumstance, NLMF under impulse noisy circumstance will be employed according to the characteristics of impulse noise. The output of NLMF is treated as the temporary denoised image which offers a large number of examples to train a redundant dictionary by K-SVD dictionary learning method. Then, for an image patch extracted from the noisy image, it is coded sparsely over the trained dictionary with the impulse noise replaced by the corresponding values from the obtained temporary denoised image. Lastly, the clean image patch can be reconstructed by multiplying the sparse coding coefficient and the redundant dictionary. All the restored image patches are combined together to get the final restored image. This proposed method is verified to generate a better denoising performance compared with NLMF or SRDT. Besides, compared with some typical methods, the proposed method has an obvious improvement of denoising performance for texture images. The structure of this paper is as follows. In Sect. 2, the impulse noise model is firstly given. In Sect. 3, we describe the new denoising framework in details. Section 4 includes the useful experiments to verify the effectiveness of the proposed method and some discussion is given in Sect. 5. Section 6 contains a conclusion of the whole paper.

2   Impulse Noise Model

The appearance of impulse noise is attributed to errors generated in noisy sensors and communication channels. As described before, it just corrupts the image pixels with a certain proportion and the remaining pixels are kept clean. Let Ω_n be the noisy pixel space and Ω_n^c be the clean pixel space. Suppose that a noisy image Y with impulse noise is with the size of $M \times N$. The corresponding clean image is X. (i,j) represents the pixel location in the image space Ω, $(i,j) \in \Omega \equiv \{1,\ldots,M\} \times \{1,\ldots,N\}$. Then, we have the following model:

$$Y(i,j) = \begin{cases} X(i,j), & \text{with probability } 1-p \\ n(i,j), & \text{with probability } p \end{cases}. \tag{1}$$

Here p is the noise ratio of impulse noise occupying in Ω. $n(i,j)$ is the impulse value which has no any relationship with the original value. Usually, there are two categories about impulse noise. One is fixed-valued impulse noise which is also called "salt-and-pepper noise" because $n(i,j)$ has the extreme value like 0 or 255 for an 8-bit digital image. The other type is random-valued impulse noise. That is to say, $n(i,j)$ may be the any value between 0 and 255. All $n(i,j)s$ are distributed uniformly in the range of intensity. In this situation, some impulse noise may be very close to the true values so that the accurate detection and restoration for these pixels are more difficult. In this paper, we focus on the denoising problem of random-valued impulse noise.

3   A New Denoising Framework

3.1   Description of the Denoising Framework

Our proposed whole denoising framework is given as Fig. 1. This framework includes the following three parts. Firstly, the noisy image Y is input into NLMF and then NLMF outputs a temporary denoised image X_0. At the same time, the noise space Ω_n and its complementary set Ω_n^c are determined in the part. Secondly, an adaptive redundant dictionary D is learned based on the examples extracted from X_0. Thirdly, the true values in Ω_n are estimated with the help of sparse representation. Y is splitted into the overlapped image patches. Then, each patch is coded by D to form a sparse coefficient. In order to overcome the negative effect of impulse noise on the sparse coding, we replace the impulse noise in each patch by the corresponding values from X_0. Finally, a denoised patch is obtained by multiplying the coefficient and D. All denoised patches are combined together to output a final denoised image $\hat{X}$. Next, we describe the details of this framework.

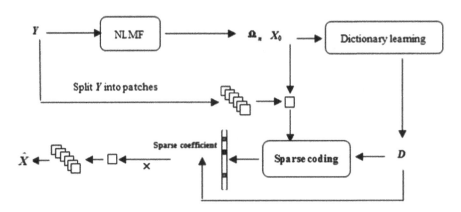

Fig. 1. The proposed image denoising framework

3.2   Details of the Denoising Framework

The core idea of NLMF is that estimating the true value by weight averaging of non-local similar pixels surrounding the objective pixel. However, in the circumstance of impulse noise, we cannot use the original NLMF directly. Fortunately, our previous work [19] solved this problem. In [19], the weight in the filtering model is adjusted according to the feature of impulse noise. Then, it is adaptive to the input data well and the denoising performance is better than that of some traditional methods. We name the filter as RVNLM. Therefore, we can employ it directly into the new denoising framework and get a temporary denoised image X_0. At the same time, the noise space Ω_n and clean pixel space Ω_n^c can be also determined based on the pixel weight.

In order to obtain a better denoised image beyond X_0, we need to further employ the technique of sparse representation. Let y_p^{ij} be an image patch extracted from Y with (i, j) as the top left corner. The size of y_p^{ij} is $\sqrt{h} \times \sqrt{h}$. Arrange y_p^{ij} to be a column vector y^{ij}, $y^{ij} \in \mathbb{R}^{h \times 1}$. For convenience, we use R^{ij} to represent an operating matrix to extract a patch and turn it into a vector. Then, $y^{ij} = R^{ij}Y$. According to the theory of sparse representation [20], the natural signal y^{ij} can be represented by the linear combination of several atoms of a redundant dictionary. Let D be the redundant dictionary, $D \in \mathbb{R}^{h \times l}$ ($h < l$). Each column d_i ($i = 1, 2, \ldots, l$) in D is called an atom. Then, we can get the sparse coefficient by sparse coding as follows:

$$\hat{\alpha}^{ij} = \arg\min_{\alpha^{ij}} \left\| \alpha^{ij} \right\|_0, \ s.t. \left\| y^{ij} - D\alpha^{ij} \right\|_2^2 \leq T. \tag{2}$$

Here, $\|\cdot\|_0$ is the l_0 norm which calculates the number of non-zero values in a vector. T is the error tolerant between y^{ij} and $D\alpha^{ij}$. Through sparse coding, $\hat{\alpha}^{ij}$ can be obtained and then the true signal is reconstructed by $\hat{x}^{ij} = D\hat{\alpha}^{ij}$. Usually, the redundant dictionary D can be obtained by employing analytic function set or training on the related examples. In our denoising framework, we extract the image patches from X_0 and use K-SVD [21] dictionary learning algorithm to get D which is more adaptive than the analytic dictionary like DCT dictionary. Back to the formula (2), we need to use some pursuit techniques to get $\hat{\alpha}^{ij}$ such as orthogonal matching pursuit (OMP) technique [22]. However, because of the interference by impulse noise in y^{ij}, any pursuit technique will fail to solve formula (2) unless the impulse noise is restrained in sparse coding or replaced by the right values. Fortunately, the temporary denoised image X_0 can offer the approximate right values to replace the impulse noise. Therefore, we first mark the impulse noise according to the obtained noise space. Denote the labeling matrix by $\boldsymbol{B}$. Then, $\boldsymbol{B}$ can be got by:

$$B(i,j) = \begin{cases} 0, & (i,j) \in \Omega_n \\ 1, & (i,j) \in \Omega_n^c \end{cases} \tag{3}$$

Next, we change the formula (2) as follows to overcome the negative effect caused by impulse noise:

$$\hat{\alpha} = \arg\min_{\alpha^{ij}} \left\| \alpha^{ij} \right\|_0, \ s.t. \left\| (y^{ij} \otimes R^{ij} B + R^{ij} X_0 \otimes (\mathbf{1} - R^{ij} B)) - D\alpha^{ij} \right\|_2^2 \leq T. \qquad (4)$$

Here, $\mathbf{1}$ is the column vector with the size of h and every element is one. Note that $y^{ij} \otimes R^{ij} B$ is totally same with $R^{ij} X_0 \otimes R^{ij} B$. Therefore, the formula (4) can be simplified as:

$$\hat{\alpha}^{ij} = \arg\min_{\alpha^{ij}} \left\| \alpha^{ij} \right\|_0, \ s.t. \left\| R^{ij} X_0 - D\alpha^{ij} \right\|_2^2 \leq T. \qquad (5)$$

In order to pursuit a good sparse coefficient, we set T by $h \cdot 5^2$ because there is no obvious noise in $R^{ij}X_0$. Using the formula (5), the nonlocal similarity information in the spatial domain is naturally merged into the sparse coding. It can generate $\hat{\alpha}^{ij}$ closer to the true vector and then promote to reconstruct a better signal by $\hat{x}^{ij} = D\hat{\alpha}^{ij}$. Lastly, all the $\hat{x}^{ij}s$ together generate the final denoised image $\hat{X}$.

Use P to represent a set of coordinates which contains the locations of top-left pixels of all the overlapping patches. Next, we summarize the whole denoising algorithm in Table 1.

4   Experiment and Results

In our experiment, several typical images are chosen into the test. They are "Barbara", "Lena", "Boat", "Pentagon" and "Pepper". Each one is the 8-bit grey image with the size of 512×512. They are shown in Fig. 2.

Table 1. Our proposed denoising algorithm

Input: a noisy image Y corrupted by random-valued impulse noise.
Output: a denoised image $\hat{X}$.
Step 1: Operate RVNLM filter for Y and get a temporary denoised image X_0. At the same time, the noise space Ω_n and clean pixel space Ω_n^c are also determined.
Step 2: Train an adaptive overcomplete dictionary D based on the examples extracted from X_0.
Step 3: Split Y into the overlapped image patches and code each patch by $\{\hat{\alpha}^{ij}\} = \arg\min_{\alpha^{ij}} \|\alpha^{ij}\|_0, \ s.t. \| R^{ij} X_0 - D\alpha^{ij} \|_2^2 \leq T, \ ij \in P$.
Step 4: Each denoised patch is reconstructed by multiplying $\hat{\alpha}^{ij}$ and D. Then, all denoised patches are combined together by $Z = \sum_{ij \in P} (R^{ij})^T D\hat{\alpha}^{ij}$. Simultaneously, an important matrix W is formed by $W = \sum_{ij \in P} (R^{ij})^T R^{ij}$ to represent a diagonal matrix that weights every pixel in the outcome based on the number of contributions it gets from the overlapped patches.
Step 5: The final denoised image is obtained by the following formula: $\hat{X}(i,j) = \begin{cases} Y(i,j), (i,j) \in \Omega_n^c \\ \dfrac{Z(i,j)}{W(i,j)}, (i,j) \in \Omega_n \end{cases}, \ (i,j) \in \Omega.$

Fig. 2. Test images. (From left to right, they are Barbara, Lena, Boat, Pentagon, Pepper.)

Before testing the image denoising performance of the proposed method, we corrupt the images by random-valued impulse noise with 10%–50% noise ratio to simulate the different noise circumstance. Besides, some traditional or related algorithms are also implemented for comparison. They are ACWMF [5], Tri-Filter [7], IDPVM [11] and RVNLM [19]. The quantitative indexes to measure the denoising performance are PSNR (Peak Signal-to-Noise Ratio) which is obtained by $10 \log_{10} 255^2 / (1/MN) \sum_{(i,j) \in \Omega} (\hat{X}(i,j) - X(i,j))^2$ and MSSIM (Mean Structure Similarity Index Measure) described in [23]. When the denoised image $\hat{X}$ is closer to the original image X, the value of PSNR is higher and MSSIM is closer to 1.

Tables 2, 3 and 4 list the quantitative denoising results about different algorithms under the noise level $p = 10\%$, 30% and 50%. The bold data is the best value in the corresponding column. Besides, in order to compare the denoised results visually, we choose some denoised image groups to show in Figs. 3, 4 and 5. They are denoised Barbaras when $p = 10\%$, denoised Pentagons when $p = 30\%$ and denoised Boats when $p = 50\%$. Based on the comparison from data and images, we get the following analysis.

Firstly, we focus on the comparison between Trifilter and RVNLM. The core idea of the two methods is weighted average. The difference is how to choose the pixels participating in filtering. RVNLM searches the similar pixels within the nonlocal region and includes more useful pixels so that it generates better denoised results especially for the texture images. For example, when $p = 10\%$, the average improvement of PSNR is 4 dB. From the observation about Figs. 3, 4 and 5(c) and (e), we can see that the denoised images obtained by TriFilter are blurry and some important details are lost. In contrast, the edges and textures are preserved well in the denoised images obtained by RVNLM especially for Barbara.

Secondly, we concentrate on the comparison between IDPVM and our method. As is known to all, DPVM is a customized model to remove impulse noise. There are lots of papers to prove its effectiveness and robustness [9–11]. IDPVM is an improved model for coping with random-valued impulse noise and can generate better denoised image. Unfortunately, DPVM just utilizes the local information to construct the image prior of piecewise smoothness. Therefore, when it processes the texture images, the nonlocal useful information cannot be used. From the data in Tables 2, 3 and 4, we discover that IDPVM is inferior to our method except for Lena. For Barbara, the value of PSNR of our method surpasses IDPVM over 4 dB when $p = 10\%$ and 0.7 dB when $p = 50\%$. Comparing Fig. 3(d) and (f), we find that there are some cracked textures existing in the denoised image obtained by IDPVM.

Table 2. The denoised results when the ratio of random-valued impulse noise is 10% (PSNR, MSSIM)

Denoising methods	Barbara 18.82, 0.4199	Lena 19.30, 0.3184	Boat 19.40, 0.3900	Pentagon 19.66, 0.4047	Pepper 18.42, 0.2922
ACWMF	26.93, 0.9186	37.55, 0.9732	32.89, 0.9529	27.78, 0.7370	35.30, 0.9652
Tri-Filter	24.47, 0.7677	33.29, 0.9046	28.85, 0.8263	27.97, 0.7546	31.86, 0.8834
IDPVM	27.31, 0.9264	**38.74,** 0.9788	33.38, 0.9576	28.01, 0.7451	35.77, 0.9704
RVNLM	30.94, 0.9628	37.72, 0.9732	33.84, 0.9497	27.63, 0.7453	36.32, 0.9589
Proposed algorithm	**31.37,** **0.9637**	38.14, 0.9687	**34.12,** **0.9690**	**28.85,** **0.7980**	**36.33,** **0.9719**

Table 3. The denoised results when the ratio of random-valued impulse noise is 30% (PSNR, MSSIM)

Denoising methods	Barbara 14.12, 0.1910	Lena 14.47, 0.1156	Boat 14.52, 0.1576	Pentagon 15.25, 0.1733	Pepper 13.69, 0.1070
ACWMF	23.54, 0.7361	28.00, 0.7978	26.28, 0.7801	25.14, 0.6253	26.32, 0.7547
Tri-Filter	23.11, 0.6428	28.26, 0.8012	25.09, 0.6639	25.32, 0.5820	27.77, 0.8074
IDPVM	25.03, 0.8478	**33.16,** 0.9314	**29.59,** **0.8900**	26.58, 0.6852	31.35, 0.9145
RVNLM	26.05, 0.8807	32.39, 0.9303	28.54, 0.8802	26.29, 0.6792	31.02, 0.9248
Proposed algorithm	**26.30,** **0.8856**	32.95, **0.9334**	28.83, 0.8814	**26.97,** **0.7156**	**31.37,** **0.9267**

Table 4. The denoised results when the ratio of random-valued impulse noise is 50% (PSNR, MSSIM)

Denoising methods	Barbara 11.85, 0.1056	Lena 12.24, 0.0615	Boat 12.33, 0.0846	Pentagon 13.14, 0.0925	Pepper 11.49, 0.0566
ACWMF	18.83, 0.4129	20.75, 0.4324	20.34, 0.4627	21.40, 0.4302	19.06, 0.3802
Tri-Filter	22.37, 0.5907	26.22, 0.7454	23.61, 0.5895	24.11, 0.5025	25.60, 0.7505
IDPVM	23.32, 0.7271	**29.91,** **0.8805**	26.19, 0.7668	25.62, 0.6284	28.04, 0.8561
RVNLM	23.94, 0.7726	29.46, 0.8662	26.15, 0.7812	25.60, 0.6418	28.47, 0.8610
Proposed algorithm	**24.00,** **0.7645**	29.69, 0.8678	**26.24,** **0.7720**	**25.93,** **0.6581**	**28.65,** **0.8637**

Thirdly, we focus on the comparison between RVNLM and our method. As described before, we want to employ sparse representation technique to obtain a better denoised image beyond the temporary denoised image X_0 got by RVNLM. Now, we can verify the rightness of the thought. From the data and images, we can see that no

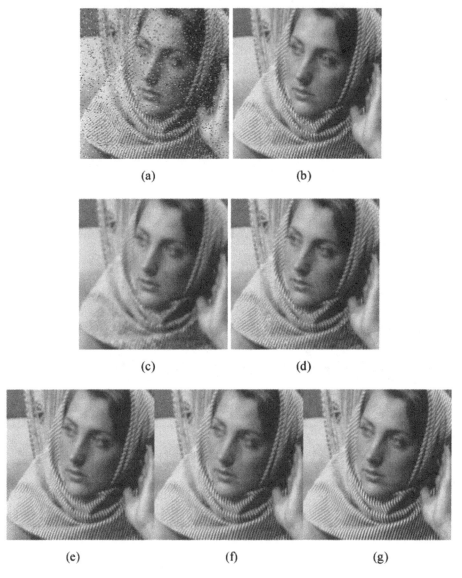

(a)　　　　　　　　　(b)

(c)　　　　　　　　　(d)

(e)　　　　　　(f)　　　　　　(g)

Fig. 3. The denoised Barbara images when $p = 10\%$. (a) is the noisy Barbara with 10% random-valued impulse noise. (b) is the denoised image got by ACWMF. (c) is the denoised image got by TriFilter. (d) is the denoised image got by IDPVM. (e) is the denoised image got by RVNLM. (f) is the denoised image got by our proposed method. (g) is the original Barbara.

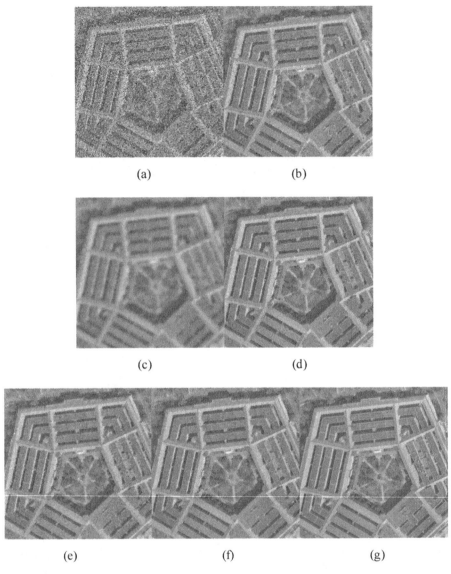

(a)   (b)

(c)   (d)

(e)   (f)   (g)

Fig. 4. The denoised Pentagon images when $p = 30\%$. (a) is the noisy Pentagon with 30% random-valued impulse noise. (b) is the denoised image got by ACWMF. (c) is the denoised image got by TriFilter. (d) is the denoised image got by IDPVM. (e) is the denoised image got by RVNLM. (f) is the denoised image got by our proposed method. (g) is the original Pentagon.

matter which image is and which noise level is, our method can output the better denoised image than that from RVNLM. When p is 10%, 30% and 50%, the average increase of PSNR is 0.5 dB, 0.4 dB and 0.2 dB respectively.

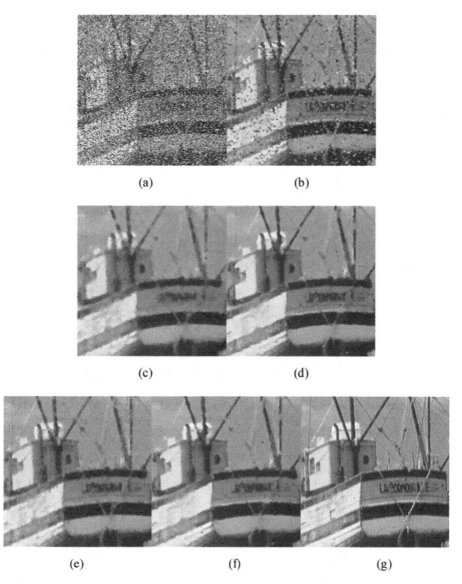

(a)   (b)

(c)   (d)

(e)   (f)   (g)

Fig. 5. The denoised Boat images when $p = 50\%$. (a) is the noisy Boat with 50% random-valued impulse noise. (b) is the denoised image got by ACWMF. (c) is the denoised image got by TriFilter. (d) is the denoised image got by IDPVM. (e) is the denoised image got by RVNLM. (f) is the denoised image got by our proposed method. (g) is the original Boat.

Based on the previous experimental data, we find that IDPVM performs better when denoising *Lena* and our method obtains superior denoised results for *Barbara*. Next, we choose other six natural images as the objective denoising images to further compare IDPVM and our method when p varies from 10% to 50%. These objective images are shown in Fig. 6. Some have rich textures like House. Some have rich details like Baboon. Some own the mixed flat and texture region like Bird and Lady. The denoising results (PSNRs and MSSIMs) when $p = 10\%$, 30%, 50% are listed in Table 5. The last row is the average promotion or decline values of PSNR and MSSIM

Fig. 6. Six natural images to be the objective denoising images to compare IDPVM and our method. From left to right, they are Baboon, Bird, House, Lady, Mushroom and Window.

Table 5. The denoising results (PSNRs and MSSIMs) between IDPVM and our proposed method when $p = 10\%$, 30%, 50%.

Objective images	$p = 10\%$		$p = 30\%$		$p = 50\%$	
	IDPVM	Our method	IDPVM	Our method	IDPVM	Our method
Baboon	23.85, 0.7331	25.59, 0.8173	22.28, 0.6485	21.92, 0.6472	20.58, 0.4756	20.72, 0.5078
Bird	35.84, 0.9861	37.22, 0.9826	31.71, 0.9455	30.06, 0.9475	27.61, 0.9077	28.27, 0.8989
House	28.46, 0.9477	32.48, 0.9692	25.96, 0.8895	24.40, 0.8625	22.99, 0.7866	23.14, 0.7824
Lady	37.40, 0.9726	37.03, 0.9472	33.08, 0.9157	33.12, 0.8993	30.27, 0.8387	30.07, 0.8113
Mushroom	32.60, 0.9575	33.90, 0.9584	28.77, 0.8869	28.46, 0.8687	25.27, 0.7485	25.67, 0.7341
Window	37.23, 0.9861	38.49, 0.9864	32.10, 0.9481	32.19, 0.9513	27.94, 0.8946	29.24, 0.9009
Average	+1.55, +0.0130		−0.62, −0.0122		+0.41, −0.0045	

between the two methods in the corresponding noise ratio. "+" represents that our method has the promotion. "−" represents that our method has the decline. We can easily observe that when the noise ratio p is low like 10%, our proposed denoising method surpasses IDPVM a lot for other five images except Lady. When p rises to 50%, our method is still better than IDPVM except Lady. However, in the noise circumstance $p = 30\%$, IDPVM performs better in most cases except Window. Therefore, we can conclude that our proposed method is more suitable for denoising natural images with rich texture and details. Besides, the applied noise ratios are limited in the range of $p <= 20\%$ and $p >= 50\%$. Otherwise, IDPVM can be employed for better denoising.

5 Some Discussion

In our denoising scheme, we train a redundant dictionary D based on the temporary denoised image X_0 and we call it an adaptive dictionary. Undoubtedly, when the noise level is low like $p = 10\%$, X_0 is close to the clean image so that the trained dictionary is adaptive to represent the objective signal. However, with the increase of p, RVNLM has no ability to restore an image close to the original one. There are some blurry details existing in X_0. In this kind of condition, D trained on X_0 may be not a good choice. Here, we design an experiment which uses another two dictionaries to replace the trained dictionary. One is the redundant DCT dictionary and the other is a global redundant dictionary got by learning on the examples from many clear natural images. Then, we compare the restoration performances under different dictionaries. In Table 6, we see that when $p = 50\%$, the trained dictionary has no superiority but it is not bad. In other words, generating D through training on the examples from X_0 is a universal and safe choice in our denoising scheme.

Besides, we test the time consumption of our method and some competing methods like IDPVM and RVNLM for denoising *Lena* and *Barbara*. Our denoising scheme includes three parts: RVNLM filtering to get X_0, generating the redundant dictionary and denoising the image by sparse representation technique. In order to balance the denoising performance and time consumption, we set some parameters with the suitable values. Moreover, according to the observation from Table 6, we adjust the denoising scheme as follows. When $p < 30\%$, we employ the trained dictionary. When $p >= 30\%$, we just utilize the analytical dictionary to save the denoising time. The calculating platform is MATLAB 2016 with 2.6-GHz Intel(R) Core(TM) i5-3230M CPU and 4.0 GB internal storage. The time consumption is listed in Table 7. From it, we can see that our proposed method sometimes consumes less time than IDPVM when $p = 50\%$ and obtain better denoised results for texture image. Moreover, our proposed method consumes less than 200 s in most cases and it is not a problem in the conditions of today's high-performance computing.

Table 6. Comparison the restoration performances under different dictionaries (PSNR, MSSIM)

Image	P	DCT dictionary	Global dictionary	Adaptive dictionary
Barbara	10%	31.21, 0.9632	31.06, 0.9605	**31.37, 0.9637**
	30%	26.26, 0.8854	26.24, 0.8829	**26.30, 0.8856**
	50%	**24.02, 0.7682**	23.98, 0.7632	24.00, 0.7645
Boat	10%	33.92, 0.9383	33.82, 0.9369	**34.12, 0.9690**
	30%	28.82, 0.8811	28.82, 0.8811	**28.83, 0.8814**
	50%	26.26, 0.7732	**26.26, 0.7733**	26.24, 0.7720
Lena	10%	37.92, 0.9687	37.87, 0.9681	**38.14, 0.9687**
	30%	32.88, 0.9330	32.92, 0.9331	**32.95, 0.9334**
	50%	29.74, 0.8689	**29.75, 0.8685**	29.69, 0.8678

Table 7. CPU consuming time (seconds) of three denoising algorithms.

Image	p	IDPVM	RVNLM	Our method
Lena	10%	77	58	132
	30%	104	79	93
	50%	196	104	113
Barbara	10%	83	98	286
	30%	114	101	146
	50%	183	114	146

6   Conclusion

In this paper, we attempt to combine the nonlocal means filter and sparse representation denoising technique into a unified framework. In order to maximize the advantages of the two techniques, we use RVNLM customized in the impulse noise circumstance to generate a temporary denoised image which offers the patch examples to train an adaptive redundant dictionary. Besides, over the adaptive dictionary, we code sparsely for the image patch of the initial denoised image and obtain the sparse coefficient closer to the real one. Then, a good denoised patch is reconstructed by multiplying the sparse coefficient and dictionary. All the denoised patches are combined together and generate the final denoised image. The extensive experimental data show that our method is effective and can obtain better denoising performance than several typical algorithms. Especially when processing texture images, our method performs much better.

Acknowledgment. This work was supported by the National Natural Science Foundation of China (Grant Nos. 61401379 and 61571376); the General Project of Educational Commission of Sichuan Province in China (Grant No. 14ZB0107); the LongShan Academic Talent Research Support Plan of Southwest University of Science and Technology (Grant No. 17LZX648).

References

1. Gabriela, G., Thomas, B., Marcelo, B., et al.: A decomposition framework for image denoising algorithms. IEEE Trans. Image Process. **25**(1), 388–399 (2016)
2. Xie, Q., Zhao, Q., Meng, D., et al.: Multispectral images denoising by intrinsic tensor sparsity regularization. In: IEEE Conference on Computer Vision and Pattern Recognition (2016)
3. Chen, C., Liu, L., Chen, L., et al.: Weighted couple sparse representation with classified regularization for impulse noise removal. IEEE Trans. Image Process. **24**(11), 4014–4026 (2015)
4. Gonzalez, R.C., Woods, R.E.: Digital Image Processing. Prentice Hall, New York (2002)
5. Chen, T., Wu, H.R.: Adaptive impulse detection using center-weighted median filters. IEEE Signal Process. Lett. **8**(1), 1–3 (2001)
6. Dong, Y., Xu, S.: A new directional weighted median filter for removal of random-valued impulse noise. IEEE Signal Process. Lett. **14**(3), 193–196 (2007)
7. Garnett, R., Huegerich, T., Chui, C., et al.: A universal noise removal algorithm with an impulse detector. IEEE Trans. Image Process. **14**(11), 1747–1754 (2005)
8. Nikolova, M.: A variational approach to remove outliers and impulse noise. J. Math. Imag. Vis. **20**, 99–120 (2004)
9. Chan, R.H., Hu, C., Nikolova, M.: An iterative procedure for removing random-valued impulse noise. IEEE Signal Process. Lett. **11**(12), 921–924 (2004)
10. Chan, R.H., Hu, C., Nikolova, M.: Salt-and-pepper noise removal by median type noise detectors and detail-preserving regularization. IEEE Trans. Image Process. **14**(10), 1479–1485 (2005)
11. Zhou, Y.Y., Ye, Z.F., Huang, J.J.: Improved decision-based detail-preserving variational method for removal of random-valued impulse noise. IET Image Process. **6**(7), 976–985 (2012)
12. Buades, A., Col, B., Morel, J.M.: A non-local algorithm for image denoising. In: Proceedings of IEEE International Conference on Computer Vision and Pattern Recognition, pp. 60–65 (2005)
13. Wu, J., Tang, C.: Random-valued impulse noise removal using fuzzy weighted non-local means. Signal Image Video Process. **8**(2), 349–355 (2014)
14. Mairal, J., Elad, M., Sapiro, G.: Sparse representation for color image restoration. IEEE Trans. Image Process. **17**(1), 53–69 (2008)
15. Xiao, Y., Zeng, T., Yu, J., et al.: Restoration of images corrupted by mixed Gaussian-impulse noise via l1–l0 minimization. Pattern Recogn. **44**, 1708–1720 (2011)
16. Dong, W., Zhang, L., Shi, G., et al.: Nonlocally centralized sparse representation for image restoration. IEEE Trans. Image Process. **22**(4), 1620–1630 (2013)
17. Dabov, K., Foi, A., Katkovnik, V., et al.: Image denoising by sparse 3-D transform-domain collaborative filtering. IEEE Trans. Image Process. **16**(8), 2080–2095 (2007)
18. Wang, Y.Q.: A note on the size of denoising neural networks. SIAM J. Imag. Sci. **9**(1), 275–286 (2016)
19. Zhou, Y., Zang, H., Zhao, J., et al.: Image recovering algorithm for impulse noise based on nonlocal mean filter. Appl. Res. Comput. **33**(11), 3489–3494 (2016)
20. Elad, M.: Sparse and Redundant Representations From Theory to Applications in Signal and Image Processing. Springer, New York (2010). https://doi.org/10.1007/978-1-4419-7011-4
21. Aharon, M., Elad, M., Bruckstein, A.: K-SVD: an algorithm for designing overcomplete dictionaries for sparse representation. IEEE Trans. Signal Process. **54**(11), 4311–4322 (2006)
22. Li, S., Chen, W., Yang, J., et al.: Fast OMP algorithm based on Bayesian test for multiple measurement vectors model. J. Electron. Inf. Technol. **38**(7), 1731–1737 (2016)
23. Wang, Z., Bovik, A.C., Sheikh, H.R., et al.: Image quality assessment: from error visibility to structural similarity. IEEE Trans. Image Process. **13**(4), 600–612 (2004)

Joint Classification Loss and Histogram Loss for Sketch-Based Image Retrieval

Yongluan Yan, Xinggang Wang$^{(\boxtimes)}$, Xin Yang, Xiang Bai, and Wenyu Liu

School of Electronic Information and Communications,
Huazhong University of Science and Technology,
1037 Luoyu Road, Wuhan 430074, Hubei Province, People's Republic of China
xgwang@hust.edu.cn

Abstract. We study the problem of content-based image retrieval using hand drawn sketches. The problem is very challenging since the low-level visual features of sketch and image have a large variance. Recent studies show that learning deep features that utilize high-level supervision is a feasible solution of this problem. We propose a new network structure with a joint loss by combining a simple classification loss with a robust histogram loss to learn better deep features for both sketch and image. The joint loss method has nearly no parameters to tune; it can not only learn the difference between image/sketch samples from different semantic class but also capture the fine-grained similarity between image/sketch samples in the same semantic class. In the experiments, we show the proposed method obtains excellent performance in real-time on the standard sketch-based image retrieval benchmark.

Keywords: Sketch · Histogram loss · Image retrieval · Deep learning

1 Introduction

Sketch-based image retrieval (SBIR) is an important problem that is attractive in both computer vision and computer graphics. In computer vision, sketch and image have different low-level visual cues; finding visual representation or designing a computer vision system to match sketch and image is a meaningful research topic. In computer graphics, sketch-based image retrieval has many fancy applications, such as MindFinder[1], shoe search, furniture design [1]. Thus, it is important to find a robust method to solve this problem.

Before the era of deep learning, there are two popular methods for SBIR. The first one is to extract sketch/edge from the image, and then perform sketch to image retrieval by shape matching methods. The second one is to extract local image descriptors and encode the image descriptors to generate a vector representation of both image and sketch. The local image descriptors can be SIFT [2] or HOG [3]. But these methods are not robust enough since the variation measured by the low-level visual features between image and sketch is so large.

---

[1] http://research.microsoft.com/en-us/projects/mindfinder.

© Springer International Publishing AG 2017
Y. Zhao et al. (Eds.): ICIG 2017, Part I, LNCS 10666, pp. 238–249, 2017.
https://doi.org/10.1007/978-3-319-71607-7_21

Deep learning is more robust for this problem because it produces high-level semantic features. But the conventional deep features are not suitable for the sketch-based image retrieval task, such as the deep feature of AlexNet [4] trained in the ImageNet dataset [5]. Deep features for SBIR are learned from sketch and image data with instance-level or category-level annotations. Wang et al. firstly proposed a sketch-image dataset that contains category-level annotations in [6]; then Yu et al. proposed a sketch-image dataset with instance-level annotations in [1]. Using these annotations, the deep network for SBIR is trained using the batch contains both sketches and images; classification loss and triplet loss are utilized by [1,6] respectively. In this paper, we develop a new deep network structure that takes the advantages of both [1,6]; the network is supervised by both classification loss and embedding loss; furthermore, we adopt a more advanced embedding loss named histogram loss - it has nearly no parameters to tune and achieves excellent performance. The histogram loss is recently proposed in [7]; when training the network, histogram loss computes two similarity distributions for positive similarities and negative similarities respectively; the positive similarity means the similarity between two training samples from the same class, and the negative similarity means the similarity between two training samples from different classes; in the end, the histogram loss minimizes the intersection between the positive similarity distribution and the negative similarity distribution.

In the experiments, we validate the proposed method on the standard SBIR benchmark, i.e., M.Eitz-SBIR dataset [8]. The experimental results show that the joint loss function outperforms each of the individual loss, and the proposed deep feature obtains the state-of-the-art performance on this benchmark.

2   Related Work

Since there are more and more tablets and smart phones with pen as input, it is much easier for people to show his idea using sketch. Recognizing sketch is becoming more important in many AI applications. Previous SBIR methods can be divided into three folds: (1) SBIR using shape matching methods aims on matching the query sketch to the edge map of natural image, such as [9–13]. (2) SBIR using image descriptors, such as SIFT [14] and the dense stroke feature [15], and typically a bag of word model is adopted to aggregate the image descriptors into a compact representation for both sketch and image. (3) SBIR using deep learning features, which use supervised deep convolutional neural networks to learn representations for sketch and image, such as [6,16–18]. In detail, the contrastive loss [16,17] is used for sketch to 3D shape retrieval and sketch to image retrieval in [18,19] respectively. In [6], classification loss is used to learn deep representation, and it needs a balanced number of training data for each category. In [1], triplet loss is used since for each instance there is a limited number of training samples. Our work includes both classification loss and histogram loss [7] which is suitable for a small number of training samples per category.

Learning deep embeddings is widely used in many visual applications beyond of SBIR, for example, face recognition, person re-identification, fine-grained recognition, online product search etc. The histogram loss method [7] adopted has been proven to be more powerful than triplet loss [20,21] and the lifted structure similarity softmax (LSSS) loss [22].

3   Methodology

In this section, we give detailed descriptions of the proposed method for SBIR. Inspired by the histogram loss method in [7], our method estimates two distributions of similarities for a pair of positive and negative samples, then minimizes the probability of the case that the similarity score in a positive pair is lower than that in a random negative pair. We follow the trend of recent work which utilizes the CNN model combines it with the classification loss and the histogram loss to learn a cross-domain embedded feature [1,6,18,19,23].

3.1   Network Architecture

Given a query sketch s and a set of candidate nature images $\{p_j\}_{j=1}^{M} \in P$, SBIR focuses on computing the similarity between s and p. We use deep CNN model as feature extractor for both s and p. Without loss of generality, we denote the CNN feature extractor as $f_\theta(\cdot)$.

Due to the semantic gap between nature images and sketches, it is difficult to train a CNN model which works well in both sketch and image domains. In recent work, [18,23] focused on using a network with heterogeneous branches for the two domains, whereas [1,19] trained a network with multiple identity branches for free-hand sketches and edge maps extracted from nature images by the structural edge detector [24]. Unlike the previous works, we propose to learn deeply embedded features that represent both nature images and sketches well.

TU-Berlin dataset [14] is a widely-used sketch dataset containing 20,000 sketches, and HUST SI dataset [6] is composed of 31,824 nature images from the web. We extract edge maps from these nature images by using the edge detector in [24]. Then we obtain a mixed dataset with 20,000 sketches, 31,824 nature images, and 31,824 edge maps from nature images to train our model.

Deep models have the ability to learn high-level descriptions for input data. Here AlexNet [4], which is trained in the ImageNet dataset [5] consisting of $1,000$ common object images, is adopted as our pre-trained model. Different from [6], we not only use the traditional 'softmax' classification loss but also adopt the histogram loss that encourages our model to be more sensitive to fine-grained sketch-to-image similarities. The framework is illustrated in Fig. 1.

3.2   Classification Loss

We define a batch of examples as $X = \{x_1, x_2, \ldots, x_n\}$ and a deep convolutional network as $f_\theta(\cdot)$, where θ represents learnable parameters of the network. As our

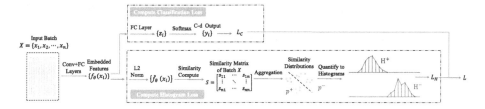

Fig. 1. The proposed deep convolutional network supervised by the classification loss and the histogram loss.

training dataset is composed of C common categories, the embedded features $\{f_\theta(x_i)\}$ can be classified by a fully-connected layer (we can regard it as a classifier) with C neurons. The output of the fully-connected layer z_i is fed into a C-way softmax layer which produces a distribution y_i over the C class in Eq. (2). The classification loss L_C over a batch of n examples can be calculated as in Eq. (1), where t_i is the class label of ith example.

$$L_c(T, Y) = -\sum_{i=1}^{n} L_c(t_i, y_i) = -\sum_{i=1}^{n}\sum_{c=1}^{C} t_{ic} \log(y_{ic}) \tag{1}$$

$$y_{ic} = \text{softmax}(z_{ic}) = \frac{e^{z_{ij}}}{\sum_{t=1}^{C} e^{z_{it}}} \tag{2}$$

3.3 Histogram Loss

Histogram loss is inspired by the Quadruplet-based loss [25,26] which computes similarities/distances of positive pairs and negative pairs. However, the potential problem of the quadruplet-based loss is that there are an even larger number of all quadruplets than of all triplets for large-scale training dataset, leading to rare usage of this loss. As a consequence, [7] proposed a histogram loss which is regarded as an efficient quadruplet-based loss and almost in a parameter-free manner.

We use $f_\theta(\cdot)$ to convert the input samples $X = \{x_1, x_2, \ldots, x_n\}$ to the embedded features $\{f_\theta(x_i)\}$. After performing $L2$-normalization, the embedded features can be represented as $\{\hat{f}_\theta(x_i)\}$. We match elements to each other to form a dense similarity matrix $S = \{s_{ij} = \left\langle \hat{f}_\theta(x_i), \hat{f}_\theta(x_j) \right\rangle\}$, which shows how similar they are. And the label $m_{ij} \in \{+1, -1\}$ indicates whether x_i and x_j is similar (from the same class) or not. Two similarity sets $S^+ = \{s_{ij}|m_{ij} = +1\}$ and $S^- = \{s_{ij}|m_{ij} = -1\}$ for positive and negative pairs are aggregated to estimate the probability distributions p^+ and p^-, respectively. In addition, the elements of two sets are bounded to $[-1; +1]$ for the sake of task simplification. By this means, we can acquire two distributions and convert them to R-dimensional histograms H^+ and H^- with uniformly spaced bins (the step of bins Δ is $\frac{2}{R-1}$).

The rth bin h_r^+ of the histogram H^+ is computed as in Eq. (3).

$$h_r^+ = \frac{1}{|S^+|} \sum_{(i,j):m_{ij}=+1} \delta_{i,j,r} \tag{3}$$

where (i,j) is a positive pair in the batch and $\delta_{i,j,r}$ can be assigned as in Eq. (4).

$$\delta_{i,j,r} = \begin{cases} (s_{ij} - t_{r-1})/\Delta, & \text{if } s_{ij} \in [t_{r-1}; t_r], \\ (t_{r+1} - s_{ij})/\Delta, & \text{if } s_{ij} \in [t_r; t_{r+1}], \\ 0, & \text{otherwise} \end{cases} \tag{4}$$

Meanwhile, H^- is estimated in the same way.

Consequently, we employ two distributions p^+ and p^- to calculate the probability of the case that the similarity score in a random negative pair is higher than that in a random positive pair, and it can be represented as in Eq. (5).

$$L_h(X) = \sum_{r=1}^{R} (h_r^- \sum_{q=1}^{r} h_q^+) \tag{5}$$

where L_h is our histogram loss for the batch X.

3.4 Optimization

We adopt the joint supervision of the classification loss L_c and the histogram loss L_h for learning deep features. The formulation is given in Eq. (6).

$$L = L_c + L_h \tag{6}$$

In order to optimize this network, it is crucial to update weights of this proposed network. Indeed, it is easy to do the back-propagation of classification loss. Here, the gradients of the histogram loss L_c with respect to h_r^+ and h_r^- are computed in Eq. (7):

$$\begin{array}{l} \frac{\partial L_h}{\partial h_r^+} = \sum_{q=1}^{r} h_q^+ \\ \frac{\partial L_h}{\partial h_r^-} = \sum_{q=1}^{r} h_q^- \end{array} \tag{7}$$

Furthermore, the back-propagation gradients for similarities s_{ij} can be derived as shown in Eq. (8).

$$\frac{\partial h_r^+}{\partial s_{ij}} = \begin{cases} \frac{+1}{\Delta|S^+|}, & \text{if } s_{ij} \in [t_{r-1}; t_r], \\ \frac{-1}{\Delta|S^-|}, & \text{if } s_{ij} \in [t_r; t_{r+1}], \\ 0, & \text{otherwise,} \end{cases} \tag{8}$$

For $\frac{\partial h_r^-}{\partial s_{ij}}$, it is computed in a similar way. Finally, given $\frac{\partial s_{ij}}{\partial \hat{f}_\theta(x_i)} = \hat{f}_\theta(x_j)$ and $\frac{\partial s_{ij}}{\partial \hat{f}_\theta(x_j)} = \hat{f}_\theta(x_i)$, the loss can be back-propagated to the individual samples, and then further into the deep embedding network.

4   Experiment

In this section, we perform experiments to test the proposed method on the task of SBIR and compare it to the previous methods.

4.1   Dataset

TU-Berlin dataset [14] has 20,000 non-expert sketches, divided into 250 common object categories, e.g., bicycle, car. In each category, there are 80 sketches of 1111×1111 size are drawn by the human.

HUST SI dataset [6] contains 31,824 nature images of 250 categories, corresponding to TU-Berlin sketch classes. For each category, there are at least 80 nature images in various sizes.

M.Eitz-SBIR [8] dataset is the retrieval set. This dataset contains 31 sketches and each sketch is associated with 40 nature images. We query a sketch in its 40 related nature images and obtain a ranking list of the nature images. And we compute the Kendall's rank correlation coefficient [8] to evaluate the performance of the proposed method. This evaluation criteria will be briefly reviewed in Sect. 4.3.

In order to learn deep features suitable for sketches and nature images, we combine TU-Berlin, HUST SI, and edge maps of HUST SI as mixed training data. M.Eitz-SBIR dataset is served as the retrieval dataset.

4.2   Experimental Settings

Our deep learning model is based on a widely used pre-trained model AlexNet [4], which is designed for 1000 common object categories of the ImageNet classification task [5]. AlexNet contains 8 layers: the first five ones are convolutional layers and the remaining layers are fully-connected layers. Each convolutional layer is followed by a ReLU layer, and some of them are also followed by a local normalization layer and max-pooling layer. The 6th layer and the 7th layer both includes 4096 neurons, and the 8th layer outputs 1000 nodes for 1000-category classification. As is referred in Sect. 3.3, only the first 7 layers of AlexNet are employed in our model to extract deep features, and we use these features to compute the histogram loss. With deep features as input, a new fully-connected layer with 250 neurons outputs the class distributions. And the classification loss is calculated based on these class distributions. No matter it is sketch or image, it is resized into 227×227 to extract its deep feature.

We use the open source Keras [27] toolbox to train our models. Weights of the last fully-connected layer are initialized using a glorot-uniform distribution [28]. Biases are all initialized to be 0. The initial learning rate is set to 0.001, divided it by 10 at the 15th epoch and the 30th epoch. And mini-batch size is assigned to 256. The size of histogram bins is set to 100. Meanwhile, the weight decay is 0.0005.

Table 1. Comparison with the results (using Kendall's rank correlation coefficient) of different data pre-process strategies on M.Eitz-SBIR dataset. The best result is in bold.

Training data	Without data-aug	With data-aug
Sketch	0.373	0.347
Sketch + image	0.434	0.471
Sketch + image + edge-map	0.479	**0.497**

4.3 Evaluation

We perform our retrieval experiments on the M.Eitz-SBIR dataset with the Kendall's rank correlation coefficient [8] as the evaluation criteria. As is referred in [8], the Kendall's rank correlation coefficient τ is proposed to determine how similar two ranking lists are. So we compare the ranking list of our proposed method to the user ranking which is regarded as "ground-truth". τ can take values in the range $[-1, 1]$, with -1 indicating a reversed list, 0 indicating two ranking lists are independent, and 1 indicating two lists are in a same order.

A SBIR system may produce the same score for two images, thus possibly producing tied pairs. Therefore, a variation of the Kendall's rank correlation coefficient is used. This variation is denoted as τ_b and defined as Eq. (9):

$$\tau_b = \frac{n_c - n_d}{[(N - U)(N - V)]^{\frac{1}{2}}} \tag{9}$$

where n_c and n_d denote the number of concordant and discordant pairs, respectively. $N = n(n-1)/2$ means the number of possible pairs in a set of n distinct elements, $U = \frac{1}{2}\sum_{i=1}^{t} t_i(t_i - 1)/2$ means the number of tied pairs in the baseline ranking list, and $V = \frac{1}{2}\sum_{i=1}^{u} u_i(u_i - 1)/2$ represents the number of tied pairs in the ranking list of our proposed method.

4.4 Results

Training data pre-process strategies. We employ different strategies of data pre-process to train our model. Firstly, we discuss on the influence of different mixing strategies of training data. (1) *Only using Sketches*: 20, 000 sketches in TU Berlin are used to train our model directly. (2) *Mixing the sketches and nature images*: We combine TU Berlin with HUST SI dataset as the training data. (3) *Mixing the sketches, nature images, and edge maps*: Following [6], edge maps of the HUST SI dataset are added to training data. We extract edge maps by the structural edge detector and binary them with the threshold of 0.9.

Data augmentation (data-aug) is widely used to boost the performance of deep learning system. Here, we compare the experimental results with data augmentation to those without data augmentation. The data augmentation method applied in this article is briefly introduced as follows: For training data, we resize a image/sketch to the size 256×256, then randomly crop a 227×227

Table 2. Comparison with the results of different size of histogram bins on M.Eitz-SBIR dataset.

Size of histogram bins	Correlation coefficient
100	**0.497**
50	0.494
25	0.492
10	0.483

patch from the resized image and randomly horizontally flip the patch during the network training. To obtain fast retrieval speed, for retrieval images, no data-augmentation is done.

As is shown in Table 1, performing data augmentation for mixed data of TU Berlin, HUST SI and edge maps of HUST SI achieves the best performance. Due to the similar appearance between sketches and edge maps from the same category, edge maps can bridge the common characteristic of them. In contrast, if a model is trained without edge maps, it is hard to fill the semantic gap and learn the same feature extractor for sketches and images. When only applying sketches as the input, the features extracted by the model are only suitable for sketches but not suitable for nature images. So mixing sketches, nature images, and edge maps are superior to other two strategies of using training data.

Parameter study of the histogram loss. As is referred in Sect. 3.3, the size of histogram bins is the only tunable parameter of the histogram loss. It determines whether histograms are coarse or fine-grained. In order to estimate similarity distributions p^+ and p^-, we transform a training batch of examples to a dense matrix of pairwise similarities. Then the distributions are quantized to fixed-length vectors. If the batch size is too small, the similarity distributions may not model the real distributions. Only keeping large batch size can provide the data independence.

We perform experiments when the size of histogram bins is equal to 100, 50, 25, 10 ($\Delta = 0.01, 0.02, 0.04, 0.1$). And the batch size is fixed to 128. Table 2 illustrates that we get similar results if the number of histogram bins is set to 100, 50 and 25. However, if the size of histogram bins is too small, the correlation coefficient value will drop. Therefore, we set the size of histogram bins as 100 and the batch size as 128.

Comparison with the state-of-the-art methods. We make a comparison with previous work in Table 3. As is mentioned in Sect. 4.4, it discusses the data pre-process of training data and the size of histogram bins. Following our best setting, our proposed method achieves the state-of-the-art result, which outperforms SHOG [8], Key-shape [29], cross-domain method [6], etc. Meanwhile, we conduct comparison experiments that the model trains only with classification loss or histogram loss.

Table 3. Comparison with results of different method on M.Eitz-SBIR dataset. In the table, hist, classification and joint respectively represents the network trained only with histogram loss, only with histogram loss and with the joint loss.

Method	Correlation coefficient
SHOG [8]	0.277
Words-of-Interest [30]	0.313
Key-shape [29]	0.289
Min-Hash [31]	0.336
Content-aware [32]	0.352
Cross-domain [6]	0.477
Ours (hist)	0.451
Ours (classification)	0.441
Ours (joint)	**0.497**

Table 3 explains that our model with the joint loss is superior to that with a single classification or histogram loss. The advantage of joint loss is that it learns the category semantics and fine-grained details at the same time. Moreover, some samples of the SBIR results are shown in Fig. 2. We list the top 10 retrieval results of our proposed method for 8 query sketches. The first column denotes the Kendall's rank correlation coefficient score τ_b of each query sketch which is given in second column. If τ_b is closer to 1, it means that this retrieval result is in better performance. Conversely, it represents a bad retrieval result. In Fig. 2, we can find that the correlation coefficient score of second row and fifth row are lower than other rows. In second row, query sketch is an image of two people and should retrieval group photos. However, it is easily confused by images that contain many people, like 2th and 3th retrieval results. Query sketch in fifth row is a building with some windows, but we retrieval several images that contain a sign or a door actually. It indicates that our proposed method can not distinguish buildings from other rectangular objects. However, it still makes sense, because buildings have rectangular shape inside.

4.5   Running Cost

All of our experiments run on a PC with a NVIDIA GeForce GTX 1080 GPU (8 GB) and 32 GB RAM. It takes about 7 h for training (nearly 25,000 iterations, 45 epochs). During testing, it will take about 17 ms to preform one retrieval, including the time of feature extraction of query sketch and feature comparison. It meets the requirement of real-time application. The source code for reproducing results is available upon acceptance.

Fig. 2. The top 10 retrieval results of the proposed method. Each row shows a retrieval result. The first column and second column means the correlation coefficient score and query image respectively.

5   Conclusion and Future Work

For the problem of SBIR, the proposed deep network jointly trained using classification loss and histogram loss is able to learn superior deep features. The joint loss is better than the single loss; it could be applied in tasks which need to learn deep embeddings. In addition, we will study how to design network structure that is more suitable for sketch recognition and generating an image from a sketch using generative adversarial networks in the future.

References

1. Yu, Q., Liu, F., Song, Y.-Z., Xiang, T., Hospedales, T.M., Loy, C.-C.: Sketch me that shoe. In: Proceedings of the IEEE Conference on Computer Vision and Pattern Recognition, pp. 799–807 (2016)
2. Lowe, D.G.: Distinctive image features from scale-invariant keypoints. Int. J. Comput. Vis. **60**(2), 91–110 (2004)
3. Dalal, N., Triggs, B.: Histograms of oriented gradients for human detection. In: IEEE Computer Society Conference on Computer Vision and Pattern Recognition, CVPR 2005, vol. 1, pp. 886–893. IEEE (2005)
4. Krizhevsky, A., Sutskever, I., Hinton, G.E.: Imagenet classification with deep convolutional neural networks. In: Advances in Neural Information Processing Systems, pp. 1097–1105 (2012)

5. Russakovsky, O., Deng, J., Su, H., Krause, J., Satheesh, S., Ma, S., Huang, Z., Karpathy, A., Khosla, A., Bernstein, M., et al.: Imagenet large scale visual recognition challenge. Int. J. Comput. Vis. **115**(3), 211–252 (2015)
6. Wang, X., Duan, X., Bai, X.: Deep sketch feature for cross-domain image retrieval. Neurocomputing **207**, 387–397 (2016)
7. Ustinova, E., Lempitsky, V.: Learning deep embeddings with histogram loss. In: Advances in Neural Information Processing Systems, pp. 4170–4178 (2016)
8. Eitz, M., Hildebrand, K., Boubekeur, T., Alexa, M.: Sketch-based image retrieval: benchmark and bag-of-features descriptors. IEEE Trans. Vis. Comput. Graph. **17**(11), 1624–1636 (2011)
9. Olsen, L., Samavati, F.F., Sousa, M.C., Jorge, J.A.: Sketch-based modeling: a survey. Comput. Graph. **33**(1), 85–103 (2009)
10. Eitz, M., Hildebrand, K., Boubekeur, T., Alexa, M.: A descriptor for large scale image retrieval based on sketched feature lines. In: SBIM, pp. 29–36 (2009)
11. Cao, Y., Wang, C., Zhang, L., Zhang, L.: Edgel index for large-scale sketch-based image search. In: IEEE Conference on Computer Vision and Pattern Recognition, pp. 761–768 (2013)
12. Parui, S., Mittal, A.: Similarity-invariant sketch-based image retrieval in large databases. In: Fleet, D., Pajdla, T., Schiele, B., Tuytelaars, T. (eds.) ECCV 2014. LNCS, vol. 8694, pp. 398–414. Springer, Cham (2014). https://doi.org/10.1007/978-3-319-10599-4_26
13. You, X., Peng, Q., Yuan, Y., Cheung, Y.-M., Lei, J.: Segmentation of retinal blood vessels using the radial projection and semi-supervised approach. Pattern Recogn. **44**(10), 2314–2324 (2011)
14. Eitz, M., Hays, J., Alexa, M.: How do humans sketch objects? ACM Trans. Graph. **31**(4), 44 (2012)
15. Ma, C., Yang, X., Zhang, C., Ruan, X., Yang, M.-H., Omron Coporation: Sketch retrieval via dense stroke features. In: British Machine Vision Conference (BMVC), vol. 2, p. 3 (2013)
16. Hadsell, R., Chopra, S., LeCun, Y.: Dimensionality reduction by learning an invariant mapping. In: 2006 IEEE Computer Society Conference on Computer Vision and Pattern Recognition, vol. 2, pp. 1735–1742. IEEE (2006)
17. Chopra, S., Hadsell, R., LeCun, Y.: Learning a similarity metric discriminatively, with application to face verification. In: IEEE Computer Society Conference on Computer Vision and Pattern Recognition, CVPR 2005, vol. 1, pp. 539–546. IEEE (2005)
18. Wang, F., Kang, L., Li, Y.: Sketch-based 3D shape retrieval using convolutional neural networks. In: Proceedings of the IEEE Conference on Computer Vision and Pattern Recognition, pp. 1875–1883 (2015)
19. Qi, Y., Song, Y.-Z., Zhang, H., Liu, J.: Sketch-based image retrieval via Siamese convolutional neural network. In: 2016 IEEE International Conference on Image Processing (ICIP), pp. 2460–2464. IEEE (2016)
20. Wang, J., Song, Y., Leung, T., Rosenberg, C., Wang, J., Philbin, J., Chen, B., Wu, Y.: Learning fine-grained image similarity with deep ranking. In: Proceedings of the IEEE Conference on Computer Vision and Pattern Recognition, pp. 1386–1393 (2014)
21. Hoffer, E., Ailon, N.: Deep metric learning using triplet network. In: Feragen, A., Pelillo, M., Loog, M. (eds.) SIMBAD 2015. LNCS, vol. 9370, pp. 84–92. Springer, Cham (2015). https://doi.org/10.1007/978-3-319-24261-3_7

22. Oh Song, H., Xiang, Y., Jegelka, S., Savarese, S.: Deep metric learning via lifted structured feature embedding. In: Proceedings of the IEEE Conference on Computer Vision and Pattern Recognition, pp. 4004–4012 (2016)
23. Sangkloy, P., Burnell, N., Ham, C., Hays, J.: The sketchy database: learning to retrieve badly drawn bunnies. ACM Trans. Graph. (TOG) **35**(4), 119 (2016)
24. Dollár, P., Zitnick, C.L.: Fast edge detection using structured forests. IEEE Trans. Pattern Anal. Mach. Intell. **37**(8), 1558–1570 (2015)
25. Law, M.T., Thome, N., Cord, M.: Quadruplet-wise image similarity learning. In: Proceedings of the IEEE International Conference on Computer Vision, pp. 249–256 (2013)
26. Zheng, W.-S., Gong, S., Xiang, T.: Reidentification by relative distance comparison. IEEE Trans. Pattern Anal. Mach. Intell. **35**(3), 653–668 (2013)
27. Chollet, F.: Keras (2015). https://github.com/fchollet/keras
28. Glorot, X., Bengio, Y.: Understanding the difficulty of training deep feedforward neural networks. In: AISTATS, vol. 9, pp. 249–256 (2010)
29. Saavedra, J.M., Bustos, B.: Sketch-based image retrieval using keyshapes. Multimedia Tools Appl. **73**(3), 2033–2062 (2014)
30. Luo, X., Guo, W.-J., Liu, Y.-J., Ma, C.-X., Song, D.: A words-of-interest model of sketch representation for image retrieval
31. Bozas, K., Izquierdo, E.: Large scale sketch based image retrieval using patch hashing. In: Bebis, G., et al. (eds.) ISVC 2012. LNCS, vol. 7431, pp. 210–219. Springer, Heidelberg (2012). https://doi.org/10.1007/978-3-642-33179-4_21
32. Liang, S., Zhao, L., Wei, Y., Jia, J.: Sketch-based retrieval using content-aware hashing. In: Ooi, W.T., Snoek, C.G.M., Tan, H.K., Ho, C.-K., Huet, B., Ngo, C.-W. (eds.) PCM 2014. LNCS, vol. 8879, pp. 133–142. Springer, Cham (2014). https://doi.org/10.1007/978-3-319-13168-9_14

Correlation Based Identity Filter: An Efficient Framework for Person Search

Wei-Hong Li[1], Yafang Mao[2], Ancong Wu[1], and Wei-Shi Zheng[2(✉)]

[1] School of Electronics and Information Technology, Sun Yat-sen University,
Guangzhou, China
{liweih3,wuancong}@mail2.sysu.edu.cn
[2] School of Data and Computer Science, Sun Yat-sen University, Guangzhou, China
maoyf5@mail2.sysu.edu.cn, zhwshi@mail.sysu.edu.cn

Abstract. Person search, which addresses the problem of re-identifying a specific query person in whole candidate images without bounding boxes in real-world scenarios, is a new topic in computer vision with many meaningful applications and has attracted much attention. However, it is inherently challenging because the annotations of pedestrian bounding boxes are unavailable and we have to identify find the target person from the whole gallery images. The existence of many visually similar people and dramatic appearance changes of the same person arising from the great cross-camera variation such as illumination, viewpoint, occlusions and background clutter also leads to the failure of searching a query person. In this work, we designed a Correlation based Identity Filter (CIF) framework for re-identifying the query person directly from the whole image with high efficiency. A regression model is learnt for obtaining a correlation filter/template for a given query person, which can help to alleviate the accumulated error caused by doing detection and re-identification separately. The filter is light and can be obtained and applied to search the query person with high speed with the utilization of Block-Circulant Decomposition (BCD) and Discrete Fourier Transform (DFT) techniques. Extensive experiments illustrate that our method has the important practical benefit of searching a specific person with a light weight and high efficiency and achieves better accuracy than doing detection and re-identification separately.

Keywords: Person search · Correlation based Identity Filter
Regression · Pedestrian detection · Person re-identification

1 Introduction

Person re-identification (re-id) aims to re-identify the same person across disjoint camera views in multi-camera system. It has drawn intensive attention in the computer vision society in recent decades with many important applications in video surveillance and multimedia, such as criminals detection and cross-camera tracking. However, person re-id by visual matching is particularly challenging

© Springer International Publishing AG 2017
Y. Zhao et al. (Eds.): ICIG 2017, Part I, LNCS 10666, pp. 250–261, 2017.
https://doi.org/10.1007/978-3-319-71607-7_22

because of the existence of many visually similar people and appearance variances of the same people resulting from great cross-camera variation such as viewpoints, poses, illumination, occlusions, resolutions and background clutter.

In current person re-id literature, numerous benchmarks and algorithms have been proposed in recent years and the performance on these benchmarks have been improved substantially. However, in the development of a person re-id systems for real-world applications, a challenge remained unsolved. The person re-id system with practice applications mainly consists of two components, including pedestrian detection and person re-id. Bulk of existent person re-id benchmarks and models only focus on the matching task with assumption that all persons in images have been perfectly detected and cropped manually. More sepecifically, these works proposed models to re-identify a query person by matching it with cropped pedestrians in the gallery instead of seaching from the whole image. In real-world scenarios, perfectly annotated pedestrian bounding boxes are unavailable in surveillance system. To manually annotate pedestrian is extremely costly and impractical, and existent pedestrian detectors inevitably produce false alarms, misdetections, and misalignments which would compromise the person re-id performance. This makes it unable to directly apply current person re-id algorithms to real-world tasks.

In order to overcome these challenges, developing a method that can jointly detect the pedestrian and match the query person, known as person search, is a new branch of person re-id and has been investigated by a few work. Existent person search methods are dominated by end-to-end deep CNN networks [15,17] which consist of two parts: (1) generating candidate Pedestrian boxes in images by region proposal network and extracting features of these boxes by ROI pooling; (2) matching the query image and these boxes by calculating pairwise euclidean distances.

In contrast to existent person re-id methods, person search algorithms have to jointly detect a pedestrian and match the query person. Some inevitable false alarms, misdetections and misalignments would harm the person search performance. Therefore, in this work, we reformulate the person search as a regression task so that the model which is learnt for obtaining a correlation filter/template for a given query person, can help to alleviate the accumulated error caused by doing detection and re-identification separately. And we can develop a Correlation based Identity Filter (CIF) framework that can efficiently re-identify the query person from the whole gallery image. The regression score represented as a confidence map is utilized to measure the similarity between a candidate and the query person, and to reflect the potential of a candidate being a pedestrian. This is also unique as compared with these person search methods.

More specifically, for a given query person, a great amount of training samples, which contains samples of the query person, other identities and background, are collected by dense sampling. We further generate labels for these samples so that the regression model we learn on such training data is capable of re-identify the query person over a whole image and distinguishing a pedestrian from the background. In practice, the regression weight can be ghastly solved by adopting the Block-Circulant Decomposition technique, which is equivalent to obtaining a correlation filter/template for a given query person. In testing procedure, when a gallery image is presented, we extract samples with various scales at all locations. And we evaluate the potential of a candidate matched with the query person and meanwhile being a pedestrian by the learnt regression weight, which can be seen as a spatial filtering operation over the gallery images.

Since the regression weight is light and the Discrete Fourier Transform technique can be employed to accelerate the spatial filtering operation, our CIF can fastly search the query person in the whole gallery images.

In summary, we make following contributions. (1) We develop a Correlation based Identity Filter (CIF) framework for person search. In our development, we consider reformulating the person search which needs to jointly handle two tasks (i.e., pedestrian detection and person re-id) as a regression task. For an image of the given query person, the regression model we learn can be used for matching the query person with the candidates at all locations and meanwhile judging whether the candidates is a pedestrian or not. (2) Since we extract the training and testing samples by the cycle shift, the learning process is equivalent to obtaining a correlation filter and then can be accelerated by the Block-Circulant Decomposition technique. This makes our framework flexibly and fastly learn the correlation based identity filter for the given query person. Due to the fact that the regression weight is light and we employ the Discrete Fourier Transform technique to accelerate the spatial filtering operation, our CIF can fastly search the query person in the whole gallery images even though we have to match numerous candidate samples with the query person.

2   Related Work

Person Re-identification. A large number of models for person re-identification problem have been proposed in literature, including feature learning [9,13,18], distance metric learning [6,8–11,19], and deep learning [1,7,16]. These methods focus on improving matching accuracy with assumption that the pedestrian images are well detected and cropped.

Person Search. Person search is a new topic in computer vision and has been investigated by only a few works [15,17]. Existent works [15,17] mainly proposed a kind of end-to-end deep CNN networks which are able to jointly handle two tasks: (1) generating candidate pedestrain boxes in images by region proposal network and extracting features of these boxes by ROI pooling; (2) matching the query image and these boxes by calculating pairwise euclidean distances. Instead of focusing on designing a good CNN network for better feature representation for person search, in this work, we consider formulating a shallow framework that detects and matches the query person on the whole gallery images jointly by regression. In particular, we proposed to learn a correlation based identity filter that is capable of re-identifying the query person on a whole image and distinguishing a pedestrian from the background, which differs from other person search methods. Although our framework has to be retrained when a new query is given, the weight of our CIF is light and can be learnt fastly with the use of Block-circulant Decomposition and Discrete Fourier Transform techniques.

Correlation Filter. Recently, Correlation Filter have shown its effectiveness and efficiency in object tracking [4] and pedestrian detection [3], and has attracted increasing attention. Henriques et al. [4] proposed the kernel correlation filter for high-speed object tracking, which is the fastest object tracker so far. Valmadre et al. [14] developed an end-to-end trainable correlation filter network for object tracking which obtained improved performance on several tracking benchmarks. Henriques et al. [3] proposed to adapt the correlation filter for efficient pedestrian beyond hard negative mining. In contrast to these work, we formulate the person search that is to re-identify the query person on the whole gallery images as a regression task, and then correlation filter, the effective and efficient technique, can be well adopted for person search.

3 Approach

In this work, we present a Correlation based Identity Filter (CIF), a new and efficient framework, for person search. Given an image of one query person, we first collect a large training set which consists a lots of training samples and their

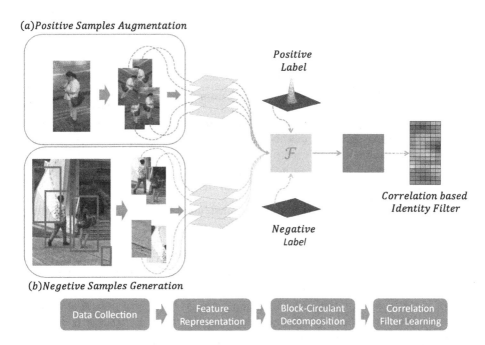

Fig. 1. An illustration of the training procedure of our CIF. In this figure, the yellow rectangle represents the Discrete Fourier transform (DFT) and the red one means the Inverse Discrete Fourier transform (IDFT). (Better viewed in color).

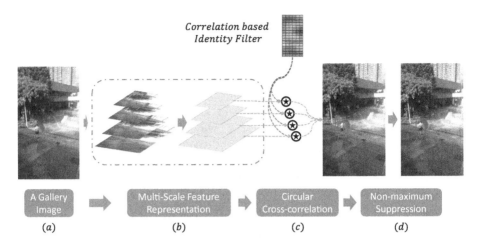

Fig. 2. An illustration of the testing procedure of our CIF. In this figure, the ⋆ denotes the circular cross-correlation.

labels. We further learn a regression model over this training set, which is equivalent to learning a correlation based identity filter which encodes the identity information of the query person and the invariant information of the pedestrian. Finally, the regression model is employed to re-identify the query person over the whole gallery images, which can be seen as a spatial filtering operation by the identity filter on the images. An illustration of the training procedure and the one of the testing pipeline is shown in Figs. 1 and 2, respectively.

3.1 Cropping Original Patches and Dense Sampling

Instead of utilizing the patch inside the annotated bounding box of all pedestrians as the training samples, in this work, we consider cropping dense samples from the surrounding area of each person. Since dense sampling results in a vast quantity of hard samples, it can help to alleviate the drifting problem in pedestrian detection [3] and enhance the ability of discriminate different identities.

Cropping Original Patches. First of all, instead of randomly extracting training samples over the whole training images, we crop an image patch which centers on the center of the bounding box of the person. And the sizes of these patches are larger than the sizes of their bounding box. We further rotate the patch of the query person with different angles so as to alleviate the impact of rare images of the query person. These image patches containing persons are utilized to captured the discriminative information between the query person and other identities. Moreover, in order to distinguish the difference between a pedestrian and the background clutter, as shown in Fig. 1(b), some background patches are also cropped randomly. For convenience of description, we denote each of cropped patches as $\mathbf{x}_i \in \mathcal{R}^d (i = 1, 2, \cdots, M)$ and called original patches.

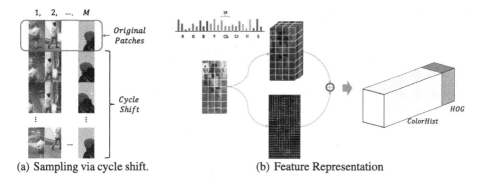

(a) Sampling via cycle shift.   (b) Feature Representation

Fig. 3. Sampling and feature representation. (Better viewed in color).

Dense Sampling by Cycle Shift. From each of original patches, we extract L samples by cycle shift (Fig. 3(a)) which can be efficiently handled by Discrete Fourier Transform (DFT) techniques proposed in [4]. For notational simplicity, the samples generate from the patch $\mathbf{x}_i$ are denoted by a sample matrix $\tilde{\mathbf{X}}_i = \mathcal{F}^{-1}(diag(\mathcal{F}(\mathbf{x}_i))) \in \mathcal{R}^{d \times L}$, where $\mathcal{F}(\cdot)$ denotes the forward DFT, $\mathcal{F}^{-1}(\cdot)$ is the Inverse DFT and $diag(\cdot)$ is a diagonalization operator. And then we generate labels $\tilde{\mathbf{Y}}_i \in \mathcal{R}^L$, which is a column vector, for these samples. In particular, the samples where the query person is at the center of the sample are annotated by 1 and others are labelled by 0. Therefore, we collect the shifted samples of all cropped patches as a large scale training sample set and denote them as a large sample matrix $\tilde{\mathbf{X}} = [\tilde{\mathbf{X}}_1, \tilde{\mathbf{X}}_2, \ldots, \tilde{\mathbf{X}}_M] \in \mathcal{R}^{d \times N}$, where each column $\tilde{\mathbf{x}}_i$ is a $d-$dimensional vector representing a sample that obtained by cycle shift and $N = M \times L$. And a label vector $\tilde{\mathbf{Y}} = [\tilde{\mathbf{Y}}_1^T, \tilde{\mathbf{Y}}_2^T, \cdots, \tilde{\mathbf{Y}}_M^T]^T \in \mathcal{R}^N$, where each element $\tilde{\mathbf{y}}_i$ that is a label corresponding to $\mathbf{x}_i$, is also generated.

3.2 Learning Identity Filter

Further, we consider the person search as a regression task, and then we fomulate a function $f(\tilde{\mathbf{x}}) = \mathbf{w}^T \tilde{\mathbf{x}}$ to measure the potential of a candidate or a sample can be matched with the query person and meanwhile is a pedestrian. In other words, for each query person, we aim at learning a sole identity filter $\mathbf{w}$ that can not only distinguish a pedestrian from an image but also identify whether a candidate is the query person or not.

Concretely, based on the previous collected data, we seek a solution $\mathbf{w}$ that minimizes the squared error over samples $\tilde{\mathbf{x}}_i$ and their generated regression label $\tilde{\mathbf{y}}_i$,

$$\min_{\mathbf{w}} \sum_{i=1}^N L(f(\tilde{\mathbf{x}}_i), \tilde{\mathbf{y}}_i) + \lambda ||\mathbf{w}||^2, \tag{1}$$

where $L(f(\tilde{\mathbf{x}}_i), \tilde{\mathbf{y}}_i)$ is a loss function. In this work, we exploit the squared epsilon-insensitive loss:

$$L(f(\tilde{\mathbf{x}}_i, \tilde{\mathbf{y}}_i)) = max(0, |\mathbf{w}^T \tilde{\mathbf{x}}_i - \tilde{\mathbf{y}}_i| - \epsilon)^2. \tag{2}$$

The above formulation Eq. 1 then can be expressed in its dual form:

$$\min_{\alpha}\frac{1}{2}\sum_{i=1}^{N}\sum_{j=1}^{N}\alpha_i\alpha_j\tilde{\mathbf{x}}_i^T\tilde{\mathbf{x}}_j + \sum_{i=1}^{N}(\frac{1}{2}\lambda\alpha_i^2 - \alpha_i\tilde{\mathbf{y}}_i + \epsilon|\alpha_i|). \tag{3}$$

We can rewrite the Eq. 3 as:

$$\min_{\alpha}\frac{1}{2}\alpha^T\mathbf{G}\alpha + \frac{\lambda}{2}\alpha^T\alpha - \alpha^T\tilde{\mathbf{Y}} + \epsilon|\alpha|, \tag{4}$$

where $\mathbf{G} = \tilde{\mathbf{X}}^T\tilde{\mathbf{X}}$.

The relationship between the solution of Eq. 1 and the one of Eq. 4 is $\mathbf{w} = \tilde{\mathbf{X}}\alpha$. Although the covariance matrix $\mathbf{G}$ is extremely large, in this work, we exploit the Block-circulant Decomposition proposed in [3] to fastly obtained the matrix $\mathbf{G}$ so that $\mathbf{w}$ can be learnt with high efficiency.

3.3   Search the Query Person

When a gallery image $\mathbf{z}$ is presented, we apply the previous learnt correlation based identity filter on the whole image to search the query person. First of all, we construct a pyramid of multi-scale image representation (Fig. 2(b)) to account for large scale change of person appearance such as the scale of the person. Then the learnt correlation based identity filter of the query person is applied on the feature of one layer of the pyramid and produce confidence map where each element reflects the similarity of the query person and a candidate and the propability of a candidate is a pedestrian by circular cross-correlation.

More specifically, we denote the testing image as $\mathbf{z}$ and we can generate a large amount of candidate by dense sampling and denote these samples as a sample $\tilde{\mathbf{Z}} \in \mathcal{R}^{d \times K}$, where each column $\tilde{\mathbf{z}}_i$ is a candidate. Therefore, the potential that a candidate is the query person and meanwhile is a pedestrian can be calculated by:

$$f(\tilde{\mathbf{Z}}) = \mathbf{w}^T\tilde{\mathbf{Z}}. \tag{5}$$

Fortunately, although dense samples are extracted, the above equation can be calculated fastly by circular cross-correlation:

$$f(\tilde{\mathbf{Z}}) = \mathbf{w}^T \star \mathbf{z} = \mathcal{F}^{-1}(diag(\mathcal{F}(\mathbf{w})^*) \odot diag(\mathcal{F}(\mathbf{z}))), \tag{6}$$

where $\odot$ is a element-wise operator, $\star$ denotes the circular cross-correlation and $\mathcal{F}(\mathbf{w})^*$ is a complex-conjugate.

Intuitively, evaluating $f(\tilde{\mathbf{Z}})$ at all locations can be seen as a spatial filtering operation over the image patch $\mathbf{z}$. Finally, the candidate with highest confidence map score is selected as a pedestrian that is most likely to be the query person.

4   Experiment

In this section, extensive experiments are conducted on CUHK-SYSU person search dataset [17] for evaluation of our proposed method and some baseline.

4.1 Dataset and Evaluation Protocols

We evaluate our method and other baselines on CUHK-SYSU person search dataset proposed by [17]. This dataset contains 18, 184 images where 96, 143 pedestrians bounding boxes are annotated. The test set consists of 6,978 images of 2900 persons, and for each of the test person, one image was selected as the query. Besides, different queries have different galleries, and a set of protocols were defined in [17] with the gallery size ranging from 50 to 4000. We followed the standard evaluation settings [17] for performing a fair comparison with existent methods. The mean Average Precision (mAP) and Rank$-k$ matching rate of different methods are reported to show the effectness and efficiency of our methods.

4.2 Implementation Details

Feature Representation. Color Histogram (ColorHist) is a kind of widely used feature in person re-id, while Histogram of Oriented Gradient (HOG) is one of best hand-craft feature for pedestrian detection. Since we aim at learning a filter that is able to detect a person that is matched with the query person, in this work, we proposed to represented each training image patches and the gallery images by the combination feature of ColorHist and HOG (Fig. 3(b)). For a given data, the feature is then represented as a $s_1 \times s_2 \times 159$ cube, where the value of s_1 and s_2 rely on the size of the image.

Table 1. Comparison results of different methods.

Gallery size	Detector	Method	mAP (%)	Rank-1 (%)	Rank-5 (%)	Rank-10 (%)	Rank-20 (%)
50	SSD	Euclidean	39.33	40.83	56.76	63.86	71.03
		KISSME	36.71	38.07	52.55	59.45	66.03
		XQDA	36.99	38.45	53.07	59.86	66.66
	GT	Euclidean	48.46	51.24	65.24	70.76	77.59
		KISSME	46.95	49.76	63.14	69.48	75.24
		XQDA	47.43	50.48	63.31	69.55	75.69
		CIF (Ours)	45.41	52.38	61.21	63.55	65.31
100	SSD	Euclidean	35.01	37.07	51.55	57.76	64.66
		KISSME	32.37	34.62	47.76	52.83	59.69
		XQDA	32.75	35.17	48.07	53.34	60.17
	GT	Euclidean	43.69	47.24	59.76	64.59	70.69
		KISSME	42.33	46.28	57.28	63.34	69.59
		XQDA	42.58	46.38	57.59	63.55	69.76
		CIF (Ours)	43.35	50.48	59.07	61.31	63.59

Compared methods. Since the practice person search algorithms have to process two tasks: (1) pedestrian detection; (2) person re-id. In this work, we modified SSD [12], a fast state-of-the-art object detector, for pedestrian detection and train it on Caltech Pedestrian Detection Benchmark [2]. The modified SSD obtain a comparable performance on Caltech Benchmark and is adopted as a baseline detector. Besides, the ground-truth annotation pedestrian bounding boxes are also utilized as a ground-truth detector, called GT. For evaluation of our method, we compared three different person re-id methods: (1) Euclidean which match the query person using the Euclidean distance; (2) KISSME [5]; (3) XQDA [9]. Therefore, 6 methods are formed: (1) SSD + Euclidean; (2) SSD + KISSME; (3) SSD + XQDA; (4) GT + Euclidean; (5) GT + KISSME; (6) GT + XQDA. All experiments were implemented on an Intel E5-2650 v3 2.30 GHz CPU with 256 GB RAM.

4.3   Results

Compared with other methods. We report comparison results of our CIF and other methods in Table 1. The results shows that our CIF surpass the three methods whose detector are SSD, and can ourperform or approximate the performance of those methods which based on the ground-truth annotation bounding boxes. Firstly, this indicates that our CIF is able to detect a person that is matched to the query person with high probability. Compared to the methods which match the query person with candidates provided by ground-truth bounding boxes, our proposed method is able to distinguish a pedestrian from the background.

Table 2. Results of our CIF on CUHK-SYSU person search dataset.

Gallary size	mAP (%)	Rank-1 (%)	Rank-5 (%)	Rank-10 (%)	Rank-20 (%)
50	45.41	52.38	61.21	63.55	65.31
100	43.35	50.48	59.07	61.31	63.59
500	32.05	38.28	46.48	49.21	51.79
1000	29.80	35.97	43.83	46.90	49.24
2000	28.33	34.15	41.70	44.48	47.22
4000	25.90	31.41	40.50	42.57	43.56

Evaluation with various gallery sizes. We evaluate our proposed method and other methods on the CUHK-SYSU person search dataset with different gallery size and the results are shown in Table 2 and Fig. 4. It is evidence that the performance of all methods including our proposed method decreases when the gallery size increases. However, CIF also outperform methods which match the query person with the candidates detected by SSD and can surpass or approximate the ones based on ground-truth annotation bounding boxes.

Visual Results. We also shows some visual experimental results in Fig. 5. It is evidence that our proposed method is capable of re-identifying the query person from the gallery image although some inherent challenges such as the change

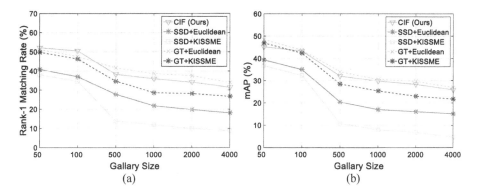

Fig. 4. Comparison of different methods with various gallery size (Better viewed in color).

Fig. 5. Some visual result of our CIF. For each query person, one query image and its rank−k images are shown in each row.

of appearance (Fig. 5(a), (d)), background clutter (Fig. 5(b), (c)) and the visual similarity of different persons (Fig. 5(e)) exist.

Searching speed. For evaluating the speed of person search when applying all methods, we measured the mean frames per second (Mean FPS). All methods are conduct on the original gallery images without resize operation. In particular, our CIF can runs at 5.3 frames per second with CPU while other methods (i.e., SSD + Euclidean, SSD + KISSME and SSD + XQDA) operate at only 0.17 FPS. Besides, CIF takes only 30 seconds to learn on training data for each query person before being applied on test images for searching for the target people. This results illustrate that our CIF can fastly find the query person from a whole image.

5   Conclusion

The main contribution is to first cast the person search as a regression task and develop a Correlation based Identity Filter framework for fast person search. A regression model is learnt for obtaining a correlation filter/template for a given query person, which can help to alleviate the accumulated error caused by doing detection and re-identification separately. Finally, the regression model is employed to re-identify the query person over the whole gallery images with high efficiency, which can be seen as a spatial filtering operation by the identity filter on the images. This all forms the proposed CIF. Extensive evaluations reported CUHK-SYSU person search dataset have shown the efficient performance of CIF.

References

1. Ahmed, E., Jones, M., Marks, T.K.: An improved deep learning architecture for person re-identification. In: CVPR (2015)
2. Dollar, P., Wojek, C., Schiele, B., Perona, P.: Pedestrian detection: an evaluation of the state of the art. TPAMI **34**(4), 743–761 (2012)
3. Henriques, J.F., Carreira, J., Caseiro, R., Batista, J.: Beyond hard negative mining: efficient detector learning via block-circulant decomposition. In: ICCV (2013)
4. Henriques, J.F., Caseiro, R., Martins, P., Batista, J.: High-speed tracking with kernelized correlation filters. TPAMI **37**(3), 583–596 (2015)
5. Koestinger, M., Hirzer, M., Wohlhart, P., Roth, P.M., Bischof, H.: Large scale metric learning from equivalence constraints. In: CVPR (2012)
6. Köstinger, M., Hirzer, M., Wohlhart, P., Roth, P.M., Bischof, H.: Large scale metric learning from equivalence constraints. In: CVPR (2012)
7. Li, W., Zhao, R., Xiao, T., Wang, X.: DeepReID: deep filter pairing neural network for person re-identification. In: CVPR (2014)
8. Li, Z., Chang, S., Liang, F., Huang, T.S., Cao, L., Smith, J.R.: Learning locally-adaptive decision functions for person verification. In: CVPR (2013)
9. Liao, S., Hu, Y., Zhu, X., Li, S.Z.: Person re-identification by local maximal occurrence representation and metric learning. In: CVPR (2015)
10. Liao, S., Li, S.Z.: Efficient PSD constrained asymmetric metric learning for person re-identification. In: ICCV (2015)
11. Lisanti, G., Masi, I., Del Bimbo, A.: Matching people across camera views using kernel canonical correlation analysis. In: ICDSC (2014)
12. Liu, W., Anguelov, D., Erhan, D., Szegedy, C., Reed, S., Fu, C.-Y., Berg, A.C.: SSD: single shot multibox detector. In: Leibe, B., Matas, J., Sebe, N., Welling, M. (eds.) ECCV 2016. LNCS, vol. 9905, pp. 21–37. Springer, Cham (2016). https://doi.org/10.1007/978-3-319-46448-0_2

13. Ma, B., Su, Y., Jurie, F.: Covariance descriptor based on bio-inspired features for person re-identification and face verification. Image Vis. Comput. **32**(6), 379–390 (2014)
14. Valmadre, J., Bertinetto, L., Henriques, J.F., Vedaldi, A., Torr, P.H.: End-to-end representation learning for correlation filter based tracking. In: CVPR (2017)
15. Xiao, J., Xie, Y., Tillo, T., Huang, K., Wei, Y., Feng, J.: IAN: the individual aggregation network for person search. arXiv preprint arXiv:1705.05552 (2017)
16. Xiao, T., Li, H., Ouyang, W., Wang, X.: Learning deep feature representations with domain guided dropout for person re-identification. In: CVPR (2016)
17. Xiao, T., Li, S., Wang, B., Lin, L., Wang, X.: Joint detection and identification feature learning for person search. arXiv preprint arXiv:1604.01850 (2017)
18. Yang, Y., Yang, J., Yan, J., Liao, S., Yi, D., Li, S.Z.: Salient color names for person re-identification. In: Fleet, D., Pajdla, T., Schiele, B., Tuytelaars, T. (eds.) ECCV 2014. LNCS, vol. 8689, pp. 536–551. Springer, Cham (2014). https://doi.org/10.1007/978-3-319-10590-1_35
19. Zheng, W.S., Gong, S., Xiang, T.: Person re-identification by probabilistic relative distance comparison. In: CVPR (2011)

An Online Approach for Gesture Recognition Toward Real-World Applications

Zhaoxuan Fan[1], Tianwei Lin[1], Xu Zhao[1(✉)], Wanli Jiang[2], Tao Xu[2], and Ming Yang[1]

[1] Department of Automation, Shanghai Jiao Tong University, Shanghai, China
zhaoxu@sjtu.edu.cn
[2] Connected and Automated Driving Lab, BMW China Services Ltd., Shanghai, China

Abstract. Action recognition is an important research area in computer vision. Recently, the application of deep learning greatly promotes the development of action recognition. Many networks have achieved excellent performances on popular datasets. But there is still a gap between researches and real-world applications. In this paper, we propose an integrated approach for real-time online gesture recognition, trying to bring deep learning based action recognition methods into real-world applications. Our integrated approach mainly consists of three parts. (1) A gesture recognition network simplified from two-stream CNNs is trained on optical flow images to recognize gestures. (2) To adapt to complicated and changeable real-world environments, target detection and tracking are applied to get a stable target bounding box to eliminate environment disturbances. (3) Improved optical flow is introduced to remove global camera motion and get a better description of human motions, which improves gesture recognition performance significantly. The integrated approach is tested on real-world datasets and achieves satisfying recognition performance, while guaranteeing a real-time processing speed.

Keywords: Gesture recognition · Action recognition · Online Real-time

1 Introduction

Human action recognition is a very energetic area in computer vision field, with a great potential in practical applications. In recent years, deep learning has shown its superior capability over conventional methods in many image based tasks, in terms of both performance and speed. Same trend also can be seen in video based problems [1–4]. Specifically, recently some deep learning based methods [5–9] are proposed to solve action recognition problem.

Among these works, two-stream CNNs [10] is a typical and successful method, which achieves excellent performance on mainstream datasets. Stacked optical

© Springer International Publishing AG 2017
Y. Zhao et al. (Eds.): ICIG 2017, Part I, LNCS 10666, pp. 262–272, 2017.
https://doi.org/10.1007/978-3-319-71607-7_23

flow images are used to represent temporal information and the still frame images are used to represent spatial information of action sequences. Based on this idea, two CNNs are trained separately on temporal and spatial data. The scores of these two CNN streams are combined by late fusion. Because of the salient performance of two-stream CNNs, some related improved method are proposed in different ways. Feichtenhofer et al. [11] propose to use CNNs to fuse outputs of two CNN streams. Zhang et al. [12] significantly improve the recognition speed by replacing optical flow with enhanced motion vector. Singh et al. [13] add two additional CNN streams in target bounding box and combine the multi-stream CNNs with LSTM network. These state-of-the-art deep learning methods have achieved excellent performances on public datasets like UCF101 and HMDB51. However, most of the current methods are offline and concentrate on limited public datasets, so they are not completely applicable for real-world applications.

In this paper, we propose an integrated real-time online gesture recognition approach toward real-world applications. Our initial motivation is to recognize traffic police gestures from a moving vehicle. Gesture can be considered as a subset of action. For gesture recognition method, we adopt the concepts of temporal and spatial information of actions from two-stream CNNs [10], and further simplify the network to fit our requirements. In real applications, major difficulty comes from the uncertain environments, which bring about many disturbances from the background and other objects in scene. So target localization is a natural choice to reduce these disturbances. In our approach, target detection and tracking are utilized to allow us focusing on the bounding area of the target. In this way, the disturbances from external background are maximally eliminated. Another problem raised in many scenarios is the global change in optical flow caused by camera motion, which is disadvantageous for gesture recognition. We introduce the improved optical flow method from iDT [14] as assistance to fix this problem.

In sum, there are three main contributions in this paper. Firstly, we propose a framework for real-world applications of gesture recognition. Target localization and optical flow improvement are introduced to solve real-world difficulties efficiently. Secondly, the integrated approach is designed and streamlined to perform real-time online recognition. In our test, it costs about 55 ms–85 ms per recognition for videos of different resolutions, which is qualified for real-time recognition with commonly used frame sampling method. Thirdly, we collect a new action dataset for traffic police gestures, which will be released with this paper later.

2   Approach

Our integrated approach mainly consists of three parts, namely, gesture recognition network, target localization and optical flow improvement, as shown in Fig. 1. The following sections will discuss about these three parts respectively.

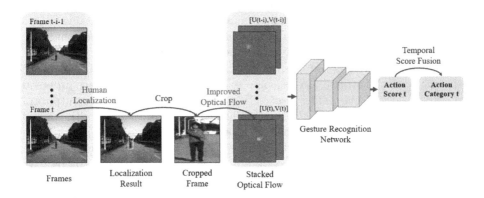

Fig. 1. Overall framework of the integrated approach. For a raw frame, target localization is performed to get target area. In target area, improved optical flows are computed as the features for recognition. Optical flow images are then stacked to feed into gesture recognition network. The network's output is post-processed by temporal fusion to give a final gesture label.

2.1   Gesture Recognition Network

Two-stream CNNs method fuses spatial and temporal information simultaneously to recognize actions and achieves state-of-the-art performance on popular public datasets. Its architecture contains two separate recognition networks, which perform spatial and temporal recognition separately and are then combined by certain fusion method. The spatial stream uses still frames, while the temporal stream uses optical flow image sequence to recognize actions [10].

Although the combination of spatial and temporal information achieves good performance, in our work, we decide to only use the temporal stream to recognize gestures in our approach, motivated by the following two reasons. (**1**) The temporal network alone is able to give a relatively satisfying recognition performance. The reduction of spatial network and late fusion network causes a small decrease on accuracy but saves a lot of time. (**2**) In popular datasets like UCF101, the videos are collected from all kinds of sources, and the difference of appearance features between different videos are significant, so spatial stream works well in this situation. But in real-world environments and especially in our target scenarios, the difference between still frames of different gestures are not significant and the spatial stream usually performs not as good as expected.

So the final recognition network only takes optical flow stream for gesture recognition. The deep CNN network in our approach is implemented with a VGG-16 net. It takes stacked optical flow images of $L = 10$ frames as a $2L$ dimension input (x, y directions). For one frame F_t in a video, the optical flow images $[U_i, V_i]$ of its previous L frames, $[F_{t-L+1}, F_{t-L+2}, ..., F_t]$, are stacked to represent the temporal feature of this frame, as $[U_{t-L+1}, V_{t-L+1}, U_{t-L+2}, V_{t-L+2}, ..., U_t, V_t]$. The stacked optical flow images are then fed into the network for recognition. To further improve recognition performance, temporal pooling is used to post-process the output scores. The gesture label of current frame is determined by the average score of last K frames.

2.2   Target Localization

In real-world applications, the environment is usually very complicated and noisy, making it difficult to recognize gestures from the whole image. Target localization is a good solution to this problem. In our approach, target detection and tracking methods are used to make sure only focusing on the target. In this way, recognition is performed only in the bounding box of the target. Target location is beneficial to gesture recognition in two ways. (1) Target location makes it possible to focus on the target, therefore maximally eliminates the impacts from environment. This guarantees the applicability of recognition algorithm in various environments. (2) Focusing on target area makes the motions of body parts more significant, therefore is helpful to improve recognition performance.

For now, our methods are based on single target scenarios. A Single Shot MultiBox Detector (SSD) [15] network is applied to detect target in scene. SSD is a superior state-of-the-art detection network and is very efficient in terms of speed and accuracy, therefore is very suitable for our task. Then KCF [16] algorithm is used to track the detected target. KCF is a tracking algorithm with extremely high speed and satisfying performance. In application, when tracking moving targets for a long time, micro errors may gradually accumulate, causing inaccurate tracking results. To solve this, SSD detector is set to re-detect target and re-initialize KCF tracker with refreshed target location at a certain time interval. The choice of SSD and KCF reduces time cost in target detection and tracking procedure at a large extent, while giving a satisfactory tracking performance.

2.3   Optical Flow Improvement

In many real scenarios, the camera is not fixed, which causes global changes in optical flow inevitably. We introduce the optical flow improvement method from iDT [14] to eliminate the influences from global camera motion in order to get a better description of actions from optical flow images. By doing so, the algorithm adapts well to moving camera scenarios.

Usually, the global motion between two adjacent frames are small, and the relation between two frames can be assumed as a homography. To estimate the homography, SURF features are extracted to find the correspondence between these two frames, after which the homography is estimated robustly using RANSAC algorithm [14].

The SURF matches obtained on the whole image include matches from human motions, which actually are disturbances for estimating global camera motion. So we use the bounding box obtained from target localization to remove the matches from human region. This reduces disturbances from moving targets and guarantees the correctiveness of homography computation, which gives an accurate description about global motion maximally.

With the homography matrix, the two frames are rectified to eliminate camera motion before calculating optical flow. Figure 2 shows the comparison of optical flow images. We can see that the application of target localization and optical flow improvement significantly enhance the final optical flow. The optical flow of target motion is subtle in the original whole image, and interfered by optical flows caused by global motion, e.g. the optical flows of the lamp and trees. After target localization and optical flow improvement, the optical flow images distinctly describes the target motion in target area, while other irrelevant optical flows are eliminated.

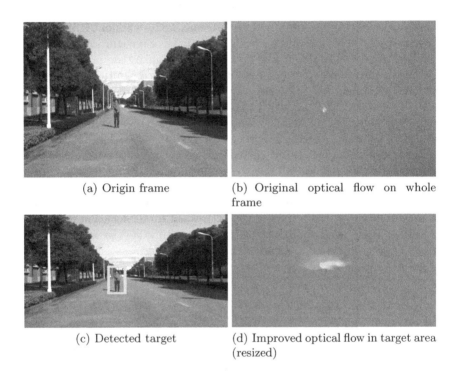

(a) Origin frame

(b) Original optical flow on whole frame

(c) Detected target

(d) Improved optical flow in target area (resized)

Fig. 2. Comparison of optical flow images. In the original optical flow image, the optical flow of target is subtle, and there are false optical flows caused by camera motion, such as the optical flow of the lamp and trees on the left. After target localization and optical flow improvement, the optical flow of target is obviously enhanced.

2.4   Integration

The methods presented above are integrated to make an applicable real-time online gesture recognition algorithm. The overall procedure for online gesture recognition is described in Fig. 1. For a new frame in a video to be recognized, the following procedure is applied: (1) Localize target in the frame. (2) Compute improved optical flow in target bounding box. (3) Feed stacked optical flow images into gesture recognition network. (4) Temporal fuse the outputs over previous K results and to get the final recognition result.

3   Experiments

In this section, the components involved in our approach are evaluated separately in several aspects. The experiments are implemented based on Caffe [17] and MatConvNet [18].

3.1   Datasets

The experiments are conducted on 3 datasets, TPG (Traffic Police Gesture), UCF101 [19] and NATOPS (Naval Air Training and Operating Procedures Standardization) [20].

TPG. TPG is a dataset collected by us for our task of recognizing Chinese traffic police gestures. For now, it contains two traffic police gestures, *stop* and *pullover*. Other random gestures are also collected as an *other* gesture class, which is mainly used as negative samples. The dataset consists of videos collected from still cameras and moving cameras. For convenience, in our experiments the gestures are further divided into 3 subclasses, HandUp, HandDown and WaveHorizon. Including "Other" class of random gestures, the dataset consists of over 2 h videos of 4 classes. These videos are split into more than 2000 clips, with approximately 500 clips per class. Videos in TPG have a high resolution with 1440×1080. Figure 3 shows some example frames in TPG dataset.

UCF101. UCF101 is a popular dataset for action recognition research. It contains 13320 realistic videos of 101 classes, which are mostly of 341×256

(a) Pullover	(b) Stop	(c) Other

Fig. 3. Example frames from TPG dataset

resolution. UCF101 is a universal action dataset and not specifically collected for gesture recognition. So we select 24 classes from its original 101 classes, making it more appropriate for gesture recognition. The selected UCF24 mainly contains subjects with a clear body or upper body in video.

NATOPS. NATOPS is a dataset of US naval aircraft handling signals. It contains 24 gestures, with 400 samples for each gesture. The videos are recorded with a stereo camera, which produces 320×240 resolution images. The dataset contains RGB images, depth maps and mask images.

3.2   Evaluation on Online Method

Our online method is evaluated on TPG and UCF101 dataset. The experiment is conducted without target localization and optical flow improvement. It simply evaluates online method's performance. For TPG, training and test sets are split as 5:1, in terms of subject. The recognition network is trained on extracted optical flow data. For UCF101, training and test sets are split according to its official split 1 and the model provided by [11] is used in this experiment.

For online test, the recognition is performed at every incoming frame in a test video, and recognition result of every frame is counted for final accuracy calculation. Different averaging schemes are tested. For offline test, as the baseline, each test video gets a single recognition result and this result is counted for accuracy calculation. In offline test, 25 random frames are sampled uniformly in a test video and recognized, and the scores of these 25 frames are averaged to give a single label for the whole test video.

The experiment results are shown in Table 1. As can be seen, the online method causes a decrease in accuracy, but is still acceptable. The reason for the decrease is that, offline test samples 25 frames evenly in the video and gets a comprehensive description about the whole action. While for the online method, only a limited clip of action information is available at every time instant for recognition. Another results is that, for online test, the average schemes could improve accuracy but the improvement is not salient. So, to speed up response time for online recognition, $K = 5$ score averaging scheme is adopted in our approach.

Table 1. Accuracy results of online method experiment

Method	TPG	UCF101
Offline method	0.9238	0.8625 [11]
Online method (K = 1)	0.8124	0.7000
Online method (K = 5)	0.8137	0.7197
Online method (K = 10)	0.8151	0.7386

3.3 Evaluation on Target Localization and Optical Flow Improvement

In this part, the effectiveness of target localization (TL) and optical flow improvement (OFI) in gesture recognition is evaluated. The experiments are performed on TPG and UCF24. Training and test sets of UCF24 are still split according to its official split 1.

For each dataset, two CNNs are trained and compared. One network, as the baseline, is trained and tested on the original optical flow images of the raw videos. The other network is trained on optical flow images obtained with target localization and optical flow improvement. The test is performed offline, same as the offline test method in Sect. 3.2.

The experiment results are shown in Table 2. From the comparison, we can see that target localization and optical flow improvement effectively increases accuracy on TPG dataset, but causes a small decrease on UCF24. The main reason for the decrease on UCF24 is that most of the actions in UCF24 are not exactly gestures but interactions with objects, such as balls and instruments. In this case, the application of target localization only concentrates on humans but leaves out the objects in the interactions, which causes the information deficiency. But for TPG dataset, the target localization brings significant performance improvement, because target localization effectively extracts target from environment and enhances optical flow from target motion. The result indicates that target localization is an effective method to enhance recognition performance in gesture area, especially in real-world scenarios.

Table 2. Accuracies of target localization (TL) and optical flow improvement (OFI) experiment

Method	TPG	UCF24
Offline test on original video	0.9238	0.9824
Offline test with TL and OFI	0.9887	0.9573

3.4 Evaluation on Overall Integrated Approach

The integrated online gesture recognition approach, which combines online recognition pipeline, target localization and optical flow improvement, is evaluated on three datasets, TPG, UCF24 and NATOPS, respectively. The online and offline tests are executed in the same way as introduced in Sect. 3.2.

For TPG and UCF24, our approach is compared with the temporal stream (TS) of two-stream CNNs [10], which is an offline method. For NATOPS dataset, our approach is compared with the extended online LDCRF method proposed in [21]. The LDCRF method utilizes all three kinds of data in NATOPS (RGB image, depth image and mask image) to recognize gestures, while only the RGB images of NATOPS are used in our approach.

Table 3 shows the comparison results, we can see that our integrated app-roach achieves satisfactory performance compared with baselines. The perfor-mance decrease in UCF24 is reasonable as we have analyzed in the previous sections. The reason for the relatively poor performance on NATOPS is that the gestures in this dataset contains many subtle hand movements and many pairs of gestures only differ in minor ways like thumb up or down. In this case, the optical flow feature used in our approach is not micromesh enough to capture these indistinctive differences. So our approach is better at gestures with big body motions, like traffic police gestures.

Table 4 shows our speed performance on three datasets. What is important is that our approach guarantees a real-time implementation of the algorithm, which is critical for online recognition in real applications. The average time cost per frame of our approach are about 55 ms–85 ms for low resolution videos (UCF24 and NATOPS) and high resolution videos (TPG) respectively. The processing speed is qualified for real-time recognition with frame sampling, which is a com-monly used method to eliminate information redundancy in gesture sequences. The result shows that our integrated approach works well for real-time online gesture recognition task.

Table 3. Accuracy comparison on three datasets

Method	TPG	UCF24	NATOPS
TS of two-stream CNNs [10]	0.9238	0.9824	-
Extended online LDCRF [21]	-	-	0.7537
Our integrated approach	0.9498	0.8927	0.7277

Table 4. Speed performance of our approach on different datasets

Dataset	TPG	UCF24	NATOPS
Video resolution	$1440 \times, 1080$	$341, \times, 256 \, (most)$	$320, \times, 240$
Time cost (ms/frame)	85	67	55

4   Conclusion

In this paper, we propose an integrated online gesture recognition approach. The approach assembles online gesture recognition network, target localization and optical flow improvement. It is applicable in real-world environment and mov-ing camera situation. Evaluations on several datasets show that the integrated approach gives a satisfying recognition accuracy while guaranteeing real-time processing speed.

Acknowledgement. This research has been supported by the funding from NSFC (61673269, 61375019, 61273285).

References

1. Karpathy, A., Toderici, G., Shetty, S., et al.: Large-scale video classification with convolutional neural networks. In: Proceedings of the IEEE Conference on Computer Vision and Pattern Recognition, pp. 1725–1732 (2014)
2. Xu, Z., Yang, Y., Hauptmann, A.G.: A discriminative CNN video representation for event detection. In: Proceedings of the IEEE Conference on Computer Vision and Pattern Recognition, pp. 1798–1807 (2015)
3. Weinzaepfel, P., Harchaoui, Z., Schmid, C.: Learning to track for spatio-temporal action localization. In: Proceedings of the IEEE International Conference on Computer Vision, pp. 3164–3172 (2015)
4. Park, E., Han, X., Berg, T.L., et al.: Combining multiple sources of knowledge in deep cnns for action recognition. In: 2016 IEEE Winter Conference on Applications of Computer Vision (WACV), pp. 1–8. IEEE (2016)
5. Ji, S., Xu, W., Yang, M., et al.: 3D convolutional neural networks for human action recognition. IEEE Trans. Pattern Anal. Mach. Intell. **35**(1), 221–231 (2013)
6. Gkioxari, G., Girshick, R., Malik, J.: Contextual action recognition with R*CNN. In: Proceedings of the IEEE International Conference on Computer Vision, pp. 1080–1088 (2015)
7. Ijjina, E.P., Mohan, C.K.: Human action recognition based on motion capture information using fuzzy convolution neural networks. In: 2015 Eighth International Conference on Advances in Pattern Recognition (ICAPR), pp. 1–6. IEEE (2015)
8. Sun, L., Jia, K., Yeung, D.Y., et al.: Human action recognition using factorized spatio-temporal convolutional networks. In: Proceedings of the IEEE International Conference on Computer Vision, pp. 4597–4605 (2015)
9. Song, J., Shen, H.: Beyond frame-level CNN: saliency-aware 3D CNN with LSTM for video action recognition. IEEE Signal Process. Lett. **24**(4), 510–514 (2016)
10. Simonyan, K., Zisserman, A.: Two-stream convolutional networks for action recognition in videos. In: Advances in neural information processing systems, pp. 568–576 (2014)
11. Feichtenhofer, C., Pinz, A., Zisserman, A.: Convolutional two-stream network fusion for video action recognition. In: Proceedings of the IEEE Conference on Computer Vision and Pattern Recognition, pp. 1933–1941 (2016)
12. Zhang, B., Wang, L., Wang, Z., et al.: Real-time action recognition with enhanced motion vector CNNs. In: Proceedings of the IEEE Conference on Computer Vision and Pattern Recognition, pp. 2718–2726 (2016)
13. Singh, B., Marks, T.K., Jones, M., et al.: A multi-stream bi-directional recurrent neural network for fine-grained action detection. In: Proceedings of the IEEE Conference on Computer Vision and Pattern Recognition, pp. 1961–1970 (2016)
14. Wang, H., Schmid, C.: Action recognition with improved trajectories. In Proceedings of the IEEE International Conference on Computer Vision, pp. 3551–3558 (2013)
15. Liu, W., Anguelov, D., Erhan, D., Szegedy, C., Reed, S., Fu, C.-Y., Berg, A.C.: SSD: single shot multibox detector. In: Leibe, B., Matas, J., Sebe, N., Welling, M. (eds.) ECCV 2016. LNCS, vol. 9905, pp. 21–37. Springer, Cham (2016). https://doi.org/10.1007/978-3-319-46448-0_2
16. Henriques, J.F., Caseiro, R., Martins, P., et al.: High-speed tracking with kernelized correlation filters. IEEE Trans. Pattern Anal. Mach. Intell. **37**(3), 583–596 (2015)
17. Jia, Y., Shelhamer, E., Donahue, J., et al.: Caffe: convolutional architecture for fast feature embedding. In: Proceedings of the 22nd ACM International Conference on Multimedia, pp. 675–678. ACM (2014)

18. Vedaldi, A., Lenc, K.: Matconvnet: convolutional neural networks for MATLAB. In: Proceedings of the 23rd ACM international conference on Multimedia, pp. 689–692. ACM (2015)

19. Soomro, K., Zamir, A.R., Shah, M.: UCF101: a dataset of 101 human actions classes from videos in the wild. arXiv preprint arXiv:1212.0402 (2012)

20. Song, Y., Demirdjian, D., Davis, R.: Tracking body and hands for gesture recognition: NATOPS aircraft handling signals database. In: 2011 IEEE International Conference on Automatic Face and Gesture Recognition and Workshops (FG 2011), pp. 500–506. IEEE (2011)

21. Song, Y., Demirdjian, D., Davis, R.: Continuous body and hand gesture recognition for natural human-computer interaction. ACM Trans. Interact. Intell. Syst. (TiiS) **2**(1), 5 (2012)

A Novel Pavement Crack Detection Approach Using Pre-selection Based on Transfer Learning

Kaige Zhang[(✉)] and Hengda Cheng

Utah State University, Logan, UT 84341, USA
{kg.zhang,hd.cheng}@aggiemail.usu.edu

Abstract. Most of the existing pavement image crack detection methods cannot effectively solve the noise problem caused by the complicated pavement textures and intensity inhomogeneity. In this paper, we propose a novel fully automatic crack detection approach by incorporating a pre-selection process. It starts by dividing images into small blocks and training a deep convolutional neural network to screen out the non-crack regions in a pavement image which usually cause lots of noise and errors when performing crack detection; then an efficient thresholding method based on linear regression is applied to the crack-block regions to find the possible crack pixels; at last, tensor voting-based curve detection is employed to fill the gaps between crack fragments and produce the continuous crack curves. We validate the approach on a dataset of 600 (2000 × 4000-pixel) pavement images. The experimental results demonstrate that, with pre-selection, the proposed detection approach achieves very good performance (recall = 0.947, and precision = 0.846).

Keywords: Pavement crack detection · Transfer learning
Convolutional neural network · Linear regression

1 Introduction

Road maintenance plays an important role in safe driving. The world's road network has reached 64,285,009 km and the United States has 6,586,610 km [1]. It needs a huge cost for maintenance and upgrade of such immense road network. Pavement crack is one of the most common road distresses and is also the most important information to be collected in road management system.

During the last three decades, researchers have paid a lot of attention to automatic pavement crack detection using various image processing methods. Reference [2] gives a comprehensive summaries about existing pavement cracking detection methods. Intensity thresholding was used in the early approaches widely because it is fast and straightforward; however, due to the complexity of pavement textures at different scales and non-uniform illuminance, thresholding cannot achieve good performance [3]. A dynamic optimization method was utilized to detect pavement cracks and showed good performance, but the time complexity is too high [4]. Shi *et al.* [5] proposed a method named "CrackForest" which applied random structured forest [6] to crack detection and achieved good performance; they use the distribution differences of the statistical feature

© Springer International Publishing AG 2017
Y. Zhao et al. (Eds.): ICIG 2017, Part I, LNCS 10666, pp. 273–283, 2017.
https://doi.org/10.1007/978-3-319-71607-7_24

histogram and statistical neighborhood histogram to discriminate true cracks from noises; but it cannot remove the noises which connected to the true crack regions. In addition, Cheng et al. [7, 8] used fuzzy logic and neural network to find the proper thresholds and segment the darker crack pixels from the background; Zou et al. [9] used tensor voting to find the local maximum as the crack seeds and to build the minimal spanning tree to represent the actual crack pattern; Wang et al. [10] proposed a wavelet-based method which uses different scales of wavelet transformation information to detect pavement cracks; Zalama et al. [11] used visual features extracted by Gabor filters for road crack detection; Oliveira and Correia [12] developed an automatic detection system based on an unsupervised pattern recognition method; and Song et al. [13] proposed a dual-threshold method for pavement crack detection. All these methods achieved some success in their cases, but still cannot get a satisfying performance considering both the detection accuracy and time complexity; especially, on different datasets. Two main problems still exist in current approaches: (1) they are sensitive to image noise, and would produce lots of false positives which cause a low precision; and (2) most of the approaches can only produce discontinuous crack fragments because of their sensitivity to non-uniform intensity.

For the last ten years, deep learning has achieved great success and obtained better performance in solving many problems [14] comparing to the traditional hand-crafted feature extraction methods [15, 16]; and transfer learning showed great advantage in training complex deep neural network [17, 18]. Zhang et al. [19] designed a 6-layer convolutional neural network to do crack detection using the dataset captured by a cell-phone. The major problems of this approach are: it used the cellphone captured images which are easy to process due to the high quality and less noise; however, they are far from the practice, that makes the work less useful; the generalization ability of the network architecture is weak, and it is hard to process different datasets containing actual industry images; and using patch-wise classification [20, 21] for pixel-level/pixel-wise detection is unrealistic due to its huge time complexity.

To solve the above problems, we proposed a novel pre-selection method to remove most noise by discarding the non-crack image regions which can reduce the false positives significantly in later crack detection; then an efficient thresholding method based on linear regression is proposed to segment crack-block regions; and in order to overcome the discontinuous fragment problem existing in most thresholding methods, tensor voting based curve detection is employed to fill the gaps between crack fragments successfully. The experimental results demonstrate the effectiveness of the proposed approach.

2   Proposed Method

The main idea of this work is doing a pre-selection to screen out most non-crack areas in an image before crack detection. We first divide the images into small crack blocks and train a deep convolutional neural network to classify the crack/non-crack blocks which are used to divide the pavement image area into crack/non-crack regions; the generic knowledges learned from ImageNet dataset [22] is transferred to train the network successfully; then a linear model is built to quickly find the best thresholds and segment the crack-block regions of the image; likewise, the segmented results contain many crack fragments; therefore, tensor voting based curve detection method is finally applied to fill the gaps between crack fragments and produce the real long crack curves refer Fig. 1 for an overview of the proposed method.

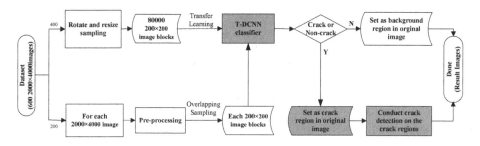

Fig. 1. Flowchart of the proposed method

2.1 Preprocessing

Different from Zhang's dataset [19], our pavement images are captured by single line-scan industry camera. The camera could scan 4 m wide road area into a 4000-pixel wide line, and store a 2000 × 4000-pixel image for every 2000 lines. Due to different lighting conditions, the illuminance along the scanning line could be different which may cause the non-uniform intensity levels in different columns, see Fig. 2 (left). The column-wised illuminance balancing from [11] is performed to eliminate the non-uniform gray levels. The mean value of each column is set to 128.

Fig. 2. Original low-quality pavement image captured by a vehicle running at 100 km/h (left) and the illuminance balanced image (right).

2.2 T-DCNN Pre-selection

To conduct pre-selection, a transfer leaning-based deep convolutional neural network (T-DCNN) is trained to classify the crack and non-crack image blocks. 600 (2000 × 4000-pixel) crack images with low similarity are selected from 30,000 images. Among them, 400 images were used to yield the training set of 40,000 crack and 40,000 non-crack blocks (200 × 200-pixel). The other 200 images were used to yield the test set of 20,000 crack and 20,000 non-crack blocks. In order to make the dataset with more variability, we use both image resize and image rotation to augment the dataset. These two methods can efficiently expand the variability of the dataset because: (1) crack has the property of direction invariance, since a crack changes its direction, it is still a crack; and (2) different cracks may have different widths, and the pavement textures might have different coarse levels; therefore, the resized images (we used 90%, 95%, 100%, 105% and 110% of the original images, respectively) can also be used to generate the image blocks.

For training the network using transfer learning, three issues need to be considered: what knowledge could be transferred; how to transfer the knowledge and when to transfer [17]. The knowledge learned by a multi-layer neural network contains plenty of knowledge from the source task, but not all of them are useful for different tasks. In deep convolutional neural networks, low-level layers learned more generic features, e.g. edges or color blobs, which occur regardless of the exact cost function and image dataset [17, 18]. Those features could be utilized to build different kinds of parts and produce various objects. Middle and high-level knowledges contain more information specified by the source task which have weaker transferability.

In our case, only the basic generic knowledge is transferred from the pre-trained model using ImageNet dataset [22], see Fig. 3. The reasons are: (1) the pattern of crack is relatively simple; therefore, the generic knowledge could be used to extract the crack successfully (the feature maps in Fig. 4 proves this assumption); (2) the pattern of crack has low similarity with the natural objects like dog, cat, etc.; therefore, the middle and high level knowledges are useless and we do not transfer them. The related fine-tuning details are described in experiment section.

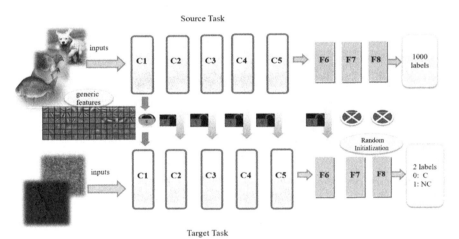

Fig. 3. Transfer the ImageNet generic knowledge. C1, C2, ..., and C5 are convolution layers; F6, F7 and F8 are fully connected layers; the green lock shows that the generic features are transformed directly without change during training; the red unlocked locks are for fine tuning, which means that they transfer the weights and allow them to be relearned during training; and the weights of last two fully connected layers are randomly initialized and trained from scratch. (Color figure online)

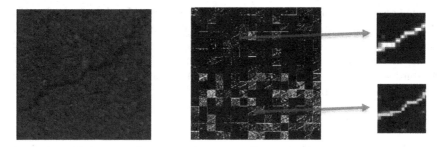

Fig. 4. An image block sample with crack (left) and the related feature maps (right) after convolution layer 5 of the T-DCNN (see Fig. 3 about the network architecture). It is noticed that many of the feature maps show the crack pattern as the original image which supports the assumption that generic knowledge transferred from ImageNet could be used to extract the crack pattern and perform the classification.

Before doing the crack detection, a pavement image is firstly divided into small blocks; then the trained network is used to classify the image blocks as crack/non-crack blocks and divide the image area into crack and non-crack regions at the same time. In order to get more accurate crack regions, the image blocks are sampled every 100 pixels with overlap between sample blocks. Then, most of the non-crack regions are discarded so that the crack detection could be done by only focusing on the crack regions, see Fig. 5.

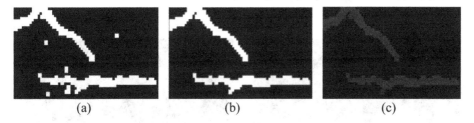

(a)   (b)   (c)

Fig. 5. Crack and non-crack regions classified using T-DCNN pre-selection. (a) Result after the pre-selection: the white regions are those classified as crack regions and the black regions are non-crack regions. (b) Result after removing false positive crack regions in (a) whose size is smaller than 3 times of the block-size. (c) The image only focuses on the crack regions.

2.3 Crack Detection

After T-DCNN pre-selection, the proposed detection method is applied to the crack regions for obtaining the detection results. Since crack pixels are usually darker than non-crack pixels, we segment the crack-block regions using intensity-thresholding method and find the possible crack pixels. A linear model is built by using linear regression to find the best threshold for each crack block. The best threshold is defined as the threshold which maximizes the F_1-measure $\left(\dfrac{2 * precison * recall}{precision + recall} \right)$ [26] of the segmented result against the ground truth of each crack block. In our experiment, the segmented results using thresholds from M − 30 to M + 30 (M is the mean value of the block) are stored and compared with the ground truth to find the best threshold for each crack block (best thresholds of 4,000 different crack blocks are used to build the model). Then the initial model is built with mean (M), standard deviation (SD), smoothness (SM), third momentum (TM) and uniformity (UF) [21] as the predictors; and the best threshold (T) as the response variable:

$$T = \beta_0 + \beta_1 M + \beta_2 SD + \beta_3 SM + \beta_4 TM + \beta_5 UF \qquad (1)$$

Then LASSO [24] is used to find the most significant predictors. In our case, M, SD and TM were selected as the most significant predictors, and the prediction model is:

$$T = 1.21 * M - 1.31 * SD + 6.83 * TM - 2.51 \qquad (2)$$

Focusing on the crack-block regions, we calculate the best threshold using Eq. (2) and apply the thresholding to obtain the thresholded image; after that, the noise removing operation is employed to eliminate small noises; there are many discontinuous crack fragments after the above steps; therefore, the tensor voting-based curve detection [25] is employed to fill the gaps between the crack fragments and produce the elongated crack curves. Note that some small gaps are produced by using the maximum formula from examining the orthogonal along the curve [27]; then a morphology close operation [23] is conducted and the noise fragments smaller than experiment-determined value 40 pixels are removed to generate the final results. Refer Figs. 6 and 7 about the related results.

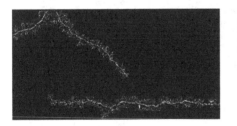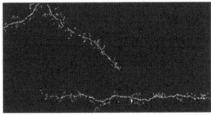

Fig. 6. Thresholded image after T-DCNN pre-selection (left) and the result removing small noises less than 30 pixels (right).

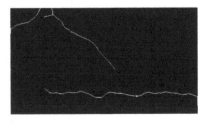

Fig. 7. Tensor voting based curve detection result (left) and noise fragments removed result (right).

3   Experiment

The experiments are performed using an HP Z220 workstation with 8G memory; a Nvidia QuadroK4000 GPU is used for training and testing the deep convolutional neural network. The models are built with software package Caffe [28]; Matlab R2014a is used as the programming tool.

3.1   Dataset and Metrics

The dataset is obtained from the images captured by a line-scan camera. The camera is set at a height of 2.3 m on the top of a vehicle and could scan 2 m × 4 m road area to generate an image of 2000 × 4000-pixel, i.e., a road area of 1 mm^2 corresponds to 1 pixel. Furthermore, the capturing vehicle is able to run at 100 km/h without frame loss which is hard to achieve by using cellphone camera. The speed also makes it usable for actual engineering application to capture huge amount of images of highways. To process this kind of images is more challenging due to low resolution and high noise.

Pre-selection performances (Table 1) of four different methods were evaluated based on recall, accuracy and the converge time for different convolutional neural network models are also present using number of iterations/epochs. We also compared the proposed method with the current state-of-the-art method in [5]; the performances are evaluated using recall, precision and F_1-measure $\left(\dfrac{2 * precison * recall}{precision + recall} \right)$. The precision and recall can be computed on true positive (TP), false negative (FN) and false positive (FP) by the following way:

$$\text{Precision} = \frac{\text{True positives}}{\text{True positives} + \text{False positives}} \tag{3}$$

$$\text{Recall} = \frac{\text{True positives}}{\text{True positives} + \text{False negatives}} \tag{4}$$

Table 1. Pre-selection performances of different methods on test set.

Method	Recall	Accuracy	# of iterations before convergence
Network in [19]	0.933	0.513	Not converge
Hog + SVM	0.920	0.683	N/A
Network in [22] without fine-tuning	0.921	0.886	6100
Fine-tune the network in [22]	**0.997**	**0.943**	**400**

3.2   Fine-Tuning ImageNet-Based Model

The architecture of the network in Fig. 3 is adopted from [22], which is pre-trained with Caffe [28] using ImageNet dataset. The fine-tuning strategies are as follows: the generic knowledge from first convolution layer are transferred directly without any change during training; base learning rate is changed from 0.01 to 0.001; the test iteration is set as 100, which means that for each time the network calculates the average accuracy of 100 iterations; min-batch for each iteration is set as 200; learning policy is for every "step size" (100 is used) iterations, the learning rate decreases to:

$$base\_lr * gamma^{floor\left(\frac{iter}{step}\right)} \tag{5}$$

where $base\_lr$ is the base learning rate, $gamma$ is the decreasing factor (set as 0.2), $iter$ is the current iteration time and $step$ is the step size; "weight decay" used to update the back-propagate gradient is set as 0.005; all the weights of the convolution layers are copied from the source pre-trained network; weights of the last 2 fully-connected layers are set randomly; the number of outputs from the last layer is set to 2 which stands for the crack and non-crack categories; and the max iteration is set to 40000.

Considering the efficiency and accuracy, 200 × 200-pixel image blocks are used as the training and test sets. During training, a test operation was performed every 100 iterations; finally, we obtained a 0.943 pre-selection accuracy after 40000 iterations on the test set; however, we found that the network had already reached the best performance after 400 iterations and changed little from 400 to 40000 iterations.

3.3 Experimental Results

The 6-layer network in [19] is trained using our dataset. The classification accuracy stayed on low level without change after 200 iterations (see Table 1); the recall is 0.933 and the accuracy is very low (0.513) which means most non-crack blocks are classified as crack blocks wrongly. The method using Hog (histogram of oriented gradients) with cell sizes of 32 × 32-pixel and 16 × 16-pixel as feature extractor and SVM (support vector machine) with Gaussian kernel as the classifier is also tested; the recall is 0.920, but the accuracy is 0.683 because the non-crack blocks with complicated textures cannot be discriminated from the crack blocks by only using statistical features. In addition, we also did the pre-selection operation by training the network in [22] without fine-tuning; 0.921 recall and 0.886 accuracy were achieved; however, it used 6100 iterations to converge to the results which cost a lot of time than using transfer learning (converged to 0.997 recall and 0.943 accuracy after only 400 iterations). The results demonstrate that the transfer leaning-based method using the deep convolutional neural network in [22] is easy-to-train and has good generality; furthermore; and transferring the generic features to classify the crack patterns is effective.

For evaluation of the detection performance, ground truths of the 200 test images are manually marked. Due to the manually marked difference, the detected pixels located in no more than 6 pixels away from manually marked ground truth are considered as true positives. We compared the detection performance with state-of-the-art approach CrackForest in [5]; as shown in Table 2, CrackForest achieved quite low precision (0.506) and F_1-measure (0.620) because many noises cannot be removed effectively, especially it fails to cope with the noises connected to the true crack regions; benefit from the T-DCNN pre-selection, the proposed approach achieved very good performance (see Table 2). Please refer the related results in Fig. 8.

Table 2. Crack detection evaluation.

Method	Recall	Precision	F_1-measure
CrackForest	0.801	0.506	0.620
Proposed	**0.947**	**0.846**	**0.894**

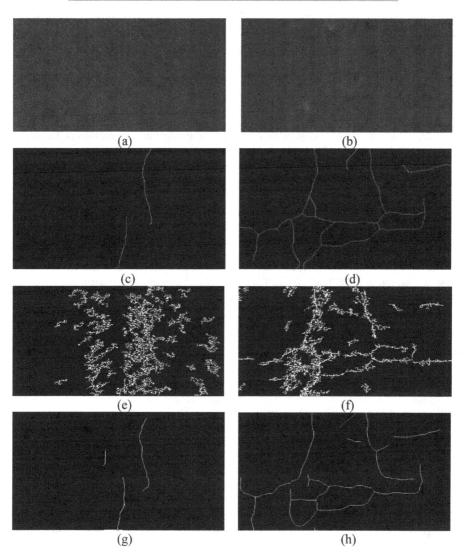

Fig. 8. Comparison of different methods on the challenging images. (a) and (b) are original images; (c) and (d) are the manually marked ground truths; (e) and (f) are the detection results of CrackForest; (g) and (h) are the results of proposed method.

4 Conclusion

In this paper, we proposed a novel fully automatic crack detection approach by incorporating a transfer learning-based pre-selection which significantly reduced the number of false positives from the noisy non-crack image regions; an efficient thresholding method based on linear regression is also developed to quickly segment the crack-block regions and find the possible crack pixels; moreover, tensor voting based curve detection method is employed to link the non-continuous crack fragments and extract the crack curves successfully. The proposed method achieves better performance comparing to the current state-of-the-art approach "CrackForest". In the future, we will design an intelligent detection system which can detect more kinds of complex distresses under different road conditions.

References

1. C.I.A.: The world fact book. https://www.cia.gov/library/publications/resources/the-world-factbook/. Accessed 15 March 2017
2. Zhang, K., Cheng, H.D., Zhang, B.: Unified approach to pavement crack and sealed crack detection using pre-classification based on transfer learning. J. Comput. Civil Eng. (2017). https://doi.org/10.1061/(ASCE)CP.1943-5487.0000736
3. Koutsopoulos, H.N., Sanhouri, I.E., Downey, A.B.: Analysis of segmentation algorithms for pavement distress images. J. Transp. Eng. 119(6), 868–888 (1993)
4. Tsai, Y.C., Kaul, V., Mersereau, R.M.: Critical assessment of pavement distress segmentation methods. J. transportation Eng. 136(1), 11–19 (2010)
5. Shi, Y., Cui, L., Qi, Z., Meng, F., Chen, Z.: Automatic road crack detection using random structured forest. IEEE Trans. Intell. Transp. Syst. 17(12), 3434–3445 (2016)
6. Dollar, P., Zitnick, C.L.: Structured forest for fast edge detection. In: Proceedings of the IEEE ICCV, Sydney, pp. 1841–1848 (2013)
7. Cheng, H.D., Chen, J., Glazier, C., Hu, Y.G.: Novel approach to pavement crack detection based on fuzzy set theory. J. Comput. Civil Eng. 13(4), 270–280 (1999)
8. Cheng, H.D., Wang, J., Hu, Y., Glazier, C., Shi, X., Chen, X.: Novel approach to pavement cracking detection based on neural network. J. Transp. Res. Board 1764(13), 119–127 (2001)
9. Zou, Q., Cao, Y., Li, Q., Mao, Q., Wang, S.: CrackTree: automatic crack detection from pavement images. Pattern Recogn. Lett. 33(2012), 227–238 (2012)
10. Wang, K., Li, Q., Gong, W.: Wavelet-based pavement distress image edge detection with a trous algorithm. J. Transp. Res. Rec. 2024, 24–32 (2000)
11. Zalama, E., Gomez-Garcia-Bermejo, J., Medina, R., Llamas, J.: Road crack detection using visual features extracted by Gabor filters. Comput. Aided Civil Infrastruct. Eng. 29(5), 342–358 (2014)
12. Oliveira, H., Correia, P.L.: Automatic road crack detection and characterization. IEEE Trans. Intell. Transp. Syst. 14(1), 155–168 (2013)
13. Song, H.X., Wang, W.X., Wang, F.P., Wu, L.C., Wang, Z.W.: Pavement crack detection by ridge detection on fractional calculus and dual-thresholds. Int. J. Multimedia Ubiquit. Eng. 10(4), 19–30 (2015)
14. LeCun, Y., Bengio, Y., Hinton, G.: Deep learning. Nature 512(28), 436–444 (2015)
15. Dalal, N., Triggs, B.: Histograms of oriented gradients for human detection. In: Proceedings of the IEEE Conference on Computer Vision and Pattern Recognition, San Diego (2005)

16. Zhou, R., Kaneko, S., Tanaka, F.: Early detection and continuous quantization of plant disease using template matching and support vector machine algorithms. In: Proceedings of the IEEE Symposium on Computing and Networking, Japan, pp. 300–304 (2013)
17. Pan, S.J., Yang, Q.: A survey on transfer learning. IEEE Trans. Knowl. Data Eng. **22**(10), 1345–1359 (2010)
18. Oquab, M., Bottou, L., Laptev, I., Sivic, J.: Learning and transferring mid-level image representations. In: Proceedings of the IEEE Conference on Computer Vision and Pattern Recognition, Columbus, pp. 1717–1724 (2014)
19. Zhang, L., Yang, F., Zhang, Y.D., Zhu, Y.J.: Road crack detection using deep convolutional neural network. In: Proceedings of the IEEE Conference on Image Processing, Phoenix, pp. 3708–3712 (2016)
20. Hariharan, B., Arbeláez, P., Girshick, R., Malik, J.: Simultaneous detection and segmentation. In: Fleet, D., Pajdla, T., Schiele, B., Tuytelaars, T. (eds.) ECCV 2014. LNCS, vol. 8695, pp. 297–312. Springer, Heidelberg (2014). https://doi.org/10.1007/978-3-319-10584-0_20
21. Pinheiro, P.H., Collobert, R.: Recurrent convolutional neural networks for scene labeling. In: Proceeding of International Conference on Machine Learning, Beijing, pp. 82–89 (2014)
22. Krizhevsky, A., Sutskever, I., Hinton, G.E.: ImageNet classification with deep convolutional neural network. In: Proceeding of Neural Information Processing Systems, Nevada (2012)
23. Gonzalez, R.C., Woods, R.E., Steven, S.L.: Digital Image Processing Using Matlab. Addison-Wesley, Boston (2009)
24. Sheather, S.J.: A Modern Approach to Regression with R. Springer, Heidelberg (2009). https://doi.org/10.1007/978-0-387-09608-7
25. Medioni, G., Tang, C.: Tensor voting: theory and applications. In: Proceedings of the 12th Congress Francophone AFRIF-AFIA de Reconnaissance des Formes et Intelligence Artificielle (2000)
26. Power, D.: Evaluation: from precision, recall and F-measure to ROC, informedness, markedness and correlation. J. Mach. Learn. Technol. **2**(1), 37–63 (2011)
27. Linton, T.: Tensor voting. https://www.mathworkcia.gov/library/publications/resources
28. Jia, Y.: Caffe: an open source convolutional architecture for fast feature embedding (2013). http://caffe.berkeleyvision.org/

Learning Local Instance Constraint
for Multi-label Classification

Shang Luo[1,2], Xiaofeng Wu[1,2], Bin Wang[1,2(✉)], and Liming Zhang[1,2]

[1] Key Laboratory for Information Science of Electromagnetic Waves,
Fudan University, Shanghai, China
{sluo15,xiaofengwu,wangbin,lmzhang}@fudan.edu.cn
[2] Research Center of Smart Networks and Systems, School of Information
Science and Technology, Fudan University, Shanghai, China

Abstract. Compared to single-label image classification, multi-label image classification outputs unknown-number objects of different categories for an input image. For image-label relevance in multi-label classification, how to incorporate local information of objects with global information of label representation is still a challenging problem. In this paper, we propose an end-to-end Convolutional Neural Network (CNN) based method to address this problem. First, we leverage CNN to extract hierarchical features of input images and the dilated convolution operator is adopted to expand receptive fields without additional parameters compared to common convolution operator. Then, one loss function is used to model local information of instance activations in convolutional feature maps and the other to model global information of label representation. Finally, the CNN is trained end-to-end with a multi-task loss. Experimental results show that the proposed proposal-free single-CNN framework with a multi-task loss can achieve the state-of-the-art performance compared with existing methods.

Keywords: CNN · Multi-label classification · Multi-task

1 Introduction

Single-label image classification, which just outputs a dominant label from a predefined label set for an input image, has been studied during the past years. However, real-world images mostly contain multiple objects of different categories, thus multi-label image classification needs to be considered for real-world images and usually it is a more complex and challenging task.

In recent years, Convolutional Neural Network (CNN) [1] has achieved great success in single-label image classification [2–4]. Inspired by this, recent state-of-the-art works for multi-label image classification are mainly involved with CNN and these methods can be generally categorized into two types: based on proposals and based on

---

This work was supported in part by the National Natural Science Foundation of China under Grant 61572133.

Y. Zhao et al. (Eds.): ICIG 2017, Part I, LNCS 10666, pp. 284–294, 2017.
https://doi.org/10.1007/978-3-319-71607-7_25

multi-network. The first type of methods [5–7] has a multi-stage pipeline in training phase that first generate object proposals for an input image, and then makes predictions from features extracted by a CNN for each proposal. Although proposal based methods can produce high quality proposals, most of these proposals are redundant and thus proposal selection is required to reduce computation. The second type of methods [7, 8] trains a fusion model of multiple CNNs or CNN combining with Recurrent Neural Network (RNN). These multi-network models usually have more parameters to tune and in practice are harder to converge. Moreover, combination of local information of objects and global information of label representation is not considered in these methods.

To address the problems above, in this paper we propose a proposal-free single-CNN based multi-label classification framework with a multi-task loss. Firstly, a CNN is used to extract hierarchical features for an input image. By directly taking an image as input instead of multiple region proposals, the redundant proposal extraction process is avoided. Secondly, the dilated convolution operation is adopted to expand receptive fields without additional parameters compared to common convolutional operation, which will benefit further global information representation. Thirdly, inspired by [9], with stronger activations in convolutional feature maps of higher layers generally corresponding to positions of object instances in the image, bounding box annotation (ground-truth rectangle tightly enclosed an object) of each instance can be considered as local constraint information with strong label. To leverage this insight into multi-label classification, the CNN model is trained with a multi-task loss composed of two loss functions: one is to model local information of instance activations in convolutional feature maps and the other model global information of label representation.

The main contributions of our work can be briefly summarized as follows:

- An end-to-end proposal-free method with single-CNN framework for multi-label image classification is proposed.
- The dilated convolution operation is adopted to expand receptive fields for aggregating multi-scale contexture information without additional parameters.
- A multi-task loss is utilized to leverage local information of object instances and global information of label representation to enhance the discriminative capability of CNN.

The rest of this paper is organized as follows. The proposed method is given in Sect. 2, in which the basic structure of CNN, the dilated convolution operator and the multi-task loss are described in details. Section 3 shows experimental results on two widely used datasets and the performance comparisons of the proposed method with the state-of-the-art methods. Finally, concluding remarks are drawn in Sect. 4.

2 Our Method

To address the multi-label image classification problem, we propose an end-to-end proposal-free single-CNN based framework with a multi-task loss. Figure 1 shows that our method comprises three main parts: hierarchical feature learning of CNN (ConvNet in Fig. 1), local instance constraint on convolutional feature maps (loss1 in Fig. 1) and global presentation in label space for classification (loss2 in Fig. 1). Contributing to hierarchical feature learning, the basic structure of CNN and the dilated convolution operation are separately described in Subsects. 2.1 and 2.2, and a multi-task loss composed of two loss functions is elaborated in Subsect 2.3.

2.1 Basic Structure of Convolutional Neural Network

A CNN is generally composed of several convolutional and pooling layers (denoted as C layers and P layers) to extract hierarchical features from the original inputs or receptive fields, subsequently with several fully connected layers (denoted as FC layers) followed for specific tasks, as shown in Fig. 2.

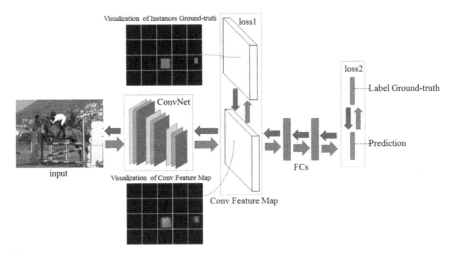

Fig. 1. Framework of the proposed method with a multi-task loss (loss1 represents local instance constraint and loss2 represents global representation in label space). Blue arrows indicate forward computation and red arrows indicate backward computation in CNN. Red rectangles in input represent bounding box annotations. Black dashed lines show description of output in CNN. (Color figure online)

Assumed that a CNN is constructed with L layers and the output of the l - th layer is denoted as $\mathbf{I}^l$, where $l \in \{1, 2, \ldots, L\}$, layer, specifically $\mathbf{I}^0$ denotes the input data. As shown in Fig. 2, the input data is connected locally to a convolutional where a 2-D convolution operation is performed with convolutional kernels $\mathbf{W}_l^c$ and a bias term $\mathbf{b}_l^c$ is added to the resultant feature maps. To model nonlinearities in CNN, an activation function $\partial(\cdot)$ is generally performed following convolutional layers. Then, a pooling operation pool$(\cdot)$ is usually followed to achieve shift-invariance by reducing the resolution of the feature maps. The general C-P block of CNN can be formulated as

$$\mathbf{I}^l = \text{pool}(\partial(\mathbf{I}^{l-1} * \mathbf{W}_l^c + \mathbf{b}_l^c), \tag{1}$$

where $*$ denotes the convolution operation. After some C-P blocks, hierarchical features are further transformed into 1-D feature vector by the FC layers. The FC layers connect all neurons in the previous layer to each singe neuron of the current layer to generate global semantic information. Denoting weight as $\mathbf{W}_l^{fc}$ and bias as $\mathbf{b}_l^{fc}$, an FC layer computation can be formulated as follows:

$$\mathbf{I}^l = \partial(\mathbf{I}^{l-1} \bullet \mathbf{W}_l^{fc} + \mathbf{b}_l^{fc}) \tag{2}$$

The output of the last FC layer is usually fed to an output layer using certain operations for specific tasks, for example, softmax operation is used for multi-class classification. Suppose we have N desired input-output pairs $\{(x^n, y^n); n \in [1, 2, \ldots, N]\}$, where x^n is the n - th input data and y^n is its corresponding target label and t^n is the corresponding output of CNN. Denoting θ as all the parameters of CNN, the loss of CNN can be computed as

$$L = \frac{1}{N} \sum_{n=1}^{N} \ell(\theta; y^n, t^n) \tag{3}$$

Training a CNN can be seen as an optimization of function mapping, i.e., to minimize the loss of CNN, and generally, stochastic gradient descent (SGD) is used to find the best fitting set of parameters.

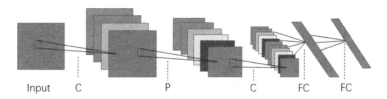

Input   C   P   C   FC   FC

Fig. 2. Common CNN architecture with convolution layers (C), pooling layers (P) and fully connected layers (FC).

2.2   Dilated Convolutional Neural Network

Compared to common convolution operation, the dilated convolution operator is used to gain context information like cross-layer connection in [10]. Unlike the deconvolutional layer [10], with dilation rate [11] in CNN, the dilated convolution operation can apply the same convolutional kernel at different scales without additional memory and loss of information. Combining with proper parameter stride and padding in convolution operation, the dilated convolution operation can be used for multi-scale context information, which is demonstrated to be superior to cross-layer connection [12].

Considering one-dimensional convolution operator with a kernel $\omega[m]$ of length M for a 1-D input signal $x[i]$, the output $y[i]$ is defined as

$$y[i] = \sum_{m=1}^{M} x[i + d \cdot m]\omega[m], \tag{4}$$

where d is the dilation rate for input sampling. Thus common convolution operation can be seen as a special case of dilated convolution with a dilation rate of 1. In practice, as shown in Fig. 3, the dilated convolution operator with kernel size of $k \times k$ and dilation rate of d just inserts $d - 1$ zeros between consecutive filter values, transforming kernel size of k to $k + (k - 1)(d - 1)$ without additional computation and memory.

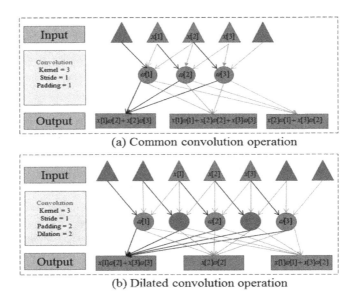

(a) Common convolution operation

(b) Dilated convolution operation

Fig. 3. Illustration of common convolution operation and dilated convolution operation in one dimension. (a) Common convolution (dilation rate of 1). (b) Dilated convolution (dilation rate of 2, insert zero between adjacent filter values).

Due to dilation rate in convolution operation, the effective kernel size increases, but the number of filter parameters remains the same because of insertion of zero values. By aggregating dilated convolution in a chain of layers with proper stride and padding, a CNN can produce feature maps with desired resolution and larger receptive fields, which contains more context information and benefits for semantic representation.

2.3   Multi-task Loss

The proposed single-CNN framework is trained with a multi-task loss composed of two loss functions. The first loss L_{act} involves a $H \times W \times C$ convolutional feature maps, in which each $H \times W$ plane represents an activation map of the category. The second loss L_{cls} involves a discrete probability over C categories.

Each input image is labeled with a multi-label ground-truth and instances ground-truth. A multi-task loss L is used to jointly train for multi-label classification:

$$L = L_{act} + \lambda L_{cls}, \tag{5}$$

where the hyper-parameter λ controls the balance between the two task losses.

Local Instance Constraint. As discovered in [9], CNN can learn hierarchical features due to its deep architecture, and higher complex features are sensitive to local structures in the input images. Following these works, we propose a loss function that considers precise instance location and activation values in convolutional feature maps, allowing the network to capture local structures of each individual object instance.

Based on [12], the dilated convolution operator described in Sect. 2.2 is employed to expand receptive fields, and after the last convolution operation, a 1×1 convolutional layer with the same number of filters as the number of categories is adopted. In this way, as shown in Fig. 1, each plane of convolutional feature maps stands for one specific category, thus higher activations in specific feature map indicate higher existing probability of the category. For local instance constraint, a Euclidean distance based loss function is adopted for penalizing the position with no object and constraining the activation values where there are objects corresponding to the category. Thus, for N training samples, the loss function L_{act} is Euclidean distance between convolutional feature map $f^{c,i}$ and sum of instance bounding box masks $\sum_{t=1}^{T(c,i)} b_t^{c,i}$ over C categories, which can be expressed as:

$$L_{act} = \sum_{i=1}^{N} \sum_{c=1}^{C} \left\| f^{c,i} - \sum_{t=1}^{T(c,i)} b_t^{c,i} \right\|, \tag{6}$$

where $b_t^{c,i} \in \{0, 1\}$ (1 indicates the position with instances and 0 indicates the position without instance) is the t - th instance bounding box mask for category c and $T(c, i)$ is the number of instances in the category c in the i - th image. There may exist overlapped instances in each individual category and we encoded its overlapped regions of instances by summing all of the individual binary masks to make the loss function L_{cls} surely aware of the higher activation values of objects.

Global Label Representation. For global representation, previous works mainly choose Euclidean distance [6, 7] or cross-entropy [8] for distance metric, but no work discusses pros and cons of the two metric learning for multi-label image classification. For each input image with a ground-truth class label **u** and predicted class label **v**, by adopting Euclidean distance the loss function L_{cls} can be defined as:

$$L_{cls} = \frac{1}{N} \sum_{i=1}^{N} \sqrt{\sum_{c=1}^{C} (u^{c,i} - v^{c,i})^2}, \tag{7}$$

and by adopting cross-entropy the loss function L_{cls} can be defined as:

$$L_{cls} = -\frac{1}{N} \sum_{i=1}^{N} \sum_{c=1}^{C} (u^{c,i} \log v^{c,i}), \tag{8}$$

where $u^{c,i}$ is the ground-truth label indicator for category c for i - th image and $v^{c,i}$ corresponds to its prediction. The two losses will be compared in Subsect 3.3.

3   Experimental Results

3.1   Datasets and Baseline

Our method is evaluated on the VOC datasets [13], which is widely used as benchmark datasets for multi-label object recognition task. Following [5–8], VOC 2007 and VOC 2012 are chosen as our experimental datasets, which has been split into 3 parts: TRAIN, VAL and TEST. Like [6–8], we take TRAIN and VAL as our training datasets and TEST for model evaluation. Details of these datasets are shown in Table 1, in which the 20 classes are *airplane (aero), bike, bird, boat, bottle, bus, car, cat, chair, cow, table, dog, horse, motorbike (motor), person, plant, sheep, sofa, train and television (tv)*. The evaluation metric is average precision (AP) and mean average precision (mAP). In particular, for VOC 2007 TEST, the scores are evaluated with standard VOC evaluation package and for VOC 2012 TEST, the scores are evaluated on VOC evaluation server.

Table 1. Datasets information.

Dataset	#TRAINVAL	#TEST	#Classes
VOC 2007	5011	4952	20
VOC 2012	11540	10991	20

We compare the proposed method with several state-of-the-art approaches [6–8, 15–17, 19] in terms of metric mAP and the results are shown in Sect. 3.3.

3.2   Parameters Configuration

Our CNN architecture is based on VGG16 [3], which is pre-trained on ImageNet. Following DeepLab [12], layer fc6 and fc7 are converted into convolutional layers and the dilated convolution operator is employed in layers conv5_1, conv5_2, conv5_3, and fc6. More details of CNN architecture can be seen in Table 2. We fine-tune the VGG model from [12] using SGD with initial learning rate 10^{-5}, 0.9 momentum,

0.0005 weight decay through caffe deep learning framework [14]. The hyper-parameter in λ Eq. 5 is set to 1 in all experiments.

3.3 Multi-label Classification Results

Multi-label Image Classification on VOC 2007. Table 3 reports our experimental results compared with the state-of-the-arts on VOC 2007. In the upper part of Table 3 above the double strike, we compared with those methods without using bounding box annotations for training, while the lower part shows the methods with bounding box information. For the state-of-the-art methods, INRIA [15] and FV [16] are hand-crafted based methods, and CNN-SVM [17] uses OverFeat [18] as a feature extractor, and the rest are CNN-based methods mainly fine-tuning pre-trained models on ImageNet.

Table 2. CNN architecture of the proposed method.

No.	Convolution					Pooling
	Kernel	Stride	Padding	Dilation	#Filter	
1	3	1	1	1	64	No
2	3	1	1	1	64	Yes
3	3	1	1	1	128	No
4	3	1	1	1	128	Yes
5	3	1	1	1	256	No
6	3	1	1	1	256	Yes
7	3	1	1	1	512	No
8	3	1	1	1	512	No
9	3	1	1	1	512	Yes
10	3	1	2	2	512	No
11	3	1	2	2	512	No
12	3	1	2	2	512	Yes
13	4	1	4	6	4096	No
14	1	1	1	1	4096	No
15	1	1	1	1	20	No

Table 3. Average precision (AP in %) comparison for the state-of-the-art methods on VOC 2007 TEST. The upper part shows the results of methods without using ground-truth annotations and the lower part shows methods with bounding box information.

	aero	bike	bird	boat	bottle	bus	car	cat	chair	cow	table	dog	horse	motor	person	plant	sheep	sofa	train	tv	mAP
INRIA[15]	77.2	69.3	56.2	66.5	45.5	68.1	83.4	53.6	58.3	51.1	62.2	45.2	78.4	69.7	86.1	52.4	54.4	54.3	75.8	62.1	63.5
FV[16]	75.7	64.8	52.8	70.6	30.0	64.1	77.5	55.5	55.6	41.8	56.3	41.7	76.3	64.4	82.7	28.3	39.7	56.6	79.7	51.5	58.3
CNN-SVM[17]	88.5	81.0	83.5	82.0	42.0	72.5	85.3	81.6	59.9	58.5	66.5	77.8	81.8	78.8	90.2	54.8	71.1	62.6	87.4	71.8	73.9
I-FT[6]	91.4	84.7	87.5	81.8	40.2	73.0	86.4	84.8	51.8	63.9	67.9	82.7	84.0	76.9	90.4	51.5	79.9	54.1	89.5	65.8	74.4
HCP-1000C[6]	95.1	**90.1**	92.8	89.9	51.5	80.0	**91.7**	91.6	57.7	77.8	70.9	89.3	89.3	85.2	93.0	64.0	85.7	62.7	94.4	78.3	81.5
CNN-RNN[8]	**96.7**	83.1	**94.2**	**92.8**	61.2	82.1	89.1	**94.2**	64.2	**83.6**	70.0	**92.4**	**91.7**	84.2	**93.7**	59.8	**93.2**	75.3	**99.7**	**78.6**	84.0
PRE-1000C[19]	88.5	81.5	87.9	82.0	47.5	75.5	90.1	87.2	61.6	75.7	67.3	85.5	83.5	80.0	95.6	60.8	76.8	58.0	90.4	77.9	77.7
d-CNN	90.2	85.5	88.5	87.5	53.7	80.7	85.0	85.4	60.3	73.0	78.0	82.9	84.8	81.9	88.6	65.4	82.9	73.8	90.1	76.7	79.7
CNN-L-GE	91.1	86.0	89.1	87.0	55.3	83.4	88.6	88.4	67.5	77.8	80.0	86.2	86.8	85.1	92.0	65.4	83.2	78.1	92.5	77.9	82.1
CNN-L-GC	91.7	87.9	89.8	88.6	**61.3**	**84.0**	90.1	88.4	**71.3**	83.3	**82.4**	89.2	89.6	**86.9**	93.4	**71.0**	85.8	**79.6**	93.8	**78.6**	84.3

From Table 3 it can be seen that the CNN-based methods outperform the hand-crafted methods with a large margin of more than 10%, which indicates that hierarchical features of CNN greatly benefits for image representation. PRE-1000C [19] fine-tunes pre-trained models on ImageNet with limited VOC data. Compared with PRE-1000C, 2% improvement can be achieved by our d-CNN (CNN with dilated convolution operation) which takes advantage of dilated convolution operator to learn more semantic information. HCP-1000C [6] is a proposal-based method that relies on proposal extraction method to prepare input patches. Compared with HCP-1000C, both our CNN-L-GE (CNN with local instance constraint and global representation of Euclidean distance) and CNN-L-GC (CNN with local instance constraint and global representation of cross-entropy metric) get higher mAP, which shows a positive effect on multi-task learning because the two tasks, separately involving with local and global information, influence each other through shared parameters. In terms of loss function measuring global representation, cross-entropy achieves a further 2.2% performance than that of Euclidean distance, which verifies the discovery that Euclidean distance is not suitable for distance metric of sparse data in high dimension [20]. Compared with the state-of-the-art method CNN-RNN that uses CNN and RNN to model label dependency and image-label representation, our CNN-L-GC with only one network achieves competitive performance, which demonstrates the effectiveness of the multi-task learning both the local and global information. In particular, the proposed method outperforms the state-of-the-art methods with a large margin when the objects are nearly squared (i.e., *bus*, *chair*, *table*, *motor*, *plant*, and *sofa*), mainly due to local instance constraint from bounding box annotations.

Multi-label Image Classification on VOC 2012. Table 4 reports our experimental results compared with the state-of-the-art methods on VOC 2012. Similar to Table 3, we compare with methods without using bounding box annotations in the upper part and methods with bounding box information in the lower part.

Table 4. Average precision (AP in %) comparison for the state-of-the-art methods on VOC 2012 TEST. The upper part shows the results of methods without using ground-truth annotations and the lower part shows methods with bounding box information.

	aero	bike	bird	boat	bottle	bus	car	cat	chair	cow	table	dog	horse	motor	person	plant	sheep	sofa	train	tv	mAP
I-FT[6]	94.6	74.3	87.8	80.2	50.1	82.0	73.7	90.1	60.6	69.9	62.7	86.9	78.7	81.4	90.5	45.9	77.5	49.3	88.5	69.2	74.7
HCP-1000C[6]	**97.7**	83.0	**93.2**	87.2	59.6	88.2	81.9	94.7	66.9	81.6	68.0	93.0	88.2	87.7	92.7	59.0	85.1	55.4	93.0	77.2	81.7
HCP-2000C[6]	97.5	84.3	93.0	89.4	62.5	90.2	84.6	**94.8**	69.7	**90.2**	74.1	**93.4**	**93.7**	88.8	93.3	59.7	**90.3**	61.8	94.4	78.0	84.2
PRE-1000C[19]	93.5	78.4	87.7	80.9	57.3	85.0	81.6	89.4	66.9	73.8	62.0	89.5	83.2	87.6	95.8	61.4	79.0	54.3	88.0	78.3	78.7
PRE-1512C[19]	94.6	82.9	88.2	84.1	60.3	89.0	84.4	90.7	72.1	86.8	69.0	92.1	93.4	88.6	**96.1**	64.3	86.6	62.3	91.1	79.8	82.8
FeV[7]	96.8	**87.8**	88.7	87.2	**63.8**	**92.3**	86.2	92.3	72.4	82.0	76.0	91.9	90.3	90.3	95.2	61.2	82.6	65.6	92.8	**84.4**	84.0
CNN-L-GE	91.1	86.0	89.1	87.0	55.3	83.4	**88.6**	88.4	67.5	77.8	**80.0**	86.2	86.8	85.1	92.0	**65.4**	83.2	**78.1**	92.5	77.9	82.1
CNN-L-GC	**97.7**	85.2	91.1	**90.0**	62.7	91.7	86.1	94.4	**75.8**	84.5	79.7	92.8	92.4	**91.9**	**96.1**	64.9	85.7	77.2	**95.4**	82.6	**85.9**

The multi-label classification results on VOC 2012 in terms of mAP are consistent with those in Table 3. Compared with HCP-2000C [6] pre-trained on ImageNet with 2000 categories and PRE-1512C [19] pre-trained on ImageNet with 1512 categories, our CNN-L-GC pre-trained on ImageNet with only 1000 categories outperforms the two state-of-the-art methods by 1.7% and 3.1%. Compared with the state-of-the-art proposal-based FeV [7] with two-stream CNN, our CNN-L-GC has an improvement of 1.9%. Similar to results on VOC 2007, the proposed method takes advantage of squared objects because of local instance constraint with bounding box annotations.

4   Conclusions

In this paper, we presented an end-to-end proposal-free single-CNN based method multi-label image classification framework with a multi-task loss. Without region proposals extraction, the training phase of our work is a single-stage pipeline. Compared with the existing works, our method adopted the dilated convolution operation to expand receptive fields without additional parameters. Further, the proposed method utilized instance constraint for local information and cross-entropy metric for global information representation at the same time to leverage a multi-task learning for boosting the discriminative capacity of CNN. The experimental results on VOC 2007 and VOC 2012 showed that the proposed method achieved the state-of-the-art performance.

References

1. LeCun, Y.: Gradient based learning applied to document recognition. Proc. IEEE **86**(11), 2278–2323 (1998)
2. Krizhevsky, A.: ImageNet classification with deep convolutional neural networks. In: Advances in Neural Information Processing Systems, pp. 1097–1105. Nips Foundation, San Diego (2012)
3. Simonyan, K.: Very deep convolutional networks for large-scale image recognition. International Conference on Learning Representations, pp. 1–14 (2015)
4. He, K.: Deep residual learning for image recognition. In: IEEE Conference on Computer Vision and Pattern Recognition, pp. 770–778. IEEE, New Jersey (2016)
5. Girshick, R.: Rich feature hierarchies for accurate object detection and semantic segmentation. In: IEEE Conference on Computer Vision and Pattern Recognition, pp. 580–587. IEEE, New Jersey (2014)
6. Wei, Y., et al.: CNN: single-label to multi-label. arXiv preprint (2014). arXiv:1406.5726
7. Yang, H.: Exploit bounding box annotations for multi-label object recognition. In: IEEE Conference on Computer Vision and Pattern Recognition, pp. 280–288. IEEE, New Jersey (2016)
8. Wang Jiang, F: CNN-RNN: A unified framework for multi-label image classification. In: IEEE Conference on Computer Vision and Pattern Recognition, pp. 2285–2294. IEEE, New Jersey (2016)
9. Zeiler, M.D., Fergus, R.: Visualizing and understanding convolutional networks. In: Fleet, D., Pajdla, T., Schiele, B., Tuytelaars, T. (eds.) ECCV 2014. LNCS, vol. 8689, pp. 818–833. Springer, Cham (2014). https://doi.org/10.1007/978-3-319-10590-1_53
10. Long, J.: Fully convolutional networks for semantic segmentation. In: IEEE Conference on Computer Vision and Pattern Recognition, pp. 3431–3440. IEEE, New Jersey (2015)
11. Yu, F.: Multi-scale context aggregation by dilated convolutions. International Conference on Learning Representation, pp. 1–13 (2016)

12. Chen, L.C., et al.: Deeplab: semantic image segmentation with deep convolutional nets, atrous convolution, and fully connected CRFS (2014). arXiv preprint arXiv:1412.7062
13. Everingham, M.: The pascal visual object classes (voc) challenge. Int. J. Comput. Vis. **88**(2), 303–338 (2010)
14. Jia, Y.: Caffe: convolutional architecture for fast feature embedding. In: ACM international conference on Multimedia, pp. 675–678. ACM, New York (2014)
15. Harzallah, H.: Combining efficient object localization and image classification. In: International Conference on Computer Vision, pp. 237–244. IEEE, New Jersey (2009)
16. Perronnin, F., Sánchez, J., Mensink, T.: Improving the fisher kernel for large-scale image classification. In: Daniilidis, K., Maragos, P., Paragios, N. (eds.) ECCV 2010. LNCS, vol. 6314, pp. 143–156. Springer, Heidelberg (2010). https://doi.org/10.1007/978-3-642-15561-1_11
17. Sharif Razavian A.: CNN features off-the-shelf: an astounding baseline for recognition. In: IEEE Conference on Computer Vision and Pattern Recognition, pp. 806–813. IEEE, New Jersey (2014)
18. Sermanet, P.: Overfeat: integrated recognition, localization and detection using convolutional networks. In: International Conference on Learning Representations, pp. 1–16 (2014)
19. Oquab, M.: Learning and transferring mid-level image representations using convolutional neural networks. In: IEEE Conference on Computer Vision and Pattern Recognition, pp. 1717–1724. IEEE, New Jersey (2014)
20. Aggarwal, C.C., Hinneburg, A., Keim, D.A.: On the surprising behavior of distance metrics in high dimensional space. In: Van den Bussche, J., Vianu, V. (eds.) ICDT 2001. LNCS, vol. 1973, pp. 420–434. Springer, Heidelberg (2001). https://doi.org/10.1007/3-540-44503-X_27

Disparity Refinement Using Merged Super-Pixels for Stereo Matching

Jianyu Heng, Zhenyu Xu, Yunan Zheng, and Yiguang Liu[(✉)]

Vision and Image Processing Lab (VIPL), College of Computer Science,
SiChuan University, Chengdu 610065, People's Republic of China
liuyg@scu.edu.cn, lygpapers@aliyun.com

Abstract. The traditional disparity refinement methods cannot get highly accurate disparity estimations, especially pixels around depth boundaries and within low textured regions. To tackle this problem, two novel stereo refinement strategies are proposed: (1) merging super-pixels into stable region to maintain continuity and accuracy of the same disparity; (2) optimizing the co-operative relations between adjacent regions. Then we can obtain high-quality and high-density disparity maps. The quantitative evaluation on Middlebury benchmark shows that our algorithm can significantly refine the results obtained by local and non-local methods.

Keywords: Stereo matching · Disparity refinement · Super-pixels
Region optimization

1 Introduction

Stereo matching has been one of the key problems in computer vision for years. Recently, most of publications [1–4] have been focused on solving this problem. And the segment-based methods [7–9] have attracted more and more attention due to their good performances for years.

Most segment-based stereo matching algorithms follow the four-step pipeline [5]: First, matching cost computation; Second, cost aggregation; Third, disparity computation/optimization; Fourth, disparity refinement. Traditional disparity refinement methods, involving left-right consistency checking [10], hole filling [11], and median filtering [12, 13], could not provide highly accurate disparity estimation. Yoon et al. [14] adopted adaptive supporting-weight approach for correspondence search to refine the local aggregation results. Yang [15] firstly proposed the non-local aggregation method and refined the non-local results with minimum spanning tree (MST). Based on Yang's method, Mei et al. [16] proposed a segment-tree (ST) structure for non-local cost aggregation, they enhanced the disparity values, with a depth-color segmentation method extended from a classic graph-based segmentation method [17]. The region-based methods [18, 19], presented to further improve the disparity estimation, can get better results especially in low textured regions.

In this paper, we propose a stereo refinement algorithm based on merging super-pixels (MSP). Our algorithm includes the following seven steps: First, estimating the initial disparity values with a local or non-local method and locating the

© Springer International Publishing AG 2017
Y. Zhao et al. (Eds.): ICIG 2017, Part I, LNCS 10666, pp. 295–305, 2017.
https://doi.org/10.1007/978-3-319-71607-7_26

super-pixels with a depth-color segmentation method from stereo images; Second, estimating the robust information of each super-pixel by voting; Third, searching for the supporting neighbors of each super-pixel; Fourth, merging super-pixels into region based on the correlation of adjacent super-pixels; Fifth, updating the information of each region and finding out unreliable regions; Sixth, correcting unreliable region with its supporting region; Seventh, assigning disparity value for each pixel with considering the disparity of the correlative region.

In general, our paper makes these main contributions: (1) we merge super-pixels into stable region, then the disparity of each pixel can be estimated by considering the constraint on smoothness of the correlative region to maintain the continuity of the same disparity. (2) we apply the optimization of the cooperative relations between adjacent regions to reduce the unreliable disparity values and obtain the high-quality depth boundaries.

2   Obtaining Raw Cost Aggregation and Initial Disparities

2.1   Obtaining Cost and Disparity in Pixel Domain

First of all, we employ some local or non-local algorithms to obtain the raw cost aggregation and initial disparity values. These algorithms always poorly use WTA strategy to select disparities from multiple candidates and the disparity estimation obtained by these algorithms is not accurate enough. Later, the accuracy will be improved by our algorithm.

2.2   Over-Segment Based on Color-Depth

Segment-based algorithms usually assume that disparity values vary smoothly in each segment and the depth discontinuities only occur on segment boundaries. But in practice, over-segment based on color-depth is preferred and the assumption is not al-ways met. In this paper, we use efficient graph-based image segmentation [16, 17]. Figure 1 shows the disparity map of the Teddy stereo pair and the segmentation result of the left image produced by the method in [16]. In this paper, we call the over-segmentation super-pixel.

2.3   Cross-Checking Test

At first, a local or non-local cost aggregation method runs the left and the right image as reference images in turn to obtain two corresponding disparity maps. In order to eliminate the outlier in disparity map and obtain robust disparity estimation of each segmentation, the cross-checking test is applied. Then the occlusions and matching errors in the disparity map can be obtained, they are all called unreliable pixels in this paper. After cross-checking, the cost volume is refined according to [15]. Let D denotes the disparity map, a new cost value is computed for each pixel p at each disparity level d as:

$$C_1^n(p) = \begin{cases} |d - D(p)|, & p \ is \ stable \ and \ D(p) > 0 \\ 0, & otherwise \end{cases} \tag{1}$$

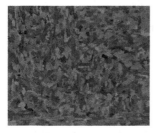 

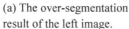

(a) The over-segmentation result of the left image.

(b) The initial disparity map.

Fig. 1. The segmentation result of the left image by using color-depth based over-segmentation method and the disparity map of the Teddy stereo pair by using segment-tree stereo matching algorithm [16]. (Color figure online)

3 Robust Super-Pixels Merging

The super-pixels are sensitive to unreliable pixels and they are correlative rather than individual. If the super-pixel is handled solely, the disparity values around the boundary between adjacent regions, which have the same disparity may be discontinuous. In this paper, an effective approach of merging super-pixels to stable region is proposed to resolve this problem.

3.1 Voting the Information of Super-Pixel

Before merging, the information of super-pixels should be obtained by voting. The information contains RGB values, disparity and the message whether the super-pixel is unreliable or not. The process of voting robust information can be expressed as:

First, the RGB values of super-pixel are estimated by using RGB values of all pixels within the region. And the RGB values of each super-pixel are respectively determined by voting a one-dimensional histogram, where the x-coordinate is the value of one of the three channels, and the y-coordinate is the count number of values. After sorting the histogram and smoothing operation by a Gaussian filter, the value of each individual channel is finally estimated by the maximum of the corresponding histogram;

Second, the disparity of each super-pixel is estimated in a similar way by getting rid of unreliable pixels.

Third, if the number of unreliable pixels in a super-pixel is more than a given per-cent of the number of all pixels within the super-pixel, we regard this super-pixel as an unreliable super-pixel and assign true (denotes the super-pixel is unreliable) for the message of this super-pixel. Let W_{occ} denotes the percent.

3.2 Supporting Neighbors Selection

In order to get rid of piecewise smooth, the super-pixels should be merged to stable region by considering the supporting neighbors of each super-pixel. Let $W_i(S_p)$ denotes the weight of the correlation between the super-pixel S_p and its neighboring super-pixel S_i. Considering the difference of disparity and color between super-pixels S_p and S_i. The ratio α, which denotes the ratio of common border lengths to perimeter, can be written as:

$$\alpha = \frac{N_i}{N_{all}} \qquad (2)$$

where N_i denotes the length of the boundary between super-pixel S_p and S_i. And N_{all} denotes the perimeter of super-pixel N_i. Thus, $W_i(S_p)$ can be written as:

$$W_i(S_p) = \alpha \frac{\left| D_r(S_p) - D_r(S_i) \right| \cdot \sigma_s}{\sigma_c} = (1 - \alpha) \frac{I_r(S_p) - I_r(S_i)}{\sigma_c} \qquad (3)$$

where S_i covers all neighbors of super-pixel S_p. σ_s and σ_c are two variables, which can self-adapt in terms of the disparity range and color range, to normalize I_r and D_r to the range [0, 1]. D_r denotes the disparity of super-pixel and I_r denotes the RGB values of super-pixel.

Here, it is worthy of attention that the proposed approach just depends on the con-textual information of the adjacent super-pixels and no ambiguity or artificial factor exists.

The supporting neighbors are selected by minimizing the set of $W_i(S_p)$, $i = 1, 2 \ldots n$. Due to the several minimum (because of equal) at the same time, the supporting neighbors of super-pixel S_p are consist of all neighboring super-pixels, which can minimize the $W_i(S_p)$.

3.3 Merging Super-Pixels to Stable Region

This step aims to obtain stable region by merging super-pixels and it is divided into the following three cases:

(a) If two neighboring super-pixels are both reliable super-pixel and their disparities are equal, then merge the two super-pixels;

(a) The merged super-pixels   (b) The first iteration disparity
result of the left image.   map.

Fig. 2. The first iteration: merging the super-pixels and then estimating the disparity map based on the merged result.

(b) If the two super-pixels are both unreliable or one is unreliable region, the other is not and one is the supporting neighbor of the other one, then merge the two super-pixels;

(c) The rest conditions will not be merged. If a super-pixel was not merged with any other super-pixel, it should be regarded as a stable region. We merge the super-pixels by using a forest structure. (The forest construction algorithm, which regards super-pixel as pixel, is similar to the ST structure algorithm in [16].)

Figure 2 gives the super-pixels merged result of the left image and the disparity map with first iteration. The experimental results show that the new segmentations are stable and our method performs well in disparity estimation.

4 The Principle of Unreliable Region Optimization

The unreliable pixels have great effects on disparity estimation. In this section, we propose a new method to deal with unreliable pixels by optimizing the unreliable region. As described in Sect. 3, before optimizing, the information and the supporting neighbors of each region must be updated.

The principles of unreliable region optimization are as follows:

(a) Considering each unreliable region's supporting neighbors, if there is a supporting neighbor which is a reliable region, or an unreliable region which has already been optimized, then we regard the supporting neighbor as a supporting region;

(b) If there is no supporting region of unreliable region S_u, we select the neighbor which can minimize $W_i(S_u)$ from all neighbors of S_u to be a supporting region;

(c) If an unreliable region has more than one supporting region, selecting the supporting region with the minimum of disparity. And then we regard the selected supporting region as the final supporting region;

(d) Assigning the final supporting region disparity for the correlative unreliable region disparity. And then set a label, which denotes the unreliable region has been optimized, to this unreliable region. Applying the four steps to all unreliable regions until each of them have been set an optimized label.

5 Depth Hypotheses Generation

In this section, we obtain the accurate disparity map by two steps. First, we adopt the constraint on smoothness to reduce the effect of spurious disparity estimation. Second, the iterative refinement is employed to enhance the accuracy of the disparity map.

5.1 The Constraint on Smoothness of Region

In order to reduce effects on spurious disparity estimation, we consider the smooth-ness of stable region. Usually, the depth discontinuity occurs around the boundaries of regions. Thus, the method, used to solve the smoothness problem, assigns the disparity value for each pixel by selecting the disparity from the correlative stable region disparity, which can minimize the cost aggregation. The optimal disparity value of pixel p within super-pixel S_p can be written as:

$$\varphi_d(p) = \min_{d_i}\left(D^A_{d_i}(p)\right), d_i \in \left[D_r(S_p) - \Delta d, D_r(S_p) + \Delta d\right] \qquad (4)$$

where Δd is a variable which determines the range of stable region disparity. If it is too small, the correct cost value may be excluded and if it is too large, the effects of spurious cost values may not be reduced. Thus we apply an adapting formulation for computing Δd, the formulation can be written as:

$$\Delta d = \frac{R}{\gamma} \qquad (5)$$

where R denotes the disparity range of image and γ is a constant which is set to six in all of our experiments. According to Eq. (4), the disparity value of pixel p is d which minimizes $D^A_{d_i}(p)$.

5.2   Enhancement with Iteration

After estimating the accurate disparity values, we can use iterative refinement to enhance the disparity estimation. As shown in Fig. 3, in the first iteration, disparity value with the best cost value is selected for each pixel, and then the robust typical disparity value can be voted for each stable region. In the next iteration, refining the disparity values by re-computing the steps from 2 to 7 based on the last iteration disparity map. New stable regions are determined and their information is updated. The best disparity values of pixels are selected only among the represent disparity value of the correlative stable regions. The final disparity values can be assigned after two iterations.

(a) The merged super-pixels   (b) The second iteration dis-
result of the left image.   parity map.

Fig. 3. The second iteration: merge super-pixels and then estimate the disparity map based on the merged result.

Figure 3 shows the second iteration segmentation result of the left image. Obviously, the experimental result performs better than the result in the first iteration (Fig. 2). In addition, in order to verify the robustness of the proposed algorithm, Fig. 4 shows the merged results of the rest stereo image pairs in the Middlebury data sets [6].

Fig. 4. The image from top to bottom is the merged super-pixels results of Tsukuba, Venus and Cones.

6   Experimental Results

The local algorithm [14] and the non-local algorithm [16] proved to be the top performer on Middlebury benchmark [6], but the results of this paper demonstrates that quantitative disparity map estimated by these algorithms can be improved by the proposed algorithm·(MSP).

All experiments in this paper strictly follow a local stereo matching pipeline [5]. The specific descriptions are as follows:

(a) Cost computation: The same cost used in the local method [14] and non-local method [16], is adopted in all our experiments. It is a blending of truncated color difference and truncated gradient difference.

(b) Cost aggregation: Two cost aggregation methods are evaluated with various stereo data sets: local aggregation with adaptive supporting-weight (AW) [14], non-local aggregation with enhanced ST (Segment-tree) [16].

(c) Disparity optimization: WTA (Winner-Take-All) operation is adopted in all experiments. This method simply chooses the disparity for each pixel with the minimal aggregated cost.

(d) Disparity refinement: Based on the result of (c), applying the merged super-pixel (MSP) refinement algorithm to enhance the performance. Two parameters require to be set in this method, the parameter k is set to 0.03 and W_{occ} is set to 0.4. The final disparity map can be obtained by only iterating the proposed algorithm twice.

The disparity maps of all four stereo pairs in the Middlebury data sets computed by local method [14] are presented in Fig. 5(a). And the disparity maps obtained by the proposed algorithm, and based on the resulting disparity maps in Fig. 5(a), with different iterations, are presented in Fig. 5(b)–(c). Obviously, Fig. 5(b)–(c) show that their results are more accurate than the result in Fig. 6(a). Thus, it proves that the proposed method (MSP) is available to enhance the performance of local methods. Similarly, the proposed method (MSP) is effective to improve the performance of non-local methods. Visual comparisons in Fig. 5 show that the proposed refinement method performs better within the low textured regions. For instance, the region near the hand of teddy bear (the third row of Fig. 5) is estimated inaccurate with cost computation method (the first step of stereo matching pipeline). Both the local and non-local cost aggregation methods cannot correct these errors, but the proposed method can obtain the accurate disparity values through optimizing the unreliable region with its supporting region. Moreover, the method is more accurate around depth boundaries, such as the boundaries of the newspaper in Venus data set (the second row of Fig. 5). Errors around

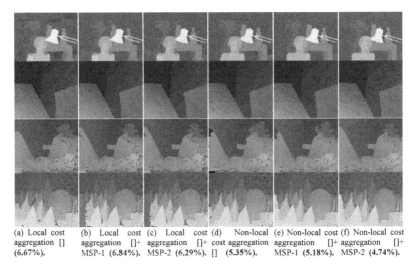

(a) Local cost aggregation [] (6.67%).　(b) Local cost aggregation []+ MSP-1 (6.84%).　(c) Local cost aggregation []+ MSP-2 (6.29%).　(d) Non-local cost aggregation [] (5.35%).　(e) Non-local cost aggregation []+ MSP-1 (5.18%).　(f) Non-local cost aggregation []+ MSP-2 (4.74%).

Fig. 5. Experimental results using the Middlebury data sets [6]: Tsukuba, Venus, Teddy and Cones. (a) is the disparity map obtained by using the local cost aggregation algorithm [14]. (b)–(c) are the refined results of (a) by applying MSP-1 and MSP-2 refinement method proposed in Sect. 2, respectively. (d) is the disparity map obtained by employing the non-local cost aggregation [16]. And (e)–(f) are the refined results of (d) by applying MSP-1 and MSP-2 refinement method, respectively. The bold numbers under the images are the average errors (percentages of bad pixels) which show that the significant improvement of quantitative evaluation with local and non-local stereo matching method by employing the proposed refinement method. The corresponding quantitative evaluation is summarized in Table 1. Visual comparison of the disparity maps using the local or non-local cost aggregation method without MSP or not shows that the proposed refinement method performs better around depth boundaries. For instance, the disparity estimations around the boundaries of the newspaper (the second row) in (b)–(c) or (e)–(f) are more accurate than in (a) or (d). Moreover, note that the proposed refinement can also enhance the performance in low textured regions. For example, the disparity estimations within the low texture region near the hand of teddy bear (the third row) in (b)–(c) or (e)–(f) are more accurate than in (a) or (d).

depth boundaries are mostly due to noises and would cause inconsistency, the method corrects the errors by merging super-pixels to stable region and assign the disparity value for each pixel by considering the constraint on smoothness of stable region. More details are presented in Figs. 6 and 7. According to the comparisons of the disparity estimation within zoom-in regions in Figs. 6 and 7, MSP-2 performs completely better

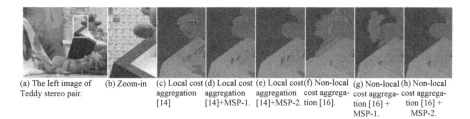

(a) The left image of   (b) Zoom-in   (c) Local cost (d) Local cost (e) Local cost(f) Non-local (g) Non-local (h) Non-local
Teddy stereo pair.   aggregation   aggregation   aggregation   cost aggrega- cost aggrega- cost aggrega-
                                            [14]   [14]+MSP-1.   [14]+MSP-2.   tion [16].   tion [16] +   tion [16] +
                                                                                                       MSP-1.   MSP-2.

Fig. 6. (a) The left image of Teddy stereo pair from Middlebury data sets [6]. (b) The zoom-in region of yellow box. (c) The result of the local cost aggregation [14]. (d) The refined result of (c) by employing MSP once. (e) The refined result of (c) by employing MSP twice. (f) The result of the non-local cost aggregation [16]. (g) The refined result of (f) by employing MSP once. (h) The refined result of (f) by employing MSP twice. Visible comparison of the results in low textured region, (d)–(e) are more accurate than (c) and (g)–(h) are more accurate than (f), shows that the proposed refinement method is significantly available to reduce the efforts of spurious disparity values estimated by local or non-local method. (Color figure online)

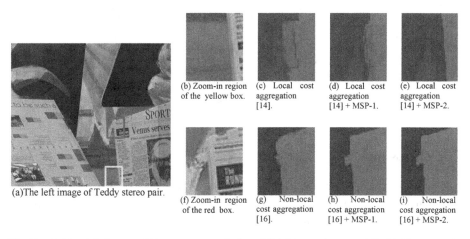

(b) Zoom-in region   (c) Local cost   (d) Local cost   (e) Local cost
of the yellow box.   aggregation   aggregation   aggregation
                     [14].   [14] + MSP-1.   [14] + MSP-2.

(a)The left image of Teddy stereo pair.

(f) Zoom-in region   (g)   Non-local   (h)   Non-local   (i)   Non-local
of the red box.   cost aggregation   cost aggregation   cost aggregation
                     [16].   [16] + MSP-1.   [16] + MSP-2.

Fig. 7. (a) The left image of Venus stereo pair from Middlebury data sets [6]. (b) The zoom-in region of the yellow box. (c) The result of the local cost aggregation [14]. (d) The refined result of (c) by employing MSP once. (e) The refined result of (c) by employing MSP twice. (f) The zoom-in region of the red box. (g) The result of the non-local cost aggregation [16]. (h) The refined result of (g) by employing MSP once. (i) The refined result of (g) by employing MSP twice. Visible comparison of the results around depth boundaries, (d)–(e) are more accurate than (c) and (h)–(i) are more accurate than (g), shows that the proposed refinement method is significant available to improve the accuracy of the results estimated by local or non-local method. (Color figure online)

than local and non-local methods, with more accurate estimation both in low textured regions (shown in Fig. 6) and around depth boundaries (shown in Fig. 7).

The running time of the algorithm is related to the number of iterations. By using a PC with CPU of PM 2.5G, the total time for processing the stereo pair of Tsukuba is about 2 s. Here, the number of iterations is 2, and the time for image segmentation is about 1 s. The comparisons between the proposed refinement method and local method [14] or non-local method [16] are shown in Table 1. The average error of local method is reduced by 0.38% (from 6.67% to 6.29%) through applying the proposed method. And the rank is increased by 18.3 (from 79.5 to 61.2). The average error of non-local method [16] is reduced by 0.61% (from 5.35% to 4.74%) through using the proposed method. And the rank is increased by 13.4 (from 37.7 to 24.3). It is clear to see the significant improvement of quantitative evaluation when we replace local and non-local stereo matching method with our novel refinement method.

Table 1. Quantitative evaluation of six methods (AW [14], AW [14] + MSP-1, AW [14] + MSP-2, ST [16], ST [16] + MSP-1, ST [16] + MSP-2) on the standard middle-bury benchmark [6] with error threshold 1. The percentages of the erroneous pixels in nonocc./all/disc. regions are used to evaluate the performance of the method. The disparity estimation using local [14] or non-local [16] method with MSP-1 is slightly more accurate than only using [14] or [16], while MSP-2 outperforms the other methods with the best overall accuracy.

Algorithm	Avg. rank	Avg. error	Tsukuba			Venus			Teddy			Cones		
			Nonocc	All	Disc	Nonocc	All	Disc	Nonocc	All	Disc	Nonocc	All	Disc
AW [14]	79.5	6.67	**1.38**	1.85	**6.90**	0.71	1.19	6.13	7.88	13.3	18.6	**3.97**	**9.79**	**8.26**
AW [14] + MSP-1	76.9	6.84	1.44	1.69	7.52	0.28	0.54	3.38	7.49	15.0	18.9	4.28	11.4	10.1
AW [14] + MSP-2	**61.2**	**6.29**	1.43	**1.69**	7.49	**0.17**	**0.32**	1.89	**7.30**	**12.6**	**18.4**	4.09	10.5	9.70
ST [16]	37.7	5.35	1.25	1.68	6.69	0.20	0.30	**1.77**	6.00	11.9	15.0	2.77	**8.82**	7.81
ST [16] + MSP-1	32.1	5.18	1.09	1.48	**5.83**	0.15	0.28	1.97	5.75	12.8	14.0	2.57	8.92	7.37
ST [16] + MSP-2	**24.3**	**4.74**	**1.09**	1.48	5.85	**0.15**	**0.27**	1.90	**4.76**	**9.98**	12.9	2.49	8.84	**7.11**

7   Conclusion

This paper proposed a novel refinement algorithm for stereo matching, permits us to obtain the high-quality and high-density disparity map of a scene from its initial disparity estimation. Its novelty is reflected in the following two aspects: Novelty 1, presenting the method of merging super-pixels into stable region. Novelty 2, dealing with unreliable pixels by optimizing the unreliable region.

The advantage of this algorithm lies in that it is able to restrain and correct errors both in low textured regions and around depth boundaries, making us obtain the high-quality and high-density disparity map.

In the near future, we will focus on testing the algorithm with more challenging stereo data sets and various local or non-local cost aggregation methods.

References

1. Zbontar, J., LeCun, Y.: Computing the stereo matching cost with a convolutional neural network. In: Proceedings of the IEEE Conference on Computer Vision and Pattern Recognition, pp. 1592–1599 (2015)
2. Sinha, S.N., Scharstein, D., Szeliski, R.: Efficient high-resolution stereo matching using local plane sweeps. In: Proceedings of the IEEE Conference on Computer Vision and Pattern Recognition, pp. 1582–1589 (2014)
3. Zhang, K., Fang, Y., Min, D., et al.: Cross-scale cost aggregation for stereo matching. In: Proceedings of the IEEE Conference on Computer Vision and Pattern Recognition, pp. 1590–1597 (2014)
4. Shi, C., Wang, G., Yin, X., et al.: High-accuracy stereo matching based on adaptive ground control points. IEEE Trans. Image Process. 24(4), 1412–1423 (2015)
5. Scharstein, D., Szeliski, R.: A taxonomy and evaluation of dense two-frame stereo correspondence algorithms
6. Scharstein, D., Szeliski, R.: Middlebury stereo evaluation
7. Mei, X., Sun, X., Dong, W., et al.: Segment-tree based cost aggregation for stereo matching. In: Proceedings of the IEEE Conference on Computer Vision and Pattern Recognition, pp. 313–320 (2013)
8. Muninder, V., Soumik, U., Krishna, G.: Robust segment-based stereo using cost aggregation. In: Proceedings of International Conference on British Machine Vision Conference (2014)
9. Wang, H.W., Chang, M.W., Lin, H.S., et al.: Segmentation based stereo matching using color grouping. In: ACM SIGGRAPH 2014 Posters, p. 73. ACM (2014)
10. Cochran, S.D., Medioni, G.: 3-D surface description from binocular stereo. TPAMI 14, 981–994 (1992)
11. Birchfield, S., Tomasi, C.: A pixel dissimilarity measure that is insensitive to image sampling. TPAMI 20, 401–406 (1998)
12. Mühlmann, K., Maier, D., Hesser, J., Männer, R.: Calculating dense disparity maps from color stereo images, an efficient implementation. IJCV 47, 79–88 (2002)
13. Rhemann, C., Hosni, A., Bleyer, M., Rother, C., Gelautz, M.: Fast cost-volume filtering for visual correspondence and beyond. In: CVPR (2011)
14. Yoon, K.J., Kweon, I.S.: Adaptive supporting-weight approach for correspondence search. PAMI 28(4), 650–656 (2006)
15. Yang, Q.: A non-local cost aggregation method for stereo matching. In: CVPR, pp. 1402–1409 (2012)
16. Mei, X., Sun, X., Dong, W., et al.: Segment-tree based cost aggregation for stereo matching. In: 2013 IEEE Conference on Computer Vision and Pattern Recognition (CVPR), pp. 313–320. IEEE (2013)
17. Felzenszwalb, P.F., Huttenlocher, D.P.: Efficient graph based image segmentation. IJCV 59(2), 167–181 (2004)
18. Klaus, A., Sormann, M., Karner, K.: Segment-based stereo matching using belief propagation and a self-adapting dissimilarity measure. In: 18th International Conference on Pattern Recognition, ICPR 2006, vol. 3, pp. 15–18. IEEE (2006)
19. Wang, Z.F., Zheng, Z.G.: A region based stereo matching algorithm using cooperative optimization. In: IEEE Conference on Computer Vision and Pattern Recognition, CVPR 2008, pp. 1–8. IEEE (2008)
20. Felzenszwalb, P.F., Huttenlocher, D.P.: Efficient graph based image segmentation. IJCV 59(2), 167–181 (2004)

Deep Scale Feature for Visual Tracking

Wenyi Tang, Bin Liu[✉], and Nenghai Yu

CAS Key Laboratory of Electromagnetic Space Information,
University of Science and Technology of China, Hefei, China
flowice@ustc.edu.cn

Abstract. Recently, deep learning methods have been introduced to the field of visual tracking and gain promising results due to the property of complicated feature. However existing deep learning trackers use pre-trained convolution layers which is discriminative to specific object. Such layers would easily make trackers over-fitted and insensitive to object deformation, which makes tracker a good locator but not a good scale estimator. In this paper, we propose deep scale feature and an algorithm for robust visual tracking. In our method, object scale estimator is made from lower layers from deep neural network and we add a specially trained mask after convolution layers, which filters out potential noise in this tracking sequence. Then, the scale estimator is integrated into a tracking framework combined with locator made from powerful deep learning classifier. Furthermore, inspired by correlation filter trackers, we propose an online update algorithm to make our tracker consistent with changing object in tracking video. Experimental results on various public challenging tracking sequences show that our proposed framework is effective and produce state-of-art tracking performance.

1 Introduction

Visual tracking plays one of the most fundamental role in the field of computer vision, due to it has wide range of applications, such as safety surveillance, intelligent city system and vision-based self-driving cars. Visual tracking is model-free, which means given a bounding box of target in the first frame, the tracker would estimate its position and scale in the next frames of video with none prior knowledge related to this sequence. It lacks training samples and every sequence is of great difference. Although visual tracking has been researched for years, it still has a lot of challenging problems need solve, including occlusion, scale variation, illumination change and object deformation [27].

Object tracking algorithms are of two categories: generative and discriminative. Generative algorithms learn a high-dimension feature space to describe target and locate the target by minimizing the reconstruction error in thousands of potential regions. Discriminative algorithm builds a metric to minimize the distance between target in consequence frames and target in the first frame and maximize the distance between target and background. These approaches have been developed to gain better performance. However, classical methods

© Springer International Publishing AG 2017
Y. Zhao et al. (Eds.): ICIG 2017, Part I, LNCS 10666, pp. 306–315, 2017.
https://doi.org/10.1007/978-3-319-71607-7_27

utilize artificial features, such as Histogram of oriented gradients (HoG) [4], Local binary patterns (LBP) [18] to describe texture information, or appearance model. These features cannot represent complicated structure and show deeper information of object and background.

Convolutional Neural Network (CNN), which could learn sophisticated features from original image data, has been adopted in tracking as well. Inspired by transfer learning [19] used in other computer vision field, for example, object detection [8,21] and semantic segmentation [17], they transfer convolutional layers pre-trained at ILSVRC2012 ImageNet [16] classification dataset. These pre-trained layers have excellent ability of generalization and relieve the lack of training sample in tracking partly.

Those aforementioned trackers, which use highly-deep convolution layers, simply ignore the lack of training samples in model-free tracking. Since the output of deep convolution layers is quite sparse and overfitted to some parts of target, these features might not suit to scale estimate job. It is quite straightforward for us to get features from shallow layers to estimate the current target scale. But, this raises another problem, that shallower layers mean more noise from background and such noise would interfere the scale estimator. So we need learn a mask after the shallow network and filter out noise from background.

In this paper, we propose a tracking framework based on deep scale feature (DSF), which consists of two parts. One based on deeper CNN decides the center of current target at current time. The other one based on shallow CNN learns the target appearance and generates estimation to object size. Recent deep learning trackers usually has only one network and ignore the immanent contradiction between two different tasks, locator and scale estimator. Because, the scale estimation task requires the net sensitive to appearance change, while locator demands invariance feature. Different from these approaches, the locator of our method is relived from the task of estimating the scale variance and built from deeper networks. On the other hand, the scale estimator is not that deep.

The contribution of our method can be summarised as:

(1) We propose a self-learnt mask algorithm and deep scale feature to describe the appearance model of target.
(2) We propose a visual tracking framework consisting of two neural networks, which has state-of -art performance.

The rest of the paper is organised as follows. In Sect. 2, we first review related work. The details of the proposed method are illustrated in Sect. 3. In Sect. 4, we would presents and discuss the experimental results on a tracking benchmark. Section 5 provides conclusions.

2   Related Work

Widely used tracking-by-detection [15] framework consists of two models: appearance model to tell the target shape and motion model to tell the center of target. There are two kinds of appearance model, generative and discriminative.

Generative model mainly focuses on reconstruction error of target candidates. These methods utilizes raw pixel information [1] or sparse subspace [13] to describe the appearance model. Discriminative model finds the most discriminative feature to distinguish object from background. Online learning framework based on structured SVM [10], multiple instance learning [2] and correlation filters [5,7] are adopted and they performs better than generation models. DCF-based tracker initially uses low level feature, such as HOG feature [5]. Resent DCF-based trackers [6] utilize CNN as robust feature extractor. [5] proposes an algorithm to estimate the scale changes based on the Gaussian model and [24] reimplements it by deep features.

As the development of hardware, plenty of algorithms of computer vision have been invented based on neural network. So do they in model-free tracking. In [9], two-stream structure is proposed to build a classifier-based tracker. Pre-trained on auxiliary images, [26] presents an auto-encoder tracker. To reduce over-fitting, [24] uses a complicated sequential ensemble learning strategy. [20] tries to use multi-level feature from stacks of convolutional networks (Fig. 1).

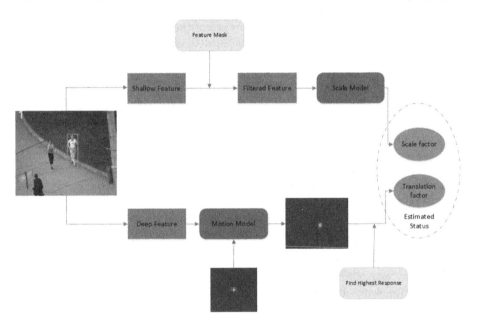

Fig. 1. The structure of proposed algorithm. Our algorithm consists of three main steps: (1) extract robust features from convolutional layers; (2) detect the object center; (3) estimate the scale change

3   Proposed Method

3.1   Deep Network Output When Tracking

Before describing the details of proposed deep scale feature tracker, we first analyse output of deep convolution layers in the field of tracking. When a deep convolution network, like VGG [22] or ResNet [11], tries to classify an object, it first uses its convolution kernels to slide across the object and produces heat maps indicating what kernels response to this structure. After the last convolutional layer, VGG would connect all its heat map unit to all the unit of fully connection layer to learn every unit's contribution to the final decision. However, as described in [25], if we transfer these layers to tracking jobs, the most neurons of last convolution layer are nearly zero. These neurons are highly sparse and discriminative to specific object. Since max pooling layer is partly shift invariance, these sparse activated neurons might not change much when object varies in scale. Therefore, we should remove some max pooling layers, and choose feature extractor not quite deep. Thus, we choose layers before conv4_3 of VGG as base feature extractor.

On the other side, deeper convolution layer has more semantic information in object categories, the shallower layer has more structure information in texture. These inactivated or dead neurons of shallow layer however, might become activated when object is occluded by background or new object, which has similar texture structure, appears in the receptive field. These unexpected activated neurons would interfere scale estimator. We should learn a mask to shut down these potential noisy neurons.

3.2   Deep Feature Mask

As mentioned before, we should find those potential noisy deep feature from 512 channels of conv4_3 layer. Simply speaking, the self-learnt mask should disable those neurons which output similar pattern activations between object and background. Because we would append several layers after conv4_3 to estimate current scale. As a result, we should take the discriminative ability of newly appended layers. So the simplest way of disabling those sensitive to everything neurons is not our choice. This is because, these neurons might output easy-to-distinguish pattern between object and background. Inspired by [25], the proposed deep mask method is based on a target heat map regression model. This model is conducted on conv4_3 layers of VGG and consists of a convolutional layer without any nonlinear activation layer. It takes the feature maps of conv4_3 to be masked as input to predict the target heat map g, which is a compact 2-D centeredtarget of ground truth as used in [5]. The model is trained by minimizing the following loss function:

$$L = \|G(F_t) - g\|^2 + \lambda \Sigma \|w\|^2 \tag{1}$$

G function is the newly added layers. If fed with the feature maps F of conv4_3 of whole frame at the time, it would produce a 2-D heat map. The parameter λ balances importance of L2 loss and regularization term.

After back-propagation converges, we select the feature maps according to their output at the location of object and background. If $\mathbf{f}_i$ represents the i-th feature maps F of conv4_3, the heat map difference can be computed by masked out the i-th feature map $\hat{G}_i$ then minus g. Then we define the importance I_i of the element $\mathbf{f}_i$ as its difference with target map and can be computed as follows:

$$I_i = \|\hat{G}_i - g\|^2 \qquad (2)$$

All the 512 feature maps are sorted in the descending order by their importance. The K selected feature maps have the top-K importance others are masked out. In our experiments, we choose 300 as K and only do mask learning at the first frame and tracker performs quite well.

3.3   Deep Scale Feature

The proposed deep scale feature is based on conv4_3 from VGG with deep feature mask, which simultaneously sense more low-level information and avoid possible noisy from similar object categories. Next, we would describe the scale estimator and how it works.

The scale estimator is constructed on top of conv4_3 layers with learnt mask and consists of a fully-connected layer with one neuron, which produces the scale variance factor. At the first frame, after mask has been built, we crop the object rectangle in different sizes with a step of 1.02 as suggested in [5]. Then, the scale estimator is trained with these feature map from different size with stochastic gradient descent (SGD) algorithm.

When tracking, the tracker firstly uses locator to determine current center and crop rectangle area around object with size of last frame. Secondly, the cropped image patch is interfered by scale estimator and update the scale coefficient accordingly. Since target could change a lot in the same sequence, the tracker would update scale estimator periodically.

3.4   Locator Construction

According to foremost analysis, the locator should use such features as discriminative as possible. Therefore, we choose one of the best CNN classifiers as feature extractor. The locator is based on the Res4a layers of ResNet-51, then add two convolutional layers and one rectifier activation between them.

We follow the approach of discriminative correlation filter to train our model, which is trained by minimizing the following loss function:

$$L = \|F(I) - g\|^2 + \lambda \Sigma \|w\|^2 \qquad (3)$$

F function is the position-CNN. If fed with image patch I, it would produce a 2-D heat map. g is the target heat map which has a compact 2-D Gaussian shaped peak centerred at the center. The parameter λ balances importance of L2 loss and regularization term. At the first frame, in order to learn context information around the object, we crop rectangle two times larger than ground truth bounding box and modify target heat map g accordingly.

During tracking, image patch around last position is input into locator and we get the current object center which has the largest confidence in the heat map. The locator parameters are updated in the same way as scale estimator.

3.5   Tracking Algorithm

Algorithm 1. Deep scale feature tracking algorithm

Input: The initial bounding box $bbox_1$
Output: current bounding box $bbox_t$
1: Initialize mask with Eq. (1) and Eq. (2)
2: Initialize locator and scale estimator
3: **repeat**
4:    Crop region I_t centered at last location and two time larger in size
5:    Use *locator* to estimate current center $center_t$ of target.
6:    **if** confidence higher than threshold **then**
7:        Crop region I_t' centered at $center_t$ with the same size as I_t.Pass I_t' through
          scale estimator, produce current scale factor
8:        Update object location
9:    **else**
10:       current location equals last location
11:   **end if**
12:   **if** location changes and tracker has process 10 frames **then**
13:       Update locator and scale estimator
14:   **end if**
15: **until** The sequence ends

Overview. The overall tracking procedure is presented in Algorithm 1.

Tracking and Update. We use locator to get the center of object, while use scale estimator to track scale variance. Assuming heat map of locator is current possibility distribution and the confidence of each candidates equals the value of heat map. And we find the maximum confidence and convert relative position to pixel position.

To balance periodic update and poorly samples, we propose one update criteria: high locator confidence. The criteria is measured by ways as in [25], we treat the maximum heat map value as current confidence. If it is less than a threshold 0.1, we would stop parameter update. Once scale or size needs update, they vary by one step (1.02 for scale and ratio).

4   Experiment

4.1   Experiment Setup

The proposed framework is implemented in Caffe [14] with MATLAB R2016a and runs at 0.5 frames per second. Our tracker runs on a PC with 3.0 GHz i7-X5960 CPU and TITAN X GPU. All of networks are trained with SGD solver at learning rate 1e−7 with momentum of 0.9.

Our tracker is evaluated on 12 public challenging video sequences, containing plenty sort of challenging factors, such as fast motion, scale and illumination change, background clutter and object occlusion. We compare our tracker result with 10 state-of-art trackers, consisting of 4 deep learning based trackers, including FCNT [25], SiamFC [3], SINT [23], STCT [24], 3 DCF-based trackers, including SRDCF [7], DeepSRDCF [6], HDT [20] and 3 classic trackers, including Struck [10], MEEM [28], MUSTer [12]. For the fairness, we adopt the source codes or result files provided by the authors.

4.2   Experiment Result

Two common used metrics are applied for quantitative evaluation: Central Location Error (CLE) and Overlap Rate (OR). CLE is defined as the Euclidean distance between center of $Bbox_G$ and $Bbox_T$, where $Bbox_G$ is the ground-truth bounding box and $Bbox_T$ is the bounding box produced by trackers. OR is defined as $OR = \frac{Bbox_T \cap Bbox_G}{Bbox_T \cup Bbox_G}$.

Quantitative Evaluation. We use the precision plot and the success plot, as shown in Fig. 2, to evaluate average performance of trackers on every sequence. The precision plot demonstrates the percentage of frames where the distance between the predicted target location and the ground truth location is within a given threshold. Whereas the success plot illustrates the percentage of frames where OR between the predicted bounding box and the ground truth bounding box is higher than a threshold. The area under curve (AUC) is used to rank the tracking algorithms in each plot. As shown in Fig. 2 and Tables 1 and 2, our method achieves the superior performance in terms of both evaluation metrics compared to state-of-art trackers. Especially, STCT tracker utilizes similar structure as proposed algorithm, but STCT does not consider deep feature mask at scale and uses highly sophisticated framework compared to proposed method. If we exam those not-well-performed sequences, we would some common properties, like out-of-plane rotation in Coke, shape deformation in Basketball and similar object in Car4 and Deer. These factors undermine the power of CNN feature to estimate scale, which is complicated 2-D coarse-grained feature and cannot handle 3-D and fine-grained changes well.

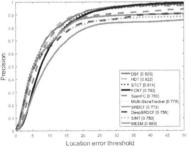
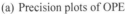
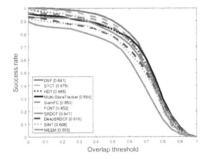

(a) Precision plots of OPE   (b) Success plots of OPE

Fig. 2. Result curve

Table 1. Comparison of 11 trackers on 12 video sequences in terms of central location error (in pixels). Red fonts indicate the best performance while the blue fonts indicate the second best.

	FCNT	SRDCF	SiamFC	MEEM	SINT	Struck	HDT	MUSTer	DeepSRDCF	STCT	DSF
Deer	7.7	4.0	5.5	4.5	5.3	5.3	5.1	7.2	4.6	4.3	4.8
Basketball	10.3	10.8	22.9	8.5	19.1	118.3	3.3	4.8	19.8	3.9	5.3
Car4	4.7	1.7	5.6	18.0	3.3	8.7	7.4	1.9	1.8	2.7	5.3
Coke	11.0	18.9	11.3	11.0	7.5	12.1	10.2	15.1	14.9	15.1	13.4
FaceOcc1	22.3	14.8	11.7	16.4	13.8	18.8	17.4	14.3	12.9	18.3	19.2
Football	8.6	5.7	6.3	88.9	210.9	17.3	5.8	14.8	6.2	7.4	6.8
Jogging-2	15.3	3.7	6.1	8.2	4.1	107.7	2.9	4.8	5.7	6.4	2.8
Woman	9.5	4.8	14.9	4.1	11.1	4.2	10.9	9.4	3.7	8.6	3.5
CarScale	10.6	19.7	15.4	30.1	31.5	36.4	29.9	18.7	25.2	15.2	15.3
Subway	5.1	2.6	3.3	4.1	3.6	4.5	2.6	2.2	3.0	3.0	2.4
MountainBike	6.4	9.0	6.1	13.2	10.3	8.6	8.4	8.1	9.7	12.6	7.2
MotorRolling	12.5	247.1	87.9	170.9	24.0	145.7	14.1	110.4	200.8	18.2	17.1
Avg	10.3	28.6	16.4	31.5	28.7	40.6	9.8	17.6	25.7	9.6	8.6

Table 2. Average overlap rate. Red fonts indicate the best performance while the blue fonts indicate the second best.

	FCNT	SRDCF	SiamFC	MEEM	SINT	Struck	HDT	MUSTer	DeepSRDCF	STCT	DSF
Deer	0.71	0.81	0.73	0.75	0.71	0.74	0.75	0.75	0.77	0.76	0.75
Basketball	0.67	0.53	0.57	0.66	0.64	0.20	0.85	0.75	0.39	0.78	0.71
Car4	0.82	0.87	0.78	0.46	0.78	0.49	0.49	0.90	0.88	0.84	0.75
Coke	0.66	0.51	0.58	0.65	0.63	0.67	0.65	0.52	0.52	0.56	0.54
FaceOcc1	0.64	0.76	0.76	0.75	0.75	0.73	0.74	0.76	0.79	0.71	0.77
Football	0.56	0.66	0.70	0.34	0.14	0.53	0.68	0.54	0.65	0.61	0.69
Jogging-2	0.67	0.71	0.70	0.63	0.75	0.20	0.79	0.75	0.60	0.74	0.78
Woman	0.69	0.67	0.54	0.71	0.62	0.73	0.74	0.69	0.72	0.67	0.64
CarScale	0.52	0.73	0.69	0.41	0.54	0.41	0.41	0.68	0.69	0.72	0.74
Subway	0.63	0.76	0.75	0.68	0.68	0.65	0.76	0.72	0.73	0.75	0.79
MountainBike	0.77	0.69	0.76	0.60	0.63	0.71	0.70	0.73	0.69	0.61	0.78
MotorRolling	0.58	0.09	0.37	0.10	0.52	0.15	0.52	0.29	0.10	0.51	0.56
Avg	0.66	0.65	0.66	0.56	0.62	0.52	0.67	0.67	0.63	0.69	0.70

5 Conclusion

In this paper, we have proposed a robust tracking framework based on deep scale feature. To make the tracker sensitive to scale variance and robust against noises, a type of mask is learnt from the first frame and is used to filter out potential noisy feature maps. To estimate current scale factor, we train a fully-connected layer with one neuron right after masked feature map. Last but not least, a periodic update scheme is proposed to trade off between poorly tracking result and object changes. We have tested out method on 12 different challenging sequences and experiment results show the superiority of proposed algorithm compared to 10 state-of-art trackers.

Acknowledgements. This work is supported by the National Natural Science Foundation of China (Grant No. 61371192), the Key Laboratory Foundation of the Chinese Academy of Sciences (CXJJ-17S044) and the Fundamental Research Funds for the Central Universities (WK2100330002).

References

1. Adam, A., Rivlin, E., Shimshoni, I.: Robust fragments-based tracking using the integral histogram. In: 2006 IEEE Computer Society Conference on Computer vision and pattern recognition, vol. 1, pp. 798–805. IEEE (2006)
2. Babenko, B., Yang, M.H., Belongie, S.: Visual tracking with online multiple instance learning. In: IEEE Conference on Computer Vision and Pattern Recognition, CVPR 2009, pp. 983–990. IEEE (2009)
3. Bertinetto, L., Valmadre, J., Henriques, J.F., Vedaldi, A., Torr, P.H.S.: Fully-convolutional Siamese networks for object tracking. In: Hua, G., Jégou, H. (eds.) ECCV 2016. LNCS, vol. 9914, pp. 850–865. Springer, Cham (2016). https://doi.org/10.1007/978-3-319-48881-3_56
4. Dalal, N., Triggs, B.: Histograms of oriented gradients for human detection. In: IEEE Computer Society Conference on Computer Vision and Pattern Recognition, CVPR 2005, vol. 1, pp. 886–893. IEEE (2005)
5. Danelljan, M., Häger, G., Khan, F., Felsberg, M.: Accurate scale estimation for robust visual tracking. In: British Machine Vision Conference, Nottingham, 1–5 September 2014. BMVA Press (2014)
6. Danelljan, M., Hager, G., Shahbaz Khan, F., Felsberg, M.: Convolutional features for correlation filter based visual tracking. In: Proceedings of the IEEE International Conference on Computer Vision Workshops, pp. 58–66 (2015)
7. Danelljan, M., Hager, G., Shahbaz Khan, F., Felsberg, M.: Learning spatially regularized correlation filters for visual tracking. In: Proceedings of the IEEE International Conference on Computer Vision, pp. 4310–4318 (2015)
8. Girshick, R.: Fast R-CNN. In: IEEE International Conference on Computer Vision (ICCV), December 2015
9. Gladh, S., Danelljan, M., Khan, F.S., Felsberg, M.: Deep motion features for visual tracking. arXiv preprint arXiv:1612.06615 (2016)
10. Hare, S., Golodetz, S., Saffari, A., Vineet, V., Cheng, M.M., Hicks, S.L., Torr, P.H.: Struck: structured output tracking with kernels. IEEE Trans. Pattern Anal. Mach. Intell. **38**(10), 2096–2109 (2016)
11. He, K., Zhang, X., Ren, S., Sun, J.: Deep residual learning for image recognition. In: Proceedings of the IEEE Conference on Computer Vision and Pattern Recognition, pp. 770–778 (2016)
12. Hong, Z., Chen, Z., Wang, C., Mei, X., Prokhorov, D., Tao, D.: Multi-store tracker (muster): a cognitive psychology inspired approach to object tracking. In: Proceedings of the IEEE Conference on Computer Vision and Pattern Recognition, pp. 749–758 (2015)
13. Jia, X., Lu, H., Yang, M.H.: Visual tracking via adaptive structural local sparse appearance model. In: 2012 IEEE Conference on Computer vision and pattern recognition (CVPR), pp. 1822–1829. IEEE (2012)
14. Jia, Y., Shelhamer, E., Donahue, J., Karayev, S., Long, J., Girshick, R., Guadarrama, S., Darrell, T.: Caffe: convolutional architecture for fast feature embedding. arXiv preprint arXiv:1408.5093 (2014)

15. Kalal, Z., Mikolajczyk, K., Matas, J.: Tracking-learning-detection. IEEE Trans. Pattern Anal. Mach. Intell. **34**(7), 1409–1422 (2012)
16. Krizhevsky, A., Sutskever, I., Hinton, G.E.: Imagenet classification with deep convolutional neural networks. In: Advances in Neural Information Processing Systems, pp. 1097–1105 (2012)
17. Long, J., Shelhamer, E., Darrell, T.: Fully convolutional networks for semantic segmentation. In: Proceedings of the IEEE Conference on Computer Vision and Pattern Recognition, pp. 3431–3440 (2015)
18. Ojala, T., Pietikainen, M., Maenpaa, T.: Multiresolution gray-scale and rotation invariant texture classification with local binary patterns. IEEE Trans. Pattern Anal. Mach. Intell. **24**(7), 971–987 (2002)
19. Oquab, M., Bottou, L., Laptev, I., Sivic, J.: Learning and transferring mid-level image representations using convolutional neural networks. In: IEEE Conference on Computer Vision and Pattern Recognition (CVPR), June 2014
20. Qi, Y., Zhang, S., Qin, L., Yao, H., Huang, Q., Lim, J., Yang, M.H.: Hedged deep tracking. In: Proceedings of the IEEE Conference on Computer Vision and Pattern Recognition, pp. 4303–4311 (2016)
21. Ren, S., He, K., Girshick, R., Sun, J.: Faster R-CNN: towards real-time object detection with region proposal networks. In: Advances in neural Information Processing Systems, pp. 91–99 (2015)
22. Simonyan, K., Zisserman, A.: Very deep convolutional networks for large-scale image recognition. arXiv preprint arXiv:1409.1556 (2014)
23. Tao, R., Gavves, E., Smeulders, A.W.: Siamese instance search for tracking. In: Proceedings of the IEEE Conference on Computer Vision and Pattern Recognition, pp. 1420–1429 (2016)
24. Wang, L., Ouyang, W., Wang, X., Lu, H.: STCT: sequentially training convolutional networks for visual tracking. In: 2016 IEEE Conference on Computer Vision and Pattern Recognition (CVPR), pp. 1373–1381, June 2016
25. Wang, L., Ouyang, W., Wang, X., Lu, H.: Visual tracking with fully convolutional networks. In: Proceedings of the IEEE International Conference on Computer Vision, pp. 3119–3127 (2015)
26. Wang, N., Li, S., Gupta, A., Yeung, D.Y.: Transferring rich feature hierarchies for robust visual tracking. arXiv preprint arXiv:1501.04587 (2015)
27. Wu, Y., Lim, J., Yang, M.H.: Online object tracking: a benchmark. In: IEEE Conference on Computer Vision and Pattern Recognition (CVPR) (2013)
28. Zhang, J., Ma, S., Sclaroff, S.: MEEM: robust tracking via multiple experts using entropy minimization. In: Fleet, D., Pajdla, T., Schiele, B., Tuytelaars, T. (eds.) ECCV 2014. LNCS, vol. 8694, pp. 188–203. Springer, Cham (2014). https://doi.org/10.1007/978-3-319-10599-4_13

TCCF: Tracking Based on Convolutional Neural Network and Correlation Filters

Qiankun Liu[1,2], Bin Liu[1,2(✉)], and Nenghai Yu[1,2]

[1] Key Laboratory of Electromagnetic Space Information,
Chinese Academy of Sciences, Hefei, China
[2] School of Information Science and Technology,
University of Science and Technology of China, Hefei, China
`flowice@ustc.edu.cn`

Abstract. With the rapid development of deep learning in recent years, lots of trackers based on deep learning were proposed, and achieved great improvements compared with traditional methods. However, due to the scarcity of training samples, fine-tuning pre-trained deep models can be easily over-fitted and its cost is expensive. In this paper, we propose a novel algorithm for online visual object tracking which is divided into two separate parts, one of them is target location estimation and the other is target scale estimation. Both of them are implemented with correlation filters independently while using different feature representations. Instead of fine-tuning pre-trained deep models, we update correlation filters. And we design the desired output of correlation filters for every training sample which makes our tracker perform better. Extensive experiments are conducted on the OTB-15 benchmark, and the results demonstrate that our algorithm outperforms the state-of-the-art by great margin in terms of accuracy and robustness.

Keywords: Visual object tracking · Correlation filter · CNN

1 Introduction

As one of the popular branches of computer vision, visual object tracking has been widely used in various fields, such as military strike, traffic control, security system, human-computer interaction and so on, and it has been rapidly developed thanks to the development of deep learning in recent years. Single-target tracking can be described as follow: an arbitrary target is given by a bounding box in the first frame and the trackers give predicted bounding box in subsequent frames. Although great progress has been made in past decades, visual object tracking is still a challenging task to handle with owning to complicated and volatile interferences like illumination variation, scale variation, partial or full occlusion, motion blur, background clutters and deformation.

The features that can effectively distinguish target from its surrounding background play significant role in visual tracking. Trackers [10,12,16,17,30,31] based on hand-crafted features have solved mentioned challenges more or less

© Springer International Publishing AG 2017
Y. Zhao et al. (Eds.): ICIG 2017, Part I, LNCS 10666, pp. 316–327, 2017.
https://doi.org/10.1007/978-3-319-71607-7_28

to some extent and can run at a high speed. But hand-crafted features are usually specially designed for certain scenarios, so they are less accurate or robust when faced with more complex scenarios, which can lead to tracking failure. Recently, lots of trackers [4,21,23,24,27,28] based on deep learning methods have been proposed and made a great progress in terms of accuracy and robustness. These trackers all use features that extracted by Convolutional Neural Networks (CNNs) as the representation of tracking target.

Apart from advantages of CNNs, there exist some thorny issues to handle with. For example, a numerous amount of annotated samples are required for supervised training of deep CNNs which have millions of parameters. And the lack of training samples becomes more severe for online visual object tracking since there is only one annotated sample provided in the first frame of each video. What's more, the computation of features extracted by CNNs is more complex than hand-crafted features. Correlation filters, which transform convolution into multiplication to accelerate processing speed, have been widely used in tracking [5,10,24], but the desired output of correlation filters in these trackers are either the same for all training samples or designed improperly which reduces the correlation between filters and tracking targets.

In this paper, we divide tracking into two parts, one of them is target location estimation, and the other is target scale estimation. Both of them are implemented by correlation filters. On the training stage, we design the desired output of correlation filters carefully to get more superior filters. The contributions of this paper are summarized as follows: (i) we comprehensively analyze the diversity of the features from different layers in a CNN as well as the difference between hand-crafted features and the features extracted by CNNs. And we design two correlation filters to utilize these features effectively; (ii) we proposed a novel tracker based on these correlation filters for single-target tracking which just need to update correlation filters dynamically instead of fine-tuning pretrained deep models. We conducted extensive experiments on OTB-15 benchmark [29] dataset and the results demonstrate that our algorithm outperforms several state-of-the-art trackers.

The rest of this paper is organized as follows. Section 2 reviews related work about our algorithm. Section 3 introduces our algorithm thoroughly and Sect. 4 represents the experimental results of our evaluation on different trakers. Finally, Sect. 5 makes a conclusion on our work in this paper.

2   Related Work

The usage of features extracted by CNNs has shown great effectiveness for computer vision tasks in recent years, such as segmentation [8], classification [20], and gained considerable improvements. However, the computation complexity of extracting these features is much higher than hand-crafted features, and some scholars have done lots of research to improve computational efficiency. Correlation filters, which have played a significant role in signal processing since the 80's [15,22] and solved myriad objective functions in the Fourier domain, are widely used in visual tracking to speed up trackers owning to their high computational efficiency.

In [6], Bolme *et al.* proposed a new type of correlation filter called Average of Synthetic Exact Filters (ASEF), and performed well in some specific tasks [6,7]. However, a large number of samples are required for the training of ASEF. In the next year, Bolme *et al.* modified ASEF and proposed Minimum Output Sum of Squared Error (MOSSE) filter for tracking [5], which achieved remarkable performance at a high processing speed. Both ASEF and MOSSE filters are single-channel correlation filters. Henriques *et al.* [14] proposed an analytic model which is named KCF for datasets consisted of thousands of translated patches using the concept of circulant matrices. For linear regression, this model is equivalent to a correlation filter, but it is also suitable for non-linear regression. What's more, KCF can be extend to multi-channel correlation filter. The work in [19] also did some research on multi-channel correlation filters which make it possible for correlation filters to be more widely used.

Danelljan *et al.* proposed a concise tracker called DSST [10] based on correlation filters which inspired us to do our research. The highlight of DSST is its approach for scale estimation. But according to our observation of DSST, we found that the desired outputs of correlation filters are designed improperly, which will be explained in detail in Sect. 3. The tracker HDT [24] exploits features from different layers in a CNN by a correlation filter for localizing tracking target. But HDT is limited to only location estimation which leads to poor performance in video sequences with severe scale variations. What's more, the desired output of correlation filter is fixed since the first frame, which worsen its performance.

3   Tracking Based on CNN and Correlation Filters

Here, we will describe our algorithm TCCF (Tracking based on CNN and Correlation Filters) thoroughly. Before that, we first introduce the features used for target location estimation and scale estimation.

3.1   Feature Selection

Hand-crafted features, take HOG [9] features for example, do well in representing the texture and edge of tracking target. As shown in Fig. 1, different targets are all described clearly by HOG features[1]. But the drawback of hand-crafted features is that they can not distinguish tracking target between objects that are in the same category effectively (refer to the feature map locating at the intersection of third row and second column).

Recently, some deep CNN models [20,25,26] trained on ImageNet [11] have been widely used in many computer vision tasks and achieved great success.

---

[1] The HOG feature map is visualized with the aid of Pitor's Computer Vision Matlab Toolbox: https://pdollar.github.io/toolbox/.

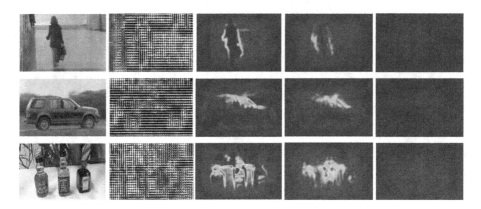

Fig. 1. Feature maps for different tracking targets. From left to right: the first column are input images, the second one are visualized HOG feature maps, the rest are feature maps extracted by VGG-16 from conv2-2, conv3-3 and conv4-3 layers respectively, and the feature map from a layer presented here is the average of all channel feature maps.

The features extracted by CNNs are more discriminative than hand-crafted (refer to Fig. 1). What's more, features extracted by a CNN vary from layers to layers. As shown in Fig. 1, shallower layers capture generic information of the target, while deeper layers capture semantic information of the target. Wang *et al.* also did some research on these differences between different layers [27].

Here, our tracking algorithm is divided into two parts, one of them is target location estimation, and the other is target scale estimation. The two parts are implemented independently. Since features extracted by CNNs can separate target from background more effectively than hand-crafted features, and there are some diversities between features from different layers, so they will be used by a correlation filter to implement location estimation. Once the location of tracking target is determined, hand-crafted (to be exact, HOG) features are used by another correlation filter to complete scale estimation since they do better in representing the texture and edge of target than features extracted by CNNs.

3.2 Correlation Filters

The structure of our proposed method is shown in Fig. 2, tracking online is divided into two parts here. Location Correlation Filter (LCF) is used for location estimation, while Scale Correlation Filter (SCF) is used for scale estimation. Both LCF and SCF are multi-channel correlation filters. Here, we make an introduction to the multi-channel correlation filter used in our algorithm.

Let x^t, which is a multi-channel signal, denote the features extracted from the given training sample, y^t denote the desired output of correlation filter and f^t denote the correlation filter we want to get. The upper case variants $X^t = \mathcal{F}(x^t)$, $Y^t = \mathcal{F}(y^t)$ and $F^t = \mathcal{F}(f^t)$, where $\mathcal{F}(\cdot)$ denote the Discrete

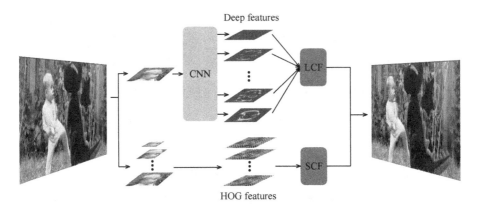

Fig. 2. The structure of TCCF.

Fourier Translation (DFT). y^t is artificially pre-defined according to the specific problem we are handling with. The correlation f^t is an ensemble of C weak filters, where C is the number of channels. In the Fourier domain, F^t can be computed by minimizing:

$$F^t = arg\min_{F^t} ||Y^t - \sum_{c=1}^{c=C} F_c^t \odot X_c^t||^2 + \lambda \sum_{c=1}^{c=C} ||F_c^t||^2 \qquad (1)$$

where the subscript index c denote the component in c_{th} channel. The parameter λ in the second term on the right is the regularizer and the symbol $\odot$ denote element-wise product. The solution to Eq. (1) is:

$$F_c^t = \frac{Y^t \odot \bar{X}_c^t}{\sum_{c=1}^{c=C} X_c^t \odot \bar{X}_c^t + \lambda} \qquad (2)$$

where the division is performed element-wise and $\bar{X}_c^t$ denote the complex conjugation of X_c^t. Obviously, the first term in the denominator is the power spectrum of x^t. From Eq. (2) we can find that once the training sample x^t and the regularizer λ are determined, the filter is directly controlled by y^t.

Given a testing sample t, we first transform it to the Fourier domain to obtain T, then the response of t can be computed by:

$$r = \mathcal{F}^{-1}(\sum_{c=1}^{c=C} T_c \odot F_c^t) \qquad (3)$$

where $\mathcal{F}^{-1}(\cdot)$ is the inverse of DFT (IDFT).

In order to simplify our proposed model and reduce the cost of computation, we adopt an incremental update method as other researchers do in [5,10,24], which only use current frame to partially update previous correlation filters when tracking online. Given the t_{th} frame in a video sequence, let p^t and s^t

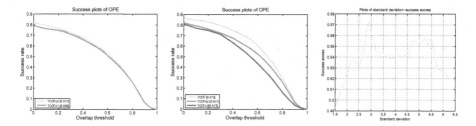

Fig. 3. Left: Average success plots of two trackers. Middle: Average success plots of three trackers. Right: The curve between average success scores and standard deviation of y_s^t.

denote the position and size of target in this frame, which are predicted by the tracker. F^t is updated as follows:

$$F_c^t = \frac{A^t}{B^t} = \frac{(1-\eta)A^{t-1} + \eta\hat{A}^t}{(1-\eta)B^{t-1} + \eta\hat{B}^t} \tag{4}$$

where

$$\hat{F}_c^t = \frac{\hat{A}^t}{\hat{B}^t} = \frac{Y^t \odot \bar{X}_c^t}{\sum_{c=1}^{c=C} X_c^t \odot \bar{X}_c^t + \lambda} \tag{5}$$

and the parameter η is the learning rate of correlation filters.

Location Correlation Filter: Since features extracted by a pre-trained CNN are used in LCF, so x^t and f^t are three dimensional, which means $x^t, f^t \in \Re^{M \times N \times C}$. Let $y_l^t \in \Re^{M \times N}$ denote the desired output of LCF and it is a 2-D Gaussian shape distribution which is determined by the mean μ_l^t and standard deviation δ_l^t. Suppose features from K convolution layers are used in our algorithm, there will be K independent correlation filters in LCF, which means:

$$\text{LCF} = \{F^{k,t}|k = 1, 2, \dots, K\} \tag{6}$$

each $F^{k,t}$ has a weight w^k, and $\sum_{k=1}^{k=K} w^k = 1$. The location of target predicted by $F^{k,t}$ is the coordinate (m^k, n^k) of the maximum value in r^k. The ultimate location of target is computed as follows:

$$(m, n) = \sum_{k=1}^{k=K} w^k \cdot (m^k, n^k) \tag{7}$$

the symbol $\cdot$ denote the product of two scalars. Once the ultimate location of target is predicted, there will be a loss between (m^k, n^k) and (m, n), which implies the stability of $F^{k,t}$. And the weight w^k is updated according to the stability of $F^{k,t}$. Please refer to [24] for more information.

TCCF	SiamFC	HDT	CSK	FCNT	KCF	DSST	STCT	L1APG	Frag

Fig. 4. Qualitative results of the proposed TCCF tracker and other 9 trackers on a subset of OTB-15 benchmark. From left to right and top to bottom: *Basketball*, *Biker*, *BlurOwl*, *CarDark*, *Bolt*, *Car*1, *RedTeam*, *Deer*, *Walking*2, *Human*4, *Singer*2, *Surfer*. Two frames of each video are presented here.

It should be noted that the mean of y_l^t is set to 0 and the standard deviation δ_l^t is proportional to the target size s^t, i.e.:

$$\delta_l^t \propto s^t \tag{8}$$

which means the desired output y_l^t of location correlation filter is controlled by δ_l^t and it is dynamically updated to adjust to the scale variation of target. While in HDT [24] and DSST [10], the desired outputs of correlation filters are fixed since the first frame in a video sequence, which has a negative impact on the performance of trackers. Suppose we choose a reference system ϕ in the image from the perspective of tracking target and the target make a translation distance D in ϕ. Now we jump out of the image and choose a reference system ϕ' in the screen from the respective of observer and the target make a translation distance D' in ϕ'. Since the location estimation is completed in ϕ' and it's a common sense that the larger s^t is, the larger D' will be when D is a constant and vice versa, which means the location estimation is relevant to the size of target.

Scale Correlation Filter: In order to implement scale estimation, we pre-define a set of scale factors $\{\alpha_l = \theta^{\lceil \frac{L}{2} \rceil - l} | l = 1, 2, \ldots, L\}$, where $\theta > 1$ is the step for scale transformation. Given a training sample, we first extract L rectangles of interest with the size $\alpha_l \cdot s^t$, where s^t denote the size of target in this training sample. Then we get a feature map $M^t \in \Re^{C \times L}$ from these rectangles of interest with each collum in M^t corresponding to one rectangle. Let $x_c^t \in \Re^{1 \times L}$ denote the c_{th} row vector in M^t, and y_s^t denote the desired output of SCF, then SCF can be obtained by Eq. (2). y_s^t is 1-D Gaussian shaped distribution with its mean $\mu_s^t = 0$. And the target size s' in testing sample is determined by:

$$s' = \alpha_i \cdot s^t \tag{9}$$

where α_i is the scale factor and i is the index of the maximum value in the response r.

Inspired by the effectiveness of dynamical update of y_l^t, we keep y_s^t dynamically updated like Eq. (8), but experimental results demonstrate that the dynamical update of y_s^t reduces the performance of tracker which is opposite of what we have expected.

Here we give an explanation. Unlike location estimation which is implemented in ϕ', the scale estimation is just to find an optimal scale factor α_i which is independent with ϕ and ϕ'. Since the scale variation between two consecutive frames is small, which means the probability of severe scale variation between two consecutive frames is much lower and vice versa, so y_s^t is independent with the size of target but relative to the number of scale factors L:

$$\delta_s^t \propto L \tag{10}$$

Table 1. Average precision scores on different attributes: Illumination Variation (IV), Occlusion (OCC), Deformation (DEF), Out-of-Plane Rotation (OPR), Background Clutters (BC), Scale Variation (SV), Motion Blur (MB), Fast Motion (FM), Out-of-View (OV), Low Resolution (LR), In-Plane Rotation (IPR).

Trackers / Attributes	CSK	Frag	L1APG	Staple	DSST	KCF	FCNT	HDT	SiamFC	STCT	TCCF
IV	0.405	0.256	0.295	0.251	0.545	0.667	0.712	0.803	0.686	0.737	0.815
OCC	0.368	0.336	0.392	0.323	0.546	0.609	0.693	0.743	0.629	0.732	0.738
DEF	0.341	0.289	0.338	0.286	0.487	0.582	0.688	0.760	0.560	0.734	0.731
OPR	0.363	0.342	0.340	0.314	0.505	0.598	0.740	0.745	0.678	0.717	0.759
BC	0.460	0.317	0.366	0.308	0.565	0.623	0.689	0.766	0.635	0.762	0.797
SV	0.348	0.306	0.347	0.298	0.567	0.568	0.709	0.787	0.717	0.761	0.755
MB	0.325	0.302	0.342	0.247	0.670	0.573	0.698	0.780	0.703	0.768	0.757
FM	0.302	0.321	0.317	0.279	0.630	0.529	0.635	0.763	0.697	0.719	0.745
OV	0.252	0.330	0.350	0.207	0.475	0.441	0.635	0.651	0.688	0.594	0.611
LR	0.380	0.306	0.409	0.360	0.509	0.558	0.716	0.756	0.859	0.741	0.805
IPR	0.389	0.320	0.405	0.329	0.566	0.587	0.763	0.803	0.697	0.705	0.753
Overall	0.406	0.342	0.392	0.328	0.579	0.611	0.742	0.804	0.693	0.770	0.796

4   Experiments

The proposed algorithm is implemented in MATLAB with Caffe framework [18] and runs at 3.5 fps on a Ubuntu 14.04.3 machine with a 3.0 GHz Intel i7-5960x CPU and a Nvidia GM2000 TITAN X GPU. The VGG-16 is used as the pretrained CNN in our experiments, and the last 6 convolutional layers are used to extract features. We use $L = 33$ and $\theta = 1.02$ for scale estimation. And the learning rate η is set to 0.00902.

We use one-passe-evaluation (OPE) metric on the first 50 video sequences in OTB-15 benchmark [29] to evaluate different trackers. According to different challenging factors, such as illumination variation, occlusion, deformation and so on, there are 11 attributes tagged to these video sequences, which make it possible to evaluate these trackers thoroughly.

Inspired by DSST [10], we first construct two naive trackers TCCFn1 and TCCFn2 based on LCF to illustrate the effectiveness of the dynamical update of y_l^t. The y_l^t in TCCFn1 is fixed since the first frame, and the y_l^t in TCCFn2 is dynamically updated according to Eq. (8). As shown on the left in Fig. 3, there are 1.2% improvements in TCCFn2 which demonstrates the effectiveness of dynamical update of y_l^t. We also construct another tracker TCCFn3 where the y_l^t and y_s^t both are dynamically updated. The success scores of TCCFn2 and TCCFn3 are shown in the middle in Fig. 3, from where we can figure out that the dynamical update of y_s^t reduces the performance of tracker. To find the optimal y_s^t according to Eq. (10), we conduct extensive experiments using variable-controlling method and get a graphic which is shown on the right in Fig. 3, from where we find the optimal standard deviation of y_s^t and then we construct the optimal tracker TCCF as depicted in the middle in Fig. 3.

We compare our proposed TCCF tracker with other ten trackers, CSK [13], Frag [1], L1APG [2], Staple [3], DSST [10], KCF [14], FCNT [27], HDT [24], SiamFC [4], STCT [28]. And We do qualitative and quantitative evaluation on these trackers. Among them, qualitative results are shown in Fig. 4, from where we can figure out that our approach efficiently handles some challenging factors, such as deformation, motion blur, scale variation, background cluster and so on. Quantitative results are shown in Tables 1 and 2. We compared these trackers for every attribute. In Table 1, all the values are obtained at the threshold of 20 pixels. In Table 2, all the values are computed using the metric AUC (Area Under Curve). The first, second and third best trackers are highlighted in red, green and blue, respectively. From Tables 1 and 2, we can find that our TCCF performs well in different attributes, which demonstrates the effectiveness of our correlation filters.

We also use the precision and success plots to evaluate all trackers in Fig. 5. The precision plots demonstrate the percentage of frames where the distance between the ground truth center of target and the predicted center of target is within a given threshold. The success plots demonstrate the percentage of frames where the overlap ratio between the ground truth bounding box and the predicted bounding box is higher than a given threshold. Comparing TCCF with DSST, we can figure out that there are 21.7% and 15.2% improvements in the precision and success scores. While compared with STCT, TCCF gets 2.6% and 0.6% improvements in the precision and success scores. When comparing TCCF with HDT, although HDT gets 0.8% improvements in the precision scores, TCCF gets 5.9% improvements in the success scores. The plots in Fig. 5 demonstrate that our TCCF tracker achieves the best overall performance than other trackers.

Table 2. Average success scores on different attributes: Illumination Variation (IV), Occlusion (OCC), Deformation (DEF), Out-of-Plane Rotation (OPR), Background Clutters (BC), Scale Variation (SV), Motion Blur (MB), Fast Motion (FM), Out-of-View (OV), Low Resolution (LR), In-Plane Rotation (IPR).

Attributes \ Trackers	CSK	Frag	L1APG	Staple	DSST	KCF	FCNT	HDT	SiamFC	STCT	TCCF
IV	0.318	0.201	0.235	0.172	0.399	0.433	0.486	0.500	0.484	0.570	0.587
OCC	0.269	0.252	0.277	0.190	0.377	0.396	0.473	0.486	0.458	0.514	0.510
DEF	0.267	0.235	0.248	0.178	0.357	0.400	0.482	0.487	0.407	0.544	0.506
OPR	0.271	0.261	0.248	0.197	0.355	0.396	0.503	0.486	0.487	0.513	0.532
BC	0.344	0.246	0.294	0.215	0.416	0.417	0.474	0.501	0.466	0.579	0.574
SV	0.266	0.238	0.253	0.192	0.402	0.352	0.474	0.479	0.528	0.545	0.541
MB	0.274	0.265	0.263	0.196	0.495	0.395	0.505	0.524	0.536	0.587	0.571
FM	0.257	0.268	0.252	0.202	0.477	0.370	0.469	0.510	0.536	0.553	0.557
OV	0.214	0.258	0.253	0.146	0.365	0.327	0.459	0.441	0.509	0.455	0.457
LR	0.242	0.201	0.267	0.217	0.308	0.297	0.415	0.415	0.616	0.491	0.568
IPR	0.296	0.265	0.305	0.216	0.397	0.389	0.519	0.523	0.519	0.507	0.552
Overall	0.310	0.265	0.292	0.200	0.421	0.403	0.508	0.514	0.509	0.567	0.573

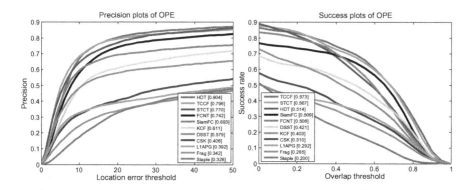

Fig. 5. Average precision plots and success plots of different trackers tested over 50 video sequences. On the left, trackers are ranked according to the precision score at the threshold of 20 pixels. On the right, trackers are ranked according to the area under curve.

5 Conclusion

In this paper, we proposed a novel algorithm for online visual object tracking based on CNN and correlation filters (TCCF). The pre-trained VGG-16 [25] is the only one CNN used in our algorithm and it is kept fixed when tracking online, so the algorithm just need to update correlation filters dynamically instead of fine-tuning pre-trained deep models, which means the structure of our algorithm is simple and compact. TCCF is consisted with two separate component entities: location estimation and scale estimation. Both of them are implemented by correlation filters independently while using different feature representations. The results of extensive experiments demonstrate that our algorithm outperform the state-of-the-art by a great margin in terms of accuracy and robustness.

Acknowledgement. This work is supported by the National Natural Science Foundation of China (Grant No. 61371192), the Key Laboratory Foundation of the Chinese Academy of Sciences (CXJJ-17S044) and the Fundamental Research Funds for the Central Universities (WK2100330002).

References

1. Adam, A., Rivlin, E., Shimshoni, I.: Robust fragments-based tracking using the integral histogram. In: 2006 IEEE Computer Society Conference on Computer vision and pattern recognition, vol. 1, pp. 798–805. IEEE (2006)
2. Bao, C., Wu, Y., Ling, H., Ji, H.: Real time robust l1 tracker using accelerated proximal gradient approach. In: 2012 IEEE Conference on Computer Vision and Pattern Recognition (CVPR), pp. 1830–1837. IEEE (2012)
3. Bertinetto, L., Valmadre, J., Golodetz, S., Miksik, O., Torr, P.H.: Staple: complementary learners for real-time tracking. In: Proceedings of the IEEE Conference on Computer Vision and Pattern Recognition, pp. 1401–1409 (2016)
4. Bertinetto, L., Valmadre, J., Henriques, J.F., Vedaldi, A., Torr, P.H.S.: Fully-convolutional siamese networks for object tracking. In: Hua, G., Jégou, H. (eds.) ECCV 2016. LNCS, vol. 9914, pp. 850–865. Springer, Cham (2016). https://doi.org/10.1007/978-3-319-48881-3_56
5. Bolme, D.S., Beveridge, J.R., Draper, B.A., Lui, Y.M.: Visual object tracking using adaptive correlation filters. In: 2010 IEEE Conference on Computer Vision and Pattern Recognition (CVPR), pp. 2544–2550. IEEE (2010)
6. Bolme, D.S., Draper, B.A., Beveridge, J.R.: Average of synthetic exact filters. In: IEEE Conference on Computer Vision and Pattern Recognition, CVPR 2009, pp. 2105–2112. IEEE (2009)
7. Bolme, D.S., Lui, Y.M., Draper, B.A., Beveridge, J.R.: Simple real-time human detection using a single correlation filter. In: 2009 Twelfth IEEE International Workshop on Performance Evaluation of Tracking and Surveillance (PETS-Winter), pp. 1–8. IEEE (2009)
8. Caelles, S., Maninis, K.K., Pont-Tuset, J., Leal-Taixé, L., Cremers, D., Van Gool, L.: One-shot video object segmentation. arXiv preprint arXiv:1611.05198 (2016)
9. Dalal, N., Triggs, B.: Histograms of oriented gradients for human detection. In: IEEE Computer Society Conference on Computer Vision and Pattern Recognition, CVPR 2005, vol. 1, pp. 886–893. IEEE (2005)
10. Danelljan, M., Häger, G., Khan, F.S., Felsberg, M.: Accurate scale estimation for robust visual tracking. In: British Machine Vision Conference, pp. 65.1–65.11 (2014)
11. Deng, J., Dong, W., Socher, R., Li, L.J., Li, K., Fei-Fei, L.: Imagenet: a large-scale hierarchical image database. In: IEEE Conference on Computer Vision and Pattern Recognition, CVPR 2009, pp. 248–255. IEEE (2009)
12. Hare, S., Golodetz, S., Saffari, A., Vineet, V., Cheng, M.M., Hicks, S.L., Torr, P.H.: Struck: structured output tracking with kernels. IEEE Trans. Pattern Anal. Mach. Intell. **38**(10), 2096–2109 (2016)
13. Henriques, J.F., Caseiro, R., Martins, P., Batista, J.: Exploiting the circulant structure of tracking-by-detection with kernels. In: Fitzgibbon, A., Lazebnik, S., Perona, P., Sato, Y., Schmid, C. (eds.) ECCV 2012. LNCS, vol. 7575, pp. 702–715. Springer, Heidelberg (2012). https://doi.org/10.1007/978-3-642-33765-9_50

14. Henriques, J.F., Caseiro, R., Martins, P., Batista, J.: High-speed tracking with kernelized correlation filters. IEEE Trans. Pattern Anal. Mach. Intell. **37**(3), 583–596 (2015)
15. Hester, C.F., Casasent, D.: Multivariant technique for multiclass pattern recognition. Appl. Opt. **19**(11), 1758–1761 (1980)
16. Hong, Z., Chen, Z., Wang, C., Mei, X., Prokhorov, D., Tao, D.: Multi-store tracker (muster): a cognitive psychology inspired approach to object tracking. In: Computer Vision and Pattern Recognition, pp. 749–758 (2015)
17. Jia, X.: Visual tracking via adaptive structural local sparse appearance model. In: IEEE Conference on Computer Vision and Pattern Recognition, pp. 1822–1829 (2012)
18. Jia, Y., Shelhamer, E., Donahue, J., Karayev, S., Long, J., Girshick, R., Guadarrama, S., Darrell, T.: Caffe: convolutional architecture for fast feature embedding. In: Proceedings of the 22nd ACM International Conference on Multimedia, pp. 675–678. ACM (2014)
19. Kiani Galoogahi, H., Sim, T., Lucey, S.: Multi-channel correlation filters. In: Proceedings of the IEEE International Conference on Computer Vision, pp. 3072–3079 (2013)
20. Krizhevsky, A., Sutskever, I., Hinton, G.E.: Imagenet classification with deep convolutional neural networks. In: Advances in Neural Information Processing Systems, pp. 1097–1105 (2012)
21. Li, H., Li, Y., Porikli, F.: DeepTrack: learning discriminative feature representations online for robust visual tracking. IEEE Trans. Image Process. **25**(4), 1834–1848 (2016)
22. Mahalanobis, A., Kumar, B.V., Casasent, D.: Minimum average correlation energy filters. Appl. Opt. **26**(17), 3633–3640 (1987)
23. Nam, H., Han, B.: Learning multi-domain convolutional neural networks for visual tracking. In: Proceedings of the IEEE Conference on Computer Vision and Pattern Recognition, pp. 4293–4302 (2016)
24. Qi, Y., Zhang, S., Qin, L., Yao, H., Huang, Q., Lim, J., Yang, M.H.: Hedged deep tracking. In: Proceedings of the IEEE Conference on Computer Vision and Pattern Recognition, pp. 4303–4311 (2016)
25. Simonyan, K., Zisserman, A.: Very deep convolutional networks for large-scale image recognition. arXiv preprint arXiv:1409.1556 (2014)
26. Szegedy, C., Liu, W., Jia, Y., Sermanet, P., Reed, S., Anguelov, D., Erhan, D., Vanhoucke, V., Rabinovich, A.: Going deeper with convolutions. In: Proceedings of the IEEE Conference on Computer Vision and Pattern Recognition, pp. 1–9 (2015)
27. Wang, L., Ouyang, W., Wang, X., Lu, H.: Visual tracking with fully convolutional networks. In: Proceedings of the IEEE International Conference on Computer Vision, pp. 3119–3127 (2015)
28. Wang, L., Ouyang, W., Wang, X., Lu, H.: STCT: sequentially training convolutional networks for visual tracking. In: Proceedings of the IEEE Conference on Computer Vision and Pattern Recognition, pp. 1373–1381 (2016)
29. Wu, Y., Lim, J., Yang, M.H.: Object tracking benchmark. IEEE Trans. Pattern Anal. Mach. Intell. **37**(9), 1834–1848 (2015)
30. Zhang, K., Zhang, L., Liu, Q., Zhang, D., Yang, M.-H.: Fast visual tracking via dense spatio-temporal context learning. In: Fleet, D., Pajdla, T., Schiele, B., Tuytelaars, T. (eds.) ECCV 2014. LNCS, vol. 8693, pp. 127–141. Springer, Cham (2014). https://doi.org/10.1007/978-3-319-10602-1_9
31. Zhang, L., Lu, H., Du, D., Liu, L.: Sparse hashing tracking. IEEE Trans. Image Process. **25**(2), 840–849 (2016). A Publication of the IEEE Signal Processing Society

PPEDNet: Pyramid Pooling Encoder-Decoder Network for Real-Time Semantic Segmentation

Zhentao Tan[1,2], Bin Liu[1,2(✉)], and Nenghai Yu[1,2]

[1] Key Laboratory of Electromagnetic Space Information,
Chinese Academy of Sciences, Hefei, China
[2] School of Information Science and Technology,
University of Science and Technology of China, Hefei, China
flowice@ustc.edu.cn

Abstract. Image semantic segmentation is a fundamental problem and plays an important role in computer vision and artificial intelligence. Recent deep neural networks have improved the accuracy of semantic segmentation significantly. Meanwhile, the number of network parameters and floating point operations have also increased notably. The real-world applications not only have high requirements on the segmentation accuracy, but also demand real-time processing. In this paper, we propose a pyramid pooling encoder-decoder network named PPEDNet for both better accuracy and faster processing speed. Our encoder network is based on VGG16 and discards the fully connected layers due to their huge amounts of parameters. To extract context feature efficiently, we design a pyramid pooling architecture. The decoder is a trainable convolutional network for upsampling the output of the encoder, and fine-tuning the segmentation details. Our method is evaluated on CamVid dataset, achieving 7.214% mIOU accuracy improvement while reducing 17.9% of the parameters compared with the state-of-the-art algorithm.

Keywords: Semantic segmentation · Pyramid pooling · Real-time

1 Introduction

Image semantic segmentation is to divide an image into several regions with each region having the same semantic implication. Over the years, researchers have proposed many powerful algorithms, which can be roughly grouped into two categories: traditional approaches and deep convolutional neural network (DCNN) based approaches. Traditional approaches rely on low-level vision cues, such as Normalized cut [24]. They are not suitable for complex scenes due to their limited performance. By contrast, recent approaches have achieved remarkable success by applying deep convolutional neural network to this pixel-level labeling task [6,18,19,30]. DCNN is applied to classification tasks in the early days, such as handwritten digit recognition, image classification and object detection. Recently, the availability of large scale well annotated datasets and

© Springer International Publishing AG 2017
Y. Zhao et al. (Eds.): ICIG 2017, Part I, LNCS 10666, pp. 328–339, 2017.
https://doi.org/10.1007/978-3-319-71607-7_29

computationally-powerful machines have pushed forward the development of deep convolutional neural network. Moreover, it has been widely proved that the well-trained DCNN models [12,25,26] pretrained on these large scale datasets can be transferred to other vision tasks, like image semantic segmentation. For better performance, deeper and larger convolutional neural networks are explored [15,21,29], requiring more computing resources and inference time.

However, the real-world applications such as augmented reality wearables, self-driving vehicles and other automatic devices have a strong demand for image semantic segmentation algorithms that can process in real-time. Taking self-driving vehicles as an example, the complex traffic environment requires autopilot system can deal with emergency timely and effectively. Obviously, the existing architectures can not meet this requirement [7,10,21,29]. To solve this problem, several neural networks have been proposed to balance the segment accuracy and inference time, such as SegNet [1] and ENET [23]. These networks pay more attention to complex segmentation tasks such as in road and indoor scenes, and achieve a fast segmentation speed at the cost of accuracy.

In this paper, we propose a new convolutional neural network architecture which achieves higher segmentation accuracy and faster inference speed. Our network is primarily motivated by the road scene dataset [4] which requires modeling both appearance and shape, understanding the context between different classes such as the road surface and the side-walk. The main contributions of this paper can be summarized as follows: (1) we propose a new DCNN-based network architecture which reduces the model size notably; (2) we explore a well-designed pyramid pooling architecture to extract contextual information; (3) we build a practical system for semantic segmentation which outperforms existing approaches with similar processing speed [1,19,23].

The rest of this paper is organized in the following order. In Sect. 2 we review the related work about image semantic segmentation. In Sect. 3 we introduce the pyramid pooling encoder-decoder network architecture and discuss the advantages of this architecture. In Sect. 4, we evaluate our network empirically and compare it with other networks. Finally, we give a conclusion on our work in Sect. 5.

2   Related Work

With the development of convolutional neural networks, image semantic segmentation has achieved unprecedented performance recently. Fully convolutional neural network (FCN) [19] was the first algorithm used in PASCAL VOC 2012 segmentation tasks [9]. This method was based on VGG16 and changed its fully connected layers to convolutional ones. Pre-trained on ImageNet [2], FCN can extract the features of object efficiently and outperform all previous methods. This successful attempt encouraged other researchers to exploit deep network architecture for better segmentation results.

The direct prediction of FCN based methods are usually in low resolution. To obtain high resolution predictions, many recent methods focus on refining

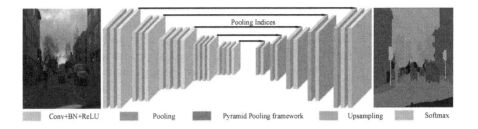

Fig. 1. The architecture of pyramid pooling encoder-decoder network

the low resolution predictions. DeepLab-CRF [6] performed bilinear upsampling of the score map to the input image size and applied the fully connected conditional random fields [14] to refine the object boundary. The work in [21] trained deconvolutional layers to upsample the low resolution predictions. CRF-RNN [30] applied a recurrent neural network to replace conditional random fields for end-to-end training. To reduce the computation time, Liu et al. [18] and Lin et al. [15] both designed an efficient approximate inference algorithm for fully connected CRF models. The network proposed in [5] extracted the edge feature maps and applied a discriminatively trained domain transform so as to combine it with the score maps from FCN. The networks such as [16,22,28] used context information for finer segmentation results. These networks achieve high score in image semantic segmentation challenges like PASCAL VOC 2012 [9], but can not meet the requirement of real-world application because of their large network architectures.

Unlike employing the whole CNNs directly, SegNet [1] discarded the fully connected layers of VGG16, so as to reduce the number of parameters. Furthermore, this network only stored the max-pooling indices in the encoder to its corresponding upsampling layers. As a result, SegNet had a great performance both on segmentation accuracy and processing speed. Another network, named ENET [23], focused on real-time image segmentation and chose to pre-train it's own encoder network in ImageNet classification task to avoid overlarge network architecture. Tested on an NVIDIA Titan X GPU, ENET achieved the fastest implementation speed, more than 100 fps. However, the high segmentation speed was built at the sacrifice of segmentation accuracy.

3   Network Architecture

Our network architecture PPEDNet (Pyramid Pooling Encoder-Decoder Network) is shown in Fig. 1. It consists of a large encoder network, a corresponding small decoder network followed by a pixel-wise classification layer. The encoder corresponds to the feature extractor that transforms the input image to multidimensional feature representation, whereas the decoder is a shape generator that produces segmentation result from the features extracted from the encoder. Following the process of image segmentation, we first present the encoder network and then the decoder network.

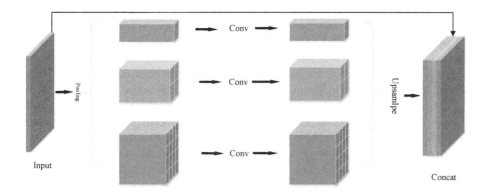

Fig. 2. Pyramid pooling model

3.1   Encoder Network

Feature extraction is the premise and core of pixel-wise classification. Thus, a powerful encoder network is of great importance. Our feature extraction framework is based on VGG16 which is a very successful image classification network. Therefore, we can initialize the training process from weights trained for classification on large datasets [2]. Each *encoder* in the encoder network performs convolution with a filter bank to produce a set of feature maps. They are then batch normalized. Following that, an element-wise rectified-linear non-linearity (ReLU) max $(0, x)$ is performed. Max pooling with a 2×2 window and stride 2 (non-overlapping window) is used to result in a large input image context (spatial window) for each pixel in the feature maps. Different from the original VGG network, we remove the fully connected layers because these layers consume too many parameters. Besides, the most significant change is that we have designed a pyramid pooling framework.

Most convolutional neural networks like FCN [19] and DeepLab [6] only predict each pixel independently, without considering context relationship between each receptive field. This limits the ability of diverse scenes understanding, and networks in [6,19] may usually make mistakes when there exists similar appearance inter class. Although some post-processing methods such as conditional random field, can calculate the pairwise potential and smooth noisy segmentation maps, the complicated inference operations reduce the processing speed severely. Liu et al. [17] tried to learn global context with global average pooling, and yielded encouraging improvement. Compared with the Parsenet [17], pyramid pooling model has a stronger ability of extracting and combining different regional characteristics.

The pyramid pooling model is shown in Fig. 2. The input is high-level feature maps, which in our network is the output of Conv5-1 of VGG16. Then, three different pyramid scales are used to extract different sub-region features from the input feature maps, forming pooled representation for different locations. The outputs of different levels of the pyramid pooling model contain feature maps of different sizes. We use 1×1 convolutional operation after each pyramid pooling layer to adjust the weights of every channel. To concatenate these feature maps with the original one, a direct upsampling operation is used to resize the low-dimensional feature maps, producing the desired feature map via bilinear interpolation. Finally, different levels of feature maps are concatenated as a hybrid multi-scale context input for further convolutional layers. Compared to other multi-scale pooling modules, our pyramid pooling model extracts the multi-scale feature maps in the same high-level maps, and concatenates these new contexts directly without several 3×3 convolutional operations. This makes the raw hybrid multi-scale context with the same resolution, which provides strong evidence for classification.

The number of pyramid pooling levels and sizes can be modified according to how many sub-regional contexts we want to combine. Considering the input images of CamVid dataset with a resolution of 480×360 (Width, Height), the feature maps which are the input of the pyramid pooling model (30×23) are too small to be divided into many levels. So, our pyramid pooling model has three levels with bin sizes of 1×1, 2×2, and 4×4. Furthermore, we note that road scene images could always be divided into three parts: the road in the middle and the buildings on the two sides. A three-level pyramid pooling model with sizes of 1×1, 3×2, and 6×4 should be more reasonable. For convenience, we name these two frameworks as the original pyramid pooling and the attentional pyramid pooling respectively. Inspired by Zhao et al. [29], we choose average pooling as the type of pooling operation. With the pyramid pooling model, our network extracts an effective global context for pixel-level scene parsing.

3.2   Decoder Network

With several layers of max-pooling, low-resolution feature maps from the encoder network have a loss of spatial resolution, which is unbeneficial to segmentation. Thus, we need an appropriate method to upsample these feature maps to dense high-resolution segmentation image with the same size as original input image. Recent work has pursued two directions to address localization challenge. The first approach is to employ information from multiple layers in the network [19] or a super-pixel representation [20] to optimise the edge segmentation. The second approach is to design a trainable decoder network to learn deconvolution [1,21]. These decoder networks are always the mirror of the encoder networks.

In our method, we propose an asymmetric encoder-decoder network that is different from the one presented in [1]. This is motivated by the idea that the encoder network should extract the appearance and shape features, providing strong evidence for classifier. By contrast, decoder network is only required to restore the resolution of the input feature maps and fine-tune the segmentation

details. To explore the influence of decoder network on segmentation performance, we choose SegNet [1] as the baseline, and try three different decoder
networks. First, we remove the deconv3-3, deconv4-3 and deconv5-3 convolutional layers in SegNet. Then, only one convolutional layer is retained between
two upsampling layers. Further more, we try to replace the convolutional layers
with the bottleneck architecture presented in ENET [23] for its success. Different from the original bottleneck, we make some changes which are shown in
Fig. 3. Figure 3(a) is the original convolutional block, it consists of three parts,
a 3 × 3 convolutional layer, a batch normalization layer and a rectified linear
unit. Figure 3(b) is the bottleneck module which has two branches. On the right
of the branch includes three convolutional layer: a 1 × 1 projection that reduces
the channels of feature maps, a main convolutional layer with 3 × 3 kernels, and
a 1 × 1 expansion that resizes the channels. On the left of the branch is a 1 × 1
adjustion matches the number of the channels. The details of the experiment are
shown in Sect. 4. As a result, we choose the second approach for the balance of
accuracy and speed.

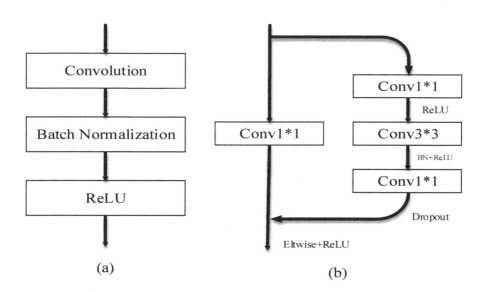

(a)   (b)

Fig. 3. The comparison of convolutional module. (a) Original convolutional block. (b)
Bottleneck module.

Another noteworthy point is that the *decoder* in the decoder network upsam-
ples its input feature maps using the memorized max-pooling indices from the
corresponding encoder feature maps. Inspired by SegNet [1], we only store the
max-pooling indices, i.e., the location of the maximum feature value in each
pooling window is memorized for each encoder feature map. For intuitive comparison, we inference DeconvNet [21] which applies this upsamle technology, and
the required memory is reduced greatly (from 1872M to 1174M).

4 Experiments

We conduct experiments on CamVid dataset [4]. This dataset consists of 367 training and 233 testing RGB images at 960×720 resolution. There are eleven different classes such as tree, car, building, etc.[1] To reduce the computational requirements, we reshape the image to 480×360 before training.

Table 1. Comparison of decoder variants.

Model	GA/%	CAA/%	mIoU/%	IM/MB	MS/MB	IS/FPS
SegNet	87.462	69.531	**56.984**	1038	112.4	13
SegNet-1	**87.492**	71.116	56.893	987	92.1	14.3
SegNet-2	87.445	70.956	56.89	**873**	71.3	**16.8**
SegNet-3	69.993	58.958	39.834	1235	**59.4**	11.3

4.1 Decoder Variant

We train three different decoder variants described in Sect. 3 on CamVid dataset. Inspired by SegNet [1], the encoder weights are initialized by VGG16 model pre-trained on ImageNet classification challenge, the decoder weights are initialized using the technique in [11]. All the variants are trained using stochastic gradient descent (SGD) [3] with a fixed learning rate of 0.001 and momentum of 0.9. Before each epoch, the training set is shuffled and each mini-batch (4 images) is then picked in order to ensure that each image is used only once in each epoch. The weighted cross-entropy loss is used as loss function for training the network. There is a need to balance the weights since there is too many differences between the number of each class in the set. The balance strategy is named median frequency balancing [8], which is assigned to calculate the ratio of the median of class frequency on the entire training set, implying larger classes have smaller weights while smaller classes have higher weights. To compare the three different decoder variants quantitatively, we use six commonly used performance measures: global accuracy (GA) measures the percentage of pixels that are correctly classified in the entire dataset, class average accuracy (CAA) is the predictive accuracy over all classes, mean intersection over union (mIoU) is a more stringent metric than class average accuracy since it penalizes false positive predictions, inference memory (IM) is the memory requirement to segment images, model size (MS) means the number of parameters and inference speed (IS) tests the segmentation efficiency.

The experiment results are illustrated in Table 1. There are three decoder variants named SegNet-1, SegNet-2 and SegNet-3. SegNet-1 removes the deconv3-3, deconv4-3 and deconv5-3 convolutional layers. SegNet-2 only retains

---

[1] The twelfth class contains unlabeled data, which is ignored while training.

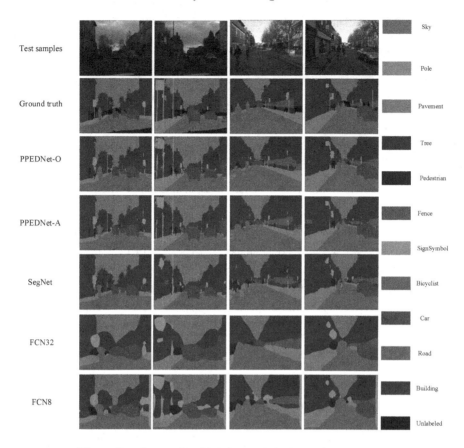

Fig. 4. Results on CamVid day and dusk test/val samples.

one convolutional layer between two upsampling layers. SegNet-3 is based on SegNet-2 and replaces the convolutional layers with the bottleneck architecture in the decoder. Compared with the baseline (SegNet), SegNet-2 reduces 34.6% model size, accelerates more than 3 fps and has only 0.094% mIoU loss. It is notable that when it comes to global accuracy and class average accuracy, SegNet-1 even has better performance than the baseline. This suggests that some parameters in decoder layers are redundant for upsample. However, the huge successful bottleneck architecture in ENET [23] has a poorer performance, reduce 17.15% mIoU, 17.47% global accuracy and 10.57% class average accuracy. Further more, this architecture pluses feature map with the lower one, which infinitely increasing the required inference memory, thus probably making slower inference speed.

Table 2. The comparison of accuracy among different classes.

Model	Sky	Building	Pole	Road	Pavement	Tree	SignSymbol	Fence	Car	Pedestrian	Bicyclist
SegNet	93.11	87.82	35.15	94.21	86.07	81.16	56.07	39.41	80.84	71.90	39.10
ENET	95.1	74.7	35.4	95.1	86.7	77.8	51.0	51.7	82.4	67.2	34.1
ReSeg	93.0	86.8	35.6	98.0	87.3	84.7	48.6	20.9	87.3	63.3	43.5
FCN32	90.27	74.39	10.22	74.05	84.65	80.73	40.47	54.83	80.83	53.03	46.45
FCN8	89.24	71.85	25.66	87.90	82.59	82.31	65.58	52.22	79.61	74.90	55.72
PPED-O	94.10	88.51	48.37	96.84	87.79	87.93	57.89	52.00	83.17	72.17	60.42
PPED-A	94.66	90.73	40.30	97.17	87.68	86.53	53.27	50.87	81.41	73.01	62.05

Table 3. Quantitative comparison of semantic segmentation on the CamVid test set when trained on its original train set.

Model	GA/%	CAA/%	mIoU/%	IM/MB	MS/MB	IS/FPS
SegNet	87.462	69.531	56.984	1038	112.4	13
FCN32	77.535	62.720	46.441	1271	512.4	12.1
FCN8	80.94	69.78	50.50	1290	512.5	11.7
PPED-O	89.956	**75.382**	63.294	884	92.3	**16.4**
PPED-A	**90.310**	74.334	**64.198**	884	92.3	16.2

4.2   Comparison

We compare our network with ENET [23], ReSeg [27], FCN × 32 and FCN × 8 [19] on the test set for their fine segment accuracy and inference speed. All the compared network architectures are trained on the original CamVid train set with 367 RGB images. The objective is to understand the performance of these architectures when trained on the same dataset. We add batch normalization [13] layers after each convolutional layer in order to end-to-end train the network. To provide a controlled benchmark we use the same SGD solver [3] with a fixed momentum of 0.9, the learning rate is unfixed for different convergence speed between these networks. A mini-batch size of 4 is set to ensure all architectures can be trained on an NVIDIA Titan X GPU and dropout of 0.5 is added for some deeper convolutional layers to prevent overfitting. VGG16 pre-trained model parameters are used in order to accelerate convergence and other layers' weights are initialized using the technique in He et al. [11]. There is no limit for maximum epoch, and all architectures are trained until no further performance increase is observed.

The results in Table 2 show the accuracy of each class that belongs to different architectures. ENET performance is provided by [23] while the data of ReSeg is provided by Visin [27]. Our network have two versions which are introduced in Sect. 3. PPED-O uses the original pyramid pooling framework, and PPED-A is with the attentional pyramid pooling framework. Both our two networks use the second decoder variant described in Sect. 3 as their decoder. It is clear that our networks get the highest accuracy in six of the categories. Some classes like pole and bicyclist on which SegNet and ENET get a poor segmentation result, are much better segmented by our networks. Different pyramid pooling models also influence the segmentation accuracy. Attention pyramid pooling outperforms in five classes which exactly distribute on the left, middle and right of an image. It is notable that particular designed pooling focuses on these three regions, making finer segmentation of some objects like pedestrian and road. But for other classes, especially someone which is between buildings and the road, original pyramid pooling has better performance. Table 3 shows more performance metrics, and our network outperforms existing state-of-the-art algorithms in all the metrics. Our model obtain a 17.9% less of parameters than SegNet, and accelerates implementation speed more than 3 images per second. For more detailed comparison, attention pyramid pooling has better performance in global accuracy and mIoU. But compared in class average accuracy, original pyramid pooling is better. The qualitative comparisons of our network predictions with other deep architectures can be seen in Fig. 4. It is clear that our proposed architecture has a stronger ability to segment smaller classes in road scenes.

5   Conclusion

We propose a novel neural network architecture for complex scene image semantic segmentation. The main motivation is the need of an efficient method for road scene understanding which works well in terms of both accuracy and computational time. For this objective, we propose a pyramid pooling encoder-decoder network architecture. We compare it with others in the metrics of mean of intersection over union (mIoU), inference memory, model size and particularly processing speed. The experimental results reveal both 7.214% mIoU improvement and more than 3 fps acceleration compared with existing state-of-the-art algorithm, SegNet [1].

Acknowledgement. This work is supported by the National Natural Science Foundation of China (Grant No. 61371192), the Key Laboratory Foundation of the Chinese Academy of Sciences (CXJJ-17S044) and the Fundamental Research Funds for the Central Universities (WK2100330002).

References

1. Badrinarayanan, V., Kendall, A., Cipolla, R.: Segnet: a deep convolutional encoder-decoder architecture for image segmentation. arXiv preprint arXiv:1511.00561 (2015)
2. Berg, A., Deng, J., Fei-Fei, L.: Large scale visual recognition challenge (ILSVRC) (2010). http://www.image-net.org/challenges/LSVRC
3. Bottou, L.: Large-scale machine learning with stochastic gradient descent. In: Lechevallier, Y., Saporta, G. (eds.) Proceedings of COMPSTAT 2010, pp. 177–186. Physica-Verlag, Heidelberg (2010). https://doi.org/10.1007/978-3-7908-2604-3_16
4. Brostow, G.J., Fauqueur, J., Cipolla, R.: Semantic object classes in video: a high-definition ground truth database. Pattern Recogn. Lett. **30**(2), 88–97 (2009)

5. Chen, L.C., Barron, J.T., Papandreou, G., Murphy, K., Yuille, A.L.: Semantic image segmentation with task-specific edge detection using CNNs and a discriminatively trained domain transform. In: Proceedings of the IEEE Conference on Computer Vision and Pattern Recognition, pp. 4545–4554 (2016)
6. Chen, L.C., Papandreou, G., Kokkinos, I., Murphy, K., Yuille, A.L.: Semantic image segmentation with deep convolutional nets and fully connected CRFs. arXiv preprint arXiv:1412.7062 (2014)
7. Chen, L.C., Yang, Y., Wang, J., Xu, W., Yuille, A.L.: Attention to scale: Scale-aware semantic image segmentation. In: Proceedings of the IEEE Conference on Computer Vision and Pattern Recognition, pp. 3640–3649 (2016)
8. Eigen, D., Fergus, R.: Predicting depth, surface normals and semantic labels with a common multi-scale convolutional architecture. In: Proceedings of the IEEE International Conference on Computer Vision, pp. 2650–2658 (2015)
9. Everingham, M., Eslami, S.A., Van Gool, L., Williams, C.K., Winn, J., Zisserman, A.: The pascal visual object classes challenge: a retrospective. Int. J. Comput. Vis. **111**(1), 98–136 (2015)
10. Ghiasi, G., Fowlkes, C.C.: Laplacian pyramid reconstruction and refinement for semantic segmentation. In: Leibe, B., Matas, J., Sebe, N., Welling, M. (eds.) ECCV 2016. LNCS, vol. 9907, pp. 519–534. Springer, Cham (2016). https://doi.org/10.1007/978-3-319-46487-9_32
11. He, K., Zhang, X., Ren, S., Sun, J.: Delving deep into rectifiers: surpassing human-level performance on imagenet classification. In: Proceedings of the IEEE International Conference on Computer Vision, pp. 1026–1034 (2015)
12. He, K., Zhang, X., Ren, S., Sun, J.: Deep residual learning for image recognition. In: Proceedings of the IEEE Conference on Computer Vision and Pattern Recognition, pp. 770–778 (2016)
13. Ioffe, S., Szegedy, C.: Batch normalization: accelerating deep network training by reducing internal covariate shift. arXiv preprint arXiv:1502.03167 (2015)
14. Lafferty, J., McCallum, A., Pereira, F., et al.: Conditional random fields: probabilistic models for segmenting and labeling sequence data. In: Proceedings of the Eighteenth International Conference on Machine Learning, ICML, vol. 1, pp. 282–289 (2001)
15. Lin, G., Shen, C., van den Hengel, A., Reid, I.: Efficient piecewise training of deep structured models for semantic segmentation. In: Proceedings of the IEEE Conference on Computer Vision and Pattern Recognition, pp. 3194–3203 (2016)
16. Lin, G., Shen, C., van den Hengel, A., Reid, I.: Exploring context with deep structured models for semantic segmentation. arXiv preprint arXiv:1603.03183 (2016)
17. Liu, W., Rabinovich, A., Berg, A.C.: Parsenet: looking wider to see better. arXiv preprint arXiv:1506.04579 (2015)
18. Liu, Z., Li, X., Luo, P., Loy, C.C., Tang, X.: Semantic image segmentation via deep parsing network. In: Proceedings of the IEEE International Conference on Computer Vision, pp. 1377–1385 (2015)
19. Long, J., Shelhamer, E., Darrell, T.: Fully convolutional networks for semantic segmentation. In: Proceedings of the IEEE Conference on Computer Vision and Pattern Recognition, pp. 3431–3440 (2015)
20. Mostajabi, M., Yadollahpour, P., Shakhnarovich, G.: Feedforward semantic segmentation with zoom-out features. In: Proceedings of the IEEE Conference on Computer Vision and Pattern Recognition, pp. 3376–3385 (2015)
21. Noh, H., Hong, S., Han, B.: Learning deconvolution network for semantic segmentation. In: Proceedings of the IEEE International Conference on Computer Vision, pp. 1520–1528 (2015)

22. Pan, T., Wang, B., Ding, G., Yong, J.H.: Fully convolutional neural networks with full-scale-features for semantic segmentation (2017)
23. Paszke, A., Chaurasia, A., Kim, S., Culurciello, E.: ENet: a deep neural network architecture for real-time semantic segmentation. arXiv preprint arXiv:1606.02147 (2016)
24. Shi, J., Malik, J.: Normalized cuts and image segmentation. IEEE Trans. Pattern Anal. Mach. Intell. **22**(8), 888–905 (2000)
25. Simonyan, K., Zisserman, A.: Very deep convolutional networks for large-scale image recognition. arXiv preprint arXiv:1409.1556 (2014)
26. Szegedy, C., Liu, W., Jia, Y., Sermanet, P., Reed, S., Anguelov, D., Erhan, D., Vanhoucke, V., Rabinovich, A.: Going deeper with convolutions. In: Proceedings of the IEEE Conference on Computer Vision and Pattern Recognition, pp. 1–9 (2015)
27. Visin, F., Ciccone, M., Romero, A., Kastner, K., Cho, K., Bengio, Y., Matteucci, M., Courville, A.: ReSeg: a recurrent neural network-based model for semantic segmentation. In: Proceedings of the IEEE Conference on Computer Vision and Pattern Recognition Workshops, pp. 41–48 (2016)
28. Wang, P., Chen, P., Yuan, Y., Liu, D., Huang, Z., Hou, X., Cottrell, G.: Understanding convolution for semantic segmentation. arXiv preprint arXiv:1702.08502 (2017)
29. Zhao, H., Shi, J., Qi, X., Wang, X., Jia, J.: Pyramid scene parsing network. arXiv preprint arXiv:1612.01105 (2016)
30. Zheng, S., Jayasumana, S., Romera-Paredes, B., Vineet, V., Su, Z., Du, D., Huang, C., Torr, P.H.: Conditional random fields as recurrent neural networks. In: Proceedings of the IEEE International Conference on Computer Vision, pp. 1529–1537 (2015)

A New Kinect Approach to Judge Unhealthy Sitting Posture Based on Neck Angle and Torso Angle

Leiyue Yao, Weidong Min[✉], and Hao Cui

School of Information Engineering, Nanchang University, Nanchang 330031, China
minweidong@ncu.edu.cn

Abstract. Sitting posture has a close relationship with our health, keeping right sitting posture is important for people to avoid chronic diseases. However, automatic unhealthy sitting posture detection system is rare, especially for those based on computer vision technology. This paper proposes a new method of judging unhealthy sitting posture based on neck angle and torso angle detection using Kinect sensor. The method tracks neck angle and torso angle as two representative features from the depth image in a given period of time to judge whether the sitting posture is healthy or not. Experimental results show that the proposed method can judge sitting posture effectively for different unhealthy sitting types. Compared with the existing methods of action recognition, our method only needs a Kinect sensor without any other wearable sensors and is time efficient and robust because of only calculating two angles.

Keywords: Sitting posture judgment · Neck angle · Torso angle · Depth image

1 Introduction

Sitting is one of the most common postures in daily activities. Unhealthy sitting postures will inevitably increase the risk of musculoskeletal disorders [1] while good sitting posture is helpful for children growth and eyesight protection. For these and many more other reasons, the number of researchers on sitting posture correction is getting larger and larger over recent years. With the development of computer science and electronic sensors, automatic unhealthy sitting posture detection methods give help for us to form a good sitting habit. In general, these methods can be divided into two types, methods based on wearable devices and methods based on computer vision.

Mattmann et al. [2] researched on recognizing 27 upper body postures using a garment with strain sensors. The method of Harms et al. [3] recognized 21 human exercise postures through a smart shirt system (SMASH) with acceleration sensors. Karantonis et al. [4] used a waist-mounted tri-axial accelerometer system to classify human movement status. The approach of Jeong et al. [5] used a 3-axis accelerometer to monitor human's activity volume and recognize emergent situations. Barba et al. [6] aimed at creating a sensor capable of providing detection measures at the least possible cost. Although the above wearable sensors approaches gathered sufficient information to detect, classify and recognize human activities and worked well in posture detection and recognition, they have some obvious disadvantages. The wearable systems can be a

© Springer International Publishing AG 2017
Y. Zhao et al. (Eds.): ICIG 2017, Part I, LNCS 10666, pp. 340–350, 2017.
https://doi.org/10.1007/978-3-319-71607-7_30

source of inconvenience or discomfort. Moreover, the wearable devices can be worn gradually or damaged due to external factors such as being squeezed or pressed, which lead to failure to collect information.

Due to these main disadvantages of the wearable device based approaches, the methods based on computer vision become a hot topic in recent researches. The computer vision based methods need no wearable devices and extract features from videos using image processing technologies. Li and Chen [7] researched on recognizing human postures including standing, sitting, kneeling and stooping through analyzing 10 parameters extracted from video frames. Boulay et al. [8, 9] proposed a 3D human-body-posture recognition method to recognize standing, sitting, lying down and stooping by comparing horizontal and vertical projections of human body with their corresponding predefined 3D human posture models. A method proposed by Wang et al. [10] used background subtraction on the depth image created by Kinect sensor to extract a silhouette contour of a human, and determined different type of activities using a pre-trained LVQ (Learning Vector Quantization) neural network.

Among the computer vision methods, approaches based on machine learning, deep learning and neural network are popular and work well in posture recognition. Althloothi et al. [11] presented a shape representation and kinematic structure, and used the MKL (Multiple Kernel Learning) technique at the kernel level for human activity recognition. Ruizhi and Lingqiao [12] achieved posture estimates by encoding each local descriptor, named as trajectorylet in their method, using a discriminative trajectorylet detector set which is selected from a large number of candidate detectors trained through exemplar-SVMs. Because of environmental problems and intrinsic noise, videos of similar actions may suffer from huge intra-class variations. Jalal et al. [13] solved these problems by introducing the ELS-TSVM (Energy-based Least Square Twin Support Vector Machine) algorithm. Jiayu et al. [14] proposed an abstract and efficient motion tensor decomposition approach to compress and reorganize the motion data. Together with a multi-classification algorithm, the approach is able to efficiently and accurately differentiate various postures. Vina and Mohamad [15] proposed a distribution-sensitive learning method based on RVM (Relevance Vector Machine) to recognize pose-based human gesture and solve imbalanced data problem. The gesture recognition method of Liu et al. [16] constructed a 3D2CNN (3D-based Deep Convolutional Neural Network) to directly learn spatio-temporal features, and then computed a joint based feature vector named JointVector for each sequence using the simple position and angle information between skeleton joints. Li et al. [17] proposed a feature learning approach based on SAE (Sparse Auto-Encoder) and principle component analysis for recognizing human gestures. Leng et al. [18] proposed a novel 3D model recognition mechanism based on DBM, which can be divided into two parts, the feature detection based on DBM and the classification based on semi-supervised learning method.

Since the depth image provides more information than color image, more and more researchers pay special attention to detect and recognize human postures and activities through analyzing the depth image. Kinect sensor is widely used because of its competitive price and exceptional performance in skeleton tracking. Ibañez et al. [19] proposed a lightweight approach to recognize gestures with Kinect through utilizing approximate string matching. In literatures [20–23], several other methods based on the depth image and Kinect sensors have been proposed for fall detection. Manghisi et al. [24] developed a semi-automatic evaluation software based on Kinect V2 to detect awkward postures in real time. Since depth image is unaffected by illumination of the environment and shadows, Wang et al. [25] proposed a new method based on depth image for human shape object detection and a combined method to recognize five postures. In literatures [26], spatiotemporal features created by RGB-D video sequences are used for human tracking and activity recognition. Alwani et al. [27] calculated joint angles by using the skeleton information to describe the sequences of actions. A Hidden Markov Model was used to classify actions. With the help of skeleton data and 3D joint positions, there are lots of new method emerged in the field of action recognition and classification. However, as for judging whether an action is correct or not, few attentions are paid to this research field.

As discussed above in details, the wearable based approaches have some limitations, while the deep learning based approaches based on computer vision are time consuming and depend on training data sets. To alleviate these issues, this paper presents a new method based on neck angle and torso angle detection in depth images to effectively recognize unhealthy sitting posture. The neck angle and the torso angle are the most representative two features of unhealthy sitting posture [28], therefore they are adopted as the criteria of sitting posture judgment in our approach. Being different from the wearable device based approaches and the deep learning based approaches, our approach only need a Kinect sensor without any other wearable sensors and is time efficient and robust because of only calculating two angles. Moreover, only usage of depth image ensures privacy protecting in some senses.

The following parts of this paper are organized as follows. Section 2 describes our proposed method of unhealthy sitting posture judgment. Section 3 discussed the experiments and results of our approach. Conclusions are given in Sect. 4.

2   Our New Approach for Unhealthy Sitting Posture Detection

2.1   Sitting Posture Modeling and Feature Extraction

Before judging the unhealthy sitting posture, criterions which can be used to differentiated healthy sitting posture and unhealthy sitting posture should be built first. In this paper, PEO (Portable Ergonomic Observation Method) [29] is adopted to model sitting posture. Thanks to the clear definition of unhealthy sitting posture in PEO, two representative features, i.e. the neck angle and the torso angle, can be extracted from the model. Figure 1 shows the comparison of healthy and unhealthy sitting gesture.

Figure 1(a) shows the typical healthy sitting gesture where two angles, the neck angle and the torso angle, are taken into consideration regarding whether the upper body and the head line up with the gravity direction, respectively. The neck angle is the angle between the vector from the head to the neck and the gravity vector. The torso angle is the angle between the vector from the neck to the spine base and the gravity vector. Unhealthy sitting gesture can be identified when the value of either of these two angles is larger than a given threshold 20°. McAtamney et al. [28] proved that the sitting posture

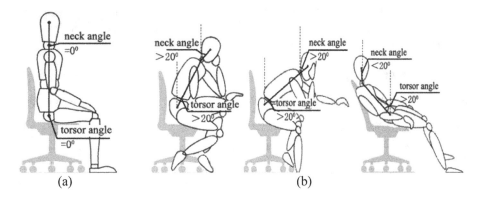

Fig. 1. Sitting posture model. (a) Healthy sitting gesture. (b) Three typical unhealthy sitting gestures.

is unhealthy when the torso angle is over 20°. Figure 1(b) shows three typical unhealthy sitting gestures.

Since sitting, especially sitting for work, is an activity occupying a long period of time, unhealthy sitting posture cannot be simply judged by one or two frames containing abnormal postures. In our proposed method, we take a certain period of time as a unit of measurement and calculate the ratio of unhealthy frames to total frames. When the ratio is larger than a given threshold, it is detected as the unhealthy sitting posture. Detailed algorithm is elaborated in Sect. 2.3.

2.2 Key Joints Acquisition and Angles Calculation

It is a hard work to estimate the joints of one's body in a RGB image. However, the depth image created by Kinect 2.0 sensor provides not only 3D information but also 25 joints information of a person when the person stands and 10 joints information when the person sits.

Every joint contains three-dimensional information and its tracking state. Although the spin joint cannot be tracked, it can be estimated by Kinect program. To calculate the neck angle and the torso angle discussed in Sect. 2.1, three joints of head, shoulder-center and spin, are adopted to fulfill this task. Formulas (1) and (2) are used to calculate the following two vectors. One is the vector from head to shoulder-center ($\overrightarrow{HSc}$). Another vector is from shoulder-center to spin ($\overrightarrow{ScSp}$).

$$\overrightarrow{HSc} = (X_h - X_{sc}, Y_h - Y_{sc}, Z_h - Z_{sc}) \tag{1}$$

$$\overrightarrow{ScSp} = (X_{Sc} - X_{Sp}, Y_{Sc} - Y_{Sp}, Z_{Sc} - Z_{Sp}) \tag{2}$$

Here, $H(X_h, Y_h, Z_h)$, $Sc(Xs_c, Ys_c, Zs_c)$ and $Sp(Xs_p, Ys_p, Zs_p)$ mean the position of head, shoulder-center and spin in three-dimensional space, respectively.

As shown in Fig. 2(a), both angles are formed through the gravity vector. We take the neck angle as an example to explain the way we calculate its value. Figure 2 shows the detailed steps.

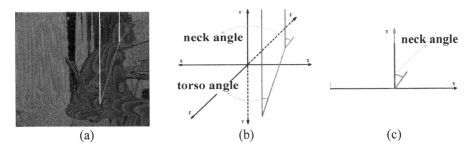

(a)   (b)   (c)

Fig. 2. Extracting the neck angle and the torso angle features from a depth image. (a) Depth image of a typical unhealthy sitting posture. (b) Vectors and angles in 3D space. (c) neck angle transformed in 2D plane

Firstly, once a person is detected, vector $\overrightarrow{HSc}$ can be extracted from the frame. Figure 2(a) shows the vector line which is calculated and drawn in depth image. Figure 2(b) is its presentation in 3D coordinate.

Secondly, according to vector translation theory in solid geometry, point Sc in $\overrightarrow{HSc}$ can be moved to the origin coordinate, and the vector can be presented in 2D coordinate. Figure 2(c) shows its final status.

Thirdly, since the gravity vector is always vertical to the ground, any point on y-axis and the origin coordinate can be used to form the gravity vector. To keep gravity vector and $\overrightarrow{HSc}$ in the same 2D plane, the position of gravity point in 3D coordinate can be defined as $G(Xsc, 0, Zxc)$, where the values in x-axis and z-axis are the same as shoulder-center. The gravity vector can be calculated using formula (3).

$$\overrightarrow{GSc} = (Xg - X_{Sc}, Yg - Y_{Sc}, Zg - Z_{Sc}) \tag{3}$$

Since Xg and Zg are the same as Xsc and Zxc, formula can also be simplified as follows in formula (4).

$$\overrightarrow{GSc} = (0, -Y_{Sc}, 0) \tag{4}$$

Forthly, when two vectors have been defined, the neck angle can be calculated using formula (5).

$$\cos(\alpha) = \cos(\overrightarrow{HSc}, \overrightarrow{GSc}) = \frac{\overrightarrow{GSc} \cdot \overrightarrow{HSc}}{|\overrightarrow{GSc}| \times |\overrightarrow{HSc}|} \tag{5}$$

These 4 steps elaborated above can also be used to calculate the torso angle in the same way.

2.3 Algorithm and Implementation

In our experiments, we used Kinect with 30 frames per second. Sitting is such an activity that does not change dramatically in a certain period of time. Therefore, there is no need to analyze every frame and calculate the angles. To reduce computational load, we extract and analyze one frame per 100 ms in our proposed method. Figure 3 shows the general block diagram.

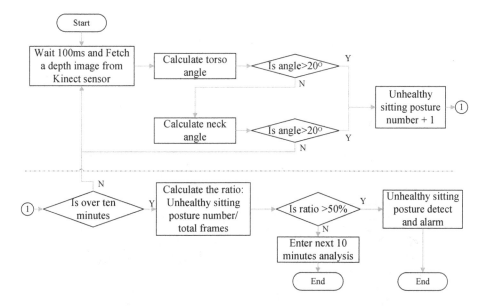

Fig. 3. General block diagram of our approach (Color figure online)

The general block can be divided into two parts. The upper portion above the red line in Fig. 3 shows the key steps of extracting the two angles in our algorithm. Once a person comes into the scene, the program starts to track the person. Every other 100 ms, a depth image will be extracted for neck angle and torso angle calculating. The number of total frame adds 1 and unhealthy sitting posture frames add 1 only when neck angle or torso angle is larger than 20°. Compare with neck, torso shows more times in unhealthy sitting posture, therefore torso angle is first calculated, while neck angle is calculated only when torso angle is less than 20°. In most cases, this order can reduce half computational load.

The lower portion under the red line in Fig. 3 shows the key steps of applying the criteria of unhealthy sitting posture judgment. Since sitting posture is an activity occupying a long period of time, the unhealthy posture is judged every 10 min. That is to say, every 10 min the UFR (Unhealthy Frame Ratio, i.e., the ratio of unhealthy frames to the total frames) is calculated and compare with the given threshold. If the ratio is larger than a given threshold 50%, the 10 min sitting posture is judged as unhealthy, or else it is healthy.

3 Experiment and Results

Our method was implemented using VisualStudio2013 + emgu.cv3.1 + Kinect on a PC using an Intel Core i7-4790 3.60 GHz processor, 8 GB RAM clocked at 1.333 GHZ. All tests were captured from a Kinect 2.0 sensor in BMP format of 640 × 480 resolution. The tests consist of 5 different types of sitting postures which include 3 healthy sitting posture videos and 30 unhealthy sitting posture videos in 4 different types. Since 10 min sitting posture supervision is too long, which can be compressed and simulated in a shorter period of time without losing generality and correctness of our experiments. All videos in our experiments are kept in 1 min for saving experimental time.

Before calculating neck angle and torso angle, the pre-work which should be guaranteed is finding out the position of three joints in depth image. Figure 4 shows that our proposed method is able to find out the exact position of head, shoulder-center and spin. However, the Kinect sensor should be installed properly because installing in a too high or too low position will have strong effect on the accuracy of joints recognition.

(a)   (b)

Fig. 4. Three joints in one's skeleton when sitting. (a) healthy sitting posture; (b) unhealthy sitting posture.

Since sitting is a long time activity. Single frame or only a few frames containing unhealthy sitting posture cannot be the basis of judgment. For example, stretching and twisting are common activities during sitting. Therefore, we take the proportion of unhealthy sitting posture frames as the criterion. Figure 5 shows the angles' change curves of a typical unhealthy sitting posture in 1 min video, which contains 201 frames in total, in where there are 130 unhealthy frames and 71 healthy frames. The UFR reaches 61.9%.

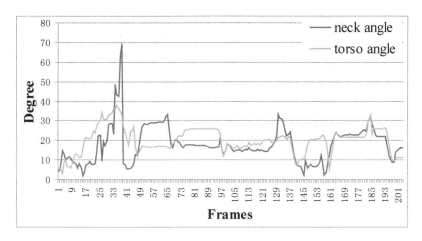

Fig. 5. The angles' change curve of a typical unhealthy sitting posture video.

For most situation, unhealthy sitting posture always accompany with excessive tilt torso. Figure 6 shows angles' change curves in 4 typical unhealthy sitting postures.

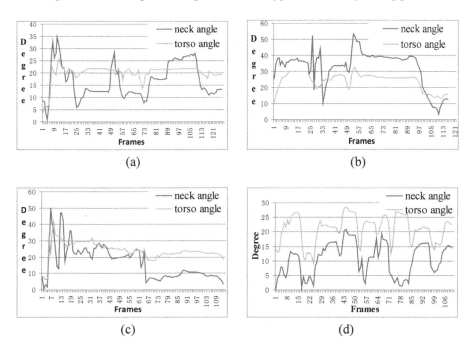

Fig. 6. Typical unhealthy sitting postures. (a) Reading with head down (UFR: 68.6%). (b) Right leaning on the chair (UFR: 84.6%). (c) Sprawling in the chair (UFR: 89.5%). (d) Sitting with body moving right to left (UFR: 68.5%).

According to the line charts in Fig. 6, it can be inferred that for most situations neck angle is not necessary to be calculated. Because when neck angle bends over 20°, torso angle always reaches its given threshold. Therefore, it is an efficient way to reduce the computational load by calculating torso angle first.

Comparing our method with wearable device approach and deep learning approach, our approach has advantages in real-time calculation and robustness because of its low cost for computing representative features. Our experiment results indicate that the method effectively detected unhealthy sitting postures, and distinguished healthy sitting postures from unhealthy sitting postures. Table 1 shows the detailed information of the experiments.

Table 1. Statistics for sitting posture judgments

Sitting posture types	Sample numbers	Correct identification of sitting posture	Accuracy
Healthy sitting posture	3	3	100%
Lean against the chair	5	5	100%
Lean forward	5	5	100%
Lean backward	5	5	100%
Sitting with body moving	15	11	73.3%

Only 4 unhealthy sitting postures of the type "sitting with body moving" could not be detected correctly. Upon reviewing the records of these 4 videos, we found out that the person in these 4 test videos changed his postures too frequently to accord with human common sitting posture. Therefore, although the accuracy of "sitting with body moving" is only 73.3%, it can be anticipated that our method will work even better in the practical use.

4   Conclusions

In this paper, we proposed a new and fast method of unhealthy sitting posture judgment which is based on the neck angle and the torso angle using depth image captured from a Kinect sensor. In our method only two angles need to be calculated, so it is robust and of high time efficiency. The torso angle is calculated first and used in the judgment. In most situations, when the neck angle reaches the given threshold, it is usually accompanied with a high value of torso angle. Judging sitting posture in this way can further reduce computational load. Experimental results show that the proposed method can judge sitting posture effectively for different unhealthy sitting types. Compared with the existing wearable device based approaches and the deep learning based approaches, our method only needs a Kinect sensor without any other wearable sensors and is time efficient and robust because of only calculating two angles. What is more, our method is based on published medical findings of unhealthy sitting posture judgment condition, and therefore having solid theoretical foundation.

In the future work, we will investigate using deep learning methods to further improve the accuracy of our current method. Moreover, the unhealthy sitting posture judgment criteria and our proposed algorithm may be extended to other methods using other types of video cameras such as the more common-used monocular camera.

Acknowledgments. This research was supported by the National Natural Science Foundation of China under Grant 61662044 and the Natural Science Foundation of Jiangxi Province, China under Grant 20161ACB20004.

References

1. Lis, A.M., Black, K.M., Korn, H., Nordin, M.: Association between sitting and occupational LBP. Eur. Spine J. **16**(2), 283–298 (2007)
2. Mattmann, C., Amft, O., Harms, H., Clemens, F., Clemens, F.: Recognizing upper body postures using textile strain sensors. In: 11th IEEE International Symposium on Wearable Computers, MA, Boston, pp. 29–36 (2007)
3. Harms, H., Amft, O., Roggen, D., Troster, G.: Rapid prototyping of smart garments for activity-aware applications. J. Ambient Intell. Smart Environ. **1**(2), 87–101 (2009)
4. Karantonis, D.M., Narayanan, M.R., Mathie, M., Lovell, N.H., Celler, B.G.: Implementation of a real-time human movement classifier using a triaxial accelerometer for ambulatory monitoring. IEEE Trans. Inf Technol. Biomed. **10**(1), 156–167 (2006)
5. Jeong, D.U., Kim, S.J., Chung, W.Y.: Classification of posture and movement using a 3-axis accelerometer. In: International Conference on Convergence Information Technology, pp. 837–844. IEEE (2007)
6. Barba, R., de Madrid, Á.P., Boticario, J.G.: Development of an inexpensive sensor network for recognition of sitting posture. Int. J. Distrib. Sens. Netw. **11**(8), 1–13 (2015)
7. Li, C.C., Chen, Y.Y.: Human posture recognition by simple rules. In: IEEE International Conference on Systems, Man and Cybernetics, pp. 3237–3240 (2007)
8. Boulay, B., Bremond, F., Thonnat, M.: Posture recognition with a 3D human model. In: The IEE International Symposium on Imaging for Crime Detection and Prevention, pp. 135–138. IET (2005)
9. Boulay, B., Brémond, F., Thonnat, M.: Applying 3D human model in a posture recognition system. Pattern Recogn. Lett. **27**(7), 1788–1796 (2006)
10. Wang, W.J., Chang, J.W., Haung, S.F., Wang, R.J.: Human posture recognition based on images captured by the kinect sensor. Int. J. Adv. Robot. Syst. **13**(2), 1–16 (2016)
11. Althloothi, S., Mahoor, M.H., Zhang, X., Voyles, R.M.: Human activity recognition using multi-features and multiple kernel learning. Pattern Recogn. **47**(5), 1800–1812 (2014)
12. Qiao, R., Liu, L., Shen, C., Hengel, A.V.D.: Learning discriminative trajectorylet detector sets for accurate skeleton- MARK based action recognition. Pattern Recogn. **66**(6), 202–212 (2017)
13. Nasiri, J.A., Charkari, N.M., Mozafari, K.: Energy-based model of least squares twin support vector machines for human action recognition. Sig. Process. **104**(6), 248–257 (2014)
14. Chen, J., Qiu, J., Ahn, C.: Construction worker's awkward posture recognition through supervised motion tensor decomposition. Autom. Constr. **77**(1), 67–81 (2017)
15. Ayumi, V., Fanany, M.I.: Distribution-sensitive learning on relevance vector machine for pose-based human gesture recognition. In: The Third Information Systems International Conference, pp. 527–534 (2015)
16. Liu, Z., Zhang, C., Tian, Y.: 3D-based deep convolutional neural network for action recognition with depth sequences. Image Vis. Comput. **55**(11), 93–100 (2016)

17. Li, S.Z., Yu, B., Wu, W., Su, S.Z., Ji, R.R.: Feature learning based on SAE–PCA network for human gesture recognition in RGBD images. Neurocomputing **151**(5), 565–573 (2015)
18. Leng, B., Zhang, X., Yao, M., Xiong, Z.: A 3D model recognition mechanism based on deep Boltzmann machines. Neurocomputing **151**(3), 593–602 (2015)
19. Ibañez, R., Álvaro, S., Teyseyre, A., Rodriguez, G., Campo, M.: Approximate string matching: a lightweight approach to recognize gestures with Kinect. Pattern Recogn. **62**(2), 73–86 (2017)
20. Mastorakis, G., Makris, D.: Fall detection system using Kinect's infrared sensor. Real-Time Image Proc. **9**(4), 635–646 (2014)
21. Rougier, C., Auvinet, E., Rousseau, J., Mignotte, M., Meunier, J.: Fall detection from depth map video sequences. In: Abdulrazak, B., Giroux, S., Bouchard, B., Pigot, H., Mokhtari, M. (eds.) ICOST 2011. LNCS, vol. 6719, pp. 121–128. Springer, Heidelberg (2011). https://doi.org/10.1007/978-3-642-21535-3_16
22. Kwolek, B., Kepski, M.: Fuzzy inference-based fall detection using Kinect and body-worn accelerometer. Appl. Soft Comput. **40**(3), 305–318 (2016)
23. Gasparrini, S., Cippitelli, E., Spinsante, S., Gambi, E.: A depth-based fall detection system using a Kinect® sensor. Sensors **14**(2), 2756–2775 (2014)
24. Manghisi, V.M., Uva, A.E., Fiorentino, M., Bevilacqua, V., Trotta, G.F., Monno, G.: Real time RULA assessment using Kinect v2 sensor. Appl. Ergon. **2**(1), 1–11 (2017)
25. Wang, W.J., Chang, J.W., Haung, S.F., Wang, R.J.: Human posture recognition based on images captured by the Kinect sensor. Int. J. Adv. Rob. Syst. **13**(1), 1–16 (2016)
26. Kamal, S., Jalal, A.: A hybrid feature extraction approach for human detection, tracking and activity recognition using depth sensors. Arab. J. Sci. Eng. **41**(3), 1043–1051 (2016)
27. Alwani, A.A., Chahir, Y., Goumidi, D.E., Molina, M., Jouen, F.: 3D-posture recognition using joint angle representation. In: Laurent, A., Strauss, O., Bouchon-Meunier, B., Yager, R.R. (eds.) IPMU 2014. CCIS, vol. 443, pp. 106–115. Springer, Cham (2014). https://doi.org/10.1007/978-3-319-08855-6_12
28. Mcatamney, L., Corlett, E.N.: RULA: a survey method for the investigation of work-related upper limb disorders. Appl. Ergon. **24**(2), 91–99 (1993)
29. Fransson-Hall, C., Gloria, R., Kilbom, A., Winkel, J., Karlqvist, L., Wiktorin, C.: A portable ergonomic observation method (PEO) for computerized on-line recording of postures and manual handling. Appl. Ergon. **26**(2), 93–100 (1995)

Using Stacked Auto-encoder to Get Feature with Continuity and Distinguishability in Multi-object Tracking

Haoyang Feng[✉], Xiaofeng Li, Peixin Liu, and Ning Zhou

School of Communication and Information Engineering,
University of Electronic Science and Technology of China, Chengdu, China
haoyang_feng@std.uestc.edu.cn

Abstract. Good feature expression of targets plays an important role in multi-object tracking (MOT). Inspired by the self-learning concept of deep learning methods, an online feature extraction scheme is proposed in this paper, based on a conditional random field (CRF). The CRF model is transformed into a certain number of multi-scale stacked auto-encoders with a new loss function. Features obtained with our method contain both continuous and distinguishable characteristics of targets. The inheritance relationship of stacked auto-encoders between adjacent frames is implemented by an online process. Features extracted from our online scheme are applied to improve the network flow tracking model. Experiment results show that the features by our method achieve better performance compared with other handcrafted-features. The overall tracking performance are improved when our features are used in the MOT tasks.

Keywords: Feature · Multi-object tracking · Stacked auto-encoder
Continuity · Distinguishability

1 Introduction

Robust detection and tracking of video sequence is one of the key task of computer vision. Multiple object tracking (MOT) is one of the hot spot. It links multiple independent targets of interest in each frame with their precursors or successors through feature association methods into complete trajectories.

Recent years, with the great progress in object detection [5,9], tracking-by-detection has become one of the mainstream in MOT tasks. The detection output in each frame is given as a prior knowledge at the first step. Then, some data association and global optimization methods are applied to connect the discrete detections into trajectories. One of the state-of-the-art global data association method is based on a network flow paradigm. Zhang et al. were the first one who formulated the MOT problem as finding a maximum posterior probability and transformed it into a min-cost network flow problem [13]. Pirsiavash et al. developed it and used a dynamic programming algorithm to improve efficiency [8].

© Springer International Publishing AG 2017
Y. Zhao et al. (Eds.): ICIG 2017, Part I, LNCS 10666, pp. 351–361, 2017.
https://doi.org/10.1007/978-3-319-71607-7_31

However, as a sequence of images, higher-order information among adjacent frames was ignored. Traditional tracking methods are unable to achieve more robust results in complex scenes since they only extract static and superficial features. Considering about this, Butt and Collins added higher-order tracking smoothness constraints, such as constant velocity [3]. On the other hand, usual handcrafted-features are not efficient enough. New features extracted by a deep neural network are successfully applied in single target tracking [11,14]. Different from single object tracking, in MOT tasks, different targets of same category are of interesting, such as pedestrian individuals in a surveillance application. It is not just to connect the same target, but also to distinguish others. However, traditional features and classification methods are not efficient for this purpose since they are usually based on characteristics of categories.

In this paper, we originally propose a new online feature extraction scheme which is appropriate for tracking-by-detection framework of MOT. The new scheme is based on a conditional random field (CRF) model whose potential functions are implemented by a certain number of multi-scale stacked auto-encoders. The loss function of the auto-encoders is formulated with constraints of the continuity and the distinguishability of targets. The continuity also implies the inheritance relationship of a stacked auto-encoders between frames and it relates to the high-order information of a trajectory. We apply our new features into a classical network flow method [8] on MOT and reach a better result which demonstrates the benefit of our feature extraction scheme.

The rest of the paper is as follows. Section 2 describes the CRF model of the online feature extraction scheme. Multi-scale stacked auto-encoder, the new loss function and the online approach are discussed in Sect. 3. Section 4 explains how we utilize the new feature into a network flow method and why it works. Section 5 presents experiments on the performance of obtained features and MOT tasks. Finally, conclusions are drawn in Sect. 6.

2   Conditional Random Field Model

Our online feature extraction scheme is based on a CRF model. Target detections at different frames, as conditions, are abstracted as an observation set $X = \{x_1^1, x_1^2, \cdots, x_k^{j-1}, x_k^j, x_k^{j+1}, \cdots, x_m^n\}$, where x_k^j donates the jth detection at frame k. Correspondingly, Let $Y = \{y_1^1, y_1^2, \cdots, y_k^{j-1}, y_k^j, y_k^{j+1}, \cdots, y_m^n\}$ be the state set, where y_k^j is the feature expression of x_k^j. The feature extraction problem for MOT can be formulated as a maximum conditional probability problem in CRF as follows,

$$\underset{Y,\theta}{\operatorname{argmax}} \, P(Y|X,\theta) \tag{1}$$

where θ represents all of the undetermined parameters in the model. The conditional probability is defined as a normalized product of all the potential functions based on their corresponding maximal cliques $\{y_{k-1}^j, y_k^j\}$ for $k \in \{2, 3, \cdots, m\}$,

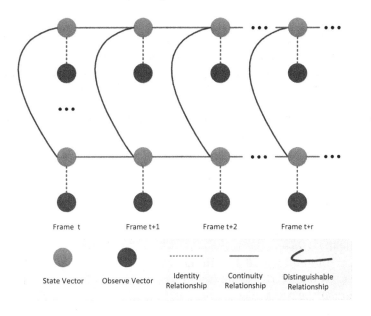

Fig. 1. Conditional random field model. (Color figure online)

or $\{y_k^j, y_k^l\}$ for $j \neq l$, and it is given by,

$$p(Y|X, \theta) = \frac{1}{Z} \prod_j \prod_k (\psi_1(y_{k-1}^j, y_k^j) \prod_{l \neq j} \psi_2(y_k^j, y_k^l)) \tag{2}$$

where $\psi_1(y_{k-1}^j, y_k^j)$ and $\psi_2(y_k^j, y_k^l)$ are the potential functions of maximal cliques respectively, and Z is a normalization factor.

Figure 1 shows two different targets and their features at frame $t, t+1, \cdots,$ $t+r$ as a sketch. Two types of maximal cliques are displayed as red and blue edges respectively. The potential functions can be expressed in an exponential form,

$$\psi_1(y_{k-1}^j, y_k^j) = \exp(I(y_k^j, x_k^j) + \lambda S(y_{k-1}^j, y_k^j, x_{k-1}^j, x_k^j)) \tag{3}$$

and,

$$\psi_2(y_k^j, y_k^l) = \exp(I(y_k^j, x_k^j) + \mu D(y_k^j, y_k^l, x_k^j, x_k^l)) \tag{4}$$

where $I(y_k^j, x_k^j)$ represents the identity relationship between observations and features, $S(y_{k-1}^j, y_k^j, x_{k-1}^j, x_k^j)$ and $D(y_k^j, y_k^l, x_k^j, x_k^l)$ describe the sequential characteristic and distinguishable property of features respectively.

Realized that any nonlinear function can be fitted with a deep neural network, we utilize a multi-scale stacked auto-encoder f_k^j to implement the product of the potential functions in (2) and to obtain the optimal extraction of the features.

$$\psi(y_{k-1}^j, y_k^j) \prod_{l \neq j} \psi(y_k^j, y_k^l) = f_k^j \tag{5}$$

3   Approach

We transform the maximum conditional probability problem on (1) to an online training process of a certain number of stacked auto-encoders by modeling the product of potential functions by (5). For each detection, an auto-encoder is trained according to a new loss function we proposed, which considers three of the relations in (3) and (4). An online training process is used which is initialized in the first several frames and runs iteratively in following frames. The structure of auto-encoder, our new loss function and the online training are presented below.

3.1   Auto-encoder Structure

Compared with many handcrafted-ones, features learned by an unsupervised model, especially a deep learning model, tells more about the fundamental or inner property of an object [6,12]. Recent studies [10] have shown that stacked auto-encoder, as one of the widely used unsupervised deep learning model, is capable to grasp the most generic and intrinsic feature of the interest. In light of [14], the internal feature of each detection is extracted by a two-layer stacked auto-encoder similar in [11,14].

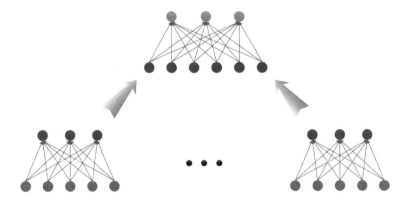

Fig. 2. Multi-scale stacked auto-encoder structure. (Color figure online)

As shown in Fig. 2, the two-layer stacked auto-encoder is modeled by one input layer (red) and two feature expressing layers (blue and yellow). At the input layer, different patches from each area given by its detection bounding box are reshaped into vectors with three RGB channels. The vector passes the first layer weight matrix and a nonlinear function to generate a feature responses of local characteristics. Then, the local responses are cascaded together and are sent into the second layer to learn the global information.

In [11], PCA whitening and pooling method is applied in the deep network to decrease the dimensionality of feature vectors. We adjust the number of neurons in each feature expressing layer to get computational efficiency and maintain a similar performance.

3.2 New Loss Function

We formulate a new loss function of the multi-scale stacked auto-encoder by adding two regulation terms as follows,

$$L = \underset{W}{\operatorname{argmin}} \left|\left| x_i - W^T W x_i \right|\right|_2$$
$$+ \alpha \left|\left| h(W x_i^{old}) - h(W x_i) \right|\right|_2$$
$$+ \beta \sum_{j \neq i}^{N-1} \left|\left| h(W x_i) - h(W x_j) \right|\right|_2 \qquad (6)$$

where x_i donates the input vector of encoder, W the weight matrix, and h a sigmoid transportation. Both the first and the second layer auto-encoders are trained by this minimum function. The three terms are explained below.

Identity. The first term in Eq. (6) is the standard loss term of an auto-encoder, learning the intrinsic feature of a detection. It represents the identity relationship in Eqs. (3) and (4).

Continuity. In the second term in Eq. (6), x_i^{old} and x_i are inputs in the previous and current frame respectively. α is a weight parameter. This term guarantees the high similarity between features of the same target in two adjacent frames. In this way, the continuity of target in (3) is introduced in the output features.

The inheritance strategy of stacked auto-encoder also contribute to the continuity characteristic. In this strategy, The stacked auto-encoder on current detection inherits previously results from the nearest detection at the frame before, which has a great chance to be the same target compared with current detection. However, this constraint is not necessarily one hundred percent correct. A appropriate weight parameter α in (6) controls the feature similarity error from mistaken inheritance within an acceptable limit.

Distinguishability. In the third term, x_j indicates the other targets in the same frame and N is the number of detections. In order to differentiate other targets, we set β a negative number and treat it as a penalty term. It forces the extracted features between different targets to keep away from each other as much as possible. It represents the distinguishable property in Eq. (4).

3.3 Online Learning

In our online learning system, multi-scale stacked auto-encoders are trained by solving (6) with the Stochastic Gradient Descent (SGD) algorithm [2]. The first several frames are used to train the multi-scale stacked auto-encoders with randomly initialized weight matrix and they will reach a relatively stable state. At that time, the original input will pass the auto-encoder and obtain the final feature expression at current frame. Then through inheritance relation expounded above, the weight matrix of each auto-encoder is transmitted to the next frame and fine tuned by new comers. Thus, the feature expressions will be computed frame by frame.

4   New Feature in Network Flow

In this section, we are going to describe details on utilizing the new features extracted by our online system and explaination on improving MOT performance with solving network flow problem.

The min-cost network flow paradigm to solve MOT problem in [8] was formulated as,

$$
\mathcal{F}^* = \underset{\mathcal{F}}{\operatorname{argmin}} \sum_i C_{in}(i) f_{in}(i) + \sum_i C_{out}(i) f_{out}(i) \\
+ \sum_i C_{det}(i) f_{det}(i) + \sum_{i,j} C_t(i,j) f_t(i,j)
\tag{7}
$$

where the total flow set $\mathcal{F}$ is a solution of all the indicator variables $f_{in}(i)$, $f_{out}(i)$, $f_{det}(i)$, $f_t(i,j)$ in the network. $f_{in}(i)$, $f_{out}(i)$ and $f_{det}(i)$ indicate whether detection i is a start or an end or belongs to a trajectory respectively. For each trajectory, $f_t(i,j)$ determines whether detection j is right behind detection i. Costs $C_{in}(i)$ and $C_{out}(i)$ define the probability of a target belongs to the start or end of one trajectory. The detection cost $C_{det}(i)$ is linked to the score that detection i was given by the detector. It represents a confidence of whether the target is a real one. $C_t(i,j)$, as the connection cost, describes the probability of two detections i and j belong to the same trajectory.

In [8], all the costs $C_{in}(i)$, $C_{out}(i)$, $C_{det}(i)$ and $C_t(i,j)$ are defined with off-line trained certain values. With the specificity of each video sequences, constant costs will end up with solutions which are not very robust. They can not adjust diverse kinds of MOT scenes. In addition, [8] only use some arbitrary or simply considered constraints to shrink the solution space down. For example, some edges from detection i to j in the network are deleted when detection j is not at the next frame or has no space overlap with detection i. These measures indeed speeds up the algorithm to find optimal flow effectively, but may ignore better result for the reason of over simple and tough constraints.

In our method, in order to make the model more accurately and self-adaptive to video sequences in difference of kinds, the detection similarity computed from new features is mapped into a variable cost which replaces $C_t(i,j)$ as a certain value originally. With high confidential detection similarity calculated from features with continuity and distinguishability, it will take less costs to associate same target and distinguish others. Furthermore, to find the optimal solution with higher reliability, we set a similarity threshold to cut down the searching space. Once the similarity computed from two new detections features is less than the threshold, the edge between two detections will be deleted. Location change, size change and overlap ratio are also considered into the determination. Each fact is assigned a particular weight to adjust the impact on the final decision. Besides, we do not insist that the two detections with an edge must be in adjacent frames, and relax the constraint to an appropriate frame gap. Thus, some lost then reappeared detections due to occlusion get their chances to connect with former trajectories.

5   Experiment

In this section, we first evaluate the feature quality from our online feature extraction scheme based on multi-scale stacked auto-encoder in TUD-Crossing video sequence [1], which is widely used to check the tracking performance in MOT tasks. The continuity and distinguishability of the extracted feature are revealed by comparing with some other handcrafted-features utilized in MOT. The influence of weight parameters in loss function (6) is also explained and analyzed. Finally, we apply our feature extraction into a typical network flow method which is called DP_NMS [8] as discussed in Sect. 4, and test the overall tracking performance on a series of video sequences on MOT2015 benchmark [7].

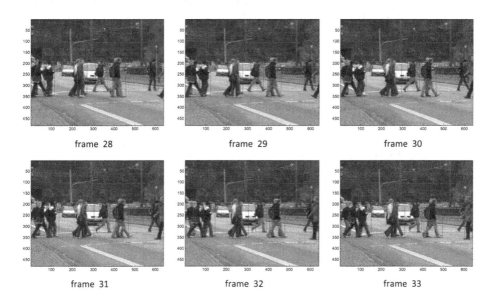

Fig. 3. TUD-Crossing detection result.

5.1   Continuity and Distinguishability

Figure 3 shows the detections in several frames in the TUD-Crossing. Our feature extraction scheme is applied in the video of 200 frames and similarity performance of features is evaluated. The similarity is measured with Bhattacharyya distance which is commonly used in video tracking [4].

Table 1 presents the similarity of features for the rightmost target between adjacent frames in frame 28, 29 and 30, as shown in Fig. 3. The last column computes the average similarity of this target in the whole video sequence. Clearly, the feature from our online learning method provides the highest similarity and keeps best consistent in consecutive frames. High similarity for the same targets means good continuity.

Table 1. Continuity of features

Method	Frame 28–29	Frame 29–30	Frame 30–31	Average
Hist RGB	0.898	0.895	0.870	0.907
Hist HSV	0.641	0.637	0.782	0.776
Our method	**0.920**	**0.996**	**0.939**	**0.974**

Table 2 presents the similarity of features between the rightmost target and three other targets in frame 28, 29 and 30, respectively. The last column shows the average diversity which is the difference between similarity of identical targets and different targets. Our method achieves the highest diversity compared with two other handcrafted-features, so it provides the best distinguishability.

Table 2. Distinguishability of features

Method	Frame 28–29	Frame 29–30	Frame 30–31	Diversity
Hist RGB	0.786	0.772	0.783	
	0.691	0.678	0.703	0.148
	0.704	0.667	0.687	
Hist HSV	0.385	0.401	0.342	
	0.343	0.362	0.314	0.381
	0.235	0.242	0.227	
Our method	0.331	0.383	0.337	
	0.332	0.380	0.336	**0.621**
	0.332	0.379	0.337	

Table 3 illustrates the influence of the weight parameters in loss function (6). The first row lists a suitable pair, where $\alpha = 0.15$ and $\beta = -0.5$. When β

increases to -0.1, as the second row in the table, the diversity between different targets will decrease to a low level. Though increasing in α seems to raise it back, as shown in the third row, it can not adapt the situation in other frames, such as in Table 4.

Table 3. Influence of weight parameter

Weight	α	β	Avr identity	Avr diversity
$pair_1$	0.15	-0.5	0.974	0.621
$pair_2$	0.15	-0.1	0.953	0.520
$pair_3$	0.2	-0.15	**0.986**	**0.641**

Also shown in Table 4, at frame 32, there is an wrong inheritance of auto-encoder for the rightmost, which is unavoidable since the detections cannot be absolutely correct. When the weight factor α holds a leading role ($pair_3$ for example), the identity similarity will be on a high level and the two targets are not easy to be distinguished. It is good practice to keep α below a proper limit ($pair_1$ for example) to separate them apart and maintain the high continuity simultaneously.

Table 4. Wrong inheritance and weight parameters

Method	Frame 31–32	Frame 32–33
Hist RGB	0.799	0.870
Hist HSV	0.719	0.731
$pair_1$	**0.162**	0.934
$pair_2$	0.257	0.861
$pair_3$	0.770	**0.989**

5.2   Tracking Perfomance

We apply our feature extraction scheme in the DP_NMS model in [8], as expound in Sect. 4. Evaluations are carried out on several widely used MOT video sequences on MOT2015 benchmark for the original [8] and the improved method. The results are presented in Table 5. In the evaluation, our own detections and ground truths are used for PETS and TUD-Crossing, while public data from MOT2015 benchmark [7] are used for the other two videos. From the results, it is clear that our scheme promotes the performance of the MOT system effectively on most of the evaluating indicators on the classical network flow solution. And there is no doubt that the new detection features extracted from our scheme can also help to promote most of the MOT method based on tracking-by-detection paradigm.

Table 5. Tracking performance

Video sequence	Method	MOTA	MOTP	GT	MT	PT	ML	FP	FN	ID	FM	Rcll	Prcn
PETS	DP_NMS	44.8	67.1	10	0	8	2	**109**	527	92	44	60.0	87.9
	Improved	**67.3**	**68.6**	10	**7**	**3**	**0**	110	**254**	**67**	**36**	**80.7**	**90.6**
TUD-Crossing	DP_NMS	75.7	95.7	13	13	0	0	9	84	159	**16**	**91.9**	99.1
	Improved	**87.0**	95.7	13	13	0	0	**8**	**82**	**35**	17	91.1	**99.2**
ADL-Rundle-6	DP_NMS	26.4	**73.5**	24	0	12	12	111	3500	75	**54**	30.1	93.1
	Improved	**27.0**	73.4	24	0	**13**	**11**	**109**	**3474**	**73**	55	**30.6**	**93.4**
TUD-Stadtmitte	DP_NMS	52.5	65.7	10	3	5	2	**47**	472	30	**24**	59.2	**93.6**
	Improved	**53.7**	65.7	10	3	**6**	**1**	54	**455**	**26**	26	**60.6**	92.8

6   Conclusion

An online feature extraction system built on a CRF model is proposed in this paper, which requires both the continuity and distinguishability. The CRF model is transformed into a certain number of multi-scale stacked auto-encoders with new loss function to get feature expression of targets. New features extracted from our online scheme are applied to improve the network flow tracking model. Experiments have shown better performance compared with other handcrafted-features and obtain a good performance promotion on MOT tasks with our feature extraction.

References

1. Andriluka, M., Roth, S., Schiele, B.: People-tracking-by-detection and people-detection-by-tracking. In: IEEE Conference on Computer Vision and Pattern Recognition, pp. 1–8 (2008)
2. Bottou, L.: Large-scale machine learning with stochastic gradient descent. In: Lechevallier, Y., Saporta, G. (eds.) Proceedings of COMPSTAT 2010, pp. 177–186. Physica-Verlag, Heidelberg (2010). https://doi.org/10.1007/978-3-7908-2604-3_16
3. Butt, A.A., Collins, R.T.: Multi-target tracking by lagrangian relaxation to min-cost network flow. In: IEEE Conference on Computer Vision and Pattern Recognition, pp. 1846–1853 (2013)
4. Comaniciu, D., Ramesh, V., Meer, P.: Real-time tracking of non-rigid objects using mean shift. In: IEEE Conference on Computer Vision and Pattern Recognition, p. 2142 (2000)
5. Forsyth, D.: Object detection with discriminatively trained part-based models. IEEE Trans. Pattern Anal. Mach. Intell. **32**(9), 1627–1645 (2010)
6. Krizhevsky, A., Sutskever, I., Hinton, G.E.: Imagenet classification with deep convolutional neural networks. In: Pereira, F., Burges, C.J.C., Bottou, L., Weinberger, K.Q. (eds.) Advances in Neural Information Processing Systems, vol. 25, pp. 1097–1105. Curran Associates, Inc. (2012). http://papers.nips.cc/paper/4824-imagenet-classification-with-deep-convolutional-neural-networks.pdf
7. Lealtaix, L., Milan, A., Reid, I., Roth, S., Schindler, K.: Motchallenge 2015: towards a benchmark for multi-target tracking (2015)

8. Pirsiavash, H., Ramanan, D., Fowlkes, C.C.: Globally-optimal greedy algorithms for tracking a variable number of objects. In: Computer Vision and Pattern Recognition, pp. 1201–1208 (2011)
9. Ren, S., He, K., Girshick, R., Sun, J.: Faster R-CNN: towards real-time object detection with region proposal networks. IEEE Trans. Pattern Anal. Mach. Intell. **39**(6), 1137–1149 (2017)
10. Vincent, P., Larochelle, H., Bengio, Y., Manzagol, P.A.: Extracting and composing robust features with denoising autoencoders. In: International Conference, pp. 1096–1103 (2008)
11. Wang, L., Liu, T., Wang, G., Chan, K.L., Yang, Q.: Video tracking using learned hierarchical features. IEEE Trans. Image Process. **24**(4), 1424–1435 (2015)
12. Zeiler, M.D., Fergus, R.: Visualizing and understanding convolutional networks. In: Fleet, D., Pajdla, T., Schiele, B., Tuytelaars, T. (eds.) ECCV 2014. LNCS, vol. 8689, pp. 818–833. Springer, Cham (2014). https://doi.org/10.1007/978-3-319-10590-1_53
13. Zhang, L., Li, Y., Nevatia, R.: Global data association for multi-object tracking using network flows. In: IEEE Conference on Computer Vision and Pattern Recognition, pp. 1–8 (2008)
14. Zou, W.Y., Ng, A.Y., Zhu, S., et al.: Deep learning of invariant features via simulated fixations in video. In: Advances in Neural Information Processing Systems, vol. 25, pp. 3212–3220 (2012)

Vehicle Detection Based on Superpixel and Improved HOG in Aerial Images

Enlai Guo, Lianfa Bai, Yi Zhang, and Jing Han[✉]

Jiangsu Key Laboratory of Spectral Imaging and Intelligent Sense,
Nanjing University of Science and Technology, Nanjing 210094, China
njusthanjing@163.com

Abstract. A method is introduced in this paper, which could be applied for vehicle detection in aerial images. In considering of the stable scale and structure feature of vehicles in aerial images, the method is divided into three steps: region extraction based on SLIC and contour shrinking, feature extraction with improved HOG and classification using SVM with RBF kernel function. Compared to the original HOG algorithm, SLIC is employed to reduce the time cost of the sliding window in the proposed method. Both vehicle and other object could be contained in one patch acquired from SLIC. To ensure that pixels in each patch for feature extraction belong to the same category, contours of the patches are shrunk towards its own center after the segmentation using SLIC. The 31-dimensional feature based on HOG is applied as the feature describer. The average time cost of the proposed method is 20.7 ms. The effectiveness of the proposed method is indicated by the detection results shown in experiments.

Keywords: Vehicle detection · Aerial images · Improved HOG · SVM

1 Introduction

Vehicle detection is a major task in target recognition. Methods based on deep learning are the most popular vehicle detection algorithms based on large datasets. In real application, some special environment cannot provide adequate data to constitute a dataset with enough samples. Therefore, it's still necessary to develop algorithms based on artificially designed features.

As a feature describer, histogram of oriented gradient (HOG) was proposed in [1] by Dalal and Triggs in 2005. HOG is based on evaluating well-normalized local histograms of image gradient orientations in a dense grid [1]. Cooperating with support vector machine (SVM), HOG is widely used in different image processing tasks.

Deformable part model (DPM) proposed in [2] is a successful algorithm, which achieved the best result in the PASCAL challenge in 2007, 2008 and 2009. As a further improvement to the method based on HOG and SVM, DPM achieved a double accuracy against the best algorithm in the 2006 challenge. A variety of detection tasks could be fulfilled by using DPM.

© Springer International Publishing AG 2017
Y. Zhao et al. (Eds.): ICIG 2017, Part I, LNCS 10666, pp. 362–373, 2017.
https://doi.org/10.1007/978-3-319-71607-7_32

Feature pyramid is made use of to realize multi-scale detection. Meanwhile, deformable part thought is employed to acquire better performance in deformed object like pedestrian. Because of those two factors mentioned, convolution operation is taken for several times in generating the final score map. The computational complexity of DPM is improved significantly by multiple convolution operations. According to [2], two seconds are demanded in processing an image using DPM. In practice, DPM needs to be simplified to realize real-time detection.

In aerial images, the scale of vehicles is fixed to some degree. As for vehicles, structure feature is relatively stable. In consideration of the characteristics, both feature pyramid and deformable part thought of DPM is unnecessary for vehicle detection in aerial images.

In order to provide regions for feature extraction and classification, sliding windows are put to use in the HOG algorithm proposed in [1]. Dense grids are the basic point in HOG, which brings the consequence of low time efficiency. To reduce the time cost, the sliding window method is replaced by region extraction based on SLIC and contour shrinking in the proposed method. The 31-dimensional feature describer proposed delivered in [3] is applied in our model to further improve the detection precision of our model.

The algorithm proposed in this paper consists of three steps: region extraction based on SLIC and contour shrinking, feature extraction and classification, which will be introduced in the follow section.

2 Model Based on Superpixel Segmentation and Improved HOG

The method is given in detail in this section. A three-stage method is proposed to detect the vehicles in aerial images in this paper.

Superpixel is applied to provide segmentation result of the raw aerial image firstly. Both vehicle and other object could be contained in the same patch obtained from SLIC. To ensure that each cell for feature extraction contains only vehicle or other objects, contours of the patches are shrunk towards its own center.

Then feature vectors are extracted to represent different patches obtained in the first step. The feature describer used in our method is a variation of HOG proposed in [3]. The scale of each feature vector should be controlled in the same range by normalizing.

In the last stage, SVM is employed in order to classify the feature vectors into two different classes. The basic unit of the detection result is the patch obtained through SLIC and contours shrinking. Each patch contains several cells. The category of a patch is produced by means of voting mechanism. The categories of vectors within a patch are utilized to vote with the same weight. When the voting result achieves equal, the patch will be determined as a negative sample. According to the classification, the patches belong to vehicle could be discriminated from others which the irrelevant objects are consisted of. The result of vehicle detection is produced by the form of bounding boxes eventually. The proposed model for vehicle detection in aerial images is shown in Fig. 1.

Compared to the traditional HOG algorithm, two characteristics are contained in the proposed method: 1. region extraction based on SLIC and contour shrinking, 2. the improved feature describer employed to extract feature. Details will be discussed in Sects. 2.1 and 2.2. The computational procedure of the proposed model is delivered entirely in the form of pseudocode in Sect. 2.3.

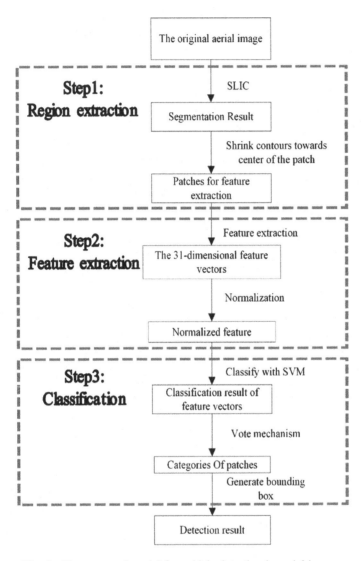

Fig. 1. The proposed model for vehicle detection in aerial images.

2.1   Region Extraction Based on SLIC and Contour Shrinking

HOG describer is regarded as a sliding-window object detector. Sliding-window is employed in most HOG based methods like the algorithms delivered in [1, 4, 5]. To reduce the time cost, superpixel segmentation is applied in this paper to generate patches for feature extraction. As a replacement to sliding-window, the original image could be segmented into subregions according to the similarity between pixels by using superpixel segmentation.

The superpixel segmentation could be categorized into two classes: graph-based algorithms and gradient-ascent-based methods. Normalized cuts was presented by [6] as the first practical superpixel segmentation method. Since then, many superpixel algorithms were successively proposed, such as Graph cuts, Watershed, Turbopixel and SLIC. Simple linear iterative clustering (SLIC) is employed in this paper.

SLIC was proposed in [7]. Compare to other superpixel algorithms, SLIC has the advantage that could obtain compact, uniform and following image edges. At the meantime, high time efficiency is relatively achieved by SLIC. SLIC is an algorithm improved on K-means clustering algorithm with a new distance measurement and limited search range. SLIC completes the clustering process in terms of a vector with 5-dimension. Combined the coordinates $[x, y]$ in RGB color space and color $[l, a, b]$ the CIELAB color space, each pixel could be represented as $[l, a, b, x, y]$. By measuring the distance between pixels, clustering result could be obtained. Two parameters K and C need to be fixed as number of superpixels and compact coefficient, respectively. Applied to different algorithms, the parameters of SLIC should be determined through the specific circumstances.

In this step, the original aerial image is segmented into several parts. A parallel algorithm called gSLICr was proposed by Ren in [8], which employed Compute Unified Device Architecture (CUDA) to accelerate the SLIC algorithm delivered in [7]. Applying the gSLICr, patches could be generated as shown in Fig. 2. The number of superpixels is set as 50 according to experiments, while the compact coefficient is set as 5.6. Number of iterations is chosen as 50. Relatively speaking, patches belong to the vehicle are separated from other objects accurately.

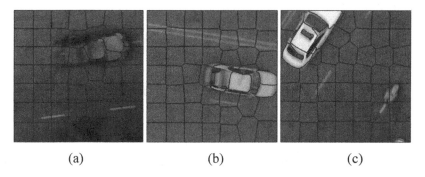

| (a) | (b) | (c) |

Fig. 2. Segmentation results of three samples. (a) Sample A (b) Sample B (c) Sample C (Color figure online)

As shown in Fig. 2(a) and (b), both vehicle and other object could be contained in one patch. Contour shrinking is adopted to ensure that each cell for feature extraction contains only vehicle or other objects as far as possible.

Plenty experiments are conducted to analyze the patches obtained with SLIC. The conclusion is drawn that most pixels inside a patch belong to one category and the pixels been mistaken are close to the contour. To remove the interference of pixels segmented into the wrong patch, the contours of the patches are shrunk towards its own center. The coordinates of pixels in the contours could be acquired through the result of SLIC. In the meantime, the normal direction is approximated to eight directions. The values of coordinates in the contours are along the approximated normal direction towards its center.

According to the result patches obtained through this step, feature expression of different patches will be extracted.

2.2   Feature Extraction

As a highly applied feature describer, the effectiveness of HOG has been proved. In last step, the time cost is been reduced by applying SLIC. The defect of reducing detecting window is also remarkable. It's necessary to use an improved feature to ensure detection effect.

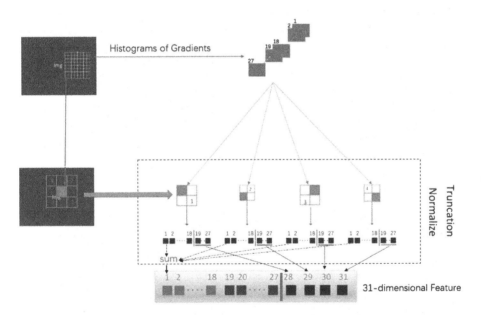

Fig. 3. The calculation process of the 31-dimensional feature vector.

An improved feature describer based on HOG was introduced in the DPM algorithm by [3]. Figure 3 shows the process of calculating the vector of 31-dimensional feature. In order to achieve perfect performance in different kinds of objects as many as possible, the feature vector is constituted by both contrast sensitive and contrast insensitive information. The feature vector F could be defined as:

$$F = \{f_i\}, i \in [1, 31] \tag{2.1}$$

where f_i represents contrast sensitive feature, when $i \in [1, 18]$; f_i represents contrast insensitive feature, when $i \in [19, 27]$.

The cell is normalized and truncated to 4 cells in the diagonal domain individually. In consideration of contrast sensitive and contrast insensitive gradient feature, a matrix of 4 * (18 + 9) is formed as follow:

$$\begin{bmatrix} a_{11} & \cdots & a_{1i} \\ a_{21} & \cdots & a_{2i} \\ a_{31} & \cdots & a_{3i} \\ a_{m1} & \cdots & a_{mi} \end{bmatrix}, \begin{cases} i \in [1, 27] \\ m \in [1, 4] \end{cases} \tag{2.2}$$

where i represents the dimension of the gradient histograms. f_i could be further expressed as:

$$f_i = \begin{cases} \sum_{m=1}^{4} a_{mi}, i \in [1, 27] \\ \sum_{j=29}^{27} a_{ij}, i \in [28, 31] \end{cases} \tag{2.3}$$

Thus, feature vectors are ready for next operation. The experiments delivered in follow sections indicate the effect of the 31-dimensional feature on improving the detection accuracy.

2.3 Computational Procedure of the Proposed Model

The computational procedure is delivered in detail in Table 1.

The final position of vehicle could be acquired through the proposed model. The detection results are delivered in Fig. 4.

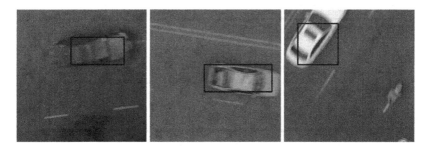

Fig. 4. Detection results of samples used in Fig. 1

Table 1. Computational procedure.

Algorithm parameters: N -number of pixels, K -number of superpixel, C -compact coefficient, d_{shrink} -distance of contour shrinking

---

Step 1: Region extraction based on SLIC and contour shrinking

1. SLIC

Calculate label $l(i)$ of pixel i through distance D' between pixels and cluster center:

$$D' = \sqrt{(\frac{d_s}{S})^2 * C^2 + (d_c)^2}$$

$$S = \sqrt{N/K}$$

$$d_s = \sqrt{(x_m - x_n)^2 + (y_m - y_n)^2}$$

$$d_c = \sqrt{(I_m - I_n)^2 + (a_m - a_n)^2 + (b_m - b_n)^2}$$

---

2. Contour shrinking

2.1 Mark the set of coordinates C_{ori} in the original contours through label $l(i)$:

    set $CoordinateIndex=0$

    for pixel $i(x, y)$ do

      if $l(i) \mathrel{!=} l(j)$, where j are the pixels around pixel i

        set $C_{ori}(CoordinateIndex)=(x_i, y_i)$;

        $Dir(CoordinateIndex) = direction(i)$;

        $CoordinateIndex=CoordinateIndex + 1$;

      end if

    end for

2.2 shrink the original contour to obtain the set C_{final} of final contours:

    for each coordinate (x_i, y_i) in C_{ori} do

      $C_{final}(index) = (x_{index} \pm d_{shrink}, y_{index} \pm d_{shrink})$,

      the operational symbol is set according to $Dir(index)$

    end for

Step 2: Feature extraction

1. Cells extraction

    for each shrunk contour obtained through C_{final} do

      obtain cells inside contour

    end if

---

2. Calculate feature vector (Eq.2.3)

Step 3: Classification using SVM with RBF kernel function

1. Classify the feature vector of each cell

$$Category(cell) = SVM.predict(feature\_vector)$$

---

2. Vote mechanism

$$Category(patch) = \sum Category(Cell\_inside\_Patch)$$

---

3. Draw bounding boxes

3 Experiments and Results

3.1 Parameter Analyze

Two groups of experiments are introduced in this section to analyze critical factors involved in the model.

Firstly, feature describer is a major factor related to the separability of data. A vehicle would be segmented into several parts by SLIC. Inconsistent characteristics are shown by different parts of the segmented vehicle. The improved HOG performed excellently in experiments. Both contrast sensitive HOG and contrast insensitive HOG are employed individually in compared experiment, in order to verify the effectiveness of the 31-dimensional features. As shown in Fig. 5, the improved feature achieves the best performance in our model.

Secondly, the choice of kernel function in SVM is very critical related to the performance of the classifier directly. The RBF kernel function is the first choice mentioned in [9]. Figure 6 shows the different performance with four kinds of kernel function. The best results are achieved by the RBF kernel function.

In summary, the improved HOG feature is proved to be practical in the proposed method.

3.2 Performance Analyze

To validate the effectiveness of the proposed model, several experiments are carried in this section. The experiments delivered in this paper is based on the desktop with Intel Core I7-4790 CPU. All the model been tested is built with OpenCV under release mode.

The performance of DPM [2] and the original HOG algorithm [1] is presented as compared experiments. The threshold of scores is the most important parameter in DPM, which is been set as 2.5 in order to make sure that DPM achieves its best performance in the compared experiment. There are five parameters in the original HOG algorithm: size of window, stride of window, size of block, stride of block, size of cell and number of orientation bin, which are set to (64, 64), (3, 3), (16, 16), (8, 8), (8, 8) and 9. All the samples tested in the experiments are in the size of 300 * 300.

The average time cost of the original HOG algorithm, DPM and the proposed method is shown in Table 2. To compare the performance of detection, detection results are shown in Fig. 7.

The average time cost on the detection process is 20.7 ms. The detection algorithm achieves 48.3 FPS with the image size of 300 * 300, which is much faster than DPM and the original HOG algorithm.

In summary, the results shown in this section verify the effectiveness of the model introduced in this paper.

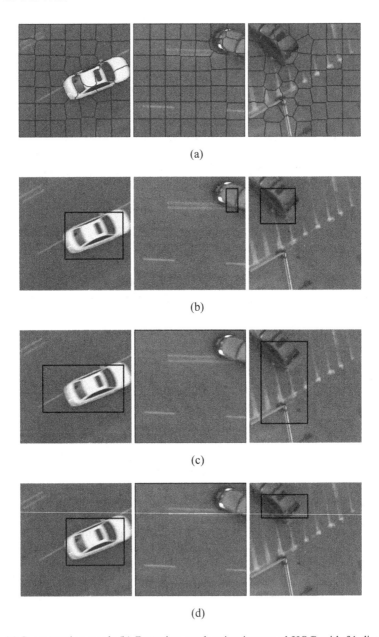

(a)

(b)

(c)

(d)

Fig. 5. (a) Segmentation result (b) Detection result using improved HOG with 31-dimensional feature (c) Detection result using HOG with 18-dimensional contrast sensitive feature (d) Detection result using HOG with 9-dimensional contrast insensitive feature.

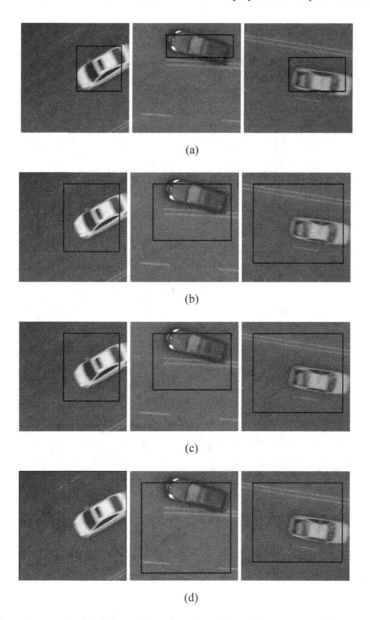

(a)

(b)

(c)

(d)

Fig. 6. Detection result with different SVM kernel (a) SVM with RBF kernel function (b) SVM with linear kernel function (c) SVM with polynomial kernel function (d) SVM with sigmoid kernel function.

Table 2. Average time cost.

Model	DPM	The original HOG	The proposed method
Average time cost	0.2716 s	0.1338 s	0.0207 s

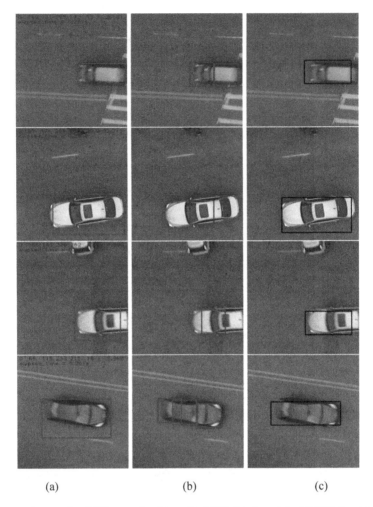

| (a) | (b) | (c) |

Fig. 7. Detection result of different algorithms (a) DPM (b) the original HOG algorithm (c) the proposed method

4   Conclusions

A method is presented in this paper, which could be applied for vehicle detection in aerial images. As shown in Sect. 3.2, the average time cost of the proposed method is 20.7 ms. Using SLIC to replace the sliding window method achieves satisfactory time cost. And the 31-dimensional feature based on HOG has been proved to be effective as the feature describer in the proposed model. SVM with RBF kernel function could achieve the best classification result compares to the SVM with linear, polynomial or sigmoid kernel function.

Meanwhile, several patches belong to vehicle are not classified into the 'vehicle' category. Further improvement needs to be done to obtain the more precise bounding boxes used as the detection results.

Acknowledgment. This work was supported by the Natural Science Foundations of China (61373061 and 61501235). This work was supported by the Fundamental Research Funds for the Central Universities (30915011335).

References

1. Dalal, N., Triggs, B.: Histograms of oriented gradients for human detection. In: IEEE Computer Society Conference on Computer Vision and Pattern Recognition, pp. 886–893. IEEE Computer Society (2005)
2. Felzenszwalb, P., Mcallester, D., Ramanan, D.: A discriminatively trained, multiscale, deformable part model. In: IEEE Computer Society Conference on Computer Vision and Pattern Recognition, pp. 1–8. DBLP (2008)
3. Felzenszwalb, P.F., Girshick, R.B., Mcallester, D., et al.: Object detection with discriminatively trained part-based models. IEEE Trans. Pattern Anal. Mach. Intell. 32(9), 1627–1645 (2014)
4. Wang, X., Han, T.X., Yan, S.: An HOG-LBP human detector with partial occlusion handling. In: IEEE International Conference on Computer Vision, pp. 32–39. IEEE (2010)
5. Creusen, I.M., Wijnhoven, R.G.J., Herbschleb, E., et al.: Color exploitation in hog-based traffic sign detection. In: IEEE International Conference on Image Processing, pp. 2669–2672. IEEE (2010)
6. Shi, J., Malik, J.: Normalized cuts and image segmentation. IEEE Trans. Pattern Anal. Mach. Intell. 2(8), 888–905 (2000)
7. Achanta, R., Shaji, A., Smith, K., et al.: SLIC superpixels compared to state-of-the-art superpixel methods. IEEE Trans. Pattern Anal. Mach. Intell. 34(11), 2274–2282 (2012)
8. Ren, C.Y., Prisacariu, V.A., Reid, I.D.: gSLICr: SLIC superpixels at over 250 Hz. arXiv preprint arXiv:1509.04232 (2015)
9. Hsu, C.-W., Chang, C.-C., Lin, C.-J.: A practical guide to support vector classification. Technical report, Department of Computer Science, National Taiwan University (2003)

Scalable Object Detection Using Deep but Lightweight CNN with Features Fusion

Qiaosong Chen[✉] (iD), Shangsheng Feng (iD), Pei Xu (iD), Lexin Li (iD), Ling Zheng (iD),
Jin Wang (iD), and Xin Deng (iD)

Chongqing Key Laboratory of Computational Intelligence,
Chongqing University of Posts and Telecommunications, Chongqing, China
chenqs@cqupt.edu.cn

Abstract. Recently, deep Convolutional Neural Network (CNN) is becoming more and more popular in pattern recognition, and have achieved impressive performance in multi-category datasets. Most object detection system include three main parts, CNN features extraction, region proposal and ROI classification, just like Fast R-CNN and Faster R-CNN. In this paper, a deep but lightweight CNN with features fusion is presented, and our work is focused on the improvement of the features extraction part in Faster R-CNN framework. Inspired by recent technical innovation structures, such as Inception, HyperNet and multi-scale construction, the proposed network is able to result in lower computation consumption with considerable deep layers. Besides, the network is trained with the help of data augmentation, fine-tune and batch normalization. In order to apply scalable with features fusion, there are different sampling methods for different layers, and various size kernel to extract both global and local features. Then fuse these features together, which can deal with diverse size object. The experimental results shows that our method have achieved better performance than Faster R-CNN with VGG16 on VOC2007, VOC2012 and KITTI datasets while maintaining the original speed.

Keywords: Deep CNN · Features fusion · Multi-scale · Object detection

1 Introduction

Object detection and classification is a hot topic in the field of computer vision. Recently, object detection and classification have got widely applications in many aspects, such as intelligent transportation, video surveillance and robot environment awareness. As a core part of object detection and classification, deep learning has achieved great success in this area, but there are still some problems that make it become a challenging task, such as the complexity of image scene, the non-uniform of image shooting angle, object occlusion, and different postures of the same object or small size object.

For object detection and classification, the traditional machine learning method basically exists four stages: sliding window, features extraction, features selection and features classification. The heated research area are features extraction (How to enhance the ability of expression and anti-deformation ability), and features classification (How

© Springer International Publishing AG 2017
Y. Zhao et al. (Eds.): ICIG 2017, Part I, LNCS 10666, pp. 374–385, 2017.
https://doi.org/10.1007/978-3-319-71607-7_33

to improve the accuracy and speed of the classifier). Researchers have proposed various of features and classifiers, there are some representative features (Haar [1], HOG [2], SIFT [3], SURF [4], etc.) and classifiers (Adaboost [5], SVM [6], DPM [7], etc.).

The traditional object detection method uses the characteristics of manual design, and the accuracy of traditional object detection can not meet the actual requirements even with the best non-linear classifier for feature classification. There are three short-comings in the designing of characteristics: (a) Hand-crafted features are low-level features, which lack of expression of the object. (b) The separability of designed features is poor, which will result in a higher classification error rate. (c) It is difficult to choose a single feature applied to multi-category datasets.

In order to extract better features, Hinton presented Deep Learning [8] in 2006, the using of deep neural network from a large number of data can automatically learn high-level features. Compared with the hand-crafted features, the learning features of deep learning is richer, and the ability of expression is stronger. With continuous development in Deep Learning, the researchers have found that the accuracy based on CNN for objection detection can be greatly improved. Not only the convolution neural network can extract high-level features and improve the expression of features, but also combine feature extraction, feature selection and feature classification into the same model. In training by end-to-end, function optimization from the overall can enhance the separa-bility of features. Especially in the past three years, Deep Learning has become more popular in the major pattern recognition competition, and achieved better and better performance, speed and accuracy have been greatly improved. This paper has three main contributions: (1) Proposed a deep but lightweight network model. (2) Adapted the multi-scale structure that can learn both global and local parts features, and then combine them to a new feature which has better ability to express. (3) The features fusion and multi-scale structure are added to the pre-trained VGG16 [9] model. The experimental results shows that the proposed method achieved better performance than original VGG16 model.

The rest of this paper is organized as follows. In Sect. 2, we review some related works. Section 3 introduces details of the designed network model, and Sect. 4 is presentation of the experimental results and evaluation. Finally, we conclude our work and arrange the future work in Sect. 5.

2   Related Work

Object detection can be divided into two categories, one is the early traditional machine learning methods, the other is the rise of Deep Learning in recent years. In this section, we generalize the development of these two methods.

2.1   Traditional Machine Learning

In 2004, Viola and Jones [1] proposed a new feature named Haar-like with cascade Adaboost classifier for face detection, it shows a great speed advantage compared with other methods at the same period. Therefore it also attracted many researchers in the feature design, cascade structure, boosting algorithm three aspects of in-depth research at the same time. Next year, Dalal and Triggs [2] proposed a local image texture called Histograms of Oriented Gradient (HOG), and combined it with Support Vector Machine (SVM) for pedestrian detection. With the development of HOG, Deformable Parts Model (DPM) [7] appeared, and also won the championship for three consecutive years at The Pascal Visual Object Classes (VOC) Challenge. Due to the fact that DPM considers well for local and global relationships, it has got higher detection accuracy and better performance. Although the above methods have achieved great performance, their development are limited by the limitations of hand-crafted design features and redundant time caused by sliding window.

2.2 Current Deep Learning

In 1998, Lécun et al. [10] proposed famous LeNet-5 model. It includes convolution layer, Relu layer, polling layer and the final innerproduct layer, and these layers have been still used, the network is also considered to be the first true sense of the convolution neural network. In 2012, Krizhevsky et al. [11] proposed AlexNet model, and have got lower ten percentage points than the previous year champion in ImageNet Large Scale Visual Recognition Competition (ILSVRC). This year is called the turning point of Deep Learning, marking the Deep Learning to take off. With the development of Deep Learning, some famous model like ZF [12], VGG [9], GoogleNet [13], and ResNet [14] are proposed.

In past three years, Deep Learning has got rapid development. Li et al. [15] proposed a kind of cascade convolution neural network named Cascade CNN. It contains six independent networks, three for the classification of the network, the other three for the bounding box regression. Cascading ideas can combine weak classifiers for higher accuracy, but the 6 networks of this paper are separated and can not be trained by end-to-end. So Qin et al. [16] proposed a joint training cascade convolution neural network for face detection, it has maintained the advantages of cascade and trained by end-to-end. In [17], Can and Fan proposed a multi-scale network named MS-CNN, it can detect different size objects at the same time. GoogleNet [13] uses Inception structure to make the network deeper, and the training parameters less. Ren et al. [18] proposed a network based on region proposal network (RPN) called Faster R-CNN, it decomposes the object detection problem into two subproblems. Firstly, the RPN network generates proposal bounding boxes, and uses these bounding boxes as input to the R-CNN. Because the RPN and R-CNN networks share the convolution feature, so the detection time is reduced and the detection accuracy is higher. Although RPN can reduce the detection time, the time is still too long. Aiming at this problem, YOLO [19] is an approach proposed by Redmon and Divvala. It removes the RPN network, can further reduce the detection time, but reduce the accuracy a little. On the basis of Faster R-CNN and YOLO framework, many classical methods are proposed by related researchers, such as FCN [20], PVANET [21], SSD [22] and YOLO9000 [23]. It is worth mentioning that our work is also based on the Faster R-CNN framework.

3   The Proposed Scalable Object Detection Method

In this section, we present the details of the proposed Scalable object detection method. Firstly, we describe the overall framework, next elaborate the feature fusion part of the pre-training model, and then expound the multi-scale structure. Finally, we present the training details.

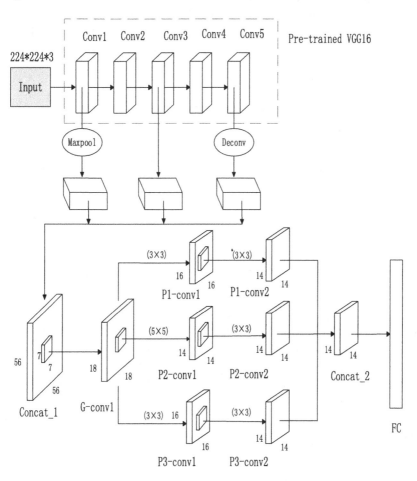

Fig. 1.   Scalable object detection architecture. The network takes an input image of size 224 × 224, (1) combine the downsampling of Conv1, Conv3 and upsampling of Conv5 feature maps of pre-trained VGG16 model to carry out Concat_1, (2) behind the Concat_1, there is a global convolution name G-Conv1, (3) and then divided into three equal local parts named as Pi-Conv1 (i = 1, 2, 3), finally combine the Pi-Conv2 (i = 1, 2, 3) to get the Concat_2

3.1 The Overall Framework

The proposed scalable object detection architecture is showed in Fig. 1, and the details of the parameters of the network are given in Table 1. Initially, a 224 × 224 image is forwarded through the convolutional layers of pre-trained VGG16, and the features maps are produced. We aggregate hierarchical feature maps and then compress them into a uniform space, namely Concat_1. There is a global convolution with the kernel size of 7 × 7 to get global features, and a cascaded multi-scale structure consists of three parts for extracting local features, we combine the three local part feature maps to get the layer Concat_2. Finally, the innerproduct layer outputs detection classification results. Besides, each convolution layer is followed by a normalizing layer using local response normalization (LRN) and RELU layer.

Table 1. Detail parameters of the network

Name	Type	Kernel size	Stride/pad	Output
Conv1_1	Convolution	3 × 3	1/1	224 × 224 × 64
Conv1_2	Convolution	3 × 3	1/1	224 × 224 × 64
Pool1	Maxpool	2 × 2	2/0	112 × 112 × 64
Conv2_1	Convolution	3 × 3	1/1	112 × 112 × 128
Conv2_2	Convolution	3 × 3	1/1	112 × 112 × 128
Pool2	Maxpool	2 × 2	2/0	56 × 56 × 256
Conv3_1	Convolution	3 × 3	1/1	56 × 56 × 256
Conv3_2	Convolution	3 × 3	1/1	56 × 56 × 256
Conv3_3	Convolution	3 × 3	1/1	56 × 56 × 256
Pool3	Maxpool	2 × 2	2/0	28 × 28 × 512
Conv4_1	Convolution	3 × 3	1/1	28 × 28 × 512
Conv4_2	Convolution	3 × 3	1/1	28 × 28 × 512
Conv4_3	Convolution	3 × 3	1/1	28 × 28 × 512
Pool4	Maxpool	2 × 2	2/0	14 × 14 × 512
Conv5_1	Convolution	3 × 3	1/1	14 × 14 × 512
Conv5_2	Convolution	3 × 3	1/1	14 × 14 × 512
Conv5_3	Convolution	3 × 3	1/1	14 × 14 × 512
Down	Maxpool	4 × 4	4/0	56 × 56 × 128
Up	Deconvolution	4 × 4	4/0	56 × 56 × 128
Concat_1	Concat			56 × 56 × 512
G-Conv1	Convolution	7 × 7	3/1	18 × 18 × 512
P1-Conv1	Convolution	3 × 3	1/0	16 × 16 × 128
P1-Conv2	Convolution	3 × 3	1/0	14 × 14 × 128
P2-Conv1	Convolution	5 × 5	1/0	14 × 14 × 256
P2-Conv2	Convolution	3 × 3	1/1	14 × 14 × 256
P3-Conv1	Convolution	3 × 3	1/0	16 × 16 × 128
P3-Conv2	Convolution	3 × 3	1/0	14 × 14 × 128
Concat_2	Concat			14 × 14 × 512

3.2 The Features Fusion Structure

We initialize the parameters of Conv1 to Conv5 layers according to the pre-trained model VGG16. Because of subsampling and pooling operations, these feature maps are not in the same dimension. In order to combine different levels of feature maps, we have different sampling methods for different layers. A max pooling layer is added on Conv1 to get its downsampling, a deconvolution layer is added on Conv5 to carry out its upsampling. It makes them and Conv3 into a unified space, and finally combines them to generate Concat_1. But why is Conv1, Conv3 and Conv5, because their characteristics are the largest different. If the feature difference is not big, the effect of fusion will be reduced.

The lower feature maps are the details of the information, it is conducive for bounding box regression. And the higher feature maps are semantic information, which is good for classification. When we combine these two type features together, we can get better performance. The experimental results will be a good proof, so it is effective.

3.3 Multi-scale Structure

There is a global convolution on Concat_1 layer named G-Conv1 with the kernel size of 7×7, because different sizes of the convolution of the kernel field is not the same, the characteristics of the extraction is also not the same. The kernel of size 7×7 can extract global features, and it is divided into three equal local convolution parts. According to the Inception structure, the network has kernel with size 5×5 and 3×3, each different parts is designed to learn different local features. While getting the local feature maps Pi-Conv2 $(i = 1, 2, 3)$, we combine the three part feature maps to get the concatenation layer Concat_2. So we can obtain both global and local features at the same time.

3.4 Training Details

- **Data augmentation:** Data augmentation is an indispensable technique in Deep Learning, it can manually increase the training data, and effectively inhibit the over-fitting. To apply data augmentation, we resize the shorter side to 600, and do the same as the short side of the scale operation on long side. Then we randomly crop a small patch 224×224 around objects from the whole image, and each sample is horizontally flipped.
- **Faster R-CNN:** Faster R-CNN combines the region proposal network and the detection network into a unified network, including two independent networks, one is RPN, the other one is R-CNN. RPN is used to predict the region proposal of input image with the three scales (128, 256, 512) and three kinds of aspect ratio (1:1, 1:2, 2:1), the mechanism of mapping is called anchor, each convolution produces 9 anchor. IOU (Intersection-over-union) of these achor and ground-truth is less than 0.3 as negative (background) and greater than 0.7 as positive (foreground). If it does not belong to the above, the proposal bounding box will be lost. The remaining bounding

boxes are used as input to the R-CNN, and the two networks share the convolution feature.

- **Fine-Tune:** The pre-trained VGG16 is used to initialize the parameters of Conv1 to Conv5 layers, and the learning rate is set to 0. So we can reduce a lot of training parameters. The rest of the convolution layers are initialized with Xaiver, and set the bias terms to 0. The last innerproduct layer layers is randomly initialized with Gaussian distributions with the standard deviations of 0.01 and 0.001, and also set the bias terms to 0.
- **SGD parameters:** We set global learning rate 0.001. The RPN and RCNN both have 40000 iterations, after 30000 iterations, we lower the learning rate to 0.0001 to train more iterations. Following standard practice, we use a momentum term with weight 0.9 and weight decay factor of 0.0005.

4   Experiments and Evaluation

In our experiments, The proposed method is evaluated on VOC2007, VOC2012 and KITTI datasets. The PASCAL Visual Object Classes Challenge is well known in the field of pattern recognition competitions, the VOC dataset has also become a standard dataset for object detection and classification, so it is shown that the VOC dataset can well explain the advantage and disadvantage of our method. Compared with the VOC dataset, KITTI has more small objects, occlusion situation is serious and the shooting angle is different. Experimental results also have proved that the performance on VOC is better, some detection examples of different datasets are showed in Fig. 2. Our experimental environment is NVIDA GTX1070 with Caffe, because of the limitation of experimental environment, all our experimental results are lower than original paper. But it does not affect the comparison results, it can still explain the results.

4.1   Datasets

- **VOC2007:** VOC2007 is a dataset containing 20 categories. Images are from our daily life scenes; Image size is around 500×375. It includes a total of 9963 images, 5011 training images and 4952 test pictures, 24640 annotated objects.
- **VOC2012:** Compared with VOC2007, occlusion flag is added to annotations and action classification is presented, the number of images increased to 11530, including 27450 annotated objects.
- **KITTI:** KITTI is a vehicle pedestrian dataset containing a total of 9 categories, including 7481 training images and 7518 test images, image size is around 1250×375.

4.2   VOC2007 and VOC2012 Results

Loss, accuracy and precision are three important indicators in the field of object detection and classification. The loss value can reflect whether the training situation of the model is stable, accuracy reflect the ability to judge the whole of the model, include both

(a) VOC2007+VOC2012

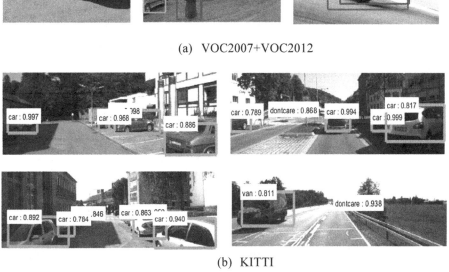

(b) KITTI

Fig. 2. Results on different datasets. (a) VOC2007 + VOC2012, (b) KITTI Datasets

positive and negative samples. And precision only reacts to the ability of the model to judge the positive samples. The Eqs. (1) and (2) are mathematical expressions of accuracy and precision. TP and FP respectively mean True Positive and False Positive, TN and FN respectively mean True Negative and False Negative. We use these three indicators to evaluate the experiment, and do it also in KITTI.

$$\text{Accuracy} = \frac{\text{TP} + \text{TN}}{\text{TP} + \text{FP} + \text{TN} + \text{FN}} \tag{1}$$

$$\text{Precision} = \frac{\text{TP}}{\text{TP} + \text{FP}} \tag{2}$$

Figure 3 shows the comparisons of loss and accuracy, from this picture we can see that the loss of our method is lower while accuracy is higher. Besides, when we only add the features fusion structure (Faster Rcnn + Fusion) or multi-scale structure (Faster Rcnn + MS), the loss also lower than original Faster R-CNN with VGG16, and the accuracy is higher. It indicates that the features fusion and multi-scale structure which we add are valid. Table 2 shows our results compared with other methods in average precision (AP) and Frames Per Second (FPS) values. Because our work is based on the Faster R-CNN framework, the FPS of our method is lowest with 5, but we enhance the mean AP (mAP). Compared with other methods, our mAP is higher than YOLO but little lower than SSD500. And for single classes, our AP value is higher or lower. The reason is that different network structures perform differently for different object scene, such as different object size and pose. We combine different levels of feature maps, and use different convolution kernels in the multi-scale structure, so we have got a higher mAP on the whole. However, there is no single-scale features targeted for individual special classes, AP value may be lower. In general speaking, we have achieved better performance than original VGG16 model, and keep the speed at the same time.

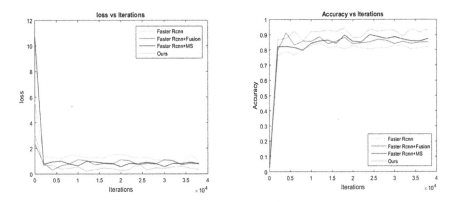

Fig. 3. Loss and accuracy on VOC2007 + VOC2012

4.3 KITTI Results

Just as we can see in the Fig. 4, we have got lower loss and higher accuracy the same as VOC2007 and VOC2012. It indicates that the feature fusion and multi-scale structure which we add is valid once again. Table 3 shows the results of mAP and FPS, we have got a higher mAP than Faster R-CNN and YOLO, but little lower than SSD500. Compared with the results on VOC2007 and voc2012, all the mAP are lower and FPS are identical. The reason is that there is more small size object in KITTI dataset, and occlusion situation is serious.

Table 2. Results on VOC2007 + VOC2012 (with IOU = 0.7)

Method	Faster R-CNN	YOLO	SSD500	HyperNet	Proposed
Tv	52.7	45.3	68.3	61.6	63.5
Bird	67.5	52.7	71.5	49.5	85.3
Boat	46.1	33.9	54.6	46.3	42.5
Bottle	42.2	19.4	47.2	48.8	52.4
Bus	66.7	62.6	77.4	72.2	61.2
Table	49.1	42.8	54.8	51.3	44.5
Cat	73.6	71.5	85.2	64.4	83.1
Chair	43.9	35.9	52.0	32.7	58.3
Cow	68.2	54.4	75.4	60.6	64.9
Car	65.4	51.2	77.1	66.9	78.7
Dog	74.3	71.3	83.7	59.1	87.6
Horse	73.7	66.1	80.3	63.8	85.8
Aero	74.9	71.8	84.6	61.8	70.2
Plant	36.5	24.4	44.9	26.7	49.1
Person	67.4	58.2	80.6	55.9	79.4
Sheep	62.3	46.7	72.7	62.4	76.8
Sofa	54.4	48.5	61.5	57.1	69.3
Train	73.6	67.1	82.9	62.2	68.9
mbike	70.8	64.6	81.2	54.6	84.4
Bike	71.3	62.3	78.1	62.9	81.6
mAP	61.7	52.5	70.7	56.0	69.4
FPS	5	32	14	5	5

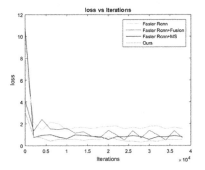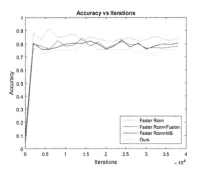

Fig. 4. Loss and accuracy on KITTI

Table 3. Results on KITTI (with IOU = 0.7)

Method	Faster R-CNN	YOLO	SSD500	HyperNet	Proposed
Tram	49.1	42.6	57.3	45.5	58.9
Car	69.4	60.2	74.5	64.7	78.3
Person_sitting	45.2	37.9	56.1	42.3	41.8
Pedestrian	63.5	55.8	70.2	60.2	60.6
Truck	57.4	49.3	61.6	54.3	66.7
Cyclist	64.9	57.2	73.3	62.1	62.3
Dontcare	56.3	48.4	64.1	51.9	63.8
Misc	38.5	34.6	43.8	39.5	51.2
Van	45.8	36.5	49.7	41.6	54.1
mAP	54.5	47.0	61.2	51.3	59.7
FPS	5	32	14	5	5

5   Conclusion

In this paper, we proposed a unified multi-scale network with features fusion, through combining different levels of feature maps, we can obtain advantage of both high and low-level maps, multi-scale structure can detect object of different sizes. Experimental results show that we have got a higher mAP as a whole on the VOC2007, VOC2012 and KITTI datasets, and maintained the original speed. We also analyzed the experimental results, compared with other mainstream methods, it illustrates the advantages and disadvantages of our approach. In the future work, our main focus is how to further improve the detection speed and achieve real-time performance, it is better to enhance the mAP at the same time.

Acknowledgements.   This work was partially supported by the National Natural Science Foundation of China (No. 61403054), and the Fundamental and Frontier Research Project of Chongqing under Grant No. cstc2014jcyjA40001.

References

1. Viola, P., Jones, M.: Rapid object detection using a boosted cascade of simple features. In: Proceedings of the 2001 IEEE Computer Society Conference on Computer Vision and Pattern Recognition, CVPR 2001, vol. 1, pp. 511–518. IEEE Xplore (2001)
2. Dalal, N., Triggs, B.: Histograms of oriented gradients for human detection. In: IEEE Computer Society Conference on Computer Vision and Pattern Recognition, CVPR 2005, pp. 886–893. IEEE (2005)
3. Lowe, D.G.: Distinctive image features from scale-invariant keypoints. Int. J. Comput. Vis. **60**, 91–110 (2004)
4. Li, J., Zhang, Y.: Learning surf cascade for fast and accurate object detection. In: Proceedings of the IEEE Conference on Computer Vision and Pattern Recognition, pp. 3468–3475 (2013)

5. Freund, Y., Schapire, R.E.: A decision-theoretic generalization of on-line learning and an application to boosting. In: Vitányi, P. (ed.) EuroCOLT 1995. LNCS, vol. 904, pp. 23–37. Springer, Heidelberg (1995). https://doi.org/10.1007/3-540-59119-2_166
6. Vapnik, V.: The Nature of Statistical Learning Theory, pp. 988–999. Springer, New York (1995). https://doi.org/10.1007/978-1-4757-3264-1
7. Felzenszwalb, P.F., Girshick, R.B., McAllester, D., Ramanan, D.: Object detection with discriminatively trained part-based models. IEEE Trans. Pattern Anal. Mach. Intell. **32**, 1627–1645 (2010)
8. Lecun, Y., Bengio, Y., Hinton, G.: Deep learning. Nature **521**, 436–444 (2015)
9. Simonyan, K., Zisserman, A.: Very deep convolutional networks for large-scale image recognition. In: Computer Science (2014)
10. Lécun, Y., Bottou, L., Bengio, Y.: Gradient-based learning applied to document recognition. Proc. IEEE **86**, 2278–2324 (1998)
11. Krizhevsky, A., Sutskever, I., Hinton, G.E.: ImageNet classification with deep convolutional neural networks. In: International Conference on Neural Information Processing Systems, pp. 1097–1105. Curran Associates Inc. (2012)
12. Zeiler, M.D., Fergus, R.: Visualizing and understanding convolutional networks. In: Fleet, D., Pajdla, T., Schiele, B., Tuytelaars, T. (eds.) ECCV 2014. LNCS, vol. 8689, pp. 818–833. Springer, Cham (2014). https://doi.org/10.1007/978-3-319-10590-1_53
13. Szegedy, C., Liu, W., Jia, Y.: Going deeper with convolutions. In: IEEE Conference on Computer Vision and Pattern Recognition, CVPR 2014, pp. 1–9 (2014)
14. Szegedy, C., Ioffe, S., Vanhoucke, V.: Inception-v4, inception-ResNet and the impact of residual connections on learning. In: IEEE Conference on Computer Vision and Pattern Recognition (2016)
15. Li, H., Lin, Z., Shen, X.: A convolutional neural network cascade for face detection. In: IEEE Conference on Computer Vision and Pattern Recognition, pp. 5325–5334 (2015)
16. Qin, H., Yan, J., Li, X.: Joint training of cascaded CNN for face detection. In: IEEE Conference on Computer Vision and Pattern Recognition, pp. 3456–3465. IEEE Computer Society (2016)
17. Cai, Z., Fan, Q., Feris, R.S.: A unified multi-scale deep convolutional neural network for fast object detection. In: IEEE Conference on Computer Vision and Pattern Recognition (2016)
18. Ren, S., He, K., Girshick, R.: Faster R-CNN: towards real-time object detection with region proposal networks. In: IEEE Transactions on Pattern Analysis & Machine Intelligence, p. 1 (2015)
19. Redmon, J., Divvala, S., Girshick, R.: You only look once: unified, real-time object detection. In: IEEE Conference on Computer Vision and Pattern Recognition, CVPR 2015, pp. 779–788 (2015)
20. Long, J., Shelhamer, E., Darrell, T.: Fully convolutional networks for semantic segmentation. In: IEEE Conference on Computer Vision and Pattern Recognition, pp. 3431–3440 (2015)
21. Kim, K.H., Hong, S., Roh, B.: PVANET: deep but lightweight neural networks for real-time object detection. In: IEEE Conference on Computer Vision and Pattern Recognition (2016)
22. Liu, W., Anguelov, D., Erhan, D., Szegedy, C., Reed, S., Fu, C.-Y., Berg, A.C.: SSD: single shot MultiBox detector. In: Leibe, B., Matas, J., Sebe, N., Welling, M. (eds.) ECCV 2016. LNCS, vol. 9905, pp. 21–37. Springer, Cham (2016). https://doi.org/10.1007/978-3-319-46448-0_2
23. Redmon, J., Farhadi, A.: YOLO9000: better, faster, stronger. In: IEEE Conference on Computer Vision and Pattern Recognition (2016)

Object Tracking with Blocked Color Histogram

Xiaoyu Chen, Lianfa Bai, Yi Zhang, and Jing Han[(✉)]

Jiangsu Key Laboratory of Spectral Imaging and Intelligent Sense,
Nanjing University of Science and Technology, Nanjing 210094, China
njusthanjing@163.com

Abstract. Object deformation and blur are challenging problems in visual object tracking. Most existing methods increase the generalization of the features to decrease the sensitivity of spatial structure or combine statistical feature and spatial structure feature. This paper presents a novel approach to add structure characteristics to color histograms with blocked color histogram (BCH) to increase the robustness of trackers based on color histogram especially in deformation or blur problems. The proposed approach works by computing color histograms of every blocks extracted from given boxes. We strengthen structure characteristics by separating the whole box to several parts and use the color histogram of the individual parts to track, then weighting the results, and the result shows that this improves the performance compared to the methods using the whole color histogram. We also use double layer structure to speed up the method with the necessary accuracy. The proposed method gets good score in VOT2015 and VOT2016.

Keywords: Visual tracking · Blocked color histogram · Double-layer structure
Mean shift

1 Introduction

Visual object tracking problems have recently achieved great progress. However, it is still difficult to create a generic tracker due to some complex factors in the real world such as deformation, motion blur, fast motion, partial occlusion, illumination variation, background clutter and scale variations. Most recent methods attempt to reduce the effect of deformation, motion blur by weakening the structure features or adding statistical features.

Recent years, researchers are focusing on discriminative learning methods, and many excellent methods are proposed, such as TLD [9], KCF [4], and DSST [5]. Nevertheless, the same problems are remained to be solved. Discriminative learning models are prefer structure features such as HOGs or LBP. Also, they often increase the generalization ability by decreasing the spatial discrimination, but achieve limited success. Discriminative learning methods has been widespread adopted in visual tracking with well-engineered features such as HOG. These methods have been shown to achieve great performance but also bring much computation.

We all know that color histogram is statistical feature containing no spatial structure information, so it is good at object deformation and blur problems with invariance of

© Springer International Publishing AG 2017
Y. Zhao et al. (Eds.): ICIG 2017, Part I, LNCS 10666, pp. 386–396, 2017.
https://doi.org/10.1007/978-3-319-71607-7_34

color distribution, but not good at the problems with interference and occlusion. So it is easy to think of increasing the spatial expression of color histogram, and the basic method is to block the object in space.

Mean shift was originally proposed by Fukunage in 1975, and developed by Yizong Cheng with kernel functions [7]. Mean shift is still popular method widely applied in visual tracking, segment, clustering, because of its simplicity. However, the methods based on mean shift are prone to local minima if there are some of the target features in the background, because it is very sensitive to clutter inference, illumination changes and the influence of background. Therefore Comaniciu et al. further proposed background-weighted histogram (BWH) to decrease the interference from background. Recently Fouad Bousetouane et al. combine the texture and color features as the target model to make it robust to these problems [2].

There are also many other attempts. DAT [1] uses the distractor-aware object model which employs a color histogram based Bayes classifier to explicit suppression of regions with similar colors. Staple [3] combines HOG features and a global color histogram in a ridge regression framework to describe the object. Similar methods also include CSK [14] and LSHT [15]. Both of them outperform many more complex trackers in multiple benchmarks. So it is possible to use features containing both spatial structure and color distribution to achieve better performance.

Stated thus, we propose a method based on color matching modeling color histograms in blocks, which enhances the ability of statistical features by separating the object region into blocks, and we argue that methods based on non-training method with blocked statistical features can also achieve state-of-the-art performance.

As shown in Fig. 1. Color histogram focuses on statistical result, but neglect spatial structure. Template models (like HOG) depend on the spatial configuration of the object and perform poorly when the object changes rapidly. Our methods add spatial characteristics to color histograms by separating the object to four blocks. Proposed method is proved to have more powerful spatial expression ability than classic mean shift (up) [7], and more robust to DSST [5] to fast deformation or blur.

Fig. 1. Comparison of our method and classic mean shift [7] and DSST [5]

2 Proposed Approach

2.1 Mean Shift with Blocked Color Histogram

Classic mean shift method [7] for tracking computes the vector of local mean maxima point by estimating the distribution of samples. The mean shift vector is defined as

$$M_h(x) \equiv \sum_{x_i \in S_k} d_i * (x_i - x) \tag{1}$$

In witch x is the position of center point, x_i is the position of sampled points, d_i is the distribution density of position x_i, S_k is the searching space.

The object model of d_i is defined by

$$\begin{cases} q_u = C \sum_{i=0}^{n} K\left(\left\|z_i^*\right\|^2\right) \delta\left[b(z_i) - u\right] \\ C = \dfrac{1}{\sum_{i=0}^{n} K\left(\left\|z_i^*\right\|^2\right)} \\ z_i^* = \left(\dfrac{(x_i - x_0)^2 + (y_i - y_0)^2}{x_0^2 + y_0^2}\right)^{0.5} \end{cases} \tag{2}$$

In witch z_i^* represent normalized position relative to center point (x_0, y_0), $K(*)$ is kernel function, $b(z_i)$ represent witch bin of color histogram the pixel of z_i belong to u is the index of color histogram ($u = 1, 2, \ldots m$) [8].

At t frame, initializing the search box with last searching result position f and computing color histogram candidate model is described as

$$p_u(f) = C \sum_{i=0}^{n} K\left(\left\|\frac{f - z_i}{h}\right\|^2\right) \delta\left[b(z_i) - u\right] \tag{3}$$

In witch h represent window size of kernel function.

In this paper, we adopt Bhattacharyya coefficient [10] as similarity measure:

$$\rho(p, q) = \sum_{i=0}^{m} \sqrt{p_u(f) q_u} \tag{4}$$

If we divide the searching space into four pieces, we will get four color histograms. However when compute the four color histograms, we found that the histogram is very sparse especially when the searching box is small, and it is hard to get a reasonable similarity map. So to increase the success rate for histograms matching, we add the histogram of the full searching box to each histogram of block, and it is proved to work, robustness increasing and iterations decreasing. The q_u will be changed to four parts:

$$
\begin{cases}
qlu_u = C_1 \sum_{i=0}^{n/4} K\left(\|z_i^*\|^2\right) \delta\left[b(z_i) - u\right] + C_1 \sum_{i=0}^{n} K\left(\|z_i^*\|^2\right) \delta\left[b(z_i) - u\right] \\
qld_u = C_1 \sum_{i=n/4}^{n/2} K\left(\|z_i^*\|^2\right) \delta\left[b(z_i) - u\right] + C_1 \sum_{i=0}^{n} K\left(\|z_i^*\|^2\right) \delta\left[b(z_i) - u\right] \\
qru_u = C_1 \sum_{i=n/2}^{n*3/4} K\left(\|z_i^*\|^2\right) \delta\left[b(z_i) - u\right] + C_1 \sum_{i=0}^{n} K\left(\|z_i^*\|^2\right) \delta\left[b(z_i) - u\right] \\
qrd_u = C_1 \sum_{i=n*3/4}^{n} K\left(\|z_i^*\|^2\right) \delta\left[b(z_i) - u\right] + C_1 \sum_{i=0}^{n} K\left(\|z_i^*\|^2\right) \delta\left[b(z_i) - u\right]
\end{cases} \tag{5}
$$

And $p_u(f)$ will be also divided:

$$
\begin{cases}
plu_u(f) = C_1 \sum_{i=0}^{\frac{n}{4}} K\left(\left\|\frac{f - z_i}{h}\right\|^2\right) \delta\left[b(z_i) - u\right] + C \sum_{i=0}^{n} K\left(\left\|\frac{f - z_i}{h}\right\|^2\right) \delta\left[b(z_i) - u\right] \\
pld_u(f) = C_1 \sum_{i=\frac{n}{4}}^{\frac{n}{2}} K\left(\left\|\frac{f - z_i}{h}\right\|^2\right) \delta\left[b(z_i) - u\right] + C \sum_{i=0}^{n} K\left(\left\|\frac{f - z_i}{h}\right\|^2\right) \delta\left[b(z_i) - u\right] \\
pru_u(f) = C \sum_{i=n/2}^{n*3/4} K\left(\left\|\frac{f - z_i}{h}\right\|^2\right) \delta\left[b(z_i) - u\right] + C \sum_{i=0}^{n} K\left(\left\|\frac{f - z_i}{h}\right\|^2\right) \delta\left[b(z_i) - u\right] \\
prd_u(f) = C \sum_{i=n*3/2}^{n} K\left(\left\|\frac{f - z_i}{h}\right\|^2\right) \delta\left[b(z_i) - u\right] + C \sum_{i=0}^{n} K\left(\left\|\frac{f - z_i}{h}\right\|^2\right) \delta\left[b(z_i) - u\right]
\end{cases} \tag{6}
$$

Correspondingly, the similarity measure will be changed to

$$
\rho(p, q) = \sum_{i=0}^{m} \sqrt{plu_u(f)qlu_u} + \sum_{i=0}^{m} \sqrt{pld_u(f)qld_u} + \\
\sum_{i=0}^{m} \sqrt{pru_u(f)qru_u} + \sum_{i=0}^{m} \sqrt{prd_u(f)qrd_u} \tag{7}
$$

Then we approximate the mean shift vector of similarity and start to search to the maxima point.

As shown in Fig. 2. The object is described by four individual color histograms which extracted from the four blocks of selected box respectively. And at t frame the searching box can be described in the same way. Then we compute the similarity of histograms of corresponding blocks and map the similarity to the spatial pixels. Finally we get the similarity map which can be used to compute mean shift vector. The histogram may be sparse which is not good for similarity measure, we also add the whole box color histogram to each.

Dividing the box into four is to add structure information to the object representation. Thus, the more blocks it is divided the more structure it will have, however, the more blocks make each block itself smaller, leading the representation more sparse and the amplitude of histograms lower, which reduce the effective information of each block, so we choose four as the blocks number.

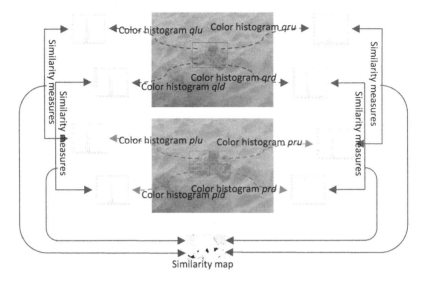

Fig. 2. Schematic diagram of blocked color histogram matching

2.2   Speed up with Double-Layer Structure

Four blocks bring more computation as well. First, the one histogram is changed into four and now four histograms need to be compute. Second, the bigger size means more points to be considered. Third more color levels will make the color histograms more sensitive, and it will be harder to get stable similarity map. Besides, smaller block means more sparse color histogram, and lower success rate of histogram matching, leading to more iterations. We propose a double-layer structure in which the first layer is more lightweight with smaller input and fewer color levels, the second more complex with bigger input and more color levels. And it appears to converge faster to the maxima point of similarity.

We set the iterating stopping condition of both layers as that module value of mean shift vectors of all four blocks smaller than a threshold which means the position of searching box is approaching to the maxima point when we get the box as the searching result of current frame. The second layers input position is the result of the first layer. We did not add scale prediction in this method, so the size of searching box will not change.

As is shown in Fig. 3. Searching process will go through two layers. First layers extract four histograms from resized input with 512 color levels, and shift by computing the mean shift vector. After iterating, second layer continue to search with searching box of original size and histogram with 4096 color levels. By searching with a rough model and a fine model, the method will achieve better performance with relatively less time (Table 1).

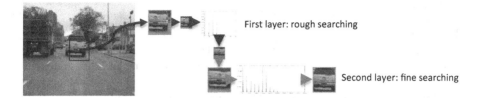

Fig. 3. Schematic diagram of double layer structure

Table 1. The algorithm process

Algorithm Proposed tracking method: processing at t frame
Input:
ImageI_t.
Previous target position l_{t-1} and scale s.
Reference histograms q, qlu, qld, qru, qrd.
Output:
Estimated target positionl_t.
Histograms preparation
1: Extract a cropped patch from I_t at l_{t-1} and scale s
2: Separate the patch to four blocks z_k, $(k = 1, 2, 3, 4)$
3: Compute the color histograms for rough and fine searching.
Rough searching
4: Compute the rough similarity ρ_r according to (7)
5: Searching for the rough position l_r from l_{t-1} by mean shift iterations.
Fine searching
6: Compute the fine similarity ρ_r according to (7)
7: Searching for the fine position l_t from l_r by mean shift iterations.

3   Evaluation

The approach proposed in this paper is implemented in Matlab. We perform the experiments on an Intel Core i7-7700 K 4.20 GHz CPU with 16 GB RAM.

Datasets. We employ all sequences of VOT2015 [11] and VOT2016 [12]. The sequences also contain challenging problems such as illumination variation, motion blur, background clutter and occlusion.

Evaluation Methodology. We use vot-toolkit to evaluate our method and follow the protocol of the VOT benchmark challenges. The performance of our approach is quantitatively validated by Accuracy-Robustness rank plot and expected overlap.

3.1   Model Analysis

Selection of Reference Model
Many tracking algorithms face a choice when select object model. Algorithms like DSST [5] and KCF [4] choose last few predicted results as the new model. This strategy do better in illumination changing or occlusion problems. However the error will accumulate, and the accumulated error will lead to the low overlap or even lost the target. We use the labeled box at the first frame which is the only manual intervention during the whole tracking process. This method make the box always point to true object, but also bring problems when the color distribution is changing severely.

Benefits from Blocked Color Histograms
As explained in Sect. 2.1, the blocked color histogram contain both the overall statistical characteristics and spatial structure characteristics, so it has better performance than those methods simply based on structure features such as DSST [5], KCF [4] and CT [6] especially in deformation and blur problems. Besides, the performance approaches to DAT [1] which also adopts color histogram and trains a discriminative object model with Bayes classifier.

The same situation also appear in motion change problem. The proposed method and color histogram based method DAT [1] have better performance than the others when motion changes.

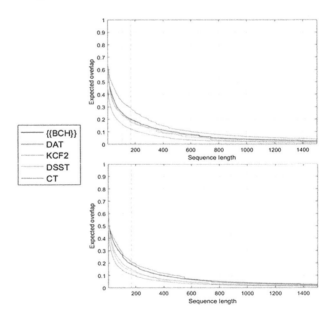

Fig. 4. Expected overlap in sequence with cameral motion problem (up) and motion change problem (down).

As shown in Fig. 4. Proposed method is outperforming those methods simply using structure features. We can see that the expected overlap of our method is higher than

KCF2 [4], DSST [5], CT [6] all during the sequence length in the problems of camera motion and motion change problems. And DAT [1] which also use color histograms has good performance too.

Efficiency
We perform the blocked color histogram with double layers structure mean shift, the first layer running 10 iterations and second layer 10 iterations, and the average speed is up to 20 fps. The most computation is determined by the image size, the scale of histogram, and the iterations. After 10 iteration, the searching box will not find the maxima point, where we make a tradeoff of accuracy and efficiency.

3.2 Results of VOT2015 and VOT2016 Benchmark

The Visual Object Tracking challenge VOT benchmark aims at comparing short-term single-object visual trackers that do not apply pre-learned models of object appearance. We select some recent state-of-art methods as compared algorithms, including the winner of VOT2014 challenge [13], DSST [5], KCF [4] which are based on popular correlation filters, CT [6] based on sparse representation and compressive sensing and STC based on spatial weight function.

The accuracy of a tracker on a sequence in VOT2015 [11] is defined as the average per-frame overlap between the predicted box r_t and the ground truth box r_{GT} with the intersection-over-union criterion:

$$S_t = \frac{|r_t \cap r_{GT}|}{|r_t \cup r_{GT}|} \tag{8}$$

The robustness of a tracker is defined as the number of failures over the sequence, with a failure determined to have occurred when S_t comes zero. Since the benchmark is focusing on short-term tracking, a tracker will be automatically reinitialized to the ground truth five frames after the failure.

Figure 5 shows the tracking results of six sequences of VOT2015. These sequences contain the situations with deformation, illumination changing, interference, and blur problems. The result demonstrate that the proposed method has good performance facing these problems. For example, in sequence car1, the object is blurred and the road has similar color distribution with the object, methods like CT [6] and DAT [1] can hardly keep up with the object, while our method has better robustness. In sequence motocross2, where object deforms rapidly, but keep the color distribution, our method has better overlap compared with the others. In sequence racing, when shadow covers the car, our method also has competitive performance.

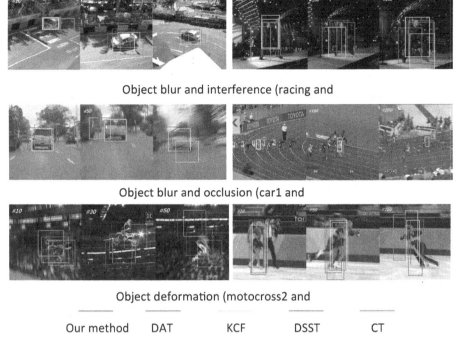

Object blur and interference (racing and

Object blur and occlusion (car1 and

Object deformation (motocross2 and

Our method   DAT   KCF   DSST   CT

Fig. 5. A visualization of tracking results of our method, and state-of-art visual trackers DAT [1], DSST [5], KCF [4], CT [6] on six benchmark sequences.

As we do not add scale adaptive part, the method performs not well in overlap index when there is a scale variation of the object, but the robustness remains good. As shown in Fig. 6. We see the result of challenge of VOT2015 and VOT 2016. Our method has good performance. Our method has better robustness than most compared methods, which means mean shift method based on BCH has good performance overall.

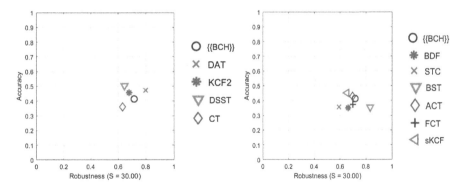

Fig. 6. Accuracy-Robustness rank plot with compared methods for report challenge of VOT2015 (left) and VOT2016 (right). Our method is BCH. Better trackers are closer to the top right corner.

4   Conclusion

We propose a generic object tracking method based on color features. To overcome the drifting problem, we adopt the blocked color histogram, which remain spatial structure characteristics. The result of VOT benchmark also demonstrate that our method have better performance than those simply based on spatial structure features or statistical features, especially in deformation and blur problems. Benefiting from double layer structure, the method is up to 20 fps. Overall, our method is suitable for the application with need for high efficiency and in which it is robust to color. Further, we will implement blocked color histogram with more complex strategy instead of mean shift to enhance the searching efficiency and robustness as there have been some smarter method for optimization.

Acknowledgment. This work was supported by the Natural Science Foundations of China (61373061 and 61501235). This work was supported by the Fundamental Research Funds for the Central Universities (30915011335).

References

1. Possegger, H., Mauthner, T., Bischof, H.: In defense of color-based model-free tracking. In: Computer Vision and Pattern Recognition, pp. 2113–2120. IEEE (2015)
2. Bousetouane, F., Dib, L., Snoussi, H.: Improved mean shift integrating texture and color features for robust real time object tracking. Vis. Comput. **29**(3), 155–170 (2013)
3. Bertinetto, L., Valmadre, J., Golodetz, S., Miksik, O., Torr, P.H.S.: Staple: complementary learners for real-time tracking, **38**(2), 1401–1409 (2016)
4. Henriques, J.F., Rui, C., Martins, P., Batista, J.: High-speed tracking with kernelized correlation filters. IEEE Trans. Pattern Anal. Mach. Intell. **37**(3), 583–596 (2014)
5. Danelljan, M., Häger, G., Khan, F.S., Felsberg, M.: Accurate scale estimation for robust visual tracking. In: British Machine Vision Conference, pp. 65.1–65.11 (2014)
6. Zhang, K., Zhang, L., Yang, M.-H.: Real-time compressive tracking. In: Fitzgibbon, A., Lazebnik, S., Perona, P., Sato, Y., Schmid, C. (eds.) ECCV 2012. LNCS, vol. 7574, pp. 864–877. Springer, Heidelberg (2012). https://doi.org/10.1007/978-3-642-33712-3_62
7. Cheng, Y.: Mean shift, mode seeking, and clustering. IEEE Trans. Pattern Anal. Mach. Intell. **17**, 790–799 (1995). IEEE Xplore
8. Comaniciu, D., Meer, P.: Mean shift: a robust approach toward feature space analysis. IEEE Trans. Pattern Anal. Mach. Intell. **24**, 603–619 (2002)
9. Kalal, Z., Mikolajczyk, K., Matas, J.: Tracking-learning-detection. IEEE Trans. Pattern Anal. Mach. Intell. **34**(7), 1409–1422 (2012)
10. Kailath, T.: The divergence and Bhattacharyya distance measures in signal selection. IEEE Trans. Commun. Technol. **15**(1), 52–60 (1967)
11. Kristan, M., Matas, J., Leonardis, A., Felsberg, M., Cehovin, L., Fernandez, G., et al.: The visual object tracking VOT2015 challenge results. In: ICCV, vol. 6, pp. 564–586 (2015)
12. Yeung, D.Y., Wang, N., Li, S.: The visual object tracking VOT2016 challenge results (2016)
13. Kristan, M., et al.: The visual object tracking VOT2014 challenge results. In: Agapito, L., Bronstein, Michael M., Rother, C. (eds.) ECCV 2014. LNCS, vol. 8926, pp. 191–217. Springer, Cham (2015). https://doi.org/10.1007/978-3-319-16181-5_14

14. Danelljan, M., Khan, F.S., Felsberg, M., Weijer, J.V.D.: Adaptive color attributes for real-time visual tracking. In: Computer Vision and Pattern Recognition, pp. 1090–1097. IEEE (2014)
15. He, S., Yang, Q., Lau, R.W.H., Wang, J., Yang, M.H.: Visual tracking via locality sensitive histograms. In: Computer Vision and Pattern Recognition, vol. 9, pp. 2427–2434. IEEE (2013)
16. Zhang, W.Z., Ji, J.G., Jing, Z.Z., Jing, W.F., Zhang, Y.: Adaptive real-time compressive tracking. In: International Conference on Network and Information Systems for Computers, pp. 236–240 (2015)
17. Maresca, M.E., Petrosino, A.: Clustering local motion estimates for robust and efficient object tracking. In: Agapito, L., Bronstein, Michael M., Rother, C. (eds.) ECCV 2014. LNCS, vol. 8926, pp. 244–253. Springer, Cham (2015). https://doi.org/10.1007/978-3-319-16181-5_17
18. Montero, A.S., Lang, J., Laganiere, R.: Scalable kernel correlation filter with sparse feature integration. In: IEEE International Conference on Computer Vision Workshop, pp. 587–594. IEEE (2016)

Deep Networks for Single Image Super-Resolution with Multi-context Fusion

Zheng Hui, Xiumei Wang$^{(\boxtimes)}$, and Xinbo Gao

School of Electronic Engineering, Xidian University, Xi'an 710071, China
zheng_hui@aliyun.com, wangxm@xidian.edu.cn, xbgao@mail.xidian.edu.cn

Abstract. Deep convolutional neural networks have been successfully applied to image super resolution. In this paper, we propose a multi-context fusion learning based super resolution model to exploit context information on both smaller image regions and larger image regions for SR. To speed up execution time, our method directly takes the low-resolution image (not interpolation version) as input on both training and testing processes and combines the residual network at the same time. The proposed model is extensively evaluated and compared with the state-of-the-art SR methods and experimental results demonstrate its performance in speed and accuracy.

Keywords: Convolutional neural networks · Super-resolution Multi-context fusion

1 Introduction

Aim to recover a high-resolution (HR) image from the corresponding low-resolution (LR) image, single image super-resolution (SR) has been utilized in the area of computer vision for several decades. Typical image SR methods can be roughly categorized into three kinds, i.e., interpolation-based, reconstruction-based, and learning-based [1].

Recently, learning-based SR methods using convolutional neural network (CNN) have demonstrated notable progress. Dong *et al.* first proposed a CNN-based SR method known as SRCNN, which learns a mapping from LR to HR in an end-to-end manner and shows the state-of-art performance in accuracy and visual. A neural network that closely mimics the sparse coding approach for image SR is proposed by Wang et al. [2]. Kim *et al.* proposed a very deep neural network with residual architecture to exploit contextual information over large image regions [3].

Although the CNN-based models mentioned above have achieved good performance, there are two main issues should not be neglected. First, most of existing methods upscale a single low-resolution image to the desired size using bicubic interpolation before applying the network for prediction. This pre-processing step increases unnecessary computational cost and often results in visible reconstruction artifacts. Several approaches are observed to perform better which

© Springer International Publishing AG 2017
Y. Zhao et al. (Eds.): ICIG 2017, Part I, LNCS 10666, pp. 397–407, 2017.
https://doi.org/10.1007/978-3-319-71607-7_35

accelerate SRCNN directly by learning from the LR image and embedding the resolution change into the network [4]. These method, however, use relatively small networks and cannot learn complicated mappings well due to the limited network capacity. In addition, most methods rely on the context information of small image regions. These ways don't make full use of the information of large image regions.

To solve the aforementioned issues, we propose a Multi-context Fusion Super-Resolution Network (MFSR) based on a cascade of convolutional neural networks (CNNs) and a residual network. Note that very deep CNN model would increase the model capacity, but it would introduce more parameters which is infeasible on the scene requiring the higher speed. Thus, an architecture with trade-off between accuracy and speed is essential for practical applications. In this paper, we adopt the suitable network width (namely the number of filters in a layer) to reduce the amounts of parameters. Experiments prove that the proposed model can achieve both state-of-the-art PSNR and SSIM results and visually pleasant results.

2   Related Work

Lately, many convolutional neural network based SR methods have been proposed in the papers. So, we focus on recent convolutional neural networks based SR approaches.

2.1   Convolutional Neural Network for Image Super-Resolution

The SRCNN [1] aims at learning an end-to-end mapping, which takes the low-resolution image Y as input and directly outputs the high-resolution one $F(Y)$. This model contains three layers: patch extraction and representation, non-linear mapping and reconstruction. The VDSR network [3] demonstrates significant improvement over SRCNN [1] by increasing the network depth from 3 to 20 convolutional layers. To speed-up the training, VDSR suggests the residual-learning CNN and uses high learning rates. To achieve real-time performance, the FSR-CNN network [4] takes the LR image as input and enlarges feature maps by using transposed convolution.

2.2   Residue Learning

It is pointed by [3] that enabling residue learning during network training results in a faster convergence as well as a better performance in the final result. Kim *et al.* point out carrying the input to the end is conceptually similar to what an auto-encoder does. In this way, the network concentrates on the learning of residual image, so that the convergence rate is significantly decreased. To facilitate residue learning in our network, we up-sample the input LR image with bicubic interpolation algorithm, then add it to the output of the transposed convolutional layer.

Our approach builds upon existing CNN-based SR algorithms with a main difference. We joint residual learning and multi-context fusion learning by using convolutional and transposed convolutional layers.

3 Proposed Method

In this section, we describe the design methodology of the proposed multi-context fusion learning network.

3.1 Network Architecture

We propose to construct the network by using a series of convolutional layers, as shown in Fig. 1. Our model takes an LR image as input (rather than interpolated version of the LR image) and predicts a residual image. The proposed model has two parts, feature extraction and image reconstruction.

Feature Extraction. We use n cascaded containers, one convolutional layer and one transposed convolutional layer upsampling the extracted features. Each

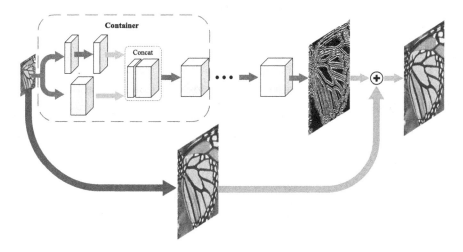

Fig. 1. The overview of our proposed method. Red arrows indicate convolutional layers. The blue straight arrow indicates transposed convolutional layer and the blue curved arrow indicates the combination of the split operation and convolutional operation, namely split operation is performed first and then convolutional operation is deployed. The purple arrow denotes bicubic interpolation operator and the green arrow denotes element-wise addition operator. Orange arrows and 'Concat box' represent data flow from orange arrows to 'Concat box' to accomplish feature maps fit together in channel dimension. We cascade n containers (broken blue box) repeatedly. A low-resolution (LR) image goes through our network and transforms into a high-resolution (HR) image. (Color figure online)

container has two parallel paths, which are used as multi-context fusion features extractor. One path contains two cascaded convolutional layers and each convolutional layer has 16 filters of spatial sizes 3×3, the other path has one convolutional layer with 32 filters of spatial sizes 3×3. Two 3×3 layers bring receptive field with the same size as one 5×5 layer. Each of our containers uses receptive fields of different sizes for taking context information on the larger image regions and the smaller image regions into account simultaneously and can be regarded as local context fusion unit. Here, sub-networks in each container adopt two different depths which means to combine contextual feature information on both shallow sub-network and deep sub-network. And then, one 3×3 layer with 48 filters merges these extracted feature maps and takes the results as the next container's input. And a convolutional layer with 64 filters of size 3×3 is followed by the last container mainly increase the dimension of previous extracted features. The last layer on this stage adopts one transposed convolutional layer with 1 filter of size 9×9 to upsample and aggregate the previous generated feature maps. Then the output is the predicted residual image.

Image Reconstruction. On this stage, the input coarse image is upsampled by the customized bicubic upscaling layer. The upsampled image is then combined (using element-wise summation) with the predicted residual image from the feature extraction stage to produce a high-resolution output image.

3.2   Loss Function

Mean square error (MSE) is employed as the loss function to train the network, and our optimization objective can be expressed as

$$\min_{\Theta} \sum_i \left\| MFSR\left(I_y^{(i)}; \Theta\right) - I_x^{(i)} \right\|_2^2, \tag{1}$$

where $I_y^{(i)}$ and $I_x^{(i)}$ are the i-th pair of LR/HR training data, and $MFSR\left(I_y; \Theta\right)$ denotes the HR image for I_y predicted using the MFSR model with parameter set Θ. All the parameters are optimized through the standard back-propagation algorithm.

4   Experiments

In this section, we first explain the implementation details in the experiments and then compare the MFSR with state-of-the-arts on four benchmark datasets to demonstrate the effectiveness of our proposed method.

4.1   Implementation Details

In the proposed model, we initialize the convolutional filters using the method of He *et al.* [5]. The size of the transposed convolutional filter is 9×9 and the weight is initialized from bilinear interpolation kernel. For the activation function after each convolution layer, we suggest the use of Parametric Rectified Linear Unit (PReLU) [5] instead of the commonly-used Rectified Linear Unit (ReLU). We pad zeros around the boundaries before applying convolution to keep the size of all feature maps. As the training is implemented with the *caffe* package [6], the transposed convolution filter will output a feature map with $(s-1)$-pixel cut on the border (s is the stride of kernel namely magnification). As to the number of the containers, we set $n = 7$ to achieve the trade-off between performance and the execution time.

We use 91 images from Yang *et al.* [7] and 200 images from Berkeley Segmentation Dataset [8] as our training data. The optimization is conducted by the mini-batch stochastic gradient descent method with a batch size of 64, momentum of 0.9, and weight decay of $1e-4$. The learning rate is initially set to $1e-4$ and fixed during the whole training phase. In addition, data augmentation (rotation, scaling and flipping) is used.

Table 1. Quantitative evaluation of state-of-art SR algorithms: average PSNR/SSIM for scale 2×, 3× and 4×. Red text indicates the best and blue text indicates the second best performance.

Algorithm	Scale	Set5 PSNR / SSIM	Set14 PSNR / SSIM	BSD100 PSNR / SSIM	Urban100 PSNR / SSIM
Bicubic	2	33.66 / 0.9299	30.24 / 0.8688	29.56 / 0.8431	26.88 / 0.8403
A+	2	36.54 / 0.9544	32.28 / 0.9056	31.21 / 0.8863	29.20 / 0.8938
SRCNN	2	36.66 / 0.9542	32.45 / 0.9067	31.36 / 0.8879	29.50 / 0.8946
SelfExSR	2	36.49 / 0.9537	32.22 / 0.9034	31.18 / 0.8855	29.54 / 0.8967
RFL	2	36.54 / 0.9537	32.26 / 0.9040	31.16 / 0.8840	29.11 / 0.8904
FSRCNN	2	37.00 / 0.9558	32.63 / 0.9088	31.50 / 0.8906	29.85 / 0.9009
MFSR	2	**37.71 / 0.9593**	**33.13 / 0.9132**	**31.94 / 0.8965**	**30.80 / 0.9143**
Bicubic	3	30.39 / 0.8682	27.55 / 0.7742	27.21 / 0.7385	24.46 / 0.7349
A+	3	32.59 / 0.9088	29.13 / 0.8188	28.29 / 0.7835	26.03 / 0.7973
SRCNN	3	32.75 / 0.9090	29.28 / 0.8209	28.41 / 0.7863	26.24 / 0.7989
SelfExSR	3	32.58 / 0.9093	29.16 / 0.8196	28.29 / 0.7840	26.44 / 0.8088
RFL	3	32.43 / 0.9057	29.05 / 0.8164	28.22 / 0.7806	25.86 / 0.7900
FSRCNN	3	33.16 / 0.9140	29.43 / 0.8242	28.52 / 0.7893	26.42 / 0.8064
MFSR	3	**33.76 / 0.9217**	**29.82 / 0.8318**	**28.82 / 0.7976**	**27.06 / 0.8266**
Bicubic	4	28.42 / 0.8104	26.00 / 0.7027	25.96 / 0.6675	23.14 / 0.6577
A+	4	30.28 / 0.8603	27.32 / 0.7491	26.82 / 0.7087	24.32 / 0.7183
SRCNN	4	30.48 / 0.8628	27.49 / 0.7503	26.90 / 0.7101	24.52 / 0.7221
SelfExSR	4	30.31 / 0.8619	27.40 / 0.7518	26.84 / 0.7106	24.79 / 0.7374
RFL	4	30.14 / 0.8548	27.24 / 0.7451	26.75 / 0.7054	24.19 / 0.7096
FSRCNN	4	30.71 / 0.8657	27.59 / 0.7535	26.96 / 0.7128	24.60 / 0.7258
MFSR	4	**31.49 / 0.8841**	**28.08 / 0.7686**	**27.29 / 0.7254**	**25.11 / 0.7513**

Our model is tested on four benchmark data sets, which are Set5 [9], Set14 [10], BSD100 [11] and Urban100 [12]. The ground truth images are downscaled by bicubic interpolation to generate LR/HR image pairs for both training and testing databases. We convert each color image into the YCbCr color space and only process the luminance channel with our model, and bicubic interpolation is applied to the chrominance channels, because the visual system of human is more sensitive to details in intensity than in color.

4.2   Comparisons with the State-of-the-arts

We compare the proposed MFSR with 5 state-of-the-art SR algorithms: A+ [13], SRCNN [1], SelfExSR [12], REL [14] and FSRCNN [4]. Table 1 shows the average PSNR and SSIM [15] of the results by different SR methods. It can be observed that the proposed method achieves the best SR performance in all experiments.

Figure 2 shows visual comparisons on image "butterfly" with a scale factor of 3×. Our method accurately reconstructs the very thin line on the butterfly. We observe that methods using the bicubic upsampling for pre-processing generate results with noticeable artifacts. In contrast, our approach effectively suppresses such artifacts. Similarly, in Figs. 3, 6 and 7, contours are clean in our method whereas they are severely blurred or distorted in other methods.

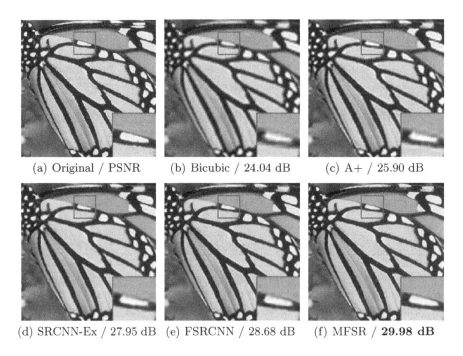

(a) Original / PSNR   (b) Bicubic / 24.04 dB   (c) A+ / 25.90 dB

(d) SRCNN-Ex / 27.95 dB   (e) FSRCNN / 28.68 dB   (f) MFSR / **29.98 dB**

Fig. 2. The "butterfly" image from the Set5 dataset with an upscaling factor 3.

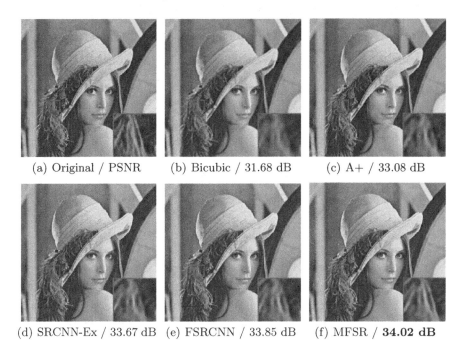

(a) Original / PSNR   (b) Bicubic / 31.68 dB   (c) A+ / 33.08 dB

(d) SRCNN-Ex / 33.67 dB   (e) FSRCNN / 33.85 dB   (f) MFSR / **34.02 dB**

Fig. 3. The "lenna" image from the Set14 dataset with an upscaling factor 3.

4.3   Execution Time

Our network is implemented using the Python interface of *Caffe* package [6] and is trained and tested on a machine with 4.2 GHz Intel i7 CPU (32G RAM) and Nvidia TITAN X (Pascal) GPU (12G Memory). Table 2 shows the execution time of our model on Set5, Set14, BSD100 and Urban100 by using CPU implementation and GPU implementation. The speed of the proposed MFSR using GPU is much faster than that of using CPU. Figure 4 shows the trade-offs between the

Table 2. Comparison of the execution time (sec) of our method on the 4 benchmark datasets with CPU implementation and GPU implementation.

CPU / GPU	Scale	Set5	Set14	BSD100	Urban100
CPU	2	0.832	1.589	1.004	5.267
GPU	2	0.015	0.018	0.010	0.041
CPU	3	0.254	0.523	0.341	1.746
GPU	3	0.012	0.013	0.007	0.023
CPU	4	0.147	0.301	0.187	0.972
GPU	4	0.009	0.010	0.005	0.016

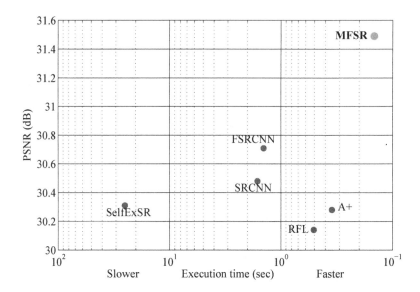

Fig. 4. The average PSNR and the average inference time for upscaling factor 4× on Set5. SRCNN and FSRCNN use the public slower MATLAB implementation of CPU. Our MFSR uses the matcaffe implementation of CPU.

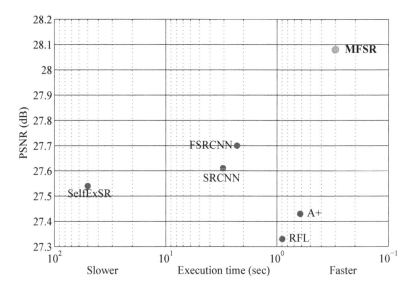

Fig. 5. The average PSNR and the average inference time for upscaling factor 4× on Set14. All methods use CPU implementation.

run time and performance on Set5 for 4 × SR. We measure the run time of all methods on CPU. Similarly, from Fig. 5, we can see that the proposed MFSR generates SR images efficiently and accurately on Set14 with scaling factor 4.

(a) Original / PSNR   (b) Bicubic / 23.71 dB   (c) A+ / 25.03 dB

(d) SRCNN-Ex / 27.04 dB   (e) FSRCNN / 27.11 dB   (f) MFSR / **28.05 dB**

Fig. 6. The "ppt3" image from the Set14 dataset with an upscaling factor 3.

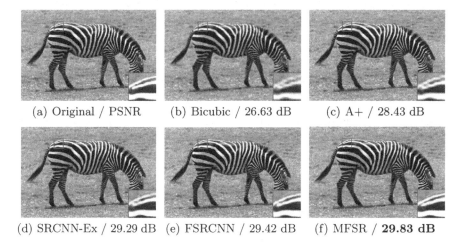

(a) Original / PSNR   (b) Bicubic / 26.63 dB   (c) A+ / 28.43 dB

(d) SRCNN-Ex / 29.29 dB   (e) FSRCNN / 29.42 dB   (f) MFSR / **29.83 dB**

Fig. 7. The "zebra" image from the Set14 dataset with an upscaling factor 3.

5   Conclusions

In this work, we investigate a deep convolutional network for single image super-resolution. Our method presents the multi-context fusion leaning and combine it with residual learning. MFSR is compared with several state-of-art SR methods (both DL and non-DL) in our experiments, and shows a visible performance advantage both quantitatively and perceptually. In the future, this approach of image super-resolution will be explored to facilitate other image restoration problems such as denoising and compression artifacts reduction.

Acknowledgments. This work was supported in part by the National Natural Science Foundation of China under Grant 61472304, 61432014 and U1605252.

References

1. Dong, C., Loy, C.C., He, K., Tang, X.: Image super-resolution using deep convolutional networks. TPAMI **38**(2), 295–307 (2015)
2. Wang, Z., Liu, D., Yang, J., Han, W., Huang, T.: Deep networks for image super-resolution with sparse prior. In: ICCV, pp. 370–378 (2015)
3. Kim, J., Lee, J.K., Lee, K.M.: Accurate image super-resolution using very deep convolutional networks. In: CVPR, pp. 1646–1654 (2016)
4. Dong, C., Loy, C.C., Tang, X.: Accelerating the super-resolution convolutional neural network. In: Leibe, B., Matas, J., Sebe, N., Welling, M. (eds.) ECCV 2016. LNCS, vol. 9906, pp. 391–407. Springer, Cham (2016). https://doi.org/10.1007/978-3-319-46475-6_25
5. He, K., Zhang, X., Ren, S., Sun, J.: Delving deep into rectifiers: Surpassing human-level performance on imagenet classification. In: ICCV (2015)
6. Jia, Y., Shelhamer, E., Donahue, J., Karayev, S., Long, J., Girshick, R., Guadarrama, S., Darrell, T.: Caffe: convolutional architecture for fast feature embedding. In: ACM MM, pp. 675–678 (2014)
7. Yang, J., Wright, J., Huang, T.S., Ma, Y.: Image super-resolution via sparse representation. TIP **19**(11), 2861–2873 (2010)
8. Martin, D., Fowlkes, C., Tal, D., Malik, J.: A database of human segmented natural images and its application to evaluating segmentation algorithms and measuring ecological statistics. In: ICCV (2001)
9. Bevilacqua, M., Roumy, A., Guillemot, C., AlberiMorel, M.L.: Low-complexity single-image super-resolution based on nonnegative neighbor embedding. In: BMVC (2012)
10. Zeyde, R., Elad, M., Protter, M.: On single image scale-up using sparse-representations. In: Boissonnat, J.-D., Chenin, P., Cohen, A., Gout, C., Lyche, T., Mazure, M.-L., Schumaker, L. (eds.) Curves and Surfaces 2010. LNCS, vol. 6920, pp. 711–730. Springer, Heidelberg (2012). https://doi.org/10.1007/978-3-642-27413-8_47
11. Arbelaez, P., Maire, M., Fowlkes, C., Malik, J.: Contour detection and hierarchical image segmentation. TPAMI **33**(5), 898–916 (2011)
12. Huang, J.B., Singh, A., Ahuja, N.: Single image super-resolution from transformed self-exemplars. In: CVPR, pp. 5197–5206 (2015)

13. Timofte, R., De Smet, V., Van Gool, L.: A+: adjusted anchored neighborhood regression for fast super-resolution. In: Cremers, D., Reid, I., Saito, H., Yang, M.-H. (eds.) ACCV 2014. LNCS, vol. 9006, pp. 111–126. Springer, Cham (2015). https://doi.org/10.1007/978-3-319-16817-3_8

14. Schulter, S., Leistner, C., Bischof, H.: Fast and accurate image upscaling with super-resolution forests. In: CVPR, pp. 3791–3799 (2015)

15. Wang, Z., Bovik, A.C., Sheikh, H.R., Simoncelli, E.P.: Image quality assessment: From error visibility to structural similarity. TIP **13**(4), 600–612 (2004)

Chinese Handwriting Generation by Neural Network Based Style Transformation

Bi-Ren Tan[1,2], Fei Yin[1], Yi-Chao Wu[1,2], and Cheng-Lin Liu[1,2(✉)]

[1] National Laboratory of Pattern Recognition (NLPR),
Institute of Automation of Chinese Academy of Sciences, Beijing 100190, China
{biren.tan,fyin,yichao.wu,liucl}@nlpr.ia.ac.cn
[2] University of Chinese Academy of Sciences, Beijing, China

Abstract. This paper proposes a novel learning-based approach to generate personal style handwritten characters. Given some training characters written by an individual, we first calculate the deformation of corresponding points between the handwritten characters and standard templates, and then learn the transformation of stroke trajectory using a neural network. The transformation can be used to generate handwritten characters of personal style from standard templates of all categories. In training, we use shape context features as predictors, and regularize the distortion of adjacent points for shape smoothness. Experimental results on online Chinese handwritten characters show that the proposed method can generate personal-style samples which appear to be naturally written.

Keywords: Handwriting generation · Style transformation
Neural network learning

1 Introduction

Handwriting synthesis is important for many applications, such as computer font personalization, data enhancement for training recognition systems, handwriting-based communication. The synthesis of personal-style handwriting is one of the most important research problems in this field. Its goal is to generate handwritten characters in the same style as the target writer. This is particularly useful for Chinese handwriting, which is known for the large number of characters (e.g. 27,533 categories for GB18030-2000) and the complex characters structures. It is hard for a person to write thousands of characters to make a personal font library, and instead, it is desirable to generate large number of stylized characters by learning from a small number of written characters. The challenge of synthesis is how to grasp the personal style of specific writer, and how to generate stylized characters with smooth shape.

The problem of handwriting modeling and synthesis has been studied for a long time, and there are many related works in the literature. The methods of

© Springer International Publishing AG 2017
Y. Zhao et al. (Eds.): ICIG 2017, Part I, LNCS 10666, pp. 408–419, 2017.
https://doi.org/10.1007/978-3-319-71607-7_36

handwriting synthesis can be generally divided into three groups: perturbation-based generation, fusion-based generation, statistical model-based generation.

The perturbation-based methods generate new characters by changing the geometric characteristics of original samples, such as size, stroke thickness, tilt and so on [1,2]. However, this approach is not suitable for synthesizing of personal-style handwritten characters, since the synthesized samples may be unnatural due to random and non-calibrated parameter settings.

Fusion-based methods combine existing samples into new synthesized ones [3–5]. They are more suitable for composing words from letters. The methods of [6–8] tried to split Chinese characters into strokes and then generate new characters by recombining the strokes. As an example Zhou et al. [9] developed a system to construct the shapes of 2,500 simplified Chinese character by recombining radicals of 522 characters written by a user, and thus built a small-scale Chinese font library in the users' handwriting style. The challenge of this method lies in accurate segmentation of character components, which is the key to make the combined characters look more natural and smooth.

Statistical model-based methods capture the statistics of natural handwriting variations between different styles. A common modeling method [3] is to obtain the mapping relation between the sample points of corresponding character templates, and then obtain the displacement of the matched sample points. Then a new style character can be generated from the statistical model by moving the sample points of the standard template. Lian et al. [10] presented a system to automatically generate a handwriting font library in the user's personal style with huge amounts of Chinese characters by learning variation of stroke shape and layout. However, this method relies on the precise locating and matching each stroke on the characters.

To generate personal-style handwritten characters flexibly with reduced human efforts, this paper proposes a learning-based method to online personal-style handwriting generation. We take some given characters written by an individual as training samples, and use a neural network to learn the personal style (transformation function) after corresponding the samples points between the handwritten characters and standard templates. The transformation function is then used to generate stylized samples of all categories by transforming standard templates. We validated our algorithm on online Chinese handwritten characters, and the experimental results show that the proposed method can generate qualified handwriting characters of specific personal-styles when learning transformation from only 300 handwritten samples.

The remainder of this paper is organized as follows. Section 2 describes the proposed handwriting generation method. Section 3 introduces the character style transform algorithm based on neural network. Section 4 presents experimental results and Sect. 5 concludes the paper.

2   Handwriting Generation Method

We work with online Chinese handwritten characters, as it is easier to extract stroke trajectories from online characters, and it is trivial to generate offline

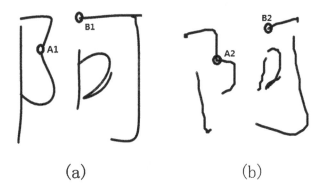

Fig. 1. Examples of online character samples. (a) is the standard template; (b) is the personal-style handwritten character. A1, A2 and B1, B2 are two pairs of corresponding points.

character images from online characters. To generate stylized handwritten characters for a large category set from a small number of handwritten samples, we have standard temples (such as carefully written samples or printed characters) for all the categories in a set (say, GB2312-80 or GB18030-2000). The handwritten samples are matched with the corresponding standard temples to get the correspondence of stroke points, and transformation function is learned by neural networks from the correspondence. The learned transformation is applied to the standard templates of all categories to generate stylized handwritten characters. In Fig. 1, we show a pair of corresponding characters where (a) is the standard template and (b) is a personal handwritten character. In the following, we describe the procedures of character sample points matching and the measure of matching distance. The style transformation method is detailed in Sect. 3.

2.1   Sample Points Matching

This task aims to obtain the corresponding relation between two sets of sample points. The problem of point set registration has been studied for a long time. There are many available algorithms for point set matching. In this paper, we choose the TPS-RPM algorithm [11] to implement registration between standard and target point set. Specifically, $C_x = (p_{x_1}, \cdots, p_{x_n})$ represents an online standard character with n sample points, and $C_y = (p_{y_1}, \cdots, p_{y_m})$ is the target character with m points.

The TPS function can be used to simulate the non rigid deformation by decomposing the spatial transformation into a global affine transformation and a local non rigid transformation. Generally speaking, this point matching process is divided into two steps. Firstly, we modify matching matrix $\{M_{ij}\}$, under the current transformation parameter (d, w); Secondly, we make the matching matrix unchanged and estimate the TPS parameters. Under the framework of the deterministic annealing technique, these two steps are iterated until convergence with the gradual decline of the control temperature T. In this process, the author obtained the matching matrix and the TPS parameters by minimizing the following objective functions:

$$E_{TPS}(M, d, w) = \sum_{i=1}^{m}\sum_{j=1}^{n} M_{ij}\|p_{x_i} - p_{y_j}d - \phi w\|^2 + \lambda\text{trace}(w^T\phi w), \quad (1)$$

where M_{ij} represents the matching probability between sample point p_{x_i} and p_{y_j}, d and w is the affine and non rigid transformation parameter, respectively.

2.2 Matching Distance Between Characters

The online characters are represented as combined of strokes $C = (S_1, S_2 \ldots S_N)$, where S_N is the Nth stroke of character C, and the strokes can be seen as a set of ordered points $S = (p_1, p_2 \ldots p_M)$. The similarity between two characters is defined as the average distance of matching points. Sect. 2.1, we describe the matching method between two corresponding characters C_1 and C_2, where $C_1 = (p_1{}^{C1}, p_2{}^{C1} \ldots p_n{}^{C1})$, $C_2 = (p_1{}^{C2}, p_2{}^{C2} \ldots p_m{}^{C2})$, the corresponding matching point set of C_1 is $C_{\text{match}} = (p_1{}^{M12}, p_2{}^{M12} \ldots p_n{}^{M12})$, the average matching distance between C_1 and C_2 define as follow:

$$d_{12} = \frac{1}{n}\sum_{i=1}^{n}\sqrt{(p_i{}^{C1} - p_i{}^{M12})^2}, \quad (2)$$

where the value of d_{12} determines the similarity of C_1 and C_2. The problem of calculating the similarity between two characters thus become that of computing the distance between two sets of matching points.

3 Style Transformation Learning

Give a number of personal-style handwritten characters as training samples, our method first match each training sample with its standard template of same category and get the corresponding pairs of sample points. We then use a neural network to learn the transformation function from the sample points of training samples to those of standard templates. Shape context features are extracted from the neighborhood of each sampled point as predictors (inputs of the neural network). And to guarantee the smoothness of generated samples, we propose multiple sampled points regression taking into account the spatial relationship between the points.

3.1 Sample Point Context Feature Extraction

In our learning model, we use shape context features as predictors, and regularize the distortion of adjacent points for shape smoothness. In this paper the shape context feature [12] is obtained by analyzing the distribution of the peripheral sample points. For example, in Fig. 2 we take a sample point in the standard

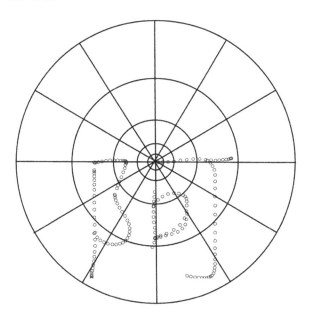

Fig. 2. Obtain the shape context feature of sample point.

character as the center of a circle whose radius equals to the width of the character, then we divide the circular region into 60 bins, so that we can obtain the distribution histogram of the sample points as 60 dimensional context features. Based on the statistical distribution of sample points, the shape context feature can describe the global information of a character. To solve specific problems, we can change the number of bins to obtain the most suitable of shape context feature in the experiment.

3.2 Single Points Regression

We first introduce single point regression model which predicts the displacement of only one point. In this model, the features of sample point consist of position information and context information. They are represented by the coordinates of the sample point and its 120 dimensional shape context feature. The two dimensional coordinates of target point are the outputs of FNN, and its structure was experimentally chosen as $I * H_1 * H_2 * H_3 * O = 122 * 100 * 100 * 100 * 2$, where I, H and O represent the input, hidden and output layers, respectively. Besides, the mean square error of the output coordinates is used as the network loss function:

$$L = \frac{1}{2m} * \sum_m (Y - Y_o)^2. \tag{3}$$

However, from the experimental results, the performance of single point regression model didn't meet our expectation because some synthesized characters were distorting. This is due to drastic change of relative position between adjacent points. To solve this problem, we need to smooth each stroke by a post-processing. Let $C^D = (S_1^D, S_2^D \ldots S_n^D)$ represent a deformed character composed of n strokes, and $S_K^D = (p_1^D, p_2^D \ldots p_m^D)$ is its Kth stoke which is consisted of m regression points. The following is the smoothing process of S_K^D:

1. Calculate the new coordinates of every point:

$$p_j^{new} = \begin{cases} p_1^D & j = 1 \\ \left(p_{j-1}^D + p_j^D + p_{j+1}^D\right)/3 & 1 < j < m \\ p_m^D & j = m. \end{cases} \quad (4)$$

2. Repeat step 1until the stroke look natural, usually we only need to repeat 3 times. It should be noted that each stroke is smoothed independently.

Experimental results show that adding the position constraint of adjacent points is an effective method to improve the synthetic quality of strokes. Further, in the following section we will try to regularize the distortion of adjacent points for shape smoothness in the training process.

3.3 Multi-point Regression

In training the neural network to fit multiple samples points simultaneously, the spatial relationship between the points is considered to smooth the deformation of stroke shape. We first consider to restrict the relative position of two adjacent points. Because of the proximity of these two input points, they have a similar shape context feature, so we just need to choose one of their shape context as the common feature. Usually we take the first point as the center point and the second point as a constraint point. The 120 dimensional shape context feature of center point and the coordinates of adjacent points consist as the inputs of Neural Network. The structure of network is changed as $I * H_1 * H_2 * H_3 * O = (120 + 2 * N) * 100 * 100 * 100 * (2 * N)$, where N represents the number of input sample points. The objective function of double point regression model becomes as follows:

$$L = \frac{1}{2m} * \sum_m (Y - Y_o)^2 + w * \frac{1}{2m} * \sum \left((p_{y_1} - p_{y_2}) - (p_{yo_1} - p_{yo_2})\right)^2, \quad (5)$$

where Y are the real coordinate of matching points, Y_o is the output of the network, p_{y_1}, p_{y_2} and p_{yo_1}, p_{yo_2} represent two pairs of adjacent points respectively. In (5), the first term is the mean square error, the second term is the penalty term for the change of relative position working as smoothness constraints.

Double point regression restricts the relative position of two adjacent points by controlling their displacement, however, it limits only one direction. In order to further strengthen the smoothness constraints, we constraint the displacement in both ahead and hinder directions. Therefore, we need to use the coordinate of front and rear points as constraint information.

We assume that $X = \left(p_{x_{c-n}}, p_{x_{c-n+1}}, \cdots, p_{x_c}, \cdots, p_{x_{c+n-1}}, p_{x_{c+n}} \right)$ is a section of stroke within standard character, p_{x_c} is the center of this section which contains of $2n + 1$ points. We use coordinates of X and the shape context of center point as the input of network.

The matching point set of X is $Y = \left(p_{y_{c-n}}, p_{y_{c-n+1}}, \cdots, p_{y_c}, \cdots, p_{y_{c+n-1}}, p_{y_{c+n}} \right)$, Y is the target output of network.

The optimal solution is obtained by minimizing the following objective functions:

$$L = \frac{1}{2m} * \sum_m (Y - Y_o)^2 + w * \frac{1}{2m} * \sum \left((Y - p_{y_c}) - (Y_o - p_{y_{oc}}) \right)^2, \quad (6)$$

where $(Y - p_{y_c}) - (Y_o - p_{y_{oc}})$ is the penalty term for the change of position relative to center point, and Y_o whose center point is $p_{y_{oc}}$ represents the actual output of network.

4   Experiments

In the experiment, we collected different styles of personal handwritten character sets, each of which has 6,763 characters. We chose one of the well written online character sets as the standard template, and selected one of the remaining sets as the target personal-style.

However, sometimes it is difficult to collect a carefully written samples set and not all handwritten characters qualify as standard characters directly. To solve this problem, we need to normalize the handwritten characters again. The printed Song typefaces are ideal for standard character set, but we can't obtain the stroke trajectories information of printed characters directly. Inspired by Thin Plate Spline deformation [11], we normalize the standard templates by single character deformation. In the Sect. 2.1, we can obtain the deformation functions parameters of two characters during point matching. To normalize one standard character, we first calculate the deformation of corresponding points between an online handwritten character and the stroke trajectory of its corresponding printed character, and then estimate the TPS transformation parameters. Finally, we use the TPS transformation function to deform the shape of character template, and then we can obtain an online character with standard Song typeface style. Figure 3 shows the normalization effect.

Fig. 3. Normalize each template character. (a) are handwritten characters; (b) are normalization results.

We took 300 standard characters and their corresponding target characters as the training samples. We normalized the template character to the same size by keeping the width to height ratio. It was better when the training set was composed of different structural characters. Then we matched the corresponding sample point between different style character templates using TPS point registration algorithm and extracted the 120 dimensional shape context information of each sample point. Finally we learned the transformation function by neural network. Then we used the transformation function to generate stylized samples of all categories by transforming standard templates. Following are the results of our experiments.

4.1 Deformation Effect of Different Learning Models

We compared the synthesis performance of different learning models according to direct observation and matching distance. In the experiment, we set the constraint coefficient $w = 2$, several characters generated by different models are shown in Fig. 4. In this Figure, we could intuitively find that the generated characters are similar to the target temple in both size and layout structure. That proves our regression model is effective and feasible. By contrast we can also find that the performance of multi-point models are better than single point model. In the next experiment, We will further compare the learning performance of each model by calculating the matching distance of sample points.

In Table 1, we show the change of average matching distance of 100 pairs of corresponding characters from different models. D_{ori} is the average matching point distance between original standard character and target character, and D_{def} is the average matching point distance between deform character and target character.

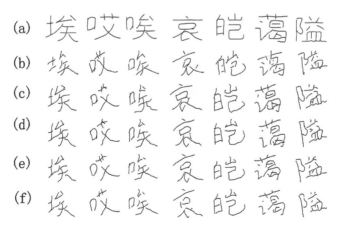

Fig. 4. Compare the generating results with different methods when $w = 2$. (a) are the standard characters, (b) are the target characters, (c), (d), (e), (f) are synthesis results of 1 point, 2 points, 3 points and 5 points regression respectively.

Table 1. The change of average matching distance.

Distance	1 point	2 points	3 points	5 points
D_{ori}	0.15145	0.15145	0.15145	0.15145
D_{def}	0.08765	0.07445	0.06522	0.05644

Fig. 5. The effect of smoothness regularization in five-point regression model. (a) Standard templates; (b) target personal-style characters; (c) generated characters without smoothness regularization; (d) generated characters with smoothness regularization.

Comparing the change of matching distance between standard characters and target characters, we further prove our conclusions that multi point regression model can effectively utilize the local features of sample points, and synthesize characters with higher quality.

In the multiple points regression model, shape context features are extracted from the neighborhood of each sampled point as inputs of the neural network, and the distortion of adjacent points are regularized for shape smoothness. In order to illustrate the effect of smoothness constraint, we do a comparative experiment on 5 points regression model. Figure 5 shows the results of smoothness constraint in five point regression model. Obviously, the generated characters appear to be more smooth and natural after adding constraints. This is obviously due to the constraints of the relative position between neighbor points prevent the occurrence of outliers during the sample points regression.

4.2 Generating Characters of Different Writing Styles

Finally, we compared the generated samples of different styles base on five-point regression model to validate the effectiveness of our algorithm. In the experiment, four personal-style handwriting sets were selected, we take one of them as the standard template and the other three as the target style. We take 300 pairs of templates as training samples for each style.

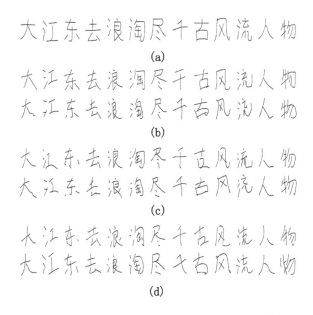

(a)

(b)

(c)

(d)

Fig. 6. Generated characters of three different personal styles. (a) Samples of standard template; (b), (c), (d) the target style characters and the synthetic characters, in every pictures, the first row represent the target character and the second row represent the synthetic characters.

Table 2. Average distance of matching points.

Style	Training set		Test set	
	D_{ori1}	D_{def1}	D_{ori2}	D_{def2}
Style1	0.12684	0.0501	0.1362	0.07354
Style2	0.1193	0.04458	0.1244	0.08225
Style3	0.1356	0.6257	0.1343	0.07903

According to the comparative experiments, we find that the generated characters are obviously different from the standard template, however, they have the same stroke features and structure characteristics as the target style. Figure 6 shows the generated results of different personal-style characters, none of these samples had appeared in the training set. Table 2 shows the matching distance of each style. The matching distance between standard characters and target characters become smaller after deforming which means that similarity between characters becomes higher. This is consistent with the observation of the human eye. The generated results proves that our model is effective in learning different styles with a small training set.

5   Conclusion

This paper proposes a novel learning-based approach to generate personal-style handwriting by style transformation. We learn the transition function between writing styles by predicting the displacement of the sample points. In order to synthesize high quality handwriting characters, we use shape context features as predictors, and regularize the distortion of adjacent points for shape smoothness. The experimental results demonstrated that our algorithm can learn the handwriting style and generate natural target style characters from a small number of training samples. However, in the course of the experiment, we also find the limitations of our method. For example, it was still a difficult task for us to simulate a writing style of rapid cursive. Besides, our algorithm is verified on the online character, further, we can try to extend this method to synthesis the writing trajectories of offline characters by adding the information of stroke width.

Acknowledgment. This work has been supported by the National Natural Science Foundation of China (NSFC) Grant No. 61573355.

References

1. Varga, T., Bunke, H.: Off-line handwritten textline recognition using a mixture of natural and synthetic training data. In: Proceedings of the 17th International Conference on Pattern Recognition, vol. 2, pp. 545–549 (2004)
2. Varga, T., Bunke, H.: Perturbation models for generating synthetic training data in handwriting recognition. In: Marinai, S., Fujisawa, H. (eds.) Machine Learning in Document Analysis and Recognition. SCI, vol. 90, pp. 333–360. Springer, Heidelberg (2008). https://doi.org/10.1007/978-3-540-76280-5_13
3. Wang, J., Wu, C., Xu, Y.-Q., Shum, H.-Y., Ji, L.: Learning-based cursive handwriting synthesis. In: Proceedings of Eighth International Workshop on Frontiers in Handwriting Recognition, pp. 157–162 (2002)
4. Wang, J., Wu, C., Xu, Y.-Q., Shum, H.-Y.: Combining shape and physical models for online cursive handwriting synthesis. Int. J. Doc. Anal. Recogn. (IJDAR) **7**(4), 219–227 (2005)

5. Guyon, I.: Handwriting synthesis from handwritten glyphs. In: Proceedings of the Fifth International Workshop on Frontiers of Handwriting Recognition, pp. 140–153 (1996)
6. Zong, A., Zhu, Y.: StrokeBank: automating personalized Chinese handwriting generation. In: AAAI, pp. 3024–3030 (2014)
7. Xu, S., Jin, T., Jiang, H., Lau, F.C.: Automatic generation of personal Chinese handwriting by capturing the characteristics of personal handwriting. In: AAAI (2009)
8. Shin, J., Suzuki, K.: Interactive system for handwritten-style font generation. In: Fourth International Conference on Computer and Information Technology, pp. 94–100 (2004)
9. Zhou, B., Wang, W., Chen, Z.: Easy generation of personal Chinese handwritten fonts. In: International Conference on Multimedia and Expo (ICME), pp. 1–6 (2011)
10. Lian, Z., Zhao, B., Xiao, J.: Automatic generation of large-scale handwriting fonts via style learning. In: SIGGRAPH ASIA 2016 Technical Briefs, p. 12 (2016)
11. Chui, H., Rangarajan, A.: A new point matching algorithm for non-rigid registration. Comput. Vis. Image Underst. 89(2), 114–141 (2003)
12. Belongie, S., Malik, J., Puzicha, J.: Shape matching and object recognition using shape contexts. IEEE Trans. Pattern Anal. Mach. Intell. 24(4), 509–522 (2002)

Text Detection Based on Affine Transformation

Xiaoyue Jiang, Jing Liu[✉], Yu Liu, Lin Zhang, and Xiaoyi Feng

Northwestern Polytechnical University, Xi'an, China
ljing@mail.nwpu.edu.cn

Abstract. Text detection and recognition plays an important roles in many computer vision based systems, since text can provide explicit content information. In natural scene, variations of scale, rotation and position are the main challenges for text detection and recognition algorithms. Thus, rectified text region is required for most text recognition algorithm. In this paper, we proposed a text detection method which can provide accurate text region. With the external quadrilateral of text region, the affine parameters can be estimated. Consequently, the distorted text region can be rectified according to the affine parameters. The proposed method can provide more accurate detection result for text region. In addition, it can enhance the performance of text recognition. The experiments show the effectiveness of the proposed method.

Keywords: Text detection · Affine transformation · MSER · SWT
Inertia spindle

1 Introduction

In recent years, with the development of Internet and the popularity of digital cameras and mobile phones, images and video resources are full of people's lives. The study of understanding the content of videos or image has become hotspots in Multimedia Information technology. The text in the videos and images contains rich semantic information, which is an important clue for understanding the content of images and videos. Detecting and recognizing the text in such images or videos is of great significance in many fields such as image understanding, video content analyzing and content based image or video retrieval. For text recognition, it can meet a certain degree of application requirements, and many companies have also released some commercial software packages [1, 2]. However when it is used in a natural scene, the performance will degrade. One of the key reasons is that the accuracy of the text detection reduces, thus the overall performance of the character recognition system decreases as well. Usually, a rectangular box is used to label the text region. However, due to complex background and different view position, text in images maybe shown in different position, orientation and scale. Thus, a rectangular box always cannot mark the text region accurately. Consequently, the distorted text image will also influence the performance of text recognition algorithms. Therefore a robust text detection and system should detect text in arbitrary position and orientation accurately.

The current text detection methods can be summarized as three categories as [3], gradient-based methods, the connected region-based methods and texture based

© Springer International Publishing AG 2017
Y. Zhao et al. (Eds.): ICIG 2017, Part I, LNCS 10666, pp. 420–431, 2017.
https://doi.org/10.1007/978-3-319-71607-7_37

methods. Always, the text area is rich of edges, while the background region has relatively less edges. Based on this feature, edges are used to determine the existence of text. Some popular edge detectors are applied for the text detection, such as Sobel edge detector, Harris corner detector. However, when the background become complex, the edge features bring a lot of false alarms [4].

Text detection based on the connected region mainly utilizes the similarity of some features in a local region, such as the character stroke width and color [5–9]. With color-based feature, it can detect the text in different directions, but it is sensitive to the change of environment. Maximum Extreme Stability region (MSER) algorithms [10–12] consider the variance of local features to determine the region that has similar features. The MSER detector is invariant to rotation, scale and affine. It can effectively detect the text in variable view and scale.

For texture feature, Yi and Tian [13] proposed a text detection algorithm based on the gradient, color and geometric characteristics of characters. They concatenated the characters with similar features into the text area. The texture feature of text area is considered to be different from that of background. Zhao et al. [14] applied the theory of wavelet transform to extract the texture information from images. They divided the image into multiple patches and classified each patch into text region and background according to the texture feature.

Images can be taken from any position, thus text in image can appear in any pose. However, text detection method only use rectangular box to label text region which always includes a lot of background region. In this paper, we proposed a text detection method to detect text and label the text region more accurately. With the quadrilateral label for text region, the inertial spindle is used to estimate the affine parameters for text region. Then text regions can be rectified according to affine transform, where the rectified text can be recognized more accurately.

2 Text Detection

Given an image, to localize the text region precisely is the first step to guarantee the performance of the whole text recognition system. For each character, they share some similar features, such as color and texture. Thus, we applied the region-based feature to detect the text. However, the region-based feature will also introduce some false alarms. Then geometric feature and stroke width are used further for the purification of candidate region. With all these initial character detection results, a quadrilateral is introduced to local the text region accurately. The procedure of text detection in shown in Fig. 1.

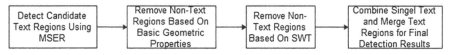

Fig. 1. The flow chart of text detection

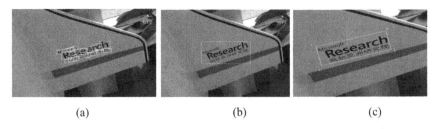

| (a) | (b) | (c) |

Fig. 2. Bounding box for text region. (a) bounding box for each character from text detection, (b) maximal external bounding box, (c) adjusted bounding box.

In order to detect all the possible text regions, region-based feature, MSER [10] is applied. The principle of MSER is based on watershed algorithm. The increment of the threshold is similar to rising the water level. As the water rises, some shallow valleys will be flooded. If you look down from the sky, the earth is divided into two parts, land and water, which is similar to the binary image. In image, the connect regions that has low variance in features will be merged together. Its mathematical definition is as follows:

$$\Delta q_i = |Q_{i+\Delta} - Q_{i-\Delta}|/|Q_i| \tag{1}$$

where Q_i denotes a certain connection region when the threshold is i, Δ is a minimal change of the gray scale threshold, and q_i is the changing rate of the region Q_i when the threshold value is i. When q_i is a local minimum, then Q_i is the maximum stable extremum region. MSER is robust to affine transformation, thus it can effectively detect the text in the case of perspective transformation and scale change.

Although the MSER can pick out most of the text, but it can also include some parts without text. Non-text area can be discarded by examining the properties of the candidate region. Due to the geometric properties of text region, the width-to-height ratio, eccentric and Euler number are applied. Eccentricity is defined as the ratio between the main axis and the auxiliary axis of the image area. The Euler number is the total number of objects in the image minus the total number of holes in those objects.

Besides geometric feature, the stroke width is another robust feature. The text areas tend to have a smaller stroke width variation than non-text areas. Thus we applied stroke width detector (SWT) [15] to calculate the stroke width for candidate regions. The variance of stroke width is used to determine the existence of text.

3   External Bounding Box Estimation

After text detection, each candidate character will be labeled by a rectangle box. Always text region is represented by the maximal external box of all the candidate text region, as shown in Fig. 2(b). However, it includes many background and cannot represent the orientation of the text region, which is useful for further affine transform. In this section, we will introduce the proposed method for accurate external bounding box estimation as shown in Fig. 2(c).

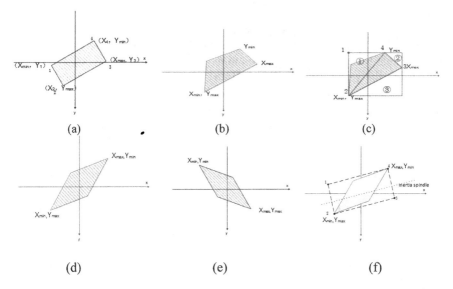

Fig. 3. Three different cases to determine the external bounding box. (a) the condition of quadruple extreme points; (b), (c) the condition of triple extreme points and the external bounding box for it; (d), (e) two possible conditions for twin extreme points, (f) the external bounding box for twin extreme points case.

In order to determine the affine parameters, we need to find an accurate bounding box to represent the contour of text region. To determine the bounding box, the four corner points of the quadrilateral should be decided according to the distribution of characters. Since the bounding box of each character has presented the position of each character, the corners of the bounding box for each character are used to determine the external quadrilateral. In fact, we find the extreme points from all the corners of character bounding box, naming the maximal and minimal horizontal position as X_{min}, X_{max}, and maximal and minimal vertical position as Y_{min}, Y_{max}. According to the distribution of these extreme points, there are three different cases to determine the external quadrilateral.

3.1   Quadruple Extreme Points

In this case, the four extreme points are not coincided together. That is, each extreme point represents one corner of external bounding box, as shown in Fig. 3(a). Then the external quadrilateral can be determined directly by these four points. With the external bounding box, the parameters of affine transform can be estimated. The details about affine transform will be introduced in Sect. 4.

3.2   Triple Extreme Points

In this condition, two extreme value appears in one points, and the other two extreme value appears in two different points. Thus, the four extreme value can determine three points of external bounding box, as shown in Fig. 3(b). With three points, a triangle can be determined. Then the forth point should be determined by the distribution of characters. First an external rectangular can be found for the three extreme points defined triangle by drawing lines parallel to axis through the triangle points. Then the region inside the rectangular is divided into four sub-regions, and there are three sub-regions outside the triangle. Then the forth point should lie in the region where most characters stay. Here the density of character can be described by the density of corner points of character bounding boxes. Then the character density of these three sub-regions is calculated and compared. The corner point of the sub-region that has the maximum character is selected as the forth point for the external quadrilateral. Figure 3 (c) shows a solution for triple extreme points.

3.3   Twin Extreme Points

In this condition, the four extreme points can only determine two corner points because of the coincidence of extreme points, as shown in Fig. 3(d), (e). Then we need to determine another two points for the external quadrilateral, which is based on the distribution of characters. In fact, the inertia spindle of the detected characters represents the main orientation of text region. Thus we propose to use the direction of inertia spindle to determine the other two points of the external bounding box. For each of the extreme points, two lines that are parallel and appendicular to the inertia spindle can be set, respectively. Then the intersection of two sets of lines can determine the other two corner points of the external bounding box, as shown in Fig. 3(f).

Similarly, the calculation of inertia spindle of text region also can be based on the corner points of character bounding box. Let C represents a set of corners (x_i, y_i), $i = 1, 2, \ldots, N$ where N is the total number of corners of the detected character bounding boxes. The centroid point of all the corners is defined as $(\bar{x}, \bar{y})$. Then the moment of inertia for corner points C is defined as

$$G_c = \sum_{i=1}^{N} [(xi - \bar{x})^2 + (yi - \bar{y})^2]$$ (2)

The moment of inertia for corner set C against the straight line L with angle θ is defined as

$$G_\theta = \sum_{i=1}^{N} [(xi - \bar{x}) \sin \theta - (yi - \bar{y}) \cos \theta]^2$$ (3)

The inertia spindle is defined as the angle $\hat{\theta}$ which make the moment of inertial G_θ minimal as

$$\hat{\theta} = \arg \min G_\theta$$ (4)

Then let the derivative of inertia moment G_θ equal to zero, as $G'_\theta = 0$

$$G'_\theta = 2 \sum_{i=1}^{N} [(xi - \bar{x}) \sin \theta - (yi - \bar{y}) \cos \theta] \cdot [(xi - \bar{x}) \cos \theta - (yi - \bar{y}) \sin \theta]$$
$$= \sum_{i=1}^{N} [(xi - \bar{x})^2 - (yi - y)^2] \sin 2\theta - 2 \sum_{i=1}^{N} (xi - \bar{x})(y_i - \bar{y}) \cos 2\theta \tag{5}$$

then

$$\tan 2\hat{\theta} = \frac{2 \sum_{i=1}^{N} (xi - x)(yi - y)}{\sum_{i=1}^{N} [(xi - \bar{x})^2 - (y_i - \bar{y})^2]} \tag{6}$$

Let $m_{20} = \sum_{i=1}^{N} (x_i - x)^2$, $m_{02} = \sum_{i=1}^{N} (y_i - y)^2$, $m_{11} = \sum_{i=1}^{N} (x_i - \bar{x})(y_i - \bar{y})$, then Eq. (5) can be written as,

$$\tan 2\hat{\theta} = \frac{2m_{11}}{m_{20} - m_{02}} \tag{7}$$

Because

$$\tan 2\theta = \frac{2 \tan \theta}{1 - \tan^2 \theta} \tag{8}$$

Then bring Eq. (9) into Eq. (3), we can get

$$m_{11} \tan^2 \hat{\theta} + (m_{20} - m_{02}) \tan \hat{\theta} - m_{11} = 0 \tag{9}$$

$$\tan \hat{\theta}_{1,2} = \frac{-(m_{20} - m_{02}) \pm \sqrt{(m_{20} - m_{02})^2 + 4m_{11}^2}}{2m_{11}} \tag{10}$$

For the two orientation $\hat{\theta}_{1,2}$, the one makes the second derivative of G_θ greater than zero is selected as the direction of inertia spindle. Then the inertia spindle can be described as the line passing through centroid point with the direction of $\hat{\theta}$

$$y_i - \bar{y} = (x_i - \bar{x}) \tan \hat{\theta} \tag{11}$$

Let $\rho = \tan \hat{\theta}$, then the other two points of the external bounding box can be determined by the intersection of parallel and perpendicular lines to direction ρ through extreme points. Equations 14–17 are the equations for four lines.

$$y_1 = \rho(x - x_{max}) + y_{min}; \quad y_2 = -\frac{1}{\rho}(x - x_{max}) + y_{min}$$
$$y_3 = \rho(x - x_{min}) + y_{max}; \quad y_4 = -\frac{1}{\rho}(x - x_{min}) + y_{max} \tag{12}$$

Solve the Eq. 17, the coordinates of the other two corners of the external bounding box can be calculated as,

$$\left(\frac{\rho^2 x_{\min} + \rho(y_{\min} - y_{\max}) + x_{\max}}{\rho^2 + 1}, \frac{\rho^2 y_{\min} + \rho(x_{\max} - x_{\min}) + y_{\max}}{\rho^2 + 1}\right) \tag{13}$$

$$\left(\frac{\rho^2 x_{\max} + \rho(y_{\max} - y_{\min}) + x_{\min}}{\rho^2 + 1}, \frac{\rho^2 y_{\max} + \rho(x_{\min} - x_{\max}) + y_{\min}}{\rho^2 + 1}\right) \tag{14}$$

4 Affine Transformation

After the external bounding box is calculated, the parameters for affine transform should be estimated first, then the affine transform will be applied to rectify the distorted text region.

4.1 Affine Parameter Estimation

According to imaging principle, the original text will be projected to image plane. For two parallel lines l_1, l_2 in image plane, where $l_i : a_i x + b_i y + c_i = 0 (i = 1, 2)$. The text plane (r_1, s_1, t_1) can be represented as

$$\begin{pmatrix} r_1 \\ s_1 \\ t_1 \end{pmatrix} = \frac{1}{\sqrt{a_1^2 + b_1^2}} \begin{pmatrix} b_1 \\ -a_1 \\ 0 \end{pmatrix} \tag{15}$$

If l_1, l_2 are not parallel in the image plane, and the vanishing point is (x_1, y_1), then the original text plane (r_1, s_1, t_1) can be represented as

$$\begin{pmatrix} r_1 \\ s_1 \\ t_1 \end{pmatrix} = \frac{1}{\sqrt{x_1^2 + y_1^2 + f^2}} \begin{pmatrix} x_1 \\ y_1 \\ f \end{pmatrix} \tag{16}$$

where f is the focus length of the camera. Then with two set of lines in the image plan, for example the two sets of lines of the external bounding box, the original text plane can be determined, as

$$\begin{pmatrix} r_3 \\ s_3 \\ t_3 \end{pmatrix} = \begin{pmatrix} r_1 \\ s_1 \\ t_1 \end{pmatrix} \times \begin{pmatrix} r_2' \\ s_2' \\ t_2' \end{pmatrix} \tag{17}$$

where (r_2', s_2', t_2') is determined by another pair of lines in image plane.

4.2 Affine Correction

With the estimation for the original text plane, we can rectify the distorted text in the image plane. Figure 4 shows the relationship between the text plane and image plane. The mapping from a point (X_t^0, Y_t^0, Z_t^0) on the text plane $O_t X_t Y_t Z_t$ to a point (x_i, y_i) of the image plane can be written as follows:

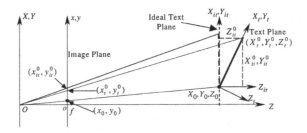

Fig. 4. The projection of text to image

$$
\begin{pmatrix} x_t^0 \\ y_t^0 \end{pmatrix} = \begin{pmatrix} f & 0 \\ 0 & f \end{pmatrix} \begin{pmatrix} \dfrac{X_{it}^0 + X_0}{Z_{it}^0 + Z_0} \\ \dfrac{Y_{it}^0 + Y_0}{Z_{it}^0 + Z_0} \end{pmatrix} \tag{18}
$$

where

$$
\begin{pmatrix} X_{it}^0 \\ Y_{it}^0 \\ Z_{it}^0 \end{pmatrix} = \begin{pmatrix} r_1 & r_2 & r_3 \\ s_1 & s_2 & s_3 \\ t_1 & t_2 & t_3 \end{pmatrix} \begin{pmatrix} X_t^0 \\ Y_t^0 \\ Z_t^0 \end{pmatrix} \tag{19}
$$

In order to reconstruct the front view of the text plane, we can use the affine transformation to correct.

$$
\begin{pmatrix} x_{it}^0 \\ y_{it}^0 \end{pmatrix} = \begin{pmatrix} f & 0 \\ 0 & f \end{pmatrix} \begin{pmatrix} \dfrac{X_t^0 + X_0}{Z} \\ \dfrac{Y_t^0 + Y_0}{Z_0} \end{pmatrix} \tag{20}
$$

In the text plane, $Z_t^0 = 0$. Since the origin point (X_0, Y_0, Z_0) of $O_t X_t Y_t Z_t$ and $O_{it} X_{it} Y_{it} Z_{it}$ is mapped to the same point (x_0, y_0) in the image panel, we can get

$$
x_0 = f \frac{X_0}{Z_0}, y_0 = f \frac{Y_0}{Z_0} \tag{21}
$$

Then the correction can be done by Eq. (22)

$$x_{it}^0 = x_0 + f \frac{\begin{vmatrix} x_0 - x_t^0 & r_2 f - t_2 x_t^0 \\ y_0 - y_t^0 & s_2 f - t_2 y_t^0 \end{vmatrix}}{\begin{vmatrix} r_1 f - t_1 x_t^0 & r_2 f - t_2 x_t^0 \\ s_1 f - t_1 y_t^0 & s_2 f - t_2 y_t^0 \end{vmatrix}}, \quad y_{it}^0 = y_0 + f \frac{\begin{vmatrix} r_1 f - t_1 x_t^0 & x_0 - x_t^0 \\ s_1 f - t_1 y_t^0 & y_0 - y_t^0 \end{vmatrix}}{\begin{vmatrix} r_1 f - t_1 x_t^0 & r_2 f - t_2 x_t^0 \\ s_1 f - t_1 y_t^0 & s_2 f - t_2 y_t^0 \end{vmatrix}} \quad (22)$$

That is for each point on the image plane, it can be mapped to a new position according to the affine transform. In order to make the image more consistent, the bilinear interpolation method is applied to reconstruct the rectified text images.

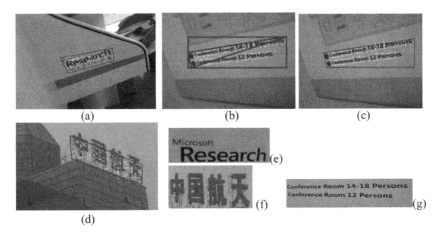

Fig. 5. Rectified results. (a) bounding box for quadruple extreme points case. (b), (c) bounding box for triple extreme points case. (d) bounding box for twin extreme points case. (e), (f), (g) rectified results for (a), (d), (b), respectively.

5   Experimental Results

We used the MSRA-TD500 database [16] to test the performance of the algorithm. This dataset contains 500 indoor and outdoor natural images. The indoor images are mainly signs, doorplates and caution plates while the outdoor images are mostly guide boards and billboards in complex background. The resolutions of the images vary from 1296×864 to 1920×1280. Some of the rectified results in different cases are shown in Fig. 5. We can see the proposed method can provide accurate detection for text region in different conditions. With the external quadrilateral of text region, the parameters of affine transform can be estimated precisely and consequently distorted images can be rectified. For Fig. 5(d), the corner points mainly lies in the middle of text region. Thus the detected text region is shifted. However, the inertia spindle still provides the main direction of the test, and consequently it can be rectified as shown in Fig. 5(f).

In order to quantify the effectiveness of the detection algorithm, the commonly used accuracy rate (P), recall rate (R) and F-score (Eq. 23) are applied

$$P = \frac{tp}{tp + fp} \times 100\%, \ R = \frac{tp}{tp + fn} \times 100\% \tag{23}$$

$$F = 2 \frac{P \times R}{P + R} \tag{24}$$

where tp is the area of the text region correctly detected in the image, fp is the non-text area in the image that is erroneously detected, that is, the false detection area. fn represents the text area that is not detected in the scene image. F score is the harmonic mean of precision and recall rate. The proposed method (TD-Affine) is test on the MSRA-TD500 database, it achieved precision rate of 0.58 and recall rate of 0.62. Compared with other methods as shown in Table 1, the proposed method keeps a high recall rate which is achieved by the MSER method. Then geometric and stroke width feature are used to remove false alarms. The final text region is determined due to different distributions of character. Since we try to keep the main direction of text region, but not the exact test region, therefore the precision rate still can be improved. Keeping the main direction is useful for the estimation of affine transformation. Figure 6 shows more results of affined rectified images. For the first two rows, all the text are in the same direction, then the proposed method can re-project the text to the frontal view. But when text are in different directions, as the third row, the global inertia spindle is balanced among local regions. Thus the proposed method cannot adjust each local region. Similarly, when the background is complex, as the forth row, it will also influence the correct estimation of inertia spindle for the text region. According the wrongly estimated affine parameters results in the wrongly rectification.

In order to shown the effectiveness of affine correction, we also performed text recognition experiments on the dataset. We used the ABBYY Finereader [17] to recognize the text. Table 2 shows the performance of text recognition with and without affine correction. From the results, we can see that the proposed affine parameter estimation and correction method can improve the text recognition rate. The proposed method mainly consider the main direction of text region, even when the detection region is not so accurate, the parameters of affine transform still can be accurately estimated. Consequently, the distorted images can be rectified precisely.

Table 1. Comparison of text detection results on MSRA-TD500

Algorithm	Precision	Recall	F-score
TD-Affine (proposed)	0.58	0.62	0.60
TD-ICDAR [16]	0.53	0.52	0.52
Epshtein et al. [9]	0.25	0.25	0.25
Chen and Yuille [6]	0.05	0.05	0.05

Table 2. Text recognition results on MSRA-TD500

	Precision	Recall	F-score
Before affine	0.76	0.75	0.75
After affine	0.82	0.84	0.83

Fig. 6. More results for affine rectification. The left column shows the character detection results, the right column shows the corresponding rectified results.

6 Conclusion

Text always provide important context information for images. In order to realize the text detection and recognition in natural environment, this paper proposed an affine transform based test detection algorithm. Since text detection is always an essential prerequisite for text recognition, providing high quality images for recognition is necessary. Thus we not only try to detect the location of text but also try to estimate the distortion of text region. In this paper, we utilize the MSER and SWT algorithms to detect the text area, and then combines the inertial spindle with some known extreme points to find the four vertices of the outer quadrilateral of the text area. Affine parameters can be obtained based on the four vertices, which will be used for affine rectification for distorted text. As a result, the text recognition rate can be improved significantly with the rectified text input.

References

1. Ou, W., Zhu, J., Liu, C.: Natural scene text positioning. J. Chin. Inform. Process. **18**(5), 42–47 (2004)
2. Maio, D., Maltoni, D., Cappelli, R., et al.: Fingerprint verification competition. Trans. Pattern Anal. Mach. Intell. **24**(3), 402–412 (2002)
3. Ye, Q., Doermann, D.: Text detection and recognition in imagery: a survey. IEEE Trans. Patten Anal. Mach. Intell. **37**(7), 1480–1500 (2014)
4. Jiang, X., Lian, J., Xia, Z., Feng, X., Hadid, A.: Fast Chinese character detection from complex scenes. In: The Sixth International Conference on Image Processing Theory, Tools and Applications (IPTA 2016) (2016)
5. Wu, H., Zhao, Y., Li, X., Zou, B., Zou, R.: Natural scene text detection based on color clustering. J. Central South Univ. (Sci. Technol.) **6**(7), 1672–7207 (2015)
6. Chen, X., Yuille, Y.: Detecting and reading text in natural scenes. In: Proceedings of CVPR (2004)
7. Wang, W., Fu, L., Gao, W., Huang, Q., Jiang, S.: Superimposed text detection method based on stroke character. Chin. J. Image Graph. **12**(019), 1354–1361 (2015)
8. Liu, Y., Xue, X., Lu, H., Guo, Y.: A video character detection algorithm based on edge detection and line feature. J. Comput. **03**(18), 0254–4164 (2015)
9. Epshtein, B., Ofek, E., Wexler, Y.: Detecting text in natural scenes with stroke width transform. In: Computer Vision and Pattern Recognition, pp. 2963–2970. IEEE (2010)
10. Matas, J., Chum, O., Urban, M., et al.: Robust wide—baseline stereo from maximally stable extremal regions. Image Vis. Comput. **22**(10), 761–767 (2004)
11. Tang, Y., Bu, W., Wu, X.: Multi-level MSER natural scene text detection. J. Zhejiang Univ. (Eng. Sci.) **50**(6), 135–1140 (2016)
12. Dai, J.: MSER-based text detection method. Tianjin Normal University (2014)
13. Yi, C., Tian, Y.: Text string detection from natural scenes by structure-based partition and grouping. IEEE Trans. Image Process. **20**(9), 2594–2605 (2011)
14. Zhao, M., Li, S., Kwok, J.: Text detection in images using sparse representation with discriminative dictionaries. Image Vis. Comput. **28**(12), 1590–1599 (2010)
15. Song, W., Xiao, J.: Natural scene text detection method based on stroke width transform. Comput. Eng. Appl. **49**(9), 190–192 (2013)
16. Yao, C., Bai, X., Liu, W., Ma, Y., Tu, Z.: Detecting texts of arbitrary orientations in natural images. In: IEEE Conference on Computer Vision and Pattern Recognition. IEEE Computer Society, pp. 1083–1090 (2012)
17. Richards, M.: ABBYY FineReader 9. APC (2008)

Visual Servoing of Mobile Robots with Input Saturation at Kinematic Level

Runhua Wang[1(✉)], Xuebo Zhang[1(✉)], Yongchun Fang[1(✉)],
and Baoquan Li[2(✉)]

[1] Tianjin Key Laboratory of Intelligent Robotics,
Institute of Robotics and Automatic Information System (IRAIS),
Nankai University, Tianjin 300071, China
zhangxuebo@nankai.edu.cn
[2] School of Electrical Engineering and Automation,
Tianjin Polytechnic University, Tianjin 300387, China

Abstract. This paper addresses the eye-in-hand visual servoing problem of mobile robots with velocity input saturation. A class of continuous and bounded functions is applied for the saturated visual servoing control design. The asymptotical convergence to zero of pose errors is proven using Lyapunov techniques and LaSalle' s invariance principle. Simulation results are provided to show that the proposed controller can stabilize the mobile robot to the desired pose under the velocity saturation constraints.

Keywords: Visual servoing · Mobile robots · Input saturation
Kinematic level

1 Introduction

The research on mobile robots with visual perception is very popular and mainly focuses on SLAM [1], visual odometry (VO) [2], visual servoing [3], and so on. In particular, visual servoing is one of the hot topics and includes visual stabilization [5,6] and visual tracking [7,8]. In this paper, we address the problem of eye-in-hand visual stabilization for mobile robots, which means driving the mobile robot from an initial pose to a desired one using real time image feedback [9,10].

There are several challenges in the problem of visual stabilization for mobile robots. Nonholonomic constraint is a key difficulty according to the famous Brockett' s necessary condition [11], which means that there is no continuous and time-invariant control for the stabilization of mobile robots. For the monocular camera-robot system, the image depth is unknown which results in more complicated controller design [12,13]. In addition, the limit of the camera field of view [14], uncalibrated camera extrinsic and intrinsic parameters [15,16], state and input saturation [17] are also critical issues in the study of visual servoing

---

B. Li—This work is supported in part by National Natural Science Foundation of China under Grants 61573195 and 61603271.

Y. Zhao et al. (Eds.): ICIG 2017, Part I, LNCS 10666, pp. 432–442, 2017.
https://doi.org/10.1007/978-3-319-71607-7_38

for mobile robots. Particularly, the control input saturation is a quite realistic problem from a practical point of view. This is because the actual actuators of the mobile robots always have maximum output values and thus the control input of mobile robots is impossible to be greater than this maximum level. If the control design takes no consideration of the input saturation constraint, the visual servoing process may be failed in the case that the computed ideal input of mobile robots exceeds the actuator output limit. Therefore, it is necessary to ensure the designed control input of mobile robots always satisfies the input saturation constraint during the whole visual servoing process.

There are some literatures related to the input saturation control of mobile robots. In [18], a framework of saturated stabilization and tracking control for wheeled mobile robots is proposed based on the passivity. In [19], Huang et al. address the problem of global tracking and stabilization for mobile robots with input saturation at the torque level. Specifically, the bounds of control torques can be converted into the function of design parameters and reference trajectories. Thus, proper parameters can be determined to ensure the bounds of control inputs to be within the saturation level. In [20], Chen presents a robust stabilization controller for a class of nonholonomic mobile robots with torque saturation limits, in which the finite-time theory and backstepping-like method are used. The work in [21] designs a switching controller to solve the input saturation problem of mobile robots. The work in [22] also applies the switch function for the saturated control design. The above mentioned methods are important references to solving the stabilization problem of mobile robots. However, there has been no approaches to deal with the visual servoing of mobile robots with input saturation.

In this paper, a visual servoing approach for eye-in-hand mobile robots is proposed with velocity input saturation. Specifically, the vision-based system model for eye-in-hand wheeled mobile robots is firstly established. Then, a class of continuous and bounded functions is defined. Next, based on Lyapunov techniques and the property of those functions, the visual servoing controller is designed for mobile robots under the velocity input saturation. The convergence to zero of the closed-loop system states is proven using LaSalle's invariance principle. Though the image depth of feature points is unknown, there is no need to design the parameter updating law, as shown in the rigorous stability proof. Thus, the main contribution of this paper is extending the stabilization method in [18] to the problem of eye-in-hand visual servoing for mobile robots in the presence of both unknown depth and velocity input saturation.

The rest of the paper is organized as follows. The vision-based system model is established in Sect. 2. The saturated velocity controller design and the closed-loop stability analysis are demonstrated in Sect. 3. Simulation results are provided in Sect. 4 to validate the effectiveness of the proposed controller. Finally, the conclusion is summarized in Sect. 5.

2   System Model Development

Figure 1 is the top view of the eye-in-hand wheeled mobile robot system. The mobile robot frame $\mathcal{F}_C$ coincides with the camera frame for the simplicity of

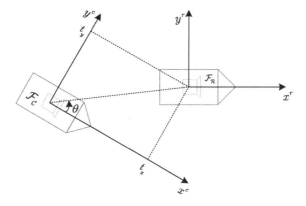

Fig. 1. Current and desired poses of the eye-in-hand mobile robot system

analysis. x^c axis is along the direction of the camera optical and z^c axis is outwardly perpendicular to the paper. $\mathcal{P}$ is a static point within the field of the camera view. We assume that the mobile robot moves on the $x^c y^c$ plane and there is no movement along the z^c direction.

2.1 System Modeling in 3D Space

Assuming that the current pose of the mobile robot is $\mathcal{F}_C$ and the desired one is $\mathcal{F}_R$ as Fig. 1 shows, the purpose of the control design is to drive the mobile robot to $\mathcal{F}_R$ from its initial pose $\mathcal{F}_C$. The coordinate of $\mathcal{P}$ is represented as $\boldsymbol{P}_C = [x_C(t)\ y_C(t)\ z_C(t)]^{\mathrm{T}}$ in $\mathcal{F}_C$. Then, $\boldsymbol{P}_C$ will change with the movement of the mobile robot as a result of the motion of $\mathcal{F}_C$. The dynamics of $\boldsymbol{P}_C$ can be formulated as $\dot{\boldsymbol{P}}_C = -\boldsymbol{V} - \boldsymbol{W} \times \boldsymbol{P}_C$, where $\boldsymbol{V} = [v(t)\ 0\ 0]^{\mathrm{T}}$ and $\boldsymbol{W} = [0\ 0\ w(t)]^{\mathrm{T}}$, with $v(t) \in \mathbb{R}$ and $w(t) \in \mathbb{R}$ denoting the linear velocity and angular velocity of the mobile robot, respectively. Thus, it is obtained that

$$\dot{x}_C = w y_C - v, \quad \dot{y}_C = -wx. \tag{1}$$

Then, rewriting (1) into the matrix form, we have

$$\begin{bmatrix} \dot{x}_C \\ \dot{y}_C \end{bmatrix} = w \begin{bmatrix} 0 & 1 \\ -1 & 0 \end{bmatrix} \begin{bmatrix} x_C \\ y_C \end{bmatrix} - \begin{bmatrix} 1 & 0 \\ 0 & 1 \end{bmatrix} \begin{bmatrix} v \\ 0 \end{bmatrix}. \tag{2}$$

Besides, $\theta(t) \in (-\pi,\ \pi]$ in Fig. 1 denotes the rotational angle between $\mathcal{F}_C$ and $\mathcal{F}_R$. Based on the knowledge of kinematics, we have

$$\dot{\theta} = w. \tag{3}$$

Since point $\mathcal{P}$ can be chosen arbitrarily within the field of the camera view, without loss of generality, we can just choose the origin of $\mathcal{F}_R$ as the static point. Therefore, we have

$$x_C(t) = t_x(t), \quad y_C(t) = t_y(t). \tag{4}$$

Substituting (4) into (2), it is obtained that

$$\begin{bmatrix} \dot{t}_x \\ \dot{t}_y \end{bmatrix} = w \begin{bmatrix} 0 & 1 \\ -1 & 0 \end{bmatrix} \begin{bmatrix} t_x \\ t_y \end{bmatrix} - \begin{bmatrix} 1 & 0 \\ 0 & 1 \end{bmatrix} \begin{bmatrix} v \\ 0 \end{bmatrix}. \tag{5}$$

In the system model (5), the translation $t_x(t)$, $t_y(t)$ between the current pose and the desired one can not be fully reconstructed through 2-D images with an unknown 3-D scene model. To be able to design the visual servoing controller, it is necessary to transform the model (3) and (5) into a form containing completely measurable state variables using pose estimation techniques. The next subsection will discuss this problem in detail.

2.2   Vision-Based System Model

The visual servoing of mobile robots means that real time images of feature points are feedback so that relative pose errors in 3D space of the mobile robot can be computed using some pose estimation techniques. Then, the control input of the mobile robot is calculated according to those pose errors. With the proper control input, the mobile robot gradually regulates to the desired pose. In this paper, homography matrix decomposition method is applied for the pose estimation [4, 12]. Then, the rotation angle $e_\theta(t)$ and scaled translation $e_x(t) \in \mathbb{R}$, $e_y(t) \in \mathbb{R}$ between $\mathcal{F}_R$ and $\mathcal{F}_C$ can be obtained as

$$e_\theta = \theta, \quad e_x = \frac{t_x}{d^*}, \quad e_y = \frac{t_y}{d^*}, \tag{6}$$

where $d^* \in \mathbb{R}^+$ is an unknown positive constant denoting the distance between the origin of $\mathcal{F}_R$ and the reference plane. Substituting (6) into (3) and (5), the vision-based system model of the mobile robot is established as

$$\dot{e}_\theta = w, \tag{7}$$

$$\begin{bmatrix} \dot{e}_x \\ \dot{e}_y \end{bmatrix} = w \begin{bmatrix} 0 & 1 \\ -1 & 0 \end{bmatrix} \begin{bmatrix} e_x \\ e_y \end{bmatrix} - \frac{1}{d^*} \begin{bmatrix} 1 & 0 \\ 0 & 1 \end{bmatrix} \begin{bmatrix} v \\ 0 \end{bmatrix}. \tag{8}$$

In the above model (7) and (8), $e_\theta(t)$, $e_x(t)$ and $e_y(t)$ are completely measurable, while d^* is unknown. Rewriting (7) and (8) as a simpler form, we have

$$\dot{e}_\theta = w, \tag{9}$$

$$\dot{e}_y = -w e_x, \tag{10}$$

$$\dot{e}_x = w e_y - \frac{1}{d^*} v, \tag{11}$$

In addition, the actual linear and angular velocities of the mobile robot are subjected to the saturation constraints as follows:

$$|v(t)| \le v_{max}, \quad |w(t)| \le w_{max} \tag{12}$$

where v_{max}, w_{max} are two positive constants, denoting the known the saturation level of the linear and angular velocities, respectively. The goal is to design linear velocity controller $v(t)$ and angular velocity controller $w(t)$ under the constraints (12) to drive the mobile robot from the initial pose to the desired one.

3   Saturated Velocity Control Design

The purpose of this section is to show that, by applying a class of continuous and bounded function, the eye-in-hand visual stabilization controller for mobile robots under the velocity input saturation can be obtained in the presence of unknown depth information. The asymptotical convergence to zero of the closed-loop system states is proven using Lyapunov techniques and LaSalle's invariance principle.

Firstly, a set of continuous and bounded functions is defined as follows:

$$\Phi_r = \{\phi : R \to R | \phi \text{ is continuous and } -r \le \phi(x) \le r$$
$$\forall x \in R, x\phi(x) > 0 \text{ for all } x \ne 0\} \tag{13}$$

Specific examples of the function $\phi(x)$ in Φ_r include

$$\phi(x) = \frac{2rx}{1 + x^2}, \quad \phi(x) = rtanh(x). \tag{14}$$

Generally, $\phi(x) = rtanh(x)$ is mostly used for saturated controller design according to the previous works [18, 20, 23].

Based on this, the linear velocity controller can be designed for the (e_x, e_y)-subsystem. Define a Lyapunov candidate function

$$V = \frac{1}{2}d^* e_x{}^2 + \frac{1}{2}d^* e_y{}^2. \tag{15}$$

Taking the time derivative of V and substituting (10) and (11) into it, we have

$$\dot{V} = -e_x v. \tag{16}$$

Inspired by the property of the function $\phi(x)$ in (13), the controller $v(t)$ is just defined as

$$v(t) = k_1 tanh(e_x), \tag{17}$$

where k_1 is a positive constant and $k_1 \le v_{max}$, such that

$$\dot{V} = -k_1 e_x tanh(e_x) \le 0. \tag{18}$$

Thus, it is concluded that e_x and e_y are bounded. Besides, we know that $|v(t)| \le k_1 \le v_{max}$.

For the e_θ-subsystem, the angular controller $w(t)$ can be designed as

$$w(t) = -k_2 tanh(e_\theta) + k_3 tanh(e_y) sint \tag{19}$$

where $k_2, k_3 > 0$. Considering the saturation constraint of the angular velocity, it should also satisfy that $k_2 + k_3 \le w_{max}$ and $k_2 > k_3$.

Substituting (19) into (9), we have

$$\dot{e}_\theta = -k_2 tanh(e_\theta) + k_3 tanh(e_y) sint. \tag{20}$$

For the closed-loop angular subsystem given in (20), the left two terms represent an asymptotical stable system and the last term can be seen as additive disturbance. Therefore, if $\lim\limits_{t\to\infty} e_y = 0$, it can be obtained that $\lim\limits_{t\to\infty} e_\theta = 0$.

Next, the asymptotical convergence analysis of the closed-loop system states will be given.

Theorem 1. Considering the open-loop system (9)–(11) with control laws (17) and (19), the system states can uniformly asymptotically converge to zero under the input saturation (12).

Proof: Following LaSalle's invariance principle, it is known that any bounded trajectory goes to the largest invariant set E. If E contains only one equilibrium point $x = 0$, $x = 0$ is asymptotically stable.

Then, substituting (17) and (19) into the open-loop model (9)–(11), it is obtained that

$$\dot{e}_\theta = -k_2 tanh(e_\theta) + k_3 tanh(e_y) sint,$$
$$\dot{e}_y = [k_2 tanh(e_\theta) - k_3 tanh(e_y) sint] e_x,$$
$$\dot{e}_x = [-k_2 tanh(e_\theta) + k_3 tanh(e_y) sint] e_y - \frac{1}{d^*} k_1 tanh(e_x). \tag{21}$$

For the (e_x, e_y)-subsystem, let $\dot{V} = 0$. Then, we have

$$-k_1 e_x tanh(e_x) = 0. \tag{22}$$

Thus, it is obtained that

$$e_x = 0. \tag{23}$$

We claim that

$$E = \left\{ (t, e_x, e_y, e_\theta) \in \phi^1 \times R^3 | e_x = e_y = 0 \right\}. \tag{24}$$

The above conclusion can be proven by contradiction. If $E = \{(t, e_x, e_y, e_\theta) \in \phi^1 \times R^3 | e_x = e_y = 0\}$ is not the largest invariant set, then there exists a trajectory $(t, e_x(t), e_y(t), e_\theta(t))$ that $e_x(t) = 0 \ \forall t \geq 0$ but $e_y(t) \neq 0$ for each t in the open subset I of $[0, \infty)$. Thus, it is obtained that $e_x \equiv 0, \dot{e}_x \equiv 0$. From (21), it is seen that $\dot{e}_y = 0$ and it is concluded that e_y is a nonzero constant e_y^*. For the (e_θ, e_y)-subsystem, we have

$$\dot{e}_\theta e_y + \dot{e}_x = -\frac{1}{d^*} k_1 tanh(e_x) \equiv 0. \tag{25}$$

Because $\dot{e}_x \equiv 0$, it can be obtained that $\dot{e}_\theta e_y = \dot{e}_\theta e_y^* \equiv 0$. Hence, it implies that $\dot{e}_\theta \equiv 0$ and thus $e_\theta = e_\theta^*$. Substituting $e_y = e_y^*$, $e_\theta = e_\theta^*$ into (21), we have

$$-k_2 tanh(e_\theta^*) + k_3 tanh(e_y^*) sint \equiv 0. \tag{26}$$

Fig. 2. The scene of visual servoing for mobile robots

Obviously, the above equation is not established, which leads to a contradiction. Consequently, the set $E = \{(t, e_x, e_y, e_\theta) \in \phi^1 \times R^3 | e_x = e_y = 0\}$ is the largest invariant set. That is,

$$\lim_{t \to \infty} e_x = 0, \quad \lim_{t \to \infty} e_y = 0. \tag{27}$$

Combining (20), it can be concluded that

$$\lim_{t \to \infty} e_\theta = 0. \tag{28}$$

Thus, the asymptotical stability of the closed-loop system is completed. It is concluded that the mobile robot can be asymptotically stabilized to the desired pose under the control (17), (19) and control inputs always satisfy the input saturation constraints (Fig. 2). ∎

Remark: In the vision based open-loop system (9)–(11), though the image depth d^* is unknown, the proposed saturated velocity controller is irrelevant to it and only contains measurable system states, as shown in the control design process and stability analysis. Thus, the design of parameter updating law for d^* can be avoided and the complexity of the saturated controller can be greatly reduced.

4   Simulation Results

In this section, simulation results are provided to validate the effectiveness of the proposed eye-in-hand visual servoing controller under the saturation constraints. We use MATLAB/Simulink model to simulate the real visual servoing process of the nonholonomic mobile robot. The monocular camera model is adopted and the image size is assumed as 960×540 pixels. The linear and angular velocity saturation levels are assumed as $v_{max} = 1.5\,\mathrm{m/s}$ and $w_{max} = 1\,\mathrm{rad/s}$, respectively.

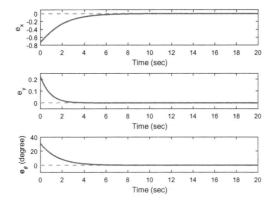

Fig. 3. States of the vision based closed-loop system

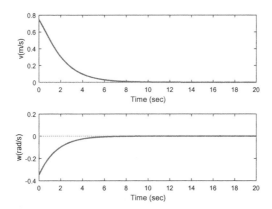

Fig. 4. Linear and angular input velocities of the mobile robot

The initial pose of the mobile robot is $(-1.5\,\text{m}, 0.37\,\text{m}, 31°)$ and the desired one is $(0, 0, 0)$. The control parameters are given as $k_1 = 1.2, k_2 = 0.7, k_3 = 0.2$.

Figure 3 shows the evolution of the closed-loop system states. It can been seen that the scaled translation errors e_x, e_y and the rotation error e_θ all asymptotically converge to zero, which implies that the mobile robot is successfully driven to the desired pose from the initial one. The velocity control inputs are illustrated in Fig. 4. Obviously, the linear velocity input and the angular velocity input of the mobile robot both satisfy the saturation constrains. Figure 5 displays the trajectories of four feature points in the image space. The stars and the circular points denote the desired and initial image, respectively. We see that four points move along their trajectories with the movement of the mobile robot and finally coincide with the desired image. Thus it can be concluded that the mobile robot achieves the pose regulation. Figure 6 shows the path of the mobile robot during the visual servoing process. It intuitively demonstrates that the mobile robot is stabilized to the desired pose.

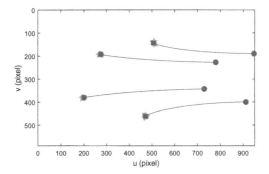

Fig. 5. The trajectories of the feature points in the image space

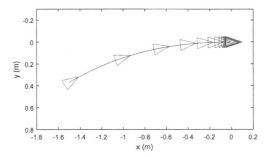

Fig. 6. The path of the mobile robot

In summary, the simulation results verify that the proposed controller (17), (19) is effective for the visual stabilization of mobile robots with the velocity input saturation.

5   Conclusion

In this paper, a saturated eye-in-hand visual servoing controller is proposed for nonholonomic mobile robots with unknown image depth. A class of continuous and bounded functions is applied for the velocity controller design. The asymptotic stability of the closed-loop system is proven using Lyapunov techniques and LaSalle's invariance principle. Simulation results are provided to show the good performance of the controller. In the future, we will take the dynamics of mobile robots into consideration and try to design the saturated visual servoing controller at acceleration level.

References

1. Fuentes-Pacheco, J., Ruiz-Ascencio, J., Rendón-Mancha, J.M.: Visual simultaneous localization and mapping: a survey. Artif. Intell. Rev. **43**(1), 55–81 (2015)

2. Liu, Y., Xiong, R., Wang, Y., Huang, H., Xie, X., Liu, X., Zhang, G.: Stereo visual-inertial odometry with multiple Kalman filters ensemble. IEEE Trans. Ind. Electron. **63**(10), 6205–6216 (2016)
3. Mariottini, G.L., Oriolo, G., Prattichizzo, D.: Image-based visual servoing for nonholonomic mobile robots using epipolar geometry. IEEE Trans. Robot. **23**(1), 87–100 (2007)
4. Zhang, X., Fang, Y., Liu, X.: Motion-estimation-based visual servoing of nonholonomic mobile robots. IEEE Trans. Robot. **27**(6), 1167–1175 (2011)
5. Fattahi, M., Vasegh, N., Momeni, H.: Stabilization of a class of nonlinear discrete time systems with time varying delay. Control Sci. Inf. Eng. **10**(8), 181–208 (2014)
6. Zhang, X., Fang, Y., Sun, N.: Visual servoing of mobile robots for posture stabilization: from theory to experiments. Int. J. Robust and Nonlinear Control **25**(1), 1–15 (2015)
7. Chen, X., Jia, Y., Matsuno, F.: Tracking control for differential-drive mobile robots with diamond-shaped input constraints. IEEE Trans. Control Syst. Technol. **22**(5), 1999–2006 (2014)
8. Wang, K., Liu, Y., Li, L.: Visual servoing trajectory tracking of nonholonomic mobile robots without direct position measurement. IEEE Trans. Robot. **30**(4), 1026–1035 (2014)
9. Chaumette, F., Hutchinson, S.: Visual servo control. Part I: basic approaches. IEEE Robot. Autom. Mag. **13**(4), 82–90 (2006)
10. Li, B., Fang, Y., Hu, G., Zhang, X.: Model-free unified tracking and regulation visual servoing of wheeled mobile robots. IEEE Trans. Control Syst. Technol. **24**(4), 1328–1339 (2016)
11. Brockett, R.: The early days of geometric nonliear control. Automatica **50**(9), 2203–2224 (2014)
12. Fang, Y., Dixon, W., Dawson, D., Chawda, P.: Homography-based visual servo regulation of mobile robots. IEEE Trans. Syst. Man Cybern. Part B-Cybern. **35**(5), 1041–1050 (2005)
13. Siradjuddin, I., Tundung, S., Indah, A.: A real-time model based visual servoing application for a differential drive mobile robot using beaglebone black embedded system (IRIS). In: IEEE International Symposium on Robotics & Intelligent Sensors, pp. 186–192 (2015)
14. Fang, Y., Liu, X., Zhang, X.: Adaptive active visual servoing of nonholonomic mobile robots. IEEE Trans. Ind. Electron. **20**(1), 241–248 (2012)
15. Li, B., Fang, Y., Zhang, X.: Visual servo regulation of wheeled mobile robots with an uncalibrated onboard camera. IEEE Trans. Mechatron. **21**(5), 2330–2342 (2016)
16. Zhang, X., Fang, Y., Li, B., Wang, J.: Visual servoing of nonholonomic mobile robots with uncalibrated camera-to-robot parameters. IEEE Trans. Ind. Electron. **64**(1), 390–400 (2017)
17. Ke, F., Li, Z., Xiao, H., Zhang, X.: Visual servoing of constrained mobile robots based on model predictive control. IEEE Trans. Syst. Man Cybern. Syst. **47**, 1428–1438 (2016)
18. Jiang, Z., Lefeber, E., Nijmeijer, H.: Saturated stabilization and tracking of a nonholonomic mobile robot. Syst. Control Lett. **42**(5), 327–332 (2001)
19. Huang, J., Wen, C., Wang, W., Jiang, Z.: Adaptive stabilization and tracking control of a nonholonomic mobile robot with input saturation and disturbance. Syst. Control Lett. **62**(3), 234–241 (2013)
20. Chen, H.: Robust stabilization for a class of dynamic feedback uncertain nonholonomic mobile robots with input saturation. Int. J. Control Autom. Syst. **12**(6), 1216–1224 (2014)

21. Chen, H., Zhang. J.: Semiglobal saturated practical stabilization for nonholonomic mobile robots with uncertain parameters and angle measurement disturbance. In: IEEE Control and Decision Conference, pp. 3731–3736 (2013)
22. Izumi, K., Tanaka, H., Tsujimura, T.: Nonholonomic control considering with input saturation for a mobile robot. In: Conference of the Society of Instrument and Control Engineers of Japan, pp. 1173–1172 (2016)
23. Su, Y., Zheng, C.: Global asymptotic stabilization and tracking of wheeled mobile robots with actuator saturation. In: IEEE International Conference on Robotics and Biomimetics (ROBIO), pp. 345–350 (2010)

Fabric Defect Detection Algorithm Based on Multi-channel Feature Extraction and Joint Low-Rank Decomposition

Chaodie Liu, Guangshuai Gao, Zhoufeng Liu, Chunlei Li$^{(\boxtimes)}$, and Yan Dong

School of Electric and Information Engineering,
Zhongyuan University of Technology, Zhengzhou 450007, Henan, China
lichunlei1979@sina.com

Abstract. Fabric defect detection plays an important role in the quality control of fabric products. In order to effectively detect defects for fabric images with numerous kinds of defects and complex texture, a novel fabric defect detection algorithm based on multi-channel feature extraction and joint low-rank decomposition is proposed. First, at the feature extraction stage, a multi-channel robust feature (Multi-channel Distinctive Efficient Robust Feature, McDerf) is extracted by simulating the biological visual perception mechanism for multiple gradient orientation maps. Second, joint low-rank decomposition algorithm is adopted to decompose the feature matrix into a low rank matrix and a sparse matrix. Finally, for the purpose of localizing the defect region, the threshold segmentation algorithm is utilized to segment the saliency map generated by sparse matrix. Comparing with the existing fabric defect detection algorithms, the experimental results show that the proposed algorithm has better adaptability and detection efficiency for the plain and patterned fabric images.

Keywords: McDerf · Joint low-rank decomposition · Fabric images
Defect detection

1 Introduction

Fabric defect detection plays an important role in the quality control of fabric products. The traditional manual detection results depend on human subjectivity to a large extent. But due to human fatigue, high labor costs, and slow inspection speed, their performance is often unreliable. Therefore, the automatic detection technology of fabric defect based on image processing has become a research focus.

The existing automatic fabric defect detection algorithms can be divided into four categories: model-based method, spectral analysis method, statistical-based method, and learning-based method [1]. (1) The model-based methods extract

© Springer International Publishing AG 2017
Y. Zhao et al. (Eds.): ICIG 2017, Part I, LNCS 10666, pp. 443–453, 2017.
https://doi.org/10.1007/978-3-319-71607-7_39

image texture features via modeling and parameter estimation techniques. The defect detection problem can be treated as a statistical hypothesis-testing problem on the statistics derived from this model. It includes Gauss Markov random field model [2], Poisson model [3] and Wold model [4]. However, the model-based methods share high computational complexity, and the detection results are not satisfactory. (2) Spectral analysis methods transform fabric images into the spectral domain and then detect the defects by some energy criterions, such as Fourier transform, wavelet transform and Gabor filter. But the detection performance depends on the selection of filter banks [5]. (3) Statistical-based methods employ the spatial distribution of gray values to detect fabric defects. However, they have the disadvantages that we should design the specific detection method for different fabric types, and they are hard to detect the defects with small size [6–8]. (4) The performance of the learning-based methods highly depends on the large scale training dataset. In addition, it is difficult to establish an effective and stable defect model through the limited training dataset because some fabric defects rarely occur, which causes the unsatisfactory results [9].

The low-rank decomposition model is consistent with the low-rank sparsity of human visual system. It can divide the image matrix into a low-rank part which corresponds to the background and a sparse matrix which corresponds to the object, and it has achieved good results in saliency detection and object detection [10–12]. For fabric images with complex texture, the background is highly redundant and the defects are saliently sparse, so the low-rank decomposition model is more suitable for the fabric defect detection than the object detection in the natural scene. Recently, we and some other researchers have exploited the low-rank decomposition model for fabric defect detection [8,13,14] and obtained good results in the fabric images with relatively simple texture. It demonstrates that it is feasible to use the low-rank decomposition model for fabric defect detection.

Effective image representation is crucial for fabric defect detection based on low-rank decomposition model, it can make the background of fabric images lie in a low-dimensional subspace, and the salient defects deviate from this subspace. Therefore, the low-rank decomposition model can easily divide the image into the background part and object part. However, the proposed fabric defect detection methods based on low-rank decomposition model adopted the traditional feature extraction methods, such as local binary pattern (LBP), Gabor filtering and histogram of oriented gradient (HOG), they cannot effectively represent the fabric image with complex texture, which lead to poor detection performance. Hence, it is necessary to propose an effective feature representation method for different fabric images. Fabric is woven by warp and weft. The normal fabric image has specific orientation information and the defects destroy the normal orientation information. For this reason, the effective extraction of orientation feature is crucial for the final detection results. However, the orientation information varies with the different fabric texture. Therefore, the multi-orientation feature should be extracted to efficiently describe the fabric texture.

In this paper, we proposed a novel fabric defect detection algorithm based on the multi-channel feature extraction and joint low-rank decomposition. First, the fabric image is filtered to generate multiple gradient orientation maps, a multi-channel robust feature is extracted by adopting the approach proposed in literature [15] by simulating the biological visual perception mechanism for multiple gradient orientation maps. Then, joint low-rank decomposition algorithm is employed to divide the multi-channel feature matrix into low-rank matrices and sparse matrices. Finally, an improved threshold segmentation algorithm is used to segment the saliency map generated by sparse matrices to localize the defective region.

2 McDerf Feature Extraction

The great progress of the visual perception mechanism research demonstrates that invariant feature extraction is one of the most important information processing tasks for the human visual system and is also a common characteristic of senior cortex cells in the process of information integration. Therefore, the feature descriptors based on the mechanism of the human visual system are more suitable to characterize the complex texture of all kinds of fabric. In the literature [15], the authors proposed a local image descriptor denoted as Distinctive Efficient Robust Feature (DERF) by modeling the response and distribution properties of the ganglion cells in the retina, it is superior to the traditional design methods based on artificial experience hand-crafted local descriptors.

In this paper, we proposed an improved multi-channel Derf denoted as McDerf to efficiently describe the orientation feature based on the DERF proposed by Weng et al. [15]. First, the gradient orientation maps generated by

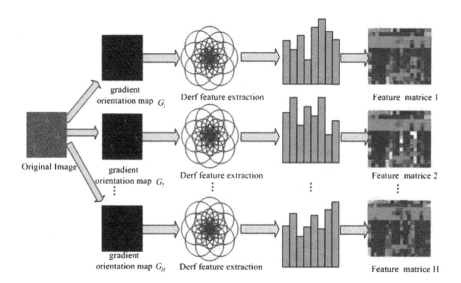

Fig. 1. Construction process of the proposed McDerf

DERF are filtered by DoG (Difference of Gaussian), respectively. And then the filtered gradient orientation maps are pooled according to the ganglion cell coding, so we can get the orientation feature matrix for each gradient orientation map respectively. It is necessary to divide the fabric image into image patches in the process of defect detection and combine the McDerf features of image patches into multiple feature matrices so as to realize the localization of the defective regions. The specific extraction process includes: (1) multi-channel Derf feature extraction; (2) feature matrix generation. The feature extraction process is shown in Fig. 1.

2.1   Multi-channel Derf Feature Extraction

Based on the Derf feature proposed in [15], we proposed the McDerf, and its construction can be described as follows.

(1) The H gradient orientation maps are calculated using Eq. (1).

$$G_o = (\frac{\partial I}{\partial o})^+, 1 \leq o \leq H \tag{1}$$

where I is the input image, o is the orientation of the derivative, $(\cdot)^+$ and is the operator such that $(a)^+ = \max(a, 0)$.

(2) Each gradient orientation map of H is convolved $S+1$ times using Gaussian kernels with different value Σ to obtain Gaussian convolution orientation maps G_o^Σ for the sake of allowing the gradients without abrupt changes under the circumstance of neighborhood slight changes, the standard deviation of the Gaussian kernel is proportional to the radius of the given neighborhood.

$$G_o^\Sigma = G_\Sigma * G_o \tag{2}$$

where G_Σ is a Gaussian kernel with scale Σ.

For each orientation of the Gaussian convolution orientation maps, the DoG convolution orientation maps is obtained by subtracting the large scale from the small scale of the two adjacent Gaussian convolution orientation maps.

$$D_o^{\Sigma_1} = G_o^{\Sigma_1} - G_o^{\Sigma_2}, \Sigma_1 < \Sigma_2 \tag{3}$$

(3) We assemble the feature vector by sampling the DoG convolution orientation maps. The sampling grid points are located in many concentric rings with different radii increasing in exponential manner, and the corresponding DoG convolution kernel scale is also increased in exponential manner, as shown in Fig. 1. Therefore, there are four parameters that determine the shape of the pooling arrangement, i.e. the radius of the region (R), number of concentric rings with different scales (S), the number of gradient orientations (H), number of grid points on each concentric ring (T). Let F_{so} represent

the single scale vector of one channel constructed of the values at location (x, y) in the DoG convolution orientation maps:

$$
\begin{aligned}
F_{so}(x, y) = [l_{1o}(x, y) \\
l_{1o}(x, y, \Sigma_1), l_{2o}(x, y, \Sigma_1) \cdots, l_{To}(x, y, \Sigma_1), \\
l_{1o}(x, y, \Sigma_2), l_{2o}(x, y, \Sigma_2) \cdots, l_{To}(x, y, \Sigma_2), \\
\vdots \\
l_{1o}(x, y, \Sigma_s), l_{2o}(x, y, \Sigma_s) \cdots, l_{To}(x, y, \Sigma_s)]
\end{aligned}
\tag{4}
$$

where $1 \le o \le H$, $l_{jo}(x, y, \Sigma)$ is location with the orientation o on different scales Σ in the orientation given by j grid point.

Researchers have recently found that the receptive field of ganglion cells can be resized to a certain extent [16–18], which results in the variable size of the receptive field. But the degree of size change is slight. Considering this modulation mechanism of receptive field of ganglion cells, we add two neighboring scales to the inherent scale of each grid point, which results in a total of three scales for each grid. However, for the grids with the smallest scale, we add the second scale to each grid, and for the grids with the largest scale, we add the reciprocal second scale. Formally, the multiple scales one channel of McDerf descriptor centered at (x, y) is defined as follows:

$$
\begin{aligned}
F_{mo}(x, y) = [l_{1o}(x, y), \\
l_{1o}(x, y, \Sigma_1), l_{2o}(x, y, \Sigma_1) \cdots, l_{To}(x, y, \Sigma_1), \\
l_{1o}(x, y, \Sigma_2), l_{2o}(x, y, \Sigma_2) \cdots, l_{To}(x, y, \Sigma_2); \\
l_{1o}(x, y, \Sigma_1), l_{2o}(x, y, \Sigma_1) \cdots, l_{To}(x, y, \Sigma_1), \\
l_{1o}(x, y, \Sigma_2), l_{2o}(x, y, \Sigma_2) \cdots, l_{To}(x, y, \Sigma_2), \\
l_{1o}(x, y, \Sigma_3), l_{2o}(x, y, \Sigma_3) \cdots, l_{To}(x, y, \Sigma_3); \\
\vdots \\
l_{1o}(x, y, \Sigma_{s-1}), l_{2o}(x, y, \Sigma_{s-1}) \cdots, l_{To}(x, y, \Sigma_{s-1}), \\
l_{1o}(x, y, \Sigma_s), l_{2o}(x, y, \Sigma_s) \cdots, l_{To}(x, y, \Sigma_s)]
\end{aligned}
\tag{5}
$$

where $1 \le o \le H$, we can extract H channel features for the fabric image.

2.2   Feature Matrices Construction

In order to localize the defective region, the fabric image is divided into N image patches with the same size. Then we extract their multi-channel features f_i^k (where i is the image patches index, $i = 1, 2, \cdots, N$, k is the channel index, $k = 1, 2, \cdots, H$) to project the normal image patches into a low-dimension subspace. All the features of the image patches are concentrated into H feature matrices $F^K = [f_1^k, f_2^k, \cdots, f_N^k]$, and then low-rank decomposition model can divide the feature matrix into low-rank part and sparse part. Finally, fabric defect detection is transformed into the low-rank decomposition of the feature matrix F, where the low-rank matrix L is the normal fabric image, the sparse matrix S corresponds to the salient object.

3   Joint Low-Rank Decomposition

For one feature matrix F^k, it can be decomposed into a low-rank matrix L_0 and a sparse matrix S_0 corresponding to the non-salient background and the salient object, respectively. It is defined as low-rank matrix recovery problem, and can be realized by the following equation:

$$\min_{L_0, S_0} \quad \|L_0\|_* + \lambda \|S_0\|_1$$
$$s.t. \quad F^k = L_0 + S_0 \tag{6}$$

where $\|\cdot\|_*$ denotes the matrix nuclear norm (sum of the singular values of a matrix), which is a convex relaxation of the rank function. $\|\cdot\|_1$ is the l_1-norm to improve the sparsity, $\lambda > 0$ is used to balance the effect of the two parts.

The above low-rank decomposition model only can model a single type of visual features, which cannot be directly used for multi-channel feature case. To combine the low-rank decomposition model with the multi-channel feature, we adopt a new solution of multi-task sparsity pursuit (MTSP) [19] for fabric defect detection, as shown in Fig. 2.

MTSP model looks for a joint sparse matrix S by solving the following convex optimization problem:

$$\min_{\substack{L_1, \cdots, L_H \\ S_1, \cdots, S_H}} \quad \sum_{k=1}^{H} \|L_k\|_* + \lambda \|S\|_{2,1}$$
$$s.t. \quad F^k = F^k L_k + S_k, k = 1, \cdots, H \tag{7}$$

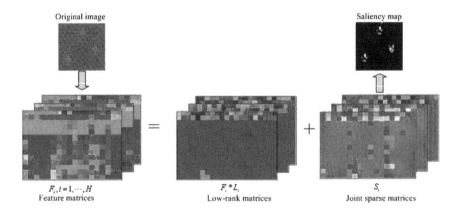

Fig. 2. Multi-task sparsity pursuit model: for a given image, we extract H orientation feature matrices $F^1, F^2, \cdots, F^H$, with F corresponding to a certain orientation of feature. Its saliency map is inferred by seeking the consistently sparse elements S from the joint decompositions of multiple feature matrices F^i into pairs of low-rank and sparse matrices.

where $\|\cdot\|_{2,1}$ is the $l_{2,1}-norm$ defined as the sum of l_2-norm of the columns of a matrix:

$$\|S\|_{2,1} = \sum_i \sqrt{\sum_j (S(j,i))^2} \tag{8}$$

The minimization of $l_{2,1}-norm$ leads the column of S to be sparsity (most of its elements are zeros). $S = [S_1; S_2; \cdots ; S_H]$ is formed by vertically concatenating $S_1, S_2, \cdots , S_H$ together along column. The integration of multiple channel features is achieved by minimizing the $l_{2,1}-norm$ of S, which requires the columns of $S_1, S_2, \cdots , S_H$ to have jointly consistent magnitudes. Since the columns in different matrices with the same index correspond to the same image patch, this method is also to encourage different features with synergistic effect to produce consistent saliency maps.

The Eq. (7) is a convex optimization problem. In this paper, we adopted the augmented Lagrange multiplier (ALM) algorithm to solve it [20]. Let $\{S_1^*, S_2^*, \cdots , S_H^*\}$ be the sparse part which is obtained by the optimal solution of the Eq. (7). We quantify the response of the sparse matrices to obtain a saliency score for the $i-$th patch P_i. And the calculation equation can be describes as follows:

$$S(P_i) = \sum_k^H \|S_k^*(:,i)\|_2 = \sum_k^H \sqrt{\sum_j (S_k^*(j,i))^2} \tag{9}$$

where $\|S_k^*(:,i)\|_2$ is the l_2-norm of the $i-$th column of S_k^*, the higher saliency score $S(P_i)$ represents the image patch i belongs to the defect with high probability. Finally, the threshold segmentation algorithm [21] is adopted to segment the saliency map generated by multiple sparse matrices to localize the defect region.

4   Experimental Results and Analysis

In order to verify the effectiveness of our algorithm for different fabric images, we randomly select several kinds of fabric defect images from the fabric image database (TILDA, patterned fabrics datasets: dot-, box-, star-patterned datasets) (including: broken end, netting multiple, hole, thick bar, thin bar, etc.). The fabric image size is 256×256, and they are divided into image patches with size of 16×16 for localizing the defect region. All experiments are implemented in the environment of Intel(R) Core(TM) i5-4570, 8 GHz CPU by using software Matlab 2011a.

We first analyze the influences of different channel. The McDerf feature with different channel is extracted for detecting the defects, and the results are shown in Fig. 3. The first column is the original fabric image, detection results are listed from the second column to the last by setting $H = 2, 4, 6, 8$. From the detection results we can see that when the number of channel is small, some detected defects are not continuous. The detection performance is improved with increasing the channel number. When the channel number is greater than 6, the

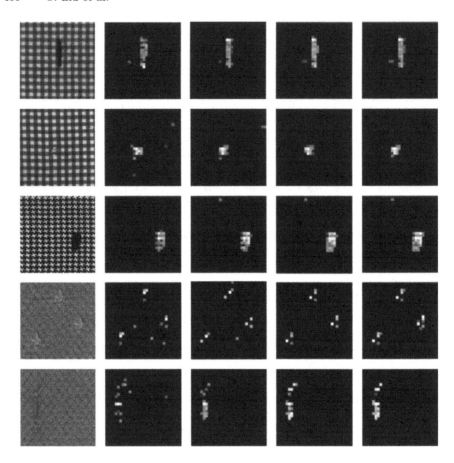

Fig. 3. The saliency detection for different channel: the first column is the original fabric image. Detection results are listed from the second column to the last by setting $H = 2, 4, 6, 8$.

detection accuracy keeps unchanged. Therefore, the channel number is set to 6 for the tradeoff between efficiency and accuracy.

In order to further verify the effectiveness of the proposed algorithm, we have compared our method with the existing saliency detection methods, such as the unified method based on low-rank matrix recovery (ULR) [22], wavelet transform method (WT) [23], histogram of oriented gradient (HOG) [13], least squares regression (LSR) [8]. The experimental results are demonstrated in Fig. 4. The first column is the original images. The detection results of ULR, WT, HOG, LSR and our method are listed from the second column to the sixth column. From Fig. 4, we can see that the results of ULR, WT and HOG methods have serious noise and error. This demonstrates that the three methods are only suitable for the fabric images with simple texture, while not for the fabric images with complex texture. For the LSR method, it can nearly localize all the defective

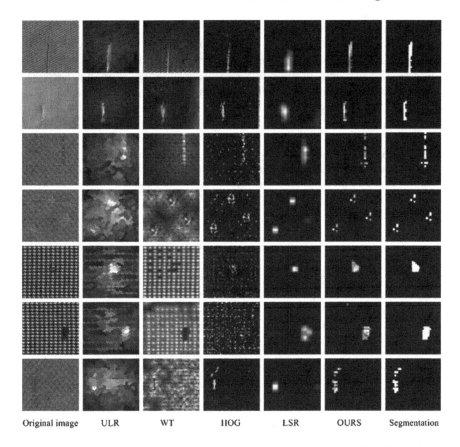

Original image   ULR   WT   HOG   LSR   OURS   Segmentation

Fig. 4. Comparison of the detection results for different methods: the first column is the original fabric images. Detection results of ULR [22], WT [23], HOG [13], LSR [8] and our method are listed from the second column to the six column, the last column is the final segmentation result generated by our method.

regions, but the defective regions are not precise enough, such as the fourth and the last image in Fig. 4. The result of our method is shown in the sixth column, and the last column is the binarization result obtained by threshold segmentation. It can be seen from Fig. 4 that our method not only precisely localize the defective region of all the fabric images, but also can outline the correct defect shape.

5   Conclusion

Fabric defect detection is a key part of quality control in the textile industry. In this paper, a novel fabric defect detection algorithm based on multi-channel feature extraction and joint low-rank decomposition is proposed. The proposed method has two contributions: (1) the multi-channel orientation features are extracted by gradient calculation and spooling technology based on the ganglion cell coding; (2) the joint low-rank decomposition technology is adopted to decompose the multiple feature matrixes into low-rank part and sparse part. The detection results are obtained by segmenting the saliency map generated by the sparse part. Experimental results demonstrate that our method can accurately detect the defect regions of various fabric defects, even for the image with complex texture.

Acknowledgement. This work was supported by the National Natural Science Foundation of China (No. 61379113), the Key Natural Science Foundation of Henan Province (1623004-10338), Science and technology innovation talent project of Education Department of Henan Province (17HASTIT019), Science and technology leader project of Zhengzhou City (131PLJRC643).

References

1. Ngan, H.Y.T., Pang, G.K.H., Yung, N.H.C.: Automated fabric defect detection: a review. Image Vis. Comput. **29**(7), 442–458 (2011)
2. Cohen, F.S., Fan, Z., Attali, S.: Automated inspection of textile fabrics using textual models. IEEE Trans. Pattern Anal. Mach. Intell. **13**(8), 803–808 (1991)
3. Brzakovic, D.P., Bakic, P.R., Vujovic, N.S., et al.: A generalized development environment for inspection of web materials. In: IEEE International Conference on Robotics and Automation, pp. 1–8 (1997)
4. Zengbo, X., Yunan, G., Xiubao, H.: Fabric detects detection with wold-based texture model and fractal theory. J. China Text. Univ. **26**(1), 6–9 (2000)
5. Yang, X., Pang, G., Yung, N.: Robust fabric defect detection and classification using multiple adaptive wavelets. IEE Proc.-Vis. Image Signal Process. **152**(6), 715–723 (2005)
6. Wen, Z., Cao, J., Liu, X., et al.: Fabric defects detection using adaptive wavelets. Int. J. Cloth. Sci. Technol. **26**(3), 202–211 (2014)
7. Li, W., Cheng, L.: New progress of fabric defect detection based on computer vision and image processing. J. Text. Res. **35**(3), 152–164 (2014)
8. Cao, J., Zhang, J., Wen, Z., et al.: Fabric defect inspection using prior knowledge guided least squares regression. Multimed. Tools Appl. **76**, 1–17 (2015)
9. Li, Y., Zhao, W., Pan, J.: Deformable patterned fabric defect detection with fisher criterion-based deep learning. IEEE Trans. Autom. Sci. Eng. **14**, 1–9 (2016)
10. Peng, H., Li, B., Ling, H., et al.: Salient object detection via structured matrix decomposition. IEEE Trans. Pattern Anal. Mach. Intell. **39**, 818–832 (2016)
11. Tang, C., Wu, J., Zhang, C., et al.: Salient object detection via weighted low rank matrix recovery. IEEE Signal Process. Lett. **24**, 490–494 (2016)
12. Yan, J., Liu, J., Li, Y., et al.: Visual saliency detection via rank-sparsity decomposition. In: IEEE International Conference on Image Processing, pp. 1089–1092 (2010)
13. Li, C., Gao, G., Liu, Z., Liu, Q., Li, W.: Fabric defect detection algorithm based on histogram of oriented gradient and low-rank decomposition. Journal of Textile Research. **38**(3), 153–158 (2017)
14. Zhang, D., Gao, G., Li, C.: Fabric defect detection algorithm based on Gabor filter and low-rank decomposition. In: Eighth International Conference on Digital Image Processing, p. 100330L (2016)

15. Weng, D., Wang, Y., Gong, M., et al.: DERF: distinctive efficient robust features from the biological modeling of the P Ganglion cells. IEEE Trans. Image Process. **24**(8), 2287–2302 (2015)

16. Kamermans, M., Hark, J., Habraken, J., et al.: The size of the horizontal cell receptive fields adapts to the stimulus in the light adapted goldfish retina. Vis. Res. **36**(24), 4105–4119 (1996)

17. Shapley, R.: Retinal physiology: adapting to the changing scene. Curr. Biol. **7**(7), R421–R423 (1997)

18. Li, Y., Li, H., Gong, H., et al.: Characteristics of receptive field encoded by synchronized firing pattern of ganglion cell group. Acta Biophys. Sin. **27**(3), 211–221 (2011)

19. Lang, C., Liu, G., Yu, J., Yan, S.: Saliency detection by multi-task sparsity pursuit. IEEE Trans. Image Process. **21**(3), 1327–1338 (2012)

20. Lin, Z., Chen, M., Wu, L., Ma, Y.: The augmented Lagrange multiplier method for exact recovery of corrupted low-rank matrices. Eprint ArXiv (2009)

21. Navalpakkam, V., Itti, L.: Search goal tunes visual features optimally. Neuron **53**(4), 605–617 (2007)

22. Shen, X., Wu, Y.: A unified approach to salient object detection via low rank matrix recovery. In: IEEE Conference on Computer Vision and Pattern Recognition, vol. 23, no. 10, pp. 853–860 (2012)

23. Imamoglu, N., Lin, W., Fang, Y.: A saliency detection model using low-level features based on wavelet transform. IEEE Trans. Multimed. **15**(1), 96–105 (2013)

Robust 3D Indoor Map Building via RGB-D SLAM with Adaptive IMU Fusion on Robot

Xinrui Meng[1,2], Wei Gao[1,2(✉)], and Zhanyi Hu[1,2]

[1] NLPR, Institute of Automation, Chinese Academy of Sciences,
Beijing 100190, China
{xinrui.meng, wgao, huzy}@nlpr.ia.ac.cn
[2] University of Chinese Academy of Sciences, Beijing 100049, China

Abstract. Building a 3D map of indoor environment is a prerequisite for various applications, ranging from service robot to augmented reality, where RGB-D SLAM is a commonly used technique. To efficiently and robustly build a 3D map via RGB-D SLAM on robot, or the RGB-D sensor mounted on a moving robot, the following two key issues must be addressed: How to reliably estimate the robot's pose to align partial models on the fly, and how to design the robot's movement patterns in large environment to effectively reduce error accumulation and to increase building efficiency. To address these two issues in this work, we propose an algorithm to adaptively fuse the IMU information with the visual tracking for the first issue, and design two robot movement patterns for the second issue. The preliminary experiments on a TurtleBot2 robot platform show that our RGB-D SLAM system works well even for difficult situations such as weak-textured space, or presence of pedestrians.

Keywords: Camera pose estimation · RGB-D · SLAM · IMU · Robot
Movement pattern · Calibration

1 Introduction

To autonomously solve several tasks by mobile robots including transportation, search and rescue, or home service, the robot needs a map of its working environment. In an indoor environment, where GPS signal is not available, Simultaneous Localization and Mapping (SLAM) method is the best way to localize the robot and map the environment. SLAM is a classical problem in robotics and other fields, concerning the simultaneous estimation of the scene structure and of the trajectory of a mobile robot within a framework using only onboard sensors. Previously many SLAM approaches relied on expensive and heavy sensors such as laser scanners, ultrasonic and sonar sensors. In recent years, visual SLAM has been substantially advanced, where the main sensor is a camera which is cheap, small and capable to provide rich information of the environment.

Visual SLAM can be performed using just a monocular camera [1–3]. The approaches perform real-time mapping, but usually reconstruct a rudimentary map of sparse point cloud. In the past few years, consumer-grade RGB-D cameras capable of delivering color and depth information in real time, e.g. the Microsoft Kinect and Asus

© Springer International Publishing AG 2017
Y. Zhao et al. (Eds.): ICIG 2017, Part I, LNCS 10666, pp. 454–465, 2017.
https://doi.org/10.1007/978-3-319-71607-7_40

Xtion Pro Live, have fostered new approaches to tackle the SLAM problem [4–6]. The approaches reconstruct dense scene models and perform real-time processing on entire images via GPU hardware.

However, even with a RGB-D sensor, if the features of the scene are sparse, such as exploring a workspace outside of the valid depths, processing a frame sequence that misses a certain amount of frames, encountering a dynamic occlusion or a low-textured workspace or dealing with blurred images due to fast camera movements, the pose tracking will fail for most visual SLAM algorithms. Using only visual sensor seems difficult to solve the above tracking failure problems. On the other end, mobile robots are nowadays equipped with inertial sensors and encoders, such as accelerometers, gyroscopes and wheel encoders. We call inertial sensors and encoders inertial measurements in the following articles. Such inertial measurements may therefore be used to improve the camera pose tracking. Note that the inertial data from mobile robot is more accurate than from mobile phone, because the robot moves in the ground plane with only 3 degrees of freedom and has a wheel encoder to calculate the translations.

In this paper, we propose an approach to integrate robot inertial measurements into an RGB-D SLAM system. By adaptively combining the visual pose with the robot IMU (Inertial Measurement Unit), we obtain a more accurate pose estimation. In addition, to build a full 3D model of the indoor scene with robot, we design and analyze two robot movement patterns for large scene to reduce the accumulated drift.

The rest of this paper is organized as follows. Section 2 reviews some relevant publications on RGB-D SLAM systems and the fusion of inertial and visual data for visual odometry. In Sect. 3, we calibrate the robot IMU pose to the camera pose in the world coordinate system. Section 4 proposes an adaptive method to combine the IMU and visual pose. Section 5 analyzes two movement patterns. The experimental findings are reported in Sect. 6. And some concluding remarks are listed in Sect. 7.

2   Related Work

With the arrival of consumer-grade RGB-D camera and the development of General-Purpose computing on Graphics Processing Units (GPGPU), real time dense 3D SLAM has received great attentions. One of the earliest RGB-D SLAM system was KinectFusion [4]. This system fuses all depth data into a volumetric model and uses Iterative Closest Point (ICP) algorithm to track the camera pose. The ICP method tracks the current depth frame against the globally fused model without feature extraction based on GPU, which reduces the estimated error and achieves real time performance. While the system is limited to small workspaces due to its volumetric representation and lacks of loop closing detector. [7, 8] replace the explicit voxel representation used by KinectFusion with an octree representation which allows to expand the workspaces. RGB-D SLAM of Endres et al. [9] was the first open-source system, which is a feature based system and estimates the camera pose by feature matching and ICP. This system achieves loop closing by pose graph optimization. Kintinuous [5] can be used for large environments by freeing up voxels as the sensor moves and the method combines dense geometric camera pose constraints with dense photometric constraints to achieve a more robust pose estimate. Similar works on dense RGB-D camera tracking were reported in [6, 10, 11], they all also estimated the camera pose on geometric and photometric information. ElasticFusion [6] builds a surfel based map of the environment and performs loop closing applying deformation graph instead of standard pose graph optimization. This map-centric method can reconstruct better quality 3D models than the previous methods which only focus on the pose accuracy.

SLAM algorithms may fail when features are scarce, e.g. when exploring a less featured scene or the robot's movement is too fast. These issues may be tackled in the mobile devices using inertial sensors. [12, 13] use a standard Extended Kalman Filter to fuse both visual and inertial measurements on a mobile phone with a monocular camera. [14, 15] combine the RGB-D visual SLAM with the inertial measurements on a mobile platform. Our approach is to integrate robot inertial measurements into an RGB-D SLAM system. The mobile robot usually moves on a planar ground so the associated pose is only of 3 degrees of freedom. And the robot has a wheel encoder which can provide more accurate estimations of translation than accelerometer. As a result, we obtain a less noisy inertial measurement such that the commonly used Kalman filter becomes unnecessary in our case.

3   Calibration Between Camera and IMU System

3.1   System Setup

We use an TurtleBot2 (Fig. 1) and a Lenovo Rescuer notebook. The laptop controls the robot's movement and collects data from Kinect. We mount the Kinect on a shelf that is 1.6 m tall, because most indoor spaces are designed for human heights. The Kinect is arranged about $25°$ down vertically to capture more scenes.

3.2   System Calibration

Using the Robot Operating System (ROS), we estimate a full robot pose with the gyroscope and the wheel encoders that come with the robot, where the rotation angles are estimated by the gyroscope and the translations are estimated by the wheel encoders. Common inertial sensors generally use the accelerometer to estimate translations, which is less accurate than using the wheel encoders. And estimating poses by inertial sensors in mobile devices [15] such as mobile phone and tablets PC always need to calculate six degrees of freedom, while in our work, robot moves on the ground plane with only three degrees of freedom including two translations along the X axis and Y axis and a rotation along the Z axis, so the robot IMU poses are more accurate and less noisy.

By monitoring the transformation between the odometer coordinate system and the robot coordinate system in ROS, we obtain the robot's IMU pose which is represented with a transformation matrix

$$\mathbf{P}_{robot} = \begin{bmatrix} \mathbf{R}_{robot}(\varphi) & \mathbf{t}_{robot} \\ 0 \quad 0 \quad 0 & 1 \end{bmatrix} \tag{1}$$

where $\mathbf{R}_{robot}$ is the rotation matrix, φ is the rotation angle around the Z axis, $\mathbf{t}_{robot} = [t_x \quad t_y \quad 0]^T$ is the translation vector.

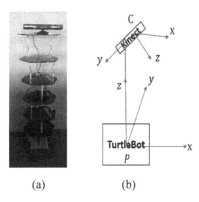

(a)   (b)

Fig. 1. The relative position between robot and camera. (a) The equipments of our system, where the robot is TurtleBot2 and the depth camera is Kinect. (b) The relationship between the robot coordinate system and the camera coordinate system, C is the camera center, P is the robot center.

The depth camera is fixed on the robot and moves together with the robot. Figure 1 shows the relative position between the robot and the camera. The initial camera coordinate system is in coincidence with the world coordinate system. We estimate the camera poses in the world coordinate system with the robot IMU poses.

Firstly, we calibrate the robot coordinate system to the camera coordinate system using a calibration checkerboard. Since the camera intrinsic parameters are known (calibrated separately), we calculate the extrinsic parameters of the camera by using the 3D to 2D matching pairs on the checkerboard. Substituting the matching pairs into the following imaging model:

$$s \begin{bmatrix} u \\ v \\ 1 \end{bmatrix} = \mathbf{K}[\mathbf{R}|\mathbf{t}] \begin{bmatrix} x \\ y \\ z \\ 1 \end{bmatrix} \tag{2}$$

where $\mathbf{K}$ is the camera intrinsic parameter matrix, $[\mathbf{R}|\mathbf{t}]$ is the camera extrinsic parameter matrix, $[u \quad v]^T$ is a 2D point in the image coordinate, $[x \quad y \quad z]^T$ is a 3D point in the robot coordinate. By the above method, we get the extrinsic parameter matrix $[\mathbf{R}|\mathbf{t}]$ and the coordinate of the camera center in the robot coordinate system $[x_c \quad y_c \quad z_c]^T = [-\mathbf{R}^T \cdot \mathbf{t}]^T$.

Secondly, we calculate the camera pose in the world coordinate system. Since the camera moves together with the robot and the robot rotates around the Z axis in the robot coordinate, the camera also rotates around this Z axis. We transform the Z axis in the robot coordinate to an axis defined as $[n_x \quad n_y \quad n_z]^T$ in the world coordinate:

$$
\begin{bmatrix} n_x \\ n_y \\ n_z \\ 1 \end{bmatrix} = [\mathbf{R}|\mathbf{t}] \begin{bmatrix} 0 \\ 0 \\ 1 \\ 0 \end{bmatrix} \tag{3}
$$

where $\begin{bmatrix} 0 & 0 & 1 & 0 \end{bmatrix}^{\mathrm{T}}$ represents the Z axis in the robot coordinate. Using this rotation axis, we calculate the rotation matrix of the camera pose in the world coordinate:

$$
\mathbf{R}_{camera}^{imu} = \begin{bmatrix} n_x^2 + \left(1 - n_x^2\right)cos\varphi & n_x n_y(1 - cos\varphi) - n_z sin\varphi & n_x n_z(1 - cos\varphi) + n_y sin\varphi \\ n_x n_y(1 - cos\varphi) + n_z sin\varphi & n_y^2 + \left(1 - n_y^2\right)cos\varphi & n_y n_z(1 - cos\varphi) - n_x sin\varphi \\ n_x n_z(1 - cos\varphi) - n_y sin\varphi & n_y n_z(1 - cos\varphi) + n_x sin\varphi & n_z^2 + \left(1 - n_z^2\right)cos\varphi \end{bmatrix} \tag{4}
$$

where φ is the rotation angle of the robot's pose. The translation of the camera pose is the position of the camera in the world coordinate, so we directly use the coordinate of the camera center to calculate the translations of the camera pose in the world coordinate:

$$
\mathbf{t}_{camera}^{imu} = [\mathbf{R}|\mathbf{t}]\, \mathbf{P}_{robot} \begin{bmatrix} x_c \\ y_c \\ z_c \\ 1 \end{bmatrix} \tag{5}
$$

Finally, we get the camera pose $\mathbf{P}_{camera}^{imu} = [\mathbf{R}_{camera}^{imu}|\mathbf{t}_{camera}^{imu}]$ in the world coordinate from the robot IMU pose.

4   Adaptively Combining IMU and Visual Pose to Enhance Tracking Robustness

One of the core issues of RGB-D SLAM algorithm is to estimate the transformation $\mathbf{T}$ between the current frame pose $\mathbf{P}_t$ and the proceeding frame pose $\mathbf{P}_{t-1}$. We base our approach on ElasticFusion [6], and aim to find the motion parameters ξ that minimize the following joint cost function:

$$
E_{track} = E_{icp} + w_{rgb} E_{rgb} \tag{6}
$$

with $w_{rgb} = 0.1$. E_{icp} is the cost over the point-to-plane error between 3D back-projected vertices:

$$
E_{icp} = \sum_k \left(\left(\mathbf{v}^k - \exp\left(\hat{\xi}\right) \mathbf{T} \mathbf{v}_t^k \right) \cdot \mathbf{n}^k \right)^2 \tag{7}
$$

E_{rgb} is the cost over the photometric error between pixels:

$$E_{rgb} = \sum_{\mathbf{u} \in \Omega} (I(\mathbf{u}, C_t) - I(\pi(\mathbf{K}exp(\xi)\mathbf{T}\mathbf{p}(\mathbf{u}, \mathcal{D}_t)), C_{t-1}))^2 \tag{8}$$

where $\mathbf{v}_t^k$ is the back-projection of the k-th vertex in the current depth image, $\mathbf{v}^k$ and $\mathbf{n}^k$ are the corresponding vertex and normal represented in the last predicted depth image. $exp\left(\hat{\xi}\right)$ is the matrix exponential. Vertices are associated using projective data association. C_t is the current color image and C_{t-1} is the last predicted color image. $I(\mathbf{u}, C)$ refers the intensity value of a pixel $\mathbf{u}$ given a color image C. $\mathbf{p}(\mathbf{u}, \mathcal{D})$ means the 3D back-projection of a point $\mathbf{u}$ given a depth map $\mathcal{D}$. $\pi(\mathbf{p})$ means the perspective projection of a 3D point $\mathbf{p}$.

To minimize the joint cost function, we use the Gauss-Newton non-linear least-squares method with a three level coarse-to-fine pyramid scheme. To solve each iteration, we calculate the least-squares solution:

$$\arg \min_{\xi} \| \mathbf{J}\xi + \mathbf{r} \|_2^2 \tag{9}$$

ElasticFusion [6] yields an improved camera transformation estimate:

$$\mathbf{T}' = \exp\left(\hat{\xi}\right)\mathbf{T} \tag{10}$$

$$\hat{\xi} = \begin{bmatrix} [\omega]_x & \mathbf{x} \\ 000 & 0 \end{bmatrix} \tag{11}$$

with $\xi = [\omega^T \mathbf{x}^T]^T, \omega, \mathbf{x} \in \mathbb{R}^3$.

In some situations, including exploring a workspace outside of the sensor's valid depths, processing a frame sequence that misses a certain amount of frames, encountering a dynamic occlusion or a low-textured workspace or dealing with blurred images due to fast camera movements, the transformation $\mathbf{T}'$ estimated in each iteration using the above visual method is always error prone. From the robot IMU, we can obtain the current frame IMU pose $\mathbf{P}_{camera,t}^{imu}$ and the last frame IMU pose $\mathbf{P}_{camera,t-1}^{imu}$. We define the transformation between $\mathbf{P}_{camera,t}^{imu}$ and $\mathbf{P}_{camera,t-1}^{imu}$ as

$$\mathbf{T}^{imu} = \mathbf{P}_{camera,t}^{imu} \cdot \left(\mathbf{P}_{camera,t-1}^{imu}\right)^{-1} \tag{12}$$

The transformation $\mathbf{T}^{imu}$ is stable which is not affected by the scene environment. Figure 2 shows the comparison of the local model using only visual method with the model using only $\mathbf{T}^{imu}$. Even a small difference of $\mathbf{T}^{imu}$ with the ground truth transformation could lead to a poor quality of the local model.

In each iteration, we define the transformation estimated by the above visual method as $\mathbf{T}^{vis} = \exp\left(\hat{\xi}\right)\mathbf{T}$. Then adaptively combining $\mathbf{T}^{vis}$ with $\mathbf{T}^{imu}$ to balance the local model quality and the stability of pose tracking:

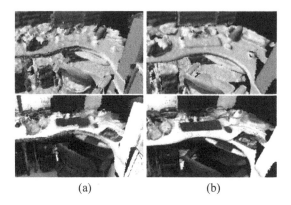

(a)   (b)

Fig. 2. Local model reconstructed by IMU and visual method. The top row shows the 3D surfel model and the bottom row shows the textured model. (a) the local model using only IMU, where the desktop becomes thicker. (b) the local model using only visual pose, the quality is better.

$$\mathbf{T}' = (1 - s \cdot d)\mathbf{T}^{vis} + (s \cdot d)\mathbf{T}^{imu} \tag{13}$$

where s is a balance scale, d is the distance between $\mathbf{T}^{vis}$ and $\mathbf{T}^{imu}$. We define the distance of $(\mathbf{T}^{vis} - \mathbf{T}^{imu})$ as its Frobenius Norm as $d = \left\| \mathbf{T}^{vis} - \mathbf{T}^{imu} \right\|_F$.

When the transformation $\mathbf{T}^{vis}$ is close to $\mathbf{T}^{imu}$, which means the pose estimated by the visual tracking is successful, we set $\mathbf{T}^{imu}$ to account for only a small part to guarantee local model quality. Conversely, if $\mathbf{T}^{vis}$ and $\mathbf{T}^{imu}$ have an obvious difference, which means the visual pose is not reliable, we set $\mathbf{T}^{imu}$ to account for a big part to correct the pose. Using the above adaptive weight setting, we find the pose tracking is always successful in our experiments and the local model quality is better than that under the fixed weight combination.

5   Robot Movement Pattern Design

Our goal is to move the robot on the floor and reconstruct the full 3D model of the indoor environment. To localize and map the scene accurately, there are several constraints on the robot movement: (1) The speed of the movement cannot be too fast, especially the rotation angular velocity cannot be too large, otherwise the pose will not be reliably estimated by the visual method. (2) The movement should have some closed loops to eliminate accumulated errors. Thanks to our above adaptive pose combination method, we can adequately handle difficult situations such as dynamic occlusion, low-textured region, and the scene outside of the range of valid depths.

If the scene is relatively small, the robot only needs to move around the room and ensure that it can be back to the starting point to achieve a closed loop. While if the scene is large, we should design some small loops in case the accumulated error is notable such that the global model error cannot be eliminated completely if a single loop is wed (Fig. 3). We use two kinds of movement patterns for the map building.

Movement Pattern 1 is to make a circular movement at each location and then move forward to the next location (Fig. 4), which is similar to [16]. But in the experiment we find each circle is an independent movement and there is no closed loop between two nearby circles, which leads to the large accumulated errors between the circles and the two local models reconstructed by two circles cannot be aligned. In addition to that, the pure rotation moves slowly and the captured data in the nearby circles are almost the same, so there are a lot of redundant data in the first movement pattern. We design Movement Pattern 2 with a bigger closed loop and the two nearby loops always overlap (Fig. 4). This movement can eliminate the accumulated error between two loops with the closed loop in the overlap region. And the system will capture streamlined data

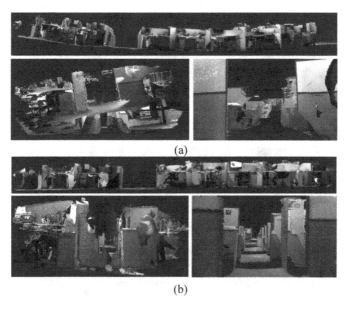

(a)

(b)

Fig. 3. Comparison of the big size loop result and the small size loop result. (a) Move in one large circle movement where the model has some distortions in the global perspective. (b) Move in Movement Pattern 2, the overall accuracy is higher.

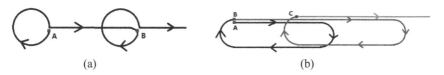

(a)   (b)

Fig. 4. Robot movement patterns in large workspace. (a) Movement Pattern 1, where A and B are the starting points of the two circles; (b) Movement Pattern 2, where the black line represents the first loop, the blue line represents the second loop and the green line represents the next loop, A B C stand for the loop starting points respectively. The overlapping region between any two different color lines is the loop closing area. (Color figure online)

because the pattern has less repeated scenes and uses more translation movements whose speed is faster than the rotation speed. The experimental results are shown in the next section.

6   Experiments

We use a TurtleBot2, a Kinect and a Lenovo Rescuer notebook with an Intel Core I5-6300HQ CPU at 2.3 Hz, 8 GB of RAM to collect the data. The test platform is a desktop with an Intel Xeon E5-1620 CPU at 3.7 GHz, 32 GB of RAM and an NVidia GeForce GTX 1060 GPU with 6 GB of memory. The Kinect receives 30 frames per second, and we collect the IMU information at the same rate. The TurtleBot2 moves at a speed of 0.2 m/s and rotates at a speed of 0.4 rad/s.

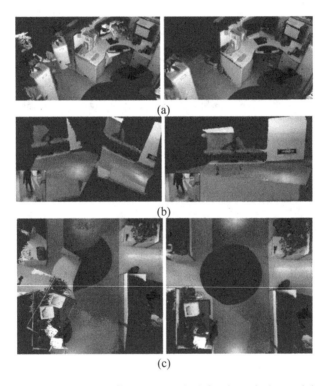

Fig. 5. The reconstructed result of difficult scene. The left column is the result by visual method without IMU information and the right column is the result with IMU fused pose. (a) The result that processes a frame sequence which misses a certain amount of frames. (b) The result that encounters dynamic pedestrians. (c) The result when explores a workspace outside of the range of the sensor's valid depths.

We carry out experiments on some difficult situation, including processing a frame sequence that misses a certain amount of frames, encountering dynamic pedestrians and an empty scene where the camera only can see the ground plane. We compare the result of the system combining IMU information with the system without IMU information in Fig. 5. With vision and IMU fused pose, the robot can go to where successfully, but without IMU fusion, the tracking is always failed.

We use the two movement patterns on the same scene, find the 3D model reconstructed by Movement Pattern 1 has many noise in the model and some parts of the model are not aligned, while Movement Pattern 2 is much better, which can be seen in Fig. 6. The underlying reason is that Movement Pattern 1 needs multiple modeling and there is no closed loop between circles. We also find that although Movement Pattern 2 has many repeated areas to close loop, the redundant data is less than that using Movement Pattern 1.

Our approach relies on robot IMU, and common RGD-D SLAM datasets such as TUM RGB-D dataset and ICL_NUIM dataset do not have IMU information, so we cannot compare with others on benchmarks. We compare the reconstruction result of our approach with ElasticFusion [6] and Kintinuous [5] on our data in Fig. 7. We do a quantity of experiments to validate our approach in different scenes (Fig. 8).

Fig. 6. Comparison of the local model using different movements. Left based on Movement Pattern 1 and right based on Movement Pattern 2.

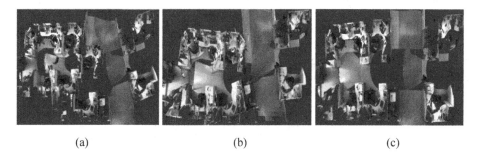

(a)   (b)   (c)

Fig. 7. Comparison of the reconstruction results by different approaches. (a) The result by ElasticFusion. (b) The result by Kintinuous. (c) The result by our approach.

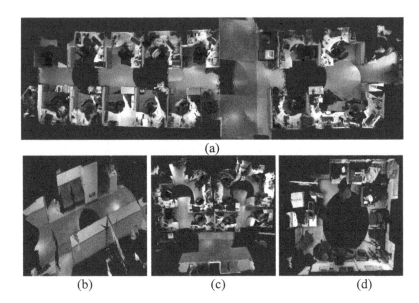

(a)

(b)   (c)   (d)

Fig. 8. Reconstructed results in different scenes. (a) A long office scene where the robot moves in Movement Pattern 2. (b) A corridor scene that both ends of the corridor are out of sensor's valid depths. (c) A large office scene with dynamic pedestrians. (d) A small office scene that the data lost several frames.

7   Conclusion

Our goal is to reconstruct the indoor scene with a RGB-D camera on a robot. To overcome the pose tracking failure problem caused by the week featured scene, we fuse the inertial measurement into the pose tracking process and an adaptive weight scheme to balance the IMU pose and the visual pose. With the movement of the robot, the pose error gradually accumulates, we should design closed loops in the movement to eliminate the errors. So we propose two movement patterns for robot and analyze the two patterns with the experiments. With our IMU combination system, we find the pose estimation is greatly improved, that we did not find any failure cases even under difficult situation. We will test our approach in more scenes such as home and restaurant and study the theoretical support for the movement patterns in future work.

Acknowledgement. This work is supported in part by the National Key R&D Program of China (2016YFB0502002), and in part by the National Natural Science Foundation of China (NSFC) (61472419).

References

1. Davison, A.J.: Real-time simultaneous localisation and mapping with a single camera. In: Proceedings of the International Conference on Computer Vision (ICCV), vol. 3, pp. 1403–1410 (2003)

2. Klein, G., Murray, D.W.: Parallel tracking and mapping for small AR workspaces. In: Proceedings of the International Symposium on Mixed and Augmented Reality (ISMAR), pp. 225–234. IEEE (2007)
3. Mur-Artal, R., Montiel, J.M.M., Tardós, J.D.: ORB-SLAM: a versatile and accurate monocular SLAM system. IEEE Trans. Robot. **31**(5), 1147–1163 (2015)
4. Newcombe, R.A., Izadi, S., Hilliges, O., Molyneaux, D., Kim, D., Davison, A.J., Kohli, P., Shotton, J., Hodges, S., Fitzgibbon, A.: KinectFusion: real-time dense surface mapping and tracking. In: Proceedings of the 2011 10th IEEE International Symposium on Mixed and Augmented Reality, ISMAR 2011, pp. 127–136. IEEE Computer Society, Washington, DC, USA (2011)
5. Whelan, T., Kaess, M., Fallon, M., Johannsson, H., Leonard, J., McDonald, J.: Real-time large scale dense RGB-D SLAM with volumetric fusion. Int. J. Robot. Res. (IJRR) **34**(4–5), 598–626 (2015). London, England
6. Whelan, T., Leutenegger, S., Salas-Moreno, R.F., Glocker, B., Davison, A.J.: ElasticFusion: dense SLAM without a pose graph. In: Proceedings of Robotics: Science and Systems (RSS) (2015)
7. Zeng, M., Zhao, F., Zheng, J., Liu, X.: A memory-efficient KinectFusion using octree. In: Hu, S.-M., Martin, R.R. (eds.) CVM 2012. LNCS, vol. 7633, pp. 234–241. Springer, Heidelberg (2012). https://doi.org/10.1007/978-3-642-34263-9_30
8. Steinbrücker, F., Kerl, C., Sturm, J., Cremers, D.: Large-scale multi-resolution surface reconstruction from RGB-D sequences. In: IEEE International Conference on Computer Vision (ICCV), pp. 3264–3271, Sydney, Australia (2013)
9. Endres, F., Hess, J., Sturm, J., Cremers, D., Burgard, W.: 3-D mapping with an RGB-D camera. IEEE Trans. Robot. **30**(1), 177–187 (2014)
10. Steinbrücker, F., Sturm, J., Cremers, D.: Real-time visual odometry from dense RGB-D images. In: Workshop on Live Dense Reconstruction with Moving Cameras at the International Conference on Computer Vision (ICCV), pp. 719–722 (2011)
11. Audras, C., Comport, A.I., Meilland, M., Rives, P.: Realtime dense RGB-D localisation and mapping. In: Australian Conference on Robotics and Automation. Monash University, Australia (2011)
12. Tanskanen, P., Kolev, K., Meier, L., Camposeco, F., Saurer, O., Pollefeys, M.: Live metric 3D reconstruction on mobile phones. In: International Conference on Computer Vision (ICCV), pp. 65–72, Sydney, Australia (2013)
13. Weiss, S., Siegwart, R.: Real-time metric state estimation for modular vision-inertial systems. In: International Conference on Robotics and Automation (ICRA), pp. 4531–4537, Shangai, China (2011)
14. Qayyum, U., Kim, J.: Inertial-kinect fusion for outdoor 3D navigation. In: Australasian Conference on Robotics and Automation (ACRA) (2013)
15. Brunetto, N., Salti, S., Fioraio, N., Cavallari, T., Stefano, L.D.: Fusion of inertial and visual measurements for RGB-D SLAM on mobile devices. In: Proceedings of the IEEE International Conference on Computer Vision Workshops, pp. 1–9 (2015)
16. Song, S., Zhang, L., Xiao, J.: Robot in a room: toward perfect object recognition in closed environments. CoRR (2015)

The Research of Multi-angle Face Detection Based on Multi-feature Fusion

Mengnan Hu⑩, Yongkang Liu⑩, and Rong Wang$^{(\boxtimes)}$⑩

Institute of Information Technology and Network Security,
People's Public Security University of China, Beijing 10038, China
361868422@qq.com

Abstract. The method of multi-angle face detection method is proposed based on fusion of Haar-like, HOG and MB-LBP features. Firstly, three Adaboost cascade classifiers for original face region detection are constructed respectively according to Haar-like, MB-LBP and HOG features, using the processed training samples of face and non-face to train the classifiers. Secondly, the preprocessing of testing sample is implemented based on skin color model, which results are the classifiers input, and then the suspected face regions and their weights are obtained. Finally, the refined face regions are selected according to the results of voting and weighted threshold. The method proposed in this paper is implemented on VS2012 platform invoking opencv function library, and the simulation experiment is carried on FDDB. To verify the effect, our method is compared with other methods based on a single feature. Results of experiments show that the proposed method has higher accuracy and better real-time performance.

Keywords: Multi-feature fusion · Multi-angle face detection
Haar-like feature · HOG feature · MB-LBP feature

1 Introduction

Video surveillance has been extensively used in the field of public security. As the face information has the advantages of unique identification and easy accessibility, face detection and tracking based on video sequence has been part of the most significant means to locate and track the criminal suspects. Human head is a 3D object, in the video image, 1D information would be dropped during the process of transformation from 3D to 2D. When different angles of 3D face are projected to 2D, different parts of the face will be stretched and compressed, leading to huge difference between different angles of 2D face. Most existing face detection methods require that the detected person must be positive. In some cases, however, due to the movement of the detected person and various imaging angles, it is difficult to obtain a frontal image. Therefore, multi-angle face detection has been one of the research hotspots.

In view of the problem of multi-angle face detection, many methods have been proposed. In some research, Haar-like features were extended differently and classifiers were constructed based on Adaboost algorithm to accomplish multi-angle face detection [1–4]. The methods based on different skin color models were proposed which

© Springer International Publishing AG 2017
Y. Zhao et al. (Eds.): ICIG 2017, Part I, LNCS 10666, pp. 466–476, 2017.
https://doi.org/10.1007/978-3-319-71607-7_41

were used for coarse detection to improve efficiency, [5, 6]. Guo proposed an Adaboost-SVM algorithm, in which features were fused with Haar-like and edge-orientation field features, and it was combined with the improved decision tree cascade structure to carry out the multi-angle face detection, [7]. But because the number of Haar-like feature is very large and it will be much larger when adapting to different angles, training process based on Haar-like feature is quite slow. So the method based on Multi-block Local Binary Pattern feature (MB-LBP) was proposed to detect human faces, [8]. Reference [9] proposed a method based on MB-LBP feature and controlled cost-sensitive Adaboost (CCS- Adaboost). Reference [10] proposed an algorithm cascading two SVM classifiers trained by HOG and LBP features respectively to implement face detection.

In this paper, the method based on multi-feature fusion to detect multi-angle face is proposed. Firstly, three Adaboost classifiers of a single feature are constructed respectively and trained by processed training samples. Secondly, preprocessed testing samples are sent into three classifiers for the original detection to get suspect face regions and their weights. Finally, the refined face regions are obtained by voting and weighted calculation. The method performance will be evaluated in terms of accuracy and efficiency.

The rest of the paper is organized as follows. The method of multi-angle face detection is discussed in Sect. 2. Simulation experiment and analysis are presented in Sect. 3. Conclusions are given in Sect. 4.

2 Method of Multi-angle Face Detection

The method of multi-angle face detection based on multi-feature fusion is divided into three parts, preprocessing, training and detection, as shown in Fig. 1.

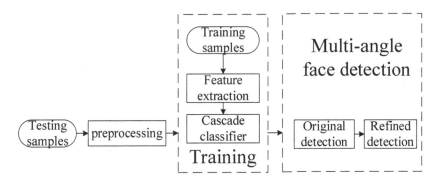

Fig. 1. Flowchart of multi-angle face detection

2.1 Preprocessing

Due to the conditions of testing samples are different, in order to reduce their effects, it is necessary for testing samples to conduct illumination compensation and histogram equalization. As testing samples contain not only human face regions but also non-face skin regions which are needed to be screened, so testing samples are normalized to 300×300 size.

The skin color feature has good clustering characteristics, and the skin color information can be separated from the background. In the YC_bC_r color space, Y represents the luminance information, C_b and C_r represents chrominance information. The conversion relation from RGB to YC_bC_r is calculated as follows:

$$\begin{bmatrix} Y \\ C_b \\ C_r \end{bmatrix} = \begin{bmatrix} 0.299 & 0.587 & 0.114 \\ -0.1687 & -0.3313 & 0.5 \\ 0.5 & -0.4187 & -0.0813 \end{bmatrix} \begin{bmatrix} R \\ G \\ B \end{bmatrix} + \begin{bmatrix} 0 \\ 128 \\ 128 \end{bmatrix} \tag{1}$$

$$\begin{bmatrix} Y \\ C_b \\ C_r \end{bmatrix} = \begin{bmatrix} 0.299 & 0.587 & 0.114 \\ -0.1687 & -0.3313 & 0.5 \\ 0.5 & -0.4187 & -0.0813 \end{bmatrix} \begin{bmatrix} R \\ G \\ B \end{bmatrix} + \begin{bmatrix} 0 \\ 128 \\ 128 \end{bmatrix} \tag{2}$$

Skin color in $C_b - C_r$ color space is aggregated into a elliptic model as in (2) and (3).

$$\frac{(x - ec_x)^2}{a^2} + \frac{(y - ec_y)^2}{b^2} = 1 \tag{3}$$

$$\begin{bmatrix} x \\ y \end{bmatrix} = \begin{bmatrix} \cos\theta & \sin\theta \\ -\sin\theta & \cos\theta \end{bmatrix} \begin{bmatrix} C_b' - C_x \\ C_r' - C_y \end{bmatrix} \tag{4}$$

where $c_x = 109.38$, $c_y = 152.02$, $\theta = 2.53$, $ec_x = 1.60$, $ec_y = 2.41$, $a = 25.39$, and $b = 14.03$. If the pixel satisfies the (2) and (3) which can be considered as skin color, it is recorded as 1, otherwise as 0 to get a binary image. Therefore, after morphology process, skin region can be obtained.

2.2   Feature Extraction

In this paper, Haar-like, MB-LBP and HOG feature is extracted respectively and multi-angle face detection classifier is constructed through training of a large number of face and non-face samples.

Haar-like feature templates consist of a simple combination of rectangles, in which there are the identical white and black rectangles, [11]. The feature value of the template is defined as the difference between the sum of pixels in the white rectangle region and it in the black rectangle region, which reflects the local change of the gray level in the image, [12]. There are three kinds of commonly used Haar-like features, edge feature, linear feature and diagonal feature, mainly representing horizontal, vertical and diagonal direction information. As the Haar-like feature is sensitive to the edge or line segments, so it's often used to distinguish the face region and non-face region. As shown in Fig. 2(a) and (b) reflects edge feature of horizontal and vertical direction respectively, Fig. 2(c) and (d) reflects linear feature of horizontal and vertical direction respectively, and Fig. 2(e) reflects the diagonal feature, [13].

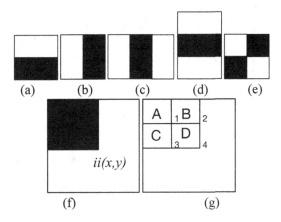

Fig. 2. Haar-like feature

The traditional method to calculate feature value is to cumulate gray value of each pixel area directly and the computation is enormous, so integral figure is used to simplify the calculation. For original image $I(x,y)$, the integral figure $ii(x,y)$ is the sum of gray values in the black areas in Fig. 2f, and it can be defined as:

$$ii(x, y) = \sum_{x' \leq x, y' \leq y,} I(x', y') \tag{5}$$

where $I(x', y')$ is the gray value of (x', y'), ii(x,y) can be got by (5) and (6),

$$s(x, y) = s(x, y - 1) + I(x, y) \tag{6}$$

$$ii(x, y) = ii(x - 1, y) + s(x, y) \tag{7}$$

where $s(x, y)$ is the sum of accumulated pixel values of each row in the original image, as in (7).

$$s(x, y) = \sum_{y' \leq y,} I(x, y') \tag{8}$$

while $s(x, -1) = 0$, $ii(-1, y) = 0$.

As shown in Fig. 2(g),the sum of gray values of area D can be calculated through ii_1, ii_2, ii_3, and ii_4. $ii_1 = A$, $ii_2 = A + B$, $ii_3 = A + C$, $ii_4 = A + B + C + D$, so $D = ii_4 + ii_1 - (ii_2 + ii_3)$.

LBP (Local Binary Pattern) feature is defined in the 3×3 neighborhood. As shown in Fig. 3(a), the gray value of center pixel in the neighborhood is the threshold value. Compared with the threshold value, if 8 adjacent gray pixel value is greater, record it as 1, else as 0 to produce an 8-bit binary number (10010110). Then it is converted to a decimal number to obtain LBP encoding (150) of the center pixel in the neighborhood, reflecting the texture information of this region, [14].

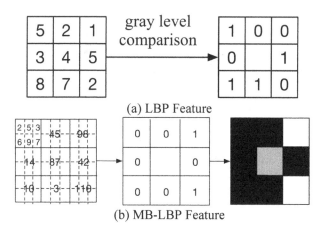

(a) LBP Feature

(b) MB-LBP Feature

Fig. 3. The process of LBP and MB-LBP feature extraction

MB-LBP (Multi Block-Local Binary Pattern) is used to improve the LBP feature. As shown in Fig. 3(b), the rectangular region is divided into image blocks which are divided into small areas, and the average gray value of the small area is regarded as the gray value of the image block. And then, LBP coding for pixel gray scale is converted into the coding for image blocks. If the image block size is 3 × 3 and the size of each small area is 1, the MB-LBP feature is the LBP feature at this time, as shown in Fig. 4. Therefore, when the image size is small, the gray value of each pixel of the image corresponds to the average gray value of the image block in the larger image, which is equivalent to extracting the MB-LBP feature. For an image size of 24 × 24, with the upper left corner of the image as the origin, with 6 × 6 pixels constituting an image block, 50% overlap between adjacent blocks, a total of 49 blocks, you can get 49 × 256 = 12544 dimensions MB-LBP feature.

HOG (Histogram of Oriented Gradient) feature can be obtained by calculating the histogram of the oriented gradient of the local image, which is used to describe the edge or gradient information of the local region. To calculate this feature, firstly, the image is

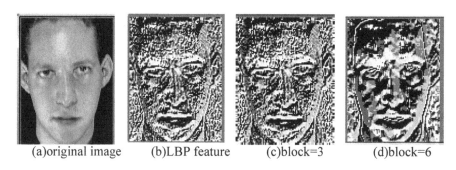

(a)original image   (b)LBP feature   (c)block=3   (d)block=6

Fig. 4. LBP and MB-LBP feature image

grayed and gamma normalized. Secondly, the gradient size and gradient direction of each pixel are computed by using the $[-1,0,1]$ and $[1,0,-1]^T$ gradient operators. Thirdly the image is divided into several small cells and $0°-360°$ is divided into nine bins. The 9D HOG feature vector of each cell unit can be obtained by accumulating weighted votes for gradient orientation over spatial cells. Blocks are composed of several cells and HOG feature of the block can be obtained by normalizing all series HOG feature vector of cells. Finally, the HOG features of all blocks are connected in series to obtain the HOG feature of the whole image. For an image size of 24×24, with the upper left corner of the image as the origin, with 3×3 pixels constituting a cell, with 2×2 cell constituting a block, 50% overlap between adjacent blocks, a total of 49 blocks, horizontal and vertical directions can get $49 \times 4 \times 9 = 1764$ dimensions HOG features respectively.

2.3   Classifier Building

Adaboost is an algorithm to linearly combine many classifiers and form a much better classifier. Firstly, dataset was trained to get weak classifiers through voting. Then, weights were set differently for each weak classifier to achieve the global optimum. Finally, according to the cascade structure, strong classifiers were obtained, [15]. As shown in Fig. 5, Adaboost cascade classifier is a coarse to fine structure, where Y represents the face area, N represents the non-face area. Three features of training samples are extracted to construct Haar-like, MB-LBP and HOG classifiers respectively.

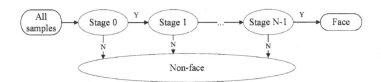

Fig. 5. Flowchart of Adaboost cascade classifier

If the classifier is based on a single feature, for the same sample, there will be a situation in which feature A can detect the face correctly while feature B cannot or feature A mistakenly regards the area as face while feature B rules it out. Therefore, in this paper, as shown in Fig. 6, a method combined three features is proposed to integrate these classifiers.

Samples will be sent to three classifiers to get suspected face areas and their weight respectively. And then, vote. When the area is detected by two classifiers at least, do the weighting. When the weight is greater than threshold, the area can be regarded as face. Voting and integrating are calculated as follows.

Firstly, classify the rectangles output by three classifiers. Record the location and weight $w_i (i \geq 0)$ of each rectangle and each rectangle corresponds to an index m_i. If the ratio of overlap areas of two rectangles is more than 0.5 of the smaller area, these two

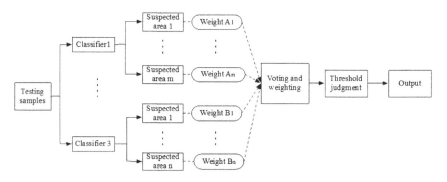

Fig. 6. Flowchart of classifier building.

rectangles are regarded as one category. Count the number of categories by traversing all rectangles and each category corresponds to an index $n_j(0 \leq j \leq i)$.

Secondly, calculate the fusion weight W_j of each category. After traversing all rectangles of each category, set the biggest weight as the original weight W_j of the category and record the index number of the corresponding rectangle. Then fuse the surplus rectangles $m_k(k \leq i)$ of each cateegory with the rectangle corresponding to the biggest weight, and calculate the proportion v of fused rectangle accounting for the larger rectangle. The fusion weight can be calculated as in (9).

$$W_j = W_j + w_k \times v \tag{9}$$

Finally, voting, weighting, and threshold decision. If the number of rectangles of each category is above one, i.e. the area is detected by at least two classifiers, calculate the integrated weight as in (10),

$$Weight = W_j^2 + num^2 \tag{10}$$

where Weight represents the total weight, W_j represents the fusion weight of the category and num represents the number of rectangles of each category. According to the threshold to determine the final output detection area.

The experiment will be carried out on the test set using four kinds of classifiers and performance will be evaluated in terms of accuracy and real-time.

3   Simulation Experiment and Result Analysis

Simulation experiment is carried out based on VS2012 platform, opencv 2.4.8. Face training samples are from CAS - PEAL database [16] and MIT database, through histogram equalization and size normalization, and 8000 pieces of which constitute the face training set. Non-face training samples are from CMU database and MIT database, through size normalization, and 24000 pieces of which constitute the non-face training set. Testing samples are from FDDB [17] including 135 images and 224 faces.

3.1 Simulation Experiment

The process of classifiers training is divided into five parts, as shown in Fig. 7, initialization, loading samples, logical judgment, computation and save. Firstly, initialize the false rate and the number of strong classifiers to 0.5 and 30. Secondly, load face samples with pos2424.vec file as positive samples and non-face samples with neg.txt as negative samples. Thirdly, judge whether the false rate and the number of strong classifiers reach the initialization. If one of them satisfy the initialization, do the fifth stage. Then, calculate the feature values and return to the second stage. Finally, save the strong classifiers information as a XML file. After training, the number of strong classifiers of three features is 15, 16, 15.

Real-time performance is evaluated by detection time, which means the time required by dealing with a single image and is obtained through processing 135 images and taking the average time. Accuracy performance is evaluated by detection rate and false rate, as shown in Table 1.

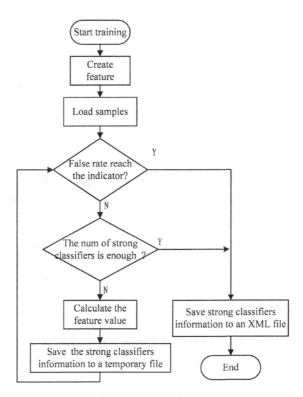

Fig. 7. Flowchart of training.

Table 1. Algorithm results

Method	Detection time (ms)	Detection rate	False rate	Miss rate
Haar-like	301.5115	95.09%	33.04%	4.91%
MB-LBP	150.4199	91.07%	16.52%	8.93%
HOG	337.5763	80.8%	17.86%	19.2%
Multi-feature fusion	0.2119	88.39%	2.11%	11.61%

3.2   Result Analysis

From Table 1, in terms of detection time: *Multi-feature fusion < MB-LBP < Haar-like < HOG*, the time of HOG required is the longest. Because during the process of classifier training, the average number of weak classifiers included in strong classifier

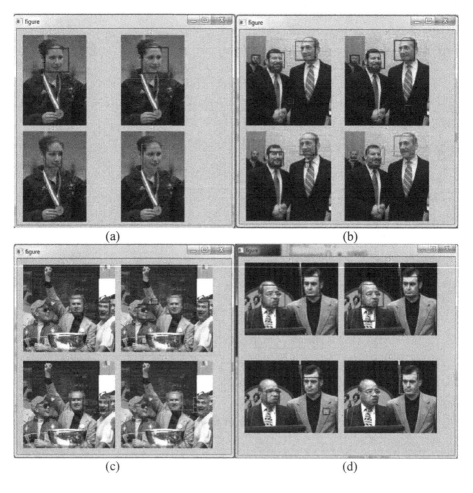

(a)   (b)

(c)   (d)

Fig. 8. Results of detection.

per layer of HOG is about 455 while it of Haar-like is 35 and it of MB-LBP is 15, detection time of HOG is the longest. In terms of detection rate: *HOG < Multi-feature fusion < MB-LBP < Haar-like*. Although after weighting and integration, compared with Haar-like and MB-LBP feature, the detection rate of Multi-feature fusion is lower and the false rate is 2.11%, filtering out most of the non-face region detected mistakenly. As shown in Figs. 8a, b, c and d is the detection result based on MB-LBP, Haar-like, HOG and Multi-feature fusion respectively.

From Fig. 8a, after weighting and integration, classifier based on Multi-feature fusion can filtrate non-face region detected by single feature, reducing the false rate, and from Fig. 8b the classifier can detect face region which single feature cannot, increasing the detection rate compared with HOG. As shown in Fig. 8c, only one classifier can detect the face region so that the there is no integrated weight calculation, and as shown in Fig. 8d, at least two single feature classifier can detect the face but the integrated weight is less than the threshold, leading to a decrease in detection rate.

It is necessary for face detection to detect the face region correctly and exclude the non-face region, so the method not only needs to ensure a higher detection accuracy but also is required to reduce the false rate as much as possible. In conclusion, the multi-feature fusion method is more suitable for multi-angle face detection.

4 Conclusion

Multi-angle face detection has grown up to a hot topic in the field of face detection. A method of multi-angle face detection based on multi-feature fusion is proposed in this paper, the effect of the method is better than the method based on single feature in the terms of real-time and accuracy, because it combined advantages of three features and has a high confidence of the refined face region through voting and weighting calculation. The results (the detection rate is 88.39% and the false rate is 2.11%) of the simulation experiment shows that the method is suitable for multi-angle face detection. In the future, the research will focus on searching a more appropriate threshold which can improve detection rate and can guarantee the false rate, and studying on applying this method to video sequence to accomplish multi-angle face detection based on video sequences.

References

1. Vural, S., Mae, Y., Uvet, H., et al.: Multi-view fast object detection by using extended haar filters in uncontrolled environments. Pattern Recogn. Lett. **33**(2), 126–133 (2012)
2. Wang, P., Zou, Y.: Multi-posture face detection real time system based on DM642. Video Eng. **37**(5), 179–182 (2013)
3. Weijian, J., Gongde, G., Zhiming, L.: An improved adaboost algorithm based on new Haar-like feature for face detection. J. Shandong Univ. **44**(2), 43–48 (2014)
4. Wang, Q.W., Ying, Z.L.: A face detection algorithm based on Haar-like t features. Pattern Recogn. Artif. Intell. **28**(1), 35–41 (2015)
5. Quanbin, L.I., Liu, J., Huang, Z.: Multi-view face detection using skin color model and FloatBoost. Comput. Eng. Appl. **49**(23), 166–169 (2013)

6. Yang, C., Sang, N., Chen, Z., et al.: Multi-view face detection method based on skin-color model and adaboost algorithm. J. Huazhong Univ. of Sci. Technol. **43**, 271–275 (2015)
7. Guo, S., Gu, G.C., Cai, Z.S., et al.: Multi-pose face detection based on feature fusion and decision tree cascade structure. J. Shenyang Univ. Technol. **34**(2), 203–208 (2012)
8. Liao, S., Zhu, X., Lei, Z., Zhang, L., Li, S.Z.: Learning multi-scale block local binary patterns for face recognition. In: Lee, S.-W., Li, S.Z. (eds.) ICB 2007. LNCS, vol. 4642, pp. 828–837. Springer, Heidelberg (2007). https://doi.org/10.1007/978-3-540-74549-5_87
9. He, Z.X., Ding, X.Q., Fang, C., et al.: Multiview face detection based on LBP and CCS-Adaboost. J. Zhejiang Univ. **47**(4), 622–629 (2013)
10. Zhang, X.L., Liu, S.X., Liu, M.H.: Face detection based on cascade support vector machine fusing multi-feature. Comput. Appl. Softw. **33**(4), 151–154 (2016)
11. Viola, P., Jones, M.: Rapid object detection using a boosted cascade of simple features. In: Proceedings of the 2001 IEEE Computer Society Conference on Computer Vision and Pattern Recognition, pp. 511–518. IEEE, Hawaii (2001)
12. Ling, G., Jiang, Z., Dong, A.M.: Application of the expansion Haar features in eye detection. J. Univ. Electron. Sci. Technol. China **39**(2), 247–250 (2010)
13. Wang, R., Hou, P.P., Zeng, Z.L.: The application of face detection and tracking method based on OpenCV. Sci. Technol. Eng. **4**(24), 15–118 (2014)
14. Ying, T.: Local binary pattern based on the directions and its application in facial expression recognition. CAAI Trans. Intell. Syst. **10**(3), 422–428 (2015)
15. Wenhao, L.I., Chen, Z.: Improved adaboost face detection algorithm. Video Eng. **38**(15), 207–212 (2014)
16. Gao, W., Cao, B., Shan, S., et al.: The CAS-PEAL large-scale chinese face database and baseline evaluations. IEEE Trans. Syst. Man Cybern. Part A Syst. Hum. **38**(1), 149–161 (2008)
17. Jain, V., Learned-Miller, E.: FDDB: a benchmark for face detection in unconstrained settings. Technical Report UM-CS-2010-009, Department of Computer Science, University of Massachusetts, Amherst, December 2010

Attention-Sharing Correlation Learning for Cross-Media Retrieval

Xin Huang, Zhaoda Ye, and Yuxin Peng[(✉)]

Institute of Computer Science and Technology, Peking University,
Beijing 100871, China
pengyuxin@pku.edu.cn

Abstract. Cross-media retrieval is a challenging research topic with wide prospect of application, aiming to retrieve among different media types by using a single-media query. The main challenge of cross-media retrieval is to learn the correlation between different media types for addressing the issue of "media gap". The close semantic correlation usually lies in specific parts of cross-media data such as image and text, which plays the key role for precious correlation mining. However, existing works usually focus on correlation learning in the level of whole media instance, or adopt patch segmentation but treat the patches indiscriminately. They ignore the fine-grained discrimination learning, which limits the retrieval accuracy. Inspired by attention mechanism, this paper proposes the attention-sharing correlation learning network, which is an end-to-end network to generate cross-media common representation for retrieval. By sharing the common attention weights, the attention of different media types can be learned coordinately. It can not only emphasize the single-media discriminative parts, but also enhance the cross-media fine-grained consistent pattern, and so learn more precious cross-media correlation to improve retrieval accuracy. Experimental results on 2 widely-used datasets with state-of-the-art methods verify the effectiveness of the proposed approach.

1 Introduction

As a key technique of information acquisition and management, multimedia retrieval has become an active research topic for decades [1], which can provide amounts of similar data with a single query. Past efforts mainly concentrate on single-media retrieval, where user query and retrieval results are of the same media type. However, with the development of multimedia and network transmission technology, multimedia data such as image, text, video and audio can be generated and found everywhere. Different media types have been merged with each other, and become the main form of big data. Under this situation, the media limitation of single-media retrieval is becoming increasingly obvious, and cross-media retrieval has become a new important retrieval paradigm.

Cross-media retrieval is proposed to retrieve data of similar semantic but different media types with a user query. Intuitively, it allows user to retrieve

© Springer International Publishing AG 2017
Y. Zhao et al. (Eds.): ICIG 2017, Part I, LNCS 10666, pp. 477–488, 2017.
https://doi.org/10.1007/978-3-319-71607-7_42

relevant texts with an image query. Different from single-media retrieval, cross-media retrieval faces the great challenge of "media gap", which means that data of different media types have different representation forms. For example, image can be represented by features based on visual information as color and texture, while text can be represented by features based on word frequency. Representations of different media types lie in different feature space, so the similarity between them cannot be directly measured. For addressing this problem, the mainstream methods of cross-media retrieval are common representation learning. The main idea is to represent data of different media types with the same type of representation, so that cross-media similarity can be directly computed by distance measurement. Based on different models, these methods can be further divided into non-DNN based learning methods [2–4] and DNN-based methods [5–8]. They all project cross-media data into one common space by learning from their correlation.

The close semantic correlation usually lies in specific parts of cross-media data. For example, the correlation between image and text can be co-existent patterns of image patches and words. The above fine-grained correlation plays the key role for precious correlation mining. However, existing works usually focus on correlation in the level of whole media instance [2,3,9], and ignore the fine-grained information. Some recent works as [10,11] adopt patch segmentation and treat the patches indiscriminately. For example, the work of [10] takes all the patches for hypergraph construction, and all the patches are equally important. However, the importances of different parts are usually different, and they can be very noisy in semantic level, limiting the effectiveness of correlation learning.

For addressing the above problem, inspired by attention mechanism [12–14], this paper proposes the attention-sharing correlation learning network (ACLN), which is an end-to-end network to generate cross-media common representation for retrieval. ACLN first extracts local features from cross-media data, and then lets them share the common attention weights, so that the attention of different media types can be learned coordinately according to pairwise correlation and semantic information. It can not only emphasize the single-media discriminative parts, but also enhance the cross-media fine-grained consistent pattern, and so learn more precious cross-media correlation to improve retrieval accuracy. Experimental results on 2 widely-used datasets with state-of-the-art methods verify the effectiveness of the proposed approach.

2   Related Work

2.1   Cross-Media Retrieval

Cross-media retrieval is designed to retrieve among different media types. As discussed in Sect. 1, the current mainstream methods can be summarized as common representation learning, including non-DNN based methods and DNN-based methods. These methods follow the idea that although representations of different media types are different, they share the same commons on semantic description. So in the semantic level, different media types can be represented in the same common space, leading to cross-media common representation.

Non-DNN based methods mainly learn linear projection for different media types. For example, canonical correlation analysis (CCA) [2] learns cross-media representation by maximizing the pairwise correlation, and is a classical baseline method for various cross-media problems as [15,16]. An alternative method is cross-modal factor analysis (CFA) [17], which minimizes the Frobenus norm of pairwise common representation. Beyond pairwise correlation, joint representation learning [3] is proposed to make use of semi-supervised regularization and semantic information, which can jointly learn common representation projections for up to five media types.

Instead of linear projection, DNN-based methods take deep neural network as the basic model for generating cross-media common representation. Recent years, DNN-based cross-media retrieval has become an active research topic, and many methods have been proposed [5,6,8,9]. For example, the architecture of Bimodal AE [5] takes two modalities as input, and has a middle code layer for common representation. CMDN [8] is proposed to simultaneously consider inter-modality and intra-modality information in a hierarchical multi-network architecture, which improves the retrieval accuracy. Wei et al. [9] propose to use CNN pre-trained with ImageNet as the feature extractor for images, and show the effectiveness of CNN feature in cross-media retrieval.

Existing methods usually focus on correlation in the level of whole media instance [2,3,9]. They take the whole media instances as input and learn correlation among them. However, close semantic correlation usually lies in specific parts of cross-media data, instead of whole data. The above methods ignore the fine-grained information. Note that some recent works as [10,11] first adopt instance segmentation to obtain several patches for media instances, and then use these patches indiscriminately as input. However, the importances of different parts are usually different. Taking text as example, not all words or sentences are semantically discriminative and have strong correlation with other media types. Some of them can even contain noisy information, and limit the effectiveness of correlation learning.

2.2   Attention Mechanism

Attention mechanism aims to find the "important" parts within a whole media instance, which has been applied to image and language processing. For example, visual attention models can select and focus on the regions containing discriminative information, such as the work of [12] which selects the regions that by recurrent attention model for multiple object recognition. Similarly, textual attention models are proposed to find the alignments between input and output text for helping deal with long-term dependency. Such methods have been applied to problems like question answering [13] and text generation [18].

Attention mechanism has also widely-used in problems involving multimedia, such as image caption [19] and visual QA [14,20]. For example, Lu et al. [20] propose the method of co-attention, which integrates visual and textual attention to guide each other for better natural symmetry between image and question. Note that the attention weights of text and image are different in [20], and it needs image and text as input at the same time, so cannot support cross-media retrieval.

Our proposed ACLN approach takes an attention-sharing strategy for cross-media retrieval. That is to say, the inputs of image and text share the common attention weights to enhance the cross-media fine-grained consistent pattern, which helps learn better common representation for cross-media retrieval.

3　Attention-Sharing Correlation Learning

In this paper, we take image and text as examples to show the ACLN approach, while it can be applied for other media types. The overview of our ACLN is shown as Fig. 1, which can be viewed as an end-to-end architecture with three parts, namely (1) local feature extraction, (2) attention-sharing learning, and (3) common representation generation.

For training stage, there are two types of cross-media correlation considered by ACLN. The first is co-existence relationship (specifically pairwise correlation in this paper), which means that data of different media types exist as a whole and have close relevance; the second is common semantic information, which means that data in each pair have the same semantics, i.e., they share the same semantic label. For testing stage, image or text can serve as input independently, and ACLN can generate common representation for them to perform cross-media retrieval with distance measurement.

We denote training data as $D_{tr} = \{D_{tr}^I, D_{tr}^T\}$, where $D_{tr}^I = \{i_p, y_p\}_{p=1}^{n_{tr}}$, and $D_{tr}^T = \{t_p, y_p\}_{p=1}^{n_{tr}}$. i_p and t_p means p-th paired image and text data, y_p means their shared label, and n_{tr} denotes the number of training pairs. Testing data is denoted as $D_{te} = \{D_{te}^I, D_{te}^T\}$, where $D_{te}^I = \{i_p\}_{p=1}^{n_{te}}$, $D_{te}^T = \{t_p\}_{p=1}^{n_{te}}$, and n_{te} means the number of testing data. The aim of ACLN is to generate common representation for D_{te}^I and D_{te}^T.

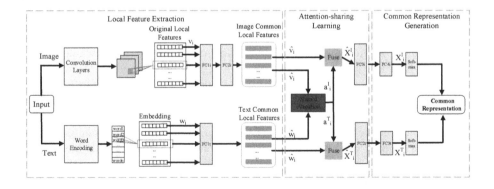

Fig. 1. An overview of our attention-sharing correlation learning network (ACLN).

3.1 Local Feature Extraction

The part of local feature extraction aims to extract the fine-grained representation for image regions and text words, and these fine-grained representations will be further fed into the attention-sharing learning part.

For a text t_p, it is encoded as 1-hot representations (vectors with only one dimension set as 1 and the others set as 0) of words and get $H(t_p) = \{w_1, ..w_T\}$ following [20], where T is the word number in t_p, $w_i \in R^{V*1}$ and V is the vocabulary size of all texts. Then we can embed each word to a representation vector as follows:

$$\hat{w}_i = W_e w_i, W_e \in R^{d_a * V} \tag{1}$$

where W_e is the weight parameters learned in the training stage of the network.

So we have the local features of text with the activation function $tanh$:

$$L(t_p) = \{tanh(\hat{w}_1), .., tanh(\hat{w}_T)\} \tag{2}$$

For an image input, we use the convolutional layers to get the image feature maps. In this paper, we take AlexNet [21] as the basic model for image. The original local features of image are denoted as $C(i_p) = \{v_1, .., v_N\}, v_i \in R^{d_i * 1}$, where the v_i is a feature vector extracted from the feature maps in spatial regions i, and N is the number of regions. Specially, we use the output of the pool5 as image local feature, and construct v_i with the value of spatial region i in each feature map. Then the local feature vectors will pass through a fully-connected layer which maps them to the same dimension as the text features (i.e., d_a here). So we have the image local features $L(i_p)$:

$$\hat{v}_i = tanh(W_{pre} v_i), W \in R^{d_a * d_i} \tag{3}$$
$$L(i_p) = \{\hat{v}_1, .., \hat{v}_N\} \tag{4}$$

where W_{pre} is the parameter of the fully-connected layer (FC1i).

At last, both the local features of images ant texts will pass through a fully-connected layer (FC2i and FC1t in Fig. 1) to convert them as *common local features*. For convenience, here we take $\hat{w}$ and $\hat{v}$ as the common local features, and have:

$$X^{\hat{w}} = tanh(W_{fc2i} \hat{w}) \tag{5}$$
$$X^{\hat{v}} = tanh(W_{fc1t} \hat{v}) \tag{6}$$

where $W_{fc2i}, W_{fc1t} \in R^{d_a * d_a}$ are the weight parameters of the fully connected layers FC2i and FC1t.

3.2 Attention-Sharing Learning

In this part, we adopt an attention-sharing structure to select the common local features which capture the correlation between two media types and then fuse to get global features.

Briefly, we adopt an attention function shared by common local features of both images and texts, and generate the attention weight vector for fusing the common local features to be the global features. Here we let $X = \{x_1, .., x_n\}$ be either the common local features of text or image for convenience, where n denotes the total number of common local features of an image or text, so we have:

$$h_i = tanh(W_a x_i) \tag{7}$$

$$a_i = \frac{e^{h_i}}{\sum_{k=1}^{n} e^{h_k}} \tag{8}$$

$$\hat{X} = \sum_{i=1}^{n} a_i x_i \tag{9}$$

where $W_a \in R^{1*d_a}$ is the weight parameter shared by all the common local features as the attention weight, which is learned to capture the fine-grained correlation between images and texts. And $\hat{X}$ is the global feature to the input X.

Note that the attention-sharing structure is to capture the fine-grained consistent patterns between different media types. Because the input is paired data, we simply assume that they share the relevant global semantics. With this in mind, we adopt the constraint that paired instances will have similar global features, letting the fusion process focus more on the local features with close correlation.

Specifically, we use the cosine similarity as the risk. For the paired global image feature $\hat{X}_i^I$ and text feature $\hat{X}_i^T$, the discrepancy of the paired feature is defined as:

$$d(\hat{X}_i^I, \hat{X}_i^T) = \frac{< \hat{X}_i^I, \hat{X}_i^T >}{\|\hat{X}_i^I\|\|\hat{X}_i^T\|} \tag{10}$$

Then we have the correlation loss as:

$$L_{corr} = \lambda \sum_{1}^{n} d(\hat{X}_i^I, \hat{X}_i^T) \tag{11}$$

where $\lambda > 0$ is a penalty parameter of the correlation loss.

3.3 Common Representation Generation

In this part, we use two fully-connected layers to obtain the final representation with the labels. Both the image and text global features will pass through two fully-connected layers and a softmax layer to generate the common representations. The semantic loss is defined as:

$$L_{Se} = \frac{1}{n} \sum_{i=1}^{n} f_s(X_i^I, L_i, \theta) + f_s(X_i^T, L_i, \theta) \tag{12}$$

where $f_s(X, L, \theta)$ is the softmax loss function:

$$f_s(X, L, \theta) = -log\frac{e^{\theta_L X}}{\sum_{j=1}^{c} e^{\theta_j X}} \tag{13}$$

where X is the output of the last fully-connected layer with an instance, L is the label of the instance, c is the total category number of the data and θ is the parameter of the network.

It should be noted that the proposed ACLN is an end-to-end network, and the correlation loss (L_{corr}) and semantic loss (L_{Se}) can be considered jointly. In training stage, by optimization with RMSProp, we can minimize the total loss to train the whole network. In the testing stage, we use the predicted probability vectors as the final common representation for performing cross-media retrieval.

4   Experiments

This section presents the experiments for verifying the effectiveness of the proposed method. We adopted 2 widely-used cross-media datasets and 7 compared methods with 2 retrieval tasks in our experiments.

4.1   Details of the Deep Architecture

In the implementation, we adopt Torch to develop our model. We use the Rnsorop optimizer with a base learning rate $4e - 4$, momentum 0.99 and weight-decay $1e - 8$, and set the batch size to be 20. Particularly, the learning rate of FC3i and FC4i is set to be $4e - 5$ on the Wikipedia dataset. The five convolutional layers of AlexNet are pre-trained with ImageNet from the Caffe Model Zoo and fine-tuned with the images in each dataset. In the training stage, the weights of the convolutional are frozen. The text local feature (and the common local feature) is a 512-dimentional vector after embedding, i.e. $d_a = 512$. The original image local feature is a 256-dimensional vector so that $d_i = 256$. We also apply dropout with probability 0.5 on each layer. We use the CosineEmbeddingCriterion layer to calculate the correlation with the margin as 0 and penalty λ as 1.

4.2   Dataset Introduction

This section introduces the 2 datasets adopted for the experiments, namely Wikipedia dataset and NUS-WIDE-10k dataset.

Wikipedia dataset [15] is widely-used for cross-media retrieval evaluation as [3,7]. It is based on "featured articles" in Wikipedia which contains 2,866 image/text pairs with 10 high-level semantic categories. In each pair, the text describes the image with several paragraphs, so they have close correlation. Following [7], the dataset is randomly split into three parts: 2,173 pairs are selected as training set, 462 pairs are selected as testing set, and 231 pairs are used for as validation set.

NUS-WIDE-10k dataset [7] is a subset of NUS-WIDE dataset [22]. NUS-WIDE dataset contains about 270,000 images with several corresponding tags which are regarded as text in the experiments. NUS-WIDE-10k dataset is constructed with 10,000 image/text pairs which are randomly selected from 10 largest categories in NUS-WIDE dataset and each category has 1,000 pairs of images and text. Following [7], the dataset is randomly split into three parts: 8,000 pairs for training, 1,000 pairs for testing and 1000 pairs for validation.

It should be noted that although the splits of these datasets have validation sets, the ACLN and compared methods don't need validation sets as input. That is to say, validation sets will not be used in the whole experiments.

4.3   Compared Methods and Input Settings

Totally 7 state-of-the-art methods are compared in the experiments: CCA [2], CFA [17], KCCA (with Gaussian kernel) [23], JRL [3], LGCFL [4], Corr-AE [7], and Deep-SM [9]. Among these, CCA, CFA, KCCA, JRL, LGCFL are non-DNN based methods, while Corr-AE and Deep-SM are DNN-based methods. Note that Deep-SM is also an end-to-end DNN-based method.

For image, the processing is end-to-end in ACLN, and it directly takes the image pixels as input. Deep-SM also takes original images as input. However, all they other methods including CCA, CFA, KCCA, JRL, LGCFL and Corr-AE can only take feature vector as input. For them we take the same fine-tuned AlexNet adopted by ACLN, and further fine-tuned to convergence with the images. Then we extract the output of the FC7 layer in the AlexNet as the feature vector. For text, ACLN also has the end-to-end processing ability, and takes the original text as input. For all the compared methods, we train a basic ACLN network which simply averages the common local features without attention and then extract the output of the FC2t layer as the feature vector.

4.4   Evaluation Metrics

Two retrieval tasks are conducted in the experiments: text retrieval by image query, and image retrieval by text query, which are briefly denoted as Image→Text and Text→Image. We first obtain the common representation for all testing images and text with all compared methods and our ACLN. Then taking Image→Text task as example, we take each image as query, and measure the cosine distance between the common representation of the query image and all texts. Finally, we get a ranking list according to the distances and then compute the mean average precision (MAP) for it to evaluate the retrieval results.

We choose MAP score as the evaluation metric because it jointly considers the precision and ranking of results, and it can be used for fair and comprehensive evaluation. The MAP scores are computed as all queries' mean of average precision (AP), and AP is computed as:

$$AP = \frac{1}{R} \sum_{k=1}^{n} \frac{R_k}{k} \times rel_k \tag{14}$$

where R denotes relevant item number in test set (according to the label in our experiments), R_k denotes the relevant item number in top k results, n denotes the test set size, and $rel_k = 1$ means the k-th result is relevant, and 0 otherwise.

4.5   Experimental Results

Table 1 shows the MAP scores in our experiments on the 2 datasets. On Wikipedia dataset, ACLN achieves the highest MAP score of 0.430. Comparing with the best compared method Deep-SM, ACLN obtains an inspiring improvement of 0.036. Similar trends can be seen on NUS-WIDE-10k dataset, where our ACLN remains the highest MAP score of 0.487. This is because that the compared methods only focus on correlation in the level of whole media instance, and ignore the fine-grained information. ACLN can not only emphasize the single-media discriminative parts, but also enhance the cross-media fine-grained consistent pattern, and so learn more precious cross-media correlation to improve retrieval accuracy.

Table 2 shows the MAP scores of our baselines and the complete ACLN. ACLN (Baseline) means that the network is trained without the attention which simply averages the common local features. ACLN (Separate Attention) means that network is trained with separate attention which adopts independent attention weights for images and text. Except for the above differences, the rest parts of the three baselines keep the same with complete ACLN.

Table 1. MAP scores of our ACLN and compared methods.

Dataset	Method	Task		
		Image→Text	Text→Image	Average
Wikipedia dataset	CCA	0.125	0.124	0.124
	Corr-AE	0.188	0.202	0.195
	CFA	0.368	0.336	0.352
	KCCA	0.340	0.316	0.328
	JRL	0.371	0.330	0.351
	LGCFL	0.390	0.321	0.356
	Deep-SM	0.441	0.347	0.394
	Our ACLN	**0.446**	**0.415**	**0.430**
NUS-WIDE -10k dataset	CCA	0.121	0.122	0.121
	Corr-AE	0.185	0.143	0.164
	CFA	0.407	0.411	0.409
	KCCA	0.402	0.427	0.415
	JRL	0.442	0.473	0.457
	LGCFL	0.421	0.440	0.431
	Deep-SM	0.465	0.445	0.455
	Our ACLN	**0.480**	**0.495**	**0.487**

Table 2. MAP scores of our ACLN and the baselines.

Dataset	Method	Task		
		Image→Text	Text→Image	Average
Wikipedia dataset	ACLN (Baseline)	0.436	0.351	0.394
	ACLN (Separate Attention)	0.429	0.396	0.413
	Our ACLN	**0.446**	**0.415**	**0.430**
NUS-WIDE -10k dataset	ACLN (Baseline)	0.458	0.454	0.456
	ACLN (Separate Attention)	0.470	0.487	0.479
	Our ACLN	**0.480**	**0.495**	**0.487**

It can be seen that the results of ACLN (Separate Attention) are better than ACLN (Baseline), which shows that the attention mechanism helps provide fine-grained clues for improving the accuracy of cross-media retrieval. The complete ACLN is even better than ACLN (Separate Attention), which shows that the attention-sharing structure enhances the cross-media fine-grained consistent pattern for higher retrieval accuracy. The above baseline experiments show the separate contribution of our ACLN architecture, and verify its effectiveness.

5   Conclusion

This paper has proposed the attention-sharing correlation learning network (ACLN), which is designed to generate cross-media common representation with fine-grained discrimination learning for cross-media retrieval. ACLN first extracts local features from cross-media data, and then lets them share the common attention weights, so that the attention of different media types can be learned coordinately according to pairwise correlation and semantic information. It can not only emphasize the single-media discriminative parts, but also enhance the cross-media fine-grained consistent pattern, and so learn more precious cross-media correlation to improve retrieval accuracy. Experimental results on 2 widely-used datasets with state-of-the-art methods verify the effectiveness of the proposed approach. The future work lies in two aspects: first, we intend to incorporate the attention learning of more than two media types into our framework; second, we will apply ACLN to other applications like image caption to further verify its effectiveness.

Acknowledgments. This work was supported by National Natural Science Foundation of China under Grants 61371128 and 61532005.

References

1. Lew, M.S., Sebe, N., Djeraba, C., Jain, R.: Content-based multimedia information retrieval: state of the art and challenges. ACM Trans. Multimedia Comput. Commun. Appl. (TOMCCAP) **2**(1), 1–19 (2006)

2. Hotelling, H.: Relations between two sets of variates. Biometrika **28**(3/4), 321–377 (1936)
3. Zhai, X., Peng, Y., Xiao, J.: Learning cross-media joint representation with sparse and semi-supervised regularization. IEEE Trans. Circ. Syst. Video Technol. (TCSVT) **24**(6), 965–978 (2014)
4. Kang, C., Xiang, S., Liao, S., Xu, C., Pan, C.: Learning consistent feature representation for cross-modal multimedia retrieval. IEEE Trans. Multimedia (TMM). **17**(3), 370–381 (2015)
5. Ngiam, J., Khosla, A., Kim, M., Nam, J., Lee, H., Ng, A.Y.: Multimodal deep learning. In: International Conference on Machine Learning (ICML), pp. 689–696 (2011)
6. Srivastava, N., Salakhutdinov, R.: Learning representations for multimodal data with deep belief nets. In: International Conference on Machine Learning Workshop (2012)
7. Feng, F., Wang, X., Li, R.: Cross-modal retrieval with correspondence autoencoder. In: ACM International Conference on Multimedia (ACM MM), pp. 7–16 (2014)
8. Peng, Y., Huang, X., Qi, J.: Cross-media shared representation by hierarchical learning with multiple deep networks. In: International Joint Conference on Artificial Intelligence (IJCAI), pp. 3846–3853 (2016)
9. Wei, Y., Lu, C., Wei, S., Liu, L., Zhu, Z., Yan, S.: Cross-modal retrieval with CNN visual features: a new baseline. IEEE Trans. Cybern. (TCYB) **47**(2), 449–460 (2017)
10. Peng, Y., Zhai, X., Zhao, Y., Huang, X.: Semi-Supervised cross-media feature learning with unified patch graph regularization. IEEE Trans. Circ. Syst. Video Technol. (TCSVT) **26**(3), 583–596 (2016)
11. Peng, Y., Qi, J., Huang, X., Yuan, Y.: CCL: cross-modal correlation learning with multi-grained fusion by hierarchical network (2017). arXiv:1704.02116
12. Ba, J., Mnih, V., Kavukcuoglu, K.: Multiple object recognition with visual attention (2014). arXiv:1412.7755
13. Kumar, A., Irsoy, O., Ondruska, P., Iyyer, M., Bradbury, J., Gulrajani, I., Zhong, V., Paulus, R., Socher, R.: Ask me anything: dynamic memory networks for natural language processing. In: International Conference on Machine Learning (ICML), pp. 1378–1387 (2016)
14. Yang, Z., He, X., Gao, J., Deng, L., Smola, A.J.: Stacked attention networks for image question answering. In: IEEE Conference on Computer Vision and Pattern Recognition (CVPR), pp. 21–29 (2016)
15. Rasiwasia, N., Costa Pereira, J., Coviello, E., Doyle, G., Lanckriet, G.R., Levy, R., Vasconcelos, N.: A new approach to cross-modal multimedia retrieval. In: ACM International Conference on Multimedia (ACM MM), pp. 251–260 (2010)
16. Ranjan, V., Rasiwasia, N., Jawahar, C.V.: Multi-label cross-modal retrieval. In: IEEE International Conference on Computer Vision (ICCV), pp. 4094–4102 (2015)
17. Li, D., Dimitrova, N., Li, M., Sethi, I.K.: Multimedia content processing through cross-modal association. In: ACM International Conference on Multimedia (ACM MM), pp. 604–611 (2003)
18. Li, J., Luong, M.-T., Jurafsky, D.: A Hierarchical Neural Autoencoder for Paragraphs and Documents. In: The Association for Computer Linguistics (ACL), pp. 1106–1115 (2015)

19. Xu, K., Ba, J., Kiros, R., Cho, K., Courville, A.C., Salakhutdinov, R., Zemel, R.S., Bengio, Y.: Show, attend and tell: neural image caption generation with visual attention. In: International Conference on Machine Learning (ICML), pp. 2048–2057 (2015)

20. Lu, J., Yang, J., Batra, D., Parikh, D.: Hierarchical question-image co-attention for visual question answering. In: Annual Conference on Neural Information Processing Systems (NIPS), pp. 289–297 (2016)

21. Krizhevsky, A., Sutskever, I., Hinton, G.E.: ImageNet classification with deep convolutional neural networks. In: Annual Conference on Neural Information Processing Systems (NIPS), pp. 1106–1114 (2012)

22. Chua, T.-S., Tang, J., Hong, R., Li, H., Luo, Z., Zheng, Y.: NUS-WIDE: a real-world web image database from National University of Singapore. In: ACM International Conference on Image and Video Retrieval (CIVR), p. 48 (2009)

23. Hardoon, D.R., Szedmák, S., Shawe-Taylor, J.: Canonical correlation analysis: an overview with application to learning methods. Neural Comput. **16**(12), 2639–2664 (2004)

A Method for Extracting Eye Movement and Response Characteristics to Distinguish Depressed People

Chao Le, Huimin Ma$^{(\boxtimes)}$, and Yidong Wang

Department of Electronic Engineering, Tsinghua University, Beijing, China
lec15@mails.tsinghua.edu.cn, mhmpub@mail.tsinghua.edu.cn

Abstract. Eye movement is an important characteristic in the field of image processing and psychology, which reflects people's attention bias. How to design a paradigm with the function of psychological discrimination to extract significant eye movement characteristic is a challenging task. In this paper, we present a novel psychology evaluation system with eye tracking. Negative and positive background images from IAPS and Google are chosen based on the Minnesota Multiphasic Personality Inventory (MMPI). Meanwhile, negative and positive face images are used as emotional foreground. The location of the face images is shown on the left or right randomly. In this paradigm, people with different psychological status have different characteristics of eye movement length, fixation points and response time. The experimental results show that these characteristics have significant discriminability and can be used to distinguish depressed and normal people effectively.

Keywords: Psycological status classification · Eye tracking
Emotional images · C-P experiment

1 Introduction

Psychological scale is commonly used to screen for psychological problems based on the theory about the attention bias of emotional disorder people [1], such as the Depression Anxiety Stress Scale (DASS) [2], Cognitive Emotion Regulation Questionnaire (CERQ) [3] and Mini International Neuropsychiatric Interview [4]. However, the scales have some shortcomings: Children may not understand the problems in scales and the subjects may deliberately choose some options which do not meet the actual status.

The research on attention bias and psychological problem by using image substitution has the advantages of objectivity and intuitive reaction. It has become an important method of psychology research but the relationship between image semantics and psychological status still remains difficulties. Anderson et al. [14] introduced text and natural scene images to capture the phenomenon of negative attraction. More elements related with image are gradually introduced into

© Springer International Publishing AG 2017
Y. Zhao et al. (Eds.): ICIG 2017, Part I, LNCS 10666, pp. 489–500, 2017.
https://doi.org/10.1007/978-3-319-71607-7_43

behavioral experiments, such as informative picture, emotional faces [5,6]. Bao et al. [7] made a novel study on the semantic mapping between MMPI and scene images, providing an affective image library and marked those images as positive or negative. Response time is widely used in psychology research as an important characteristic. Li et al. [8], Wang [12] proposed a paradigm based on natural scene images and emotional human face pictures. They used the keyboard response time to realize the distinction between different people's mental states. These studies focused on the observation of different people's responses according to the analysis about how people perceiving and dealing with image stimulation.

In addition to the keyboard, eye tracker has been used in psychological experiments in recent years. Non-contact eye movement information is directly captured with a high degree of acceptance and precision. In recent years, many scholars have adopted eye movement method to analyze problem. Bloem et al. [11] used visual images to discover the role of gaze in mental imagery and memory. Duque and Vázquez [10] used positive and negative emotional faces to observe the double attention bias in clinical depression with eye tracking.

However, these methods use the eye movement heat map or fixation points as features, while ignoring the importance of eye movement length and response time which reflect the subjects' overall status in the experiment. On the other hand, those methods based on keyboard response time may not fully reflect people's attention, since the response time is related with several factors, such as the saliency of the face expression and the age of people. The eye movement characteristics extraction, which relies on the experimental paradigm and eye movement data processing algorithm, needs to be able to reflect the subject's psychological characteristics accurately. Furthermore, the combination of keyboard and eye movement describes the people's psychological status better. The fusion of keyboard response time and eye movement reflects the unit response of subject and generate high-dimensional features, which also improve the classification accuracy.

In this paper, we present a whole set of system with a new paradigm, the face images are shown at the left or right side in the background with same probability. We collect keyboard response time of identification for emotional faces and record the eye movement during the experiment. By analyzing the collected data, we find that there exists significant discrepancies between normal and abnormal people. The accuracy of the experiment is improved compared with Li [8] and Wang [12] 's methods.

2   Experiment

2.1   Materials and Participants

We use 16 emotional face images (8 positive and 8 negative) from Taiwanese Facial Expression Image Database [16] as the foreground stimuli, 80 emotional images (40 positive and 40 negative images) chosen from ThuPIS [8] as the background scenes. All the face images are converted to gray. All the images in

ThuPIS have been choosen from IAPS [17] and Google and screened based on the Bao [7] 's method. The sample of face and scene images are shown in Fig. 1.

30 patients with depression disorder (23 males and 7 females, age Mean = 22.5, Standard Deviation = 3.86) are from two hospitals, 30 normal controls (18 males and 12 females, age M = 23.2, SD = 0.69) are university students.

Fig. 1. The example of facial expressions and scene picture. The first row is positive faces and scenes, the second row is negative faces and scenes.

2.2 Model

The whole system is divided into 4 parts as shown in Fig. 2.

Experimental paradigm. The purpose of the experiment paradigm is to observe and analyze the subjects' response data through the emotional images. Detailed content is introduced in Sect. 2.3.

Data collection. The eye movement data are collected by Tobii eye tracker, which is popular with psychological research. Eye tracker is used to record the eye movement characteristics in visual information processing. The psychological activities have a direct or indirect relationship with eye movement. Every subjects were calibrated by using the Tobii EyeX Interaction Application before the start of the test. The subjects' response time is collected by keyboard or button.

Characteristics extraction. The collected data is converted into a feature vector by a fusion algorithm which is introduced in Sect. 3.1.

Data analysis. In this system, the Support Vector Machine (SVM) [16] is used to classify normal people and depressed people, we also use SPSS (Statistical Product and Service Solutions, a software) for significance test.

2.3 Procedure

The experiment is Competing-Priming effect experiment (C-P). Compared with the former researches [7,8], it puts forward some improvements in the location of face images. The face images are shown at the left or right side in the background with same probability. The participates are required to read the instructions on the screen. Procedure of this experiment is shown in Fig. 2. First, participants are given the opportunity to practice 20 trials, then they will be asked to complete 80 formal experimental trials. At first, we present the background of scene and an emotional face appears on left or right side randomly after 500–1000 ms. Subjects need to make judgment by the button. This study focused on the competing and priming effect of the background. Eye tracking path, response time and the accuracy of each trial are recorded.

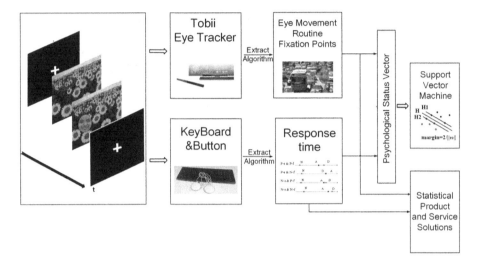

Fig. 2. The system model.

3   Reaction Characteristics Extraction

3.1   Extraction Algorithm

Eye Movement. F(x, y, z, t) is obtained at each moment by the Tobii eye tracker, indicating that the fixation point is at (x, y), and the distance from the screen to the eye is z at time t. The coordinate is shown in Fig. 3.

During a single group of experiments, the background image appears at time t_1, the foreground face appears at time t_2, the subject presses the key at time t_3. Then we construct three sets A, B, C according to these three time sets. **Set A** $= \{(x, y, t) | t_1 < t < t_2\}$, which represents the subjects' eye movement during the period from the appearance of the background to the appearance of the human face. During this time, the subjects focus on the background image, we call it cognitive period. **Set B** $= \{(x, y, t) | t_2 < t < t_3\}$, which is the period from the time when human face appears until the subjects make the decision. At this time, the subjects processed the foreground and the background images and make a button selection, we call it selective period. **Set C** $= \{(x, y, t) | t_1 < t < t_3\}$, which is the union of A and B, represents the eye movement data of whole trials.

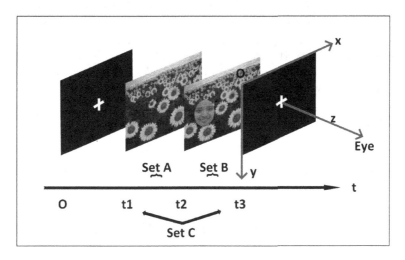

Fig. 3. Coordinate and procedure.

For a set of data with length n, $(x_1, y_1, t_1), \ldots, (x_n, y_n, t_n)$, we process the data in Fig. 4. Step 1, 2 confirm the continuity and length of data. Distance (i, i+1) is the pixel distance between point i and point i+1. Step 3 determines whether the data points are in the scope of screen. The final output is obtained by the merging of all steps.

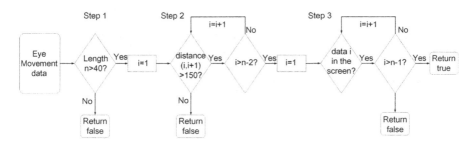

Fig. 4. Eye movement data preprocessing we need to determine the continuity and integrity of the data through three steps.

Eye movement path length is calculated as:

$$L = \sum_{i=1}^{n-1} \sqrt{(x_{i+1} - x_i)^2 + (y_{i+1} - y_i)^2}. \tag{1}$$

Salvucci and Goldberg [9] summarized some methods for calculating fixation points, including I-VT, I-HMM, I-DT, I-MST, I-AOI algorithm. In this paper we use I-VT (fast) and I-DT (accurate and robust) algorithm. I-VT algorithm calculates point-to-point velocities for each point, labels each point below velocity threshold as a fixation point and collapses consecutive fixation points into fixation groups. Velocity threshold is set to 900 pixels/second. I-DT algorithm sets dispersion threshold and duration threshold. Considering the image is a two-dimensional signal, we use Euclidean distance instead of Manhattan distance.

$$Dispersion \; D = max\sqrt{(x_i - x_j)^2 + (y_i - y_j)^2} \quad i,j \in [1, 2, \ldots n] \qquad (2)$$

The dispersion threshold is set to 30 pixels by including $1/2°$ to $1°$ of visual angle. The duration threshold is set to 83 ms (5 interval of eye tracker).

Fig. 5. The Example of eye tracking path. Every white circle represents that there is a fixation point. These 4 pictures all have positive face. The pictures show us eye movement path of normal people (first row) and depressed people (second row) (Color figure online)

The sample of eye movement path is shown in Fig. 5. The path starts from red, then changes through green to blue gradually. The human face image appears at the moment when line changes into green. That is, the red-green path is the cognitive path, the green-blue path is the selective path.

Response Time. We calculate the mean and variance of the collected data which is divided into four groups based on the combination of foreground and background. Specific algorithm is shown in Algorithm 1.

Algorithm 1. Keyboard response time preprocessing.

Require:

The set of keyboard response time (20X4).

Ensure:

The integrity and consistency of data.

1: The keyboard response time which is greater than 1200ms or less than 300ms is removed.

2: Remove the trials which are wrong judged.

3: When the total error rate is greater than 25%, the data of that experiment are removed.

4: Data of each experiment which is not fully completed are removed.

5: A trial which deviates from the mean value of the experiment more than three times the standard deviation is removed [13].

The purpose of the data preprocessing steps 1–4 is to remove the test data due to misunderstanding the experimental requirements or lack of concentration and the situation that participants were distracted in some trials. Step 5 removes abnormal test data caused by a series of external reasons, such as software abnormalities, database bugs.

We define the subscript 0 as negative, 1 as positive, 01 as the combination of negative scenes and positive face images, etc. Therefore, we obtained 4 response time and their mean value (M_{00}, M_{01}, M_{10}, M_{11}, M_M), 4 standard deviation and their mean value (STD_{00}, STD_{01}, STD_{10}, STD_{11}, STD_M).

3.2 Significance Test

We make significance test for mean time (M_{00}, M_{01}, M_{10}, M_{11}, M_M), length (L_{00}, L_{01}, L_{10}, L_{11}, L_M) and fixation points (P_{00}, P_{01}, P_{10}, P_{11}, P_M).

The independent-sample t test. T-test is to use t distribution theory to infer the probability of occurrence of the difference, so as to compare the difference between the two average. The significant for this context is the prospect of different attributes of the background and foreground, the different mental states of the people.

In the significance test, value F represents the ratio of the variance to the residual of regression model, value Sig is calculated according to value F.

3.3 SVM

We use SVM to discriminate the normal and depressed people's psychological status. The data forms achieved by our system are M_i(M_{00i}, M_{01i}, M_{10i}, M_{11i}, M_{Mi}) and their labels is $Y_i \in \{-1, 1\}$, i = 1, 2, ... N. We suppose that the first q samples are positive samples and the latter N-q samples are negative samples. There are two questions in the practical application of our system.

(i) The data collection is unbalanced between the two groups of people, depressed people's data is less than the normal people's data.

(ii) Under the condition of certain false alarm probability, the large-scale screening system needs higher accuracy of negative sample.

In view of the above problems, we need two different penalty factors C_+, C_- to substitute factor C in SVM algorithm, so the problem is:

$$min\varphi(\omega) = \frac{1}{2}\|\omega\|^2 + C_+ \sum_{i=1}^{q} \xi_i + C_- \sum_{i=q+1}^{N} \xi_i \qquad (3)$$

$$s.t. \begin{cases} Y_i(\omega \cdot M_i + b) - 1 + \xi_i \geq 0 \\ \xi_i \geq 0 \end{cases} i = 1, 2, \ldots N \qquad (4)$$

By using the Lagrangian function, the problem turns into Eqs. 5 and 6:

$$minQ(\alpha) = \frac{1}{2} \sum_{i=1}^{N} \sum_{j=1}^{N} \alpha_i \alpha_j Y_i Y_j M_i \cdot M_j \qquad (5)$$

$$s.t. \begin{cases} 0 \leq \alpha_i \leq C_+, i = 1, 2, \ldots, q \\ 0 \leq \alpha_j \leq C_-, j = q, q+1, \ldots, N \end{cases} \quad \sum_{i=1}^{N} Y_i \alpha_i = 0 \qquad (6)$$

After using the SMO algorithm iterations, we find the best set of α_i to divide the hyper plane. $C_- > C_+$ results that the weight of the negative sample is greater than the positive sample. This makes the classification hyperplane closer to the positive samples so as to achieve the purpose of screening. The same analysis is also suitable for length, fixation points and all kinds of their combinations.

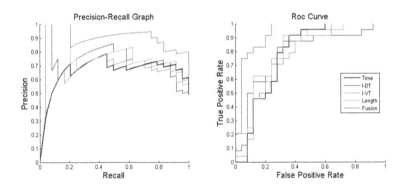

Fig. 6. The PR curve and ROC of single feature and fusion feature

4   Result

The histograms of the eye tracking length, fixation points and response time are shown in Fig. 7. The significant analysis of characteristics are shown in Tables 1, 2 and 3 (S = significant, NS = not significant).

We use these data to train a classifier through cross-validation and then to distinguish two types of people. We use these separate features and their fusion feature to train SVM models respectively. The results are shown in Table 4. The PR Curve and ROC are shown in Fig. 6. There are some inflection and turning points in the curve because of the scale of data and several classification error.

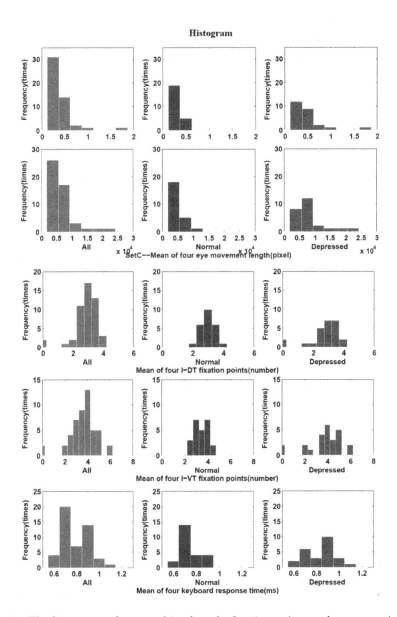

Fig. 7. The histogram of eye tracking length, fixation points and response time.

Table 1. The significant analysis of eye tracking length

Eye tracking length	Independent sample t-test			Eye tracking length	Independent sample t-test		
	F	Sig	5% level		F	Sig	5% level
L_{00}-Set C	6.267	.016	S	L_{00}-Set B	6.577	.014	S
L_{01}-Set C	3.622	.063	NS	L_{01}-Set B	4.028	.051	NS
L_{10}-Set C	5.342	.025	S	L_{10}-Set B	6.894	.012	S
L_{11}-Set C	3.159	.082	NS	L_{11}-Set B	4.058	.050	S
L_{M}-Set C	4.716	.035	S	L_{M}-Set B	5.442	.024	S

Table 2. The significant analysis of fixation points

Fixation points	I-DT independent sample t-test			I-VT independent sample t-test		
	F	Sig	5% level	F	Sig	5% level
P_{00}-Set C	5.006	.030	S	5.126	.028	S
P_{01}-Set C	4.915	.032	S	4.057	.050	S
P_{10}-Set C	4.907	.032	S	4.919	.032	S
P_{11}-Set C	3.818	.057	NS	3.945	.053	NS
P_{M}-Set C	3.460	.069	NS	4.851	.033	S

Table 3. The significant analysis of response time

Response time	Independent sample t-test		
	F	Sig	5% level
M_{00}-Set B	6.190	.016	S
M_{01}-Set B	5.287	.026	S
M_{10}-Set B	8.015	.007	S
M_{11}-Set B	.924	.341	NS
M_{00}-Set B	6.448	.014	S

Table 4. Results trained with single feature and fusion feature through cross-validation

Feature	Accuracy (%)	Recall (%)	Sensitivity (%)
Mean time	77.56	**91.67**	64
I-DT points	75.51	79.17	72
I-VT points	71.42	87.5	56
Length	79.59	91.67	68
L&I-DT&I-VT&MT $(C_{ab} = 2C_N)$	77.55	62.5	**92**
L&I-DT&I-VT&MT	**83.67**	91.67	76

5   Discussion

In this eye movement experimental paradigm, the emotional face images appear at left or right randomly. Compared with the paradigm with face images in the middle, this new method maintains the basic model of the case meanwhile promoting the psychological semantics of the task. Its advantage is obtaining better observation of the subjects' psychological status and avoiding some situations that the subjects who deliberately stare at the center of the screen to wait for the face images emerge. Moreover, the system uses the combination of the eye movement and response time improve the accuracy of classification.

After the screening of eye movement and response time data, we obtained 49 sets of data (24 normal, 25 abnormal). As shown in the histograms, the normal people's eye movement path length is shorter than the depressed people's length, which means that the depressed people need longer eye movement path in this experiment. The normal subjects' fixation points number is less than the depressed people's number, which means that the depressed people need more fixation points in this experiment. This result implies that depressed people need more attention to understand the picture. The response time of two groups is obviously a bimodal distribution, and the response time of normal people is faster than that of depressed people.

According to the results of significant analysis, most of the eye movement length, number of fixation points and response time characteristics are significant. The result indicates that these features are discriminative reflections of the subjects' psychological status. While the P_{11}-Set C, M_{11}-Set B, L_{11}-Set C, L_{01}-Set B and L_{01}-Set B aren't significant in independent sample t-test, which means there are no significant differences between the two groups in the case of positive facial stimulation or positivie background initiating. It is an powerful evidence for the negative attraction phenomenon in depressed people.

The eye movement length reflects the scanning distance of the subject's attention. The number of fixation points shows the area concerned by subjects. The keyboard response time shows the time between the stimulus presentation and the beginning of the reaction. Through cross-validation, the classification accuracy are 77.56%, 75.51%, 71.42% and 79.59% in the using of these characteristics respectively, indicating these features are discriminative. Although the accuracy of response time is not bad, its sensitivity is lower than fixation points and eye movement length. According to the trait of duration sensitive and locally adaptive, I-DT algorithm get a higher accuracy than I-VT algorithm and its sensitivity is the highest in single feature. The fusion of keyboard response time, eye movement length and fixation points improve the classification accuracy to 83.67%, what is more important is that the increase is due to sensitivity. By adjusting the penalty weights of the positive and negative samples to meet the demand of the screening system, the sensitivity increases from 76% to 92% with the expense of recall. The PR curve and the ROC also show that the fusion feature performs better than the individual features. The above results confirm the effectiveness of feature fusion in our system.

Acknowledgements. This research is supported by The National Key Research and Development Program of China (2016YFB0100901-1) and The National Natural Science Foundation of China (NSFC61171113).

References

1. Macleod, C., Mathews, A., Tata, P.: Attentional bias in emotional disorders. J. Abnorm. Psychol. **95**(1), 15–20 (1986)
2. Lovibond, S.H., Lovibond, P.F.: Manual for the depression anxiety stress scales. Psychology Foundation of Australia (1996)
3. Garnefski, N., Kraaij, V., Spinhoven, P.: Negative life events, cognitive emotion regulation and emotional problems. Personal. Individ. Differ. **30**, 1311–1327 (2001)
4. Pinninti, N.R., et al.: MINI international neuropsychiatric schedule: clinical utility and patient acceptance. Eur. Psychiatry **18**, 361–364 (2003)
5. Laeng, B., Bloem, I.M., D'Ascenzo, S., et al.: Scrutinizing visual images: the role of gaze in mental imagery and memory. Cognition **131**(2), 263–283 (2014)
6. van Harmelen, A.-L., van Tol, M.-J., Demenescu, L.R., et al.: Enhanced amygdala reactivity to emotional faces in adults reporting childhood emotional maltreatment. Soc. Cogn. Affect Neurosci. **8**(4), 362–369 (2012)
7. Bao, S., Ma, H., Li, W., et al.: Discrimination of positive facial expressions is more susceptible to affective background scenes. Int. Proc. Econ. Dev. Res. (2014)
8. Li, W., Ma, H., Wang, X., Shi, D.: Features Derived From Behavioral Experiments To Distinguish Mental Healthy People From Depressed People. Acta Press (2014)
9. Salvucci, D.D., Goldberg, J.H.: Identifying fixations and saccades in eye-tracking protocols. In: Proceedings of the 2000 Symposium on Eye Tracking Research and applications, pp. 71–78 (2000)
10. Duque, A., Vázquez, C.: Double attention bias for positive and negative emotional faces in clinical depression: evidence from an eye-tracking study. J. Behav. Ther. Exp. Psychiatry **46**, 107–114 (2015)
11. Bloem, I.M., D'Ascenzo, S., Tommasi, L.: Scrutinizing visual images: the role of gaze in mental imagery and memory. Cognition **131**, 263–283 (2014)
12. Wang, Y., Ma, H.: Identification differences among people under context of complex images. In: Bioelectronics and Bioinformatics (ISBB) (2015)
13. Bradley, B.P., Mogg, K., Millar, N., et al.: Selective processing of negative information: effects of clinical anxiety, concurrent depression, and awareness. J. Abnorm. Psychol. **104**(3), 532 (1995)
14. Anderson, E., Siegel, E.H., Bliss-Moreau, E., et al.: The visual impact of gossip. Science **332**(6036), 1446–1448 (2011)
15. Cortes, C., Vapnik, V.: Support-vector networks. Mach. Learn. **20**(3), 273–297 (1995)
16. Chen, L.F., Yen,Y.S.: Taiwanese Facial Expression Image Database. Brain Mapping Laboratory, Institute of Brain Science, National Yang-Ming University, Taipei (2007)
17. Lang, P.J., Bradley, M.M., Cuthbert, B.N.: International affective picture system (IAPS): affective ratings of pictures and instruction manual. Technical report A-8. University of Florida, Gainesville, FL (2008)

Long-Distance/Environment Face Image Enhancement Method for Recognition

Zhengning Wang[✉], Shanshan Ma, Mingyan Han, Guang Hu,
and Shuaicheng Liu

University of Electronic Science and Technology of China, Chengdu, China
zhengning.wang@uestc.edu.cn

Abstract. With the increase of distance and the influence of environmental factors, such as illumination and haze, the face recognition accuracy is significantly lower than that of indoor close-up images. In order to solve this problem, an effective face image enhancement method is proposed in this paper. This algorithm is a nonlinear transformation which combines gamma and logarithm transformation. Therefore, it is called: G-log. The G-Log algorithm can perform the following functions: (1) eliminate the influence of illumination; (2) increase image contrast and equalize histogram; (3) restore the high-frequency components and detailed information; (4) improve visual effect; (5) enhance recognition accuracy. Given a probe image, the procedure of face alignment, enhancement and matching is executed against all gallery images. For comparing the effects of different enhancement algorithms, all probe images are processed by different enhancement methods and identical face alignment, recognition modules. Experiment results show that G-Log method achieves the best effect both in matching accuracy and visual effect. Long-distance uncontrolled environment face recognition accuracy has been greatly improved, up to 98%, 98%, 95% for 60-, 100-, 150-m images after processed by G-Log from original 95%, 89%, 70%.

Keywords: Face recognition · Image enhancement
Uncontrolled environment · Long-distance

1 Introduction

In recent years, automatic face recognition has made great progress, but most efforts are focused on the situations where face images are taken at a close distance with uniform illumination in the controllable scene [1]. Face recognition accuracy greatly reduced when the scene is not controllable, especially with the increase of distance and the influence of environment. In order to better illustrate the impact of external factors on image quality, face images taken at a distance of 150 m are shown in Fig. 1 and the images taken at 1, 60, 100 and 150 m are shown in Fig. 2.

According to the Figs. 1 and 2, the characteristics of face images taken at a long distance can be summarized as: (1) the influence of illumination; (2) the loss of high-frequency components; (3) fewer facial pixels and detailed information. Generally,

© Springer International Publishing AG 2017
Y. Zhao et al. (Eds.): ICIG 2017, Part I, LNCS 10666, pp. 501–511, 2017.
https://doi.org/10.1007/978-3-319-71607-7_44

long-distance face images are captured in an uncontrolled outdoor environment. Therefore, it will be seriously affected by the illumination, as shown in the right image of Fig. 1, the face is in the shadow.

Fig. 1. The examples of face image taken at 150 m

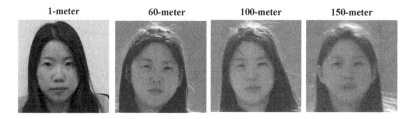

Fig. 2. The comparison of face images taken at 1, 60, 100 and 150 m, respectively

To solve the problems of image quality degradation and non-uniform illumination result from long distance, we proposed a new method to enhance the image quality and restore image detail features. In our algorithm, the nonlinear transformation is adopted, which is a combination of gamma and logarithmic transformation, giving raise to the name of the method: G-Log algorithm. By using our algorithm, both visual effect and recognition accuracy can be improved greatly.

2   Related Work

Our work is based on the LDHF database released in 2012 [2]. It contains 1-m indoor, 60-, 100-, and 150-m outdoor visible-light and near-infrared images of 100 subjects. The examples of LDHF are shown in Fig. 1. Most of the outdoor images in LDHF are influenced by the fog or the illumination, as shown in Fig. 1, the images are foggy or back-lighted.

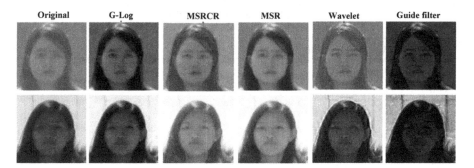

Fig. 3. Two examples enhanced facial images (from left to right): original 150-m images and images enhanced by G-Log, MSRCR, MSR, wavelet decomposition, Guild filter combined with dark channel.

Image enhancement is used to enhance the detail and useful information in the image, improve the visual effect, and purposefully emphasize the global or local features [3]. There are many existing works that focus on image enhancement, including MSRCR [4], MSR [5], wavelet decomposition [6], Guild filter [7], etc. All these algorithms are evaluated accordingly with respect to their performances of improving the recognition accuracy. Moreover, we have performed extensive experiments and summarized the results, according to the characteristics of the long-distance face, following which the G-Log is proposed. Subjective visual comparison is shown in Fig. 3. We can see that our G-Log algorithm shows the best results against others.

Recently, face recognition with Deep Learning has achieved the surprising result [8]. Therefore, to compare the difference between close-distance and long-distance images, we compare the deep feature maps. To illustrate the effect of our algorithm, we analyze the deep feature of images after enhanced by different enhancement methods, which will be described in detail in the subsequent sections.

3 Proposed G-Log Method

In this section, we firstly discuss this method in detail and analyze the effectiveness of the algorithm with respect to the improvement of image quality. Then we introduce the influence of different parameters and how to select them.

3.1 G-Log Analysis

G-Log can enhance both color and gray images. For color image, the process is identical to each channel. The algorithm is summarized in Table 1.

Firstly, the maximum and minimum pixel values of each color channel are got. We conduct the nonlinear transformation formulated as Eq. (2). This transformation is similar to the gamma transformation with some variations. When $min = 24, max = 242$, the transformation curves corresponding to different values of γ are shown in Fig. 4. When $\gamma < 1$, the curve is convex, low pixel intensity values can be stretched, which can increase the image local contrast and compress pixel areas with high intensity values.

Table 1. The details of G-Log algorithm

Algorithm   G-Log algorithm
Data: Input color image

begin

    for each $S \in \{R,G,B\}$ **do**

$$min = min_{(x,y)} S(x,y), max = max_{(x,y)} S(x,y) \tag{1}$$

$$S_{o1}(x,y) = min + (max-min) \times ((S(x,y)-min)/(max-min))^{\gamma} \tag{2}$$

$$S_{o2} = log(S_{o1}+m) \tag{3}$$

$$S_{o3} = (S_{o2}-min) \times 255/(max-min) \tag{4}$$

    end

end

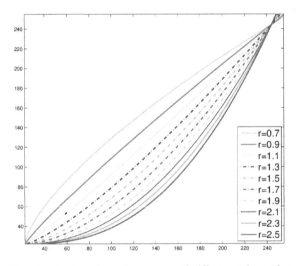

Fig. 4. The transformation curves of different values of γ

When $\gamma > 1$, the curve is concave, the transformation can stretch the range of high pixel intensity values and suppress low pixel intensity values. When the light is dark, the image pixel values are small and detailed information is lost in the low-light area. In such cases, we reduce the value γ appropriately. On the contrary, when the light is bright, we increase the value of γ appropriately. Therefore, depending on the situation of the image to be enhanced, the selection of γ may be targeted.

With the increase of the distance, the low-light area information is easier to be lost than the information in the high-light area. In order to restore the darkness information as much as possible, the next step of our method is logarithm transformation as the curve shown in Fig. 5. The low intensity area is stretched and high intensity area is compressed which can better disclose the dark-area detail. However, it can be seen that logarithm transformation largely suppresses the pixel values. Therefore, in order to make up for this defect, we make a design which add to the image a constant value m before logarithm transformation.

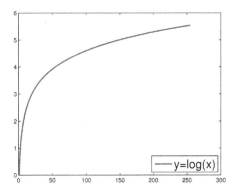

Fig. 5. The logarithm transformation curve

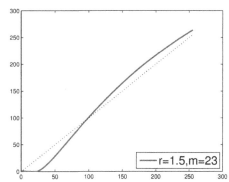

Fig. 6. The final transformation curve when $\gamma = 1.5, m = 23$ (Color figure online)

Finally, the image is normalized to 0-255 as defined in Eq. (4). To better illustrate our algorithm, we choose a specific example for the analysis: $\gamma = 1.5, m = 23$. The final transformation curve is shown in Fig. 6. The red solid line is G-Log transformation curve and the dotted line $y = x$ is drawn for the comparison. The transformation suppresses pixel values below 90 while improving the pixel value above 90. So this transformation increases image contrast by making dark-area darker and bright-area brighter. Since the pixel distribution of most detail and edge information typically lie in 50 and 200. The pixels in the middle position are more crowed, which is not conductive to the detailed information representation. This transformation mapped pixels between 40 and 170 to 0 and 200 which stretches the middle pixels and balanced image histogram.

3.2 Parameter Selection

Different parameters yield different enhanced image quality, thus affecting the final face recognition accuracy. We have done mounts of experiments to find the best parameter choice and how to choose parameters according to the original image quality. Figure 7 shows the relationship between the parameter m and the transformation curve. When γ is fixed, the transformation curve translates upward as m increases. That is, the larger the value of m, the larger image pixel value after processing. At the same time, it can be seen that as the pixel value gradually increases, the degree of pixel value increasing get smaller. This is consistent with our previous view that the information of pixel area with low levels is easier to be lost than the information in pixel area with high levels.

The relationship between parameter γ and transformation curves is shown in Fig. 8. When $\gamma < 1$, the convex degree of curve increases as γ decreases, the greater ability to stretch low pixels. When $\gamma > 1$, the curve translates downward as γ increases and stretches middle pixels in a larger degree. So, parameter m can control the global brightness of the enhanced image and parameter γ control image contrast.

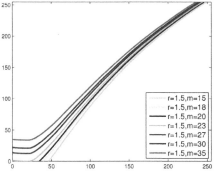

Fig. 7. The transformation curves when γ is fixed and m is changed

Fig. 8. The transformation curves when m is fixed and γ changes

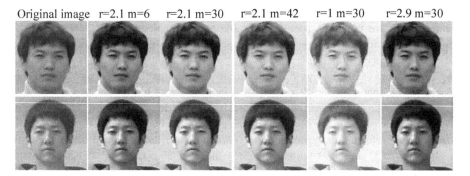

Fig. 9. Images enhanced with different parameters, the left column is original images and the rest is enhanced images with different parameters.

The increase of distance leads to low contrast of the image. If we take the influence of external factors such as illumination and weather factors out of consideration, we can properly increase the parameter m and γ. The image quality will be further reduced if we combined with the impact of all of the factors and the choice of parameters will be more complex. The influence of parameters is shown in Fig. 9 and the effect of parameters on similarity is shown in Table 2. The similarity is got by computing the cosine distance of face feature got from Convolutional Neural Network (CNN). Firstly, we get the similarity of 1-m and 150-m original images and then compare with the similarity of original 1-m and 150-m images enhanced by G-Log. From Table 2, the original image similarity of 1 m and 150 m is 0.6941. And the face image similarity can be up to 0.8218 after enhanced. Empirically, the optimal result can be attained when $\gamma \in (0.9, 1.5), m \in (14, 26)$.

Table 2. The similarities between 150-m images enhanced by different parameters and corresponding 1-m original images.

Image label	Parameter γ	Parameter m	Similarity	
			Enhanced image	Original image
The top image in Fig. 8	2.1	6	0.7963	0.6941
	2.1	30	0.8218	
	2.1	42	0.8078	
	1.0	30	0.7443	
	2.9	30	0.7824	

4 Experimental Results and Analysis

The proposed G-Log image enhancement algorithm is evaluated by face recognition accuracy, histogram and CNN feature map [9] in this section. The database we use is LDHF, including 1-, 60-, 100-, 150-m images and face recognition method is Seeta-Face Engine [10]. For the convenience, long-distance (60, 100, 150 m) face images and short distance (1 m) face images for matching are called probe and gallery images respectively. Given a probe image, the procedure of face alignment [11], enhancement and then matching is executed against all gallery images.

To compare the effect of different enhancement algorithms, all probe images are processed by different enhancement methods and the identical face alignment, recognition modules. Face recognition accuracy is shown in Table 3 and accuracy comparison of different enhancement methods is shown in Fig. 10. It can be seen that the face matching accuracy of original 150 m to 1 m is only 70% while 60 m to 1 m is up to 95%. Therefore, distance and environmental factors make a seriously influence on the face recognition. As the distance increases, recognition rate decreases significantly. After processed by G-Log algorithm, the 150-m and 100-m recognition rate are greatly improved, from 70% to 95% and 89% to 98% respectively. Compared with other algorithms involved in Fig. 10, G-Log method achieves the greatest improvement in face recognition rate. In addition, the visual effect also realizes the best result against other methods as shown in Fig. 3.

For objective performance evaluation, we compare the Cumulative Match Characteristic (CMC) curve of the matching result under different enhancement algorithms in Fig. 11. From this figure, it can be seen that G-Log algorithm achieves the best result both in 100-m and 150-m matching accuracy. The first rank recognition rate is 95% and 98% for 150-m and 100-m face images respectively and it rapidly climbs up to 98% and 98% in rank 5.

Table 3. Face recognition accuracy about different enhancement methods

Method	150-m	100-m	60-m
Original	0.70	0.89	0.95
Wavelet	0.74	0.83	0.91
Guide filter	0.71	0.90	0.94
MSR	0.83	0.89	0.93
MSRCR	0.84	0.91	0.95
G-Log	0.95	0.98	0.98

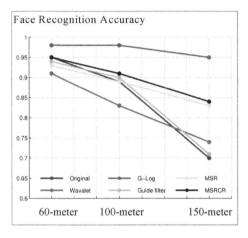

Fig. 10. Comparison of the 150-, 100-, 60-to-1 m face matching accuracy with different enhancement methods.

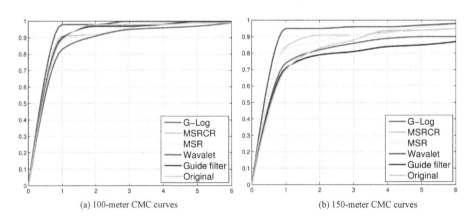

(a) 100-meter CMC curves

(b) 150-meter CMC curves

Fig. 11. CMC curves of the 100-, 150-to-1 m face matching result enhanced with different methods.

The histogram comparison is shown in Fig. 12. Except for G-Log method, MSRCR achieves the best result in face recognition accuracy in our experiment. Therefore, G-Log method is compared with MRSCR in the following experiments. It can be seen that the image histogram distribution is more uniform and the contrast is improved, after processed by G-Log method, which is helpful to the restoration of details and edge information. This method basically preserves the shape of histogram, and it does not change the corresponding relationships between pixels, so no additional noise is added.

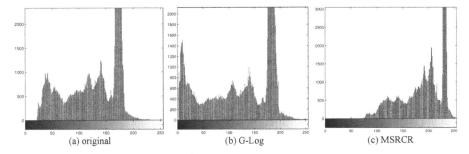

(a) original   (b) G-Log   (c) MSRCR

Fig. 12. The histogram comparison of G-Log and MSRCR

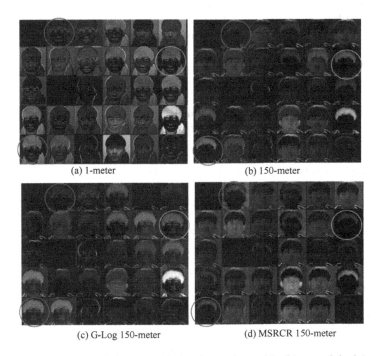

(a) 1-meter   (b) 150-meter

(c) G-Log 150-meter   (d) MSRCR 150-meter

Fig. 13. The feature maps of deep convolutional neural net: (a), (b) are original 1-m, 150-m feature maps respectively, and (c), (d) are 150-m feature maps of image enhanced by G-Log and MSRCR respectively.

In order to illustrate the effect of the G-Log algorithm on image detail recovery, the deep feature maps are shown in Fig. 13. The corresponding position of different sub-images is the same feature and the different positions of each sub-image are different feature maps. So there are 30 different feature maps of a subject shown in Fig. 13. The same subject face is used in four sub-images. Compared with the 1-m image, some of the detailed and edge information are lost in feature map of the original 150-m image. The eyes, mouth and nose features appearing in the 1-m feature map are completely degraded in the 150-m feature map as shown in circle areas in Fig. 13(a) and (b). From the sub-image (c), after processed by G-Log method, the information lost in 150 m is restored greatly. The sub-image (d) in Fig. 13 is the 150-m feature map of image enhanced by MSRCR, lost information doesn't get recovery and some noises are produced in the edge of the image.

5   Conclusion

With the increase of distance and environmental factors, non-uniform illumination, low resolution, and the influence of weather lead to a significant reduction of face recognition rate. The face matching accuracy of original 150 m and 1 m is only 70% while 60 m and 1 m is up to 95%. An effective face image enhancement algorithm G-Log has been proposed in this paper to solve these problems. By using the G-Log algorithm, the face recognition accuracy is greatly improved, from 70%, 89%, 95%, to 95%, 98%, 98% for 150-, 100-, 60-m, and the edge information, details are restored. Experiments demonstrate and confirm the effectiveness of the proposed method.

References

1. Huang, C.-T., Wang, Z., Jay Kuo, C.-C.: Visible-light and near-infrared face recognition at a distance. J. Vis. Commun. Image Represent. **41**, 140–153 (2016)
2. Huang, C.T., Wang, Z., Kuo, C.C.J.: TAEF: a cross-distance/environment face recognition method. In: 2015 IEEE Conference on Computer Vision and Pattern Recognition Workshops (CVPRW), Boston, MA, pp. 1–8 (2015)
3. Singh, R., Biswas, M.: Adaptive histogram equalization based fusion technique for hazy underwater image enhancement. In: 2016 IEEE International Conference on Computational Intelligence and Computing Research (ICCIC), Chennai, India, pp. 1–5 (2016)
4. Petro, A.B., Sbert, C., Morel, J.-M.: Multiscale retinex. Image Process. On Line (IPOL), 71–88 (2014)
5. Ma, S., Jiang, Z., Zhang, T.: The improved multi-scale retinex algorithm and its application in face recognition. In: The 27th Chinese Control and Decision Conference (CCDC 2015), Qingdao, China, pp. 5785–5788 (2015)
6. Gunawan, I.P., Halim, A.: Haar wavelet decomposition based blockiness detector and picture quality assessment method for JPEG images. In: 2011 International Conference on Advanced Computer Science and Information Systems, Jakarta, pp. 331–336 (2011)
7. Plataniotis, K.N., Androutsos, D., Venetsanopoulos, A.N.: An adaptive multichannel filter for colour image processing. Can. J. Electr. Comput. Eng. **21**(4), 149–152 (1996)

8. Gao, S., Zhang, Y., Jia, K., Lu, J., Zhang, Y.: Single sample face recognition via learning deep supervised autoencoders. IEEE Trans. Inf. Forensics Secur. **10**(10), 2108–2118 (2015)
9. Nguyen, K., Fookes, C., Sridharan, S.: Improving deep convolutional neural networks with unsupervised feature learning. In: 2015 IEEE International Conference on Image Processing (ICIP), Quebec City, QC, pp. 2270–2274 (2015)
10. Liu, X., Kan, M., Wu, W., et al.: VIPLFaceNet: an open source deep face recognition SDK. Frontiers Comput. Sci. **11**, 208–218 (2016)
11. Zhang, J., Shan, S., Kan, M., Chen, X.: Coarse-to-fine auto-encoder networks (CFAN) for real-time face alignment. In: Fleet, D., Pajdla, T., Schiele, B., Tuytelaars, T. (eds.) ECCV 2014. LNCS, vol. 8690, pp. 1–16. Springer, Cham (2014). https://doi.org/10.1007/978-3-319-10605-2_1

A Method on Recognizing Transmission Line Structure Based on Multi-level Perception

Yue Liu[1,2], Jianxiang Li[2(✉)], Wei Xu[2], and Mingyang Liu[3]

[1] State Grid Shandong Electric Power Research Institute Jinan, Jinan 250000, Shandong, China
[2] Shandong Luneng Intelligence Technology Co., Ltd., Jinan 250000, Shandong, China
jianxiang_1@126.com
[3] School of Information Science and Engineering, Lanzhou University,
Lanzhou 730000, Gansu, China

Abstract. The structure of transmission line can be recognized by processing the images captured from unmanned aerial vehicle (UAV) power inspection. That can be applied to vision based UAV intelligent inspection and the further analysis of the fault diagnosis of transmission lines. For that, a multi-level perception-based method of transmission line structure recognition is proposed. Firstly, the extracted line segments are split based on key points and then merged based on Gestalt perception theory for getting a relatively complete and independent local contour. Next the area of parallel line segments and symmetrical and crossing line segments are perceived, and then a position restraint mechanism of transmission line structure is built for the preliminary recognition. Finally, the local contour feature is used for the further recognition. In the experiment, the false rate and the missed rate of the method are verified to be lower.

Keywords: UAV inspection · Structure of transmission line · Position constraint
Local contour feature · Gestalt perception

1 Introduction

With the rapid development of UAVs technology in recent years, they are applied not only to the construction of geographic information system but also to the inspection of transmission line. Currently, UAVs are actively used by the China State Grid Corporation for improving the efficiency of visual transmission line inspection.

The research on transmission line structure is focused on the recognition of the components in the transmission line, and the image features such as shape points and characteristic points are important to the recognition of these artificial objects. SIFT feature matching [1] is a common matching method based on local feature, and the method is robust to image rotation, translation and scale transformation. But extraction error and matching error of the feature point would be high and the calculation of related data processing would be complex in natural scene of transmission lines. The shape recognition method like Fourier Descriptor [2] can reduce the influence of background noise and the sensitivity of boundary variation, Chen [3] used independent edge segments and closed contours searched by Generic Edge Token (GET) graph for object

© Springer International Publishing AG 2017
Y. Zhao et al. (Eds.): ICIG 2017, Part I, LNCS 10666, pp. 512–522, 2017.
https://doi.org/10.1007/978-3-319-71607-7_45

recognition. These shape recognition methods are only applicable to closed contour, but the extracted contours from the object in natural scene of transmission lines are usually incomplete because they are affected by background interference and mutual occlusion of the structure itself. By the study of human visual characteristics [4], this thesis can accurately identify the object according to the local contour, which shows that the local contour feature can be used to describe the object accurately. Ferrari [5] used the edge chain code to cluster K adjacent edge segments (KAS) as the local contour feature of the object. Ban [6] and Zhu [7] analyze the contour feature consisting of 2 or 3 adjacent edge segments of the object, and the semantic structure model of the contour feature is defined according to the angle between adjacent segments, segments' length and line vectors. However, these methods mainly focus on the single and significant objects (such as the insulator of transmission lines), and ignores the study on the overall structure of transmission lines. So these methods are easily affected by complex background texture and light, and more regions with similar features will be detected in the background.

The main difficulties of this paper as follows: (1) Transmission line is a kind of 3D hollow line structure, and there are a lot of occlusions in different shooting angles, so it's hard to extract the complete contour for the recognition; (2) The images taken by UAVs are greatly influenced by the background texture and the light changing, and there are many regions with similar features in the background, so it will easily cause an erroneous judgement.

2 Acquisition of Contour Segments of Transmission Line

The major objects of the recognition of transmission line structure are installed parts, and the problems mentioned above also need to be solved. An inference mechanism based on multi-level perception to recognize the structure of transmission line is proposed, and it is shown in Fig. 1.

At the bottom of image processing (Fig. 1(a)), the crossing gradient template [8] with a variable width is adopted to extract line segments. Considering that the object contour may be fused with the background, the splitting method is applied to the contour segments. Due to the influence of the light and occlusions, the extracted line segments may be discontinuous, then the line segments should be merged.

In the middle of image analysis (Fig. 1(b)), the significant characteristics are a major concern, approximate parallelism and approximate symmetrical cross. The power lines are a kind of parallel line structure, and the tower is an approximately symmetrical crossing line structure, a perception method based on blocking and clustering is proposed for perceiving these parallel and symmetrical crossing structures, and the region of the object to be recognized can be determined by both characteristic.

A high-level semantic description of image (Fig. 1(c)) is proposed to approach visual sense of human being, position constraint and local contour constraint. Analysis of the installation position of the object, a position constraint mechanism is built according to the connection of the object and power lines. Through the perception of the position constraint, the region of the object will be limited to a small area. Then combining the local contour features of the object, the structure of transmission line can be recognized semantically.

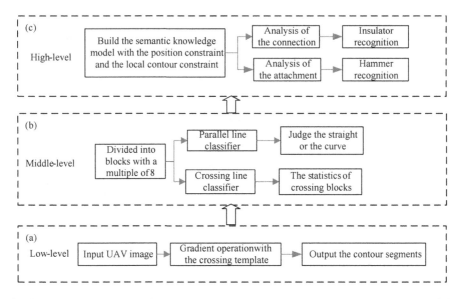

Fig. 1. The flow diagram of algorithm. (a) The low-level for image processing. (b) The middle-level for image analysis. (c) The high-level for semantic description of image

The specific recognition method is introduced in the Sects. 3, 4 and 5, the experiments and the conclusions given in Sects. 6 and 7 respectively.

3 Acquisition of Contour Segments of Transmission Line

3.1 Splitting Based on Key Points

Due to the influent of light, background texture and occlusions, the extracted line segment may be the segment with inflection point. The inflection point formed by the connection of the object contour with the background line or other parts, so the extracted segment should be divided into two segments. The detailed method of searching an inflection point as follows:

1. Each line segment are divided into *SegNumber* segments, and slopes of those are calculate by least square method, represented as: θ_1, θ_2, ... θ_s.
2. The slope angle difference between two adjacent lines is calculate, $\Delta\theta_1$, $\Delta\theta_2$, ... $\Delta\theta_{s-1}$.
3. The inflection point satisfies the following conditions:

$$abs(\Delta\theta_i) >= angle\_threshold \tag{1}$$

3.2 Merging Based on Gestalt Theory

The approximation, the co-linearity and the continuity of Gestalt perception law [9, 10] is applied in line segments merging. Therein Gestalt means when parts identified individually have different characteristics to the whole. For getting more complete contour segments of transmission line structure, the description of segments merging based on Gestalt perception law shown in Fig. 2.

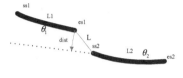

Fig. 2. Gestalt perception law calculation description

where L1 and L2 represent the lengths of two adjacent segments respectively, θ_1 and θ_2 corresponding to inclination angle of the segments.

The distance L between two adjacent segments is used to describe the approximation. If L satisfied the formula (2), it would comply with the approximation.

$$L \leq 2 \times \min(L1, L2) \tag{2}$$

If the angle variation of two adjacent segments satisfied the formula (3), it would comply with the continuity.

$$abs\left(\theta_1 - \theta_2\right) \leq T_\theta \tag{3}$$

The co-linearity is used to determine whether two segments was parallel or not, the vertical distance *dist* from the end of one segment to the other segment is a decisive factor to describe the co-linearity, as formula (4) shown.

$$dist = \frac{abs(ss_2 \times l1\_endx - l1\_endy + sl_2)}{\sqrt{ss_2^2 + 1}} \tag{4}$$

where *ss2*, *sl2* are the slope and intercept of starting end in segment 2. *l1_endx*, *l1_endy* are the coordinates of the endpoint in segment 1. If the formula (4) was satisfied, it would be a co-linearity judgment.

$$dist \leq k * \max(lw1, lw2) \tag{5}$$

Among them, *lw1* and *lw2* were line width of segment1 and segment2.

4   Perception of Significant Characteristics of Transmission Line

4.1   Perception of Parallel Structure and Symmetrical Crossing Structure

In order to detect the near parallel structure, the UAV image is divided into multiples of 8 blocks along the vertical direction, and line segments in each block are classified by the slope and the intercept. The result of the classification is the segments group which satisfies a certain condition of distance and angle, the parallel segments group. Then parallel segments group of adjacent blocks composed of a new parallel segments groups, according to the same endpoint location and the small angle difference until all the same parallel segments groups together.

Each block was divided into four equal parts horizontally for the perception of symmetrical crossing structure. Statistics is done for the number of different direction line segments in each part, including the number of horizontal line segments ($-15°$ ~ $15°$) *hnumi*; the number of upward line segments ($15°$ ~ $75°$) *upnumi*; the number of downward line segments ($-75°$ ~ $-15°$) *downnumi*; the number of vertical line segments ($>75°$ or $< -75°$) *vnumi*. If *upnumi* and *downnumi* were both higher than a present threshold, the part would belong to the symmetrical crossing part. The total number of the symmetrical crossing part is used to determine whether there exists a tower area in the image, and the region of the target object can be preliminarily determined by the perception of the tower area.

4.2   Perception of Connecting Structure and Attachment Structure

Context [5] is often used to describe the position relation between different structures in the scene. According to the structure of the transmission line, there is a position constraint of connection and attachment between the small parts and power lines, as shown in Fig. 3.

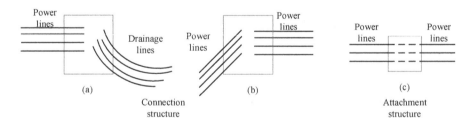

Fig. 3. Relative position of drainage line and power line in the strain tower. (a) The connection structure between power lines and drainage lines. (b) The connection structure between power lines. (c) The attachment structure between power lines.

One end of the insulator is connected with power lines, and the other end is connected with the tower. When power lines pass through the intermediate support, a strain formed by the power lines connected with the insulator, and a polyline structure presented. When power lines pass through the strain tower, the power lines are connected by a downward convex drainage line. Based on the calculation of the distance and the angle between the ends of adjacent parallel segment groups, a position constraint of connection can be established, and the insulator can be recognized around the area of the connection structure. The hammer and the spacer are installed on power lines, and an attachment is produced in the breakpoint area between the adjacent segment groups and these small parts in the image. According to the attachment structure, the recognition of the installed parts can be finished by searching along the direction of power lines.

5   The Recognition of Transmission Line Structure

5.1   The Recognition of Insulator

From the structure of the insulator, it consists of circular shaped chips joined together. Parallel arc structure is a significant feature of insulator in UAV image. Firstly, parallel line segments are extracted by different directions, and then the contour features are calculated. This coupled with the installation position of insulator in transmission line, the restraint mechanism of recognition of insulator is set up. The contour features calculation of insulator is shown in Fig. 4, the perception of parallel shape.

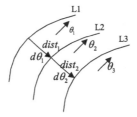

Fig. 4. Calculation of insulator parallelism

As for the parallel segments perception calculation of insulator, central points of line segments are kept in line, segments' length and the distance between adjacent segments keeping in a certain range. Orientation angle of line segment L1 and that of line segment L2 are separately represented as θ_1 and θ_2. If θ_1 and θ_2 satisfied formula (6), L1 would parallel to L2.

$$abs(\theta_1 - \theta_2) <= 2T_\theta \tag{6}$$

The orientation angle of the connecting between two center points of L1 and L2 is $d\theta_1$ and that of the connecting between center points of L2 and L3 is $d\theta_2$. If these angles satisfied the following Eq. (7), L1, L2 and L3 would be in alignment.

$$abs(d\theta_1 - d\theta_2) \leq 2.5 * T_\theta \tag{7}$$

where the parameter T_θ is a threshold for human visual perception of parallel lines.

The length of L1 and L2 are L1_len and L2_len respectively. If lengths satisfied the following Eq. (8), lengths would be in consistency.

$$abs(L1\_len - L2\_len) <= min(L1\_len, L2\_len)/3 \tag{8}$$

Considering the distance between chips of insulator less than the diameter of the chip, the distance between central points of L1 and L2 is less than the average length of L1 and L2.

$$dist <= avg(L1\_len, L2\_len) \tag{9}$$

5.2 The Recognition of Insulator

According to prior knowledge of the object to be recognized, two adjacent segments (2AS) or three adjacent segments (3AS) as the local contour feature for the object recognition, the angle and relative scale between adjacent segments are used to define the semantic model of 2AS, as shown in Fig. 5.

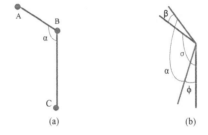

(a)   (b)

Fig. 5. 2AS segment diagram. (a) Schematic diagram of 2AS. (b) 2AS rotation angle relationship diagram.

The intersection of two approximate adjacent line segments is taken as the initial point to calculate vectors of each line segment, $\overrightarrow{BA} = r_1(x_1, y_1)$ and $\overrightarrow{BC} = r_2(x_2, y_2)$. And the angle between two vectors is also calculated. And the longest line segment is selected as the first segment to match and the length of the segment is as the normalization factor. The 2AS semantic modal can be described as formula (10).

$$\left(\frac{r_1}{L_1}, \frac{r_2}{L_1}, \alpha, 1, \frac{L_2}{L_1}\right)\left(\frac{r_1}{L_1}, \frac{r_2}{L_1}, \alpha, 1, \frac{L_2}{L_1}\right) \tag{10}$$

Local contour features (marked as a and b) of 2AS were matched from the following three aspects.

(1) The angle differences between a and b should satisfy the condition 12. θ_{thr} is a given threshold.

$$abs(\alpha^a - \alpha^b) \le \theta_{thr} \tag{11}$$

(2) The length differences of a and b should satisfy the condition 13.

$$L\_thr1 \leq \left(L_2^a/L_1^a \times L_1^b/L_2^b\right) \leq L\_thr2 \tag{12}$$

(3) the slope angle difference between two adjacent lines is calculate, $\Delta\theta_1, \Delta\theta_2, \ldots \Delta\theta_{s-1}$.

$$abs\left(\arccos\left(\frac{r_1^a \cdot r_1^b}{|r_1^a| \cdot |r_1^b|}\right) - \arccos\left(\frac{r_2^a \cdot r_2^b}{|r_2^a| \cdot |r_2^b|}\right)\right) < \theta_{thr} \tag{13}$$

Figures 6 and 7 were descriptions of local contour features of the spacer and the hammer. Local contour features of these shaped components were grouped by coding and such groups were adopted to travel the 2AS and 3AS of the clustering region traversal, and then the identification of hammer and spacer was realized.

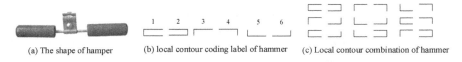

(a) The shape of hamper   (b) local contour coding label of hammer   (c) Local contour combination of hammer

Fig. 6. The description of local contour features of hammer. (a) The shape of hamper. (b) The local contour coding label of hamper. (c) The local contour combination of hamper.

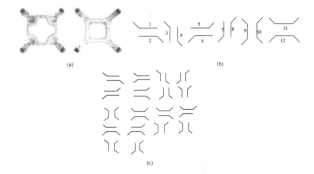

Fig. 7. The description of local contour features of spacer. (a) The shape of spacer. (b) The local contour coding label of spacer. (c) The local contour combination of spacer.

6   Experiment Result

The computer used in the experiment is Intel(R) Core(TM) i5-3470 CPU 3.20 GHz, 4 GB RAM, NVIDIA Geforce GTS 450, and the operating system is Microsoft Windows Window 7 Professional.

The recognition result of insulator is shown in Fig. 8, which is done largely through position constraint and local contour feature. Figure 1(a) is the original image, Fig. 1(b) showing the final result.

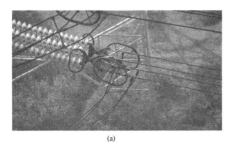 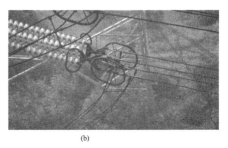

(a)   (b)

Fig. 8. A Recognition of structure of intermediate support. (a) The original image with the insulator. (b) The image with the recognized insulator.

Local contour feature is adopted in the method of Zhang [11], but the method is not suitable the case of that the insulator without obvious local contour feature and its local contour feature similar to background textures. The proposed method in this paper has made some improvements, the position constraint of the connection, the region of insulator can be inferred, as shown in Fig. 9. Statistics of the recognition result of the 2000 insulators are shown in Table 1, C_Num, F_Num, M_Num, C_Rate, F_Rate and M_Rate represent the correct recognition number, the false recognition number, the missed recognition number, the correct recognition rate, the false recognition rate and the missed recognition rate. From this table, the false rate and the missed rate of the method has been improved evidently. At last, the average running time of each image is calculated, 1.665 s, 1.689 s correspond to Zhang's method, and proposed method, respectively. By comparison, there is little difference in running time.

(a)   (b)

Fig. 9. Recognition of structure. (a) The position constraint of the connection. (b) The recognition of the insulator.

Table 1. Statics of the recognition of the insulator.

Method	C_Num	W_Num	M_Num	T_Rate	F_Rate	M_Rate
Zhang	1738	140	246	86.9%	7.01%	12.33%
Proposed	1801	114	218	90.06%	5.69%	10.94%

The recognition results of the 2000 hammers are shown in Fig. 10. For the hammer recognition method of Zhu [7], with no idea for reducing the influence of the similar structure, a comparison is made between Zhu's and the proposed in Table 2.

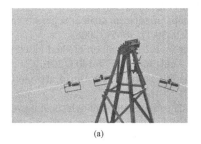 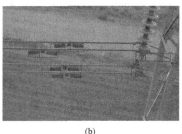

(a)   (b)

Fig. 10. A The recognition results of hamper

Table 2. Statics of the recognition of the hammer.

Method	C_Num	W_Num	M_Num	T_Rate	F_Rate	M_Rate
Zhu	1346	306	658	67.33%	15.3%	32.9%
Proposed	1608	211	152	80.42%	10.55%	7.61%

At last, the average running time of each image is calculated, 1.015 s, 0.934 s correspond to Zhu's method, and proposed method, respectively. By comparison of running time, our proposed method is a little below.

7   Conclusions

A multi-level perception-based method of transmission line structure recognition is proposed. The position mechanism of the connection and the local contour feature are used to build the semantic knowledge model of the objects recognition, and then the objects in transmission line are recognized semantically and reliably. Finally, the experimental results show that the recognition effect has been improved by the proposed method. And the proposed algorithm will be optimized under GPU in the future work for timeliness.

References

1. Zhou, Q., Zhao, Z.: Substation equipment image recognition based on SIFT feature matching. In: Proceedings of the 5th International Congress on Image and Signal Processing (CISP), pp. 1344–1347 (2012)
2. Kunttu, I., Lepisto, L., Rauhamaa, J., et al.: Multiscale fourier descriptor for shape classification. In: Proceedings of the 12th International Conference on Image Analysis and Processing, pp. 536–541 (2003)

3. Chen, H., Gao, Q.: Efficient image region and shape detection by perceptual contour grouping. In: Proceedings of IEEE International Conference on Mechatronics and Automation, vol. 2, pp. 793–798 (2005)

4. Ghosh, A., Petkov, N.: Robustness of shape descriptors to incomplete contour representations. IEEE Trans. Pattern Anal. Mach. Intell. **27**(11), 1793–1804 (2005)

5. Ferrari, V., Fevrier, L., Schmid, C., et al.: Groups of adjacent contour segments for object detection. IEEE Trans. Pattern Anal. Mach. Intell. **30**(1), 36–51 (2008)

6. Ban, X., Han, j, Lu, D., et al.: Similar circular object recognition method based on local contour feature in natural scenario. J. Comput. Appl. **36**(5), 1399–1403 (2016)

7. Zhu, M.W., Han, J., Lu, D.M., et al.: Object recognition method based on local contour feature in natural scenario. Comput. Eng. Appl. **52**(1), 162–167 (2015)

8. Wang, Y., Han, J., Chen, F., et al.: Automatic detection method of defects of power line in visual image. Comput. Eng. Appl. **47**(12), 180–184 (2011). In Chinese

9. Cheng, C., Koschan, A., Chen, C.-H., Page, D.L., Abidi, M.A.: Outdoor scene image segmentation based on background recognition and perceptual organization. IEEE Trans. Image Process. **21**(3), 1007–1019 (2012)

10. Iqbal, Q., Aggarwal, J.K.: Retrieval by classification of images containing large manmade objects using perceptual grouping. Pattern Recogn. **35**(7), 1463–1479 (2002)

11. Zhang, J., Han, J., Zhao, Y., et al.: Insulator recognition and defects detection based on shape perceptual. J. Image Graph. **19**(8), 1194–1201 (2014)

Saliency Detection Based on Background and Foreground Modeling

Zhengbing Wang, Guili Xu[✉], Yuehua Cheng, and Zhengsheng Wang

College of Automation Engineering,
Nanjing University of Aeronautics and Astronautics, Nanjing, China
guilixu@nuaa.edu.cn

Abstract. In this paper, a novel saliency detection algorithm is proposed to fuse both the background and foreground information while detecting salient objects in complex scenes. Firstly, we extract background seeds as well as their spatial information from image borders to construct a background-based saliency map. Then, an optimal contour closure is selected as the foreground region according to the first-stage saliency map. The optimal contour closure can provide a preferable description for salient object. We compute a foreground-based saliency map using the selected foreground region and integrate it with the background-based one. Finally, the unified saliency map is further refined to obtain a more accurate result. Experimental results show that the proposed algorithm can achieve favorable performance compared to the state-of-the-art ones.

Keywords: Saliency detection · Background · Foreground
Optimal contour closure

1 Introduction

Saliency detection aims at highlighting the most attractive regions in a scene. It has been further studied in recent years, and numerous computational models have been presented. As a preprocessing operation, saliency detection can benefit many other tasks, including image segmentation [9,14], image compression [4], object localization and recognition [3].

Saliency detection algorithms can be roughly divided into two categories from the perspective of information processing. The top-down approaches [13,22] driven by specific tasks need to learn the visual information of specific objects to form the saliency maps. In contrast, the bottom-up methods [5,12,19,20] usually exploit low-level cues such as color, lamination and texture to highlight salient objects. Early researches address saliency detection via heuristic principles [12], including contrast prior, center prior and background prior. Most works based on these principles exploit low-level features directly extracted from images [5,19]. They perform well in many cases, but are still unfavorable in complex scenes. Due to the shortcomings of low-level features, many algorithms are presented

© Springer International Publishing AG 2017
Y. Zhao et al. (Eds.): ICIG 2017, Part I, LNCS 10666, pp. 523–532, 2017.
https://doi.org/10.1007/978-3-319-71607-7_46

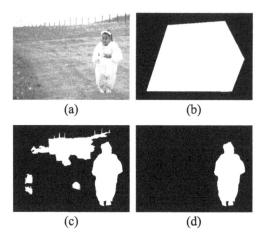

(a)   (b)

(c)   (d)

Fig. 1. Examples of foreground regions. (a) Input image, Foreground region used in (b) XIE [20], (c) BFS [17], (d) Our method.

to incorporate high-level features in saliency detection. Xie et al. [20] propose a bottom-up approach which integrates both low and mid level cues using the Bayesian framework. Some learning methods [6,16] are also presented to integrate both low and high level features to compute saliency based on parameters trained from sample images.

Recently, to achieve better performance, some object-level cues are introduced as hints of the foreground. Some examples are shown in Fig. 1. Xie et al. [20] detect the salient points in the image and a convex hull is computed to denote the approximate location of the salient object. Wang et al. [17] binarize the coarse saliency map using an adaptive threshold and select the super-pixels whose saliency values are larger than the threshold as foreground seeds. While the extracted foreground information can be used to improve performance of saliency detection, the false foreground region may have unfavorable influence.

In this paper, we propose an effective method to incorporate foreground information in saliency detection. First, we extract background seeds and their spatial information to construct a background-based saliency map. Then, several compact regions are generated using the contour information. We select the optimal one as the foreground region and calculate the foreground-based saliency map accordingly. To achieve better performance, two saliency maps are finally integrated and further refined.

2   Saliency Detection Algorithm

This section explains the details of the proposed saliency detection algorithm. In order to preserve the structural information, we over-segment the input image to generate N super-pixels [2] and use them as the minimum units. After that, a background-based saliency map is firstly constructed using the background

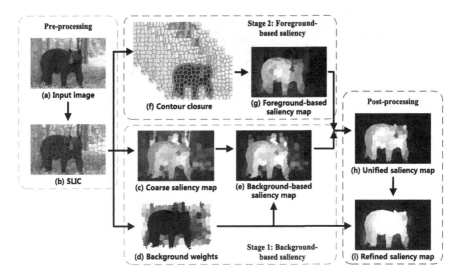

Fig. 2. Pipeline of our method, including input image pre-processing, background-based saliency, foreground-based saliency and post-processing.

information (Subsect. 2.1). We then select the optimal contour closure as the foreground region according to the first-stage saliency map and compute the foreground-based saliency map (Subsect. 2.2). Finally, these two saliency maps are integrated and further refined to form a more accurate result (Subsect. 2.3). The pipeline of our saliency detection method is illustrated in Fig. 2.

2.1   Saliency Detection via Background Information

Border regions of the image have been proved to be good visual cues for background priors in saliency detection [19]. Observing that background areas are usually connected to the image borders, we select the super-pixels along the image borders as background seeds and define the coarse saliency of super-pixels as their color contrast to the background ones. Denote the background seeds set as BG, and the coarse saliency value of super-pixel s_i is computed as

$$S_i^c = \sum_{s_j \in BG} d_c(s_i, s_j) * w_l(s_i, s_j) \tag{1}$$

where $d_c(s_i, s_j)$ is the Euclidean color distance between two super-pixels and $w_l(s_i, s_j)$ denotes the spatial weight.

As shown in Fig. 2(c), the coarse saliency map may include a large amount of background noises and is visually unfavorable. Therefore, we further consider the spatial information of the selected background seeds to define the background weight for each super-pixel, which can be used to restrain undesirable noises. The process of computing background weight is given as follows: First, we cluster the super-pixels in BG into K clusters using K-means clustering algorithm.

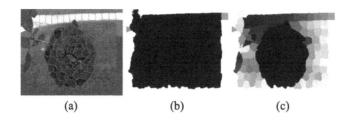

(a)   (b)   (c)

Fig. 3. Definition of background weights. (a) Background seeds clustering; (b) Background weights of the selected background seeds; (c) Background weights of the other super-pixels.

The number of clusters K is set to 3 in our experiments as shown in Fig. 3(a). For each cluster k, determine the shortest continuous super-pixel link SL_k, which contains all the super-pixels belonging to cluster k. Denote the length of this super-pixel link as L_s, and the background weight for cluster k can be calculated as

$$P_k = 1 - \exp(-\alpha(L_s + L_o)) \quad (k = 1, 2, \cdots, K) \tag{2}$$

where L_o is the number of super-pixels belonging to the other clusters in SL_k. As shown in Fig. 3(b), for each super-pixel s_j in cluster k, we assign the same value P_k to its background weight p_{s_j}. The background weights of the remainder super-pixels are determined as

$$p_{s_i} = \frac{p_{s_j^*}}{d_{geo}^*} \quad (s_i \notin BG) \tag{3}$$

where d_{geo}^* is the shortest geodesic distance from super-pixel s_i to the background seeds and s_j^* is the corresponding seed in BG.

The background-based saliency value of super-pixel s_i is finally calculated as

$$S_i^b = S_i^c * (1 - p_{s_i}) \tag{4}$$

As shown in Fig. 2(e), the background-based saliency map can be substantially improved by considering the spatial information of background seeds. However, some background regions with discriminative appearance are still incorrectly highlighted. The foreground information is therefore incorporated to suppress the background noises.

2.2   Saliency Detection via Optimal Contour Closure

The background-based saliency map can highlighted all the regions with high contrast to the background seeds but may be invalid for background noises. Some recent works [17,18,20] incorporate foreground information to restrain noises. However, the false foreground information may have unfavorable influence on saliency detection. According to the research of visual psychology [15], compact regions grouped by contour information can provide important cues for selective attention. We adopt Levinshtein et al.'s mechanism [10] to generate foreground regions. Given the contour image and the assumption that the salient contours that define the boundary of the object will align well with super-pixel boundaries, we obtain several contour closures by solving a parametric maxflow problem as shown in Fig. 4(c). We select the optimal contour closure as

$$\mathbf{x}^* = \arg\min_{\mathbf{x}^m} \sum_{i=1}^{N} |\mathbf{x}_i^m - S_i^b| + V(\mathbf{x}^m) \quad (m \le M) \tag{5}$$

where $\mathbf{x}^m$ is a binary mask, which denotes the m-th foreground region (contour closure) and M is the number of previously obtained contour closures. $V(\mathbf{x}^m)$ denotes the spatial variance of a foreground region.

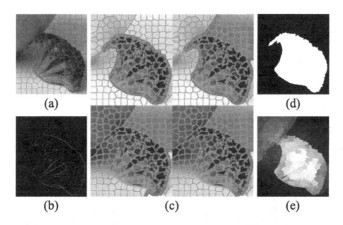

Fig. 4. Foreground-based saliency detection. (a) Super-pixels of input image; (b) Salient contours; (c) Examples of obtained contour closures; (d) Optimal contour closure; (e) Foreground-based saliency map.

The selected optimal contour closure is shown in Fig. 4(d), and we collect all the super-pixels in this contour closure to compose the foreground seeds set FG. The foreground-based saliency value of each super-pixel is computed as

$$S_i^f = \sum_{s_j \in FG} \frac{1}{d_c(s_i, s_j) + \beta d_l(s_i, s_j)} \tag{6}$$

where $d_l(s_i, s_j)$ is the spatial distance between two super-pixels.

2.3 Integration and Refinement Operation

Referring to [17], the background-based saliency map can uniformly highlight the salient object while the foreground-based one can well restrain the background noises. In order to take advantage of both the background-based saliency and the foreground-based one, we integrate two saliency maps as

$$S_i^u = S_i^b * (1 - \exp(-\theta * S_i^f)) \tag{7}$$

where θ is set to 4 in our experiments.

To obtain a better result, we further refine the unified saliency map by the energy function presented in [23]. The used energy function can not only assign large saliency value to foreground region but promote the smoothness of refined saliency map. The energy function is given as

$$\mathbf{S}^r = \arg\min_{\mathbf{S}} (\sum_{i,j=1}^{N} w_c(s_i, s_j)(S_i - S_j)^2 + \sum_{i=1}^{N} p_{s_i} S_i^2$$
$$+ \sum_{i=1}^{N} S_i^u (S_i - 1)^2) \tag{8}$$

where $w_c(s_i, s_j)$ denotes the color similarity between two adjacent super-pixels and p_{s_i} is the background weight of super-pixel s_i obtained in Subsect. 2.1. $\mathbf{S}^r = [S_1^r, S_2^r, \cdots, S_N^r]^T$ denotes the refined saliency value vector.

3   Experiments

In this section, we evaluate our algorithm on two public datasets: ASD [1] and ECSSD [21]. Both of them consist of 1000 images with pixel-wise labeled ground truth, while the ECSSD dataset is more challenging as many images contain more complex scenes. We compare our algorithm with 7 state-of-the-art methods, including IT [5], FT [1], GB [7], SF [8], XIE [20], BFS [17], and LPS [11].

To make a fair comparison, the precision-recall curve and F-measure are used for quantitative analysis. Given a saliency map, we segment it with the

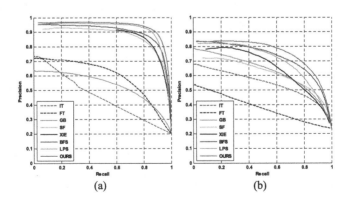

Fig. 5. Precision-recall curves of compared methods on (a) MSRA dataset, (b) ECSSD dataset.

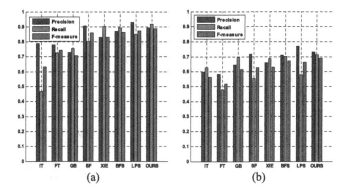

Fig. 6. Average precision, recall and F-measure of compared methods on (a) MSRA dataset, (b) ECSSD dataset.

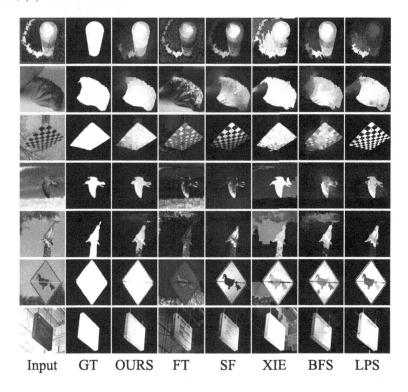

Input   GT   OURS   FT   SF   XIE   BFS   LPS

Fig. 7. Visual comparisons of our algorithm and 5 state-of-the-art methods.

thresholds ranging from 0 to 255, and compare each result with ground truth to generate the precision-recall curve. The precision-recall curves of compared methods are shown in Fig. 5, which demonstrates that our result performs better than others. To compute the F-measure, we first over-segment the original image using the mean-shift algorithm. A binary map can be obtained by a threshold,

Table 1. Average values of precision and recall for ASD and ECSSD

Methods	BFS		OURS	
Datasets	ASD	ECSSD	ASD	ECSSD
p_F	0.8197	0.6197	0.8715	0.7136
r_F	0.8726	0.7010	0.8944	0.6241

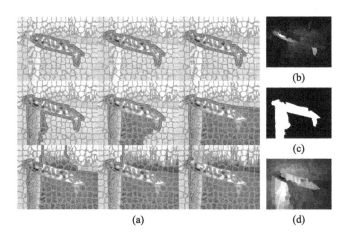

(a)   (d)

Fig. 8. Failure case of foreground region selection. (a) All the generated contour closures; (b) Background-based saliency map; (c) Selected foreground region; (d) Foreground-based saliency map.

which is set to twice the mean saliency value. For each binary map, we compute the F-measure as

$$F - measure = \frac{(1 + \gamma^2)Precision \times Recall}{\gamma^2 Precision + Recall} \qquad (9)$$

where γ^2 is set to 0.3 according to [1]. As shown in Fig. 6, our result achieves the highest recall and F-measure, although the precision is not always the best.

Figure 7 shows some visual comparison results. We note that our method can not only highlight the salient object uniformly, but well restrain the background noises. The presented algorithm achieves good performance against other state-of-the-art methods, especially in complex scenes.

The effectiveness of the proposed algorithm is partially due to the more accurate foreground information compared to the previous methods [17,18,20]. To evaluate the foreground information incorporated in the presented algorithm, we compute the precision p_F and recall r_F for our foreground regions and compare them to the Otsu segmentations used in the BFS [17]. The precision p_F and recall r_F for each foreground region are calculated as

$$\begin{cases} p_F = \frac{|R_F \bigcap R_{GT}|}{|R_F|} \\ r_F = \frac{|R_F \bigcap R_{GT}|}{|R_{GT}|} \end{cases} \qquad (10)$$

where R_F denotes the estimated foreground region and R_{GT} is the ground truth foreground region. The average values of precision and recall for each dataset is shown in Table 1. It indicates that the selected foreground regions are usually more favourable than the Otsu segmentations, since the high-level cue is incorporated.

Note that, the Levinshtein et al.'s mechanism [10] usually generates a dozen of contour closures and we select an optimal one using Eq. (5), which may not always obtain the best region. Figure 8 illustrates a failure case. Figure 8(a) presents all the contour closures generated by [10] and Fig. 8(c) is the selected contour closure. It is clear that the presented method selects an acceptable foreground region instead of the best one.

4 Conclusions

In this paper, we propose an effective method to fuse both the background and foreground information in saliency detection. To efficiently suppress the background noises, we employ two techniques: (1) the background weights defined by the spatial information of background seeds. (2) a foreground-based saliency map constructed from the optimal contour closure. The experimental results show that the presented algorithm can achieve favorable performance compared to the state-of-the-art methods.

Acknowledgments. This work is supported by the National Natural Science Foundation of China (61473148) and the Funding of Jiangsu Innovation Program for Graduate Education (KYLX16-0337).

References

1. Achanta, R., Hemami, S., Estrada, F., Susstrunk, S.: Frequency-tuned salient region detection. In: CVPR, pp. 1597–1604 (2009)
2. Achanta, R., Shaji, A., Smith, K., Lucchi, A., Fua, P., Susstrunk, S.: SLIC superpixels compared to state-of-the-art superpixel methods. IEEE TPAMI **34**(11), 2274 (2012)
3. Gao, D., Han, S., Vasconcelos, N.: Discriminant saliency, the detection of suspicious coincidences, and applications to visual recognition. IEEE TPAMI **31**(6), 989 (2009)
4. Guo, C., Zhang, L.: A novel multiresolution spatiotemporal saliency detection model and its applications in image and video compression. Oncogene **3**(5), 523–529 (2010)
5. Itti, L., Koch, C., Niebur, E.: A model of saliency-based visual attention for rapid scene analysis. IEEE TPAMI **20**(11), 1254–1259 (1998)
6. Jiang, H., Wang, J., Yuan, Z., Wu, Y.: Salient object detection: a discriminative regional feature integration approach. Int. J. Comput. Vis. **9**(4), 1–18 (2014)
7. Jonathan, H., Christof, K., Pietro, P.: Graph-based visual saliency. In: Advances in Neural Information Processing Systems, pp. 545–552 (2006)
8. Krahenbuhl, P.: Saliency filters: contrast based filtering for salient region detection. In: CVPR, pp. 733–740 (2012)

9. Lempitsky, V., Kohli, P., Rother, C., Sharp, T.: Image segmentation with a bounding box prior. In: ICCV, pp. 277–284 (2009)
10. Levinshtein, A., Sminchisescu, C., Dickinson, S.: Optimal contour closure by superpixel grouping. In: Daniilidis, K., Maragos, P., Paragios, N. (eds.) ECCV 2010. LNCS, vol. 6312, pp. 480–493. Springer, Heidelberg (2010). https://doi.org/10.1007/978-3-642-15552-9_35
11. Li, H., Lu, H., Lin, Z., Shen, X., Price, B.: Inner and inter label propagation: salient object detection in the wild. IEEE TIP **24**(10), 3176–86 (2015)
12. Liu, H., Tao, S., Li, Z.: Saliency detection via global-object-seed-guided cellular automata. In: ICIP, pp. 2772–2776 (2016)
13. Liu, T., Sun, J., Zheng, N.N., Tang, X.: Learning to detect a salient object. In: CVPR, pp. 1–8 (2007)
14. Qin, C., Zhang, G., Zhou, Y., Tao, W., Cao, Z.: Integration of the saliency-based seed extraction and random walks for image segmentation. Neurocomputing **129**(4), 378–391 (2014)
15. Qiu, F., Sugihara, T., Von Der Heydt, R.: Figure-ground mechanisms provide structure for selective attention. Nat. Neurosci. **10**(11), 1492–1499 (2007)
16. Siva, P., Russell, C., Xiang, T., Agapito, L.: Looking beyond the image: unsupervised learning for object saliency and detection. In: CVPR, pp. 3238–3245 (2013)
17. Wang, J., Lu, H., Li, X., Tong, N., Liu, W.: Saliency detection via background and foreground seed selection. Neurocomputing **152**(C), 359–368 (2015)
18. Wang, Z., Xu, G., Wang, Z., Zhu, C.: Saliency detection integrating both background and foreground information. Neurocomputing **216**, 468–477 (2016)
19. Wei, Y., Wen, F., Zhu, W., Sun, J.: Geodesic saliency using background priors. In: Fitzgibbon, A., Lazebnik, S., Perona, P., Sato, Y., Schmid, C. (eds.) ECCV 2012. LNCS, vol. 7574, pp. 29–42. Springer, Heidelberg (2012). https://doi.org/10.1007/978-3-642-33712-3_3
20. Xie, Y., Lu, H., Yang, M.H.: Bayesian saliency via low and mid level cues. IEEE TIP **22**(5), 1689–1698 (2013)
21. Yan, Q., Xu, L., Shi, J., Jia, J.: Hierarchical saliency detection. In: CVPR, pp. 1155–1162 (2013)
22. Zhang, L., Tong, M.H., Marks, T.K., Shan, H., Cottrell, G.W.: Sun: a bayesian framework for saliency using natural statistics. J. Vis. **8**(7), 1–20 (2008)
23. Zhu, W., Liang, S., Wei, Y., Sun, J.: Saliency optimization from robust background detection. In: CVPR, pp. 2814–2821 (2014)

Scale Estimation and Refinement in Monocular Visual-Inertial SLAM System

Xufu Mu, Jing Chen$^{(\boxtimes)}$, Zhen Leng, Songnan Lin,
and Ningsheng Huang

School of Optoelectronics, Beijing Institute of Technology, Beijing, China
muxufu@163.com, chen74jing29@bit.edu.cn

Abstract. The fusion of monocular visual and inertial cues has become popular in robotics, unmanned vehicle and augmented reality fields. Recent results have shown that optimization-based fusion strategies outperform filtering ones. The visual-inertial ORB-SLAM is optimization-based and has achieved great success. However, it takes all measurements into IMU initialization, which contains outliers, and it lacks of termination criterion. In this paper, we aim to resolve these issues. First, we present an approach to estimate scale, gravity and accelerometer bias together, and regard the estimated gravity as an indication for estimation convergence. Second, we propose a methodology that is able to use weight w derived from the robust norm for outliers handling, so that the estimated scale can be refined. We test our approaches with the public EuRoC datasets. Experimental results show that the proposed methods can achieve good scale estimation and refinement.

Keywords: Visual-inertial fusion · Monocular SLAM · Scale estimation

1 Introduction

The combination of vision and inertial sensors has long been a popular research field for three-dimensional structure, ego-motion estimation and visual odometry. Both monocular camera and Inertial Measurement Unit (IMU) are cheap, low-cost, low-weight and complementary. A moving camera can provide us accurate state estimation and sufficient environment 3D structure up to an unknown metric scale. While inertial sensors with high frame-rate can help us handle fast camera motion, scale ambiguity and short-term motion estimation.

Many Visual-inertial fusion strategies have been proposed, which can be divided into the loosely coupled modality and the tightly coupled one. Loosely coupled strategy is to estimate 6D pose and position separately. On the contrary, tightly coupled fusion strategy is to jointly optimize all sensor states. Most recent works concentrate on tightly-coupled visual-inertial odometry, using keyframe-based non-linear optimization [1–4] or filtering [5–8]. Non-linear optimization and tightly coupled methods have attracted much interest of researchers in recent years due to its good trade-off between accuracy and computational efficiency. This article follows this trend and focuses on the monocular unknown scale problem.

© Springer International Publishing AG 2017
Y. Zhao et al. (Eds.): ICIG 2017, Part I, LNCS 10666, pp. 533–544, 2017.
https://doi.org/10.1007/978-3-319-71607-7_47

Visual scale estimation is a research hotspot in the monocular SLAM. The early MonoSLAM [11] initializes from a target of known size, which help to assign a precise scale to the estimated map. Filter-based methods include ROVIO [12], MSCKF [5] and [13, 14], where the scale information is added to the extended Kalman filter as an additional state variable. The paper [15] proposed a maximum-likelihood estimator for the scale of the monocular SLAM system. In [16] and visual-inertial ORB-SLAM [9], the scale is estimated within the process of optimization using methods such as Gauss-Newton. While promising, taking all visual and inertial measurements for scale estimation may contain outliers, which lead to declined accuracy of scale estimation. Besides, the method introduced in [9] is lack of robust termination criterion for IMU initialization, which results in increased computation and reducing the effect of IMU information.

In this paper, we devote to solve above problems existed in [9]. The main contribution of our research work is two-fold. Firstly, we present an approach to estimate scale, gravity and accelerometer bias together, and regard the estimated gravity as an indication for identifying convergence and termination for scale estimation procedure. Secondly, we propose a keyframe-based method that uses a weighted term to reduce the influence of large residuals, which lead to scale estimation refinement.

The remainder of this article is organized as follows. In the main Sect. 2 we explain the camera model, the IMU noise models, and the kinematics models of IMU, we also give a brief introduction about IMU pre-integration technique. In Sect. 3, we describe our approach as a whole, in particular we introduce the method for scale estimation and refinement. We also propose an automatic termination criterion. Section 4 is dedicated to show the performance of our approaches and we compare them with the ground truth. We conclude the paper in Sect. 5.

2   Preliminaries

In this section, we first introduce some notation throughout this paper: the matrix $T_{EF} = [R_{EF} \quad {}_E P_F]$ represents the transformation from reference F to reference E.

Then we will introduce some preliminary knowledge about the coordinate system, the camera model, inertial sensor model, and IMU pre-integration. Figure 1 shows the situation of the camera-IMU setup with its corresponding coordinate frames. Multiple camera-IMU units represent the consecutive states at continuous time, which is convenient for understanding the following Equations in Sect. 3.1. The camera provides the pose and the unscaled position in the camera frame C. We denote the world reference frame with W and the IMU body frame B. The transformation $T_{CB} = [R_{CB} \quad {}_C P_B]$ between camera and IMU reference systems can be calibrated using Kalibr [17].

2.1   Camera Model

Here we consider a conventional pinhole-camera model [22], which any 3D point $X_C \in \mathbb{R}^3$ in the camera reference maps to the image coordinates $x \in \mathbb{R}^2$, through the camera projection function $\pi : \mathbb{R}^3 \mapsto \mathbb{R}^2$:

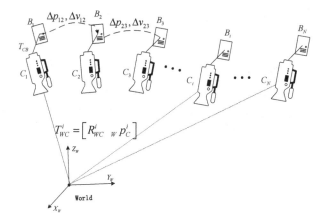

Fig. 1. The relationship between different coordinate frames and multiple states of camera-IMU

$$\pi(X_C) = \begin{bmatrix} f_u \frac{x_C}{z_C} + c_u \\ f_v \frac{y_C}{z_C} + c_v \end{bmatrix}, \quad X_C = \begin{bmatrix} x_C & y_C & z_C \end{bmatrix}^T \tag{1}$$

where $\begin{bmatrix} f_u & f_v \end{bmatrix}^T$ is the focal length and $\begin{bmatrix} c_u & c_v \end{bmatrix}^T$ is the principal point.

2.2 Inertial Sensor Model and IMU Kinematics Model

An IMU generally integrates a 3-axis gyroscope sensor and a 3-axis accelerometer sensor, and correspondingly, the measurements provide us the angular velocity and the acceleration of the inertial sensor at high frame-rate with respect to the body frame B. The IMU measurement model contains two kinds of noise: one is white noise n_t, the other is random walk noise that is a slowly varying sensor bias b_t, so we have:

$$_B\widetilde{\omega}(t) = {}_B\omega(t) + b_g(t) + n_g(t) \tag{2}$$

$$_B\widetilde{a}(t) = R_{WB}^T(t)({}_Wa(t) - {}_Wg) + b_a(t) + n_a(t) \tag{3}$$

where the $_B\widetilde{w}(t)$ and $_B\widetilde{a}(t)$ are the measured values expressed in the body frame, the real angular velocities $_Bw(t)$ and the real acceleration $_Wa(t)$ are what we need. The left subscript W denotes in the world frame. And the R_{WB} is the rotational part from the transformation $\{R_{WB} \ _WP\}$, which maps a point from sensor frame B to W. The dynamics of non-static bias b_t are modeled as a random process:

$$\dot{b}_g = n_{b_g}, \ \dot{b}_a = n_{b_a} \tag{4}$$

where the n_{b_g} and n_{b_a} are the zero-mean Gaussian White noises. Our goal is to deduce the motion of system from the output of IMU. For this purpose, we show the following IMU kinematics model [11]:

$$_W\dot{R}_{WB} = R_{WB\ B}\omega^\wedge, \quad _W\dot{v} = _Wa, \quad _W\dot{p} = _Wv \tag{5}$$

2.3   IMU Pre-integration

The IMU pre-integration technique incorporated with SLAM framework are proposed correctly in [18]. Here we give an overview of its theory and usage within monocular visual-inertial SLAM system. The pose and velocity of IMU at time $t + \Delta t$ is obtained by integrating Eq. (5):

$$R_{WB}(t + \Delta t) = R_{WB}(t)Exp(_B\omega(t)\Delta t) \tag{6}$$

$$_Wv(t + \Delta t) = _Wv(t) + _Wa(t)\Delta t \tag{7}$$

$$_Wp(t + \Delta t) = _Wp(t) + _Wv(t)\Delta t + \frac{1}{2}_Wa(t)\Delta t^2 \tag{8}$$

which assumes that $_Wa$ and $_B\omega$ maintain a constant in the time interval $[t, t + \Delta t]$. Equations (6)–(8) become function of the IMU measurements using Eqs. (2)–(3):

$$R(t + \Delta t) = R(t)Exp((\tilde{\omega}(t) - b_g(t) - n_g(t))\Delta t) \tag{9}$$

$$v(t + \Delta t) = v(t) + g\Delta t + R(t)(\tilde{a}(t) - b_a(t) - n_a(t))\Delta t \tag{10}$$

$$p(t + \Delta t) = p(t) + v(t)\Delta t + \frac{1}{2}g\Delta t^2 + \frac{1}{2}R(t)(\tilde{a}(t) - b_a(t) - n_a(t))\Delta t^2 \tag{11}$$

Here the coordinate frame subscripts is dropped for readability. In Eqs. (6)–(11) Δt is the sampling interval of the IMU. Assuming that the IMU is synchronized with the camera, and provides measurements at discrete times k. Integrating all IMU measurements between two consecutive keyframes at times $k = i$ and $k = j$, then the IMU pre-integration ΔR_{ij}, Δv_{ij} and Δp_{ij} are expressed as:

$$\Delta R_{ij} \doteq R_i^T R_j = \prod_{k=i}^{j-1} Exp((\tilde{\omega}_k - b_{gk} - n_{gk})\Delta t) \tag{12}$$

$$\Delta v_{ij} \doteq R_i^T(v_j - v_i - g\Delta t_{ij}) = \sum_{k=i}^{j-1} \Delta R_{ik}(\tilde{a}_k - b_{ak} - n_{ak})\Delta t \tag{13}$$

$$\Delta p_{ij} \doteq R_i^T(p_j - p_i - v_i\Delta t_{ij} - \frac{1}{2}g\Delta t_{ij}^2)$$
$$= \sum_{k=i}^{j-1} \left[\Delta v_{ik}\Delta t + \frac{1}{2}\Delta R_{ik}(\tilde{a}_k - b_{ak} - n_{ak})\Delta t^2 \right] \tag{14}$$

3   Scale Estimation and Refinement with a Weighted Item

In this section, we firstly introduce the process of scale estimation based on visual-inertial ORB-SLAM [9]. Since some visual-inertial measurements between two kerframes may not be exact, we propose a weighting method for outliers handling and scale estimation refinement, inspired by [10]. Next, we present a robust termination criterion for scale estimation procedure. At last, we describe the scale benchmark, which can be used to verify the accuracy of our estimated results.

3.1   Scale Estimation

In this section, we introduce the scale estimation method in details, which is able to estimate scale s, gravity $_Wg$, accelerometer bias b_a together. The full state vector X is defined as:

$$X = [s, _Wg, b_a]^T \in \mathbb{R}^{7\times 1} \tag{15}$$

In the monocular SLAM system, the camera position and 3D points are all up-to-scale. It can be solved by integrating IMU data. First we consider the following equation, which represents that it includes a visual scale s when transforming the position in the camera frame C to the IMU frame B

$$_Wp_B = s_Wp_C + R_{WC} {}_Cp_B \tag{16}$$

For two consecutive keyframe i and keyframe $i+1$, the corresponding IMU position and velocity are obtained using pre-integration Eqs. (13) and (14):

$$_Wp_B^{i+1} = {}_Wp_B^i + {}_Wv_B^i \Delta t_{i,i+1} + 0.5_Wg\Delta t_{i,i+1}^2 + R_{WB}^i(\Delta p_{i,i+1} + J_{\Delta p}^a b_a) \tag{17}$$

$$_Wv_B^{i+1} = {}_Wv_B^i + {}_Wg\Delta t_{i,i+1}^2 + R_{WB}^i(\Delta v_{i,i+1} + J_{\Delta v}^a b_a) \tag{18}$$

where Jacobian $J_{(\cdot)}^a$ denotes a first-order approximation of the effect of changing accelerometer bias. Then taking Eq. (16) into Eq. (17), it becomes:

$$s_Wp_C^{i+1} = s_Wp_C^i + {}_Wv_B^i \Delta t_{i,i+1} + 0.5_Wg\Delta t_{i,i+1}^2 + R_{WB}^i(\Delta p_{i,i+1} + J_{\Delta p}^a b_a) + (R_{WC}^i \\ - R_{WC}^{i+1})_Cp_B \tag{19}$$

To solve this linear system, we consider two relations (19) between three consecutive keyframes (Fig. 1 shows an example) and exploit the velocity relation in (18), we can get the following equations:

$$[\alpha(i) \quad \beta(i) \quad \gamma(i)]X = \psi(i) \tag{20}$$

where the visual scale s, gravity $_Wg$ and acceleration bias b_a are unknown variables. Writing keyframes i, $i+1$, $i+2$ as 1, 2, 3 for readability, we have:

$$\alpha(i) = ({}_w p_c^2 - {}_w p_c^1)\Delta t_{23} - ({}_w p_c^3 - {}_w p_c^2)\Delta t_{12} \tag{21}$$

$$\beta(i) = 0.5 I_{3\times3}(\Delta t_{12}^2 \Delta t_{23} + \Delta t_{23}^2 \Delta t_{12}) \tag{22}$$

$$\gamma(i) = R_{WB}^2 J_{\Delta p_{23}}^a \Delta t_{12} + R_{WB}^1 J_{\Delta v_{12}}^a \Delta t_{12}\Delta t_{23} - R_{WB}^1 J_{\Delta p_{12}}^a \Delta t_{23} \tag{23}$$

$$\psi(i) = (R_{WC}^1 - R_{WC}^2)c_{PB}\Delta t_{23} - (R_{WC}^2 - R_{WC}^3)c_{PB}\Delta t_{12} - R_{WB}^2\Delta p_{23}\Delta t_{12}$$
$$- R_{WB}^1\Delta v_{12}\Delta t_{12}\Delta t_{23} + R_{WB}^1\Delta p_{12}\Delta t_{23} \tag{24}$$

Stacking all relations between every three consecutive keyframes using Eq. (20), we can get a linear overdetermined equation groups. Finally, we can solve it via Singular Value Decomposition (SVD) to get the results of the scale s, gravity $_wg$, accelerometer bias b_a. Note that we can construct $3(N-2)$ equations with 7 unknowns, where N is the number of keyframes, thus we need at least 5 keyframes.

Every time a new keyframe is inserted by ORB-SLAM, the procedure runs to get new estimated values of scale, gravity and accelerometer bias. When the termination criterion is established, the estimation procedure ends up.

3.2   Weighting Method for Scale Estimation Refinement

In the Sect. 3.1, it takes all visual-inertial measurements into the scale estimation procedure, which may contain outliers, so we utilize the weight w_i to handle outliers for estimation refinement. Simply, we exploit the initial values to weight the residual in a similar way to the Huber norm [20], and define the residual as the first moment norm:

$$r_i = |C_i X_{est} - D_i| \tag{25}$$

where X_{est} is the estimated results from Sect. 3.1, C_i and D_i are from Eq. (20) for the i-th consecutive three keyframes, and defined as:

$$C_i = [\alpha(i) \quad \beta(i) \quad \gamma(i)] \tag{26}$$

$$D_i = [\psi(i)] \tag{27}$$

The weight is associated with the residual.

$$w_i = \begin{cases} 1 & r_i < threshold \\ \frac{threshold}{r_i} & otherise \end{cases} \tag{28}$$

If the measurement is obviously wrong for our scale estimate, its w_i is set to zero. And in our experiments, we set the threshold to 0.002. With the N keyframes in the process of scale estimation, we are able to build an overconstrained linear system as:

$$
\begin{bmatrix}
w_1 \cdot C_1 \\
w_2 \cdot C_2 \\
\vdots \\
w_{N-2} \cdot C_{N-2}
\end{bmatrix}
\cdot X =
\begin{bmatrix}
w_1 \cdot D_1 \\
w_2 \cdot D_2 \\
\vdots \\
w_{N-2} \cdot D_{N-2}
\end{bmatrix}
\tag{29}
$$

where C_i and D_i are from Eqs. (26) and (27) for the i-th consecutive three keyframes. Once we get the Eq. (29), the procedure runs to estimate an updated vector $\hat{X}$ by solving Eq. (29) via SVD.

3.3 Termination Criterion

In this section we propose an automatic criterion to determine when we consider the scale estimate successful. Because the norm of the nominal gravity is a constant ~ 9.8 m/s^2, we regard it as one convergence indicator. The other is that the difference of consecutive solutions X in Sect. 3.1 is under a certain threshold for several times. The visual scale estimation terminates when both conditions above are established.

3.4 Scale Benchmark

In monocular SLAM system, the translation decomposed from essential matrix is ambiguous up to an unknown scale. To obtain a globally consistent scale factor, visual-inertial ORB-SLAM system initializes mean depth of all the feature points to one. In other words, the real visual scale is determined at the start of the system initialization. Because the first two keyframes selection and the map points generation is random in the ORB-SLAM system initialization, the initial scale is not fixed. For this reason, we need to calculate the actual scale according to the ground truth data, which is extracted by Leica MS50 and motion capture system and provide us the accurate 6D pose in the IMU body reference frame B.

Once the initialization of ORB-SLAM system completes, it outcomes an initial translation t between the first two keyframes. Meanwhile, we can calculate the actual translation $_{C_1}p_{C_2}$ according to their corresponding ground truth states. Then the actual scale s is computed by the following formula:

$$
_{B_1}p_{B_2} = R_{B_1 C_2}\ _{C_2}p_{B_2} + R_{B_1 C_1}\ _{C_1}p_{C_2} + _{B_1}p_{C_1}
\tag{30}
$$

$$
s = {_{C_1}p_{C_2}}/t
\tag{31}
$$

where $_{B_1}p_{B_2}$ is the position of B_2 in the body frame B_1, B_1 and B_2 are the IMU frames corresponding to the camera frame C_1 and C_2 at the same timestamp (see Fig. 1). $R_{B_1 C_2} = R_{B_1 B_2} R_{BC}$ is computed from the orientation $R_{B_1 B_2}$ computed by the ground truth data and calibration R_{BC}.

4   Experimental Results

We conducted several experiments using the sequence $V1\_01\_easy$ and $V2\_01\_easy$ in the EuRoC dataset [21] to analyze the performance of our approach. It provides synchronized global shutter stereo images at 20 Hz with IMU measurements at 200 Hz and trajectory ground truth. We conduct the experiments in a virtual machine with 2 GB RAM.

4.1   Scale Estimation Results

The scale estimation procedure runs every time a new keyframe is inserted by ORB-SLAM [19]. Figure 2 shows the estimated scale, gravity and accelerometer bias. All variables are converged to stable values after 11 s. Figure 2(a) shows that the converged scale (~ 2.25972) is quite close to the ground truth scale (2.28132) which is the scale benchmark computed by the method that we have introduced in Sect. 3.4. Figure 2(b) indicates that the 3-axis accelerometer biases converge to almost 0. Figure 2(c) indicates that the components around x and z axes of gravity is converged quickly, and its y-axis component is converged to 9.256973 m/s^2 (near nominal gravity value). Hence the gravity direction is closed to y-axis. Figure 2(d) also shows the process of gravity estimation (depicted in blue), the green one is the nominal gravity value 9.802 m/s^2, they also come near after 11 s.

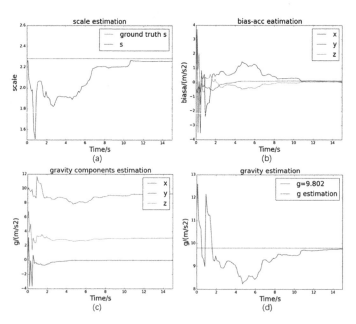

Fig. 2. The converged procedure of scale, accelerometer biases and gravity in the sequence $V1\_01\_easy$. (Color figure online)

Once we have estimated a stable and accurate scale. All 3D points in the map and the position of keyframes are updated according to the estimated scale. Figure 3(b) shows the final reconstructed sparse map, we also show a processed image in *V*1_01_*easy*.

(a)   (b)

Fig. 3. A processed image and the reconstruction from sequence *V*1_01_*easy*

4.2 The Performance of Weighted Method for Scale Estimation Refinement

We evaluated the accuracy of proposed scale estimation and refinement by comparing it with the scale benchmark computed by the method in Sect. 3.4. As can be indicated in the Tables 1 and 2: for the sequence *V*1_01_*easy* and *V*2_01_*easy*, we list the results of five tests. The second column is the scale estimation values *scale* which is almost the same as the estimated scale s of [9], and the *w_scale* is the results of estimation refinement introduced in Sect. 3.3. We show the scale benchmark in the last one. The results indicate that our scale estimation refinement method can improve the accuracy of the estimated scale.

Table 1. The results of scale estimation and refinement, compared with scale benchmark for *V*1_01_*easy*

Test number	s	Scale	w_scale	Benchmark
1	2.25409	2.25972	**2.26318**	2.28132
2	2.10896	2.12254	**2.13477**	2.35991
3	2.22838	2.24186	**2.27997**	2.27073
4	2.28314	2.34132	**2.31572**	2.26904
5	2.15126	2.16206	**2.21084**	2.26057

Table 2. The results of scale estimation and refinement, compared with scale benchmark for V2_01_easy

Test number	s	Scale	w_scale	Benchmark
1	2.79302	2.80926	**2.83144**	2.92792
2	2.52695	2.52974	**2.55774**	2.59554
3	3.02662	3.01114	**3.06962**	3.11365
4	3.16472	3.17584	**3.20926**	3.35001
5	3.41774	3.41055	**3.43063**	3.46943

4.3   The Effect of Termination Criterion

Here we test our automatic criterion to determine when we consider the scale estimation successful. In the sequence $V1\_01\_easy$, the norm of recovered gravity $_wg$ is gradually close to the nominal gravity value ~ 9.8 m/s^2, after 11 s the difference is under the threshold $(0.1\,\mathrm{m/s^2})$. And the other condition is established after the estimated scales come near for $n = 5$ times. Both conditions are established after the procedure runs about 11 s as depicted in the Fig. 3(a) and (d), and the scale estimation achieves convergence at that moment. And the converged speed in the paper [16] is 30 s, but its termination criterion is not mentioned.

5   Conclusions

In this paper, we showed our approaches for visual scale estimation and refinement. Firstly, we have presented an approach for the estimation of scale, gravity and accelerometer bias. Secondly, we proposed a weighting method for monocular visual scale estimation refinement, which utilizes weight w derived from the robust norm for outliers handling. Thirdly, we proposed an automatic way to identify convergence and termination for scale estimation procedure. We experimentally showed that the scale estimation is accurate, and the deduced weighting method further promotes the scale accuracy for the monocular visual map, and the termination criterion performs well, tested in the EuRoC dataset [21].

Acknowledgment. This research is supported by the National High Technology Research and Development Program of China (2015AA015902). We also would like to thank the authors of [19] for releasing the source code, and show my appreciation to Jing Wang for the code reproduction of the paper [9].

References

1. Leutenegger, S., Lynen, S., Bosse, M., Siegwart, R., Furgale, P.: Keyframe-based visual–inertial odometry using nonlinear optimization. Int. J. Robot. Res. **34**(3), 314–334 (2015)
2. Usenko, V., Engel, J., Stueckler, J., Cremers, D.: Direct visual-inertial odometry with stereo cameras. In: IEEE International Conference on Robotics and Automation (ICRA) (2016)
3. Forster, C., Carlone, L., Dellaert, F., Scaramuzza, D.: IMU preintegration on manifold for efficient visual-inertial maximum-a-posteriori estimation. In: Robotics: Science and Systems (RSS) (2015)
4. Concha, A., Loianno, G., Kumar, V., Civera, J.: Visual-inertial direct SLAM. In: IEEE International Conference on Robotics and Automation (ICRA) (2016)
5. Mourikis, A.I., Roumeliotis, S.I.: A multi-state constraint kalman filter for vision-aided inertial navigation. In: IEEE International Conference on Robotics and Automation (ICRA), pp. 3565–3572 (2007)
6. Jones, E.S., Soatto, S.: Visual-inertial navigation, mapping and localization: a scalable real-time causal approach. Int. J. Robot. Res. **30**(4), 407–430 (2011)
7. Wu, K., Ahmed, A., Georgiou, G., Roumeliotis, S.: A square root inverse filter for efficient vision-aided inertial navigation on mobile devices. In: Robotics: Science and Systems (RSS) (2015)
8. Lupton, T., Sukkarieh, S.: Visual-inertial-aided navigation for high-dynamic motion in built environments without initial conditions. IEEE Trans. Rob. 28(1), 61–76 (2012)
9. Mur-Artal, R., Tardós, J.D.: Visual-inertial monocular SLAM with map reuse. IEEE Robot. Autom. Lett. **2**(2), 796–803 (2017)
10. Yang, Z., Shen, S.: Monocular visual-inertial state estimation with online initialization and camera–IMU extrinsic calibration. IEEE Trans. Autom. Sci. Eng. **14**(1), 39–51 (2017)
11. Davison, A.J., Reid, I.D., Molton, N.D., et al.: MonoSLAM: real-time single camera SLAM. IEEE Trans. Pattern Anal. Mach. Intell. **29**(6), 1052 (2007)
12. Bloesch, M., Omari, S., Hutter, M., et al.: Robust visual inertial odometry using a direct EKF-based approach. In: 2015 IEEE/RSJ International Conference on Intelligent Robots and Systems (IROS), pp. 298–304. IEEE (2015)
13. Weiss, S., Achtelik, M., Chli, M., Siegwart, R.: Versatile distributed pose estimation and sensor self-calibration for an autonomous MAV. In: Proceeding of IEEE International Conference on Robotics and Automation (ICRA) (2012)
14. Weiss, S., Siegwart, R.: Real-time metric state estimation for modular vision-inertial systems. In: 2011 IEEE International Conference on Robotics and Automation (ICRA), pp. 4531–4537. IEEE (2011)
15. Engel, J., Sturm, J., Cremers, D.: Scale-aware navigation of a low-cost quadrocopter with a monocular camera. Robot. Auton. Syst. **62**(11), 1646–1656 (2014)
16. Tanskanen, P., Kolev, K., Meier, L., et al.: Live metric 3D reconstruction on mobile phones. In: Proceedings of the IEEE International Conference on Computer Vision, pp. 65–72 (2013)
17. Furgale, P., Rehder, J., Siegwart, R.: Unified temporal and spatial calibration for multi-sensor systems. In: IEEE/RSJ International Conference on Intelligent Robots and Systems (IROS), pp. 1280–1286 (2013)
18. Forster, C., Carlone, L., Dellaert, F., et al.: On-manifold preintegration for real-time visual–inertial odometry. **PP**(99), 1–21 (2016)

19. Mur-Artal, R., Montiel, J.M.M., Tardos, J.D.: ORB-SLAM: a versatile and accurate monocular SLAM system. IEEE Trans. Robot. **31**(5), 1147–1163 (2015)
20. Huber, P.J.: Robust estimation of a location parameter. Ann. Math. Statist. **35**(1), 73–101 (1964)
21. Burri, M., Nikolic, J., Gohl, P., Schneider, T., Rehder, J., Omari, S., Achtelik, M.W., Siegwart, R.: The EuRoC micro aerial vehicle datasets. Int. J. Robot. Res. **35**(10), 1157–1163 (2016)
22. Hartley, R., Zisserman, A.: Multiple View Geometry in Computer Vision, 2nd edn. Cambridge University Press, Cambridge (2004)

Crop Disease Image Recognition Based on Transfer Learning

Sisi Fang[1,2], Yuan Yuan[1], Lei Chen[1], Jian Zhang[1], Miao Li[1(✉)], and Shide Song[1]

[1] Institute of Intelligent Machines, Chinese Academy of Sciences, Hefei 230031, China
{yuanyuan,chenlei,jzhang,mli}@iim.ac.cn
[2] University of Science and Technology of China, Hefei 230026, China
fss188@mail.ustc.edu.cn

Abstract. Machine learning has been widely applied to the crop disease image recognition. Traditional machine learning needs to satisfy two basic assumptions: (1) The training and test data should be under the same distribution; (2) A large scale of labeled training samples is required to learn a reliable classification model. However, in many cases, these two assumptions cannot be satisfied. In the field of agriculture, there are not enough labeled crop disease images. In order to solve this problem, the paper proposed a method which introduced transfer learning to the crop disease image recognition. Firstly, the double Otsu method was applied to obtain the spot images of five kinds of cucumber and rice diseases. Then, color feature, texture feature and shape feature of spot images were extracted. Next, the TrAdaBoost-based method and other baseline methods were used to identify diseases. And experimental results indicate that the TrAdaBoost-based method can implement samples transfer between the auxiliary and target domain and achieve the better results than the other baseline methods. Meanwhile, the results show that transfer learning is helpful in the crop disease image recognition while the training sample is not enough.

Keywords: Image recognition · Crop diseases · Transfer learning
The spot images · Target domain

1 Introduction

Traditional methods to diagnose crop diseases, which depend on experience of agriculture experts or individual subjective consciousness who refer to some relative books, have an impact on diagnosis accuracy. Recently, the successful application of computer vision system in the area of crop disease image recognition makes up defects of conventional methods. Camargo and Smith [1] compared recognition accuracy rate of three kinds of cotton diseases by extracting different features with support vector machine (SVM), and the highest accuracy

© Springer International Publishing AG 2017
Y. Zhao et al. (Eds.): ICIG 2017, Part I, LNCS 10666, pp. 545–554, 2017.
https://doi.org/10.1007/978-3-319-71607-7_48

rate reached 90%. Li et al. [2] identified wheat stripe rust and leaf rust with SVM, which acquired a good result. Huang [3] applied artificial neural network to identify Clivia soft rot, black rot and leaf spot, and the average recognition rate ultimately got 89%. Based on rough sets theory and BP neural network, Zhang et al. [4] made four kinds of cotton diseases recognition and the average accuracy rate reached 92.72%. Nevertheless, most of these methods depend on two assumptions. First, the training and test data should be under the same distribution. Second, there should be enough labeled training samples. However, these two assumptions cannot be satisfied in many cases. In order to solve this problem, transfer learning [5] is proposed, which can improve a learner by transferring information from a relative domain to a new domain. Most proposed works mainly focused on the text domain [6–8].

In the field of image classification, the research results of transfer learning can be summarized to two main categories. The one is heterogeneous transfer learning by using related words to help image classification [9,10]. And the other one is that usually classifies images with other images from a relative domain [11]. Here, in order to solve the problem with few labeled training samples of crop diseases, combining with digital image processing technology, the paper proposed a method which introduced transfer learning to the crop disease image recognition. Took the images of five kinds of cucumber and rice diseases, for example, firstly, the spot images could be obtained after image preprocessing and segmentation. Then, the TrAdaBoost-based method was used to identify the spot images after color, texture and shape features extraction.

2   Image Acquisition and Features Extraction

2.1   Image Acquisition and Equipment

Images in this paper were collected on sunny days, using the digital single lens reflex camera of the model Canon EOS 6D. For the consideration of time and space efficiency while preserving more image details, the original images were compressed to the resolution of 600 × 400 pixels and the major disease parts were reserved with Photoshop.

2.2   Image Segmentation

Before the lesion spot image recognition, we need to segment the lesion area. There are several image segmentation methods including edge detection [12], graph theory [13] and so on. In this paper, the double Otsu algorithm [14] is used due to its universality on these five kinds of diseases. More concretely, the R component of RGB space of the original color image is selected for the first Otsu segmentation and morphological operation. As a result, the image is divided into background and non-background class. Next, after comparing different color components of the lesion area of non-background class, we carry out the second Otsu on the Cr component of YCbCr space. The spot images obtained by double Otsu are shown in Fig. 1.

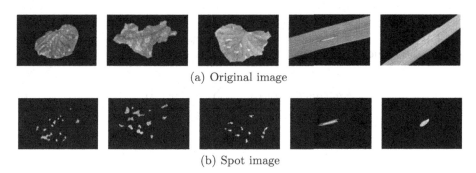

(a) Original image

(b) Spot image

Fig. 1. Segmentation results of five kinds of cucumber and rice diseases (cucumber target leaf spot, cucumber downy mildew, cucumber bacterial angular leaf spot, rice blast, rice brown spot) (Color figure online)

2.3 Feature Extraction

Color feature extraction. Since it is obviously different between the normal area and the lesion area of leaf in color, the color can be considered as an important feature. The color moment is a common method to extract color features. So we express the color distribution with average, variance and skewness. RGB and HIS are two kinds of common color spaces which consist of the component R, G, B and the component H, I, S, respectively. It is evident for the lesion areas of cucumber and rice leaf at channel B. And the component H is only one dimension value because of a conversion from gray value in RGB space to hue value in HIS space [15]. So we can calculate average, variance and skewness of B and H component according to formulas (1)–(3):

$$Average : \mu_i = \frac{1}{n} \sum_{j=1}^{n} P_{i,j}, \tag{1}$$

$$Variance : \sigma_i = (\frac{1}{n} \sum_{j=1}^{n} (P_{i,j} - \mu_i)^2)^{\frac{1}{2}}, \tag{2}$$

$$Skewness : s_i = (\frac{1}{n} \sum_{j=1}^{n} (P_{i,j} - \mu_i)^3)^{\frac{1}{3}}, \tag{3}$$

where $P_{(i,j)}$ is gray value of j pixel point at channel i and n is the number of total pixels.

Texture feature extraction. As an important indicator for the lesion area recognition, texture feature is usually expressed by GLCM (Gray Level Co-occurrence Matrix). We assume that f(x,y) is an $M \times N$ gray image whose grayscale is N_g. So the element of GLCM can be shown as:

$$P(i,j,d,\theta) = \#\{[(x_1,y_1),(x_2,y_2)] \in M \times N | f(x_1,y_1) = i, f(x_2,y_2) = j\}, \tag{4}$$

where $P(i,j,d,\theta)$ is the element of row i and j column, d is the distance between the two pixels, θ is the angle between the pixel and the abscissa axis, and $\#(x)$ is the number of the set x, and $(i,j) \in N_g \times N_g$ [15].

In the paper, we set $d = 1$. When θ is 0°, 45°, 90° and 135°, we respectively calculate the energy, the contrast and the entropy. Afterwards, we obtain their average and standard deviation. Some correlative formulas are given as:

$$Energy(Ene) : Ene = \sum_{i=0}^{N_g} \sum_{j=0}^{N_g} [p(i,j)]^2, \tag{5}$$

$$Contrast(Con) : Con = \sum_{i=0}^{N_g} \sum_{j=0}^{N_g} (i-j)^2 p(i,j), \tag{6}$$

$$Entropy(Ent) : Ent = \sum_{i=0}^{N_g} \sum_{j=0}^{N_g} p(i,j) log_2 [p(i,j)]^2, \tag{7}$$

Shape feature extraction. Because the shape of lesion areas is various for different crop diseases, it plays an important role on the lesion area recognition. We extract the shape features based on the spot boundary. Firstly, we get the binary spot image. Next, we mark every region after its boundary coordinates are found in the binary image. Finally, according to the region shape, seven parameters such as circularity, discrete index [16], inscribed circle radius, the radius ratio between the inscribed circle and circumscribed circle, rectangle, elongation and eccentricity are taken for the shape feature. Several parameters are given as follows:

$$Circularity(c) : c = \frac{4\pi A}{L^2}, \tag{8}$$

where A is the area of the spot image [17] and L is the perimeter. Obviously, the range of c is 0–1, so when $c = 1$, the spot shape is circularity.

$$Discrete\ Index(d) : d = \frac{L^2}{A}, \tag{9}$$

$$Inscribed\ Circle\ Radius(r) : r = \frac{2A}{L}, \tag{10}$$

$$Rectangle(R) : R = \frac{A}{A_R}, \tag{11}$$

where A_R is the area of smallest circumscribed rectangle, the range of R is 0–1 and when $R = 1$, the spot shape is rectangle.

Synthesizing the above features, we extract nineteen parameters as the eigenvector for the crop disease image recognition.

3   Disease Image Recognition Based on Transfer Learning

A frame for disease image recognition is shown in Fig. 2.

The purpose of transfer learning is to use the auxiliary training data under a different distribution from the less target training data to help to establish a

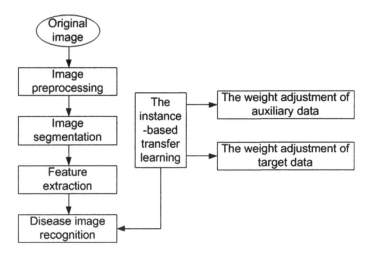

Fig. 2. The overview of disease image recognition system

reliable classification model [18]. Furthermore, if the distributions of two data sets are similar, the transfer learning based on instance works better [19]. So we introduce the instance-based transfer learning in the paper and identify cucumber and rice diseases with the TrAdaBoost-based method(TrBM).

Algorithm 1 is a holistic description of TrBM. In each iteration, on the one hand, TrBM uses Adaboost to adjust the weight of the target training data. If the sample is wrongly predicted, Adaboost will increase the weight of this sample through multiplying its weight with $\beta_t^{-|h_t(x_i)-c(x_i)|}$. On the other hand, in order to reduce the effect of the auxiliary training data which is most dissimilar to the target training data, a mechanism [19] is added to decrease its weight by multiplying its weight with $\beta^{|h_t(x_i)-c(x_i)|}$. At the same time, if the weight is less than a fixed value that we set, it will be removed. After several iterations, the target training data which is wrongly predicted and the auxiliary training data that is similar to the target training data will have larger training weights. So they will help to train a better classifier.

4   Experimental Results and Discussion

4.1   Data Sets Description

We conduct the experiments on five kinds of crop diseases, that is, cucumber target leaf spot (We shortly write as c.t.l.s.), downy mildew (c.d.m), bacterial angular leaf spot (c.b.a.l.s), rice brown spot (r.b.s) and rice blast (r.b). In addition, all the algorithms mentioned in this paper are implemented in Matlab2015a and Visual Studio 2013. We take four sets of data in Table 1 to fit transfer learning scenario after repeated attempts.

Algorithm 1. TrBM

Input: the labeled auxiliary training data set D_a, the labeled target training data set
   D_b, the unlabeled test data set, D_t the combined training data set $D = D_a \bigcup D_b$,
   a basic Learner(SVM) and the maximum number of iteration N.
   Note that, D_b and D_t are under the same distrbution.
Output: the modified learner:

$$h(x) = \begin{cases} 1, \sum_{t=N/2}^{N} ln\frac{1}{\beta_t} h_t(x) \geq \frac{1}{2}\sum_{t=N/2}^{N} ln\frac{1}{\beta_t} \\ 0, \ otherwise \end{cases}$$

1: Initialize the weight vector of D, that $w^1 = (\omega_1^1, \cdots, \omega_{p+q}^1)$,

$$\omega_i^1 \begin{cases} 1/p, \ i = 1, \cdots, p \\ 1/q, \ i = p+1, \cdots, p+q \end{cases}$$

   where p is the number of D_a, q is the number of D_b.
2: Set w_l, that is the lower limit of weight.
3: **for** $t = 1, \cdots, N$ **do**
4:    Calculate the weight distribution over D:

$$Z^t = w^t / \sum_{i=1}^{p+q} \omega_i^t$$

5:    Call Learner(SVM), get back a modified learner h_t with the combined training
      set D, the distribution Z^t and the unlabeled test set D_t.
6:    Calculate the error of h_t on D_b:

$$\varepsilon_t = \sum_{i=p+1}^{p+q} \frac{\omega_i^t |h_t(x_i) - c(x_i)|}{\sum_{i=p+1}^{p+q} \omega_i^t}$$

7:    Set $\beta = 1/(1 + \sqrt{2lnp/N})$, $\beta_t = \frac{\varepsilon_t}{1-\varepsilon_t}$, where ε_t is usually required to be less
      than $1/2$.
8:    Update the new weight vector of D:

$$\omega_i^{t+1} = \begin{cases} \omega_i^t \beta^{|h_t(x_i)-c(x_i)|}, \ i = 1, \cdots, p \\ \omega_i^t \beta_t^{-|h_t(x_i)-c(x_i)|}, \ i = p+1, \cdots, p+q \end{cases}$$

9:    Remove the weight that is less than w_l.
10: **end for**

4.2   Experimental Results and Analysis

It is necessary to normalize four data sets before the experiments. Subsequently,
we compare TrBM which uses SVM as the basic learner with other four baseline
methods. The descriptions of these five methods are shown in Table 2. Thereinto,
a linear kernel is applied in all SVMs and the nearest number of training samples
is set to 7 in all KNNs. During the experiments, a target training set D_b and a
test set D_t are under the same distribution. Table 3 presents the experimental

Table 1. Data sets description in experiment

Groups	The auxiliary training data	The number of feature vector	The target training data	The number of feature vector
Group 1	c.t.l.s & c.d.m	600	r.b.s & r.b	324
Group 2	c.d.m & r.b.s	600	c.t.l.s & c.b.a.l.s	324
Group 3	c.b.a.l.s & r.b.s	600	c.t.l.s & c.d.m	324
Group 4	c.t.l.s & c.b.a.l.s	600	r.b.s & r.b	324

Table 2. The descriptions of five methods

Methods	Labeled training data	Test data	Basic learner
SVM	D_b	D_t	SVM
SVM-T	D	D_t	SVM
KNN	D_b	D_t	KNN
KNN-T	D	D_t	KNN
TrBM	D	D_t	SVM

Table 3. Accuracy rates when the ratio is 0.04

Data Sets	SVM	SVM-T	KNN	KNN-T	TrBM
Group 1	0.8591	0.4505	0.7927	0.3754	**0.9256**
Group 2	0.6561	0.6728	0.5937	0.4601	**0.8183**
Group 3	0.7239	0.5302	0.6894	0.3694	**0.8232**
Group 4	0.8591	0.3990	0.7927	0.3392	**0.9362**

results of five methods when the ratio between the target training data and the auxiliary training data is 0.04 (Since the number of experimental data is scarce, in order to ensure reliability in experiment, the smallest ratio is set to 0.04). The performance in accuracy rate is the average of 10 repeats by random choice of the target training data and the iteration number of weight adjustment is set to 100.

From Table 3, we can see that the accuracy rates achieved by TrBM are absolutely higher than four other methods. The experimental results on four data sets are presented in Fig. 3 (Because the experimental results with SVM-T and KNN-T are much worse than other three methods, we only show SVM, KNN and TrBM results in Figure). Here, the ratio between the target and the auxiliary training data is gradually increased from 0.04 to 0.2.

In Fig. 3(a) and (d), when the ratio is less than 0.08, the performance of TrBM is better than other methods. However, as the ratio increases, the performance of TrBM is not as good as SVM, but is still better than KNN. As we know, the advantage of SVM is that it can get a better classification model when the number of the training data is not large.

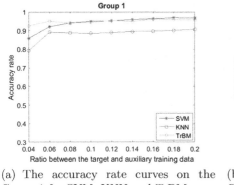
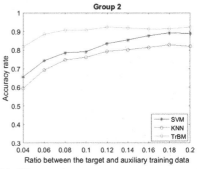

(a) The accuracy rate curves on the Group 1 for SVM, KNN and TrBM

(b) The accuracy rate curves on the Group 2 for SVM, KNN and TrBM

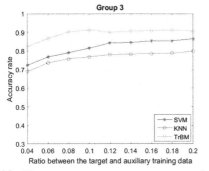
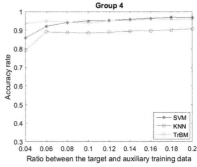

(c) The accuracy rate curves on the Group 3 for SVM, KNN and TrBM

(d) The accuracy rate curves on the Group 4 for SVM, KNN and TrBM

Fig. 3. The experimental results on four data sets

In Fig. 3(b) and (c), the performance of TrBM always exceeds the SVM and KNN when the ratio is within 0.2. Meanwhile, as the ratio increases, the results of SVM gradually approach TrBM. We believe that the auxiliary training data contain not only good knowledge, but also noisy data. When there are enough target training data to learn a good classifier, the noisy part of the auxiliary training data affect the learner.

5   Conclusions

(1) The paper proposed the instance-based transfer learning for the crop disease image recognition. After the auxiliary, target and test image pre-processing, we obtained a nineteen dimensional eigenvector for each spot image. Then, we transferred the useful auxiliary data to target data with TrBM. In short, we increased the weight of the target training data that was wrongly predicted, decrease the weight of the auxiliary training data which was most dissimilar to the target training data and remove the weight that is less than the lower limit

of weight in each iteration. Finally, we implemented comparison experiments by TrBM and four other methods on cucumber and rice diseases.

(2) The experimental results reveal that transfer learning is beneficial for the crop disease image recognition when the training sample is not enough. Especially, TrBM can implement samples transfer between two domains which are under the different distribution. In the future, we will extend transfer learning to other crop diseases image recognition.

Acknowledgments. The authors would like to thank the anonymous reviewers for their helpful reviews. The work is supported by the National Natural Science Foundation of China under No. 31501223.

References

1. Camargo, A., Smith, J.S.: Image pattern classification for the identification of disease causing agents in plants. Comput. Electron. Agric. **66**(2), 121–125 (2009)
2. Li, G.L., Ma, Z.H., Wang, H.G.: Image recognition of wheat stripe rust and wheat leaf rust based on support vector machine. J. China Agric. Univ. **17**(2), 72–79 (2012)
3. Huang, K.Y.: Application of artificial neural network for detecting phalaenopsis seedling diseases using color and texture features. Comput. Electron. Agric. **57**(1), 3–11 (2007)
4. Zhang, J.H., Qi, L.J., Ji, R.H.: Cotton diseases identification based on rough sets and BP neural network. Trans. Chin. Soc. Agric. Eng. **28**(7), 161–167 (2012)
5. Zhuang, F.Z., Luo, P., He, Q.: Survey on transfer learning research. J. Softw. **26**(1), 26–39 (2015)
6. Xie, S., Fan, W., Peng, J., Verscheure, O., Ren, J.: Latent space domain transfer between high dimensional overlapping distributions. In: Proceedings of the 18th International Conference on World Wide Web, WWW 2009, pp. 91–100. ACM, New York (2009)
7. Li, B., Yang, Q., Xue, Y.: Can movies and books collaborate? Cross-domain collaborative filtering for sparsity reduction. In: 21st International Joint Conference on Artificial Intelligence, pp. 2052–2057 (2009)
8. Jiang, J., Zhai, C.: Instance weighting for domain adaptation in NLP. In: ACL (2007)
9. Zhu, Y., Chen, Y., Lu, Z., Pan, S.J., Xue, G.R., Yu, Y., Yang, Q.: Heterogeneous transfer learning for image classification. In: Proceedings of the Twenty-Fifth AAAI Conference on Artificial Intelligence, AAAI 2011, pp. 1304–1309. AAAI Press (2011)
10. Dai, W., Chen, Y., Xue, G., Yang, Q., Yu, Y.: Translated learning: transfer learning across different feature spaces. In: Koller, D., Schuurmans, D., Bengio, Y., Bottou, L. (eds.) Advances in Neural Information Processing Systems, vol. 21, pp. 353–360 (2008)
11. Lin, Y.: Lung nodule computer-aided detection based on transfer learning (2013)
12. Tobias, B., Aura, N.Q., Wolfgang, K., Dimitar, D., Patrick, S.: Hypharea-automated analysis of spatiotemporal fungal patterns. J. Plant Physiol. **168**(1), 72–78 (2011)
13. Wang, M., Li, Y.J., Quan, X.M.: A survey on graph theory approaches of image segmentation. Comput. Appl. Soft. **31**(9), 1–12 (2014)

14. Wu, N., Li, M., Yuan, Y.: Image segmentation of cucumber target spot disease based on hybrid color space and double Otsu algorithm. J. China Agric. Univ. **21**(3), 125–130 (2016)
15. Yuan, Y., Chen, L., Wu, N.: Recognition of rice sheath blight based on image procession. J. Agric. Mech. Res. **38**(6), 84–87+92 (2016)
16. Peng, Z.: Research on cucumber disease identification based on image processing and pattern recognition technology (2007)
17. Deng, J.Z., Li, M., Yuan, Z.B.: Feature extraction and classification of tilletia diseases based on image recognition. Trans. Chin. Soc. Agric. Eng. **3**, 172–176 (2012)
18. Weiss, K., Khoshgoftaar, T.M., Wang, D.: A survey of transfer learning. J. Big Data **3**, 9 (2016)
19. Dai, W., Yang, Q., Xue, G.R., Yu, Y.: Boosting for transfer learning. In: Proceedings of the 24th International Conference on Machine Learning, ICML 2007, pp. 193–200. ACM, New York (2007)

Multi-orientation Scene Text Detection Leveraging Background Suppression

Xihan Wang[1(✉)], Xiaoyi Feng[1], Zhaoqiang Xia[1], Jinye Peng[2], and Eric Granger[3]

[1] School of Electronics and Information, Northwestern Polytechnical University,
Xi'an 710072, China
xihanwang@mail.nwpu.edu.cn

[2] School of Information Science and Technology, Northwest University,
Xi'an 710069, China

[3] Laboratoire d'imagerie, de vision et d'intelligence artificielle (LIVIA),
École de technologie supérieure, Université du Québec,
1100, rue Notre-Dame Ouest, Montréal, (QC) H3C 1K3, Canada

Abstract. Most state-of-the-art text detection methods are devoted to horizontal texts and these methods cannot work well when encountering blurred, multi-oriented, low-resolution and small-sized texts. In this paper, we propose to localize texts from the perspective of suppressing more non-text backgrounds, in which a coarse-to-fine strategy is presented to remove non-text pixels from images. Firstly, the fully convolutional network (FCN) framework is utilized to make the coarse prediction of text labeling. Secondly, an efficient saliency measure based on background priors is employed to further suppress non-text pixels and generate fine character candidate regions. The remaining candidates of character regions composite text lines, so that the proposed method can handle multi-orientation texts in natural scene images. Two public datasets, MSRA-TD500 and ICDAR2013 are utilized to evaluate the performance of our proposed method. Experimental results show that our method achieves high recall rate and demonstrates the competitive performance.

Keywords: Scene text detection · Fully Convolutional Network Background suppression · Multi-orientation texts

1 Introduction

In recent years, the extraction of information in images has attracted much attention, with the widespread application of video and image acquisition equipments. Scene text provides direct high-level semantic information and plays an important role in a variety of interesting applications [20], such as criminal investigation, visual assistant for the blinds, translators for tourists, automatic driving and navigation. Texts in uncontrolled environments may exhibit in different

© Springer International Publishing AG 2017
Y. Zhao et al. (Eds.): ICIG 2017, Part I, LNCS 10666, pp. 555–566, 2017.
https://doi.org/10.1007/978-3-319-71607-7_49

layout, language, font and size, text-like background objects, non-uniform illuminations, blur and occlusion. Consequently, text localization in natural scene is still a challenging task.

Usually, there exist two main types of conventional methods for scene text detection: sliding window based [24] and connected component (CCs) based [4,12,23]. However, the performance of these methods heavily relies on hand-crafted features. These methods may not work well under severe complexities, such as blur and low resolution. Recently, a new trend has appeared that the deep neural network based algorithms have gradually become the mainstream. State-of-the-art methods for object detection/semantic segmentation have been modified for text detection, and achieve great improvement in this field. However, most methods are specifically designed for horizontal or near-horizontal texts. The deep networks specially designed for object segmentation may not be accurate in word-level or line-level text extraction. When multiple text lines flock together, it becomes difficult to identify each individual text line (See Fig. 1(b)).

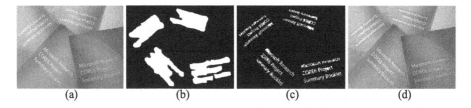

Fig. 1. Overview of our proposed algorithm: (a) Original image. (b) Prediction result of global background suppression. (c) Character candidates generation by local background suppression. (d) Result of text detection.

To overcome the above challenges, we tackle the problem of text localization from a new perspective. In this paper, we consider the character component extraction from an opposite point of view, i.e., by suppressing more non-text backgrounds. Ideally, better background suppression means better prospects of foreground detection. As illustrated in Fig. 1, an unconventional detection framework for scene text is proposed. In our method, a coarse-to-fine strategy is adopted to remove non-text pixels from global image to local regions. We use the Fully Convolutional Network (FCN) framework [11], which is suitable to generate a pixel-wise text/non-text saliency map. The map provides a powerful guidance for estimating text regions, however, this prediction is regional and it is hard to separate each instance. A saliency measure strategy is utilized to further remove the background a fine level. Then, the foreground is considered as character candidate regions and generates text lines with graph partition.

The contributions of our approach are as follows. First, we cast scene text detection as a background suppression problem and utilize a two-step framework to remove non-text pixel globally and locally. The resulting foreground regions can be considered as character-level proposals extraction. Second, an efficient saliency measure method based on background priors is presented to further suppress the non-text pixel. We use super-pixels substitute single pixels obtaining high accuracy and efficiency. This measure result allows our method to handle multi-lingual text. Third, character-to-line strategy endows the system with the ability to detect multi-oriented and curved texts.

2   Related Work

Scene text detection in natural images has received much attention and many effective methods have been presented. As mentioned, conventional methods heavily rely on manually designed features. Zhang et al. [24] directly extracted text lines from natural images by local symmetry property of character groups. A convolutional neural networks (CNN) with the powerful discrimination ability was trained to eliminate false positives. However, sliding window based methods are usually time-consuming and not suitable for multi-orientation texts. Connected component-based methods usually aim to extract character candidate regions, and then group character candidates into words or text line. Stroke Width Transform (SWT) [4], Maximally Stable Extremal Regions (MSER) [12] are two representative methods for character candidate generation as well as their subsequent works [19,22,23]. Yao et al. [19] proposed a method based on MSER for detecting text of arbitrary directions. Yin et al. [22] presented a learning framework for adaptive hierarchical clustering, in which text candidates are constructed by grouping characters based on this adaptive clustering. Wei et al. [17] captured character regions with the exhaustive segmentation method and presented a learning-based text line grouping method. These CCs-based methods obtained promising performance on a variety of standard benchmark datasets. Nevertheless, these methods may fail when character is not homogeneous or composed of broken strokes in complex backgrounds.

In recent years, deep convolutional neural networks for scene text detection [3,5–7] have been a new trend and achieved superior performance over conventional approaches. These methods use deep convolutional network mainly from two aspects: (1) learn a more robust text representation; (2) take advantage of the powerful classification ability for better eliminating false positives. Different from performing classification on local regions, Zhang et al. [25] utilized both local and global cues, and a Fully Convolutional Network (FCN) model was trained to predict the salient map. Then components are extracted based on MSER for multiple orientations text detection. Some text detection methods treat text words or lines as generic objects. Tian et al. [15] developed a vertical anchors mechanism and constructed a CNN-RNN joint-model to detect extremely challenging text. Zhong et al. [26] attempt to convert Faster-RCNN into text detection. However, those two methods may not be suitable for multi-oriented scene text detection.

The proposed algorithm is inspired by work in saliency detection [16], which aim to measure object level saliency with background priors. In this paper, we tackle the text detection from opposite thought, we focus more on the background suppression instead of text component extraction or window-based classification. Different from [16], the prior information is obtained from pixel-wise prediction maps from FCN.

3   Proposed Method

In this section, details of proposed algorithm are presented (See Fig. 2). The global background suppression is described in Sect. 3.1, character candidates extraction by local background suppression and linking of character candidates into text lines are given in Sects. 3.2 and 3.3, respectively.

3.1   Global Background Suppression

To better distinguish between foreground (text) and background (non-text), we consider this problem as a kind of pixel-labeling task. Following the general design of [18], in this paper, we apply our proposed modification architecture to label text/non-text regions in a holistic way.

Network Architecture. As shown in Fig. 2, necessary modifications are applied for fully using high-level semantic information in upper network layers. The first 5 convolutional stages are adopted from VGG-16 net [13], while the last several stages, including the 5th pooling layer and all the fully connected layers, are cut off. We focus on the last three stages, respectively conv3-3, conv4-3, conv5-3. Each stage is followed by a convolutional layer with 1×1 kernel size, and then connected to a deconvolutional layer to ensure that the outputs of all the stages have the same size as the input. The multi-level side-outputs maps are concatenated together to form the fused map with a weight layer (a convolutional layer with 1×1 kernel size). There are two reasons that prompt us to omit the first and second stages. Firstly, compared to local structures features from lower layers, our algorithm at this stage is more concerned with high-level

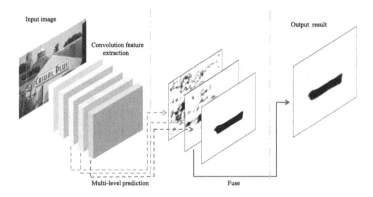

Fig. 2. Network architecture of the proposed algorithm. The first 5 convolutional stages are adopted from VGG 16-layer net, and the architectures are equivalent to making independent predictions from last three stages and fuse the results.

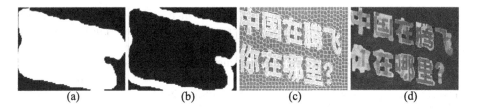

Fig. 3. Illustration of character candidates generation: (a) Prediction results of foreground region by network. (b) Designing background regions by morphological operations. (c) Super-pixel segmentation. (d) Confidence map with background suppression.

semantics semantic information in upper network layers. Secondly, different from the label data in general pixel labeling task, such as semantic segmentation and edge detection, label maps converted by ground truth are mixed with non-text background information and it will cause interference to the lower layers.

Ground Truth and Loss Function. The label maps are generated from ground truth annotations. Pixels inside the bounding box are considered as the positive regions. These pixels are marked as '1' while the background region outside the bounding box are marked as '0'.

In training phase, we use balanced cross-entropy loss to compute the errors between side-outputs and ground truth, which is introduced in [18]. Denote the ground truth for a given pixel as $y_i^* \in \{0,1\}$ and predicted value as $\hat{y}_i$, L is formulated as

$$L_s = -\beta \sum_{i \in L_s} y_i^* \log \hat{y}_i - (1 - \beta) \sum_{i \in L_s} (1 - y_i^*) \log(1 - \hat{y}_i) \tag{1}$$

where $\beta = |Y_-|/(|Y_+| + |Y_-|)$, $|Y_+|$ and $|Y_-|$ denote the number of text pixels and non-text pixels in the ground truth. In this paper, the multi-level prediction map is used to generate final prediction result through the fusion layer. The loss between the fusion output and ground truth is also using the balanced cross-entropy loss function. A binary map is generated as the result of global background suppression, and the black pixels are considered as background and the text candidate region are marked as white pixels. An example of predicted map is shown in Fig. 3(a).

3.2   Local Background Suppression

After performing global background suppression, the majority of non-text background are removed. For scene text detection, however, it is necessary to differentiate between character instances, for which two-class (text or non-text) semantic predicted are insufficient (e.g. non-text regions adjacent multiple text line are labeled as the same class with characters it make difficult to separate each instance, see Fig. 3(a)). Inspired by the works of [2,16], which aim at saliency object detection problem, two kinds of analysis about text and non-text background in scene images, namely *visual contrast analysis* and *background connectivity analysis*, is utilized to further suppress background information.

People can effortlessly capture text regions in a split second. It illustrates that the vision system is sensitive to contrast in visual signal. The first analysis is based on this rule. In other words, text in scene usually contrast strongly with their background to attract more humans attention. Specifically, the global contrast of text pixel is defined using its color contrast to all other pixels in the background. The confidence value $C(I_i)$ is defined as,

$$C(I_i) = \sum_{\forall I_b \in B} D(I_i, I_b) \tag{2}$$

where I_i is a pixel in image I and background pixel set $B\{I_b, b = 1, ..., N\}$, where N is the number of pixels in the background. $D(I_i, I_b)$ is the color distance between pixels I_i and I_b (measured in $L*a*b$ space), the sum of all distance is mapped to $[0, 1]$ by normalization. Background pixels are based on the predicted result in global background suppression stage.

Based on the contrast and predicted map prior, we further observe that most background regions close to the same character can be easily connected to their surroundings. We call it the *background connectivity*. Benefited from global prediction, the foreground regions in predicted map can be considered to contain both text and background. This suggests that we can define the background confidence of a pixel as the length of its shortest path to the foreground region boundaries, which can be obtained by computing weighted geodesic distances.

We first segment the predicted map into regions (each region contains foreground and considered as mask map). Then the boundary region is obtained with the morphological dilation operation, see Fig. 3(b). For each image region, we build an undirected weighted graph $G = \{V, E\}$. The vertex set V of nodes contains all image pixels in the foreground region and boundary region, $V = \{F\} \bigcup \{B\}$. E is a set of edges, $E \subseteq \{(v, \nu)|v, \nu \in V and v \neq \nu\}$. A path from v to ν is a sequence $P(v, \nu) = (v = p_1, p_2, ..., p_n = \nu)$. The edges $(p_i, p_{i+1}) \in E$ connect all adjacent nodes and $i = 1, 2, ..., n - 1$. The path weight $\omega(P(v, \nu))$ is defined as,

$$\omega(P(v, \nu)) = \sum_{i=1}^{n-1} D(p_i, p_{i+1}) \tag{3}$$

where $D(p_i, p_{i+1})$ is the distance between the color features of two nodes (normalized to $[0, 1]$ in $L * a * b$ space). In order to reduce the interference of similar nodes distance on path weights, a threshold τ is introduced to control the strength of adjacent nodes weight. The τ is taken as mean value of the smallest distances from all nodes with their neighbors. The distances smaller than this threshold will be equal to zero. The minimum of path weight means the shortest path from v to ν, and it characterizes the connectivity between two nodes. The background connectivity of a pixel I_i accumulates all shortest path weights from I_i to each pixel in boundary region B on the graph G. The function is given in the following manner:

$$S(I_i) = \sum_{\forall I_b \in B} \min\{\omega(P(I_i, I_b))\} \tag{4}$$

We use Johnson's [8] algorithm to find the shortest paths $\min\{\omega(P(I_i, I_b))\}$. The pixel with a lower S value in the foreground has a higher possibility of background.

Obviously, using Eqs. 2 and 5 to evaluate the value for each image pixel is an extremely inefficient process, which is too computationally expensive even for medium sized images. The key to speed up the algorithm is the use of super-pixels instead of pixels to reduce the number of pixels in the image. We extract the SLIC super-pixels [1] from image regions. Each region is re-scaled to have maximum dimension of $250 * 250$ pixels with aspect ratio unchanged. Then the mean color of super-pixels is computed and analyzed at the region level. We further incorporate its global contrast and connectivity information to increase the difference between foreground and background. Specifically, for any super-pixel region r_k, we can define $C(r_k)$ and $S(r_k)$ from Eq. 2 and 5. The background suppression result is defined as,

$$S_b(r_k) = \omega(r_k)S(r_k)(C(r_k) + \varepsilon) \tag{5}$$

where $\omega(r_k)$ is the weight of region r_k, and it is defined as $|R_+|/|R|$, $|R_+|$ denotes the count of "1" pixels which marked by predicted map and $|R|$ denotes the total count of pixels. ε controls the strength of global contrast, In our implementation, we use $\varepsilon = 0.4$. The final confidence map is shown in Fig. 3(d).

3.3 Text Lines Formation

The purpose of this stage is to form multi-oriented text lines from the remaining character candidates, which are obtained by connected component analysis. Similar to previous work in [21], we initially establish a fully connected graph G by Delaunay triangulation. In the graph, each vertex represents a character candidate region and the weight of edges model the adjacency relation between pairs of candidates. Based on the graph, a Maximum Spanning Tree is constructed. Different from method [21], we count the direction of each edge and find the main direction of the text line. The edge different from the main direction is removed. Then, the remained edges were merged to construct the original text chains. A straight line is fitted to the centroids of candidates within each chain. The single component which has similar intensities will be re-linked into a chain. The process is iterated until all text candidates have been assigned to a line. An example of text lines formation is shown in Fig. 4. In certain tasks,

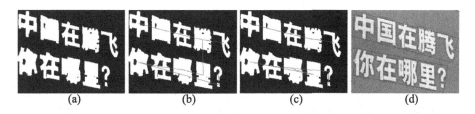

Fig. 4. Text lines formation: (a) Character candidates. (b) MST construction. (c) Text line partition. (d) Result of detection.

such as ICDAR 2013, word partition is required. Since text in images from these datasets is labelled in word level. We adopted the word partition method in [4] as it has been proven to be simple and effective.

4   Experiments and Discussions

We performed experiments on two standard benchmarks, namely, MSRA-TD 500 and ICDAR 2013 , to evaluate our algorithm, which is compared with other scene text detection methods. The training data are the union of training images from datasets. In training phase, a fixed 300×300 sliding window with half window length step is used to corp more patches from scaled images. Then we evenly rotated images to four different angles (with $90°$ angle interval). In testing, we compute the predicted map by trained model in multi-scale sliding window strategy. The detections of different scales are fused to form the final forecast. All experiments are conducted on a general computer (Intel Core i5, 3.2 GHz 4-core CPU, 8 G RAM, GeForce GTX950 and Windows 64-bit OS). At runtime, all testing images are performed at original dimension and the routine ran on a single GPU.

4.1   Datasets

Two standard datasets used to validate our scene text detection method will be introduced briefly:

MSRA-TD 500: The MSRA-TD 500 is originally proposed in [19] and it is a typical multi-orientation benchmark dataset for assessing detection algorithms. The dataset have 300 training images and 200 test images, all image are high-resolution natural scene images. Text in this dataset Contains varying directions, fonts, mixed languages, and complexity of backgrounds, these factors make the dataset have highly challenging.

ICDAR 2013: The ICDAR 2013 dataset is from the ICDAR 2013 Robust Reading Competition [10]. A total of 229 natural images were used for training, and 233 images for testing. All the text in this dataset are notable horizontal and near-horizontal, and the ground truth annotated in word level.

4.2   Experimental Results and Discussions

We adopted the evaluation method proposed by wei [17] to compare our method with other methods. We first evaluate our algorithm on MSRA-TD 500. Table 1 shows the performance comparison of different algorithms on the MSRA-TD 500 dataset. As can be seen, our method achieves the recall rate of 0.73, precision of 0.75, and f-measure of 0.74. The proposed algorithm achieves the highest recall than other methods on this dataset, the precision slightly lower than other two methods. There are two main reasons: (1) To handle some short, single characters, the global predicted map will bring more false alarms, as well as the

Table 1. Performances of different text detection methods evaluated on MSRA-TD500.

Algorithm	Precision	Recall	F-measure
Proposed	0.75	**0.73**	**0.74**
Zhang et al. [25]	**0.83**	0.67	**0.74**
Yin et al. [22]	0.81	0.63	0.71
Kang et al. [9]	0.71	0.62	0.66
Yin et al. [23]	0.71	0.61	0.66
Yao et al. [19]	0.63	0.63	0.60

Table 2. Performances of different text detection methods evaluated on ICDAR 2013.

Algorithm	Precision	Recall	F-measure
Proposed	0.82	**0.81**	0.81
Zhang et al. [25]	**0.88**	0.78	**0.83**
Wei et al. [17]	0.84	0.77	0.80
Zhang et al. [24]	0.88	0.74	0.80
Tian et al. [14]	0.85	0.76	0.80
Yin et al. [23]	0.86	0.68	0.76

not-text backgrounds which have very similar structure with text can not be easily distinguish. (2) The character candidates are still mixed with many non text regions, our proposed method currently can not filter these regions.

We then evaluate our method on ICDAR 2013, The performance of proposed algorithm evaluated on the ICDAR 2013 dataset is shown in Table 2. In this experiment, the overall performance of our algorithm is not better than other previous state-of-the-art methods, the proposed method only achieves the highest recall (0.81) among all the methods. Except we discuss in first experiments, the unsuccessful result may be due to the following reasons: (1) text in ICDAR 2013 dataset are notable horizontal and near-horizontal, most text detection algorithms are well-directed, to measure the performance of our system, text line candidates must further partitioned into words. (2) Our method is main focus on the capacity of handling multi-oriented text, the advantages of multi-oriented text detection cannot be reflected in this dataset.

Figure 5(a) shows the successful detection results of the proposed algorithm a number of challenging cases, the qualitative results show our algorithm is able to handle text instances of different orientations, fonts, and languages. The images also show that our system is robust against strong lighting and blur. However, in some certain conditions, our method may fail, for example, characters with art font, low resolution or serious blur. As shown in Fig. 5(b), we believe that our method still has room for performance improvement with the increase of training samples.

(a)

(b)

Fig. 5. Qualitative results of the proposed method: (a) Successful text detection results. (b) Some failure cases

5   Conclusions

In this work, a novel algorithm is presented for multi-oriented text detection in natural scene images. In contrast with a vast majority of the previous methods, we tackled the text extraction problem from a opposite direction. A coarse-to-fine non-text backgrounds suppress strategy was adopted to remove non-text pixels, thus is able to get better prospects foreground detection. Our algorithm can directly handle multi-oriented text from images, while most previous approaches only focused horizontal or near-horizontal text. The experiments on two public datasets demonstrated the competitive performance and effectiveness of the proposed methods.

Acknowledgment. This paper is supported by H3C Foundation of Ministry of Education of China, No. 2017A19050, the National Aerospace Science and Technology Foundation and the National Nature Science Foundation of China (No. 61702419).

References

1. Achanta, R., Shaji, A., Smith, K., Lucchi, A., Fua, P., Süsstrunk, S.: Slic superpixels compared to state-of-the-art superpixel methods. IEEE Trans. Pattern Anal. Mach. Intell. **34**(11), 2274–2282 (2012)

2. Cheng, M.M., Mitra, N.J., Huang, X., Torr, P.H., Hu, S.M.: Global contrast based salient region detection. IEEE Trans. Pattern Anal. Mach. Intell. **37**(3), 569–582 (2015)
3. Coates, A., Carpenter, B., Case, C., Satheesh, S., Suresh, B., Wang, T., Wu, D.J., Ng, A.Y.: Text detection and character recognition in scene images with unsupervised feature learning. In: 2011 International Conference on Document Analysis and Recognition (ICDAR), pp. 440–445. IEEE (2011)
4. Epshtein, B., Ofek, E., Wexler, Y.: Detecting text in natural scenes with stroke width transform. In: 2010 IEEE Conference on Computer Vision and Pattern Recognition (CVPR), pp. 2963–2970. IEEE (2010)
5. Huang, W., Qiao, Y., Tang, X.: Robust scene text detection with convolution neural network induced MSER trees. In: Fleet, D., Pajdla, T., Schiele, B., Tuytelaars, T. (eds.) ECCV 2014. LNCS, vol. 8692, pp. 497–511. Springer, Cham (2014). https://doi.org/10.1007/978-3-319-10593-2_33
6. Jaderberg, M., Simonyan, K., Vedaldi, A., Zisserman, A.: Reading text in the wild with convolutional neural networks. Int. J. Comput. Vis. **116**(1), 1–20 (2016)
7. Jaderberg, M., Vedaldi, A., Zisserman, A.: Deep features for text spotting. In: Fleet, D., Pajdla, T., Schiele, B., Tuytelaars, T. (eds.) ECCV 2014. LNCS, vol. 8692, pp. 512–528. Springer, Cham (2014). https://doi.org/10.1007/978-3-319-10593-2_34
8. Johnson, D.B.: Efficient algorithms for shortest paths in sparse networks. J. ACM (JACM) **24**(1), 1–13 (1977)
9. Kang, L., Li, Y., Doermann, D.: Orientation robust text line detection in natural images. In: Proceedings of the IEEE Conference on Computer Vision and Pattern Recognition, pp. 4034–4041 (2014)
10. Karatzas, D., Shafait, F., Uchida, S., Iwamura, M., i Bigorda, L.G., Mestre, S.R., Mas, J., Mota, D.F., Almazan, J.A., de las Heras, L.P.: Icdar 2013 robust reading competition. In: 2013 12th International Conference on Document Analysis and Recognition (ICDAR), pp. 1484–1493. IEEE (2013)
11. Long, J., Shelhamer, E., Darrell, T.: Fully convolutional networks for semantic segmentation. In: Proceedings of the IEEE Conference on Computer Vision and Pattern Recognition, pp. 3431–3440 (2015)
12. Neumann, L., Matas, J.: A method for text localization and recognition in real-world images. Comput. Vis.-ACCV **2010**, 770–783 (2011)
13. Simonyan, K., Zisserman, A.: Very deep convolutional networks for large-scale image recognition. arXiv preprint arXiv:1409.1556 (2014)
14. Tian, S., Pan, Y., Huang, C., Lu, S., Yu, K., Tan, C.L.: Text flow: a unified text detection system in natural scene images. In: IEEE International Conference on Computer Vision, pp. 4651–4659 (2016)
15. Tian, Z., Huang, W., He, T., He, P., Qiao, Y.: Detecting text in natural image with connectionist text proposal network. In: Leibe, B., Matas, J., Sebe, N., Welling, M. (eds.) ECCV 2016. LNCS, vol. 9912, pp. 56–72. Springer, Cham (2016). https://doi.org/10.1007/978-3-319-46484-8_4
16. Wei, Y., Wen, F., Zhu, W., Sun, J.: Geodesic saliency using background priors. Comput. Vis.-ECCV **2012**, 29–42 (2012)
17. Wei, Y., Zhang, Z., Shen, W., Zeng, D., Fang, M., Zhou, S.: Text detection in scene images based on exhaustive segmentation. Sig. Process.: Image Commun. **50**, 1–8 (2017)
18. Xie, S., Tu, Z.: Holistically-nested edge detection. In: Proceedings of the IEEE International Conference on Computer Vision, pp. 1395–1403 (2015)

19. Yao, C., Bai, X., Liu, W., Ma, Y., Tu, Z.: Detecting texts of arbitrary orientations in natural images. In: 2012 IEEE Conference on Computer Vision and Pattern Recognition (CVPR), pp. 1083–1090. IEEE (2012)
20. Yi, C., Tian, Y.: Scene text recognition in mobile applications by character descriptor and structure configuration. IEEE Trans. Image Process. **23**(7), 2972–2982 (2014)
21. Yin, F., Liu, C.L.: Handwritten text line extraction based on minimum spanning tree clustering. In: International Conference on Wavelet Analysis and Pattern Recognition, ICWAPR 2007, vol. 3, pp. 1123–1128. IEEE (2007)
22. Yin, X.C., Pei, W.Y., Zhang, J., Hao, H.W.: Multi-orientation scene text detection with adaptive clustering. IEEE Trans. Pattern Anal. Mach. Intell. **37**(9), 1930–1937 (2015)
23. Yin, X.C., Yin, X., Huang, K., Hao, H.W.: Robust text detection in natural scene images. IEEE Trans. Pattern Anal. Mach. Intell. **36**(5), 970–983 (2014)
24. Zhang, Z., Shen, W., Yao, C., Bai, X.: Symmetry-based text line detection in natural scenes. In: Proceedings of the IEEE Conference on Computer Vision and Pattern Recognition, pp. 2558–2567 (2015)
25. Zhang, Z., Zhang, C., Shen, W., Yao, C., Liu, W., Bai, X.: Multi-oriented text detection with fully convolutional networks. In: Proceedings of the IEEE Conference on Computer Vision and Pattern Recognition, pp. 4159–4167 (2016)
26. Zhong, Z., Jin, L., Zhang, S., Feng, Z.: Deeptext: A unified framework for text proposal generation and text detection in natural images. arXiv preprint arXiv:1605.07314 (2016)

Sparse Time-Varying Graphs for Slide Transition Detection in Lecture Videos

Zhijin Liu[1,2], Kai Li[1,2(✉)], Liquan Shen[1,2], and Ping An[1,2]

[1] School of Communication and Information Engineering, Shanghai University, Shanghai, China
kailee@shu.edu.cn
[2] Key Laboratory of Advanced Displays and System Application, Ministry of Education, Shanghai, China

Abstract. In this paper, we present an approach for detecting slide transitions in lectures videos by introducing sparse time-varying graphs. Given a lecture video which records the digital slides, the speaker, and the audience by multiple cameras, our goal is to find the keyframes where slide content changes. Specifically, we first partition the lecture video into short segments through feature detection and matching. By constructing a sparse graph at each moment with short video segments as nodes, we formulate the detection problem as a graph inference issue. A set of adjacency matrix between edges, which are sparse and time-varying, are then solved through a global optimization algorithm. Consequently, the changes between adjacency matrix reflect the slide transition. Experimental results show that the proposed system achieves the better accuracy than other video summarization and slide progression detection approaches.

Keywords: Lecture video · Slide transition
Sparse time-varying graph

1 Introduction

Nowadays, e-learning has become an important learning means to acquire knowledge. A large number of lecture videos are posted on the Internet everyday, and most of these videos are unstructured. If users want to find some specific knowledge, they usually have to browse the entire video, which is time-consuming. Therefore, it is essential to automatically extract the representative summary for lecture videos.

Detection of slides transition is a critical issue for lecture video summarization. Various lecture videos can capture the projected slides and the speaker by a pan-tilt-zoom (PTZ) camera, record the computer screen directly, or even switch from the PTZ camera to the screen recorder. During this process, the slide content may remain the same for a long time or change to others quickly, while the users have to watch the whole video to have these findings. Apparently,

Y. Zhao et al. (Eds.): ICIG 2017, Part I, LNCS 10666, pp. 567–576, 2017.
https://doi.org/10.1007/978-3-319-71607-7_50

the appearance change in the video frame does not necessarily indicate a slide transition. It is hard to tell the real slide transition from the disturbance like camera motion, camera switch, and people movement.

Unfortunately, previous approaches usually extracted slide transition keyframes by measuring the visual difference between adjacent frames. Various features such as histogram [13], SIFT [2], and wavelet [18] are chosen to describe the appearance similarity. These methods fail to deal with frames which contain people movement and camera motion, which are common noise interruption in some types of lecture video. Recently, an iterative approach has been proposed to localize the projection screen and detect the slide transition [9]. However, it is targeted for a specific type of lecture video which capture the projection screen by a single PTZ camera. Camera switches are not allowed, thus its application range is limited.

In this paper, we present an automatic approach to detect slide transitions in lecture videos by inferring sparse time-varying graphs. We first partition the video into several small segments by feature detection and matching. Inspired by the storyline summarization approach [8], we regard each segment as a node to construct a sparse time-varying graph. This graph is able to model the transition from one segment (slide) to another. After inferring the adjacency matrix of the graph through an global optimization, we analyze them to generate the slide transition keyframes robustly.

For evaluation, we collect a variety of lecture videos and compare our system with general video summarization approaches and slide progression detection method. Experimental results show that our system is able to handle several types of lecture videos and achieve the best performance.

The remainder of this paper is organized as follows. Section 2 investigates the lecture video summarization problem. Section 3 describes the system overview and general pipeline of each part. Section 4 presents the core sparse time-varying graph. Section 5 shows the experimental results and verifies the superiority of our system. Section 6 concludes this paper.

2   Related Work

In this section, we mainly review the literatures in lecture video summarization.

Many previous approaches generate the summary by measuring the appearance similarity between two adjacent frames. To compute the similarity, several features are extracted, such as color histograms, corner points, and edge information. For instance, some algorithms [10,13] leveraged color histogram to summarize lecture videos. Jeong et al. [6] detected the forward and backward slides change by a recursive pruning algorithm. However, on one hand, if there are camera motions in the lecture video, appearance difference is not always effective; on the other hand, parameter estimation for the similarity threshold is trivial.

To address these problems, some shot boundary detection approaches were proposed. For example, Zhao and Cai [21] presented a shot boundary detection algorithm based on fuzzy theory. They segmented videos into six different classes to detect shot boundary, and trained the camera movement features to avoid interference. Porter [16] designed a shot segmentation algorithm by a two-component frame differencing metric. Other classification methods introduced Support Vector Machines [20] and Neural Networks [12] to recognize shot boundaries. Recently, Li et al. [9] tracked the feature trajectories to find the slide progression frames.

Some work employed additional data to obtain a video summary, such as text embedded in lecture videos [15,19], audio signal [5,17], and electronic slides [1]. Wang et al. [19] reconstructed high-resolution video texts to detect and analyze text information for matching video clips. Ngo et al. [15] employed a foreground vs. background segmentation algorithm to obtain the projected electronic slides, and then detected and analyzed text captions to detect slide transitions. In their experiments, the camera is fixed and remain stationary, which is not universal applicable. Fan et al. [1] matched original electronic slides to presentation videos by a hidden Markov model. Since their input is the lecture video with its original electronic slides, which is not suitable for mostly lecture video summarization. In contrast, our method automatically detects slide transitions without additional data.

Our work is inspired by but different from the sparse time-varying graphs for reconstructing storyline graphs of videos and photos [7,8]. [8] used a set of photo streams to construct a storyline summary that represents the narrative structure of activities by inferring sparse time-varying graphs. The storyline can be further used for sequential image prediction. [7] proposed a scalable approach to jointly summarize a set of associated videos and images. Temporal graph analysis was also considered in [14]. The difference is that the temporal graph is used for scene modeling and detection. In our system, we introduce the temporal graphs to infer the real slide changes, while the graph in [8] is targeted to discover the common structure of an event taken by many people.

3   Problem Settings

The input to our system is a lecture video which is represented by a set of frames $\mathcal{I} = \{I^1, \cdots, I^N\}$, where N is the number of frames. The original video is first partitioned into segments that have the similar appearance through feature matching. Subsequently, by representing each segment as a node, a sparse graph at each moment is built to indicate the transition between segments. After inferring the adjacency matrix in the sparse time-varying graphs, we are able to detect slide transitions by analyzing its structure.

Video segments. SIFT features are first extracted to represent low-level visual information. With the help of feature matching, we generate a video segment by matching SIFT features in the next few frames to the first frame of current segment until the ratio of feature matches is lower than a threshold m. For instance, if video frame #2 to #10 are similar to frame #1, segment #1 consists of frame #1 to #10. Segment #2 starts from frame #11 and ends at frame whose matches ratio with respect to frame #11 is below the threshold m. To avoid parameter tuning, we adopt an adaptive technique to estimate the threshold m. Specifically, we first compute the ratio of feature matches across the whole video and compute a histogram. By estimating a Gaussian distribution $N(\mu_r, \sigma_r)$ around the peak value with maximum likelihood estimator (MLE), we naturally use $m = \mu_r + 3\sigma_r$ as the threshold to avoid empirically setting. Finally, frame $\boldsymbol{I}^i$ is described as a binary segment indicator vector $\boldsymbol{x}^i \in \Re^D$ with 1 nonzero elements, where D is the number of video segments.

Definition of graphs. The time-varying graph is defined as $\mathcal{G}^i = (\mathcal{V}, \mathcal{E}^i), i \in \{1, \cdots, N-1\}$, where each node in the vertex set $\mathcal{V}$ corresponds to a video segment (*i.e.* $|\mathcal{V}| = D$). The edge set $\mathcal{E}^i$ is encouraged to be sparse and time-varying. On one hand, sparsity is introduced to avoid unnecessary complex graph structure, and the nonzero elements indicates the strong relationship between nodes. On the other hand, $\mathcal{E}^i$ varies smoothly along with the content change over time, which is just used for slide transition detection. The slide transition detection problem is turned to the graph inference one, *i.e.*, how to obtain a set of time-specific adjacency matrix $\boldsymbol{A}^i, i \in \{1, \cdots, N-1\}$ of the edge set $\mathcal{E}^i$, which is detailed in Sect. 4.

Slide transition detection. After obtaining the sparse adjacency matrix, we analyze them to produce the slide transition keyframes. For instance, if a slide stay unchanged, the non-zero elements of matrix $\boldsymbol{A}^i$ always appear in the diagonal position, which means that the node switches to itself. However, during the slide transition period, matrix $\boldsymbol{A}^i$ differs from the previous ones and is not necessarily a diagonal one. Therefore, we are able to detect slide transitions by analyzing the nonzero elements of adjacency matrix. Due to the large amount of frames, we maintain a coarse-to-fine two-step strategy to locate the transition frame efficiently. Specifically, the whole video frames are uniformly split into multiple time intervals (such as every 10 frames), where a coarse-level adjacency matrix is first estimated. A fine-level adjacency matrix is then calculated at each frame to locate the exact time point once a slide transition is found in some certain interval. More importantly, this framework is able to neglect the disturbance such as camera motion and people movement, and reveal the real slide change.

4   Sparse Time-Varying Graphs

In this section, we first describe the graph modeling principles, and then present the optimization framework for solving such sparse time-varying graphs.

4.1   Graph Modeling

The inference of the time-varying graph is formulated as a maximum likelihood estimation problem, based on the assumption that first order Markovian is employed between the consecutive frames. We first describe the graph model in this subsection.

Given a lecture video $\mathcal{I} = \{I^1, \cdots, I^N\}$, after temporal segmenting, we rewrite it as $\mathcal{I} = \{x^1, \cdots, x^N\}$. Based on the Markovian assumption, the likelihood of the sequence is defined as

$$f(\mathcal{I}) = f(x^1) \prod_{i=1}^{N-1} f(x^{i+1}|x^i), \tag{1}$$

where $f(x^{i+1}|x^i)$ is the transition model describing the conditional transfer likelihood from frame I^i to frame I^{i+1}.

For scalability, we reasonably assume that different video segment x_m^{i+1} and x_n^{i+1}, where $m, n \in \{1, \cdots, D\}$, and $m \neq n$, are conditional independent once given x^i. Therefore, the transition likelihood is calculated over each individual dimension

$$f(x^{i+1}|x^i) = \prod_{d=1}^{D} f(x_d^{i+1}|x^i). \tag{2}$$

Naturally, we use a liner dynamic model to simplify the transition model

$$x^{i+1} = A^i x^i + \zeta, \tag{3}$$

where $\zeta \sim N(0, \sigma^2 I)$ is a Gaussian noise vector with zero mean and variance σ^2.

Combing Eqs. (2) and (3), the transition likelihood is further expressed as the probability density function of a Gaussian distribution

$$f(x_d^{i+1}|x^i) \sim N(A_{d\cdot}^i x^i, \sigma^2), \tag{4}$$

where $A_{d\cdot}^i$ denotes the d-th row of matrix A^i. Taking the logarithm of Eq. (1), the log-likelihood of the sequence is finally computed as

$$\log f(\mathcal{I}) = \log f(x^1) - \sum_{i=1}^{N-1} \sum_{d=1}^{D} \left\{ \frac{N-1}{2} \log(2\pi\sigma^2) + \frac{1}{2\sigma^2}(x_d^{i+1} - A_{d\cdot}^i x^i)^2 \right\}. \tag{5}$$

4.2 Global Optimization

The expected adjacency matrix in the graph should satisfy the following criteria: (1) it should be close to the MLE solution in Eq. (5); (2) it should only have a few nonzero elements; (3) the matrix in neighboring frames should be temporally coherent. In this subsection we show how to formulate and solve the adjacency matrix in an optimization-based framework.

Firstly, the Maximum Likelihood Estimator in Eq. (5) produces that $x^{i+1} = A^i x^i$. Due to the insufficient images at time i, the estimator suffer from high variance. Fortunately, supposing that the nearby frames should have the similar appearance, we impose the transition model on the neighboring observation pair $(x^{i+k}, x^{i-k+1}), k \in N^+$ to gather redundant constrict in the data term. Therefore, the first criterion is formulated as

$$\min_{A^i} \sum_{k=1}^{K} w_k^i (x^{i+k} - A^i x^{i-k+1})^2. \tag{6}$$

The weight coefficient w_k^i is introduced to indicate how much degree neighboring frame pair should meet the same adjacency matrix, which is defined as

$$w_k^i = \exp\left\{-\frac{(2k-1)^2}{2\sigma_t^2}\right\} \exp\left\{-\frac{||\boldsymbol{x}^{i+k} - \boldsymbol{x}^{i-k+1} - \boldsymbol{x}^{i+k+1} + \boldsymbol{x}^{i-k}||_2^2}{2\sigma_f^2}\right\}. \quad (7)$$

The former part in w_k^t is the temporal weighting of observation pair $(\boldsymbol{x}^{i+k}, \boldsymbol{x}^{i-k+1})$. As time goes on, the relation between observations is gradually weaken. Closer to time i, more contribution on the estimation $\boldsymbol{A}^i$. The latter part in w_k^i is the weighting of segment difference. If the difference between $(\boldsymbol{x}^{i+k} - \boldsymbol{x}^{i-k+1})$ and $(\boldsymbol{x}^{i+k+1} - \boldsymbol{x}^{i-k})$ is large, we think it encounters noise, and set a low weight to avoid the noise. In addition, $\sigma_t = 2$ and $\sigma_f = 0.2$ are standard deviations controlling the Gaussian kernel. $K = \min(\min(N - i - 1, i - 1), 2\sigma_t)$ is the size of the neighborhood set. In addition, this data term is the underlying explanation for being able to discard the disturbance from camera motion and people movement.

Secondly, the graph should only have a few strong connections. This is done by an ℓ_1 regularizer to control the sparsity of adjacency matrix. It not only avoids over-fitting, but also removes the weak link between nodes.

Thirdly, adjacent frames should have the similar matrix. We minimize the temporal difference $||\boldsymbol{A}^i - \boldsymbol{A}^{i-1}||_2^2$ to maintain temporal coherence.

Finally, we have the complete optimization formula for the adjacency matrix

$$\min_{\{\boldsymbol{A}^i\}} \sum_{i=1}^{N-1} \sum_{k=1}^{K} w_k^i ||\boldsymbol{x}^{i+k} - \boldsymbol{A}^i \boldsymbol{x}^{t-k+1}||_2^2 + \lambda \sum_{i=1}^{N-1} ||\boldsymbol{A}^i||_1 + \alpha \sum_{i=1}^{N-1} ||\boldsymbol{A}^{i+1} - \boldsymbol{A}^i||_2^2, \quad (8)$$

where λ and α are the weights for the sparsity term and smoothness term, respectively ($\lambda = 0.05$, and $\alpha = 0.01$ in our system). This optimization formula is significantly different from that in [8]. On one hand, in [8] each $\boldsymbol{A}^i$ suggests the common codeword transition probability of many photo streams, while we only have a single video sequence. On the other hand, they solve each $\boldsymbol{A}^i$ independently, while we employ a global optimization.

Global optimization in Eq. (8) could be solved via a lot of tools, such as coordinate descent [3]. Note that the inference of graph reduce to a weighted ℓ_1-regularized least square problem when all variables but $\boldsymbol{A}^i$ fixed. Furthermore, thanks to the assumption that each dimension of $\boldsymbol{x}^i$ are conditional independent, neighborhood selection [11] is applied to obtain each row of $\boldsymbol{A}^i$ separately. As a result, we iteratively solve the weighted lasso problem for each row of the adjacency matrix D times.

5   Results and Discussion

As shown in Fig. 1, we have collected three types of lecture video from Yale University Courses and YouTube to verify the effectiveness and superiority of our system. Type-A video is recorded with multiple cameras which allows complex

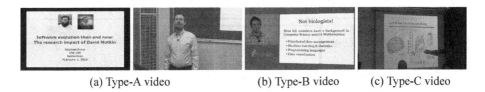

(a) Type-A video   (b) Type-B video   (c) Type-C video

Fig. 1. Three types of lecture videos in our experiments. (a) Type-A video presents complex camera motion and sudden camera switch. (b) Type-B video presents the speaker and computer screen in two regions simultaneously. (c) Type-C video presents the on-stage screen by a single camera.

camera motion and sudden camera switch, such as the switch from slide to speaker. Type-B video is also recorded with multiple cameras but shows the slide and speaker simultaneously. Type-C video captures the speaker and on-stage screen by a still camera. Both camera movement and people movement would affect the detection accuracy. Each lecture video is temporally down-sampled to 1 fps and its spatial resolution is 640×360. Video length ranges from roughly 10 min to 45 min. The parameters are fixed as stated before.

A typical detection result for Type-A lecture video is shown in Fig. 2, where slide progressions are automatically detected and marked on the timeline. Result shows that our method successfully pick out the slide content changes effectively.

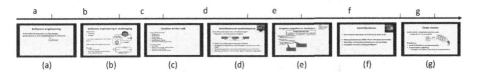

Fig. 2. Slide transition detection result by our approach for Type-A lecture video. Ticks marked on the timeline indicate the detected transition frames shown below the timeline.

We perform some quantitative evaluation to demonstrate the superiority of our system. After manually labeling the groudtruth slide change, we leverage the F_1 score as the evaluation metric

$$
F_1 = \frac{2 \times Precision \times Recall}{Precision + Recall}
$$
$$
Precision = \frac{S_c}{S_t} \qquad , \qquad (9)
$$
$$
Recall = \frac{Sc}{S_a}
$$

where S_c is the number of slides transitions correctly detected, S_t is the total number of detected slide transitions, and S_a is the total number of the actual slide transitions.

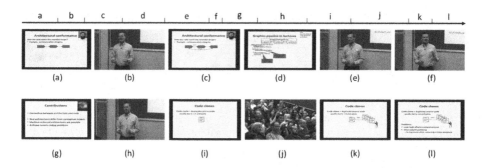

Fig. 3. Slide transition detection result by the SPD approach [9] for Type-A lecture video. Note that both camera switch and people movement are mistaken as slide transitions.

We compare our system with video summarization approach using Singular Value Decomposition (SVD) [4], shot boundary detection method using Frame Transition Parameters (FTP) [12], and recent slide progression detection method by analyzing the feature trajectories (SPD) [9]. Table 1 shows the average Precision, Recall, and F_1 score of different approaches on all types of lecture video, while detailed performance on each type of lecture video is shown in Fig. 4.

Table 1. Average performance of different methods on three types of lecture video.

	Precision	Recall	F_1 score
SVD [4]	0.997	0.439	0.571
FTP [12]	0.556	0.148	0.215
SPD [9]	0.654	0.947	0.738
Ours	0.850	0.967	**0.904**

As shown in Table 1 and Fig. 4, our system significantly outperforms these approaches in detecting slide transitions. Our system improves the F_1 score by 16.6% on average, compared with the feature trajectory-based SPD approach. In particular, our approach improves the F_1 score up to 46.8% on Type-A lecture video, where camera switch and complex motion are presented. The SPD approach would produce lots of false positives due to the sudden camera switch and frequent people movement when dealing with Type-A lecture video, which is also evidenced by Fig. 3. We also find that general SVD approach achieves a better precision but fails to discover most of the slide changes. In addition, shot boundary detection method using FTP achieves the worst performance for detecting slide transitions.

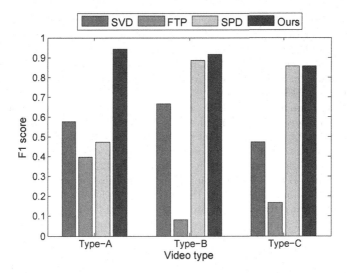

Fig. 4. Detailed performance of different methods on three types of lecture video.

6 Conclusion

In this paper, we present the sparse time-varying graph optimization approach to automatically detect slides transitions in lecture videos. By formulating the sparsity and time-varying characteristics into a global optimization framework, we are able to solve the adjacency matrix in the graphs and then detect the slide changes. Experimental results show that our system successfully summarizes lecture video by key frames and achieves the best performance. Besides the general feature matching, other specific information of lecture video, such as text title on the top of screen, could be used to further improve the performance, which will be our future work.

Acknowledgment. This work was supported by the Project of NSFC (No. 61601278, 61571285, and 61671282), the Program of Shanghai Academic Research Leader (No. 16XD1401200), and the Young Teacher Training Program of Shanghai Municipal Education Commission (No. ZZSD15117).

References

1. Fan, Q., Barnard, K., Amir, A., Efrat, A.: Robust spatiotemporal matching of electronic slides to presentation videos. IEEE Trans. Image Process. **20**(8), 2315–2328 (2011)
2. Fan, Q., Barnard, K., Amir, A., Efrat, A., Lin, M.: Matching slides to presentation videos using sift and scene background matching. In: Proceedings of ACM International Workshop on Multimedia Information Retrieval, pp. 239–248 (2006)
3. Fu, W.J.: Penalized regressions: the bridge versus the lasso. J. Comput. Graph. Stat. **7**(3), 397–416 (1998)

4. Gong, Y., Liu, X.: Video summarization using singular value decomposition. In: Proceedings of IEEE Conference on Computer Vision and Pattern Recognition, pp. 174–180 (2000)
5. He, L., Sanocki, E., Gupta, A., Grudin, J.: Auto-summarization of audio-video presentations. In: Proceedings of ACM International Conference on Multimedia, pp. 489–498 (1999)
6. Jeong, H.J., Kim, T.E., Kim, H.G., Kim, M.H.: Automatic detection of slide transitions in lecture videos. Multimed. Tools Appl. **74**(18), 7537–7554 (2015)
7. Kim, G., Sigal, L., Xing, E.P.: Joint summarization of large-scale collections of web images and videos for storyline reconstruction. In: Proceedings of IEEE Conference on Computer Vision and Pattern Recognition, pp. 4225–4232 (2014)
8. Kim, G., Xing, E.P.: Reconstructing storyline graphs for image recommendation from web community photos. In: Proceedings of IEEE Conference on Computer Vision and Pattern Recognition, pp. 3882–3889 (2014)
9. Li, K., Wang, J., Wang, H., Dai, Q.: Structuring lecture videos by automatic projection screen localization and analysis. IEEE Trans. Pattern Anal. Mach. Intell. **37**(6), 1233–1246 (2015)
10. Ma, D., Agam, G.: Lecture video segmentation and indexing. In: Proceedings of SPIE 8297, Document Recognition and Retrieval XIX, pp. 82970V–82970V-8 (2012)
11. Meinshausen, N., Bühlmann, P.: High-dimensional graphs and variable selection with the lasso. Ann. Stat. **34**(3), 1436–1462 (2006)
12. Mohanta, P.P., Saha, S.K., Chanda, B.: A model-based shot boundary detection technique using frame transition parameters. IEEE Trans. Multimed. **14**(1), 223–233 (2012)
13. Mukhopadhyay, S., Smith, B.: Passive capture and structuring of lectures. In: Proceedings of ACM International Conference on Multimedia, pp. 477–487 (1999)
14. Ngo, C.W., Ma, Y.F., Zhang, H.J.: Video summarization and scene detection by graph modeling. IEEE Trans. Circuits Syst. Video Technol. **15**(2), 296–305 (2005)
15. Ngo, C.W., Pong, T.C., Huang, T.S.: Detection of slide transition for topic indexing. In: Proceedings of IEEE International Conference on Multimedia and Expo, pp. 533–536 (2002)
16. Porter, S.V.: Video segmentation and indexing using motion estimation. Ph.D. thesis. University of Bristol (2004)
17. Repp, S., Meinel, M.: Semantic indexing for recorded educational lecture videos. In: Proceedings of IEEE International Conference on Pervasive Computing and Communications Workshops, pp. 240–245 (2006)
18. Sujatha, C., Mudenagudi, U.: A study on keyframe extraction methods for video summary. In: Proceedings of International Conference on Computational Intelligence and Communication Networks, pp. 73–77 (2011)
19. Wang, F., Ngo, C.W., Pong, T.C.: Synchronization of lecture videos and electronic slides by video text analysis. In: Proceedings of ACM International Conference on Multimedia, pp. 315–318 (2003)
20. Yuan, J., Li, J., Lin, F., Zhang, B.: A unified shot boundary detection framework based on graph partition model. In: Proceedings of ACM International Conference on Multimedia, pp. 539–542 (2005)
21. Zhao, Z.-C., Cai, A.-N.: Shot boundary detection algorithm in compressed domain based on adaboost and fuzzy theory. In: Jiao, L., Wang, L., Gao, X., Liu, J., Wu, F. (eds.) ICNC 2006. LNCS, vol. 4222, pp. 617–626. Springer, Heidelberg (2006). https://doi.org/10.1007/11881223_76

Heterogeneous Multi-group Adaptation for Event Recognition in Consumer Videos

Mingyu Yao[1], Xinxiao Wu[1(✉)], Mei Chen[2], and Yunde Jia[1]

[1] Beijing Lab of Intelligent Information Technology, School of Computer Science,
Beijing Institute of Technology, Beijing 100081, China
{yaomingyu,wuxinxiao,jiayunde}@bit.edu.cn
[2] Electrical and Computer Engineering, State University of New York at Albany,
Albany, NY 12222, USA
meichen@albany.edu

Abstract. Event recognition in consumer videos has attracted much attention from researchers. However, it is a very challenging task since annotating numerous training samples is time consuming and labor expensive. In this paper, we take a large number of loosely labeled Web images and videos represented by different types of features from Google and YouTube as heterogeneous source domains, to conduct event recognition in consumer videos. We propose a heterogeneous multi-group adaptation method to partition loosely labeled Web images and videos into several semantic groups and find the optimal weight for each group. To learn an effective target classifier, a manifold regularization is introduced into the objective function of Support Vector Regression (SVR) with an ϵ-insensitive loss. The objective function is alternatively solved by using standard quadratic programming and SVR solvers. Comprehensive experiments on two real-world datasets demonstrate the effectiveness of our method.

Keywords: Event recognition · Multi-group adaptation
Transferring learning

1 Introduction

Event recognition in consumer videos has been an active field in computer vision because of its multitude of applications in video retrieval and classification. Many existing studies [8,9,18] have shown good performances in event analysis by using a large number of labeled training videos to learn a robust classifier. Collecting sufficient videos and annotating them are labor expensive and time consuming tasks. Fortunately, Web search engines have become increasingly mature and can provide abundant loosely labeled data, which is beneficial for researchers to collect loosely labeled training data instead of manual annotation. Several methods [4,5,19] have been proposed to adapt the knowledge learned from Web domain (source domain) to consumer domain (target domain). Duan et al. [5] proposed

Y. Zhao et al. (Eds.): ICIG 2017, Part I, LNCS 10666, pp. 577–589, 2017.
https://doi.org/10.1007/978-3-319-71607-7_51

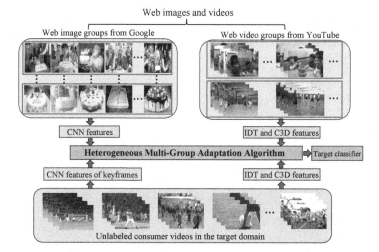

Fig. 1. An illustration of the proposed heterogeneous multi-group adaptation framework.

a domain selection machine method for event recognition in consumer videos by exploiting labeled Web images from different sources. Wang et al. [19] proposed a model to annotate the labels of target domain videos with the knowledge learned from a large number of labeled Web images and a few labeled videos. Chen et al. [4] considered temporal information and leveraged a large number of labeled Web images and videos for visual event recognition in consumer videos. However, the above methods only leverage Web images or videos according to their sources and ignore their intrinsic semantic relationships.

In this paper, we divide loosely labeled Web images and videos into several semantic groups to conduct event recognition in consumer videos where there are no labeled consumer videos. In order to comprehensively describe the events in consumer videos, we utilize several query keywords corresponding to specific classes of event in target domain to collect Web images and videos, respectively. For example, we use the keywords "birthday", "birthday cake", "birthday party", "celebration, and "anniversary" to search on the Web for images and videos related to the event "birthday. The returned images and videos of each keyword are regarded as an image group and a video group. Different group samples are represented by different types of features. The Convolutional Neural Networks (CNNs) [16] are used to represent Web image groups, and the Improved Dense Trajectories (IDT) [20] and the Convolutional 3D (C3D) [17] are used to represent Web video groups. All types of features in Web image groups and Web video groups are used to represent the consumer videos (see Fig. 1).

The downloaded images and videos by keyword search are often of poor quality and are not closely related to specific classes of event in the target domain. Therefore directly transferring the knowledge from these images and videos might lead to a negative transfer problem. To address this issue, we have developed a heterogeneous multi-group adaptation method to find the optimal weight for each group. Larger weight means that the group is more relevant to the target domain. For each group, a new classifier is learned by minimizing the distance between the new classifier and the pre-trained group classifier in terms of their weight vectors. We define the target classifier as a linear combination of these new classifiers. We further introduce a manifold regularization together with the target classifier into the objective of support vector regression with an ϵ-insensitive loss, which is based on the smoothness assumption to make two nearby target samples share the similar decision values in a high-density region. Moreover, we develop an alternating optimization algorithm where standard quadratic programming and support vector regression solvers are used to solve the target objective function, and a linear programming solver is used to find the optimal weight for each group.

The contributions of this paper are: (1) Overcome the lack of labeled videos by dividing loosely labeled Web images and videos from heterogeneous source domains into several semantic groups for event recognition in consumer videos. (2) Incorporate a manifold regularization into an ϵ-SVR based objective function to more effectively learn the target classifier.

2   Related Work

Domain adaptation has been applied for a wide variety of applications, such as event recognition [4,14,22] and object recognition [12,13,15,21,23]. Long et al. [13] proposed a transfer joint matching algorithm to learn a feature space to minimize the distance between source domain instances and target domain instances. They [14] proposed a transfer kernel learning method to directly match the distributions between source data and target data in a reproducing kernel Hilbert space. Sener et al. [15] jointly optimize the representation, target label and cross domain transformation by using deep neural networks.

The above methods [13–15] mainly cope with the single source domain setting. When training samples come from different sources, several multiple source domain adaptation methods [4,6,7] are proposed. Duan et al. [6] proposed a domain adaptation machine method to learn a target classifier by using a set of pre-learned classifiers learned from multiple source domains samples to predict the labels of the target samples. Feng et al. [7] proposed a joint weighting scheme based on smoothness assumption, which makes two similar target samples have the similar decision values and the decision values of positive labeled samples are more higher than negative labeled samples. Chen et al. [4] proposed a multi-domain adaptation with heterogeneous sources method to learn an optimal target classifier where the samples from different sources have different types of features and predict the labels of unlabeled target samples based on multiple types of features.

Different from the setting of [4] which leverages Web videos and images according to their sources, we employ the concept of group to search labeled Web images and videos related to specific event classes in consumer videos, considering their intrinsic semantic relationships. Different types of features with different dimensions are used to represent samples from Web image groups and video groups while all types of features are used to represent target domain samples. We propose an ϵ-SVR based objective function, in which a manifold regularization is introduced to enforce the target classifier to be smooth on the consumer videos. The ϵ-SVR can lead to a sparse representation of the target classifier. Our optimal problem can be efficiently solved using standard quadratic programming and SVR solvers, compared with complex cutting plane method used in [4].

3   Event Recognition Based on Heterogeneous Multi-group Adaptation

In this section, we provide a detailed description of our heterogeneous multi-group adaptation method. Following the terminology of domain adaptation, we refer to the loosely labeled Web image and video domains as heterogeneous source domains and the consumer video domain as the target domain, in which there are no labeled consumer videos.

In order to obtain training samples, we adopt keyword searching method to search images and videos from different engines (e.g., Google.com and YouTube.com) with several keywords related to each event class. The returned search result of each keyword is called a group, which is regarded as a source domain. Since the feature distributions of samples from different groups (e.g., from image groups and video groups) change significantly and the data distributions of samples from groups and target domain are also different, we address the problem of heterogeneous multi-group adaptation in this paper. The data from the g-th group for each event class is denoted as $D^g = \{(\mathbf{x}_i^g, \, y_i^g)|_{i=1}^{n_g}\}$, $g \in \{1, \ldots, G\}$, where G is the total number of groups and n_g is the total number of samples in the g-th group. Each sample $\mathbf{x}_i^g$ is assigned a label $y_i^g \in \{-1, 1\}$. All the unlabeled videos from the target domain are denoted as $D^T = \{\mathbf{z}_i^T|_{i=1}^{n_T}\}$, where n_T is the total number of target domain videos. Each video is assigned G views (i.e., $\mathbf{z} = (\mathbf{z}^{[1]}, \ldots, \mathbf{z}^{[G]})$). The g-th view $\mathbf{z}^{[g]}$ is the same view as the g-th group $\mathbf{x}^g$ and they are in the same feature space.

In the following, we use the superscript $'$ to denote the transpose of a vector or matrix. We also define $\mathbf{0}_n$ and $\mathbf{1}_n$ as the $n \times 1$ column vectors of all zeros and all ones, respectively, and define $\mathbf{I}_n$ and $\mathbf{0}_{n \times m}$ as the $n \times n$ identity matrix and $n \times m$ matrix of all zeros. Moreover, we use $\odot$ to denote the element-wise product between two vectors or two matrices.

3.1   Transfer Model

We focus on learning a robust target classifier. Inspired by [4], our target classifier f^T is formulated as

$$f^T(\mathbf{z}) = \sum_{g=1}^{G} d_g \mathbf{w}_g' \varphi(\mathbf{z}^g), \tag{1}$$

where $\mathbf{w}_g$ is the weight vector of the g-th view feature in the target domain, and $\varphi(\cdot)$ is the feature mapping function, which can induce a kernel function in the Reproducing Kernel Hilbert Space (RKHS), $k(\mathbf{x}_i, \mathbf{x}_j) = \varphi'(\mathbf{x}_i)\varphi(\mathbf{x}_j)$. d_g represents the weight of the decision values of the g-th view classifier. Chen et al. [4] expanded the regularization term in [2] as $\sum_{s=1}^{S} d_s \|\mathbf{w}_s - \gamma_s \mathbf{u}_s\|^2$, which can be applied to deal with multiple source domain setting. d_s measures the distance between the s-th view target classifier and the source classifier, and will have a larger value in case the distance is closer.

In this section, we use the expanded regularization term to penalize the complexity of the target classifier $\mathbf{f}^T$, which is minimized in our objective function. A manifold regularization $\mathbf{f}^{T'}\mathbf{Lf}^T$ is introduced to keep the target classifier smooth on the data manifold, namely, the two nearby patterns in a high-density region should share similar decision values. In order to obtain a sparse representation, we integrate the above two regularization terms into the objective of support vector regression with an ϵ-insensitive loss. We formulate our objective function as

$$\min_{\substack{\mathbf{d},\mathbf{w}_g,\gamma_g,\mathbf{f}^T \\ \xi_i^g,\xi_i^T,\xi_i^{*T}}} \frac{1}{2}\left(\sum_g d_g\|\mathbf{w}_g - \gamma_g\mathbf{u}_g\|_2^2 + \theta\sum_g \gamma_g^2\right)$$

$$+ C_T\sum_i l_\epsilon(f^T(x_i^T) - f_i^T) + C_G\sum_g\sum_i \xi_i^g + \mathbf{f}^{T'}\mathbf{Lf}^T, \qquad (2)$$

where θ, C_T, C_G are regularization parameters used for balancing different terms, and $\mathbf{d} = [d_1, \ldots, d_g]'$ is the weight vector. $\mathbf{f}^T$ is the decision values of all the target samples, denoted as $\mathbf{f}^T = [f_1^T, \ldots, f_{n_T}^T]'$, on which the graph Laplacian matrix $\mathbf{L}$ is computed. $\mathbf{L}$ is denoted as $\mathbf{L} = \mathbf{I} - \mathbf{D}^{-0.5}\mathbf{W}\mathbf{D}^{-0.5}$, where $\mathbf{W} = (W_{ij})$ and $\mathbf{D}$ is a diagonal matrix, denoted as $D_{ii} = \sum_{j=1}^n W_{ij}$. The l_2 norm of γ_g is used as a penalized term in order to avoid over-fitting. $\sum_i l_\epsilon(f^T(x_i^T) - f_i^T)$ is the empirical error of the target classifier f^T on all the target data, and l_ϵ is ϵ-insensitive loss: $l_\epsilon(t) = \begin{cases} |t| - \epsilon, & if\ |t| > \epsilon; \\ 0, & otherwise. \end{cases}$. Since ϵ-insensitive loss is non-smooth, Eq. (2) is usually transformed into a constrained optimization problem:

$$\min_{\substack{\mathbf{d},\mathbf{w}_g,\gamma_g,\mathbf{f}^T \\ \xi_i^g,\xi_i^T,\xi_i^{*T}}} \frac{1}{2}\left(\sum_g d_g\|\mathbf{w}_g - \gamma_g\mathbf{u}_g\|_2^2 + \theta\sum_g \gamma_g^2\right) + C_T\sum_i(\xi_i^T + \xi_i^{*T})$$

$$+ C_G\sum_g\sum_i \xi_i^g + \mathbf{f}^{T'}\mathbf{Lf}^T, \qquad (3)$$

$$s.t. \sum_{g=1}^G d_g\mathbf{w}_g'\varphi_g(\mathbf{z}_i^{[g]}) - f_i^T \le \varepsilon + \xi_i^T,\ \xi_i^T \ge 0, \qquad (4)$$

$$f_i^T - \sum_{g=1}^G d_g\mathbf{w}_g'\varphi_g(\mathbf{z}_i^{[g]}) \le \varepsilon + \xi_i^{*T},\ \xi_i^{*T} \ge 0, \qquad (5)$$

$$d_g y_i^g\mathbf{w}_g'\varphi_g(\mathbf{x}_i^g) \ge 1 - \xi_i^g,\ \xi_i^g \ge 0,\ \mathbf{d} \ge \mathbf{0},\ \mathbf{1}'\mathbf{d} = 1, \qquad (6)$$

where ξ_i^g is the slack variable of the g-th group training samples, ξ_i^T and ξ_i^{*T} are the slack variables of all the target samples.

3.2   Detailed Solution

In order to solve the optimization problem in Eq. (3), we introduce the Lagrangian multipliers α_i^T's, α_i^{*T}'s, α_i^g's, η_i^T's, η_i^{*T}'s and η_i^g's for the constraints in (4), (5) and (6), and then have the following Lagrangian function:

$$
\begin{aligned}
L = & \frac{1}{2} \sum_{g=1}^{G} d_g \| \mathbf{w}_g - \gamma_g \mathbf{u}_g \|_2^2 + \frac{1}{2} \theta \sum_{g=1}^{G} \gamma_g^2 + C_T \sum_{i=1}^{n_T} (\xi_i^T + \xi_i^{*T}) + C_G \sum_{g=1}^{G} \sum_{i=1}^{n_g} \xi_i^g \\
& + \mathbf{f}^{T'} \mathbf{L} \mathbf{f}^T - \sum_{i=1}^{n_T} \alpha_i^T (\varepsilon + \xi_i^T - \sum_{g=1}^{G} d_g \mathbf{w}_g' \boldsymbol{\varphi}_g(\mathbf{z}_i^{[g]}) + f_i^T) - \sum_{i=1}^{n_T} \eta_i^T \xi_i^T \\
& - \sum_{i=1}^{n_T} \alpha_i^{*T} (\varepsilon + \xi_i^{*T} + \sum_{g=1}^{G} d_g \mathbf{w}_g' \boldsymbol{\varphi}_g(z_i^{[g]}) - f_i^T) - \sum_{i=1}^{n_T} \eta_i^{*T} \xi_i^{*T} \\
& - \sum_{g=1}^{G} \sum_{i=1}^{n_g} \alpha_i^g (y_i^g d_g \mathbf{w}_g' \boldsymbol{\varphi}_g(x_i^g) - 1 + \xi_i^g) - \sum_{i=1}^{G} \sum_{i=1}^{n_g} \eta_i^g \xi_i^g .
\end{aligned}
\tag{7}
$$

By taking the derivatives of the Lagrangian function with respect to variables $w_g, \gamma_g, f^T, \xi_i^g, \xi_i^T, \xi_i^{*T}$ to zeros, Eq. (3) can be converted into the following dual form:

$$
\min_{\mathbf{d}} \max_{\boldsymbol{\alpha}^T \boldsymbol{\alpha}^{*T} \boldsymbol{\alpha}_g} \; - \frac{1}{2} \boldsymbol{\alpha}' (\sum_g d_g \tilde{\mathbf{K}}^{[g]} \odot \mathbf{yy}') \boldsymbol{\alpha} - \varepsilon \mathbf{1}'(\boldsymbol{\alpha}^T + \boldsymbol{\alpha}^{*T}) + \sum_g \mathbf{1}' \boldsymbol{\alpha}_g,
\tag{8}
$$

where $\boldsymbol{\alpha} = [\boldsymbol{\alpha}_1', \ldots, \boldsymbol{\alpha}_G', (\boldsymbol{\alpha}^T - \boldsymbol{\alpha}^{*T})']'$, and $\boldsymbol{\alpha}_g = [\alpha_1^g, \ldots, \alpha_{n_g}^g]'$, $0 \le \boldsymbol{\alpha}_g \le C_G \mathbf{1}, g = 1, \ldots, G$, $-C_T \mathbf{1} \le \boldsymbol{\alpha}^T, \boldsymbol{\alpha}^{*T} \le C_T \mathbf{1}$. The labels of training samples are defined as $\mathbf{y} = [\mathbf{y}_1', \ldots, \mathbf{y}_G', \mathbf{1}_{n_T'}]'$, where $\mathbf{y}_g = [y_1^g, \ldots, y_{n_g}^g]'$ represents the labels of the g-th group samples. $\tilde{\mathbf{K}}^{[g]}$ is the newly transformed kernel matrix computed on all the samples from the g-th group and the g-th view of target domain, which is defined as

$$
\tilde{\mathbf{K}}^{[g]} = \mathbf{K}^{[g]} + \frac{1}{\theta} \mathbf{f}^{[g]} \mathbf{f}^{[g]'} + \frac{1}{2} \begin{bmatrix} \mathbf{0} & \mathbf{0} \\ \mathbf{0} & \mathbf{L}^{-1} \end{bmatrix},
\tag{9}
$$

where $\mathbf{K}^{[g]} = \boldsymbol{\varphi}^{[g]'} \boldsymbol{\varphi}^{[g]}$, and $\boldsymbol{\varphi}^{[g]} = [\mathbf{0}_{h_g \times N(1,g-1)}, \boldsymbol{\varphi}_g, \mathbf{0}_{h_g \times N(g+1,G)}, \boldsymbol{\varphi}_T^{[g]}]$. $\boldsymbol{\varphi}_g = [\boldsymbol{\varphi}_g(\mathbf{x}_1^g), \ldots, \boldsymbol{\varphi}_g(\mathbf{x}_{n_g}^g)]$ and $\boldsymbol{\varphi}_T^{[g]} = [\boldsymbol{\varphi}_g(\mathbf{z}_1^{[g]}), \ldots, \boldsymbol{\varphi}_g(\mathbf{z}_{n_T}^{[g]})]$ are defined as the mapped feature matrices by nonlinear mapping on the samples of the g-th group and the g-th view of target domain respectively. The dimension of $\boldsymbol{\varphi}_g(\mathbf{x}^g)$ is $h_g, \boldsymbol{\varphi}_g \in R^{h_g \times n_g}$ and $\boldsymbol{\varphi}_T^{[g]} \in R^{h_g \times n_T}$. $\mathbf{f}^{[g]}$ is the decision values of $\boldsymbol{\varphi}^{[g]}$ using the g-th group classifier $f^g(\mathbf{x})$, defined as $\mathbf{f}^{[g]} = [\mathbf{0}'_{N(1,g-1)}, \mathbf{f}_g', \mathbf{0}'_{N(g+1,G)}, \mathbf{f}_T^{[g]'}]$, where $\mathbf{f}_g = [f^g(\mathbf{x}_1^g), \ldots, f^g(\mathbf{x}_{n_g}^g)]'$ and $\mathbf{f}_T^{[g]} = [f^g(\mathbf{z}_1^{[g]}), \ldots, f^g(\mathbf{z}_{n_T}^{[g]})]'$ are decision values of the g-th group and the g-th view of target domain. N(m,n) is the total number of samples between the m-th group and the n-th group.

$\tilde{\mathbf{K}}^{[g]} \odot \mathbf{yy}'$ can be rewritten as

$$\tilde{\mathbf{K}}^{[g]} \odot \mathbf{yy}' = \begin{bmatrix} \mathbf{K}_{GG}^{[g]} & \mathbf{K}_{GT}^{[g]} \\ \mathbf{K}_{TG}^{[g]} & \mathbf{K}_{TG}^{[g]} \end{bmatrix}, \tag{10}$$

where $\mathbf{K}_{GG}^{[g]} \in R^{n_g \times n_g}$, $\mathbf{K}_{GT}^{[g]} \in R^{n_g \times n_T}$, $\mathbf{K}_{TG}^{[g]} \in R^{n_T \times n_g}$, and $\mathbf{K}_{TT}^{[g]} \in R^{n_T \times n_T}$ are kernel matrices of the g-th group samples and the g-th view of target domain samples. Substituting Eq. (10) into Eq. (8), Eq. (8) can be transformed into the following form:

$$\begin{aligned} \min_{\mathbf{d}} \max_{\boldsymbol{\alpha}^T \boldsymbol{\alpha}^{*T} \boldsymbol{\alpha}_g} \quad & -\frac{1}{2} \boldsymbol{\alpha}^{G'} (\sum_g d_g \mathbf{K}_{GG}^{[g]}) \boldsymbol{\alpha}^G \\ & + \mathbf{1}' \boldsymbol{\alpha}^G - (\boldsymbol{\alpha}^T - \boldsymbol{\alpha}^{*T})' (\sum_g d_g \mathbf{K}_{TG}^{[g]}) \boldsymbol{\alpha}^G \\ & - \frac{1}{2} (\boldsymbol{\alpha}^T - \boldsymbol{\alpha}^{*T})' (\sum_g d_g \mathbf{K}_{TG}^{[g]}) (\boldsymbol{\alpha}^T - \boldsymbol{\alpha}^{*T}) - \varepsilon \mathbf{1}' (\boldsymbol{\alpha}^T + \boldsymbol{\alpha}^{*T}), \end{aligned} \tag{11}$$

where $\boldsymbol{\alpha}^G = [\boldsymbol{\alpha}_1', \dots, \boldsymbol{\alpha}_G']'$ represents the Lagrangian multipliers of all group samples.

3.3   Optimization Algorithm

In this section, we develop an alternating optimization algorithm to optimize the weight coefficient $\mathbf{d}$, dual variable $\boldsymbol{\alpha}^T$ and $\boldsymbol{\alpha}^{*T}$, and the variable $\boldsymbol{\alpha}^G$ since Eq. (11) is proved to be convergent. The optimization algorithm is divided into two steps.

Update $\boldsymbol{\alpha}^T, \boldsymbol{\alpha}^{*T}$ and $\boldsymbol{\alpha}^G$. Alternatively updating $\boldsymbol{\alpha}^T, \boldsymbol{\alpha}^{*T}$ and $\boldsymbol{\alpha}^G$ after $\mathbf{d}$ is fixed, we find Eq. (11) can be optimized via two processes. When $\boldsymbol{\alpha}^G$ is fixed, Eq. (11) has the similar form with the standard ϵ-SVR, and we can use the existing toolkit such as LIBSVM [3] to solve $\boldsymbol{\alpha}^T$ and $\boldsymbol{\alpha}^{*T}$. Once $\boldsymbol{\alpha}^T$ and $\boldsymbol{\alpha}^{*T}$ are solved, $\boldsymbol{\alpha}^G$ can be computed by using a standard quadratic programming solver. The updating processes are stopped when Eq. (11) converges to a certain value.

Update $\mathbf{d}$. After solving $\boldsymbol{\alpha}^T, \boldsymbol{\alpha}^{*T}$ and $\boldsymbol{\alpha}^G$ in each iteration of the first step, $\mathbf{d}$ can be updated with a linear programming solver.

   Alternating above two steps, Eq. (11) can quickly converge to a minimum value. Specifically, the optimization details are summarized in Algorithm 1.

   Substituting $\boldsymbol{\alpha}^T, \boldsymbol{\alpha}^{*T}, \boldsymbol{\alpha}^G$ and $\mathbf{d}$ into Eq. (1), the target classifier can be rewritten as

$$f^T(\mathbf{z}) = \sum_g d_g \boldsymbol{\beta}_g' (\boldsymbol{\varphi}^{[g]'} \boldsymbol{\varphi}_g(\mathbf{z}^{[g]}) + \frac{d_g}{\theta} \mathbf{f}^{[g]} f^g(\mathbf{z}^{[g]})), \tag{12}$$

where $\boldsymbol{\beta}_g = [(\boldsymbol{\alpha}_1 \odot \mathbf{y}_1)', \dots, (\boldsymbol{\alpha}_G \odot \mathbf{y}_G)', (\boldsymbol{\alpha}^{*T} - \boldsymbol{\alpha}^T)']'$.

Algorithm 1. Heterogeneous multi-group adaptation

---

1 Initialize $\mathbf{d}^o$, which satisfies $D = \{\mathbf{d} \mid \mathbf{d} \geq \mathbf{0}, \mathbf{1}'\mathbf{d} = 1\}, \mathbf{d}^o = \mathbf{d}^O$
2 **repeat**
3   Substitute $\mathbf{d}^o$ into Eq. (11), update $\boldsymbol{\alpha}^T, \boldsymbol{\alpha}^{*T}, \boldsymbol{\alpha}^G$
4   **repeat**
5   Initialize $\boldsymbol{\alpha}^G$, obtain optimal $\boldsymbol{\alpha}^T, \boldsymbol{\alpha}^{*T}$ by using LIBSVM [3]
6   Fixing $\boldsymbol{\alpha}^T, \boldsymbol{\alpha}^{*T}$, update $\boldsymbol{\alpha}^G$ using quadratic programming solver
7   **until** *The objective of Eq. (11) converges*
8   Substitute $\boldsymbol{\alpha}^T, \boldsymbol{\alpha}^{*T}$ and $\boldsymbol{\alpha}^G$ into Eq. (11), update $\mathbf{d}$ using linear programming solver
9      $\mathbf{d}^{o+1} \leftarrow \mathbf{d}^o$
10 **until** *The objective of Eq. (11) converges;*

---

4 Experiment

We compare our method with the baseline method employing SVM, the existing single source domain adaptation methods Transfer Joint Matching (TJM) [13] and Transfer Kernel Learning (TKL) [14], and the existing multiple source domain adaptation methods Domain Selection Machine (DSM) [5], Domain Adaptation Machine (DAM) [6], and Multi-domain Adaptation with Heterogeneous Sources (MDA-HS) [4]. All the methods are evaluated on two challenging video datasets CCV [11] and TRECVID MED 2014 [1]. We first introduce the datasets, and then describe the experimental settings. After that, we use Average Precision (AP) to evaluate the performance of all the methods and report the Mean Average Precision (MAP) for all the event classes.

4.1 Datasets and Features

CCV dataset: The CCV dataset [11] contains a training set of 4659 videos and a test set of 4658 videos annotated with 20 semantic categories. Our work focuses on event recognition, therefore, we omit videos from non-event categories (*i.e.*, "beach", "bird", "cat", "dog", and "playground"). Following [5], we merge "wedding ceremony", "wedding reception, and "wedding dance" into "wedding", "non-music performance" and "music performance" into "show", and "baseball", "basketball", "biking", "ice skating", "skiing", "soccer", "swimming" into "sports". That yields 2594 videos from 5 event classes (*i.e.*, "birthday", "parade", "show", "sports, and "wedding").

TRECVID MED 2014 Dataset: This dataset consists of 20 event classes (*i.e.*, E021-E040) and a background class, where there are around 100 videos of each event class and 4,983 videos of the background class. In our experiment, we only choose the videos from the event classes as our consumer videos.

Web Image and Video Datasets: In order to construct heterogenous multiple groups, images and videos based on keyword searching are collected from Google and YouTube search engines respectively. We downloaded the top 100 retrieved images and videos for each keyword, and ignore the invalid URLs. This gives us 2547 images and videos for the CCV dataset and 10920 images and videos for the MED dataset.

Features: We extract the CNN features for each image downloaded from Google using Caffe [10] and the VGG model provided by [16]. The output of the second fully-connected layer from the VGG network [16], a 4096-dimensional feature, is extracted as our feature descriptors. For each video in the CCV and MED datasets, we sample 5 frames per second and extract the frame level CNN descriptors. Finally, we apply average pooling on the frame descriptors of each video to generate the video level representation.

For each video in the CCV dataset and downloaded from YouTube, three types of local descriptors (*i.e.*, Histogram of Oriented Gradient, Histogram of Optical Flow and Motion Boundary Histogram) are extracted by using the source codes provided in [20]. The sampling stride is set as 16 while the other parameters are set as default values. Then, following [20], we use Fisher vector to encode these local descriptors and apply l_2 normalization. Finally, the normalized Fisher vectors of different descriptors are concatenated to generate the final video representation. For each video in the MED dataset and downloaded from YouTube, we split it into 16-frame long clips and pass these clips to the C3D network provided by [17] to extract C3D features. The final feature for each video is computed by averaging the clip features followed by an l_2 normalization.

4.2 Experimental Setup

In the experiments, we search five groups from Google and YouTube for each event class. The CCV and MED datasets are used as our target domains. We first pre-train a classifier $f^g(\mathbf{x}^g)$ for each event class on one group, where the positive samples consist of samples belonging to the corresponding event class in the corresponding group, and the negative samples are from all the samples belonging to groups of other event classes. The classifier f^g pre-trained on the g-th group is used to compute the decision values of samples from the g-th view of target domain, and the decision values of target samples are computed by averaging these decision values from all the group classifiers.

The baseline SVM is referred as SVM_A in which the decision values of target samples are computed by fusing the decision values from all the pre-trained classifiers. Since TJM and TKL are single domain adaptation methods, we extend both TJM and TKL into multi-group versions applying the same fusion strategy as SVM_A, denoted as Multi-TJM and Multi-TKL. The experiment settings of multiple source domain adaptation methods (*i.e.*, DAM, DSM, MDA-HS) are different from our experiments, therefore, we regard each group as a source domain. For DAM and DSM, we need to compute decision values of samples from each view of target domain, which are averaged as the final decision values of target samples. For all the methods, we use one-vs-all SVMs with the Gaussian kernel $K(\mathbf{x}_i, \mathbf{x}_j) = exp(-\|\mathbf{x}_i - \mathbf{x}_j\|^2)$, where γ is set as the mean of the squared

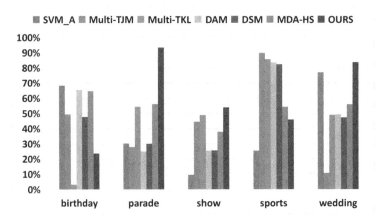

Fig. 2. Per-event APs on the CCV datasets.

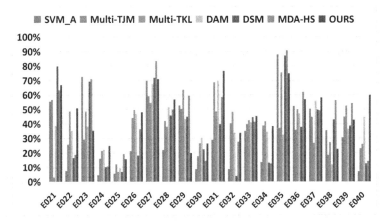

Fig. 3. Per-event APs on the MED dataset.

distance between all the training samples. The regularization parameters C_G and C_T are set as 1 and 10 respectively since target samples is more important for classification. θ and ϵ are empirically set to 0.002 and 10^{-5}, respectively.

4.3   Results

For all the methods, the per-event APs on the CCV and MED datasets are plotted in Figs. 2 and 3, and the MAPs on both datasets are showed in Table 1. It is interesting to observe that our method outperforms other methods on both datasets, which demonstrates the effectiveness of our proposed ϵ-SVR based objective function and introduced manifold regularization. There is no consistent winner among DSM, DAM and Multi-TKL in terms of MAPs, which indicates that event recognition in consumer videos from heterogeneous groups is a

Table 1. MAP (%) of all methods on the CCV and MED datasets.

Method	SVM_A	Multi-TJM	Multi-TKL	DAM	DSM	MDA-HS	Ours
CCV	42.12	44.40	48.25	49.68	46.58	53.74	60.78
MED	33.51	37.26	40.02	39.53	37.78	44.54	46.26

challenging task. SVM_A is worse than other methods, which demonstrates that adapting the knowledge learned from source domains is beneficial to learn a better classifier in target domain. MDA-HS and our method achieve relatively high performances since both methods can deal with heterogeneous features better than other methods. Our method is superior to MDA-HS in terms of computational complexity. Our method solves the objective function by using standard quadratic programming and SVR solvers. In MDA-HS, cutting-plane algorithm and multiple kernel learning are applied to solve the optimization problem, which are computationally intensive.

5   Conclusion and Future Work

In this paper, we have proposed a heterogeneous multi-group adaptation method to leverage a large number of loosely labeled Web images (from Google) and videos (from YouTube) to recognize complex events in target domain where there are no labeled videos. These images and videos are divided into several semantic groups based on different keywords corresponding to specific classes of event in the target domain. Our method can learn the weights of the classifiers from corresponding view of target domain as well as the weights of classifier learned from different groups. A manifold regularization is introduced to enforce the target classifier to be smooth on target samples.

For future work, we plan to experiment with using deep neural networks to learn discriminative deep representations for both source and target data with the intent to improve event recognition in consumer videos.

Acknowledgments. This work was supported in part by the Natural Science Foundation of China (NSFC) under Grants Nos. 61673062 and 61472038.

References

1. Trecvid med 14. http://www.nist.gov/itl/iad/mig/med14.cfm
2. Aytar, Y., Zisserman, A.: Tabula rasa: model transfer for object category detection. In: IEEE International Conference on Computer Vision, pp. 2252–2259. IEEE (2011)
3. Chang, C.C., Lin, C.J.: LIBSVM: a library for support vector machines. ACM Trans. Intell. Syst. Technol. **2**(3), 27 (2011)

4. Chen, L., Duan, L., Xu, D.: Event recognition in videos by learning from heterogeneous web sources. In: Proceedings of the IEEE Conference on Computer Vision and Pattern Recognition, pp. 2666–2673 (2013)
5. Duan, L., Xu, D., Chang, S.F.: Exploiting web images for event recognition in consumer videos: a multiple source domain adaptation approach. In: IEEE Conference on Computer Vision and Pattern Recognition, pp. 1338–1345. IEEE (2012)
6. Duan, L., Xu, D., Tsang, I.W.H.: Domain adaptation from multiple sources: a domain-dependent regularization approach. IEEE Trans. Neural Netw. Learn. Syst. **23**(3), 504–518 (2012)
7. Feng, Y., Wu, X., Wang, H., Liu, J.: Multi-group adaptation for event recognition from videos. In: 22nd International Conference on Pattern Recognition, pp. 3915–3920. IEEE (2014)
8. Ikizler-Cinbis, N., Sclaroff, S.: Object, scene and actions: combining multiple features for human action recognition. In: Daniilidis, K., Maragos, P., Paragios, N. (eds.) ECCV 2010. LNCS, vol. 6311, pp. 494–507. Springer, Heidelberg (2010). https://doi.org/10.1007/978-3-642-15549-9_36
9. Izadinia, H., Shah, M.: Recognizing complex events using large margin joint low-level event model. In: Fitzgibbon, A., Lazebnik, S., Perona, P., Sato, Y., Schmid, C. (eds.) ECCV 2012. LNCS, vol. 7575, pp. 430–444. Springer, Heidelberg (2012). https://doi.org/10.1007/978-3-642-33765-9_31
10. Jia, Y.: An open source convolutional architecture for fast feature embedding (2013)
11. Jiang, Y.G., Ye, G., Chang, S.F., Ellis, D., Loui, A.C.: Consumer video understanding: a benchmark database and an evaluation of human and machine performance. In: Proceedings of the 1st ACM International Conference on Multimedia Retrieval, p. 29. ACM (2011)
12. Long, M., Wang, J., Cao, Y., Sun, J., Philip, S.Y.: Deep learning of transferable representation for scalable domain adaptation. IEEE Trans. Knowl. Data Eng. **28**(8), 2027–2040 (2016)
13. Long, M., Wang, J., Ding, G., Sun, J., Yu, P.S.: Transfer joint matching for unsupervised domain adaptation. In: Proceedings of the IEEE Conference on Computer Vision and Pattern Recognition, pp. 1410–1417 (2014)
14. Long, M., Wang, J., Sun, J., Philip, S.Y.: Domain invariant transfer kernel learning. IEEE Trans. Knowl. Data Eng. **27**(6), 1519–1532 (2015)
15. Sener, O., Song, H.O., Saxena, A., Savarese, S.: Learning transferrable representations for unsupervised domain adaptation. In: Advances in Neural Information Processing Systems, pp. 2110–2118 (2016)
16. Simonyan, K., Zisserman, A.: Very deep convolutional networks for large-scale image recognition. arXiv preprint arXiv:1409.1556 (2014)
17. Tran, D., Bourdev, L., Fergus, R., Torresani, L., Paluri, M.: Learning spatiotemporal features with 3D convolutional networks. In: Proceedings of the IEEE International Conference on Computer Vision, pp. 4489–4497 (2015)
18. Vahdat, A., Cannons, K., Mori, G., Oh, S., Kim, I.: Compositional models for video event detection: a multiple kernel learning latent variable approach. In: Proceedings of the IEEE International Conference on Computer Vision, pp. 1185–1192 (2013)
19. Wang, H., Wu, X., Jia, Y.: Annotating videos from the web images. In: 21st International Conference on Pattern Recognition, pp. 2801–2804. IEEE (2012)
20. Wang, H., Schmid, C.: Action recognition with improved trajectories. In: Proceedings of the IEEE International Conference on Computer Vision, pp. 3551–3558 (2013)

21. Xu, Y., Fang, X., Wu, J., Li, X., Zhang, D.: Discriminative transfer subspace learning via low-rank and sparse representation. IEEE Trans. Image Process. **25**(2), 850–863 (2016)
22. Yang, X., Zhang, T., Xu, C.: Cross-domain feature learning in multimedia. IEEE Trans. Multimed. **17**(1), 64–78 (2015)
23. Yao, T., Pan, Y., Ngo, C.W., Li, H., Mei, T.: Semi-supervised domain adaptation with subspace learning for visual recognition. In: Proceedings of the IEEE Conference on Computer Vision and Pattern Recognition, pp. 2142–2150 (2015)

Margin-Aware Binarized Weight Networks for Image Classification

Ting-Bing Xu[1,2]([✉]), Peipei Yang[1], Xu-Yao Zhang[1], and Cheng-Lin Liu[1,2]

[1] National Laboratory of Pattern Recognition,
Institute of Automation of Chinese Academy of Sciences, Beijing, China
{tingbing.xu,ppyang,xyz,liucl}@nlpr.ia.ac.cn
[2] University of Chinese Academy of Sciences (UCAS), Beijing, China

Abstract. Deep neural networks (DNNs) have achieved remarkable successes in many vision tasks. However, due to the dependence on large memory and high-performance GPUs, it is extremely hard to deploy DNNs on low-power devices. For compressing and accelerating deep neural networks, many techniques have been proposed recently. Particularly, binarized weight networks, which store one weight using only one bit and replace complex floating operations with simple calculations, are attractive from the perspective of hardware implementation. In this paper, we propose a simple strategy to learn better binarized weight networks. Motivated by the phenomenon that the stochastic binarization approach usually converges with real-valued weights close to two boundaries $\{-1, +1\}$ and gives better performance than deterministic binarization, we construct a margin-aware binarization strategy by adding a weight constraint into the objective function of deterministic scheme to minimize the margins between real-valued weights and boundaries. This constraint can be easily realized by a Binary-L2 regularization without suffering from the complex random number generation. Experimental results on MNIST and CIFAR-10 datasets show that the proposed method yields better performance than recent network binarization schemes and the full precision network counterpart.

Keywords: Deep network compression · Binarized weight networks
Binary-L2 regularization

1 Introduction

Deep Neural Networks (DNNs) have been successfully applied to a wide range of vision tasks, such as object recognition [1–4], object detection [5–7] and semantic segmentation [8,9]. Despite their huge power and success, DNNs require large memory overhead and high-performance hardware for implementation, which makes it difficult to run DNNs on some resource-limited devices (e.g., Smartphone, Smart wearable devices and Embedded devices) or dedicated Deep Learning hardware directly. For instance, the famous AlexNet [1] requires about 61×10^6 parameters ($232\,\mathrm{MB}^1$) with 725 million FLoating-point OPerations

---

[1] MB: MegaBytes storage requirement.

© Springer International Publishing AG 2017
Y. Zhao et al. (Eds.): ICIG 2017, Part I, LNCS 10666, pp. 590–601, 2017.
https://doi.org/10.1007/978-3-319-71607-7_52

(FLOPs), and VGG-16 [2] involves 138×10^6 parameters (527 MB) with 15.3 billion FLOPs. Therefore, reducing the parameters of DNNs and removing most arithmetic operations are crucial problems for many real-time deployments.

To break the above bottleneck of DNNs' application on resource-limited devices, various deep model compression methods have been proposed recently. The first strategy proposes new architectures to reduce the parameters, especially in the fully-connected (fc) layer, such as GoogLenet [3], ResNet [4], Network in Network [10], SqueezeNet [11]. They replace fc layers with global average pooling layer to reduce parameters dramatically, and design diversified compact blocks (e.g., Inception module [3], "bottleneck" building block of ResNet [4], mlpconv layer [10] and Fire module [11]) to reduce parameters of convolutional layers further. Finally, the deeper and light networks are constructed for higher performance. However, such kind of light networks do not take care of the number of FLOPs (speed) adequately. For instance, the ResNet-18 [4] network still needs about 1.8 billion FLOPs to classify an image of size 224×224.

The second strategy utilizes compression techniques to remove redundant parameters [12] of the classical DNNs for less storage and faster inference, including tensor decomposition with low-rank approximation [13–15], sparse constraints [16], hash function [17], threshold based reduction with retraining [18], integration of hash trick and Huffman coding [19], etc. Though these approaches achieve significant compression ratio for fc layers, they are not well suitable for the new DNN models because the new DNNs structures (e.g., ResNet [4], SqueezeNet [11]) have discarded fc layers. While the training process is also complicated since the repetitional fine-tuned operations and difficultly recover the original accuracy produced by information loss of pre-trained models.

To obtain better compression and acceleration, the third strategy which uses lower bits to store the weight is proposed. For example, Vanhoucke et al. [20] directly replaced the 32-bit "float" with 8-bit "char" to shrink total memory footprint by 4×. Later, binarized weight networks were proposed, where the weights were approximated with binary values $\{-1, +1\}$ (in Fig. 1(a)) resulting in 32× memory saving and simple addition or subtraction operations. Soudry et al. [21] were the first to show that the binarized DNNs can obtain good accuracy by the Expectation BackPropagation (EBP) algorithm which updates the posterior distributions over real-valued weights. Courbariaux et al. [22,23] designed the BinaryConnect algorithm and BinarizedNet method by extending the probabilistic

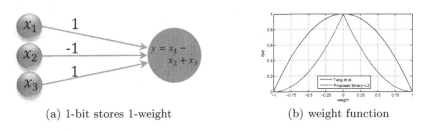

(a) 1-bit stores 1-weight   (b) weight function

Fig. 1. Binarized weight networks and weight constraint terms.

idea behind EBP algorithm, where they directly utilized binarized parameters to train Binarized Neural Networks using standard back propagation. For better performance, Rastegari et al. [24] proposed Binary-Weight-Networks and XNOR-Networks by combining optimized scale factors with binarized weights or activations. However, the overall compression rate of XNOR-Network was severely degraded because both the first and last layers were of full precision to guarantee reasonable accuracy. To address this problem, Tang et al. [25] adopted a scalar layer and new regularization term to mitigate severe accuracy drop when the last layer was also binarized, but the compression rate is still limited since the first layer is still of full precision.

In this paper, we focus on binarized weight networks which are attractive from the perspective of hardware, and study to achieve both better performance and simplicity of implementation. In the experiments of BinaryConnect [22], the stochastic binarization scheme is of better performance than deterministic binarization, but harder to implement as it needs the hardware to generate random bits. To analyse the difference between the two schemes, we carefully examine the weight distribution after the algorithm converges and find an interesting phenomenon. For the stochastic approach, all the weights gather close to the boundaries $\{-1, +1\}$ by a very small margin, while for the deterministic approach, there are considerable amount of weights scattered over the interval and some even stuck around 0, leaving a large margin to the boundaries.

This phenomenon motivates our proposed margin-aware binarization strategy which is constructed by introducing a weight constraint into the objective function of deterministic binarization to minimize the loss between real-valued weights and corresponding binarized weights (boundaries). The constraint formulated as a *Binary-L2* term gives the weights awareness of the margins to boundaries, and the proposed method can effectively improve the performance of deterministic binarization approach, which can be easily realized without random number generation. Extensive experiments demonstrate that our Binarized Weight Networks algorithm yields better performance than recent network binarization approaches and the corresponding full precision networks.

It's worth noting that although the regularization used in our method is similar to the one in [25] to some extent, the contributions of the two are obviously different in the following perspectives: (1) in Fig. 1(b), the weight gradient in our Binary-L2 term becomes stronger as it approaches 0 by a large margin to the boundaries, which shrinks the margin effectively and drives the weights towards two boundaries $\{-1, +1\}$ friendly. On the contrary, the gradient of regularization term in [25] tends to vanish around 0, and its large gradient at ± 1 is likely to stick the weights at their current binary values. (2) While the motivation in [25] is to apply a regularization on the weights, we propose the Binary-L2 based on the analysis of the discovered phenomenon, which provides a perspective on explaining why this term is effective to improve the performance. A detailed discussion on the potential mechanism behind this phenomenon is given in this paper.

The reminder of this paper is organized as follows. Section 2 presents details about our Binarized-Weight-Networks. Section 3 shows experimental results on several common datasets and the analysis. Concluding remarks will be drawn in Sect. 4.

2   Binarized Weight Networks

In the past, people thought that low-precision networks would suffer from obvious performance drop, especially under the extreme scenario: Binarized DNNs were believed to be highly destructive to the network accuracy [26]. However, recent binarized based networks [21, 22, 24] have exhibited promising results when the weights or activations of DNNs are binarized to ±1. BinaryConnect [22] algorithm constrains the weights to be only two possible values $\{-1, +1\}$ and use the binarized weights in the forward and backward propagations. To exploit the Stochastic Gradient Descent (SGD) technique to optimize the network, there is a real-valued weight corresponding to each binarized weight. In every step, the real-valued weights are updated according to the gradients of the binarized weights. Courbariaux et al. [22] explain that the constrained function of binarization can be regarded as a new regularization (a binary sampling process) for real-valued weights which is able to improve generalization capability, like Dropout [27] and DropConnect [28] operations.

Motivation: In BinaryConnect [22], there are two types of binarization operation: deterministic (det.) and stochastic (stoch.) binarization. The deterministic binarization operation constrains each real-valued weight to binary values ±1 using the following sign function:

$$w_i^b = \text{sign}(w_i) = \begin{cases} +1 & \text{if } w_i \geq 0, \\ -1 & \text{if } w_i < 0, \end{cases} \tag{1}$$

where w_i^b is the binarized weight and w_i is corresponding real-valued weight. This binarization scheme is easy to be implemented on various devices and effective in practice [22, 24]. On the other hand, the stochastic binarization requires generating random bits that is much more computationally costly and more difficult to be implemented on low-power hardware devices. However, the stochastic binarization method performs better than deterministic scheme in the experiments of BinaryConnect [22]. To explore the reason, we observe the distribution of the real-valued weights after training stage. An interesting phenomenon is observed in deterministic scheme that although a majority of weights converge to the two boundaries $\{-1, +1\}$, there are also quite a few weights scattering along the interval, leaving a large margin to the boundaries. On the contrary, in the stochastic scheme, all weights converge to two boundaries $\{-1, +1\}$ friendly with a very small margin. According to this phenomenon, we guess there may be some relationship between the margin and the performance. Thus we attempt to design a simple approach to eliminate such a margin in deterministic binarization scheme for pursuing better performance of Binarized-Weight-Networks (in Fig. 2).

Method: Through investigations, we find an analogous problem in visual similarity search field. For these algorithms, how to encode high-dimensional image data into short and effective binary codes based on hashing approaches is a crucial problem. Liong et al. [29] insert three constrained conditions into the

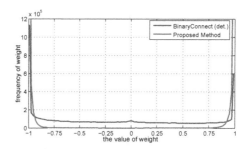

Fig. 2. Distribution of real-valued weights after training time.

objective function of DNNs to make the different bits of the learned binary vector $\mathbf{h}^b$ possess independent and discriminative properties, one of which aims at minimizing the loss between real-valued feature descriptor and the learned binary vector by the following function:

$$\min \frac{1}{2}\|\mathbf{h} - \text{sign}(\mathbf{h})\|_2^2 = \min \frac{1}{2}\|\mathbf{h} - \mathbf{h}^b\|_2^2, \tag{2}$$

where $\mathbf{h}$ denotes float values of the last fc layer and $\mathbf{h}^b$ is binarized values of $\mathbf{h}$. It is similar to our weight constraint term.

As discussed in our motivation, we are trying to get a better performance by reducing the margins between real-valued weights and the boundaries $\{-1, +1\}$, which is a similar task as the one above. Thus, we introduce a weight constraint deterministic binarization scheme. The constraint term formulated as a Binary-L2 regularization (standard norm) can effectively minimize the loss between the learned weights of DNNs and the corresponding binarized weights, which is defined as:

$$\min \frac{1}{2}\|\mathbf{W} - \text{sign}(\mathbf{W})\|_F^2 = \min \frac{1}{2}\|\mathbf{W} - \mathbf{W}^b\|_F^2$$
$$= \min \frac{1}{2}\||\mathbf{W}| - \mathbf{1}\|_{l2}^2. \tag{3}$$

Then the optimization objective function is as follows:

$$\min_{\mathbf{W}} J(\mathbf{W}) = L(\mathbf{W}^b, \mathbf{X}, \mathbf{y}) + \frac{\lambda}{2}\||\mathbf{W}| - \mathbf{1}\|_{l2}^2,$$
$$s.t. \quad \mathbf{W}^b = \text{sign}(\mathbf{W}), \tag{4}$$

where L is common loss function (such as SoftmaxLoss or HingeLoss), the second term is our Binary-L2 regularization and λ controls the balance between the two terms. $\mathbf{X}$ and $\mathbf{y}$ represents the training samples and corresponding label vector respectively. $\mathbf{W}$ is the weight tensor of the entire DNNs and $\mathbf{1}$ is the counterpart identity tensor. The first loss function (L) is minimized for high classification accuracy and the Binary-L2 term gives weights awareness to converge to the two edges $\{-1, +1\}$ friendly during parameter update for discovering better accuracy of Binarized-Weight-Networks.

Algorithm 1. SGD Training for the Binarized-Weight-Networks

Require: A minibatch of training samples $(\mathbf{X}, \mathbf{y})$, network layer number M, iterative number t, learning rate η, scaled coefficient γ, Eq. 4 is the optimization objective function, previous real-valued parameters $\mathbf{W}^{t-1}$ (weights) and $\mathbf{b}^{t-1}$ (biases).

Ensure: updated parameter $\mathbf{W}^t$ and $\mathbf{b}^t$.

1. BinaryFoward propagation:

for $m = 1$ to M layers **do**

   $\mathbf{W}_m^b = \text{sign}(\mathbf{W}_m^{t-1})$

   Compute the weighted sum $\mathbf{Z}_m$ with $\mathbf{X}_{m-1}$, $\mathbf{W}_m^b$ and $\mathbf{b}_m^{t-1}$

   Apply batch-normalization [31] and ReLU [32] to $\mathbf{Z}_m$ to obtain $\mathbf{X}_m$

end for

Compute the loss L using $\mathbf{X}_M$ and $\mathbf{y}$

2. BinaryBackward propagation:

Initialize output layer's activations gradient $\dfrac{\partial L}{\partial \mathbf{X}_M}$

for $m = M$ to 2 layers **do**

   Compute $\dfrac{\partial L}{\partial \mathbf{X}_{m-1}}$ using $\dfrac{\partial L}{\partial \mathbf{X}_m}$ and $\mathbf{W}_m^b$

end for

3. Parameter update:

for $m = 1$ to M layers **do**

   Compute $\dfrac{\partial L}{\partial \mathbf{W}_m^b}$ and $\dfrac{\partial L}{\partial \mathbf{b}_m^{t-1}}$ knowing $\dfrac{\partial L}{\partial \mathbf{X}_m}$ and $\mathbf{X}_{m-1}$

   $\mathbf{W}_m^t \leftarrow \text{clip}\left(\mathbf{W}_m^{t-1} - \eta \cdot \gamma_m \left(\dfrac{\partial L}{\partial \mathbf{W}_m^b} + \dfrac{\partial R}{\partial \mathbf{W}_m^{t-1}}\right)\right)$ // R is the new constraint

   $\mathbf{b}_m^t \leftarrow \mathbf{b}_m^{t-1} - \eta \dfrac{\partial L}{\partial \mathbf{b}_m^{t-1}}$

end for

Training Process: The entire Binarized-Weight-Networks can be trained in an end-to-end manner by back propagation (BP) algorithm and SGD optimization or Adam learning rule [30]. Same as BinaryConnect, there is a corresponding real-valued weight for each binary weight for parameter update. In every step, the previous real-valued weights are updated directly by the gradients, which are computed with respect to the binarized weights. Then the binarized weights are obtained using sign function Eq. 1. After training stage, the float weights are discarded for memory saving since the forward propagation only need binarized weights. The whole procedure is illustrated in Algorithm 1, where R denotes Binary-L2 term (the second term in Eq. 4).

Implementation Detail: Since existing deep learning platforms do not support binarized layers and Binary-L2 regularization, we need to implement binarized convolutional layer, binarized fully-connected layer and special Binary-L2 regularization based on Caffe [33] toolbox. For each real-valued weight, the Binary-L2 regularization term is continuously differentiable and its derivative is define as:

$$\frac{\partial R}{\partial w_i} = \lambda(|w_i| - 1)\text{sign}(w_i). \tag{5}$$

In addition, we also adopted several useful techniques as used in BinaryConnect algorithm [22] to achieve better Binarized-Weight-Networks. These techniques include Batch Normalization (BN), scaling the weights learning rates (γ in Algorithm 1) and clipping operation. The real-valued weights are easily updated in the range $[-1, 1]$ by these operations. The weight learning rates are scaled to enlarge the gradient magnitude with the coefficient γ from "Xavier" [34] algorithm, thus we set $\lambda\gamma = 0.0001$–0.0005 as the ratio of regularization that is similar to L2 weight decay in DNNs. Clipping operation constrains weights to $[-1, 1]$ interval for preventing weights far from the boundary $\{-1, +1\}$ overly.

3   Experiments

We conducted experiments on two widely used datasets (natural image classification task) to evaluate the effectiveness of our proposed binarization scheme with routine convolutional neural networks (CNN). In our experiments, the basic block structure of our binarized CNN contains convolutional or fully-connected layer with binarized weights, BN [31] layer and ReLU [32] activation layer. We use weights initialization of uniform distribution $[-1, 1]$, Binary-L2 regularization and Adam optimization for all Binarized-Weight-Networks, while the "Xavier" [34] initialization and Adam optimization are adopted for the corresponding full precision weight networks. The experimental settings and results are described in following.

3.1   MNIST

The MNIST [35] dataset contains handwritten digit images (0–9) including 60k training images and 10k testing images. The images are of normalized size 28×28. An architecture similar to LeNet5 [35] is used in our experiment, which is also adopted in [36] and shown in Fig. 3 (left).

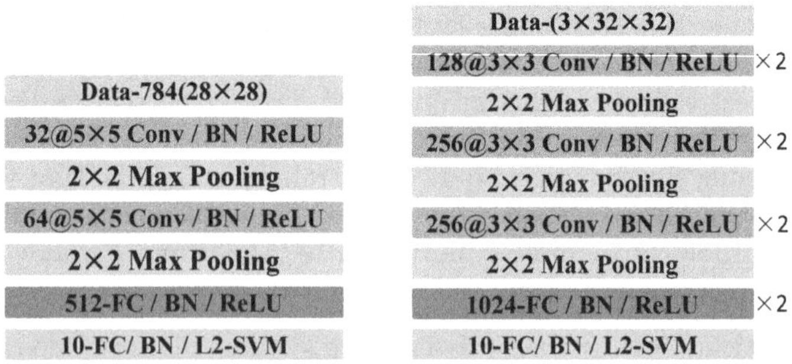

Fig. 3. Left: MNIST dataset and Right: CIFAR-10 dataset.

In this picture, the "32@5×5 Conv" denotes that a convolutional layer possess 32 convolutional kernels with size 5×5, "2×2 Max Pooling" presents a max-pooling layer with kernel size 2 and stride 2, "512-FC" is a fully connected layer with 512 output neurons, and L2-SVM indicates the square hinge loss is used as loss function (L in Eq. 4) because L2-SVM has achieved better results than Softmax on several classification dataset [37,38]. For fairness of the comparison, the same settings are adopted based on MNIST dataset as used in BinaryConnect [22] algorithm. We use the last 10000 samples of training set for validation without retraining on the validation set and do not use any data-augmentation or unsupervised pretraining. Except for our Binary-L2 regularization, no other regularizations such as Dropout or L2 regularization are used. For detailed settings (e.g., batch size, learning rate), please refer to our Caffe [33] configuration files[2]. The whole Binarized-Weight-Networks are trained from scratch and the test accuracy is reported in Table 1.

Table 1 shows that the proposed binarized method improves the accuracy by more than 1.5% compared to the recent ternary or binarized approaches, and is slightly better than corresponding full precision network. Meanwhile, our simple 4-layers binarized weight network also achieve competitive performance compared with some complex full precision networks.

Table 1. Test set accuracy for MNIST of various methods.

Method	Test accuracy (%)
Our binarized-weight-network	**99.52**
Original full precision network	**99.48**
Binary or ternary CNN models	
Ternary weight network [36]	99.35
Binary precision weight network [36]	99.05
Binary MLP models	
BinaryConnect (det.) [22]	98.71
Binarized Neural Network [23]	99.04
Full Precision MLP or CNN Models	
Maxout Networks (MLP) [39]	99.06
Deep L2-SVM (MLP) [38]	99.13
Network In Network (CNN) + Dropout [10]	99.53
Conv.maxout (CNN) + Dropout [39]	99.55
Deeply-supervised-net (CNN) + Dropout [37]	99.61

3.2   CIFAR-10

The CIFAR-10 [40] dataset consists of 32×32 colour images in 10 classes including 50000 training images and 10000 test images. Generally speaking, the dataset is preprocessed by the global contrast normalization and ZCA whitening as was used in [10,22,37,39]. We adopt the same network architecture (VGG-like in

---

[2] https://github.com/xugithub1/caffe-Binarized-Weight-Networks.

Fig. 3 right) as other binarization methods [22,23,36], where the 9-layers architecture is more simple than standard VGG-Net [2] and "×2" denotes the same two layers. To compare with previous state-of-the-art works, we also evaluate our method on this dataset with data augmentation as used in [4,37]. In the training phase, zero-padding 4 pixels on each side, and a 32×32 crop is randomly sampled from the padded image or its horizontal flip. At test time, we only use the single view of original 32×32 test image.

A comparison of our method with previous binarized or full precision approaches is shown in Table 2, and Fig. 4 exhibits test set error rate curves of several schemes. Experimental results[3] show that our binarized weight network not only obtain the new state-of-the-art accuracy compared with other binarized or ternary weight networks, but also surpass most of full precision networks including ResNet-56 structure. It indicates that the extreme low-precision networks do not destroy original network performance. On the contrary, network binarization and Binary-L2 techniques act as regularizer for improving generalization capability of original networks to some extent.

Table 2. Test set accuracy for CIFAR-10 of various methods.

Method	Test accuracy (%)
No data augmentation	
Our binarized-weight-network	**90.90**
Original full precision network	**89.66**
BinaryConnect (det.) [22]	90.10
Binary-weight-network [24]	90.12
Binarized neural network [23]	89.85
Maxout networks [39]	88.32
Network in network [10]	89.59
Deeply-supervised-net [37]	90.31
With data augmentation	
Our binarized-weight-network	**93.30**
Original full precision network	**92.89**
BinaryConnect (det.)	**91.82**
Ternary weight network [36]	92.56
Binary precision weight network [36]	90.18
Conv.maxout + dropout [39]	90.62
Network in network + dropout [10]	91.19
Deeply-supervised-net + dropout [37]	92.03
ResNet-56 [4]	93.03

---

[3] Boldface is our own experimental results.

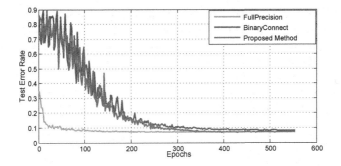

Fig. 4. Test set accuracy curves on CIFAR-10 dataset.

3.3   Compression Rates

The real compression rates of our binarized weight network are described in Table 3. We pack 32 binary-valued weight units into a single fixed32 Proto-Buffer unit [33], and other parameters such as biases and special parameters of Batch Normalization layers are still stored in float values. Finally, the proposed binarization scheme compress the float-valued similar LeNet5 (2.23 MB) and VGG-9Layer (53.5 MB) to binarized weight models whose storage requirement are 84.7 KB and 1.74 MB, respectively. The compression rates are 26.96× and 30.75×, respectively.

Table 3. The compression rates (Comp. rate) of Binarized-Weight-Networks on MNIST and CIFAR-10 datasets. 'N/Y' denotes without/with data augmentation.

Dataset	Model (full/binary)	Accuracy ('N/Y'/%)	Storage	Comp. rate
MNIST	Full	99.48	2.23 MB	1.00×
	Binary	99.52	84.7 KB	26.96×
CIFAR-10	Full	89.66/92.89	53.5 MB	1.00×
	Binary	90.90/93.30	1.74 MB	30.75×

4   Conclusion

In this paper, we present a simple yet effective algorithm for learning binarized weight deep neural network by introducing margin-aware weight constraint. The algorithm results in memory saving 32× (theoretically) compared with single-float precision models and make it possible to deploy deep neural networks on low-power devices or dedicated Deep Learning hardware. While training by back propagation algorithm and gradient decent optimization, the introduced margin-aware weight constraint brings obvious improvement of the performance with only negligible computational cost. Experimental results show that the proposed algorithm outperforms existing binarization schemes, and achieves better performance than corresponding full precision networks. The proposed binarization scheme is also robust to different network architectures on several classical image classification datasets.

Acknowledgment. This work has been supported by the National Natural Science Foundation of China (Grant No. 61633021).

References

1. Krizhevsky, A., Sutskever, I., Hinton, G.: ImageNet classification with deep convolutional neural networks. In: NIPS (2012)
2. Simonyan, K., Zisserman, A.: Very deep convolutional networks for large-scale image recognition. In: ICLR (2015)
3. Szegedy, C., Liu, W., Jia, Y., Sermanet, P., Reed, S., Anguelov, D., Erhan, D., Rabinovich, A.: Going deeper with convolutions. In: CVPR (2015)
4. He, K., Zhang, X., Ren, S., Sun, J.: Deep residual learning for image recognition. In: CVPR (2016)
5. Ren, S., He, K., Girshick, R., Sun, J.: Faster R-CNN: towards real-time object detection with region proposal networks. In: NIPS (2015)
6. Liu, W., Anguelov, D., Erhan, D., Szegedy, C., Reed, S., Fu, C., Berg, A.: SSD: single shot MultiBox detector. In: ECCV (2016)
7. Kim, K.H., Cheon, Y., Hong, S., Roh, B., Park, M.: PVANET: deep but lightweight neural networks for real-time object detection. arXiv:1608.08021 (2016)
8. Long, J., Shelhamer, E., Darrell, T.: Fully convolutional networks for semantic segmentation. In: CVPR (2015)
9. Chen, L., Papandreou, G., Kokkinos, I., Murphy, K., Yuille, A.: Semantic image segmentation with deep convolutional nets and fully connected CRFs. In: ICLR (2015)
10. Lin, M., Chen, Q., Yan, S.: Network in network. In: ICLR (2014)
11. Iandola, F., Moskewicz, M., Ashraf, K., Han, S., Dally, W., Keutzer, K.: SqueezeNet: AlexNet-level accuracy with 50x fewer parameters and <0.5 MB model size. arXiv:1602.07360 (2016)
12. Denil, M., Shakibi, B., Dinh, L., Ranzato, M., de Freitas, N.: Predicting parameters in deep learning. In: NIPS (2013)
13. Denton, E., Zaremba, W., Bruna, J., LeCun, Y., Fergus, R.: Exploiting linear structure within convolutional networks for efficient evaluation. In: NIPS (2014)
14. Jaderberg, M., Vedaldi, A., Zisserman, A.: Speeding up convolutional neural networks with low rank expansions. In: BMVC (2014)
15. Zhang, X., Zou, J., Ming, X., He, K., Sun, J.: Efficient and accurate approximations of nonlinear convolutional networks. In: CVPR (2015)
16. Zhou, H., Alvarez, J.M., Porikli, F.: Less is more: towards compact CNNs. In: ECCV (2016)
17. Chen, W., Wilson, J.T., Tyree, S., Weinberger, K.Q., Chen, Y.: Compressing neural networks with the hashing trick. In: ICML (2015)
18. Han, S., Pool, J., Tran, J., Dally, W.: Learning both weights and connections for efficient neural network. In: NIPS (2015)
19. Han, S., Mao, H., Dally, W.: Deep compression: compressing deep neural networks with pruning, trained quantization and Huffman coding. In: ICLR (2016)

20. Vanhoucke, V., Senior, A., Mao, M.: Improving the speed of neural networks on CPUs. In: Proceedings of Deep Learning and Unsupervised Feature Learning NIPS Workshop (2011)
21. Soudry, D., Hubara, I., Meir, R.: Expectation Backpropagation: parameter-free training of multilayer neural networks with continuous or discrete weights. In: NIPS (2014)
22. Courbariaux, M., Bengio, Y.: BinaryConnect: training deep neural networks with binary weights during propagations. In: NIPS (2015)
23. Courbariaux, M., Hubara, I., Soudry, D., ElYaniv, R., Bengio, Y.: Binarized neural networks: training deep neural networks with weights and activations constrained to +1 or −1. arXiv:1602.02830 (2016)
24. Rastegari, M., Ordonez, V., Redmon, J., Farhadi, A.: XNOR-Net: ImageNet classification using binary convolutional neural networks. In: ECCV (2016)
25. Tang, W., Hua, G., Wang, L.: How to train a compact binary neural network with high accuracy? In: AAAI (2017)
26. Courbariaux, M., Bengio, Y., David, J.P.: Training deep neural networks with low precision multiplications. arXiv:1412.7024 (2014)
27. Srivastava, N., Hinton, G., Krizhevsky, A., Sutskever, I., Salakhutdinov, R.: Dropout: a simple way to prevent neural networks from overfitting. J. Mach. Learn. Res. **15**, 1929–1958 (2014)
28. Wan, L., Zeiler, M., Zhang, S., LeCun, Y., Fergus, R.: Regularization of neural networks using DropConnect. In: ICML (2013)
29. Liong, V.E., Lu, J., Wang, G., Moulin, P., Zhou, J.: Deep hashing for compact binary codes learning. In: CVPR (2015)
30. Kingma, D., Ba, J.: Adam: a method for stochastic optimization. arXiv:1412.6980 (2014)
31. Ioffe, S., Szegedy, C.: Batch normalization: accelerating deep network training by reducing internal covariate shift. In: ICML (2015)
32. Nair, V., Hinton, G.: Rectified linear units improve restricted Boltzmann machines. In: ICML (2010)
33. Jia, Y., Shelhamer, E., Donahue, J., Karayev, S., Long, J., Girshick, R., Guadarrama, S., Darrell, T.: Caffe: convolutional architecture for fast feature embedding. In: Proceedings of the ACM International Conference on Multimedia (2014)
34. Glorot, X., Bengio, Y.: Understanding the difficulty of training deep feedforward neural networks. In: AISTATS (2010)
35. LeCun, Y., Bottou, L., Bengio, Y., Haffner, P.: Gradient-based learning applied to document recognition. In: Proceedings of the IEEE (1998)
36. Li, F., Liu, B.: Ternary weight networks. arXiv:1605.04711 (2016)
37. Lee, C.Y., Xie, S., Gallagher, P., Zhang, Z., Tu, Z.: Deeply-supervised nets. In: AISTATS (2015)
38. Tang, Y.: Deep learning using linear support vector machines. In: Workshop on Challenges in Representation Learning, ICML (2013)
39. Goodfellow, I.J., Warde-Farley, D., Mirza, M., Courville, A.C., Bengio, Y.: Maxout networks. In: ICML (2013)
40. Krizhevsky, A., Hinton, G.: Learning multiple layers of features from tiny images. Technical report, University of Toronto (2009)

Multi-template Matching Algorithm Based on Adaptive Fusion

Bing Li[✉], Juan Su, Dan Chen, and Wei Wu

Xi'an High-Tech Research Institution, Xi'an 710025, China
libingbenyi@163.com

Abstract. A target recognition method based on adaptive fusion of multiple matching results was proposed, in order to take advantage of the gray information and feature information in forward-looking infrared (FLIR) target recognition. On the basis of gray-value matching and feature matching, the primary decision based on the proposed adaptive analytic hierarchy process (AHP) and the secondary decision based on the overlap area and the local searching were utilized, thereby the final matching result was generated. Experimental results show that the proposed method can overcome the false matching caused by feature template matching effectively, and improve the accuracy of target matching, and especially in case of complicated background, scale difference or viewpoint difference, the proposed algorithm has better robustness.

Keywords: Image matching · AHP · Entropy-weighted method
Adaptive fusion

1 Introduction

Infrared target recognition is the key technology of infrared imaging guidance, which plays an important role in improving the performance and accuracy of the precision guidance weapon. Template matching is the main method of infrared target recognition. In the terminal guidance stage, the infrared real-time image and template are matched to obtain the relative position of the two images, thus the target identification position is achieved [1].

At present, the target recognition in IR imaging guidance mainly adopts template matching algorithm based on feature information [2], in which the templates are mostly visible image. CAO [3] used the characteristics of visible and infrared images in the shape of fuzzy similarity, and put forward an infrared and visible image matching algorithm based on the fuzzy shape context relation. Heterogeneous images matching was realized by using gradient radial angle histogram which is not affected by image gray level nonlinear transformation and image rotation [4]. Robust edge contour descriptors were proposed from the edge contour between the heterogeneous images, and the accurate matching between IR and visible images is realized [5–7]. A heterogeneous image registration is proposed based on an invariant feature designed at the pixel level, the orientation-moment, which describes the similarity of a pixel with its neighbors in different orientation [8]. Li [9] proposed a Hausdorff distance template matching method

© Springer International Publishing AG 2017
Y. Zhao et al. (Eds.): ICIG 2017, Part I, LNCS 10666, pp. 602–613, 2017.
https://doi.org/10.1007/978-3-319-71607-7_53

based on gradient phase and significant constraint to achieve the matching positioning of planar target contour. The noise statistic model [10] and the correlation filter [11] were introduced respectively, to realize the infrared small target detection under the complex background; Ming [12] took full advantage of the gradient value and gradient direction information of the pixel, and proposed an infrared target matching algorithm based on gradient vector correlation coefficient. These algorithms can realize the target recognition task well under the specific application background.

The template matching method theoretically takes the position of the peak of the correlation matrix as the matching position. However, in practical application, because of the great difference between the template and the real-time image, the real matching position usually is another peak of the correlation matrix, which leads to the failure of matching. Moreover, the template matching algorithm based on feature information is sensitive to the accuracy of feature extraction and feature matching, which loses the gray information of the image during the matching. Therefore, it is easy to have the mismatching problem when the background is complex, or when there are great differences between the real-time image and the template. If the infrared image of a typical target can simulated on the basis of the IR model, it can provide more identification information for infrared target recognition and improve the accuracy of infrared target recognition. Through SE-Workbench-IR software, Li [13] simulated the infrared images of typical target area based on the visible image, and the gray-value of the infrared simulation image is similar to the infrared real-time image.

In view of this, we propose an adaptive fusion algorithm for infrared target recognition. Firstly, the matching images are matched with gray matching and feature matching, each obtains a set of matching results; On this basis, the adaptive AHP is proposed to fuse the characteristic parameters of the two sets of matching results, and to obtain two relative best matching points; Finally, the final matching point is acquired by the secondary decision which is based on the overlap area of the matching points corresponding to the matching regions.

2 Proposed Method

As shown in Fig. 1, the proposed algorithm mainly consists of three parts: template matching based on multiple references, the primary decision based on adaptive analytic Hierarchy process, and the secondary decision of overlap region and local search.

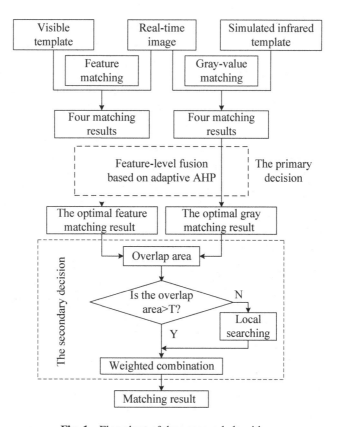

Fig. 1. Flowchart of the proposed algorithm

2.1 Template Matching Based on Multiple References

In this paper, the gray-normalized cross-correlation method and the gradient vector cross-correlation method are used as the bottom matching algorithms, which are more representative of gray matching algorithms and feature matching algorithms. The infrared simulation template and the infrared real-time image are matched by the gray-normalized cross-correlation method and the gradient vector cross-correlation method in [7] is utilized to match the visible template and the infrared real-time image. In view of the fact that the real matching position of template matching is usually located in the secondary peak of the correlation matrix, in order not to miss the true matching position, the first four peaks are retained as the candidate matching points, which participate in the subsequent fusion positioning.

As shown Fig. 2, Fig. 2(a) is IR simulation template, Fig. 2(b) are gradient feature templates obtained by the visible template in both horizontal and vertical directions, the four block diagrams in Fig. 2(c) and (d) are the matching region, in which the white block diagram area corresponds to the highest correlation coefficient, namely the theoretic matching position of the algorithm, while the other three black diagram areas correspond to the correlation coefficient secondary peaks.

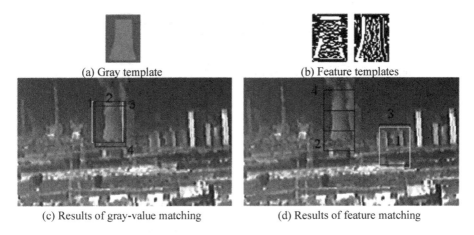

(a) Gray template   (b) Feature templates

(c) Results of gray-value matching   (d) Results of feature matching

Fig. 2. The results of image matching

However, as shown in Fig. 2(d), the best matching point of the method is the point 1 in the white block diagram, but the visual interpretation indicates that the best matching position should be the Black block diagram labeled "2", which obviously fails the feature match. Although the best matching point of the gray-scale matching shown in Fig. 2(c) is correct, there are still large deviations, so a single matching algorithm based on gray information or feature information has the problem of inaccurate matching or even mismatching.

2.2 Adaptive Analytic Hierarchy Process Based on Entropy Weight Method

For the purpose of improving the adaptability of matching accuracy and enhancing the applicability of the method, the fusion idea is introduced to optimize the matching result. The key of fusion is to set weights; And analytic hierarchy process is a classical algorithm for weighting.

Analytic Hierarchy Process (AHP) is a kind of systematic and hierarchical decision-making analysis method, which is applicable to multiple objectives or multiple schemes, quantitative and qualitative. However, the weights obtained by conventional AHP are too subjective and lack of objectivity.

In view of this, we use the entropy weight method with objectivity to improve the objectivity of the AHP, and use the improved AHP to make the primary decision on the matching results of each group to determine the best matching position in the group. The steps are as follows:

(1) Building a hierarchy model
    The hierarchy model typically consists of three layers, as shown in Fig. 3. The upper level is the target layer, which is the best matching result for the decision; The middle layer is the criteria layer, the criteria layer adopts the commonly used image matching evaluation index: correlation coefficient, RMSE and Sharpness [1]; The lowest level is the scheme layer, here is the four initial match results.

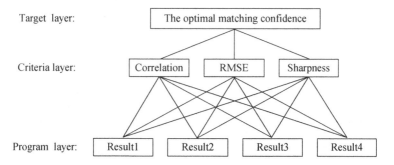

Fig. 3. Structural model of AHP

(2) Constructing Adaptive Judgment Matrix

The judgment matrix is usually constructed by paired comparison method and 1–9 comparison scale, which indicates the influence of each factor on the upper layer. However, it is concluded that the judgment matrix is too subjective, and lacks objectivity; And because of the different image data, the three indexes of the criteria layer have different influence on the result of the matching; So it is not possible to use single or multiple group of experiments to fix the values of each element in the judgment matrix.

Therefore, we use the entropy weight method with objectivity to adaptively determine the weights of these three indexes in the experiment according to the specific values of three characteristic indices in the initial matching region. This not only makes the AHP from subjective weighting to objective empowerment, but also improves the adaptive of the algorithm.

Correlation coefficient, RMSE and Sharpness have different trends: the bigger correlation coefficient and Sharpness are, the better, while the smaller RMSE is, the better. So we must first calculate the reciprocal of the RMSE index, so that the bigger the reciprocal is, the better.

Due to the three indicators have different dimension units, it's necessary to normalize of the index as shown in formula (1), where X_{ij} ($i = 1, 2, 3, 4$; $j = 1, 2, 3$) is the value of the jth indicator corresponding to the ith matching point.

$$R_{ij} = \frac{X_{ij}}{\sum_{i=1}^{4} X_{ij}} \tag{1}$$

Then, the entropy value of the jth index is given by

$$E_j = -\frac{1}{\ln 4} \sum_{i=1}^{4} \frac{R_{ij}}{\ln R_{ij}} \tag{2}$$

And the weight of the evaluation indicator is defined as

$$W_j = \frac{1 - E_j}{3 - \sum\limits_{j=1}^{3} E_j} \tag{3}$$

(3) Calculate weight vector and do consistency check

The eigenvector method is used to find the maximum eigenvalue $\lambda_{\max}$ and corresponding eigenvector of each judgment matrix, and the random consistency ratio CR of each judgment matrix is given by

$$CR = CI / RI \tag{4}$$

with RI is the average random consistency index and CI is defined as

$$CI = (\lambda_{\max} - n) / (n - 1) \tag{5}$$

where n is the order of the matrix, and the value of n in this paper is 3; The average random consistency index is based on sufficient number of random judgment matrices, and it's only related to the order of matrices, as shown in Table 1.

Table 1. Average random consistency index

n	1	2	3	4	5	6	7	...
RI	0.00	0.00	0.58	0.89	1.12	1.26	1.36	...

(4) Calculate the index comprehensive value and obtain the best match position

The comprehensive value of the corresponding indices for each initial matching point can be computed by

$$Q = X \cdot W^T \tag{6}$$

where Q is the comprehensive value matrix of the three indexes corresponding to four matching points; X is the three index value matrices corresponding to each matching point; W is the weight vector matrix of the three indices. The matching point with the maximum element value in Q is the best matching position of the primary decision. Matching results of the primary decision are shown in Fig. 4(a) and (b), and visual interpretation can illustrate that the primary decision can correct the results of the initial matching of gray-scale and feature.

(a) Result of gray-value matching   (b) Result of feature matching

Fig. 4. Matching results of the primary decision

2.3   Fusion Method Based on Overlap Region and Local Search

In order to rectify the problem of selecting the second best matching points and reducing the matching accuracy after the primary decision, the secondary decision is utilized to fuse two optimal matching points obtained in Sect. 2.2.

According to the overlap area of the two best matching regions, the corresponding secondary decision scheme is determined and the matching result is more accurate than Sect. 2.2. The secondary decision scheme are as follows:

I.   If the overlap area is larger than the threshold T, it is considered that both of the results of the two matching methods in the primary decision are accurate, and the matching result of the secondary decision is obtained directly by the weighted average of the two optimal matching points, that is, the final matching result;

II. If the overlap area is less than the threshold T, that is, the two best matching points of the primary decision are not in the same region, it is considered that the gray match result and the feature matching result have the wrong decision; then follow these steps to make the secondary decision:

① Centering on the gray matching point and feature matching point obtained in Sect. 2.2, respectively, carry out local searching in each matching graph, and record the number of matching points appearing in each search area, that is a_1 and b_1, respectively;

② Centering on the initial best matching point of gray matching and feature matching obtained in Sect. 2.1, respectively, carry out local searching in each matching graph, and record the number of matching points appearing in each search area, that is a_2 and b_2, respectively;

③ Compare with the two searching. If $a_1 \neq a_2$ and $b_1 = b_2$, the gray matching result is effective; Otherwise, the feature matching result is effective;

④ Calculate the average value of the valid results, and obtain the final matching position.

The threshold T is determined by the actual size of the template. Set the size of the template as $a * b$, the two matching results are considered to be in accordance with the requirements when the top and bottom distance $|dx|$ of the two points is less than $a/10$, and the left and right distance $|dy|$ is less than $b/10$; And the overlap area of the two matching areas is the threshold value T. The calculation shows that the relationship between the threshold value and the size of the template is $T = 0.81ab$.

Taking the matching result of Sect. 2.2 as an example, the secondary decision is made, and the result is shown in Fig. 5. In this group of experiment, the ideal matching position is (62, 123), the gray matching result and the feature matching result of the primary decision are (57, 121), and (69, 123), respectively; And the result of the secondary decision is (63, 122). Obviously, the secondary decision effectively improves the accuracy of target matching.

Fig. 5. Matching result of the secondary decision

3 Simulation Experiments and Results Analysis

The proposed algorithm has been tested on two groups of representative image sequences to evaluate the effectiveness and performance. The real-time images are obtained by infrared camera, while the reference images are simulated by Se-work-bench-IR.

3.1 Complicated Background Interference

In this group of experimental sequences, there are a large number of building disturbances in the background area, including buildings of similar shapes. The experimental results are shown in Fig. 6. Figure 6(a) are the IR simulation template and the horizontal and vertical gradient feature templates obtained by the visible template; Fig. 6(b) and (c) are the initial matching results of gray matching and feature matching, respectively, in which the white block diagram is the initial optimal matching position; Fig. 6(d) and (e) are the results of gray-scale matching and feature matching filtered by primary decision, respectively; Fig. 6(f) is final matching position of the group experiment after the secondary decision. As shown in Fig. 6, that the gray matching in the initial match is mismatched, and the result of the feature matching has a large deviation, while the decision based on the adaptive AHP corrects the matching errors in the initial match.

(a) Templates

(b) Results of gray-value matching

(c) Results of feature matching

(d) Result of gray-value matching after the
primary decision

(e) Result of feature matching after the
primary decision

(f) Matching result of the secondary decision

Fig. 6. Matching experiment in case of complicated background interference

3.2   Different Scale and Sight Interference

As shown in Fig. 7, there are some small scale difference and small angle rotation
difference between two images, including complex background environment. In Fig. 7,
part (a) are the IR simulation template and the horizontal and vertical gradient feature
templates obtained by the visible template; Fig. 7(b) and (c) are the initial matching
results of gray matching and feature matching, in which the white block diagram is the
initial optimal matching position; Fig. 7(d) and (e) are the results of gray-scale matching
and feature matching filtered by primary decision, respectively; Fig. 7(f) is final
matching position of the group experiment after the secondary decision. In this group

of experiments, the initial matching results of the feature matching are in the white block, but the actual best matching point should be in the black box labeled "3", and the primary decision failed to correct the error matching problem in the initial match, there is still a mismatching point after the decision; After the secondary decision, the position of the matching point can be corrected, and the final matching position is more accurate than before.

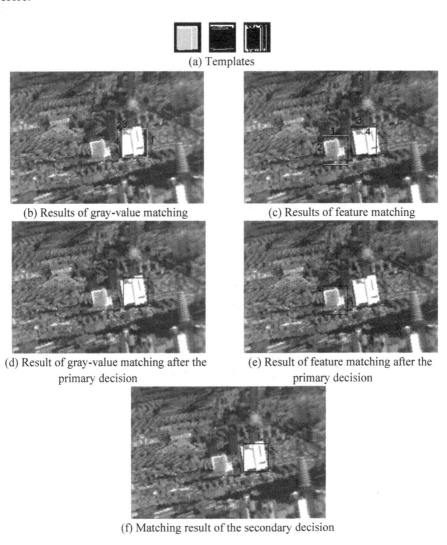

(a) Templates

(b) Results of gray-value matching

(c) Results of feature matching

(d) Result of gray-value matching after the primary decision

(e) Result of feature matching after the primary decision

(f) Matching result of the secondary decision

Fig. 7. Matching experiment in case of different scale and sight interference

The accuracy of matching points in each matching step is objectively represented by the Euclidean distance, given by

$$Ed = \sqrt{(\Delta x)^2 + (\Delta y)^2} \qquad (7)$$

with $\Delta x = |x_1 - x_0|$ and $\Delta y = |y_1 - y_0|$, where (x_0, y_0) is the ideal matching position and (x_1, y_1) is the real matching position.

In the first set of matching experiment, the template size is 33 * 44, the ideal matching position is (140, 41), and the matching result is shown in Table 2. In the second group matching experiment, the template size is 54 * 48, the ideal matching position is (135, 236), and the matching result is shown in Table 3.

Table 2. Matching results of the first experiment

	Gray matching	Feature matching	The primary decision		The secondary decision
			Gray matching	Feature matching	
Results	(151.5, 111)	(137.5, 36)	(138, 41)	(144, 43)	(141, 42)
Ed	70.94	5.59	2.00	4.92	1.00

Table 3. Matching results of the second experiment

	Gray matching	Feature matching	The primary decision		The secondary decision
			Gray matching	Feature matching	
Results	(138, 245)	(152.5, 179)	(138, 243)	(154.5, 179)	(138, 242)
Ed	9.49	59.63	7.07	60.24	6.71

It can be seen from Tables 2 and 3 that compared with the initial matching results, the Ed of matching results obtained by the primary decision is less than the initial matching result, and the matching result of the secondary decision is more accuracy than the primary decision; When the mismatching problem still occurs in the result after the primary decision, the secondary decision can correct the mismatching point well. So, the proposed algorithm can effectively correct the mismatching in single matching algorithm under the interference of the complex background and certain scale and rotation difference, and can effectively improve the matching accuracy with fully preserving the advantages of the gray matching and feature matching.

4 Conclusions

A target recognition method based on adaptive fusion of multiple matching results was proposed for the decrease in template matching performance due to the fact that the true matching position usually located in the other peak of the correlation matrix. The proposed algorithm makes full use of the gray information and feature information between the template and the infrared real-time image, takes parallel operation of two kinds of matching methods for IR real-time image; Then, the weight of each index in AHP is calculated objectively and adaptively by the entropy weighting method, and then the best matching point of each of the two matching algorithms is obtained by the primary decision; After that, the secondary decision based on overlap region and local search is utilized to rectify the mismatching, and also take advantage of the matching results of the two matching methods and improve the matching accuracy. The results of the experiment indicate that compared with the single matching method, in spite of the slightly higher of operation efficiency, the proposed algorithm has higher accuracy and higher precision; And it's more suitable for the infrared target recognition task in the complex scene, with better robustness and applicability to the scale and rotation change between heterogeneous images.

References

1. Su, J., Xu, Q.S., Liu, G.: A forward looking infrared target recognition algorithm based on edge matching. Acta Armamentarii **33**(3), 271–277 (2012)
2. Omachi, S., Omachi, M.: Fast template matching with polynomials. IEEE Trans. Image Process. **16**(8), 2139–2149 (2007)
3. Cao, Z.G., Yan, R.C., Song, Z.: Approach on fuzzy shape context matching between infrared images and visible images. Infrared Laser Eng. **37**(6), 1095–1100 (2008)
4. Li, Z., Lei, Z.H., Yu, Q.F.: Matching multi-sensor images based on gradient radius angle pyramid histogram. Acta Geodaeticaet Cartograph. Sinica **40**(3), 318–325 (2011)
5. Wang, J.W., Bai, X., You, X., et al.: Shape matching and classification using height functions. Pattern Recogn. Lett. **33**(2), 134–143 (2012)
6. Wang, P., Qu, Z.G., Wang, P., et al.: A coarse-to-fine matching algorithm for FLIR and optical satellite image registration. IEEE Geosci. Remote Sens. Lett. **9**(4), 599–603 (2012)
7. Zhao, Y.: Research on multi-modality image matching technology based on salient contour. Nanjing University of Aeronautics and Astronautics, Nanjing (2014)
8. Li, X., Zhu, Z.S., Shang, Y., et al.: Multimodal image registration based on orientation-moment. J. Nat. Univ. Defense Technol. **37**(1), 153–158 (2015)
9. Li, Z.J., Liu, S.L., Niu, Z.D., et al.: Hausdorff distance template matching method based on gradient phase and significance constraints. Infrared Laser Eng. **44**(2), 775–780 (2015)
10. Li, A.D., Lin, Z.P., An, W., et al.: Infrared small target detection in compressive domain based on self-adaptive parameter configuration. Chin. J. Lasers **42**(10), 1008003 (2015)
11. He, Y.J., Li, M., Zhang, J.L., et al.: Infrared small target detection method based on correlation filter. Acta Optica Sinica **36**(5), 0512001 (2016)
12. Ming, D.L., Tian, J.W.: Automatic infrared condensing tower target recognition using gradient vector features. J. Astronaut. **31**(4), 1190–1194 (2010)
13. Li, B., Su, J., Hao, Y.Y.: Infrared image simulation based on SE-Workbench-IR. Infrared Technol. **38**(8), 683–687 (2016)

Combining Object-Based Attention and Attributes for Image Captioning

Cong Li, Jiansheng Chen$^{(\boxtimes)}$, Weitao Wan, and Tianpeng Li

Department of Electronic Engineering, Tsinghua University, Beijing, China
{cong-li15,wwt16,ltp16}@mails.tsinghua.edu.cn,
jschenthu@mail.tsinghua.edu.cn

Abstract. Image captioning has been a hot topic in computer vision and natural language processing. Recently, researchers have proposed many models for image captioning which can be classified into two classes: visual attention based models and semantic attributes based models. In this paper, we propose a novel image captioning system which models the relationship between semantic attributes and visual attention. Besides, different from the traditional attention models which don't use object detectors and instead learn latent alignment between regions and words, we propose an object attention system which is capable to incorporate information output by object detectors and can better attend to objects when generating corresponding words. We evaluate our method on MS COCO dataset and our model outperforms many strong baselines.

1 Introduction

Thanks to the improvements on bandwidth of Internet and computation ability of computers, more and more data has been collected, and many advanced techniques for image understanding have been proposed. A fundamental problem that brings about development of these techniques is image classification whose target is to assign a label to each image. Further work have pushed its advances into progress on image captioning whose task is to not only identify objects in images, but also describe the relationship between them using language. Although image captioning has been studied for many years, the breakthrough comes from the encoder-decoder model in machine translation [4]. In machine translation, a RNN encodes a source sentence into feature vectors representation which is decoded into a target sentence by another RNN. Similarly, Vinyals et al. applies this philosophy to image captioning, an encoder CNN encodes an image into a feature representation while a decoder RNN decodes it into a sentence [18]. Further study on encoder and decoder model has branched into two directions: the visual attention based models [7,21,22] and the semantic based models [20,24].

Despite the fact that rapid developments have been achieved these years, there still exists many problems. For example, as far as we are aware of, there is no research on how to combine visual attention with high level semantic information. In this paper, we propose a new image captioning system that combines

© Springer International Publishing AG 2017
Y. Zhao et al. (Eds.): ICIG 2017, Part I, LNCS 10666, pp. 614–625, 2017.
https://doi.org/10.1007/978-3-319-71607-7_54

object attention with attributes information. Figure 1 is a overview of our model. Our contributions are as follow: (*i*) We propose a new visual attention method: object attention. Different from Xu et al. [21] which attends to different position on CNN feature map, the attention of our model is shift among different objects in the images, which is more flexible and accurate. (*ii*) We propose a novel system that unifies object attention with attributes to guide image captioning. (*iii*) we reveal the effect of depth of LSTM on image captioning. (*iv*) We evaluate our method on MS COCO dataset [3] in offline and online manners. We show that our method outperforms many previous state of the art method [5, 18, 20, 21].

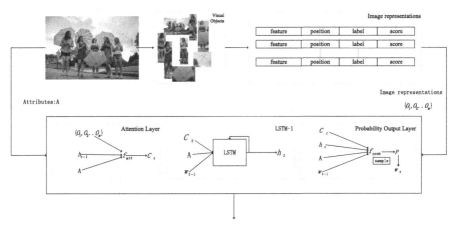

Fig. 1. A overall architecture of our model. Our model contains three parts: attention layer, LSTM, probability output layer.

2   Related Work

Objects Detection: Recently, state of the art objects detection algorithm are based on region proposal and region based convolution network method [8, 13, 16]. Faster R-CNN one of the best objects detector won the MS COCO objects detection challenge in 2015. Its detection procedure contains two stages. Firstly, RPN regresses from anchors of different size and aspect ratio to region proposals and classify proposals into two class: foreground and background. Secondly, region based convolution neural network regresses from region proposals to bbox and tries to classify objects within it. In this paper, we use Faster R-CNN to detect objects in the images, and use the features vector, class label and position information of objects in images as input into our language model to generate caption.

Image Captioning: Recent state of the art method in image captioning is based on encoder-decoder model. The encoder is CNN while the decoder is LSTM in image captioning. Vinyals et al. [18] developed a simple encoder-decoder model. It encodes an image into a fixed-length feature vector representation which is fed into LSTM in the first step as initialization to decode it into image description. However, the image feature is only sent to LSTM in the first step and will gradually vanish as LSTM generates words. gLSTM overcomes this problem by sending guiding information to LSTM as it generates words [10]. After that, Xu et al. [21] proposed attention mechanism which was very popular in image captioning and visual question answering. In attention mechanism, each time before the LSTM generates a word, the attention layer will first predict likelihood of the CNN hidden state corresponding to the word. Then it is used as attention weight and the weighted sum over CNN feature maps is computed and sent to LSTM for generating words. The process doesn't need any ground truth of attention weights and all need is images-sentence pairs. Fu et al. [7] also developed a visual attention algorithm which is based on region attention. Despite the effectiveness of attention mechanism, they don't leverage high level semantic information such as attributes. To solve the problem, You et al. [24] developed an top down and bottom up approach to combine visual image features and high level semantic attributes information, Wu et al. [20] developed a region based multi-labels classification method to predict attributes which are fed info LSTM for caption generation. Recently, Yao et al. [23] tried to combine attributes information with image feature and devises five variants of structure by sending them in different placements and time moments. In this paper, we aim at combining two recently proposed and powerful methods in image captioning: visual attention and attributes. Our method fundamentally differs from [23] in the aspect that Yao proposed five variants of structure to model relationship between image feature and attributes while our method tries to incorporate visual attention and attributes into encoder-decoder models. What's more, we devise a new visual attention method which is based on objects. Our attention method is fundamentally different from previous method [7,21] in the way that the attention in our method are computed corresponding to a set of objects in images. We argue that our object attention method is better than former attention methods because attention weights in [21] are computed at fixed-size resolution and corresponding to pre-defined positions, which is not flexible and attention weights in [7] correspond to proposals which may don't have explicit and meaningful information while our attention weights correspond to objects which are most salient parts of images and are of abundant information. What's more, proposals don't contain any class information which is very important to describe images while our models can utilize objects' position and class information which are produced by Faster R-CNN. Besides, their method don't incorporate semantic information into image captioning, while our method is able to employ attributes information to boost image captioning.

3   Model Description

Inspired by the recently popular attention method and attribute method in image captioning, we propose the object attention method and develop a new model to incorporate it and semantic attributes information into the encoder-decoder framework. The description generation process of our model shares similar spirits of human visual perception and can be divided into two phases. In the first phase, given a glimpse of the image, our model observes objects in the image and key words of it which are the most salient part of visual information and semantic information about the image respectively. In the second, our model attends to different objects while generating the sentence. We will first formulate image captioning problem, then describe each part of our model.

3.1 Problem Formulation

Image captioning is to describe an image I with a sentence S, where $S = \{w_1, w_2 \ldots w_n\}$ consisting of n words. The core idea of traditional CNN-RNN framework is to maximize the probability of generating the ground truth sentence. It can be formulated as follows:

$$\log p(S|I) = \sum_{i=1}^{n} \log p(w_i|I, w_1, w_2 \ldots w_{i-1}), \tag{1}$$

where w_i is the i_{th} word of the sentence S, $w_1, w_2 \ldots w_{i-1}$ represent words from time step 1 till $i-1$ and $p(w_i|I, w_1, w_2 \ldots w_{i-1})$ is the probability of generating word w_i given previous words $w_1, w_2 \ldots w_{i-1}$.

We adapt the traditional CNN-RNN framework by guiding it with two additional information: high level image attributes information $\mathbf{A} \in \mathbb{R}^{D_a}$ and attention context information $C_t \in \mathbb{R}^{D_C}$. We formulate image captioning problem by maximizing the equation as follows:

$$\log p(S|I) = \sum_{i=1}^{n} \log p(w_i|w_{1:i-1}, \mathbf{A}, C_t). \tag{2}$$

To be specific, given an image I, we first represents it in a sequential manner $seq(I) = \{O_1, O_2 \ldots O_m\}$ where O_1 to O_{m-1} are object representations and O_m encodes global image information by sending whole image to CNN. Then our attention layer shifts attention among different objects $\{O_1, O_2 \ldots O_m\}$ and generates attention context information C_t. Because object representations only contain local visual information and lack global semantic information of the image, we follow the weakly supervised multi-instance learning method used in [6] for semantic attributes $\mathbf{A}$ detection. At last, both context C_t and $\mathbf{A}$ are sent to LSTM and probability output layer for word generation. Our model can be seen in Fig. 1 and we will depict our attention layer, the structures of two kinds LSTM and probability output layer in Sects. 3.2, 3.3 and 3.4 respectively.

3.2 Object Attention Layer

Before generating word w_t at time step t, our attention layer attends to the object which corresponds to word w_t based on previous LSTM hidden state h_{t-1} which contains history information. Our object attention layer shares the similar spirit of soft attention in [1, 21]. However, our model is different from them. Attention weights in [21] are computed at fixed-size resolution and corresponding to pre-defined positions in an image while attention weights in our model correspond to objects, which is more flexible and accurate. Besides, Xu et al. [21] doesn't use any semantic information while we leverage the global semantic attributes information $\mathbf{A}$ to help attention layer predict attention better. Suppose we have a sequence of object representations $\{O_1, O_2 \ldots O_m\}$, image attributes $\mathbf{A}$ and previous LSTM output h_{t-1}, we adapt attention layer used in [21] to accept three inputs. It is formulated as follows:

$$C_t = \sum_{i=1}^{m} \alpha_{ti} * O_i \tag{3}$$

$$\alpha_{ti} = \frac{\exp(e_{ti})}{\sum_{i=1}^{m} \exp(e_{ti})} \tag{4}$$

$$e_{ti} = W_e * tanh(W_a \mathbf{A} + W_h h_{t-1} + W_o O_i), \tag{5}$$

where $W_e \in \mathbb{R}^{1 \times d}$, $W_a \in \mathbb{R}^{d \times d}$, $W_h \in \mathbb{R}^{d \times d}$ and $W_o \in \mathbb{R}^{d \times d}$ are parameters of the layer. According to (4), (5), our object attention layer first predicts all objects' scores α_{ti} which represents how much attention should been given to the object O_i. Then the object attention layer output C_t which represents attention context vector used to generate the word.

3.3   LSTM Structures

Recurrent neural network (RNN) has been widely used in sequence to sequence learning, such as machine translation, speech recognition and image captioning. LSTM [9] is a kind of recurrent neural network with additional four gates which are aimed at solving gradients explosion and vanishing problem. Its update process can be formulated as follows:

$$i_t = \sigma(W_{ix} x_t + W_{ih} h_{t-1}) \tag{6}$$

$$f_t = \sigma(W_{fx} x_t + W_{fh} h_{t-1}) \tag{7}$$

$$o_t = \sigma(W_{ox} x_t + W_{oh} h_{t-1}) \tag{8}$$

$$g_t = \phi(W_{gx} x_t + W_{gh} h_{t-1}) \tag{9}$$

$$c_t = c_{t-1} \odot f_t + i_t \odot g_t \tag{10}$$

$$h_t = o_t \odot \phi(c_t), \tag{11}$$

where $W_{tj}(t \in \{i, f, o, g\}, j \in \{h, x\})$ is the connection matrix; σ is the sigmoid non-linearity operator, and ϕ is the hyperbolic tangent non-linearity operator; i_t, f_t, o_t, g_t are input gate, forget gate, output gate and input modulation gate respectively; h_t, c_t are hidden state and memory cell; x_t is the input to LSTM unit; $\odot$ is the element-wise dot product operator.

Different from traditional framework, we have tried two LSTM structures and studied their effects on image captioning. In this paper, we first use the basic LSTM namely LSTM-1. Then we try its deeper version: LSTM-2 which has two layers. The detailed structures of LSTM-1 and LSTM-2 will be described in the following section.

LSTM-1. In order to incorporate context C_t, and attributes **A** into LSTM, we design a basic LSTM structure: LSTM-1. Unlike LSTM in [18,21], LSTM-1 can incorporate attributes into it. Unlike [23], LSTM-1 can make use of recently popular attention mechanism as an additional input. Here we give a detailed introduction of our basic LSTM model LSTM-1. It can be formulated as follows:

$$x_t = U_a * A + U_c C_t + U_s w_{t-1} \tag{12}$$

$$h_t = f(h_{t-1}, x_t), \tag{13}$$

where $\mathbf{A}, C_t, w_{t-1}$ are attributes, context, previous word respectively; $U_i (i \in \{a, c, s\})$ is weight matrix of LSTM-1; f represents the LSTM unit in (6)–(11).

At each step, previous word w_{t-1}, attributes **A** and context C_t are combined into a compact and abstract vector representation x_t which is sent to the LSTM unit as input to generate word w_t until an "END" is emitted. At the initial step, w_0 is set to "START", and the initial states of LSTM h_0, c_0 are predicted by an average of objects representation fed through a multi-layers perceptron. It can be formulated as follows:

$$h_0 = f_{init,h}\left(\frac{\sum_1^m o_t}{m}\right) \tag{14}$$

$$c_0 = f_{init,c}\left(\frac{\sum_1^m o_t}{m}\right), \tag{15}$$

where $f_{init,h}, f_{init,c}$ are both multi-layers perceptron and are used to predict hidden state h_0 and memory cell c_0 of LSTM at initial time step.

LSTM-2 (Two Layers of LSTM). Generally speaking, deeper networks have better ability to fit and grasp pattern in training data and performs better on more complicate task. Inspired by this philosophy, we try a deeper version of LSTM-1: LSTM-2 which is a LSTM with two layers. The state update procedure is formulated as follows:

$$x_t^1 = W_a * \mathbf{A} + W_c C_t + W_s w_{t-1} \tag{16}$$
$$h_t^1 = f^1(h_{t-1}^1, x_t^1) \tag{17}$$
$$x_t^2 = h_t^1 \tag{18}$$
$$h_t^2 = f^2(h_{t-1}^2, x_t^2) \tag{19}$$

where $\mathbf{A}, C_t, w_{t-1}$ are three inputs: attributes, context, previous generated word; f^1, f^2 are the first layer and second layer of LSTM; x_t^1 is a compact vector combing all the information of the three inputs and is fed into the first layer of LSTM; x_t^2 is the input into the second LSTM layer; h_t^1, h_t^2 are the hidden state of first LSTM and second LSTM units at time step t; W_a, W_c, w_{t-1} are embedding matrix of the LSTM-2.

3.4 Probability Output Layer

The word w_t to be generated at time step t is closely connected with history information about previous words and visual information about the image. So we design the probability output layer to incorporate information of attention context information C_t, high level attributes $\mathbf{A}$, previous word w_t and LSTM hidden state h_t to outputs probability P_t over words in vocabulary. It is represented as:

$$P_t \propto \exp(f_P(h_t, \mathbf{A}, C_t, w_{t-1})), \qquad (20)$$

where f_P is a multilayer perceptron whose weights are randomly initialized.

4 Experiments

We test our models on the most widely used image captioning dataset MS COCO [3] and evaluate them in two ways: the offline evaluation and online evaluation. For offline evaluation, we follow the split used in [11] and report results. For online evaluation, we evaluate our method on the MS COCO 2014 test server and compare our method with previous state of the art methods.

4.1 Dataset

MS COCO dataset contains 160k images which are split into 80k training images, 40k validation images and 40k testing images. Each image in the MS COCO dataset has at least five sentences which are labelled by workers.

4.2 Experimental Settings

Data Processing. We follow the data splits in [11]. We convert all captions into lower case and discard words which appears less than five times. That results in a vocabulary of 8791 words.

Training Parameter Settings. We train our model with a batch size of 100 and early stop training to prevent Overfitting after about 40000 iterations which is about 50 epochs. Our learning rate is set to 1×10^{-4} and our optimization method is Adam [12].

Inference. We use beam search method in inference stage and find that performance is best when beam size is set to 4.

Evaluation Metric. We evaluate our model with four metrics BLEU@N [15], METEOR [2], ROUGE-L [14], CIDER [17]. All metrics are computed by the code https://github.com/tylin/coco-caption which is released by MS COCO server.

4.3   Performance Comparison

We compare our method with previous state of the art method in offline and online ways. In offline evaluation manner, we compare our results with others' in Table 1 and can conclude that our method outperforms previous state of the art method by a large margin. This proves the effectiveness of the combination of two powerful mechanisms: object attention and attributes. Object attention mechanism shifts attention among different objects in the image and provides salient visual information about the word to be generated. But attention mechanism focuses on local regions and lacks global semantic information. So we provide our model with additional input: attributes information. We have also compared two variants structure Attributes + attention + LSTM-1, Attributes

Table 1. Peformance compared with state of the art image captioning method on MS COCO dataset. B1, B2, B3, B4, M, R, C are abbreviation of BLEU1, BLEU2, BLEU3, BLEU4, Meteor, ROUGE_L,CIDEr

Model	B1	B2	B3	B4	M	R	C
NIC [18]	66.6	45.1	30.4	20.3	-	-	-
LRCN [5]	62.8	44.2	30.4	21	-	-	-
Hard attention [21]	71.8	50.4	35.7	25	23	-	-
ATT [24]	70.9	53.7	40.2	30.4	24.3	-	-
Bi-LSTM [19]	67.2	49.2	35.2	24.4	-	-	-
Review-net [22]	-	-	-	29.0	23.7	-	88.6
Region-based attention [7]	72.4	55.5	41.8	31.3	24.8	53.3	95.5
Attributes + attention + LSTM-1 (ours)	**72.7**	**55.6**	**41.8**	**31.4**	**25.5**	**53.3**	**98.8**
Attributes + attention + LSTM-2 (ours)	72.4	55.5	41.6	31.2	25.0	53.2	96.6

Table 2. Performance compared with previous state of the art image captioning methods on MS COCO server (https://competitions.codalab.org/competitions/3221# results). We add subscripts to top-3 systems to indicate the ranking when compared to other methods.

Team name	B1		B2		B3		B4		M		C	
	C5	C40	C5	C40	C5	C40	C5	C40	C5	C40	C5	C40
Vinyals et al. [18]	71.3	89.5	54.2	80.2	40.7	69.4	30.9	58.7	25.4_2	34.6_2	94.3_3	94.6
Donahue et al. [5]	71.8	89.5	54.8	80.4	40.9	69.5	30.6	58.5	24.7	33.5	92.1	93.4
Wu et al. [20]	72.5	89.2	55.6_3	80.3	41.4	69.4	30.6	58.2	24.6	32.9	91.1	92.4
Xu et al. [21]	70.5	88.1	52.8	77.9	38.3	65.8	27.7	53.7	24.1	32.2	86.5	89.3
Yang et al. [22]	72.0_3	90.0_3	55.0	81.2_3	41.4_3	70.5_3	31.3_3	59.7_3	25.6_1	34.7_1	96.5_1	96.9_2
ATT_VC [24]	73.1_1	90.0_2	56.5_1	81.5_2	42.4_1	70.9_2	31.6_1	59.9_1	25.0	33.5	94.3_3	95.8_3
licongthu (ours)	73.0_2	90.8_1	56.0_2	81.9_1	41.9_2	71.0_1	31.4_2	59.9_1	25.2_3	34.0_3	96.0_2	97.2_1

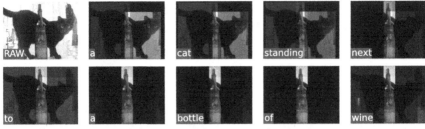

Caption: A cat standing next to a bottle of wine.

Attributes: cat, wine, bottle, black, bottle, standing, sitting, bathroom, table, glass

Caption: A woman standing on the beach holding an umbrella.

Attributes: beam, umbrella, umbrellas, women, snow, people, holding, standing, water

Caption: A group of teddy bears sitting on a table.

Attributes: bears, teddy, bear, stuff, table, room ,sitting, kitchen, group

Caption: A sailboat in the middle of the ocean.

Attributes: beam, water, boat, surfboard, wave, blue, man ,large ,white

Fig. 2. Some examples of aligning objects with words to be generated. Many words in sentence corresponds well to visual objects in the images. The brighter object mean more attention is being allocated to it. We also show the image's attributes which is able to provide global semantic information to attention layer.

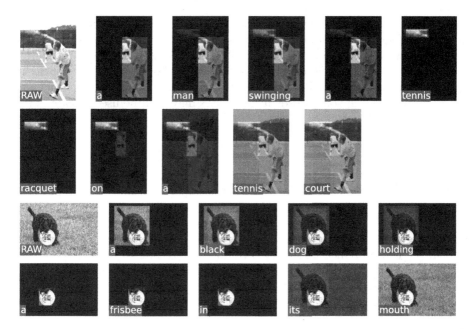

Fig. 3. More cases of attention transitions during the sentence generation

+ attention + LSTM-2. We are surprised to find that LSTM-1 outperforms its deeper version LSTM-2, which means that deeper LSTM structure are not necessarily beneficial for performance and in fact that deeper recurrent network is more difficult to train and loss drops slower. So in later online evaluation, we only report performance of our LSTM-1.

To better prove the effectiveness of our method, we have compared our method on MS COCO server and results are in Table 2. We can see that our method outperforms previous state of the art methods in many metrics especially in CIDEr [17] which is specially designed for image captioning and more convincing than other metrics which are designed for machine translation.

Results on online evaluation and offline evaluation prove the effectiveness of object attention and attribute. In fact, both the method can improve image captioning performance and unifying them can boost image captioning greatly.

4.4 Case Study and Visualization

To better show the effectiveness of our method. We have shown in Fig. 2 image attributes and the shift of attention in process of generating caption. From the first two rows, we can see that our model can align words to be generated and objects in images. Before generating words such as cat and standing, our model first attends to the region of cat in the images. While before generating words such as bottle and wine, our model attends to the region of bottle first. It has strongly proven the effectiveness of object attention method and cast light on what is happening when it generates caption. More cases of attention transitions in process of sentence generation can be seen in Fig. 3. Besides, we can also see that many words in attributes are used for captioning. Taking first image for example, many of its attributes such as cat, wine, bottle, standing appear in its final captioning. It has illustrated that attributes of images are beneficial to image captioning and some words in attributes may even be used in caption.

5   Conclusion

In this paper, we propose a new visual attention: object attention, and combine it with image attributes within two models. We compare our method with previous state of the art methods in online evaluation and offline evaluation manners. From Table 1, we can see that our method outperforms other previous state of the art method by a large margin in offline evaluation manner. From Table 2, we can see that our method achieves comparable results to other state of the art methods, and ranks top three when compared to other state of art method on all metrics. We conclude that attributes combined with object attention can greatly boost image captioning performance.

Acknowledgement. This work was supported by the National Natural Science Foundation of China under Grant 61673234.

References

1. Bahdanau, D., Cho, K., Bengio, Y.: Neural machine translation by jointly learning to align and translate. arXiv preprint arXiv:1409.0473 (2014)
2. Banerjee, S., Lavie, A.: Meteor: an automatic metric for MT evaluation with improved correlation with human judgments. In: Proceedings of the ACL workshop on intrinsic and extrinsic evaluation measures for machine translation and/or summarization, vol. 29, pp. 65–72 (2005)
3. Chen, X., Fang, H., Lin, T.Y., Vedantam, R., Gupta, S., Dollár, P., Zitnick, C.L.: Microsoft coco captions: data collection and evaluation server. arXiv preprint arXiv:1504.00325 (2015)
4. Cho, K., Van Merriënboer, B., Gulcehre, C., Bahdanau, D., Bougares, F., Schwenk, H., Bengio, Y.: Learning phrase representations using RNN encoder-decoder for statistical machine translation. arXiv preprint arXiv:1406.1078 (2014)
5. Donahue, J., Anne Hendricks, L., Guadarrama, S., Rohrbach, M., Venugopalan, S., Saenko, K., Darrell, T.: Long-term recurrent convolutional networks for visual recognition and description. In: Proceedings of the IEEE Conference on Computer Vision and Pattern Recognition, pp. 2625–2634 (2015)
6. Fang, H., Gupta, S., Iandola, F., Srivastava, R.K., Deng, L., Dollár, P., Gao, J., He, X., Mitchell, M., Platt, J.C., et al.: From captions to visual concepts and back. In: Proceedings of the IEEE Conference on Computer Vision and Pattern Recognition, pp. 1473–1482 (2015)
7. Fu, K., Jin, J., Cui, R., Sha, F., Zhang, C.: Aligning where to see and what to tell: image captioning with region-based attention and scene-specific contexts. IEEE Trans. Pattern Anal. Mach. Intell. (2016)

8. Girshick, R.: Fast R-CNN. In: Proceedings of the IEEE International Conference on Computer Vision, pp. 1440–1448 (2015)

9. Hochreiter, S., Schmidhuber, J.: Long short-term memory. Neural Comput. **9**(8), 1735–1780 (1997)

10. Jia, X., Gavves, E., Fernando, B., Tuytelaars, T.: Guiding the long-short term memory model for image caption generation. In: Proceedings of the IEEE International Conference on Computer Vision, pp. 2407–2415 (2015)

11. Karpathy, A., Fei-Fei, L.: Deep visual-semantic alignments for generating image descriptions. In: Proceedings of the IEEE Conference on Computer Vision and Pattern Recognition, pp. 3128–3137 (2015)

12. Kingma, D., Ba, J.: Adam: a method for stochastic optimization. arXiv preprint arXiv:1412.6980 (2014)

13. Li, Y., He, K., Sun, J., et al.: R-FCN: object detection via region-based fully convolutional networks. In: Advances in Neural Information Processing Systems, pp. 379–387 (2016)

14. Lin, C.: Recall-oriented understudy for gisting evaluation (ROUGE), 20 August 2005

15. Papineni, K., Roukos, S., Ward, T., Zhu, W.J.: BLEU: a method for automatic evaluation of machine translation. In: Proceedings of the 40th Annual Meeting on Association for Computational Linguistics, pp. 311–318. Association for Computational Linguistics (2002)

16. Ren, S., He, K., Girshick, R., Sun, J.: Faster R-CNN: towards real-time object detection with region proposal networks. In: Advances in Neural Information Processing Systems, pp. 91–99 (2015)

17. Vedantam, R., Lawrence Zitnick, C., Parikh, D.: Cider: consensus-based image description evaluation. In: Proceedings of the IEEE Conference on Computer Vision and Pattern Recognition, pp. 4566–4575 (2015)

18. Vinyals, O., Toshev, A., Bengio, S., Erhan, D.: Show and tell: a neural image caption generator. In: Proceedings of the IEEE Conference on Computer Vision and Pattern Recognition, pp. 3156–3164 (2015)

19. Wang, C., Yang, H., Bartz, C., Meinel, C.: Image captioning with deep bidirectional LSTMs. In: Proceedings of the 2016 ACM on Multimedia Conference, pp. 988–997. ACM (2016)

20. Wu, Q., Shen, C., Liu, L., Dick, A., van den Hengel, A.: What value do explicit high level concepts have in vision to language problems? In: Proceedings of the IEEE Conference on Computer Vision and Pattern Recognition, pp. 203–212 (2016)

21. Xu, K., Ba, J., Kiros, R., Cho, K., Courville, A., Salakhudinov, R., Zemel, R., Bengio, Y.: Show, attend and tell: neural image caption generation with visual attention. In: International Conference on Machine Learning, pp. 2048–2057 (2015)

22. Yang, Z., Yuan, Y., Wu, Y., Cohen, W.W., Salakhutdinov, R.R.: Review networks for caption generation. In: Advances in Neural Information Processing Systems, pp. 2361–2369 (2016)

23. Yao, T., Pan, Y., Li, Y., Qiu, Z., Mei, T.: Boosting image captioning with attributes. arXiv preprint arXiv:1611.01646 (2016)

24. You, Q., Jin, H., Wang, Z., Fang, C., Luo, J.: Image captioning with semantic attention. In: Proceedings of the IEEE Conference on Computer Vision and Pattern Recognition, pp. 4651–4659 (2016)

Intrinsic Image Decomposition: A Comprehensive Review

Yupeng Ma[1]([✉]), Xiaoyi Feng[1], Xiaoyue Jiang[1], Zhaoqiang Xia[1], and Jinye Peng[2]

[1] School of Electronics and Information, Northwestern Polytechnical University, Xi'an 710072, China
mayupenga@mail.nwpu.edu.cn
[2] School of Information Science and Technology, Northwest University, Xi'an 710069, China

Abstract. Image understanding and analysis is one of the important tasks in the image processing. Multiple factors influence the appearance of an object in an image. However, extracting the intrinsic images from the observer image can eliminate the environmental impact effectively and make the image understanding more accurately. The intrinsic images represent the inherent shape, color and texture information of the object. Intrinsic image decomposition is recovering shading image and reflectance image from a single input image and remains a challenging problem because of its severely ill-posed problem. In order to deal with these problems, researches have proposed various algorithms for decomposing the intrinsic image. In this paper we survey the recent advances in intrinsic image decomposition. First, we introduce the existing datasets for intrinsic image decomposition. Second, we introduce and analyze the existing intrinsic image decomposition algorithms. Finally, we use the existing algorithms to experiment on the intrinsic image datasets, and analyze and summarize the experimental results.

Keywords: Intrinsic image decomposition · Computer vision
Retinex theory · Intrinsic image dataset

1 Introduction

Image understanding and analysis is one of the important tasks in the image processing. The imaging process is influenced by various factors such as the object characteristics, the shooting environment and the conditions of the acquisition equipment. So the image processing process needs to consider many interference factors, such as shadows, discontinuity of color, and the variation of the target attitude. These interference factors have brought great challenges to the image processing algorithms, and make the existing image analysis algorithms have greater impact on the performance in complex environments. Therefore, how to improve the robustness of image analysis algorithms in complex environment has become a hot research topic in recent years.

© Springer International Publishing AG 2017
Y. Zhao et al. (Eds.): ICIG 2017, Part I, LNCS 10666, pp. 626–638, 2017.
https://doi.org/10.1007/978-3-319-71607-7_55

The appearance of an image depends on many features, such as the illumination, the shape of the surface and the surface of each surface. Each of these features contains useful information about the objects in the image. If extracting these features from an image can eliminate the environmental impact effectively and make the image understanding more accurately. In 1978, Barrow and Tenenbaum [4] called these feature images as "intrinsic image". The goal of intrinsic images decomposition is to separate an image into two layers, i.e., a reflectance image and a shading image, which multiply to form the original image. The reflectance image contains the intrinsic color, or albedo, of surface points independent of the illumination environment. The shading image consists of various lighting effects that include shadows and specular hightlights in addition to shading. The intrinsic images decomposition is expressed as

$$I(x) = R(x) \times S(x) \tag{1}$$

where $I(x)$ is the observed intensity at pixel x, $R(x)$ is the reflectance, and $S(x)$ is the shading. This decomposition of intrinsic images is of importance in both computer vision and computer graphics applications. First, the intrinsic decomposition facilitates advanced image editing in graphics applications such as re-texturing, re-color, and re-lighting. Second, the extracted intrinsic images benefit many computer vision algorithms. Shading images are preferred inputs to algorithms such as shape from shading, while reflectance images can be used for tasks such as segmentation and image white balance. Furthermore, most vision algorithms from low-level image analysis to high-level object recognition implicitly assume that its input image is a reflectance image.

One thousand years ago, humans began to solve the underconstrained problem of perceiving shape, reflectance, and illumination from a single image. Alhazen, a famous optical scientist, who noted that "Nothing of what is visible, apart from light and color, can be perceived by pure sensation, but only by discernment, inference, and recognition, in addition to sensation" [3]. When humans view a flat surface with patches of varying reflectance subject to spatially varying illumination, they are able to form a reasonably veridical percept of the reflectance in spite of the fact that a darker patch under brighter illumination may well have more light traveling from it the eyes compared to a lighter patch which is less well illuminated. Land and McCann's [21] proposed the Retinex theory in 1971, which provided a computational approach to the problem in the "Mondrian World". Retinex theory was later made practical by Horn [12], who prposed to obtain a decomposition of an image into its shading and reflectance components using the prior belief that sharp edges tend to be reflectance, and smooth variation tends to be shading. Since then, researchers have proposed various algorithms for the intrinsic image decomposition, but the problem described a challenge in computer vision which is still largely unsolved. Estimating two intrinsic components from a single input image is a fundamentally ill-posed problem: Given an input image that is composed from its reflectance and shading components, the number of unknowns is twice the number of equations. To solve this problem, further constraints are needed. Various approaches have been employed from intrinsic image decomposition.

This paper will proceed as follows. In Sect. 2, we will introduce the dataset about the intrinsic image. In Sect. 3, we will introduce intrinsic image decomposition algorithm from two aspects of reflection priors and shape priors. In Sect. 4, we analyze the performance and advantages and disadvantages of these algorithms on MIT intrinsic image dataset and IIW intrinsic image dataset. In Sect. 5 we conclude.

2   Intrinsic Image Dataset

Intrinsic image decomposition is a longstanding problem with many applications in computer vision and computer graphics. The goal of intrinsic images is to separate an image into a reflectance image and a shading image. The idea of intrinsic image decomposition was proposed in 1978 [4], however, due to the constraints of computing power, algorithm theory and lack of dataset, the research on the intrinsic image decomposition is slow. There has been significant recent progress on the problem of intrinsic image decomposition, aided by the release of the MIT Intrinsic Images dataset [10], which contains carefully constructed ground truth for images of objects. Bell et al. [5] proposed Intrinsic Images in the Wild, a large scale, public dataset for evaluating intrinsic image decompositions of indoor scenes. Laffont [18,20] proposed the first synthetic dataset that depicts a scene with complex geometry, under multiple physically-based lighting conditions for each viewpoint, with ground truth reflectance and shading images. Jiang et al. [14] propose the BOLD (Birmingham Object Lighting Dataset) surface images, which contains 10 surfaces photographed under 33 lighting conditions.

2.1   MIT Intrinsic Image Dataset

In the MIT Intrinsic Image Dataset, Grosse et al. [10] focus on one particular case: they decomposed an image into three component, which is illumination, reflectance and specular. This decomposition is expressed as

$$I(x) = R(x) \times S(x) + C(x) \qquad (2)$$

where $I(x)$ is the observed intensity at pixel x, $R(x)$ is the reflectance, and $S(x)$ is the shading, and $C(x)$ is the specular.

Fig. 1. The MIT ground-truth intrinsic image. From left to right, original image, diffuse image, shading image, reflectance image, specular image.

The MIT Intrinsic Image Dataset contribution is a set of images of real objects decomposed into Lambertian shading, reflectance, and specularities, in Fig. 1. First, Grosse separates the diffuse and specular component, they use a cross polarization approach where a polarizing filter is placed over both the light and camera. Second, they have developed two different methods for separating the diffuse component into shading and reflectance. Third, they captured diffuse images with ten more light positions using a handheld lamp with a polarizing filter. The dataset contains 20 sets of images, each set of images was taken from a single object, including diffuse image, specular image, reflectance image, shading image and 10 lighting conditions images. The diffuse image corresponds to Lambertian surface, which can be further decomposed into shading image and reflectance image. The specular image accounts for light rays that reflect directly off the surface, creating visible highlights in the image. Quantitatively comparing algorithms requires choosing a meaningful error metric. Grosse define the $LMSE$ (local mean squared error) instead of the MSE (mean squared error), because the MSE is too strict for most algorithms on the MIT Intrinsic Image Dataset. Grosse define the scale-invariant MSE for a true vector $\hat{x}$ and the estimate $\hat{x}$:

$$MSE(x, \hat{x}) = \|x - a\hat{x}\|^2 \tag{3}$$

$$a = \arg\min_a \|x - a\hat{x}\|^2 \tag{4}$$

given the true and estimated shading images S and $\hat{S}$, define $LMSE$ as the MSE summed over all local windows of size $k \times k$ and spaced in steps of $k/2$:

$$LMSE_k\left(S, \hat{S}\right) = \sum_{\omega \in W} MSE\left(S_\omega, \hat{S}_\omega\right) \tag{5}$$

$$LMSE = \frac{1}{2} \frac{LMSE_k\left(S, \hat{S}\right)}{LMSE_k\left(S, 0\right)} + \frac{1}{2} \frac{LMSE_k\left(R, \hat{R}\right)}{LMSE_k\left(R, 0\right)} \tag{6}$$

Barron [1–3] have created the MIT-Berkeley Intrinsic Image dataset, an augmented version of the MIT Intrinsic Image dataset. In the MIT-Berkeley dataset, they used photometric stereo on the additional images of each object to estimate the shape of each object and the spherical harmonic illumination for each image. For the MIT-Berkeley dataset and SIRFS algorithm, Barron and Malik [1] extended six different error metrics for each intrinsic scene property: Z-MAE is the shift-invariant absolute error between the estimated shape and the ground-truth shape. N-MAE is the mean error between our estimated normal field and ground-truth normal field, in radians. S-MSE and R-MSE are the scale-invariant mean-squared-error of our recovered shading and reflectance, respectively. RS-MSE is the error metric measures a locally scale-invariant error for both reflectance and shading. L-MSE is the scale-invariant MSE of a rendering of our recovered illumination on a sphere, relative to a rendering of the ground-truth illumination.

2.2   Intrinsic Image in the Wild (IIW) Dataset

Although the MIT dataset was the first public dataset with ground truth data, however, due to the limited scalability of the collection method, the MIT dataset contains only 20 different objects. The real-world scenes contain a rich range of shapes and materials, lit by complex illumination. Bell et al. [5] present a new, large-scale dataset of Intrinsic Images in the Wild (IIW)– real-world photos of indoor scenes, with crowdsourced annotations of reflectance comparisons between points in a scene. Instead of creating per-pixel annotations, they designed a scaleable approach to human annotation involving humans reasoning about the relative reflectance of pairs of pixels in each image. There are 4416 query points and 10645 query pairs between these point per image, over a total of 5230 images. Figuer 2, Each query to a human subject was in the form of "which point has a darker surface color?", the answer have three points: Point 1, Point 2 and About the same. They also ask users to specify there confidence in their assessment as Guessing, Probably, or Definitely. In the AMT (Amazon Mechanical Turk), they obtained 4,880,372 responses from 1381 workers which aggregated to obtain 875,833 comparisons across 5,230 photos. The IIW dataset contains over 5000 images featuring a wide variety of scenes, and has been annotated with millions of individual reflectance comparisons, this makes the dataset several orders of magnitude larger than existing intrinsic image datasets.

Fig. 2. Human judegement for an example scene.

In order to use the judgement to evaluate intrinsic image decompositions, Bell et all propose a new metric, the "weighted human disagreement rate" ($WHDR$), which measures the percent of human judgement that an algorithm disagree with, weighted by the confidence of each judgement:

$$WHDR_\delta\left(J,R\right) = \frac{\sum_i \omega_i 1\left(J_i \neq \hat{J}_{i,\delta}\left(R\right)\right)}{\sum_i \omega_i} \tag{7}$$

where R is the algorithm output reflectance layer, $\hat{J}_{i,\delta}$ is the judgement predicted by the algorithm being evaluated, and δ is the relative difference between two surface reflectance where people just begin to switch between saying "they are about the same" (E) to "one point is darker". (1 or 2).

2.3   MPI Sintel Dataset

Butler et al. [6] present the MPI Sintel Dataset in Fig. 3. This is a set of complex computer-generated images that were found to have similar statistics to natural images. The MPI-Sintel Dataset was not intended for evaluation of intrinsic image algorithms, but some papers use it for lack of a readily apparent alternative that would reproduce many of the challenge of real-world scenes, such as complex object shapes, occlusion, and complex lighting, and would be accompanied by the requisite ground truth data. It consists of 890 images from 18 scenes with 50 frames each. The dataset contains final images, clean images, albedo images and depth images. They used rendering all the scenes with uniform grey albedo on all object to created the ground-truth shading images. Chen and Koltun [7] and Narihira et al. [23] used the clean images as input, which is infinite depth of field, no motion blur, and no atmospheric effects like fog compared to final images. Fan et al. [8] regenerated the clean images with multiplication of albedo images and shading images as ground-truth.

Fig. 3. The MPI Sintel Dataset.

3   Existing Algorithm

In complex environments, one of the key technologies of robust image processing systems is how to extract the intrinsic features from target objects. Barrow and Tenenbaum [4] defined what is intrinsic images decomposition, Land and McCann's [21] Retinex theory give a solution to the intrinsic images decomposition. Since then, many researchers have been involved in how to solve the problem. Estimating two intrinsic components from a single input image is a fundamentally ill-posed problem: Given an input image that is composed from its reflectance and shading components, the number of unknowns is twice the number of equations. To solve this problem, we can use the prior knowledge and constraint condition of the target object to estimate the reflectance image and shading image respectively. We can also learn the multi-modal patterns of target objects by pattern recognition algorithm, and then classify the learning results to estimate the intrinsic image.

3.1   Image Sequence and Multiple Views

Weiss [30], who focus on a slightly easier problem: given a sequence of images where the reflectance is constant and the illumination changes, can we recover shading images and a single reflectance image. Following recent work on the statistics of natural images, he use a prior that assumes that illumination images will give rise to sparse filter outputs, and this leads to a simple, novel algorithm for recovering reflectance images. Laffont et al. [19] proposed a method to estimate intrinsic images from multiple views of an outdoor scene, in addition to reflectance, the method also generates a separate image for the sun, sky and indirect illumination.

3.2   Priors and Constraints Based on Reflectance

The reflectance, represents how the material of the object reflects light independent of viewpoint and illumination. It related to the material, color, texture, etc. of the objects. Based on the assumption of hue illumination invariant, Pan et al. [24] and Shi et al. [28] proposed the hue can also used for separating illumination information and reflection features. But, the illumination invariance of hue is established only under the condition of weak illumination variation. Under strong illumination variation, the hue is still affected by the change of illumination. For the hue instability, Tappen et al. [29] obtain a classifier for hue variation by training and learning, and realizes the separation of illumination variation and reflectance features. Finalyson et al. [9] used hue calibrated camera to capture images, re-searched a new hue space with illumination invariance. Shen et al. [26], Serra et al. [25] and Kang et al. [15] used the local continuity constraint of the hue of object's surface to estimate the reflection characteristics of objects. These algorithms mainly use the object reflection characteristics of prior and constraint to estimated the reflectance image. These priors and constraints apply to a single object, in the complex scene, the target object occlusion, shadow, the variation of the target attitude will have an impact on the algorithm. In recent years, deep learning theory has been widely used in the field of signal processing and has achieved remarkable results. With the publication of IIW (Intrinsic Images in the Wild) dataset, the dataset has a large amount of ground truth data makes the deep convolutional neural networks can be applied to the decomposition of intrinsic images. Narihira narihira2015learning used complex deep features with a simple local classification rule for lightness prediction in natural image. Zhou et al. [32] proposed a data-driven approach for intrinsic image decomposition by training a model to predict relative reflectance ordering between image patches from large-scale human annotations. Zoran et al. [33] proposed a framework that infers mid-level visual properties of an image by learning about ordinal relationships, instead of estimating metric quantities directly. For human, even the observation of gray image can also distinguish the illumination changes in the image [17]. In fact, in addition to hue features, texture also has a certain illumination invariance. Shen and Yeo [27] uses the local continuity of the texture to separate the original image into shading image and reflectance image.

In this algorithm, the texture of the pixels in the class tends to be consistent by gradually adjusting the same pixels, to achieve the purpose of separating the reflectance features. But, this algorithm of computational complexity is high.

3.3 Priors and Constraints Based on Shape and Illumination

The Retinex theory assumes that illumination is a continuous variable, and that the strong gradients change in the image are caused by reflectance characteristics. Therefore, the illumination information and reflectance characteristics can be classified by the image gradient variation as the threshold. However, the assumption that this illumination change is low frequency information is very rough, when there is occlusion or object deformation, the illumination will be mutated, which will produce high frequency illumination changes. Therefore, we need to take advantage of object shape characteristics as further constraints. Based on the Retinex theory, the shape priors and constraints are added as an additional constraint to decomposed intrinsic images. Barron [1,3] present three priors on shape: (1) a crude prior on flatness, to address the bas-relief ambiguity, (2) a prior on the orientation of the surface normal near the occluding contour, and (3) a prior on smoothness in world coordinates, based on the variation of mean curvature. Barron and Malik [3] uses those three priors on shape and two priors on reflectance in the given a known illumination to decompose intrinsic image. This lead to impressive results on MIT Intrinsic image dataset, but the method is limited to single masked objects in a scene, and problems with complex illumination remain. So, many images couldn't satisfy the requirements of this method. In recent years, with the popularity of the depth sensor, the depth information is also used as the shape priors to extract the intrinsic features. Barron and Malik [2], Chen and Koltun [7], Lee et al. [22], and Jeon et al. [13], in their papers using depth information as priors to extract intrinsic images respectively. Due to the kinect device constraints, the depth information in the natural scene cann't be obtained, which limits the application of the algorithm based on the depth information priors and constraint. Barron and Malik [2] estimated depth maps by a fully convolutional network then jointly optimizes the intrinsic factorization to recover the input image. Kim et al. [16] presented a method for jointly predicting a depth map and intrinsic images from single-image input. The model is called as JCNF (joint convolutional neural field), which jointly uses conditional random field (CRF) and convolutional neural network (CNN). The model architecture differs from previous CNNs in several ways. One is the sharing of convolutional activations and layers between networks for each task, which allows each network to account for inferences made in other networks. Another is to perform learning in the gradient domain, where there exist stronger correlations between depth and intrinsic images than in the image value domain.

4   Experiments and Result

4.1   Experiments on MIT Dataset

Quantitatively evaluating the accuracy of the intrinsic image decomposition algroithms is challenging. Thankfully, the MIT Intrinsic Image dataset provides ground-truth shading image and reflectance image for 20 objects (one object per image), and includes many additional images of each object under different illumination conditions. We selected several representative algorithms for experimental comparison. Some algorithms need to use depth maps as input, such as Barron's Scene-SIRFS [2] and Chen's algorithm [7], however, the MIT dataset does not contains depth maps. Barron [1,3] have created the MIT-Berkeley Intrinsic Images dataset, an augmented version of the MIT Intrinsic Images dataset, in which they used photometric stereo on the additional images of each object estimate the shapes of each object and the spherical harmonic illumination for each image. The MIT dataset and MIT-Berkeley dataset have the same objects and image category, includes each object's original image, diffuse image, shading image, reflectance image, specular image, and different illumination conditions image. In additional, the MIT-Berkeley contains each object's depth maps (Table 1).

Table 1. The experiment results in MIT dataset.

Algorithms	R-MSE	S-MSE	LMSE
BSA	0.0427	0.0563	0.0385
Retinex (gray)	0.048	0.033	0.0405
Retinex (color)	0.035	0.025	0.03
Weiss [30]	0.026	0.017	0.0215
Shen et al. [26]	0.045	0.0478	0.0445
Shen and Yeo [27]	0.0174	0.0236	0.0205
Barron and Malik [1]	0.02	0.0176	0.0296
Barron and Malik [2]	0.0184	0.0101	0.0227
Chen and Koltun [7]	0.0185	0.019	0.0188
Lee et al. [22]	0.0192	0.0224	0.0208
Hauagge et al. [11]	0.012	0.0095	0.011

The other difficulty in evaluation is choosing a meaningful error metric. The mean squared error (MSE) is too strict for most algorithms on the MIT dataset. Incorrectly classifying a single edge can often ruin the relative shading and reflectance for different parts of the image, and this often dominates the error scores. For this problem, we uses the local mean squared error ($LMSE$) instead of the MSE. Barron and Malik [1] present six different error metrics that have been designed to capture differnt kinds of important errors for each intrinsic scene property: *Z-MAE, N-MAE, S-MSE, R-MSE, RS-MSE, L-MSE*. These error metrics are only applicable to the Barron algorithms, we don't use these error metrics.

4.2   Experiments on IIW Dataset

In this section, we evaluate the performance of some algorithms [4,5,8,23,31] using the IIW dataset. These algorithms are based on depth convolution neural network. The IIW dataset provides 875,833 comparisons across 5,230 images, in each image, there are 4416 query points and 106 45 query pairs. This large set of pairwise comparisons has been used to benchmark several reflectance model. The weighted human disagreement rat (WHDR) [5] is proposed to measure the precent of human judgements that an algorithm disagree with (Table 2).

Table 2. The experiment results in IIW dataset.

Algorithms	WHDR(%)
Baseline (const R)	36.6
Baseline (const S)	51.6
Retinex (gray)	27.4
Retinex (color)	27.3
Bell et al. [5]	21.1
Narihira et al. [23]	18.1
Zhao et al. [31]	23.8
Zoran et al. [33]	17.9
Zhou et al. [32]	15.7

5   Conclusions

In the paper, we introduce the intrinsic image datasets and decomposition algorithms. Existing traditional algorithms are based on the Retinex theory. Those traditional algorithms using the feature of object as further priors to extract shading image and reflectance image from a single image. Such as: priors on shape, priors on hue, priors on texture. Simple use the local features of the object as priors, although achieved good results, but the application of algorithm has been limited. For example, Barron in his SIRFS`algorithm, he used priors on shape and priors on albedo to recover shape, reflectance and a spherical harmonic model of illumination. SIRFS algorithm is severely limited by its assumption that input images are segmented images of single objects, illuminated under a single global model of illumination. Natural images, in contrast, contain many shapes which may occlude or support one another, as well as complicated, spatially-varying illumination in the form of shadows, attenuation, and inter-reflection. SIRFS algorithm can't handle these images. Although Barron improves the SIRFS algorithm, the depth map is used as an additional prior for processing natural scene images. Because of the need to add additional input, the improved algorithm is not convenient to use. Traditional algorithms which based on Retinex theory have various limitations and disadvantages. In recent years, deep learning theory has been widely used in the field of single processing and has achieved remarkable results. Some researchers apply the deep learning theory in the intrinsic image decomposition and has achieved remarkable results. The neural network is obtained by deep learning, and the feature is extracted from the image instead of the traditional fixed feature.

Acknowledgements. This paper is partly supported by National Natural Science Foundation of China (Nos. 61502388 and 61702419), the National Aerospace Science and Technology Foundation and H3C foundation of ministry of education in China (No. 2017A-19050).

References

1. Barron, J.T., Malik, J.: Shape, albedo, and illumination from a single image of an unknown object. In: Computer Vision and Pattern Recognition, pp. 334–341 (2012)
2. Barron, J.T., Malik, J.: Intrinsic scene properties from a single RGB-D image. In: Computer Vision and Pattern Recognition, pp. 17–24 (2013)
3. Barron, J.T., Malik, J.: Shape, illumination, and reflectance from shading. IEEE Trans. Pattern Anal. Mach. Intell. **37**(8), 1670–87 (2015)
4. Barrow, H.G., Tenenbaum, J.M.: Recovering intrinsic scene characteristics from images. In: Hanson, A., Riseman, E. (eds.) Computer Vision Systems, pp. 3–26. Academic Press (1978)
5. Bell, S., Bala, K., Snavely, N.: Intrinsic images in the wild. ACM Trans. Graph. **33**(4), 1–12 (2014)
6. Butler, D.J., Wulff, J., Stanley, G.B., Black, M.J.: A naturalistic open source movie for optical flow evaluation. In: Fitzgibbon, A., Lazebnik, S., Perona, P., Sato, Y., Schmid, C. (eds.) ECCV 2012. LNCS, vol. 7577, pp. 611–625. Springer, Heidelberg (2012). https://doi.org/10.1007/978-3-642-33783-3_44
7. Chen, Q., Koltun, V.: A simple model for intrinsic image decomposition with depth cues. In: Proceedings of the IEEE International Conference on Computer Vision, pp. 241–248 (2013)
8. Fan, Q., Wipf, D., Hua, G., Chen, B.: Revisiting deep image smoothing and intrinsic image decomposition (2017)
9. Finlayson, G.D., Hordley, S.D., Lu, C., Drew, M.S.: On the removal of shadows from images. IEEE Trans. Pattern Anal. Mach. Intell. **28**(1), 59–68 (2006)
10. Grosse, R., Johnson, M.K., Adelson, E.H., Freeman, W.T.: Ground truth dataset and baseline evaluations for intrinsic image algorithms. In: 2009 IEEE 12th International Conference on Computer Vision, pp. 2335–2342. IEEE (2009)
11. Hauagge, D., Wehrwein, S., Bala, K., Snavely, N.: Photometric ambient occlusion for intrinsic image decomposition. IEEE Trans. Pattern Anal. Mach. Intell. **38**(4), 639–651 (2016). IEEE
12. Horn, B.K.P.: Determining lightness from an image. Comput. Graph. Image Process. **3**(4), 277–299 (1974)

13. Jeon, J., Cho, S., Tong, X., Lee, S.: Intrinsic image decomposition using structure-texture separation and surface normals. In: Fleet, D., Pajdla, T., Schiele, B., Tuytelaars, T. (eds.) ECCV 2014. LNCS, vol. 8695, pp. 218–233. Springer, Cham (2014). https://doi.org/10.1007/978-3-319-10584-0_15

14. Jiang, X., Schofield, A.J., Wyatt, J.L.: Correlation-based intrinsic image extraction from a single image. In: Daniilidis, K., Maragos, P., Paragios, N. (eds.) ECCV 2010. LNCS, vol. 6314, pp. 58–71. Springer, Heidelberg (2010). https://doi.org/10.1007/978-3-642-15561-1_5

15. Kang, X., Li, S., Fang, L., Benediktsson, J.A.: Intrinsic image decomposition for feature extraction of hyperspectral images. IEEE Trans. Geosci. Remote Sens. **53**(4), 2241–2253 (2015)

16. Kim, S., Park, K., Sohn, K., Lin, S.: Unified depth prediction and intrinsic image decomposition from a single image via joint convolutional neural fields. In: Leibe, B., Matas, J., Sebe, N., Welling, M. (eds.) ECCV 2016. LNCS, vol. 9912, pp. 143–159. Springer, Cham (2016). https://doi.org/10.1007/978-3-319-46484-8_9

17. Kingdom, F.A.: Perceiving light versus material. Vis. Res. **48**(20), 2090–2105 (2008)

18. Laffont, P.Y., Bazin, J.C.: Intrinsic decomposition of image sequences from local temporal variations. In: IEEE International Conference on Computer Vision, pp. 433–441 (2015)

19. Laffont, P.Y., Bousseau, A., Drettakis, G.: Rich intrinsic image decomposition of outdoor scenes from multiple views. IEEE Trans. Vis. Comput. Graph. **19**(2), 210–224 (2012)

20. Laffont, P.Y., Paris, S., Paris, S., Drettakis, G.: Coherent intrinsic images from photo collections. ACM Trans. Graph. **31**(6), 202 (2012)

21. Land, E.H., McCann, J.J.: Lightness and retinex theory. J. Opt. Soc. Am. **61**(1), 1 (1971)

22. Lee, K.J., Zhao, Q., Tong, X., Gong, M., Izadi, S., Lee, S.U., Tan, P., Lin, S.: Estimation of intrinsic image sequences from image+depth video. In: Fitzgibbon, A., Lazebnik, S., Perona, P., Sato, Y., Schmid, C. (eds.) ECCV 2012. LNCS, vol. 7577, pp. 327–340. Springer, Heidelberg (2012). https://doi.org/10.1007/978-3-642-33783-3_24

23. Narihira, T., Maire, M., Yu, S.X.: Learning lightness from human judgement on relative reflectance. In: Proceedings of the IEEE Conference on Computer Vision and Pattern Recognition, pp. 2965–2973 (2015)

24. Pan, S., An, X., He, H.: Intrinsic image decomposition from a single image via non-linear anisotropic diffusion. In: 2013 IEEE International Conference on Information and Automation (ICIA), pp. 179–184. IEEE (2013)

25. Serra, M., Penacchio, O., Benavente, R., Vanrell, M., Samaras, D.: The photometry of intrinsic images. In: Proceedings of the IEEE Conference on Computer Vision and Pattern Recognition, pp. 1494–1501 (2014)

26. Shen, J., Yang, X., Li, X., Jia, Y.: Intrinsic image decomposition using optimization and user scribbles. IEEE Trans. Cybern. **43**(2), 425–436 (2013)

27. Shen, L., Yeo, C.: Intrinsic images decomposition using a local and global sparse representation of reflectance. In: 2011 IEEE Conference on Computer Vision and Pattern Recognition (CVPR), pp. 697–704. IEEE (2011)

28. Shi, B., Li, Y., Xu, C.: Intrinsic image decomposition using color invariant edge. In: Fifth International Conference on Image and Graphics, ICIG 2009, pp. 307–312. IEEE (2009)

29. Tappen, M.F., Freeman, W.T., Adelson, E.H.: Recovering intrinsic images from a single image. IEEE Trans. Pattern Anal. Mach. Intell. **27**(9), 1459–1472 (2005)

30. Weiss, Y.: Deriving intrinsic images from image sequences. In: Proceedings. Eighth IEEE International Conference on Computer Vision, ICCV 2001, vol. 2, pp. 68–75. IEEE (2001)
31. Zhao, Q., Tan, P., Dai, Q., Shen, L., Wu, E., Lin, S.: A closed-form solution to retinex with nonlocal texture constraints. IEEE Transa. Pattern Anal. Mach. Intell. **34**(7), 1437–1444 (2012)
32. Zhou, T., Krahenbuhl, P., Efros, A.A.: Learning data-driven reflectance priors for intrinsic image decomposition. In: Proceedings of the IEEE International Conference on Computer Vision, pp. 3469–3477 (2015)
33. Zoran, D., Isola, P., Krishnan, D., Freeman, W.T.: Learning ordinal relationships for mid-level vision. In: Proceedings of the IEEE International Conference on Computer Vision, pp. 388–396 (2015)

Multi-instance Multi-label Learning for Image Categorization Based on Integrated Contextual Information

Xingyue Li[1(✉)], Shouhong Wan[1,2(✉)], Chang Zou[1(✉)],
and Bangjie Yin[1(✉)]

[1] School of Computer Science and Technology,
University of Science and Technology of China, Hefei 230027, China
{votelxy,kkpanda,ybj}@mail.ustc.edu.cn
[2] Key Laboratory of Electromagnetic Space Information,
Chinese Academy of Science, Hefei 230027, China
wansh@ustc.edu.cn

Abstract. In image categorization, one image is usually reshaped as a bag of instances affiliated with multiple labels, which naturally induces a paradigm of multi-instance and multi-label learning (MIMLL). Previous researches proved that the significant improvements on image categorization accuracy resulted from applying connections between labels and regions or correlations among labels, but most proposed approaches could not make full use of contextual cues. Thus we propose a brand-new MIMLL method with integrating three distinct types of contexts into a conditional random fields (CRFs) framework, which can simultaneously capture latent probability distribution of instances, spatial context among adjacent instances and correlations between instances and labels. We perform image categorization on MSRC and Corel 1000 data sets to verify our proposal. Compared with traditional and state-of-the-art MIMLL algorithms, our approach obtains the superior performance.

Keywords: Multi-instance multi-label learning · Image categorization
Conditional random fields · Contextual information

1 Introduction

Traditional single-label image categorization assumes that an image only contains objects associated with a single label, which obviously does not fit the real-world situation. Since different objects such as beach, sea and sky, belonging to different classes, can be contained in one image, it is naturally to assign the image with multiple labels to express the multiple semantic meaning of the image, which is formulated as a multi-label image categorization and is becoming a more prevailing but more challenging and complex task. Typically, multi-label categorization is treated as a set of single-label categorization tasks, for example, Boutell et al. [1] built an individual classifier for each label and the labels of a new image were determined by all of these classifiers. However, researchers found that this solution regarded each label isolated and ignored the correlations among labels, so that they proposed some approaches such

© Springer International Publishing AG 2017
Y. Zhao et al. (Eds.): ICIG 2017, Part I, LNCS 10666, pp. 639–650, 2017.
https://doi.org/10.1007/978-3-319-71607-7_56

as CLP [2] and CML-SVM [3] to exploit these correlations. Regretfully, all of them just considered an image as an indiscrete unit and only made use of global features, neglecting the fact that regions in the image greatly contribute the semantic labels, not the whole image. But under the multi-label learning framework, it is difficult to express the relationship between the whole image and its local regions precisely.

To tackle this issue, Multi-instance multi-label learning (MIMLL) applies multi-instance learning framework to multi-label problems. In multi-instance learning, an image is regarded as a bag, consisting of several instances corresponding to the regions in the image, if at least one instance is associated with a label, the image will be marked with this label, which is consistent with the situation where labels are always characterized by their corresponding regions in the image, rather than the entire image. Given a training image dataset composed of a set of bags of instances and each bag relates to multiple labels, MIMLL is to learn a classifier to predict all labels for an unseen bag [4].

In recent years, a number of effective algorithms have been presented in the field of MIMLL, the initial attempt was made by Zhou et al. [5]. They transformed the MIMLL task into a multi-instance or a multi-label learning task, which can be further transformed into a conventional learning task. Based on this, they presented two different models called MIML-Boost and MIML-SVM which achieved good performance in scene classification. Considering the issue of losing information in the degeneration process,then Zhou et al. [6] proposed D-MIMLSVM which directly tackled multi-instance multi-label (MIML) problems in a regularization framework. However, these MIMLL algorithms always neglected the contexture information hidden in the image, for example, some related objects such as "car-building" and "ship-seaboard" always appeared together in one image. To alleviate this problem, Zha et al. [7] proposed an integrated multi-label multi-instance learning approach called MLMIL based on hidden conditional random fields (HCRFS) [8] to handle the fine image classification, which simultaneously took the relationship between labels and regions, and the correlations among labels into account in the training progress. Ding et al. [4] solved the MIML problem by involving hierarchical context among instances and labels into classification model. In their work, multiple graphs were adopted to construct the instance context and a linear combination of several latent conceptions that link low level features and high level semantic labels was used to construct the label context. In addition, considering most of the existing algorithms only can deal with the moderate-sized data, Yakhnenko et al. [9] proposed DMIML and Huang et al. [10] proposed MIMLfast to efficiently handle large datasets, and both of them also exploited the correlations among labels.

Obviously, most of these existing algorithms have taken the contexture information into consideration more or less, demonstrating that the hidden contexts have a positive impact on the performance for image categorization. However, they just focused on the connections between labels and regions and the correlations among labels, but ignored other two kinds of contexts. First is the spatial context among adjacent instance. Regions in an image do not exist independently, for example, streets always appear along with the surrounding objects such as houses, cars and pedestrian and so on, which can be regarded as the spatial context. Note that this spatial context is also able to capture the correlations among labels. Second is the latent probability distribution of instances. Instances inevitably have a certain distribution in their feature space, which can reflect the similarity of instances belonging to same category. If we consider the latent probability distribution of instances, it will be helpful to better predict the corresponding label of a given instance and eventually improve the performance of image categorization.

To circumvent the limitations embedded in the existing MIMLL methods, we propose a novel approach for image categorization based on integrated contextual information, including the latent probability distribution of all instances, the spatial context among adjacent instances and the correlations between instances and labels. In our algorithm, we design a multi-instance conditional random fields (mi-CRFs) framework that can jointly model these contexts. Specifically, to model the latent probability distribution of all instances, we introduce Gaussian Mixture Model (GMM) to simulate the real distribution of positive and negative instances approximately; To express the spatial context between a certain instance and its adjacent instances, we use the proportion of labels that the instance's adjacent areas associated with; To explore the correlations between instances and labels, we give the probability that each instance belongs to a label by using multi-class support vector machine (SVM). The contributions of this paper can be summarized as follows:

(1) The mi-CRFs integrates three different terms of contextual information into model. Experimental results show that these terms are all useful and indispensable.
(2) In contrast to other MIMLL approaches, the mi-CRFs introduces GMM to construct the latent probability distribution of all instances.
(3) Besides, the mi-CRFs firstly adopts the spatial context among adjacent instances which can filter positive instances from each bag.

The remainder of this paper is organized as follows: we present the construction of three types of contexts we use in Sect. 2. The formulation of proposed mi-CRFs is described in Sect. 3. Section 4 shows our experimental results and their corresponding analysis. At last, we give the conclusion of this work in Sect. 5.

2 Construction of Contextual Information

2.1 MIMLL Formulation

For convenience, we give the framework of MIMLL first. Let $\partial \in R^d$ denotes the input instance space and $l = \{\pm 1\}^E$ denotes the set of E class labels. The target of MIMLL is to learn a function $F_{MIMLL} : 2^{\partial} \rightarrow 2^l$ from a given data set $D = \{B_i, Y_i\}_{i=1}^{N}$, where $B_i = \{x_{i,j}\}_{j=1}^{m_i} \subseteq \partial$ denotes a bag consisting of m_i instances and its corresponding labels set is $Y_i = [y_{i,1}, \ldots, y_{i,E}] \in l$. Here N is the number of bags, if B_i associates with the label e, then $y_{i,e} = 1, (e = 1, \ldots, E)$, otherwise $y_{i,e} = -1$.

2.2 Latent Probability Distribution of Instances

Theoretically, probability distribution of instances in the feature space can be illustrated in Fig. 1. Obviously, each category of instances presents as a "cluster". Different

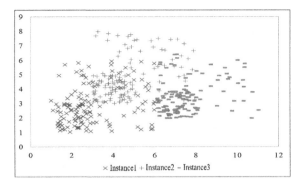

Fig. 1. Probability distribution of instances in the feature space.

clusters are formed due to the different features extracted from different categories of instances.

In opinion of probability statistics, generally, Gaussian distribution can be used to approximate the probability distribution of a given data set when we are unable to determine which one is appropriate. While a single Gaussian distribution cannot fit multiple "clusters", therefore we introduce Gaussian Mixture Model (GMM) for MIMLL, which can be defined as formula (1), assuming that $h_{i,j}(h_{i,j} \in Y_i)$ denotes the label of the instance $x_{i,j}$.

$$P(h_{i,j}|\theta) = \sum_{k=1}^{E} P(k)P(h_{i,j}|k) = \sum_{k=1}^{E} \alpha_k \phi(h_{i,j}|\theta_k) \tag{1}$$

In formula (1), E is the number of Gaussian models as well as the number of labels of the given data set, $\emptyset(h_{i,j}|\theta_k)$ is the Gaussian distribution density and α_k is the coefficient of the kth model, representing the probability of the instance $x_{i,j}$ from the kth model, the coefficients must satisfy the constraint of formula (2). In addition, $\theta_k = (\mu_k, \sigma_k^2)$ denotes the parameters of the kth model, where μ_k denotes mean and σ_k denotes standard deviation. If suitable parameters α_k, μ_k and σ_k are found, the probability distribution of instances will be determined.

$$\sum_{k=1}^{E} \alpha_k = 1 \tag{2}$$

2.3   Spatial Context Among Adjacent Instances

Figure 2 gives a detailed description of the spatial context among adjacent instances. The right is the constructed bag B_i of the image I_i, it is divided into left different objective regions, each of these regions consists of a number of dots which represent the super-pixels. Edges between dots represent the adjacent relationship. For "Car",

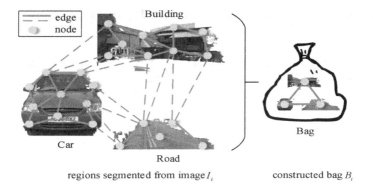

regions segmented from image I_i constructed bag B_i

Fig. 2. Example of the spatial context among adjacent instances.

super-pixels around the edge of "Car" almost belong to "Building" and "Road" which is in line with the actual situation, providing a theoretical feasibility for our model.

Here, for a given instance, we use the proportion of the labels its adjacent instances associated with to represent the spatial context. Let $I_i = \{sp_{i,j}\}_{j=1}^{m_i}$ denotes that an image I_i is segmented into m_i super-pixels and $c_{i,j}$ denotes the corresponding position the super-pixel $sp_{i,j}$ located at. First, we find out n-nearest neighbors for the super-pixel $sp_{i,j}$: $nei_{i,j} = \{sp_{i,1}^{nei}, \ldots, sp_{i,n}^{nei}\}$. And then we calculate the ratio these n-nearest neighbors belong to each category respectively according to formula (3), where $r_{i,j}^c$ denotes the ratio that n-nearest neighbors of the jth super-pixel in the image I_i belong to the label $c(c \in l)$, $[\cdot]$ is the indicator function whose value is 1 when the condition is satisfied and otherwise is 0, $count(\cdot)$ denotes the total number, and $h_{i,k}$ denotes the label of $sp_{i,k}^{nei}$.

$$r_{i,j}^c = \frac{1}{count(nei_{i,j})} \sum_{k \in nei_{i,j}} \left[h_{i,k} = c\right] \tag{3}$$

By constructing the spatial context in this manner, we can select out all possible labels of the super-pixel according to its set of n-nearest neighbors, when training the classifier for multi-label tasks. In our algorithm, we choose n as 10 because experiments show that overall performance of our algorithm on image categorization is best under this setting.

2.4 Correlations Between Instances and Labels

Correlations between instances and labels are demonstrated useful by [4, 8]. Each instance corresponds to a unique label, whose prior probability is given by the labels of the bag the instance situated in. Given the labels set Y_i of the bag B_i, one direct solution to exploit the correlation between instance $x_{i,j}$ and its label $h_{i,j}$ is to calculate the posterior probability $P(h_{i,j}|x_{i,j}, Y_i)$ and we adapt multi-class SVM to calculate it.

3 Multi-instance Conditional Random Fields Algorithm

HCFRs was proposed by Quattoni et al. [8], it is a robust algorithm aiming at exploring the labels of local regions in object detection. HCFRs considered that each observation sequence corresponded to a set of hidden variables, which represent all possible sources of the observation sequence. Inspired by HCRFs, labels of the bag B_i can be regarded as the observation sequence and labels of instances in this bag can be expressed by a set of hidden variables: $H_i = \{h_{i,1}, \ldots, h_{i,m_i}\} \in l$. In this paper, we propose a modified conditional random fields applying to MIMLL: multi-instance conditional random fields (mi-CRFs).

3.1 Algorithm Framework

The framework of proposed mi-CRFs algorithm mainly contains four steps, which is illustrated in Fig. 3.

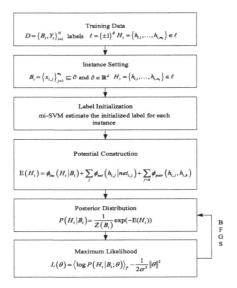

Fig. 3. Algorithm framework.

Firstly, it constructs training data set by segmenting each image into multiple super-pixels, in other words, it aims at constructing instances for bags; Secondly, it initializes the labels for each instance with the labels of its corresponding bag, and then estimates these labels to select out the most probable label for each instance by using mi-SVM [11]; Thirdly, after obtaining the estimated label for each instance, it respectively constructs the corresponding context potential for each contextual information, then, it integrates three context potentials into a total potential and gets the posterior distribution of instance labels. Lastly, it introduces BFGS [12] to maximize the likelihood of the posterior distribution obtained by the third step. After obtaining all labels of the instances in the bag, we will mark this bag with these obtained labels. Next, we begin with the details of our algorithm in Sect. 3.2.

3.2 Formulation of Mi-CRFs

Firstly, we give the definition of the integrated potential for mi-CRFs as formula (4), consisting of three parts: $\emptyset_{ins}, \emptyset_{nei}, \emptyset_{pair}$.

$$
\begin{aligned}
E(H_i) &= \sum_j \phi_{unary}(x_{i,j}) + \sum_{j<k} \phi_{pair}(x_{i,j}, x_{i,k}) \\
&= \sum_j \phi_{ins}(x_{i,j}) + \sum_j \phi_{nei}(x_{i,j}) + \sum_{j<k} \phi_{pair}(x_{i,j}, x_{i,k})
\end{aligned}
\tag{4}
$$

Secondly, we give the details of three parts in formula (4). $\emptyset_{ins}$ is an unary potential denoting the correlations between instances and labels, as illustrated in Sect. 2.2, we can give a probability for the label of each instance, so $\emptyset_{ins}$ can be defined as formula (5).

$$
\phi_{ins}(H_i|B_i, Y_i) = -\sum_j \log P(h_{i,j}|x_{i,j}, Y_i), \ 1 \leq j \leq m_i
\tag{5}
$$

$\emptyset_{nei}$ is also an unary potential but denoting the spatial context among adjacent instances. According to Sect. 2.3, to express spatial context among adjacent instances, $\emptyset_{nei}$ is illustrated in formula (6).

$$
\phi_{nei}(h_{i,j}|nei_{i,j}) = -\log r_{i,j}^c
\tag{6}
$$

$\emptyset_{pair}$ is a pairwise potential denoting the latent probability distribution of instances. It is defined as formula (7), where $\varphi_m(x_{i,j}, x_{i,k})$ denotes a Gaussian kernel, formula (8) is the specific form of $\varphi_m(x_{i,j}, x_{i,k})$, where $P_{i,j}$ represents the position of the instance $x_{i,j}$ and $P_{i,k}$ represents the position of $x_{i,k}$. By designing such a Gaussian kernel, adjacent instances can be classified to the same category. θ_α, θ_β and θ_γ are parameters of the Gaussian kernel.

$$
\phi_{pair}(h_{i,j}, h_{i,k}) =
\begin{cases}
0 & \text{if } h_{i,j} = h_{i,k}, \\
\sum_{m=1}^E \alpha_m \varphi_m(x_{i,j}, x_{i,k}) & \text{otherwise.}
\end{cases}
\tag{7}
$$

$$
\begin{aligned}
\varphi_m(x_{i,j}, x_{i,k}) &= w^{(1)} \exp\left(-\frac{|p_{i,j} - p_{i,k}|^2}{2\theta_\alpha^2} - \frac{|x_{i,j} - x_{i,k}|^2}{2\theta_\beta^2}\right) \\
&\quad + w^{(2)} \exp\left(-\frac{|p_{i,j} - p_{i,k}|^2}{2\theta_\gamma^2}\right)
\end{aligned}
\tag{8}
$$

Thirdly, CRF [13] must be constructed based on graph, here we choose full-connected graph since any pair of nodes in it has an edge connected, showing its comprehensiveness and stability. In addition, a CRF can be represented as a Gibbs distribution, general form of which is defined as formula (9).

$$P(Y_i) \propto \exp(-E(Y_i)) \tag{9}$$

In mi-CRFs, it defines a set of hidden label variables: $H_i = \{h_{i,1}, \ldots, h_{i,m_i}\} \in l$, similarly to MLMIL [7], it gets the posterior probability of the label vector Y_i of the bag B_i by combining all possible values of H_i, which is defined as formula (10), where $Z(B_i) = \sum_Y \sum_h exp(-E(Y_i, h_{i,j}))$ is the division function.

$$P(Y_i|B_i) = \sum_{j=1}^{m_i} P(Y_i, h_{i,j}|B_i) = \frac{1}{Z(B_i)} \sum_{j=1}^{m_i} \exp\big(-E\big(Y_i, h_{i,j}\big)\big) \tag{10}$$

In the task of MIML image categorization, an image corresponds to a bag and a super-pixel corresponds to an instance, mi-CRFs establishes a full-connected graph for each bag, and then obtains the corresponding potential and the expression of the posteriori probability. As well as traditional CRF [13] model, the final optimization target of mi-CRFs is to maximize the posteriori probability of the hidden sequence, which is defined in formula (11).

$$H_i^* = \arg\max_{H_i \in \{\pm 1\}^{m_i}} P(H_i|Y_i, B_i) \tag{11}$$

Now mi-CRFs is established. Since it use full-connected graph, we use Mean-field to ratiocinate and adapt BFGS [12] to optimize the parameters.

4   Experiments and Analysis

To evaluate the performance of mi-CRFs, we design a set of experiments on two data sets: MSRC and Corel 1000. In our implementation, all images are firstly segmented into several super-pixels using SLIC [14], and then a 367-dimension feature vector of each super-pixel is extracted to represent the instance, including a 3-dimension RGB, a 64-dimension color histogram and a 300-dimension dense sift histogram. As well as [7], then we perform 5-fold cross validation on each data set. For each data set, images are randomly and equally split into five parts, in addition, they must satisfy the constraint that there should be at least five positive images of each class per partition. We choose one of the five parts as the testing data set, and the other as the training set. We compare our method with several state-of-art algorithms for MIML image categorization, such as MIML-Boost [5], MIML-SVM [5], MLMIL [7], DMIML [9], CMIML [4]. And we take widely used AUC (Area Under Curve) [15] to evaluate the performance of these approaches, because of its ability to describe the probability that a randomly chosen positive sample will be ranked higher than a randomly chosen negative sample [7].

MSRC data set consists of 591 images with 23 classes. Each image is marked with at least one label on image level and also has the pixel level ground truth with its corresponding label. Note that we only use the image level ground truth to train our model. As well as [7], we consider "horse" and "mountain" as "void" because either of them only has few positive samples. Thus there are 21 labels in total. Table 1 presents the average AUC on two MSRC data set of mi-CRFs and other compared methods. Obviously, mi-CRFs achieves the best overall performance.

Table 1. Average AUC on MSRC data set of different approaches.

Algorithm	Avg. AUC
mi-CRFs	**0.960**
MIML-Boost [5]	0.842
MIML-SVM [5]	0.830
MLMIL [7]	0.910
DMIML [9]	0.914
CMIML [4]	0.909

Corel 1000 data set contains 1000 images with 10 classes. All these images have been manually marked with 1–5 labels. Table 2 presents the average AUC on Corel 1000 data set of mi-CRFs and other compared methods, and mi-CRFs also achieves the best overall performance on this data set.

Table 2. Average AUC on Corel 1000 data set of different approaches.

Algorithm	Avg. AUC
mi-CRFs	**0.969**
MIML-Boost [5]	0.796
MIML-SVM [5]	0.830
MLMIL [7]	0.913

Figure 4 gives the detailed AUC on each category of MSRC data set, as illustrated in Fig. 4, mi-CRFs achieves the best performance on most categories, but the bad performance on "car", "flower", "bird", "dog" and "boat". We find these images which mi-CRFs does not perform well on, have several common characteristics as follows: (1) One object contains too many subtypes, for example, different kinds of flowers vary in color, size, appearance and angle; Boats contains the yacht, fishing boats and canoeing, which are extremely different with each other. (2) Backgrounds of the same phyletic images are complex and varied, for example, birds can fly in the sky and on the water, and can appear on the shore and on the grass. These characteristics make it difficult for mi-CRFs to capture useful contextual information, resulting in the unsatisfied classification performance on these categories.

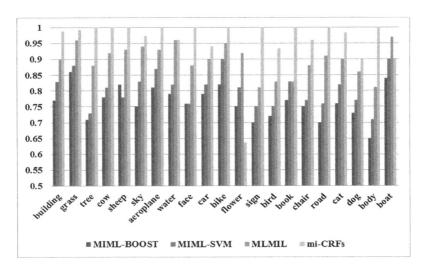

Fig. 4. AUC on each category of MSRC data set of different approaches.

In addition, in order to verify the assumption that three types of contexture information are useful and indispensable, we design two contrastive experiments and give the results on Table 3 and Fig. 5.

Table 3. Average AUC on MSRC data set of mi-CRFs with different combinations of different contexts.

Proposed Methods	Avg. AUC
mi-CRFs (no contextual potential)	0.517
mi-CRFs (no $\emptyset_{ins}$)	0.907
mi-CRFs (no $\emptyset_{nei}$)	0.820
mi-CRFs (no $\emptyset_{pair}$)	0.924
mi-CRFs	**0.960**

As can be seen from Table 3, only when mi-CRFs takes the integrated contextual information into consideration can it achieve the best performance. Average AUC of mi-CRFs will decline when losing any type of contexts, and it will decline to 0.517 when losing all contexts. Reasonable explanation for 0.517 is that, the priori information only depends on the estimated labels of instances by mi-SVM [11], has nothing to do with the features of instances and contexture information, therefore the result is close to 0.5. Apart from this, each context we use has a different influence on the performance of our model, and missing spatial context among adjacent instances leads to the largest drop by 14% compared to other two types of contexts. Figure 5 gives the detailed results on each category, showing the different impact of different contexts on different labels. Spatial context among adjacent instances is also demonstrated the most significant on most categories, while it has little influence on "dog" and "boat". Images associated with these two labels always have complex backgrounds. For example, categories of the background of dogs can be grass, road and even water, while the number of grasses almost equal to that of roads. Result of "flower" seems abnormal, maybe it has something to do with the enormous variation in color, size, appearance and angle of flowers.

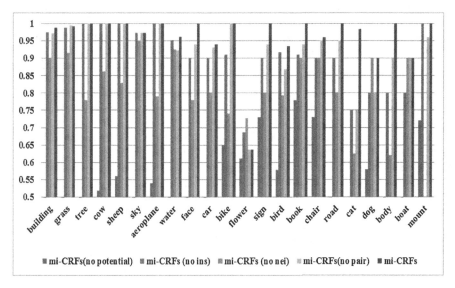

Fig. 5. AUC on each category of MSRC data set of mi-CRFs with different combinations of different contexts.

5   Conclusion

In this paper, we propose a multi-instance and multi-label framework based on combining three different types of contextual information and apply it to image categorization. Not only does our approach consider latent probability distribution of instances and spatial context among adjacent instances, it is also flexible to model correlations between instances and labels. A set of experiments based on MSRC and Corel 1000 data sets present the excellent performance of our approach and demonstrate that three types of contexts we make use of are all helpful and indispensable for the total improvements of proposed algorithm.

References

1. Boutell, M.R., Luo, J., Shen, X., Brown, C.M.: Learning multi-label scene classification. Pattern Recogn. **37**(9), 1757–1771 (2004)

2. Kang, F., Jin, R., Sukthankar, R.: Correlated label propagation with application to multi-label learning. In: IEEE Computer Society Conference on Computer Vision and Pattern Recognition, vol. 2, pp. 1719–1726. IEEE Xplore (2006)

3. Qi, G.J., Hua, X.S., Rui, Y., Tang, J., Mei, T., Zhang, H.J.: Correlative multi-label video annotation. In: International Conference on Multimedia 2007, vol. 5, pp. 17–26. DBLP, Augsburg, September 2007

4. Ding, X., Li, B., Xiong, W., Guo, W., Hu, W., Wang, B.: Multi-instance multi-label learning combining hierarchical context and its application to image annotation. IEEE Trans. Multimed. **18**(8), 1616–1627 (2016)

5. Zhou, Z.H., Zhang, M.L.: Multi-instance multi-label learning with application to scene classification. Adv. Neural. Inf. Process. Syst. **19**, 1609 (2007)

6. Zhou, Z.H., Zhang, M.L., Huang, S.J., Li, Y.F.: Multi-instance multi-label learning. Artif. Intell. **176**(1), 2291–2320 (2012)

7. Zha, Z.J., Hua, X.S., Mei, T., Wang, J., Qi, G.J., Wang, Z.: Joint multi-label multi-instance learning for image classification. In: IEEE Conference on Computer Vision and Pattern Recognition. CVPR 2008, pp. 1–8. IEEE (2008)

8. Quattoni, A., Wang, S., Morency, L.P., Collins, M., Darrell, T.: Hidden conditional random fields. IEEE Trans. Pattern Anal. Mach. Intell. **29**(10), 1848–1853 (2007)

9. Yakhnenko, O., Honavar, V.: Multi-instance multi-label learning for image classification with large vocabularies. In: BMVC, pp. 1–12 (2011)

10. Huang, S.J., Gao, W., Zhou, Z.H.: Fast multi-instance multi-label learning. In: Twenty-Eighth AAAI Conference on Artificial Intelligence (2014)

11. Andrews, S., Tsochantaridis, I., Hofmann, T.: Support vector machines for multiple-instance learning. In: Advances in Neural Information Processing Systems, pp. 577–584 (2003)

12. Liu, D.C., Nocedal, J.: On the limited memory BFGS method for large scale optimization. Math. Program. **45**(1), 503–528 (1989)

13. Lafferty, J., McCallum, A., Pereira, F.: Conditional random fields: probabilistic models for segmenting and labeling sequence data. In: Proceedings of the Eighteenth International Conference on Machine Learning, ICML, vol. 1, pp. 282–289 (2001)

14. Achanta, R., Shaji, A., Smith, K., Lucchi, A.: SLIC superpixels compared to state-of-the-art superpixel methods. IEEE Trans. Pattern Anal. Mach. Intell. **34**(11), 2274–2282 (2012)

15. Hanley, J.A., McNeil, B.J.: The meaning and use of the area under a receiver operating characteristic (ROC) curve. Radiology **143**(1), 29–36 (1982)

Book Page Identification Using Convolutional Neural Networks Trained by Task-Unrelated Dataset

Leyuan Liu[1,2], Yi Zhao[1], Huabing Zhou[2], and Jingying Chen[1(✉)]

[1] National Engineering Research Center for E-Learning,
Central China Normal University, Wuhan, China
{lyliu,chenjy}@mail.ccnu.edu.cn
[2] Hubei Key Laboratory of Intelligent Robot,
Wuhan Institute of Technology, Wuhan, China

Abstract. This paper presents a pipeline to make convolutional neural networks (CNNs) trained for another unrelated task available for book page identification. The pipeline has five building blocks: (1) An image segmentation module to separate book page from the background; (2) An image correction module to correct geometry and color distortions; (3) A feature extraction module to extract discriminative image features by a pre-trained CNN; (4) A feature compression module to reduce feature dimensions for speeding up; and (5) A feature matching module to calculate the similarity between a query image and a reference image, and then to find out the most similar reference image. The experimental results on a challenging testing dataset show that the proposed book page identification method achieves a top-5 hit rate of 98.93%.

Keywords: Book page identification · CNN · Image retrieval

1 Introduction

Nowadays, more and more printed books are accompanied by electronic resources including videos, audios, games, augmented reality and other mobile apps. However, it is not very convenient to access most of these electronic resources, as the association between printed books and electronic resources is not automatically available [1]. Take the accessing of an accompanied video for example: one should first find the right video file corresponding to the book, open it by a video player, and then repeatedly fast-forward or fast-backward to locate the exact position relevant to a certain book page. Beside the fact that this task may take an adult minutes to complete, it is often a challenge for very young children and aged people. There exists a pressing need for associating the printed books with the accompanied electronics resources to enable quick and convenient access to the electronic resources.

The major issue of associating the printed books with accompanied electronic resources is to automatically identify book pages. It is then possible to map the page to its corresponding video/audio position or to a certain scenario of an app/game via a table/database [2]. Existing page identification methods can be generally divided into three

© Springer International Publishing AG 2017
Y. Zhao et al. (Eds.): ICIG 2017, Part I, LNCS 10666, pp. 651–663, 2017.
https://doi.org/10.1007/978-3-319-71607-7_57

categories: Optical IDentification (OID), Page Identifier (PI), and Computer Vision (CV) methods.

The OID-based method usually relies on a device called "talking pen" [3], which reads and identifies invisible codes printed by infrared reflective ink. As the OID-based methods can discriminate about 600000 different codes, vast amounts of pages can be identified stably. However, this technology is hard to be popularized because high-cost ink and especially made hardware are required.

PI-based method identifies book pages by recognizing an additional page identifier printed on each page. Jeong et al. [4] print a specially designed page identifier on each page of the book, and identify book pages by comparing the characteristics of the captured page identifier with its database. Baik [5] regards the two dimensional code as an ambient media gate to the digital world, and has developed a "scan-to-watch" application to access the TV programs by scanning two dimensional codes on printed materials. Although PI-based technology can be easily integrated into mobile apps and page identifiers are quite robust for recognizing, there are two disadvantages: (1) Page identifiers more or less strip the aesthetics out of books; (2) Books without printed page identifiers cannot use PI-based method for page identification.

CV-based method treats page identification as an image retrieval problem, i.e. taking an image of a printed book page, and then finding out the most similar reference image from a registration dataset in which each reference image has already been mapped to a book page. Iwata et al. [6] use four directional features field to identify book covers for a small-scale library system. Tsai et al. [7] employ Speeded Up Robust Features (SURF) to recognize CD covers. Chae et al. [2] use a mobile phone to take sequence images of printed materials, and then retrieve the reference image from database by a keypoint-based matching and tracking method. CV-based methods don't require to print additional identifiers on books, thus this technology can be used to identify pages of any book. However, the identification accuracy of most existing CV-based methods cannot provide satisfied user experience. Recently, convolutional neural networks have made impressive progress in many fields of computer vision including image retrieval [8]. This progress make it possible to improve the performance of CV-based book page identification.

This paper presents a book page identification method based on convolutional neural networks (CNNs). As collecting and labelling millions of book page images to train a CNN is time-consuming, a pipeline is proposed to make CNNs trained by another task-unrelated dataset for book page identification. The experimental results on a challenging testing dataset show that the proposed book page identification method achieves a top-5 hit rate of 98.93%.

2   The Proposed Method

As shown in Fig. 1, the pipeline of the proposed book page identification method has five building blocks: (1) An image segmentation module to separate book page from the background; (2) An image correction module to correct geometry and color distortions; (3) A feature extraction module to extract discriminative image features by a pre-trained

CNN; (4) A feature compression module to reduce feature dimensions for speeding up; and (5) A Feature matching module to calculate the similarity between a query image and a reference image, and then to find the most similar reference image out. In the offline phase, each reference image only needs to be processed by the feature extraction module and the feature compression module to obtain a compressed feature code. The feature codes of all reference images are stored in a matrix. In the online phase, a query image is processed by all the five modules.

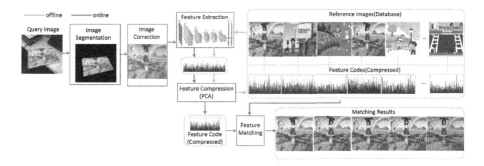

Fig. 1. The pipeline of the proposed book page identification method.

2.1   Book Page Segmentation

Background affects the performance of book page identification seriously, as abundant visual information included in background may be encoded into the feature codes by CNNs. Therefore, book pages need to be separated from background.

Many interactive image segmentation algorithms [9, 10] have been proposed in the last decade. Drawing a bounding box of an interested object, these algorithms can then separate the object from background. However, the "bounding box drawing" interaction degrades the user experience. Although some image segmentation algorithms [11, 12] can initialize the bounding box of an interested object automatically, none of them can provide real-time processing speed on mainstream smart phone and other consumer electronics.

In this subsection, a coarse-to-fine strategy is proposed to segment book page from background full automatically with real-time processing speed. As illustrated in Fig. 2, the proposed image segmentation algorithm consists of three steps: (1) Coarse segmentation to segment book page at pixel level using a fixed bounding box initialization; (2) Bounding box re-initialization to provide a more accuracy bounding box for fine segmentation; (3) Fine segmentation to obtain the final results.

A color histogram based Bayes classifier is employed to conduct coarse segmentation. Let $H_O(b)$ and $H_B(b)$ denote the b-th bin of the non-normalized histogram computed over the initial bounding box (O) and its surrounding background region (B) respectively. Additionally, let bx denote the bin b assigned to the pixel $I(x)$ at location x. Bayes rule [13] is applied to obtain the object likelihood as:

$$p(x \in O | O, B, b_x) \approx \frac{p(b_x | x \in O)p(x \in O)}{\sum\limits_{\Omega \in \{O, B\}} p(b_x | x \in \Omega)p(x \in \Omega)} \qquad (1)$$

In particular, the likelihood terms in (1) is estimated directly from color histograms, i.e. $p(b_x | x \in O) \approx H_o(b_x)/|O|$ and $p(b_x | x \in B) \approx H_B(b_x)/|B|$. Furthermore, the prior probability can be approximated as $P(x \in O) \approx |O|/(|O| + |S|)$. Thus, the Bayes classifier simplifies to:

$$p(x \in O | O, B, b_x) \approx \frac{H_O(b_x)}{H_O(b_x) + H_B(b_x)} \qquad (2)$$

The pixels of book page can be coarsely separated from background by (2) with very low computational cost. Then, a new bounding box is fitted on the coarse segmentation result using least-squares approximation. Finally, the book page is segmented by the DenseCut algorithm [10], which is a high quality image segmentation technique with a processing speed of about 15 images per second on general consumer electronics.

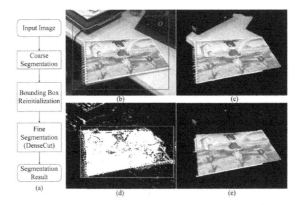

Fig. 2. Coarse-to-fine image segmentation. (a) The procedures of the proposed full automatic image segmentation algorithm. (b) An original query image with a fixed bounding box initialization. (c) Image segmentation result using the initial bounding box in (b). (d) A new bounding box is reinitialized after coarse segmentation. (e) Fine image segmentation result using the bounding box in (d).

2.2 Image Correction

There are mainly two kinds of distortions, i.e. geometry distortion and color distortion, in the original query images. If these distortions are not corrected, the performance of book page identification suffers from them significantly. In this subsection, geometry distortion and color distortion are corrected in a single pass. As illustrated in Fig. 3, the geometry distorted book page in the original query image is converted to a square one by perspective transformation, and meanwhile the distorted color of the book page is corrected to that appears under a canonical light source by chromatic adaptation.

As it is hard to make a handheld camera straight on at the plane of a book page, the rectangle book page in a query image usually distorts to quasi-quadrilateral, mainly due to perspective projection. Thus, perspective transformation is investigated to convert the quasi-quadrilateral book page to a square one. Let (x_s, y_s) denote a point in the corrected image. Perspective transformation is used to map (x_s, y_s) back to its corresponding point (x_q, y_q) in the original image:

$$
\begin{cases}
x_q = \dfrac{a_{11}x_s + a_{21}y_s + a_{31}}{a_{13}x_s + a_{23}y_s + a_{33}} \\
y_q = \dfrac{a_{12}x_s + a_{22}y_s + a_{32}}{a_{13}x_s + a_{23}y_s + a_{33}}
\end{cases}
\tag{3}
$$

where $\{a_{11}, a_{12}, a_{13}; a_{21}, a_{22}, a_{23}; a_{31}, a_{32}, a_{33} = 1\}$ are elements of the 3×3 transformation matrix. This transformation matrix needs to be computed by cues from images.

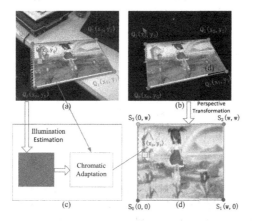

Fig. 3. An example of image distortions correction. (a) An original query image, in which the book page is distorted in both geometry and color. (b) A quadrilateral is fitted to surround the contour of the segmented book page, and is used to correct geometry distortion by perspective transformation. (c) Ambient illumination is estimated from the original image, and is used to correct colors of all pixels of the book page. (d) The corrected image of the book page.

To compute the transformation matrix, at least four point correspondences between the original image and the corrected image are needed to be established. To this end, a quadrilateral which encloses the contour of the segmented book page is fitted using least-squares approximation (see Fig. 3(b)). After that, four point correspondences, i.e. $\{(Q_0, S_0), (Q_1, S_1), (Q_2, S_2), (Q_3, S_3)\}$ in Fig. 3, are established. Then, these four point correspondences are substituted in (3), and the transformation matrix can be determined.

Color distortion in the original query image is mainly caused by ambient illumination. Once the ambient illumination is estimated, the query image can be corrected to an image that appears to be recorded under a canonical illumination using chromatic adaptation [14]:

$$
\begin{bmatrix} R_s \\ G_s \\ B_s \end{bmatrix} = \begin{bmatrix} R_q \\ G_q \\ B_q \end{bmatrix} \begin{bmatrix} \dfrac{1}{\sqrt{3}R_e} & 0 & 0 \\ 0 & \dfrac{1}{\sqrt{3}G_e} & 0 \\ 0 & 0 & \dfrac{1}{\sqrt{3}B_e} \end{bmatrix} \tag{4}
$$

where $[R_q, G_q, B_q]^T$ and $[R_s, G_s, B_s]^T$ are the pixel color in the original query image and the corrected image respectively, and $[R_e, G_e, B_e]^T$ is the ambient illumination which needs to be estimated.

Computational color constancy [14, 15] is a powerful tool for estimating ambient illumination from a single image. Exploring the tradeoff between illumination estimation accuracy and computational efficiency, the gray-edge based computational color constancy algorithm [14] is adopted. This algorithm assumes that the average edge difference in a scene is achromatic. Based on this hypothesis, the ambient illumination is estimated as:

$$
\begin{bmatrix} R_e \\ G_e \\ B_e \end{bmatrix} = \frac{1}{C} \begin{bmatrix} \left(\displaystyle\sum_{x\in[0,w),y\in[0,h)} \left(\nabla R_q(x,y) \right)^p \right)^{1/p} \\ \left(\displaystyle\sum_{x\in[0,w),y\in[0,h)} \left(\nabla G_q(x,y) \right)^p \right)^{1/p} \\ \left(\displaystyle\sum_{x\in[0,w),y\in[0,h)} \left(\nabla B_q(x,y) \right)^p \right)^{1/p} \end{bmatrix} \tag{5}
$$

where w and h are respectively the width and height of the original query image, $\nabla(\cdot)$ denotes the gradient map of the original query image, p is a parameter, and C is the normalization coefficient. In the implementation, p is set as 5.

Once the perspective transformation matrix is computed and the ambient illumination is estimated, the geometry distortion is corrected using (3) and the color distortion is corrected using (5) simultaneously.

2.3   Feature Extraction

Recently, the CNNs have achieved impressive progress in many fields of computer vision including image retrieval. The most direct way to book page identification is collecting a dataset which consists of book page images and then using it to train a CNN. So that, book pages can be identified by the trained CNN in an end-to-end way. However, to train such a CNN, a dataset which contains millions of labelled book page images is required. Collecting and labelling such a large-scale dataset is time-consuming.

Many studies [8, 16–18] have shown some qualitative evidence that the features emerging in the upper layers of the CNNs trained for object classification may serve as good descriptors for another unrelated tasks such as image retrieval. Inspired by these works, pre-trained CNNs for object classification are investigated for book page identification in this paper. Exploring the accuracy and speed trade-off of many pre-trained CNNs with different architectures [8, 16–20], the VGG Fast version (VGG-F) convolutional neural network [17] is finally adopted to identify book pages in this paper.

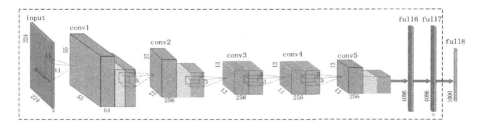

Fig. 4. The architecture of CNN used in this paper.

The architecture of VGG-F CNN is illustrated in Fig. 4. It consists of 5 convolutional layers (conv1-5) and 3 full-connected layers (full6-8). The conv1 layer employs 64 kernels of size $11 \times 11 \times 3$ to filter the $224 \times 224 \times 3$ color input images with a stride of 4 pixels. The conv2 layer takes as input the output of conv1 layer and filters it with 256 kernels of size $5 \times 5 \times 64$. The conv3, conv4 and conv5 layers all have 256 convolution kernels of size $3 \times 3 \times 256$. A max-pooling unit follows the convolution unit in layer conv1, conv2 and conv5, but does not in layer conv3 and conv4. Each of the 5 convolutional layers includes a Rectified Linear Unit (ReLU). The full-connect layers full6 and full7 are regularized using dropout, and have 4096 neurons each. The last layer full8 is the output layer and acts as a multi-way soft-max object classifier. The ILSVRC dataset [21] which contains 1.2 millions training images of 1000 object categories is used to train the VGG-F CNN.

The 4096 dimensional vector output from the full7 layer is extracted as the feature code for book page identification. For computation-saving, the full8 layer of the trained VGG-F CNN is cut off when extracting feature codes from book page images. In the offline phase, all reference images in the book page database are resized to 224×224 pixels and input into the trained CNN one by one to extract feature codes, and the extracted feature codes are stored in a matrix. In the online phase, a feature code is also extracted from the image output by the image correction module.

2.4   Feature Compression

To identify a book page, similarities between the feature code of the query image and the feature codes of all reference images are needed to be calculated. As each feature code extracted by the CNN is a 4096-dimensional vector, computing these similarities is inefficient. The most direct solution for improving the efficiency is reducing the dimensions of the feature codes. Babenko *et al.* [8] use Principle Component Analysis (PCA) to compress feature codes extracted by CNNs, and have obtained a good performance of content based image retrieval while reducing much computational cost. Encouraged by this work, PCA is employed to compress the 4096-dimensional feature codes for speeding up.

Denote the feature code extracted from an image as a vector $\mathbf{X}_i$. Suppose there are m reference images in the book page database, all of their feature codes can form a $4096 \times m$ matrix $\mathbf{M}$, i.e. $\mathbf{M} = [\mathbf{X}_1\ \mathbf{X}_2 \cdots \mathbf{X}_m]$. Then, the covariance matrix $\mathbf{\Sigma}$ of $\mathbf{M}$ can be calculated. And then, the eigen-matrix $\mathbf{U}$ can be obtained by the Singular Value Decomposition (SVD) of $\mathbf{\Sigma}$, i.e. $\mathbf{U} = \mathrm{SVD}(\mathbf{\Sigma})$. After that, the compression matrix $\mathbf{U}_d$ can be formed by selecting the first d eigen-vectors of $\mathbf{U}$. Finally, a 4096-dimensional feature code $\mathbf{X}$ can be compressed to d dimensions by:

$$\tilde{\mathbf{X}} = \mathbf{U}_d^T \mathbf{X} \tag{6}$$

where $\tilde{\mathbf{X}}$ is the compressed feature code.

In the offline phase, the feature codes of all the reference images are compressed using (6) and stored in a matrix. In the online phase, the feature code of the query image is also compressed to the d dimensions.

2.5 Feature Matching

Two kinds of search methods, i.e. exhaustive search [8] and hashing based search [22, 23], are often employed in the field of image retrieval. In most existing hashing based methods, feature codes of images are first encoded to binary hash codes by a projection and a quantization steps, then Hamming distance is adopted to calculate the distances between the pairs of the query image and each reference image. However, hashing based methods are not appropriate for applications with relatively small amount of reference images, as the computational loss for generating hash codes may outweigh the gain from computing distances. Another risk of hashing based methods is that these methods sometimes produce sub-optimal binary hash codes which will degrade the retrieval performance [24].

Taking account of the trade-off between computational cost and retrieval accuracy, exhaustive search is adopted in this paper. The procedures of exhaustive search is straightforward: (1) Compute the similarities between the query image and each reference image. (2) Rank all the reference images according to their similarities to the query image. (3) Select k top-ranking reference images as the retrieval results.

Cosine distance is adapted to measure the similarity as it experimentally achieves the best performance. Assume that $\tilde{\mathbf{X}}_i$ is the compressed feature code extracted from the query image, and $\tilde{\mathbf{X}}_j$ is the compressed feature code extracted from a reference image, then the similarity between these two images is measured by:

$$S_{i,j} = \frac{\tilde{\mathbf{X}}_i \tilde{\mathbf{X}}_j^T}{\sqrt{\tilde{\mathbf{X}}_i \tilde{\mathbf{X}}_i^T} \sqrt{\tilde{\mathbf{X}}_j \tilde{\mathbf{X}}_j^T}} \tag{7}$$

In (7), the term $\sqrt{\tilde{\mathbf{X}}_i \tilde{\mathbf{X}}_i^T}$ can be ignored as ignoring it does not change the rank of reference image j, and the term $\sqrt{\tilde{\mathbf{X}}_j \tilde{\mathbf{X}}_j^T}$ can be computed offline. Thus, the similarity can be redefined to reduce computational load while maintaining ranking results:

$$\tilde{S}_{i,j} = p_j(\tilde{\mathbf{X}}_i \tilde{\mathbf{X}}_j^T) \tag{8}$$

where $p_j = 1/\sqrt{\tilde{\mathbf{X}}_j \tilde{\mathbf{X}}_j^T}$ is computed offline. So that, only $(d + 1)$ multiplication and d addition operations are consumed for matching each reference image in the online phase.

3   Experiments

In this section, the proposed book page identification method is extensively evaluated. The experiments were conducted on a smart phone with an eight-core processor (4×2.3 GHz + 4×1.8 GHz) and 4 GB RAM, to validate that the proposed book page identification method and book-eResource association system can run on general consumer hardware. The core algorithms of the proposed book page identification method are implemented using optimized multithreaded C++ code.

To evaluate the proposed book page identification method and book-eResource association, a testing database involving 4568 book pages is collected. For each book page, a reference image is captured by a flatbed scanner, and 4 to 8 query images are taken arbitrarily by cameras on different smart phones. As a result, 4568 reference images and 25112 query images are collected in the testing dataset. When taking the query images, factors including geometry distortion, color distortion, highlight, image blur, and cluttered background have been taken into account to simulate severe usage situations.

The top-k hit rate is adopted as the metrics for quantitative evaluation:

$$\gamma_k = \frac{N_k}{N} \tag{9}$$

where N is the total testing times, and N_k is the times that the right answer is among the first k reference images considered most probable by the book page identification method.

3.1   Overall Performance

Some exemplar results of the proposed book page identification method are illustrated in Fig. 5. The results in Fig. 5(a) and (b) show that the proposed book page identification method can discriminate similar book pages. In Fig. 5(c), the proposed method does not suffer from image blur and the large highlight area in the query image. The results in Fig. 5(d) show that the proposed book page identification method does not suffer from "bad" image segmentation result due to clutter background. The results in Fig. 5(e) demonstrate that the proposed book page identification method can tolerate imperfect corrected image. The results in Fig. 5(f) and (g) show that the proposed book page identification method is not sensitive to the orientation of corrected images. In short, the proposed book page identification method achieves satisfying performance under severe usage situations including clutter background, image blur, highlight, geometry distortion and color distortion.

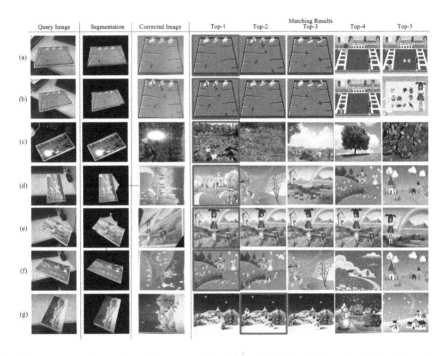

Fig. 5. The exemplar results of the proposed book page identification method. The right answers are marked with red rectangles. (Color figure online)

The proposed book page identification method is compared with the state-of-the-art end-to-end CNN based image retrieval method [8]. The CNNs used in these two method are pre-trained by the same ILSVRC dataset [21]. Both of the two methods are using a 128 dimensions feature codes compression rate in this experiment. The quantitative comparison results are shown in Table 1. The proposed book page identification method achieves a top-5 hit rate of 98.93%, while the end-to-end CNN [8] only achieves a top-5 hit rate of 55.49%.

Table 1. The hit rates of the proposed method and the end-to-end method

Methods	Hit rates (%)				
	Top-1	Top-2	Top-3	Top-4	Top-5
The proposed	97.26	98.32	98.70	98.86	98.93
End-to-end [8]	16.74	23.62	35.89	45.52	55.49

3.2   Effectiveness of the Proposed Pipeline

This experiment is designed to validate the effectiveness of the proposed pipeline. During this experiment, the image correction module is first removed, then the image segmentation module is also removed from the pipeline. To avoid interference, the feature codes are not compressed in this experiment. The hit rates after removing these two modules are shown in Table 2. From the experimental results, one can see that the book page identification method results in inferior performance when removing the image correction and image segmentation modules from the pipeline.

Table 2. The hit rates after removing modules from the pipeline

Methods	Hit rates (%)				
	Top-1	Top-2	Top-3	Top-4	Top-5
Entire pipeline	97.79	98.32	98.86	98.93	98.93
Remove IC	24.32	37.64	48.59	59.63	61.62
Remove IC & IS	17.56	24.67	37.39	47.57	58.78

IC: Image Correction, IS: Image Segmentation

3.3   Performance of Different Feature Code Compression

This experiment aims to evaluate the performance of different versions of feature codes after PCA compression to different dimensions. The top-1 to top-5 hit rates for different PCA compression rates are illustrated in Fig. 6. It demonstrates that the feature codes extracted by CNN can be compressed to 128 dimensions with slight loss of performance.

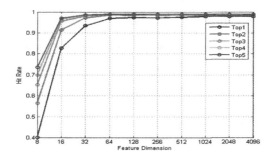

Fig. 6. The hit rates of the proposed book page identification method using different PCA compression rates.

3.4   Computation Time

The computation time is relative to the size of the query image and the dimensions of feature codes. When testing computation time in this experiment, the input query image is resized to 400 × 400 pixels for segmentation, the corrected image size is set as 224 × 224 pixels, and the feature codes are compressed to 128 dimensions. The average computation time of the entire pipeline for a query image is 430 millisecond (ms). With this period, image segmentation takes 46 ms, image correction takes 23 ms, feature code extraction takes 342 ms, feature code compression takes 2 ms, and feature matching takes 17 ms (when searching among 4568 reference images).

4   Conclusions

This paper has presented a CNN based book page identification method for associating printed books with electronic resources. A pipeline has been proposed to make CNN trained for another unrelated task available for book page identification. The pipeline has five building blocks: the image segmentation module, image correction module, CNN based feature extraction module, feature compression module, and feature matching module. Under this pipeline, the CNN trained by another task-unrelated dataset can extract effective and robust features for book page identification. The proposed book page identification method has achieved a top-5 hit rate of 98.93% on a challenging testing dataset.

Acknowledgements.   This work was supported by the National Natural Science Foundation of China (No. 41671377, 61502195), the Natural Science Foundation of Hubei Province (No. 2017CFB504), the Research Funds of CCNU from the Colleges Basic Research and Operation of MOE (Nos. CCNU17QN0003, CCNU17QN0002, CCNU2016A02020), and the Foundation of Hubei Key Laboratory of Intelligent Robot (No. HBIR201606).

References

1. Yokota, J.: From print to digital? Considering the future of picture books for children. In: Bologna: Fifty Years of Children's Books from Around the World, pp. 443–449 (2013)
2. Chae, S., Yang, Y., Choi, H., Kim, I., Byun, J., Jo, J., Han, T.: Smart advisor: real-time information provider with mobile augmented reality. In: Proceedings of the IEEE International Conference on Consumer Electronics, Las Vegas, USA, pp. 97–98, January 2016
3. Hsu, M., Chen, C.: Analysis of motivation triggers in interactive digital reading for children. Int. J. Infonomics **6**(1), 669–675 (2013)
4. Jeong, H.T., Lee, D.W., Heo, G.S., Lee, C.H.: Live book: a mixed reality book using a projection system. In: Proceedings of the IEEE International Conference on Consumer Electronics, Las Vegas, USA, pp. 680–681, January 2012
5. Baik, S.: Rethinking QR code: analog portal to digital world. Multimedia Tools Appl. **58**(2), 427–434 (2012)
6. Iwata, K., Yamamoto, K., Yasuda, M., Murata, K.: Book cover identification by using four directional features filed for a small-scale library system. In: Proceedings of the International Conference on Document Analysis and Recognition, Seattle, USA, pp. 582–586, September 2001
7. Tsai, S.S., Chen, D., Singh, J.P., Girod, B.: Rate-efficient, real-time CD cover recognition on a camera-phone. In: Proceedings of the International Conference on Multimedia, Vancouver, Canada, pp. 1023–1024, October 2008

8. Babenko, A., Slesarev, A., Chigorin, A., Lempitsky, V.: Neural codes for image retrieval. In: Fleet, D., Pajdla, T., Schiele, B., Tuytelaars, T. (eds.) ECCV 2014. LNCS, vol. 8689, pp. 584–599. Springer, Cham (2014). https://doi.org/10.1007/978-3-319-10590-1_38

9. Rother, C., Kolmogorov, V., Blake, A.: Grabcut: interactive foreground extraction using iterated graph cuts. ACM Trans. Graph. **23**(3), 309–314 (2004)

10. Cheng, M.M., Prisacariu, V.A., Zheng, S., Torr, P.H.S., Rother, C.: DenseCut: densely connected CRFs for real-time GrabCut. Comput. Graph. Forum **34**(7), 193–201 (2015)

11. Chai, Y., Lempitsky, V., Zisserman, A.: Symbiotic segmentation and part localization for fine-grained categorization. In: Proceedings of the IEEE International Conference on Computer Vision, Sydney, Australia, pp. 321–328, December 2013

12. Cheng, M.M., Mitra, N.J., Huang, X., Hu, S.M.: Salientshape: group saliency in image collections. Vis. Comput. **30**(4), 443–453 (2014)

13. Possegger, H., Mauthner, T., Bischof, H.: In defense of color-based model-free tracking. In: Proceedings of the IEEE Conference on Computer Vision and Pattern Recognition, Boston, USA, pp. 2113–2120, June 2015

14. Van De Weijer, J., Gevers, T., Gijsenij, A.: Edge-based color constancy. IEEE Trans. Image Process. **16**(9), 2207–2214 (2007)

15. Liu, L., Sang, N., Yang, S., Huang, R.: Real-time skin color detection under rapidly changing illumination conditions. IEEE Trans. Consum. Electron. **57**(3), 1295–1302 (2011)

16. Krizhevsky, A., Sutskever, I., Hinton, G.E.: ImageNet classification with deep convolutional neural networks. In: Proceedings of the Advances in Neural Information Processing Systems, Lake Tahoe, USA, pp. 1097–1105, December 2012

17. Chatfield, K., Simonyan, K., Vedaldi, A., Zisserman, A.: Return of the devil in the details: delving deep into convolutional nets. In: Proceedings of the British Machine Vision Conference, Nottingham, UK, pp. 1–12, September 2014

18. Oquab, M., Bottou, L., Laptev, I., Sivic, J.: Learning and transferring mid-level image representations using convolutional neural networks. In: Proceedings of the IEEE International Conference on Computer Vision and Pattern Recognition, Columbus, USA, pp. 1717–1724, June 2014

19. Sermanet, P., Eigen, D., Zhang, X., Mathieu, M., Fergus, R., Cun, Y.L.: Overfeat: integrated recognition, localization and detection using convolutional networks. In: Proceedings of the International Conference on Learning Representations, Banff, Canada, pp. 1–16, April 2014

20. Zeiler, M.D., Fergus, R.: Visualizing and understanding convolutional networks. In: Fleet, D., Pajdla, T., Schiele, B., Tuytelaars, T. (eds.) ECCV 2014. LNCS, vol. 8689, pp. 818–833. Springer, Cham (2014). https://doi.org/10.1007/978-3-319-10590-1_53

21. Deng, J., Dong, W., Socher, R., Li, L.J., Li, K., Fei-Fei, L.: Imagenet: a large-scale hierarchical image database. In: Proceedings of the IEEE International Conference on Computer Vision and Pattern Recognition, Miami, USA, pp. 248–255, June 2009

22. Lin, K., Yang, H.F., Hsiao, J.H., Chen, C.S.: Deep learning of binary hash codes for fast image retrieval. In: Proceedings of the IEEE Conference on Computer Vision and Pattern Recognition Workshops, Boston, USA, pp. 27–35, June 2015

23. Liu, H., Wang, R., Shan, S., Chen, X.L.: Deep supervised hashing for fast Image retrieval. In: Proceedings of the IEEE International Conference on Computer Vision and Pattern Recognition, Las Vegas, USA, pp. 2064–2072, June 2016

24. Lai, H., Pan, Y., Liu, Y., Yan, S.: Simultaneous feature learning and hash coding with deep neural networks. In: Proceedings of the IEEE Conference on Computer Vision and Pattern Recognition, Boston, USA, pp. 3270–3278, June 2015

No Reference Assessment of Image Visibility for Dehazing

Manjun Qin, Fengying Xie$^{(\boxtimes)}$, and Zhiguo Jiang

School of Astronautics, Image Processing Center, BeiHang University,
Beijing 100191, China
mnjune@163.com, xfy_73@buaa.edu.cn

Abstract. Haze affects the quality and visibility of the image. Many dehazing algorithms have been developed in recent years. However, the evaluation for the performance of the dehazing method is still not solved. The assessment is not easy to achieve since the reference image is not available. In this paper, a no reference image quality evaluation indicator is proposed to assess the visibility of a dehazed image. A multi-scale contrast feature is designed to measure the image sharpness. Considering some dehazing methods often cause under-dehazing results, a dark channel feature is employed to describe the haze residual degree of the restored image. Fusing the two features together, the final indicator that can measure the image visibility is obtained. Experimental results show that the assessment results are highly correlated with human visual perceptions and objective quality scores, which demonstrate the effectiveness and robustness of the proposed approach.

Keywords: Dehazing · Multi-scale contrast · Dark channel
Visibility assessment · No reference assessment

1 Introduction

Outdoor images captured from natural scenes are inevitably degraded under foggy weather, causing reduced contrast and faded vividness of the image [1]. Hazy images cannot meet the requirement of consumer photography and computer vision applications (e.g., object recognition, video surveillance). To address this problem, much work has been carried out to restore the image visibility. In particular, some significant progresses have been achieved in recent years. He *et al.* [2] proposed a dark channel prior to remove haze, which achieved impressive results. Tang *et al.* [3] trained a regression model to estimate the medium transmission map by extracting a set of haze-relevant features and training with Random Forest.

Despite of the remarkable progresses of image dehazing, the method of evaluating the performance of the dehazing algorithm is addressed very little. Nishino *et al.* [4] and Meng *et al.* [5] adopted the widely-used subjective analysis to conduct assessment according to their own judgements. When conducting the subjective evaluation, evaluators were more inclined to their own advantages, making

© Springer International Publishing AG 2017
Y. Zhao et al. (Eds.): ICIG 2017, Part I, LNCS 10666, pp. 664–674, 2017.
https://doi.org/10.1007/978-3-319-71607-7_58

it tough to reach a unified evaluation result. Dai and Tarel [6] invited seven students to evaluate 1500 dehazed images through visual judgements, which reduced the personal subjectivity to a certain degree.

In order to make quantitative analysis, Wu *et al.* [7] and Mai *et al.* [8] employed traditional reference Image Quality Assessment (IQA) indicators to evaluate dehazing performances, such as Mean Squared Error (MSE), Peak Signal to Noise Ratio (PSNR), and Structural Similarity (SSIM) [9]. Since haze-free images were unavailable, these metrics can only be calculated with original hazy images, leaving the evaluation results unconvincing and unreliable. To make the reference assessment feasible, Zhu *et al.* [10] synthesized hazy images and calculated these IQA indicators between dehazed and clear images. The same assessment manner can be seen in [3, 11–13]. However, such IQA indicators are mainly used to evaluate typical image distortions, like blurring and compression. They are not specially designed for haze removal, which cannot effectively and reasonably evaluate dehazing algorithms.

Hautiere *et al.* [14] paid attention to the contrast enhancement evaluation for restoration algorithms, which is a close work to dehazing evaluation. In their method, three different descriptors were developed based on the gradient of visible edges, which can be used to measure the image visibility. Fang *et al.* [15] designed an exclusive indicator for haze removal assessment, which measured the image visibility through the local band-limited contrast. However, the gradient and contrast information is very sensitive to noise. These indicators cannot give robust and accurate evaluation results in some cases.

The image visibility is an important factor for the evaluation of dehazing algorithms. In this paper, we put emphasis on the measurement of image visibility from two aspects: image sharpness and haze residual degree. The image sharpness is measured with a proposed multi-scale contrast feature, and the haze residual degree is described using the dark channel feature. Fusing the two features together, an indicator is derived to evaluate the visibility of the restored image. Experimental results demonstrate the effectiveness and robustness of the proposed method.

The remainder of the paper is organized as follows. In Sect. 2, we present the specially designed indicator to measure the visibility of the restored image. Section 3 gives the experimental results and analysis. Finally, we summarize this paper in Sect. 4.

2   The Proposed Approach

A clear restored image should have enhanced contrast and no haze disturbance. In this paper, two features are designed to describe the image sharpness and haze residual degree, respectively. With the combination of the two features, a visibility indicator is derived to rate the image clarity level.

2.1   Multi-scale Contrast Feature

Images with higher contrast are sharper in human visual perceptions. There-fore, the measurement of image contrast can indicate the image sharpness to a certain degree. Weber contrast and Michelson contrast are two popular con-trast definitions, which reflect the global contrast of the whole image. Since the restoration is usually spatial-variant, global contrast cannot make use of local information and will lead to inaccurate measurement. Local variance can aggre-gate information of all pixels and attenuate the disruption of extreme noise, which tends to be a good contrast indicator. To avoid expanding magnitude, the Root Mean Square (RMS) is more common to be used [16]. However, local RMS is sensitive to the window size selected, leading to unfixed results under different windows. To solve this problem, in this paper, a multi-scale contrast descriptor is developed, which can give stable and unified results.

For an image I, we define its contrast map as the local RMS under a non-overlapping sliding window, described as:

$$
CM(u, v) = \sqrt{\frac{1}{k^2} \sum_{x=1}^{k} \sum_{y=1}^{k} \left[I(k(u-1) + x, k(v-1) + y) - \mu(u, v) \right]^2} \tag{1}
$$

where k is the local window size, and μ is the local average value:

$$
\mu(u, v) = \frac{1}{k^2} \sum_{x=1}^{k} \sum_{y=1}^{k} I\left(k(u-1) + x, k(v-1) + y\right) \tag{2}
$$

We adopt down-sampling to generate image pyramid, denoted as $I^{(0)}, I^{(1)}, \ldots, I^{(n)}$, where $I^{(0)}$ is the initial image, $I^{(j+1)}$ is the down-sampled result of $I^{(j)}$. We call each down-sampled image a layer. In order to guarantee the image size big enough for the subsequent operations, the last layer $I^{(n)}$ should meet to:

$$
\min\left(h^{(n)}, w^{(n)}\right) \geq \xi \tag{3}
$$

where $h^{(n)}$ and $w^{(n)}$ represent the height and width of the image $I^{(n)}$, respec-tively. In this paper, ξ is fixed to 200.

Within one pyramid layer $I^{(j)}$, a set of contrast maps are generated with different window size k_i, which is defined as:

$$
k_i^{(j)} = \left\lfloor \frac{i}{m(j+1)} \min\left(\frac{h^{(j)}}{10}, \frac{w^{(j)}}{10}\right) \right\rfloor \qquad i = 1, 2, \ldots, m \tag{4}
$$

where m is the number of scales in one pyramid layer, and $\lfloor \cdot \rfloor$ indicates rounding down. In this paper, m is fixed to 3. For each image $I^{(j)}$, we produce three contrast maps, marked as $CM_1^{(j)}$, $CM_2^{(j)}$, $CM_3^{(j)}$, which consist of one octave. Note that $\left\lfloor \frac{1}{(j+1)} \min\left(\frac{h^{(j)}}{10}, \frac{w^{(j)}}{10}\right) \right\rfloor$ is the max size of local window, which ensures that the smallest size of the contrast map is at least 10×10.

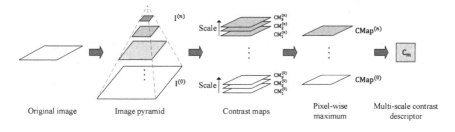

Fig. 1. An illustration for the computing of multi-scale contrast descriptor.

Since the sizes of three contrast maps in one octave are different, we resize $CM_2^{(j)}$ and $CM_3^{(j)}$ by nearest-neighbor interpolation to keep the same size with $CM_1^{(j)}$. In each pixel position, the largest value of three contrast maps is selected. Then, a new map is generated as:

$$CMap^{(j)}(u, v) = \max\left(CM_1^{(j)}(u, v), CM_2^{(j)}(u, v), CM_3^{(j)}(u, v)\right) \qquad (5)$$

Once we obtain the $CMap^{(j)}$ for the *jth* pyramid layer, the other layers' maps can be generated in the same way. Computing each map's average value and integrating them with L2 norm, the multi-scale contrast descriptor can be derived, formally defined as:

$$C_m = \left\| \left[\frac{1}{N_1}\sum_u \sum_v CMap^{(1)}(u, v), \ldots, \frac{1}{N_n}\sum_u \sum_v CMap^{(n)}(u, v)\right]^T \right\|_2 \qquad (6)$$

A detailed illustration for the computing of multi-scale contrast descriptor is shown in Fig. 1. This descriptor integrates multi-scale information through the image pyramid, which is scale-invariant along with a certain anti-noise ability.

At last, a multi-scale contrast feature that describes the contrast enhancement for a restored image is defined as:

$$MC = \frac{C_m^d}{C_m^h} \qquad (7)$$

where C_m^d and C_m^h stand for the multi-scale contrast descriptor of the dehazed image and hazy image, respectively. The multi-scale contrast feature MC can reflect the sharpness of a restored image. The larger the MC, the clearer the restored image.

2.2   Dark Channel Feature

The contrast feature can reflect image sharpness to some extent. However, when the restored images are under-dehazed, the difference of their contrast is small, and the contrast feature cannot give distinguishing measurement results.

A highly relevant feature with haze is the dark channel prior introduced by He *et al.* [2]. The prior reveals that except for the sky area, some pixels in a local haze-free region have at least one color channels with low intensities. In contrast, hazy regions do not meet this principle and have high minimum intensities among three color channels in a local patch. For a dehazed image, the more haze is removed, the more pixels meet the dark channel prior. Thus, we utilize the dark channel feature to measure the haze residual degree for under-dehazed cases.

The minimum intensity map for an image is defined as:

$$I^m(\mathbf{x}) = \min_{c \in \{r,g,b\}} (\min_{\mathbf{y} \in \Omega(\mathbf{x})} (I^c(\mathbf{y}))) \tag{8}$$

where I represents the image, I^c is one of the color channels of I, and $\Omega(\mathbf{x})$ is a local patch centered at pixel $\mathbf{x}$. The patch size is 15×15.

The average of minimum intensity map can reflect the haze residual degree for a restored image. To reduce the effect of brightness, the minimum intensity map is normalized by the sum of RGB channels. Since sky regions do not fit the dark channel prior that always have high intensities for all channels, using the minimum intensity map in sky regions will lead to wrong evaluations. Thus, we define the average of the normalized minimum intensity map in the non-sky region as the dark channel feature to describe the haze residual degree, formally described as:

$$DC = \frac{1}{\|\mathbf{S}\|} \sum_{\mathbf{x} \in \mathbf{S}} \frac{I^m(\mathbf{x})}{\sum_{c \in \{r,g,b\}} I^c(\mathbf{x}) + \varepsilon} \tag{9}$$

where $\mathbf{S}$ is the non-sky region of the image, ε is a small value to prevent the denominator from being zero, which is set to 10^{-6} in this paper. With the dark channel feature DC, under-dehazed images can be identified and evaluated. The larger the DC, the more remaining haze in the restored image.

2.3   The Proposed Visibility Indicator

The restored image should have enhanced contrast and no haze disturbance. Higher MC indicates more contrast enhancement and lower DC represents less remaining haze. Hence, the combination of the two features can reflect the visibility for a restored image. We define the visibility indicator as:

$$VI = MC - \alpha DC \tag{10}$$

where α is a parameter used to control the relative importance between the contrast feature and the dark channel feature. Bigger α gives more relative importance to DC than MC, which should happen when the restored image is under-dehazed. From this perspective, we make the parameter α self-adaptive, described as below.

Generally, dense hazy is difficult to be removed and much possible to be under-dehazed. Hence, the more dense haze pixels, the more likely the image is to be under-dehazed. According to the statistics of abundant hazy images' minimum intensity maps, the dense haze pixel should satisfy the following constraint:

$$I^m(\mathbf{x}) > 0.6 \tag{11}$$

A hazy image with more dense haze pixels should adopt higher α, and less dense pixels should use lower α. Letting r denotes the proportion of dense hazy pixels in the entire image, the parameter α is decided according to:

$$\alpha = \begin{cases} 1 & r < 0.4 \\ 2 & r \geq 0.4 \end{cases} \tag{12}$$

Another key point for the designed indicator is the calculation in sky regions. In general, sky is a challenging region to be restored by dehazing algorithms, which will introduce extra noise and halo artifacts. These introduced distortions will inevitably cause high local RMS and further lead to high MC. In addition, the sky region is also not applicable to DC feature. Therefore, to guarantee the robustness of the indicator, both MC and DC should be calculated in a non-sky mask. An automatic sky detection approach proposed in [6] is adopted here, and manual segmentation is also feasible.

The designed indicator can measure the visibility for a dehazed image. A bigger VI indicates more contrast improvement and less remaining haze, revealing a clearer dehazing result. The effectiveness and robustness of the designed indicator will be demonstrated by the following experiment section.

3   Experiments and Analysis

In order to verify the effectiveness of our proposed indicator, we collect dehazed image samples from http://www.cs.huji.ac.il/~raananf/projects/dehaze_cl/results/ by the state-of-the-art algorithms including He *et al.*'s [2], Nishino *et al.*'s [4], Meng *et al.*'s [5], Fattal's [11,17], Gibson and Nguyen [18] and Kim *et al.*'s [19] methods. Figure 2 presents some dehazing instances along with their corresponding hazy images. For each hazy image, four dehazing results with different clarity are given. Their clarity decreases gradually from left to right.

In this paper, the visibility indicator VI is proposed to assess the visibility of the dehazed image, which is the combination of multi-scale contrast feature MC and dark channel feature DC. Higher MC denotes more contrast enhancement and a sharper restored result. Lower DC indicates less remaining haze. The indicator VI can reflect the image visibility. The higher the VI, the clearer the dehazed result. Table 1 gives MC, DC and VI values for the dehazed images in Fig. 2. As can be seen, the results of the visibility indicator VI decrease progressively from (b) to (e) for all images, which give consistent evaluation results with visual judgements. Note that all the calculations are under a non-sky mask for the Buildings image in the first row, which avoids the improper increment of MC caused by noise in the sky region. For the Farmland and Red House images,

Fig. 2. (a) Hazy image. From (b) to (e) are dehazing results obtained by the method given in the bottom-right corner. Their clarity decreases gradually from left to right.

Table 1. Results of MC, DC and VI on the four groups of images in Fig. 2

Image	MC	DC	VI
Buildings (b)	2.1064	0.0174	2.0890
Buildings (c)	1.5253	0.0311	1.4942
Buildings (d)	1.2511	0.0329	1.2182
Buildings (e)	1.0122	0.0378	0.9744
Farmland (b)	4.4615	0.0018	4.4580
Farmland (c)	2.6687	0.1101	2.4486
Farmland (d)	2.3973	0.2399	1.9175
Farmland (e)	2.3166	0.3778	1.5611
Red House (b)	1.3443	0.0025	1.3418
Red House (c)	1.3410	0.0117	1.3293
Red House (d)	1.2194	0.0372	1.1822
Red House (e)	1.2088	0.1139	1.0949
City (b)	4.1607	0.0989	3.9629
City (c)	3.0824	0.1680	2.7464
City (d)	3.1116	0.2264	2.6588
City (e)	2.5960	0.2895	2.0169

MC and VI values are increasing and DC values are decreasing gradually from (b) to (e), which is consistent with the visual assessment. For the City image in the last row, MC values are not gradually decreasing, which give the wrong evaluation of image sharpness for (c) and (d). DC gives the right measurement for haze residual degree and corrects the error, leading to accurate assessment results of the final visibility indicator VI. Therefore, the dark channel feature DC can compensate the wrong evaluation of the contrast feature MC in some cases to a certain degree, which demonstrates the reasonability and effectiveness of our designed indicator.

The approach is compared with existing evaluation metrics that can measure the visibility of the dehazed image, including the image visibility descriptors e, $\bar{r}$, σ [14], and the image contrast metric C_values [15]. Higher values of these metrics indicate clearer results. Table 2 reports the results of these metrics on images shown in Fig. 2. According to the subjective assessment, the three descriptors e, $\bar{r}$, σ and the contrast metric C_values should decrease strictly from (b) to (e). However, most of their results give inconsistent evaluation results with visual perceptions. Especially for the Buildings image with noise in the sky region, these metrics' results are seriously deviated from visual observations. Compared with them, our indicator presents completely right assessment results (see Table 1), demonstrating the advantage and robustness of our approach.

Table 2. Results of e, $\bar{r}$, σ and C_values on the four groups of images in Fig. 2

Image	e	$\bar{r}$	σ	C_values
Buildings (b)	−0.0881	2.9334	7.1217	1.5703
Buildings (c)	0.0165	1.6504	4.0450	2.2721
Buildings (d)	0.0788	1.3564	0.4675	1.3585
Buildings (e)	0.3127	1.8495	0.0854	0.4557
Farmland (b)	4.3691	7.6557	5.5811	12.6983
Farmland (c)	4.9449	3.0805	0.0261	12.5452
Farmland (d)	2.9840	2.8258	0.1737	14.4442
Farmland (e)	2.7556	3.0554	0.0010	3.1626
Red House (b)	0.0789	1.8712	2.0359	2.4420
Red House (c)	0.0986	1.7776	4.3237	2.6174
Red House (d)	0.0791	1.4288	3.4712	2.8832
Red House (e)	0.0758	1.2735	0.0015	0.2963
City (b)	3.5716	5.6675	0	12.0396
City (c)	3.3414	4.0438	0.0070	5.3268
City (d)	3.3155	3.8587	0.0050	5.6014
City (e)	2.8500	3.1268	0.0160	5.1776

(a)   (b)

(c)   (d)   (e)   (f)

Fig. 3. (a) Reference image. (b) Synthetic hazy image. (c) Fattal's result. (d) He *et al.*'s result. (e) Cai *et al.*'s result. (f) Kim *et al.*'s result.

Table 3. Results of LCC and SROCC on 160 images

	e	$\bar{r}$	σ	C_values	BIQME	BRISQUE	VI
LCC	0.4212	0.6864	0.2228	0.3050	0.7682	0.4257	**0.8704**
SROCC	0.4166	0.6497	0.0273	0.3201	0.6963	0.3552	**0.8667**

To quantitatively assess the performance of the proposed approach, we test our indicator and some compared metrics using synthetic images, which include the image visibility descriptors e, $\bar{r}$, σ [14], the image contrast metric C_values [15], the image enhancement metric BIQME [20], and the general IQA metric BRISQUE [21]. We synthesize 40 hazy images using the method in [3]. Using He *et al.*'s [2], Fattal's [11], Cai *et al.*'s [13] and Kim *et al.*'s [19] methods to dehaze, $40 \times 4 = 160$ dehazed images are obtained. Figure 3 gives a dehazing instance, where (a) is the clear image (reference image), (b) is the synthetic hazy image, from (c) to (f) are the dehazing results by Fattal's [11], He *et al.*'s [2], Cai *et al.*'s [13] and Kim *et al.*'s [19] methods respectively. For a dehazed image, MSE between it and the corresponding reference image can be used as the quality ground truth for the visibility assessment. We then use two evaluation criteria to measure the linear correlation between the quality ground truth and the evaluation results of compared and our methods: Pearson linear correlation coefficient (LCC) and Spearman rank-order correlation coefficient (SROCC). The two coefficients are ranged between $[-1, 1]$, where 1 stands for total positive linear correlation, 0 is no linear correlation, and -1 represents total negative linear correlation. Considering both compared metrics and our indicator are negatively related with the MSE scores, we reverse the LCC and SROCC results to be positive values. Table 3 gives the results of the two coefficients between MSE scores and metric values on 160 images. As can be seen, the proposed indicator VI has the highest linear correlation with the quality ground truth, and outperforms the compared metrics by a large margin.

4   Conclusion

The evaluation of the dehazing method is a tough task. In this paper, the problem is addressed with a proposed indicator that can measure the visibility for the restored image. The proposed visibility indicator VI is designed from two aspects of image sharpness and haze residual degree. A multi-scale contrast feature is proposed to measure the image sharpness. Compared with traditional contrast metrics, our proposed feature integrates multi-scale information through the image pyramid, which is scale-invariant along with a certain anti-noise ability. Considering that under-dehazing happens sometimes, the contrast feature cannot give accurate assessment for this situation. The dark channel feature is adopted to reflect the haze residual degree of the dehazed image. Using a balance coefficient to fuse the two features together, the final visibility indicator is derived. Experimental results indicate that, compared with the existing relevant metrics, the proposed approach can accurately evaluate the visibility of the dehazed image with high consistency with human visual perceptions and objective quality scores.

References

1. Tan, R.T.: Visibility in bad weather from a single image. In: IEEE Conference on Computer Vision and Pattern Recognition, CVPR 2008, pp. 1–8. IEEE (2008)
2. He, K., Sun, J., Tang, X.: Single image haze removal using dark channel prior. IEEE Trans. Pattern Anal. Mach. Intell. **33**(12), 2341–2353 (2011)
3. Tang, K., Yang, J., Wang, J.: Investigating haze-relevant features in a learning framework for image Dehazing. In: Proceedings of the IEEE Conference on Computer Vision and Pattern Recognition, pp. 2995–3000 (2014)
4. Nishino, K., Kratz, L., Lombardi, S.: Bayesian defogging. Int. J. Comput. Vis. **98**(3), 263–278 (2012)
5. Meng, G., Wang, Y., Duan, J., Xiang, S., Pan, C.: Efficient image Dehazing with boundary constraint and contextual regularization. In: Proceedings of the IEEE International Conference on Computer Vision, pp. 617–624 (2013)
6. Dai, S.K., Tarel, J.P.: Adaptive sky detection and preservation in Dehazing algorithm. In: 2015 International Symposium on Intelligent Signal Processing and Communication Systems (ISPACS), pp. 634–639. IEEE (2015)
7. Wu, D., Zhu, Q., Wang, J., Xie, Y., Wang, L.: Image haze removal: status, challenges and prospects. In: 2014 4th IEEE International Conference on Information Science and Technology (ICIST), pp. 492–497. IEEE (2014)
8. Mai, J., Zhu, Q., Wu, D.: The latest challenges and opportunities in the current single image Dehazing algorithms. In: 2014 IEEE International Conference on Robotics and Biomimetics (ROBIO), pp. 118–123. IEEE (2014)
9. Wang, Z., Bovik, A.C., Sheikh, H.R., Simoncelli, E.P.: Image quality assessment: from error visibility to structural similarity. IEEE Trans. Image Process. **13**(4), 600–612 (2004)

10. Zhu, Q., Mai, J., Shao, L.: A fast single image haze removal algorithm using color attenuation prior. IEEE Trans. Image Process. **24**(11), 3522–3533 (2015)
11. Fattal, R.: Dehazing using color-lines. ACM Trans. Graph. (TOG) **34**(1), 13 (2014)
12. Mai, J., Zhu, Q., Wu, D., Xie, Y., Wang, L.: Back propagation neural network Dehazing. In: 2014 IEEE International Conference on Robotics and Biomimetics (ROBIO), pp. 1433–1438. IEEE (2014)
13. Cai, B., Xu, X., Jia, K., Qing, C., Tao, D.: Dehazenet: an end-to-end system for single image haze removal. IEEE Trans. Image Process. **25**(11), 5187–5198 (2016)
14. Hautiere, N., Tarel, J.P., Aubert, D., Dumont, E.: Blind contrast enhancement assessment by gradient ratioing at visible edges. Image Anal. Stereol. **27**(2), 87–95 (2011)
15. Fang, S., Yang, J., Zhan, J., Yuan, H., Rao, R.: Image quality assessment on image haze removal. In: 2011 Chinese Control and Decision Conference (CCDC), pp. 610–614. IEEE (2011)
16. Peli, E.: Contrast in complex images. JOSA A **7**(10), 2032–2040 (1990)
17. Fattal, R.: Single image Dehazing. ACM Trans. Graph. (TOG) **27**(3), 72 (2008)
18. Gibson, K.B., Nguyen, T.Q.: Fast single image fog removal using the adaptive wiener filter. In: 2013 20th IEEE International Conference on Image Processing (ICIP), pp. 714–718. IEEE (2013)
19. Kim, J.H., Jang, W.D., Sim, J.Y., Kim, C.S.: Optimized contrast enhancement for real-time image and video Dehazing. J. Vis. Commun. Image Represent. **24**(3), 410–425 (2013)
20. Gu, K., Tao, D., Qiao, J.-F., Lin, W.: Learning a no-reference quality assessment model of enhanced images with big data. IEEE Trans. Neural Netw. Learn. Syst. (2017)
21. Mittal, A., Moorthy, A.K., Bovik, A.C.: No-reference image quality assessment in the spatial domain. IEEE Trans. Image Process. **21**(12), 4695–4708 (2012)

Multi-focus Image Fusion Using Dictionary Learning and Low-Rank Representation

Hui Li and Xiao-Jun Wu$^{(\boxtimes)}$

School of Internet of Things Engineering, Jiangnan University,
Wuxi 214122, China
`xiaojun_wu_jnu@163.com`

Abstract. Among the representation learning, the low-rank representation (LRR) is one of the hot research topics in many fields, especially in image processing and pattern recognition. Although LRR can capture the global structure, the ability of local structure preservation is limited because LRR lacks dictionary learning. In this paper, we propose a novel multi-focus image fusion method based on dictionary learning and LRR to get a better performance in both global and local structure. Firstly, the source images are divided into several patches by sliding window technique. Then, the patches are classified according to the Histogram of Oriented Gradient (HOG) features. And the sub-dictionaries of each class are learned by K-singular value decomposition (K-SVD) algorithm. Secondly, a global dictionary is constructed by combining these sub-dictionaries. Then, we use the global dictionary in LRR to obtain the LRR coefficients vector for each patch. Finally, the $l_1 - norm$ and choose-max fuse strategy for each coefficients vector is adopted to reconstruct fused image from the fused LRR coefficients and the global dictionary. Experimental results demonstrate that the proposed method can obtain state-of-the-art performance in both qualitative and quantitative evaluations compared with serval classical methods and novel methods.

Keywords: Representation learning · Multi-focus image fusion
Dictionary learning · Low-rank representation

1 Introduction

Image fusion is an important technique in image processing community. The main purpose of image fusion is to generate a fused image by integrating complementary information from multiple source images of the same scene [1]. And the multi-focus image fusion is a branch of image fusion. For image with deep depth field which is very common, it usually contains clear (focus) and blurry (defocus) parts. With the help of multi-focus image fusion technique, the image of the same scene can be combined into a single all-in-focus image. In recent years, the image fusion technique has become an active task in image processing community, and it has been used in many fields, such as medical imaging, remote sensing and computer vision.

© Springer International Publishing AG 2017
Y. Zhao et al. (Eds.): ICIG 2017, Part I, LNCS 10666, pp. 675–686, 2017.
https://doi.org/10.1007/978-3-319-71607-7_59

Various algorithms for multi-focus image fusion have been developed over the past decades. Early image fusion methods mainly focus on non-representation learning-based methods. And the multi-scale transforms are the most commonly methods, the classical methods include discrete wavelet transform (DWT) [2], and other transform domain methods [3–5]. Due to the classical transform methods has not enough detail preservation ability, Luo et al. [6] proposed contextual statistical similarity and nonsubsampled shearlet transform based fusion method. In reference [7], Zhou et al. proposed a novel fusion method base on multi-scale weighted gradient. And this method has better detail preservation ability than above methods. Recently, the morphology which is also a non-representation learning technique was applied to image fusion. Zhang et al. [8] proposed a morphological gradient based fusion method. The focus boundary region, focus region and defocus region are extracted by different morphological gradient operator, respectively. Finally, the fused image is obtained by using an appropriate fusion strategy.

As we all know, the most common methods of representation learning are work in sparse domain. Yin et al. [9] proposed a novel sparse representation-based fusion method which use the source images as train data to obtain a joint dictionary, then use a maximum weighted multi-norm fusion rule to reconstruct fused image from the dictionary and sparse coefficients. But the detail preservation ability of this method is not well, so Zong et al. [10] proposed a fusion method based on sparse representation of classified images patches, which used the Histogram of Oriented Gradient (HOG) features to classify the image patches and learned serval sub-dictionaries. Then this method use the $l_1 - norm$ and choose-max strategy to reconstruct fused image. And the fusion method based on the joint sparse representation and saliency detection was proposed by Liu et al. [11] and obtained great fusion performance in infrared and visible image fusion. Besides the above methods, the convolutional sparse representation [12] and cosparse analysis operator [13] were also introduced to image fusion task. Recently, a fusion method based on convolutional neural network (CNN) also proposed by Liu et al. [14].

Although the sparse representation based fusion method has many advantages, the ability of capture global structure is limited. On the contrary, the low-rank representation (LRR) [15] could capture the global structure of data, but could not preservation the local structure. So in this paper, we proposed a novel multi-focus image fusion method based on dictionary learning and LRR to get a better performance in both global and local structure and this method will be introduced in next sections. The experimental results demonstrate that the proposed method can obtain very good fusion performance.

The rest of this paper is organized as follows. In Sect. 2, we give a brief introduction to related work include LRR theory and dictionary learning. In Sect. 3, the proposed dictionary learning and LRR-based image fusion method is presented in detail. The experimental results and discussions are provided in Sect. 4. Finally, Sect. 5 concludes the paper.

2   Related Work

The dictionary learning and LRR theory are two major parts in our fusion method. The LRR theory insures that we could capture the global structure of input data. And the dictionary learning processing insures the local structure information could be captured accurately.

The K-singular value algorithm (K-SVD) [16] is a standard unsupervised dictionary learning algorithm which is widely investigated in many fields. In this paper, the K-SVD algorithm is used to learn the dictionary.

The LRR theory is an important representation learning method. In reference [15], authors apply self-expression model to avoid training a dictionary and the LRR problem will be solved by the following optimization problem,

$$\min_{Z,E} ||Z||_* + \lambda ||E||_{2,1} \tag{1}$$

$$s.t., X = XZ + E$$

where X denotes the observed data matrix, $||\cdot||_*$ denotes the nuclear norm which is the sum of the singular values of matrix. $||E||_{2,1} = \sum_{j=1}^{n} \sqrt{\sum_{i=1}^{n} [E]_{ij}^2}$ is called as $l_{2,1}-norm$, $\lambda > 0$ is the balance coefficient. Equation 1 is solved by the inexact Augmented Lagrange Multiplier (ALM). Finally, the LRR coefficients matrix Z for X is obtained by Eq. 1.

3   The Proposed Image Fusion Method

In this section, dictionary learning and low-rank representation based multi-focus image fusion method is presented in detail. The framework of our method is shown in Figs. 1 and 2. The Fig. 1 is the diagram of dictionary learning processing. And Fig. 2 is the diagram of our fusion method.

3.1   Dictionary Learning

In this section, we will introduce the dictionary learning method in our fusion method. As shown in Fig. 1, for the case of two source images which are denoted as I_A and I_B respectively. Then image patches are obtained by using sliding window technique for each source image. Assume that the size of I_A and I_B is $N \times M$, the windows size is $n \times n$, and the step is s, so the patches number for each source image is $Q = \left(\lfloor(\frac{N-n}{s})\rfloor + 1\right) \times \left(\lfloor(\frac{M-n}{s})\rfloor + 1\right)$. If the source images number is two, there are altogether $2Q$ image patches.

Then the Histogram of Oriented Gradient (HOG) features [17] are used to classify these patches. In the procedure of extract HOG features, suppose that there are L orientation bins $\{\theta_1, \theta_2, \cdots, \theta_L, \}$. And $G_i(\theta_j)(j = 1, 2, \cdots, L)$ denotes the gradient value in the $j - th$ orientation bin for the $i - th$ patch P_i. Define the J_i as the class of patch P_i. The rules for classification are as follows,

$$J_i = \begin{cases} 0 & \frac{G_i max}{\sum_{j=1}^{L} G_i(\theta_j)} < T \\ J & \text{otherwise} \end{cases} \tag{2}$$

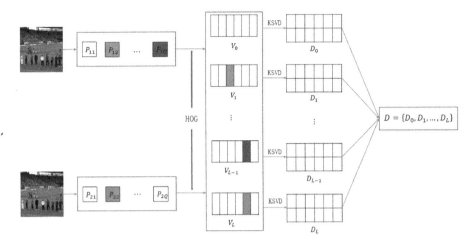

Fig. 1. The framework of sub-dictionary learning and obtain joint dictionary.

where $G_i max = \max\{G_i(\theta_i)\}$ is the maximum oriented gradient value for image patch P_i. And the index of $G_i max$ is $J = arg\max_J\{G_i(\theta_i)\}$, which represents the most dominant orientation of patch P_i. T is a threshold to determine whether the patch has certain dominant orientation or not. $J_i = 0$ means the patch does not have any dominant orientation, which implies the patch is irregular. Otherwise, the patch belongs to the category J.

After the classification, all the classified patches are reconstructed into lexicographic ordering vectors, which constitute corresponding matrix $V_j(j = 0, 1, \ldots, L)$. For each matrix V_c, the corresponding dictionary D_j is obtained by K-SVD algorithm. The sub-dictionaries $D_j(j = 0, 1, \ldots, L)$ are obtained, respectively. Then a global dictionary D is constructed by combining these sub-dictionaries, as shown in Fig. 1. This global dictionary D will be used in the procedure of image fusion and as a dictionary for LRR.

3.2   Proposed Fusion Method

In the procedure of image fusion, firstly, each source images are divided into Q image patches, as discussed in Sect. 3.1. Then all the patches are transformed into vectors via lexicographic ordering, the image patches matrix VI_A is constituted by combine these vectors. And the image patches matrix VI_B is obtained by the same operation for source image I_B.

As shown in Fig. 2, the LRR coefficients matrices Z_A and Z_B are calculated by matrices VI_A, VI_B and Eq. 3.

$$\min_{Z_C, E} ||Z_C||_* + \lambda||E||_{2,1} \tag{3}$$
$$s.t., VI_C = DZ_C + E, C \in \{A, B\}$$

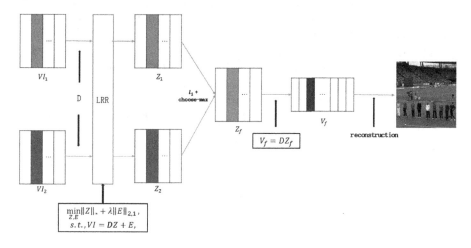

Fig. 2. The framework of proposed fusion method.

where $VI_C, C \in \{A, B\}$ donates the coefficients matrix which obtained from I_A or I_B. The dictionary D is a global dictionary obtained by combined sub-dictionaries as discussed in Sect. 3.1. Z_C is the LRR coefficients matrix for VI_C. We use the inexact ALM to solve the problem 3.

Let $Z_C i$ denotes the $i - th$ column of Z_C, where $i = \{1, 2 \ldots, Q\}$. Then $Z_C i$ is the LRR coefficients vector for corresponding image patch $P_C i$. Then we use $l_1 - norm$ and choose-max strategy to fuse the corresponding LRR coefficients vector, the fused LRR coefficients vector is obtained by Eq. 4,

$$Z_f i = \begin{cases} Z_A i & ||Z_A i||_1 > ||Z_B i||_1 \\ Z_B i & \text{otherwise} \end{cases} \tag{4}$$

Using Eq. 5, we will get fused LRR coefficients matrix Z_f.

Finally, the fused image patches matrix V_f is obtained by Eq. 5. In this formula, D is the global dictionary which is obtained by combined sub-dictionaries. And Z_f is the fused coefficients matrix which obtained by Eq. 4.

$$V_f = DZ_f \tag{5}$$

Let $V_f i$ denotes the $i - th$ column of V_f, where $i = \{1, 2 \cdots, Q\}$. Reshape the vector $V_f i$ as a $n \times n$ patch and take the patch back to its original corresponding position. And a simple averaging operation is applied to all overlapping patches to form the fused image I_F.

3.3   Summary of the Proposed Fusion Method

To summarize all the previous analyses, the procedure of the dictionary learning and Low-Rank Representation based multi-focus fusion method is described as follows:

(1) For each source image, it is divided into Q image patches by sliding window technique.

(2) A global dictionary D is obtained by combined sub-dictionaries.
   a. These image patches are classified based on HOG features in which each dominant orientation corresponds to a class.
   b. For each class, the sub-dictionary is calculated by K-SVD algorithm.
   c. These sub-dictionaries are united as a global dictionary.

(3) All the patches which from a source image are transformed into vectors via lexicographic ordering, and constitute the image patches matrix VI_A and VI_B.

(4) The LRR coefficients matrices Z_C for each source image are obtained by LRR and the learned global dictionary.

(5) The fused LRR coefficients matrix Z_f is obtained. For each corresponding column of LRR coefficients matrix, we use $l_1 - norm$ and choose-max strategy to fuse the coefficients vector.

(6) The fused image patches matrix V_f are obtained by Eq. 5.

(7) Averaging operation is applied to all overlapping patches to reconstruct the fused image I_F from V_f.

4   Experiment

This section firstly presents the detailed experimental settings and introduce the source images which we choose in our experimental. Then the fused result of proposed method and other method are analyzed.

4.1   Experimental Settings

In our paper, we choose twenty images from ImageNet in sport (http://www.image-net.org/index) as original images. Because the number of original images are too much to show all of them, so we just take an examples for these images, as shown in Fig. 3. We blur these original images with Gaussian smoothing filter (size 3×3 and $\sigma = 7$) to get twenty pairs images which contain different focus region. And the example of source images shown in Fig. 4.

Secondly, we compare the proposed method with serval typical fusion methods, including: discrete cosine transform fusion method (DWT) [2], cross bilateral filter fusion method (CBF) [18], discrete cosine harmonic wavelet transform fusion method (DCHWT) [19], sparse-representation-based image fusion approach (SR) [9], sparse representation of classified image patches fusion method (SRCI) [10]. In the fusion method SRCI, the training dictionary algorithm is K-SVD and use the Orthogonal Matching Pursuit (OMP) to get sparse coefficients.

In order to evaluate the fusion performance of fused images which obtained by above fusion methods and the proposed method, three quality metrics are utilized. These are: Average Gradient (AG), Peak Signal to Noise Ratio (PSNR) and Structural Similarity (SSIM). In particular, PSNR and SSIM are reference

Fig. 3. Six original images from the twenty original images.

Fig. 4. The example of source images which have different focus region.

image based approach and AG is non-reference approach. The fusion performance is better when the increasing numerical index of these three values.

In our experiment, the sliding window size is 8×8, the step is one pixel. The orientation bins of HOG are 6(i.e. $L = 6$). The sub-dictionary size is 128 and K-SVD algorithm is used to train sub-dictionaries. The parameter (λ) of LRR is 100.

4.2   Image Fusion Results

In this section, we use twenty pairs source images which contain different focus region to test these contrastive methods and the proposed method. The fused results are shown in Fig. 5, we choose one pair source images as an example. And the values of AG, PSNR and SSIM for twenty images are shown in Tables 1 and 2.

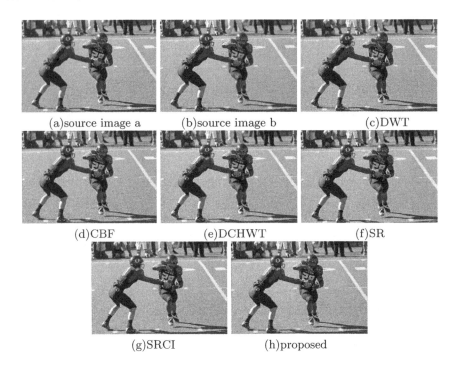

(a)source image a   (b)source image b   (c)DWT

(d)CBF   (e)DCHWT   (f)SR

(g)SRCI   (h)proposed

Fig. 5. The example of fuse results. (a) Source image a; (b) Source image b; (c) The fused image obtained by DWT; (d) The fused image obtained by CBF; (e) The fused image obtained by DCHWT; (f) The fused image obtained by SR. (g) The fused image obtained by SRCI; (h) The fused image obtained by the proposed method.

All the experiments are implemented in MTALAB R2016a on 3.2 GHz Intel(R) Core(TM) CPU with 4 GB RAM.

As shown in Fig. 5, the fused images obtained by proposed method and other fusion methods are listed. This just shows an example for the fused results which obtained by our experiment. As we can see, the proposed method has same fusion performance compare with other classical and novel fusion methods in human visual system. Therefore we mainly discus the fuse performance with the values of quality metrics, as shown in Tables 1 and 2.

The value of AG indicates the clarity of fused image, the lager value means the fused image is sharper. And the values of PSNR and SSIM denote the difference between fused image and original image. If the fused image has lager values of PSNR and SSIM, then the fused image is more similar to original image.

In Tables 1 and 2, the best results are indicated in bold and the second-best value are indicated in red. As we can see, the proposed fusion method has all best values in AG and nineteen best values and one second-best values in SSIM. And our method has fourteen best values and six second-best values in PSNR. These values indicate that the fused images obtained by the proposed method are more similar to original image and more natural than other fused images obtained by compared methods.

Table 1. The AG, PSNR and SSIM values of the compared methods and the proposed method for ten pairs source images.

		DWT	CBF	DCHWT	SR	SRCI	Proposed
Image1	AG	0.0846	0.0748	0.0812	0.0737	0.0800	**0.0862**
	PSNR	37.0188	34.8557	**37.6991**	30.8481	34.9755	37.5665
	SSIM	0.9673	0.9647	0.9699	0.9159	0.9581	**0.9745**
Image2	AG	0.1049	0.0967	0.1004	0.1004	0.0971	**0.1068**
	PSNR	36.4171	35.5492	37.0933	32.3211	34.1743	**40.0973**
	SSIM	0.9783	0.9822	0.9819	0.9461	0.9611	**0.9949**
Image3	AG	0.0943	0.0842	0.0910	0.0903	0.0886	**0.0963**
	PSNR	37.7503	35.8778	39.4640	33.9790	35.9429	**42.0192**
	SSIM	0.9823	0.9824	0.9860	0.9510	0.9750	**0.9928**
Image4	AG	0.1028	0.0912	0.0984	0.0948	0.0943	**0.1041**
	PSNR	36.9723	35.0365	38.4210	31.7981	34.8116	**41.9717**
	SSIM	0.9795	0.9803	0.9830	0.9185	0.9660	**0.9918**
Image5	AG	0.0907	0.0819	0.0862	0.0884	0.0883	**0.0924**
	PSNR	37.1535	34.9156	38.1989	33.8048	36.1505	**40.4725**
	SSIM	0.9785	0.9775	0.9811	0.9554	0.9754	**0.9891**
Image6	AG	0.0847	0.0746	0.0818	0.0802	0.0799	**0.0863**
	PSNR	**37.0322**	33.8555	36.7390	31.7423	33.8922	36.8921
	SSIM	0.9723	0.9707	0.9712	0.8968	0.9617	**0.9795**
Image7	AG	0.0757	0.0674	0.0729	0.0706	0.0714	**0.0777**
	PSNR	**37.4557**	34.3481	36.4605	32.7315	35.9622	36.0487
	SSIM	0.9741	0.9754	0.9730	0.9217	0.9719	**0.9817**
Image8	AG	0.1708	0.1560	0.1653	0.1632	0.1546	**0.1739**
	PSNR	34.0008	33.7624	36.9543	29.9209	30.3544	**40.1589**
	SSIM	0.9759	0.9794	0.9825	0.9393	0.9490	**0.9953**
Image9	AG	0.1514	0.1378	0.1459	0.1448	0.1393	**0.1543**
	PSNR	33.7263	33.2206	35.3401	30.2005	31.2392	**37.4141**
	SSIM	0.9738	0.9784	0.9796	0.9371	0.9534	**0.9916**
Image10	AG	0.1154	0.1030	0.1115	0.1115	0.1092	**0.1184**
	PSNR	36.2289	34.0351	37.7971	32.1752	34.0357	**39.7722**
	SSIM	0.9781	0.9788	0.9833	0.9345	0.9672	**0.9938**

And the values of SSIM represent the proposed method could preserve the global structure from source images, the values of AG and PSNR denote our fusion method has better performance in local structure. These experiment results demonstrate that the proposed fusion method has better performance than other fusion method.

Table 2. The AG, PSNR and SSIM values of the compared methods and the proposed method for another ten pairs source images.

		DWT	CBF	DCHWT	SR	SRCI	Proposed
Image11	AG	0.0680	0.0580	0.0604	0.0605	0.0646	**0.0702**
	PSNR	**38.3437**	34.5043	35.8079	33.1686	35.3299	36.5102
	SSIM	0.9750	0.9732	0.9668	0.9332	0.9679	**0.9779**
Image12	AG	0.1142	0.1053	0.0957	0.0958	0.1027	**0.1159**
	PSNR	35.9972	36.9215	33.2545	32.9198	33.6469	**42.1478**
	SSIM	0.9793	0.9842	0.9616	0.9340	0.9615	**0.9929**
Image13	AG	0.1109	0.0981	0.0946	0.0949	0.1029	**0.1133**
	PSNR	**35.2271**	32.9351	32.9011	31.4786	33.3810	34.9402
	SSIM	0.9694	0.9704	0.9554	0.9158	0.9565	**0.9742**
Image14	AG	0.0853	0.0754	0.0738	0.0748	0.0785	**0.0866**
	PSNR	36.0482	34.5947	34.9556	33.0427	35.3658	**39.5008**
	SSIM	0.9770	0.9789	0.9686	0.9237	0.9678	**0.9919**
Image15	AG	0.1104	0.0986	0.0977	0.0991	0.1051	**0.1140**
	PSNR	**34.5466**	31.5296	32.1961	29.8237	31.4633	33.0836
	SSIM	0.9676	0.9680	0.9602	0.9153	0.9565	**0.9734**
Image16	AG	0.1338	0.1181	0.1100	0.1081	0.1204	**0.1362**
	PSNR	34.7157	33.4927	31.4690	30.9152	32.2771	**38.4244**
	SSIM	0.9779	0.9803	0.9529	0.9034	0.9535	**0.9915**
Image17	AG	0.1947	0.1750	0.1577	0.1530	0.1692	**0.1975**
	PSNR	33.2829	30.9666	28.7314	29.7126	28.9817	**36.1011**
	SSIM	0.9748	0.9776	0.9352	0.9286	0.9420	**0.9886**
Image18	AG	0.1721	0.1578	0.1414	0.1361	0.1492	**0.1748**
	PSNR	32.6045	33.4321	29.3121	29.6468	29.3174	**37.7719**
	SSIM	0.9715	0.9786	0.9419	0.9321	0.9364	**0.9901**
Image19	AG	0.1425	0.1333	0.1101	0.1046	0.1258	**0.1437**
	PSNR	36.0427	35.9360	30.8280	32.0196	32.2789	**37.4533**
	SSIM	0.9792	0.9850	0.9353	0.9324	0.9491	**0.9873**
Image20	AG	0.0958	0.0851	0.0800	0.0834	0.0899	**0.0983**
	PSNR	36.1874	34.1353	33.1515	32.8215	34.8414	**35.9744**
	SSIM	0.9678	0.9708	0.9586	0.9134	0.9644	**0.9729**

5   Conclusions

In this paper, we proposed a novel fusion method based on dictionary learning and low-rank representation. First of all, the sliding window technique is used to divided the source images. And these image patches are classified by

HOG features. Then for each class which obtained by HOG features, we use K-SVD algorithm to train a sub-dictionary. And a global dictionary is obtained by combined these sub-dictionaries. The global dictionary and LRR are used to calculate the low-rank coefficients for each image patches. Then the fused image patches are obtained by $l_1 - norm$ and choose-max strategy. Finally, the averaging operation is applied to all overlapping patches to reconstruct the fused image. The experimental results show that the proposed method exhibits better performance than other compared methods.

References

1. Li, S., Kang, X., Fang, L., Hu, J., Yin, H.: Pixel-level image fusion: a survey of the state of the art. Inf. Fusion **33**, 100–112 (2017)
2. Ben Hamza, A., He, Y., Krim, H., Willsky, A.: A multiscale approach to pixel-level image fusion. Integr. Comput.-Aided Eng. **12**(2), 135–146 (2005)
3. Yang, S., Wang, M., Jiao, L., Wu, R., Wang, Z.: Image fusion based on a new contourlet packet. Inf. Fusion **11**(2), 78–84 (2010)
4. Wang, L., Li, B., Tian, L.: EGGDD: an explicit dependency model for multi-modal medical image fusion in shift-invariant shearlet transform domain. Inf. Fusion **19**(1), 29–37 (2014)
5. Pang, H., Zhu, M., Guo, L.: Multifocus color image fusion using quaternion wavelet transform. In: International Congress on Image and Signal Processing, pp. 543–546. IEEE (2013)
6. Luo, X., Zhang, Z., Zhang, B., et al.: Image fusion with contextual statistical similarity and nonsubsampled shearlet transform. IEEE Sens. J. **PP**(99), 1 (2017)
7. Zhou, Z., Li, S., Wang, B.: Multi-scale weighted gradient-based fusion for multi-focus images. Inf. Fusion **20**(1), 60–72 (2014)
8. Zhang, Y., Bai, X., Wang, T.: Boundary finding based multi-focus image fusion through multi-scale morphological focus-measure. Inf. Fusion **35**, 81–101 (2017)
9. Yin, H., Li, Y., Chai, Y., et al.: A novel sparse-representation-based multi-focus image fusion approach. Neurocomputing **216**(C), 216–229 (2016)
10. Zong, J.J., Qiu, T.S.: Medical image fusion based on sparse representation of classified image patches. Biomed. Sig. Process. Control **34**, 195–205 (2017)
11. Liu, C.H., Qi, Y., Ding, W.R.: Infrared and visible image fusion method based on saliency detection in sparse domain. Infrared Phys. Technol. **83**, 94–102 (2017)
12. Liu, Y., Chen, X., Ward, R., et al.: Image fusion with convolutional sparse representation. IEEE Sig. Process. Lett. **PP**(99), 1 (2016)
13. Gao, R., Voroborov, S., Zhao, H.: Image fusion with cosparse analysis operator. IEEE Sig. Process. Lett. **PP**(99), 1 (2017)
14. Liu, Y., Chen, X., Peng, H., Wang, Z.: Multi-focus image fusion with a deep convolutional neural network. Inf. Fusion **36**, 191–207 (2017)
15. Liu, G., Lin, Z., Yu, Y.: Robust subspace segmentation by low-rank representation. In: The 27th International Conference on Machine Learning (2010)
16. Aharon, M., Elad, M., Bruckstein, A.: rmK-SVD: an algorithm for designing overcomplete dictionaries for sparse representation. IEEE Trans. Sig. Process. **54**, 4311–4322 (2006)

17. Ludwig, O., Delgado, D., Goncalves, V., et al.: Trainable classifier-fusion schemes: an application to pedestrian detection. In: International IEEE Conference on Intelligent Transportation Systems, pp. 1–6. IEEE (2009)
18. Shreyamsha Kumar, B.K.: Image fusion based on pixel significance using cross bilateral filter. Sig. Image Video Process. **9**, 1–12 (2013)
19. Shreyamsha Kumar, B.K.: Multifocus and multispectral image fusion based on pixel significance using discrete cosine harmonic wavelet transform. Sig. Image Video Process. **7**, 1125–1143 (2013)

Key-Region Representation Learning for Anomaly Detection

Wenfei Yang[1,2], Bin Liu[1,2(✉)], and Nenghai Yu[1,2]

[1] Key Laboratory of Electromagnetic Space Information,
Chinese Academy of Science, Hefei, China
[2] School of Information Science and Technology,
University of Science and Technology of China, Hefei, China
flowice@ustc.edu.cn

Abstract. Anomaly detection and localization is of great importance for public safety monitoring. In this paper we focus on individual behavior anomaly detection, which remains a challenging problem due to complicated dynamics of video data. We try to solve this problem in a way based on feature extraction, we believe that patterns are easier to classify in feature space. However, different from many works in video analysis, we only extract features from small key-region patches, which allows our feature extraction module to have a simple architecture and be more targeted at anomaly detection. Our anomaly detection framework consists of three parts, the main part is an auto-encoder based representation learning module, and the other two parts, key-region extracting module and Mahalanobis distance based classifier, are specifically designed for anomaly detection in video. Our work has the following advantages: (1) our anomaly detection framework focus only on suspicious regions, and can detect anomalies with high accuracy and speed. (2) Our anomaly detection classifier has a stronger power to capture data distribution for anomaly detection.

Keywords: Anomaly detection · Auto-encoder · Mahalanobis distance

1 Introduction

Anomaly can be defined in many ways and usually observations that do not follow the expected patterns are considered as anomalies. Anomaly has a lot to do with the specific scene, which makes it difficult to define. The same pattern may be considered to be normal in one scene but considered as anomaly in another. For example, a riding person is considered to be normal among a riding group, but it may be considered to be an anomaly if the person is riding across a group of walking person. Depending on the spatial range of anomalies, anomalies can be categorized into individual behavior anomalies and group behavior anomalies. In this paper, we focus on individual behavior anomaly detection in video. And patterns that do not conform with their surroundings are considered to be

© Springer International Publishing AG 2017
Y. Zhao et al. (Eds.): ICIG 2017, Part I, LNCS 10666, pp. 687–697, 2017.
https://doi.org/10.1007/978-3-319-71607-7_60

anomalies. To be precisely, we only learn a model for the regular patterns, and those patterns that does not follow this model are classified as anomalies.

Due to the complexity of video data, direct detection of anomalies in video is nearly impossible. Most of existing work tries to solve this problem by establishing a reference model on the training videos, and test patterns that does not resemble this model is considered as anomalies. Reconstruction based mothods [4,6] classify test video with large reconstruction error as anomaly, but when meet with complicated scenes, these methods usually have a unsatisfactory performance because large scale reconstruction is impossible in complicated scenes. Feature based methods try to detect anomalies in feature space [8,21], video dynamics are encoded into feature in a selective way by the feature extraction module, features are believed to be easier to classify than raw data. These methods need a well chosen representation module and a suitable classifier. But none of existing feature based methods learn features that are targeted at anomaly detection. To handle this problem, in this paper, we propose an anomaly detection framework based on key-region representation learning.

Our anomaly detection framework consists of three parts, the first one is the video preprocessing module, the second one is the representation learning module, and the last one is the normal/abnormal classifier. We will have a brief discussion below and a detailed discussion in Sect. 3.

In this paper, a key-region selection module is proposed as the video preprocessing module. The goal of this module is to find the video patches that anomaly may appear, wiping off the influence of background patches. Subsequent modules only operate on these patches, thus it would enable the representation learning module focus on the patterns of key regions. As for the representation learning module, we adopt a variant of the auto-encoder architecture in [18], which is proposed as a robust feature extractor. Finally, we use the Mahalanobis distance as the normal/abnormal classifier, proposed in [13] as a probabilistic model in image classification task, we demonstrate that this classifier have a better ability to capture data distribution and can be adapted to an online system.

The main contribution of this paper is: (1) we propose a key-region extracting module for both training the auto-encoder and detecting anomalies. (2) we utilize a Mahalanobis distance based classifier to classify whether the test sample is anomalous or not. (3) To allow the framework to be implemented online, we introduce an online updating method for the classifier.

The rest of this paper is organized as follows: In Sect. 2, we introduce related works in anomaly detection area. In Sect. 3, we show the details of our work. In Sect. 4, We show the experimental results. In Sect. 5, we conclude our work with a brief summary.

2   Related Work

Work in this area can be mainly categorized into feature based or not feature based methods. Among the latter, reconstruction based methods were the most popular [5,11,20]. A reconstruction model was trained over regular patterns, where reconstruction error for training samples was minimized. At test time, samples with large reconstruction error were classified as anomaly. However, some researchers pointed out that reconstruction based methods tended to just remember the input [12]. While in video anomaly detection, our goal is to learn the temporal and spatial structure of video events. So predicting future frames based methods were proposed to address this problem, these methods were due to the intuition that prediction needs more information about the motion and appearance than simple reconstruction. In fact, they also pointed out that prediction based methods tended to just remember the last few frames so as to predict the next frame. Besides, due to complicated dynamics of video data, reconstruction for the whole video frames was impractical, and in practice, a sophisticated preprocessing procedure was needed.

Feature based methods [16,21] usually consist of two parts, the representation learning model and the normal/abnormal classier, as reviewed in [14]. The key is representation learning, and usually how well an anomaly detection framework could work mainly depend on the representative power of the learned features. Hand-crafted features were the main choice before neural networks become popular. In recent years, Neural networks have shown their powerful representation learning ability [17]. In anomaly detection area, most existing powerful neural networks can not be used directly. Since most of these networks need to be trained in an supervised way, and we usually do not have labelled data but only positive samples in anomaly detection task. However, auto-encoder was proved to be an effective unsupervised representation learning method, thus it was widely used in anomaly detection [4,6,15]. Auto-encoder based methods are essentially reconstruction methods, but we emphasize its representation learning ability here. To the best of our knowledge, they are still the most popular representation learning method used in anomaly detection area. In this paper, we also adopt an auto-encoder as the representation learning module.

When the representation learning is done, a normal/abnormal classifier is needed. Many classifiers were proposed to handle various problems over the years, among them, one-class SVM [9], Gaussian classifier, distance based (cluster, nearest neighbor, etc.) classifier [7] were the most frequently used classifiers. Each of them had a preference for specific data distribution, for example, linear one-class SVM was suitable for data that mainly lies in one side of a plane. In order to capture the data distribution better, we adopt Mahalanobis distance based classifier.

3   The Proposed Method

Figure 1 is an over view of our proposed anomaly detection framework. It is consisted of three parts, key-region selection module, representation learning module, normal/abnormal classifier. Below we will show the details of the three modules.

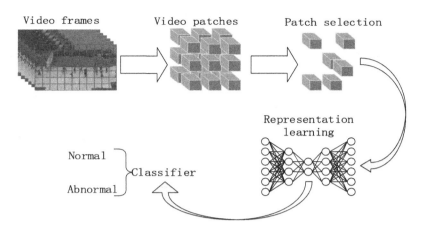

Fig. 1. An overview of our proposed anomaly detection framework.

3.1   Key-Region Selection Module

Establishing a model over raw video frames is difficult, because model complexity would be extremely high so as to model complicated video dynamics. One widely used method to handle this problem is to divide the video into small spatial-temporal patches [3,8,10,15], and subsequent operations and anomaly detection are conducted over these patches. But this method suffers a lot of problems. First, most of the patches only contain background information, which does no help for individual behavior modeling. Second, as far as our knowledge is concerned, all anomaly detection frameworks that use this method only divide video into uniform patched straightforwardly, without considering moving targets as a whole. We design our key-region selection module for the following consideration.

The key of our anomaly detection framework is the representation learning module, only features with enough representative power are learned will subsequent classifier classify the samples correctly. Reconsider our goal in anomaly detection, we want to model the moving targets' pattern, however, as shown in Fig. 1, most of the patches only contain background information. Imagine if we train our representation learning model using all these patches, our learned features may lack representative power for what we are concerned with, since most of the training patches have nothing to do with our concern. So if we can train our model only using those patches that contain moving targets, which is of our concern, the learned features will be more targeted at anomaly detection.

The goal of this module is to find the patches that contain moving targets. In this paper, we view this as a foreground/background classification problem, since they share many similarities. This module is designed based on the following two points: (1) The intensity distribution of foreground patches are different from their surrounding patches. (2) The intensity in a foreground patch is diverse while relatively simplex in a background patch.

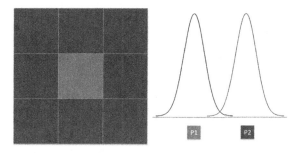

Fig. 2. An explicit show for the similarity evaluation between a patch and its surrounding patches.

We propose two kind of measures for each of the two points mentioned above respectively. Based on the first point, we use cosine distance [22] to measure the similarity between a patch and its surrounding patches.

$$SIM = \frac{P_1^T * P_2}{\| P_1 \| * \| P_2 \|} \tag{1}$$

where P_1 is a column vector, represents the intensity distribution of the patch being considered, and P_2 represents the intensity distribution of the surrounding patches. In Fig. 2, we show how a patch is evaluated in explicit way. For the second point, we use the concept entropy in information theory to measure the intensity diversity in a patch.

$$E = - \sum_{i=0}^{255} P(i) log P(i) \tag{2}$$

And we give every patch a score based on this two measures, the higher the score, the more likely it is a foreground patch.

$$Score = E - \lambda * SIM \tag{3}$$

where λ is a parameter that measures the relative importance of the two measures.

3.2 Representation Learning Module

We utilize a variation of sparse auto-encoder [18] as the representation learning module. The model architecture is shown in Fig. 3. This network transforms the input $x \in R^D$ into hidden representation $h \in R^d$ through the encoder.

$$h = f_\theta(x) = \sigma(W_1 x + b_1) \tag{4}$$

where $\theta = (W_1, b_1)$, $W_1 \in R^{D*d}$ is the weight matrix and $b_1 \in R^d$ is the bias term. σ is the sigmoid activation function.

$$\sigma(x) = \frac{1}{1 + e^{-x}} \tag{5}$$

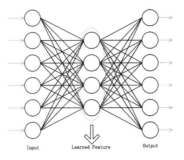

Fig. 3. Architecture of the representation learning module.

The hidden representation is then mapped into the output as a reconstruction of the input through the decoder.

$$y = g_{\theta'}(h) = \sigma(W_2 h + b_2) \tag{6}$$

where $\theta' = (W_2, b_2)$, $W_2 \in R^{d*D}$ is the weight matrix, $b_2 \in R^d$ is the bias term. σ is the same as above. For an auto-encoder, we get the optimal parameter θ and θ' by minimizing the reconstruction error between the input x and reconstruction y.

$$\theta^*, \theta'^* = \arg\min_{\theta, \theta'^*} E_{p(x)} L(x, y) \tag{7}$$

L(x,y) is the reconstruction error between x and corresponding output y. In this paper, we adopt the Euclidean Distance as the reconstruction error.

$$L(x, y) = \|x - y\| \tag{8}$$

With a training set of size m, we get θ^*, θ'^* through minimizing the objective function.

$$\theta^*, \theta'^* = \arg\min_{\theta, \theta'^*} \frac{1}{m} \sum_{i=1}^{m} L(x^i, y^i) + \sum_{j=1}^{s_j} KL(\rho \| \rho_j) \tag{9}$$

The loss function consists of two parts, where the first part is the reconstruction error introduced above. The second term serves as a sparsity constraint, it can be understood as a prior over the parameter distribution as explained in [18]. ρ is a preset activation value, usually is a number much smaller than 1. Let ρ_j be the average activation value of hidden state j over m training samples. Equation (9) is optimized through Gradient Descent.

$$\rho_j = \frac{1}{m} \sum_{i=1}^{m} a_j(x^i) \tag{10}$$

3.3   Normal/Abnormal Classifier

Most distance based methods use Euclidean Distance as a measure, these methods are based on the assumption that different dimensions of the feature are

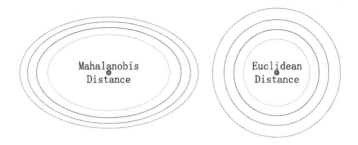

Fig. 4. Each circle represents the points that have the same distance to the center point. As is shown, Mahalanobis distance can capture dependence between different dimensions

independent. However, in practice, it's usually not the case. Mahalanobis Distance based methods do not need the isotropy assumption. We give a comparison between them in Fig. 4, here we only consider two dimensional case for visualization.

$$MahalanobisDistance = (x - \mu)^T \Sigma^{-1}(x - \mu) \tag{11}$$

μ is the mean vector of the samples, and Σ is the covariance matrix. Mahalanobis distance can be interpreted intuitively as the Euclidean distance in a non-regular coordinate system. Σ^{-1} can be decomposed into $W^T diag(\Lambda)W$, we get Eq. (12).

$$\begin{aligned} MahalanobisDistance &= (x - \mu)^T \Sigma^{-1}(x - \mu) \\ &= (W(x - \mu))^T diag(\Lambda)(W(x - \mu)) \end{aligned} \tag{12}$$

The usual way of computing μ and Σ is

$$\mu = \frac{1}{n} \sum_{i=1}^{n} x_i \tag{13}$$

$$\Sigma = \frac{1}{n} \sum_{i=1}^{n} (x_i - \mu)(x_i - \mu)^T \tag{14}$$

But this computation method can't be used in an online way, since we need to compute μ and Σ over all samples again when we get new samples, that's time-consuming and has a huge storage requirement. We introduce the method in [19] to compute them in an efficient way, thus allowing this method to be used in an online system. Denote the mean vector and covariance matrix of previous $n-1$ samples as μ_{n-1} and Σ_{n-1} respectively, when we get a new sample, the new mean vector and covariance matrix is denoted as μ_n and Σ_n, then we have the following updating methods.

$$\mu_n = \mu_{n-1} + \frac{x_n - \mu_{n-1}}{n} \tag{15}$$

$$\Sigma_n = \frac{n-1}{n} \Sigma_{n-1} + \frac{1}{n}(x_n - \mu_{n-1})(x_n - \mu_n)^T \tag{16}$$

4   Experiment Validation

4.1   Parameter Setting

The size of video patch is set to be $10 * 10 * 5$, as illustrated in [1,15]. The weight parameter in Eq. (3) is set to be 2. For the representation learning module, the number of hidden state is 100, the sparsity parameter ρ is 0.1. At the training stage, we first use a normal distribution to initial the parameter. And then the stochastic gradient descent [2] is used to train the representation learning module introduced in Sect. 3.1, and learning rate is set to be 0.5. The network takes about 4 hours to converge on an i7-5960X CPU.

4.2   Experiment Result

The experiment is implemented over the UCSD Ped2 dataset, which is the most popularly used dataset in anomaly detection. This dataset is composed of 16 training sequence and 12 test sequence. The resolution of the video is $240 * 360$, gray scale.

Here we show the experiment result of the proposed anomaly detection framework. We validate the effectiveness of our proposed patch selection module in key-region extracting in Fig. 5. As is shown in the figure, our patch selection module assigns a high score for the patch that contains our targets, while a relatively low score for the patches that only contain background information. For better visualization, we normalize the score into [0, 1] using a linear mapping.

For the performance assessment of the whole algorithm, we compare our work with [15], since we share a similar structure. We compare them using the most important evaluation indicator in anomaly detection, ROC and EER, and we also compare their running speed on our machine. The ROC curve is shown in Fig. 6, experiment shows the AUC of our work surpasses Sabokrou's by 8%. And the results of some other assessment criterions are shown in Table 1, the average processing time for one frame in our work is slightly longer than their's, since

Fig. 5. Right: the pseudo-color map of score map, yellow color represents high score and blue represents low scorewe crop the regions that have a high score. Left: we crop the corresponding regions that have a relatively high score in original image. (Color figure online)

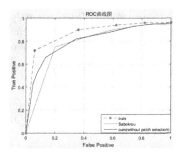

Fig. 6. ROC of our work compared to Sabokrou's work in [15]

Table 1. Comparison of our work with Sabokrou's work

	Sabokrou's work	Ours	Ours (without patch selection)
AUC	0.78	0.86	0.80
Running Time	0.36 s per frame	0.41 s per frame	0.30 s per frame
EER	0.23	0.20	0.24

our work need to go through a patch selection procedure. But compared to the gain we get in AUC, this sacrifice is worthwhile. Moreover, in order to emphasize the importance of our key-region selection module, we discard this module and experiment result shows a decline on the performance.

5 Conclusion

In this paper, we propose an anomaly detection framework, experiment shows a better performance is achieved compared to work with a similar structure. We owe this achievement to our patch selection module and mahalanobis distance based classifier, and we also introduce an online implementation method for this algorithm.

Acknowledgement. This work is supported by the National Natural Science Foundation of China (Grant No. 61371192), the Key Laboratory Foundation of the Chinese Academy of Sciences (CXJJ-17S044) and the Fundamental Research Funds for the Central Universities (WK2100330002).

References

1. Bertini, M., Del Bimbo, A., Seidenari, L.: Multi-scale and real-time non-parametric approach for anomaly detection and localization. Comput. Vis. Image Underst. **116**(3), 320–329 (2012)
2. Bottou, L.: Large-scale machine learning with stochastic gradient descent. In: Lechevallier, Y., Saporta, G. (eds.) Proceedings of COMPSTAT 2010, pp. 177–186. Springer, Heidelberg (2010). https://doi.org/10.1007/978-3-7908-2604-3_16

3. Cheng, K.W., Chen, Y.T., Fang, W.H.: Video anomaly detection and localization using hierarchical feature representation and Gaussian process regression. In: Proceedings of the IEEE Conference on Computer Vision and Pattern Recognition, pp. 2909–2917 (2015)
4. Chong, Y.S., Tay, Y.H.: Abnormal event detection in videos using spatiotemporal autoencoder. arXiv preprint arXiv:1701.01546 (2017)
5. Cong, Y., Yuan, J., Liu, J.: Sparse reconstruction cost for abnormal event detection. In: 2011 IEEE Conference on Computer Vision and Pattern Recognition (CVPR), pp. 3449–3456. IEEE (2011)
6. Hasan, M., Choi, J., Neumann, J., Roy-Chowdhury, A.K., Davis, L.S.: Learning temporal regularity in video sequences. In: Proceedings of the IEEE Conference on Computer Vision and Pattern Recognition, pp. 733–742 (2016)
7. Hu, X., Hu, S., Zhang, X., Zhang, H., Luo, L.: Anomaly detection based on local nearest neighbor distance descriptor in crowded scenes. Sci. World J. **2014** (2014)
8. Leyva, R., Sanchez, V., Li, C.T.: Video anomaly detection with compact feature sets for online performance. IEEE Trans. Image Process. (2017)
9. Li, K.L., Huang, H.K., Tian, S.F., Xu, W.: Improving one-class SVM for anomaly detection. In: International Conference on Machine Learning and Cybernetics, vol. 5, pp. 3077–3081. IEEE (2003)
10. Li, W., Mahadevan, V., Vasconcelos, N.: Anomaly detection and localization in crowded scenes. IEEE Trans. Pattern Anal. Mach. Intell. **36**(1), 18–32 (2014)
11. Lu, C., Shi, J., Jia, J.: Abnormal event detection at 150 fps in MATLAB. In: Proceedings of the IEEE International Conference on Computer Vision, pp. 2720–2727 (2013)
12. Medel, J.R., Savakis, A.: Anomaly detection in video using predictive convolutional long short-term memory networks. arXiv preprint arXiv:1612.00390 (2016)
13. Mensink, T., Verbeek, J., Perronnin, F., Csurka, G.: Distance-based image classification: generalizing to new classes at near-zero cost. IEEE Trans. Pattern Anal. Mach. Intell. **35**(11), 2624–2637 (2013)
14. Popoola, O.P., Wang, K.: Video-based abnormal human behavior recognitiona review. IEEE Trans. Syst. Man. Cybern. Part C (Appl. Rev.) **42**(6), 865–878 (2012)
15. Sabokrou, M., Fathy, M., Hoseini, M., Klette, R.: Real-time anomaly detection and localization in crowded scenes. In: Proceedings of the IEEE Conference on Computer Vision and Pattern Recognition Workshops, pp. 56–62 (2015)
16. Sabokrou, M., Fayyaz, M., Fathy, M., et al.: Fully convolutional neural network for fast anomaly detection in crowded scenes. arXiv preprint arXiv:1609.00866 (2016)
17. Simonyan, K., Vedaldi, A., Zisserman, A.: Deep inside convolutional networks: visualising image classification models and saliency maps. arXiv preprint arXiv:1312.6034 (2013)
18. Vincent, P., Larochelle, H., Bengio, Y., Manzagol, P.A.: Extracting and composing robust features with denoising autoencoders. In: Proceedings of the 25th International Conference on Machine Learning, pp. 1096–1103. ACM (2008)
19. Welford, B.: Note on a method for calculating corrected sums of squares and products. Technometrics **4**(3), 419–420 (1962)
20. Wu, C., Guo, Y., Ma, Y.: Adaptive anomalies detection with deep network, pp. 181–186 (2015)

21. Xu, D., Ricci, E., Yan, Y., Song, J., Sebe, N.: Learning deep representations of appearance and motion for anomalous event detection. arXiv preprint arXiv:1510.01553 (2015)
22. Zhang, D., Lu, G.: Evaluation of similarity measurement for image retrieval. In: Proceedings of the 2003 International Conference on Neural Networks and Signal Processing, vol. 2, pp. 928–931. IEEE (2003)

Author Index

Printed in the United States
By Bookmasters